The Legal Secretary's Guide

The Legal Secretary's Guide

Fifth Edition

Ann Cheyne

OXFORD
UNIVERSITY PRESS

This book has been printed digitally and produced in a standard specification
in order to ensure its continuing availability

OXFORD
UNIVERSITY PRESS

Great Clarendon Street, Oxford OX2 6DP

Oxford University Press is a department of the University of Oxford.
It furthers the University's objective of excellence in research, scholarship,
and education by publishing worldwide in

Oxford New York

Auckland   Cape Town Dar es Salaam   Hong Kong   Karachi
Kuala Lumpur Madrid Melbourne Mexico City   Nairobi
New Delhi Shanghai Taipei Toronto
With offices in
Argentina Austria Brazil Chile Czech Republic France Greece
Guatemala Hungary Italy Japan South Korea Poland Portugal
Singapore Switzerland Thailand Turkey Ukraine Vietnam

Oxford is a registered trade mark of Oxford University Press
in the UK and in certain other countries

Published in the United States
by Oxford University Press Inc., New York

© A. Cheyne 2005

The moral rights of the author have been asserted

Database right Oxford University Press (maker)

Reprinted 2010

Crown copyright material is reproduced under Class Licence
Number C01P0000148 with the permission of OPSI and
the Queen's Printer for Scotland.

ISBN 978-0-19-926840-5

Printed and bound by CPI Group (UK) Ltd,
Croydon, CR0 4YY

CONTENTS

Forms of address for the judiciary   349

Finding the right job   355

Addresses and telephone numbers   361

Useful web addresses   369

PREFACE

This book is intended for those who can already type and who wish to break into the more lucrative and interesting field of legal secretarial work. It is aimed at those who wish to be good legal secretaries and who wish to become involved in their work. Legal secretarial work is not only very interesting, it is fun! The more you are able to put into your job, the more you will get out of it and I have therefore endeavoured to explain not only how to do things, but also why they must be done. However, it is a guide only and not meant to be a legal textbook. It relates only to the law practised in England and Wales.

Unless I produce a series of books of encyclopaedic proportions, I cannot hope to cover everything you will come across. I have therefore covered the most-used basic forms and aspects of law and have, of necessity generalised matters. To assist you until you become familiar with legal work, I have made many cross-references throughout the book. You will see also that I repeat certain important points. After the introductory chapter, there is a glossary which includes some expressions and terms commonly used in lawyers' offices.

You may find that you will never need to refer to some parts of the book, depending on what aspect of law your firm specialises in. In the smaller firms, your duties will probably be more diverse and you may be working in many different areas of law doing everything from making the tea and ordering stationery to meeting clients and attending court.

At the end of each section there are some questions for you to test yourself on. If you find that you cannot answer them, read the section again until you are happy with your answers. Please also make sure that you read and understand all the example forms and documents shown.

Throughout the book, where persons are referred to in the masculine this includes persons in the feminine and, similarly, persons referred to in the feminine include the masculine. All names given in the examples are purely fictitious.

The law is constantly changing and the text of this book is up to date as at May 2005.

By the time you finish this book you should have sufficient knowledge to enable you to find out for yourself anything which may not be covered. I am sure you will enjoy my book and find it of assistance to you throughout your career as a legal secretary.

Ann Cheyne

ACKNOWLEDGMENTS

The author and publishers would like to acknowledge permission to reproduce the following copyright material:

Reproduced for educational purposes only by kind permission of the Solicitors Law Stationery Society Limited: Divorce forms 4 (Petition (separation: 2 years)), 7 (Certificate with regard to reconciliation), 89 (Affidavit by petitioner in support of petition), 51A (Application for Directions for trial (special procedure)), and 100 (Notice of application for decree nisi to be made absolute); Legal Services Commission form Controlled Work 1; Companies form 10; Probate form 4 (Oath for executors); Conveyancing forms LLC1, Con 29 Part 1 Standard Enquiries of Local Authority (2002 Edition), Conveyancing 29 (Short), Conveyancing 28B, Seller's Property Information Form (4th edition).

Reproduced for educational purposes only by kind permission of the Solicitors Law Stationery Society Limited and the Law Society of England and Wales: form SCS1 (Contract Incorporating the Standard Conditions of Sale (4th edition)).

The material in the following forms is subject to Crown copyright and is taken from the Court Service website at www.courtservice.gov.uk: chart showing structure of the courts, forms N1, N251, N215, N9, N9A, N9B, N225, N211, N150, N170, N265, N244, N20, N242A, Court Funds Office form 100, N243A/201, N279, N434, N252, D8A, Form A. (Please note: the Court Service has recently amalgamated with the Magistrates' Courts Service and is now known as Her Majesty's Courts Service: the new web address is www.hmcourts-service.gov.uk).

The material in the following forms is subject to Crown copyright and is taken from the Inland Revenue website at www.inlandrevenue.gov.uk: IHT205, IHT 200, D18, SDLT1. (Please note: the Inland Revenue has recently amalgamated with HM Customs and Excise and is now known as HM Revenue & Customs: the new web address is www.hmrc.gov.uk).

The material in the following forms is produced by Land Registry and is taken from the Land Registry website at www.landregistry.gov.uk. It is subject to Crown copyright. © Crown copyright material is reproduced with the permission of Land Registry: OC1, TR1, CS, OS1, SIM, AP1, FR1, DL, K15, DS1.

All forms in this book are the latest version at the time of going to press but please note that forms are updated regularly and therefore may change.

With thanks to Zarak Legal, specialist recruitment consultancy, for writing Chapter 14, 'Finding the Right Job.'

EXAMPLE DOCUMENTS

TABLE OF FORMS

Introduction

The lawyer's office

The term 'lawyer' is used here because, as you will discover when you become a legal secretary, you will encounter various people for whom you may work, and they may not all be solicitors. In solicitors' offices persons who handle cases and earn money for the firm are known as 'fee earners' or 'case handlers'.

The solicitor

The function of a solicitor is to conduct the legal affairs of his clients, give them legal advice and represent them in various matters, perhaps at court or at a tribunal. He deals direct with his clients who may come into the office to discuss matters.

The conduct of a solicitor is governed by the Law Society and only those admitted to the Roll of Solicitors can practise as solicitors. They are also officers of the Supreme Court of Judicature, i.e., the High Court, the Crown Court and Court of Appeal and, as such, come under the jurisdiction of the court.

Solicitors may practise on their own or with other solicitors as partnerships. As an ordinary partnership, liability to the public cannot be limited but, of course, firms insure (indeed, must insure) against possible claims. However, it is also now possible in certain circumstances, for firms to form limited liability partnerships or companies. Partners of a firm may be responsible not only for their own actions and those of their partners, but also for the actions of their employees. Partners in an ordinary partnership have ultimate responsibility for everything the firm does and they share in the profits of the firm. A firm of solicitors may employ other solicitors who are not partners (known as 'assistant solicitors') and may also employ barristers, legal executives, clerks and paralegals.

Some solicitors specialise in one field of law only and this mainly applies to those in large practices. There are large firms of solicitors in London and throughout the country that consist of 100 or more partners employing hundreds of solicitors and other fee earners. Some firms are even larger than this. Most of these large firms are divided into specialist departments. At the other end of the scale, particularly outside large cities, in rural areas, there are some very small firms with only one or two solicitors who deal with everything that comes their way. Often, a solicitor in a large city will have country solicitors as his clients, either because of his particular expertise or because the country practitioner requires the city practitioner to deliver papers, or attend court as his agent, within that city.

As well as their ordinary work, some solicitors do voluntary work for a law centre. There are law centres throughout England and Wales offering a free service to people who are unable to see a solicitor privately, perhaps because they cannot afford it. Law centres are supported by public funds and they usually deal with problems that might be associated with underprivileged areas, such as welfare, housing and juvenile crime.

Regulation of solicitors' practices is the responsibility of the Law Society who lay down rules for conduct, ability and the regulation of client monies. If, for example, the solicitor sells a client's house, he must put that client's money into a specified account for client monies. He may, in fact, have different sums for different clients in hand at any one time but he must always maintain accurate records of all monies held. There are various organisations within the Law Society that supervise matters relating to solicitors, e.g., the Consumer Complaints Service (formerly the Office for Supervision of Solicitors), whose function includes dealing with complaints from solicitors' clients.

Until fairly recently, solicitors could appear only before county courts and magistrates' courts, and had a limited right of audience in the High Court and Crown Court. However, they now have a more extensive right of audience by taking or being exempt from taking the Higher Courts Advocacy Qualification.

The legal executive

In previous days, solicitors employed clerks to assist with their work. These clerks carried out many different functions and gradually some clerks became very involved in carrying out legal work even though they were without formal legal qualifications. As their numbers grew and they became fairly senior members of staff, they were called managing clerks. In 1892, the Solicitors' Managing Clerks' Association was formed to represent the interests of these clerks. Examinations were introduced and various attempts were made by the Association to have a recognised status for their members.

In 1963, the Institute of Legal Executives was formed. This body governs the examination standards of those who wish to become legal executives. A Fellow of the Institute has had to pass examinations of a high standard and must have completed a certain number of years' employment with a solicitor. Fellows of the Institute can, after certain conditions have been met, set up on their own account as licensed conveyancers, dealing in property transactions. Fellows of the Institute have only a very limited right of audience in the county court and, in certain circumstances, in magistrates' courts, coroner's courts and tribunals.

The licensed conveyancer

Licensed conveyancers are persons who are not solicitors but have passed certain examinations and are registered with the Council for Licensed Conveyancers. As the name suggests, they deal with conveyancing matters (see Chapter 12) and can set up in business on their own account to deal with these matters.

The trainee solicitor

Training for the solicitors' profession is in two parts—an academic part at university, polytechnic and/or College of Law and an in-service training. This in-service training in a solicitor's office or 'training contract', as it is now called, lasts for two years. In the past, it was known as 'Articles of Clerkship' and instead of being called a 'trainee solicitor', the trainee was known as an 'articled clerk'. During the training contract, the trainee must complete a Professional Skills Course, validated by the Law Society.

During the two-year period the trainee has to undergo further courses as laid down by Law Society guidelines. He will work for fixed periods in different departments of a firm or other legal establishment.

The barrister

Barristers (also referred to as 'counsel') have traditionally not been permitted to take instructions direct from the public. The practice has been that barristers have received instructions only through a solicitor acting for a client or from certain specified professions or organisations. However, the rules have been relaxed and now, with specific conditions to be met, they may take instructions direct from the public, although certain areas of law are excluded. Most barristers specialise in a particular field of law and their work involves basically giving advice and opinions on matters of law, drafting documents and advocacy in the courts. They have a right of audience in all the courts of the land.

A large number of barristers have their 'chambers' or offices in London near the Royal Courts of Justice. They generally form a 'set' and share expenses with other barristers. There are also many barristers who have their chambers outside London, especially in large cities. Others work for organisations in the legal department of a company, or in a firm of solicitors.

You have probably heard of Queen's Counsel (QC) but perhaps do not know quite what this is. Barristers of some standing and seniority may apply to become a QC. Once a barrister becomes a QC he is entitled to wear a silk gown, and thus the expression 'taking silk' has evolved. When a QC appears in court he usually has with him another barrister who is not a QC and who is known as a 'junior' barrister, the QC being known as the 'leader'. Since 1996, solicitors have been allowed to apply to become QCs but, at the time of writing, there are only eight solicitor QCs.

Conduct of barristers is governed by the Bar Council.

The barrister's clerk

As barristers usually share the expenses of running a set of chambers, the administration of the set of chambers is also shared and this includes sharing clerks, secretaries and other staff. Because of this, a secretary may find she is typing work for two opposing sides and must be very careful not to get their work mixed up. There are normally two or three clerks, headed by a senior clerk. They deal with the administrative paperwork of the chambers, keep the barristers' diaries and negotiate fees on their behalf, ensure that barristers new to the chambers receive work, advise solicitors which barristers would be most suitable for a particular matter, and perform many other functions. They also often have responsibility for secretarial staff employed by their chambers.

Barristers' clerks do not generally have specific formal qualifications for the job, and they are represented by the Institute of Barristers' Clerks.

Lawyers not in private practice

There are many solicitors and barristers who are not in private practice. The only real difference is that those not in private practice act for one client only, that being their employer.

Many large organisations employ lawyers, either to advise generally or specifically. Among the number of such organisations are local authorities, banks, insurance companies and various government departments.

The client

The 'product' of a lawyer is advice and representation and the person who buys that product is like any other customer—he expects good quality and value, so lawyers are anxious to serve their customers (their clients) well. An essential part of this is that the client must be able to place absolute trust and confidence in the lawyer. Hence it is all-important that the client's details are *never* discussed outside the firm. In fact, solicitors can be reprimanded by the Law Society for doing so or if their employees do so. This kind of 'discretion' can be as simple as not saying to a telephone caller 'Yes, we act for X'. It is of fundamental importance that you may divulge information only with the *express authority of the client*.

The clients must always be the most important element of the work, no matter how difficult, slow or unresponsive they may be and this must be borne in mind at all times.

Categories of law

Civil law

Civil law regulates relations and activities of private citizens and/or organisations between one another. This may involve purchase of property, disputes, performance and non-performance of contracts, Wills, and so on. In fact, matters which generally are of interest only to the parties involved.

In civil law it is generally a claimant who sues or brings an action against a defendant. If the defendant is found to be liable, then judgment may be entered against him and he may be ordered to, for example, pay damages to the claimant.

Criminal law

Criminal law can be said to consist of offences committed against the State (the Crown) and action against the offender in these cases is normally taken by the Crown (usually through the police in the first instance). Private prosecutions are possible in certain circumstances.

In criminal law a prosecutor prosecutes a defendant for a criminal offence. If the defendant is found guilty, he is convicted and may be punished.

Other categories

There are other important areas of law which are not strictly either civil or criminal. These include social security, tax and family law.

Structure of the courts in England and Wales

The highest court is the House of Lords, which can hear appeals from the Court of Appeal and the High Court.

The Court of Appeal has a Criminal Division and a Civil Division. The Criminal Division can hear appeals from the Crown Court and the Civil Division can hear appeals from the High Court, county courts and tribunals.

The High Court has three divisions. The Queen's Bench Division, the Family Division and the Chancery Division. For further information on the High Court, see page 56.

Below the High Court come the county courts, which hear the majority of civil litigation claims. For further information on the county courts, see page 57.

With regard to the criminal courts, the Crown Court hears the more serious offences and can also hear appeals from magistrates' courts. Magistrates' courts hear the less serious criminal offences. They also deal with preliminary criminal proceedings before a case proceeds to the Crown Court. Magistrates' courts also deal with some family matters and act as youth courts (where the offender is under 18). For further information on the criminal courts, see page 195.

For a general overview of the court structure in England and Wales, see the chart below.

International and European law

International law

International law can be either public international or private international law. The former governs relations between states, for example, such things as treaties and wars—and is unlikely to concern you. The latter governs the relations between individuals and/or companies between different jurisdictions and is of importance to solicitors who practise international law.

Solicitors often keep lists of lawyers in other countries and one must always remember that laws of other countries may differ greatly from English law. In fact, even the laws of Scotland are different in many ways and permission must be obtained from the court to issue court proceedings in Scotland.

However, many judgments obtained outside England and Wales may be enforced within the jurisdiction. A judgment obtained in another part of the United Kingdom or in another EU Member State may be registered in the courts of England and Wales. Once the judgment has been registered, it may be enforced as though it were an English judgment. Money judgments obtained in certain other countries may be registered and enforced here in a similar way.

With regard to enforcing an English judgment outside England and Wales, the judgment may be registered with a court in another part of the UK and then enforced in that court as though it were a judgment of that court. Further, if a judgment has been obtained in England and Wales, application can be made for the judgment to be enforced in another EU country. For other countries, there may be a reciprocal agreement but, if not, then new proceedings may have to be commenced in that country.

International Court of Justice

The International Court of Justice is based in The Hague in the Netherlands and deals with legal disputes submitted to it by countries that are members of the United Nations. The

Court has dealt with matters concerning disputes over land frontiers, diplomatic relations, hostage-taking and many others. It also gives advisory opinions on legal questions submitted to it by authorised international organisations.

International Criminal Court

The International Criminal Court has been established fairly recently to deal with those accused of the most serious international crimes, such as crimes against humanity, genocide and war crimes. It is a court of last resort and can act only when national authorities are unwilling or unable to prosecute. It has jurisdiction only for crimes committed in a country which has bound itself to co-operate, or by a citizen of one of those countries, or if the United Nations Security Council refers a case to it. The Court is based in The Hague.

The Judicial Committee of the Privy Council

The Privy Council itself is part of Government and has various functions. The Judicial Committee of the Privy Council is the court of final appeal for certain Commonwealth countries. It also deals with appeals from medical and vetinary disciplinary bodies and some ecclesiastical cases, as well as having certain other legal responsibilities within the United Kingdom. The Court sits at Downing Street in London.

The European Court of Justice

One of the main tasks of the European Court of Justice (ECJ), often referred to simply as 'the European Court' (its full title is the Court of Justice of the European Communities), is to assist national courts in interpreting and applying Community law and to ensure its uniform application. Attached to the ECJ is the Court of First Instance of the European Communities (CFI) which is, in effect, a subordinate part of the ECJ. The CFI exercises at first instance the jurisdiction of the ECJ in certain specified matters. The ECJ sits in Luxembourg.

Certain actions may be brought against a Member State or against a Community institution, often by the European Commission or by another Member State, Community institution or legal or natural person. Some actions are lodged with the CFI and others are lodged direct with the ECJ. There is a right of appeal on a point of law against a judgment of the CFI to the ECJ.

Both civil and criminal courts of Member States may refer a point of European law to the ECJ if they consider that guidance is necessary before they can give judgment in a case before them. The request for guidance is known as the preliminary reference, and the answer given by the ECJ is known as the preliminary ruling. Until the ECJ has ruled on the point, the national proceedings are suspended; after the ruling is made by the ECJ, the national court applies that ruling to the case and continues to judgment.

European Court of Human Rights

The European Court of Human Rights was set up under the Convention for the Protection of Human Rights to deal with applications by an individual or a participating country that claims to be a victim of a violation of the Convention. The application may be lodged directly with the Court, which is based in Strasbourg. A legal aid scheme for applicants who cannot afford legal representation has been set up by the Council of Europe.

The Court Structure in England and Wales

The Court Service carries out the administrative and support tasks for: the Court of Appeal; the High Court; the Crown Court; the county courts; the Probate Service; and certain tribunals. The structure of the courts in England and Wales is set out below.

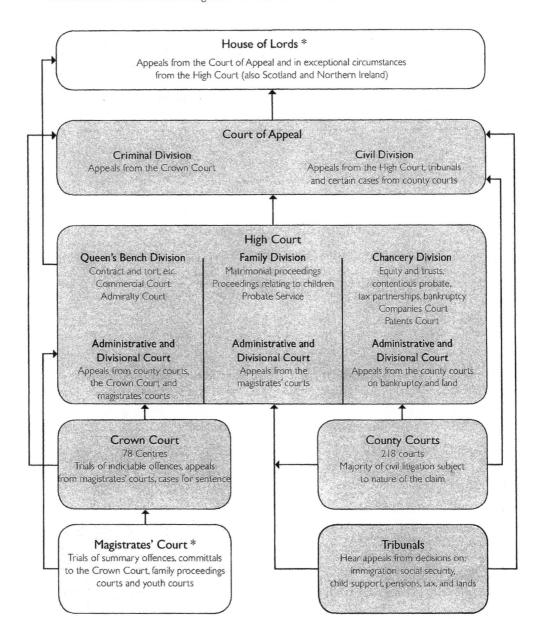

Taken from the Court Service website at www.courtservice.gov.uk
© Crown copyright

Glossary

Listed below are some of the words and terms you may encounter. You will find in law that many Latin words are used. Although you may not appreciate it at the moment, this usage is very helpful because it can eliminate the need for long definitions and explanations. If you wish to have a more comprehensive list or more detailed definitions, there are legal dictionaries available. Latin or foreign words which have not been brought into common usage in the English language are usually written in italics.

Ab initio   From the beginning. If something is void *ab initio* it means void from the beginning.

Abjuration   The renunciation by oath of a legal right or privilege.

Absolute   Final, complete, without conditions.

Act of God   An unforeseen event of natural causes, such as a flood or earthquake.

Actus reus   A guilty act.

Ad diem   To the appointed day.

Address for service   The address that a party in a civil action nominates as the address where he may be served with documents relating to the action. It does not need to be that person's own address—it is often the address of a solicitor.

Ad hoc   For a specific purpose.

Ad idem   This indicates that two or more persons are in agreement.

Ad infinitum   Endless or for ever.

Adjourned *sine die*   The adjournment of legal proceedings without fixing a date on which the proceedings will be recommenced.

Administration of estates   The management and distribution of a deceased person's estate.

Ad valorem   According to the value.

Affidavit   A written statement sworn under oath or affirmed before a solicitor or other person who is empowered to administer oaths. An affidavit may be used, in some cases, as evidence in court proceedings.

Alias   An assumed name by which a person is known.

Alibi   A defence given by a person that he was elsewhere at the time an offence was committed.

Alibi Warning/Notice   A warning given to the defendant on a trial on indictment informing him that if he intends to put forward an alibi at the trial as a defence, he should give notice of the alibi to the prosecution within the prescribed time.

Alternative Dispute Resolution   A term used to describe various methods of resolving disputes without going to court (see page 152).

Ancillary   Additional and incidental to something.

Annul   To make void or invalid.

Antecedents   A person's past history.

Anton Piller **Order**   Prior to the Civil Procedure Rules (see page 58, this was an order issued by the High Court whereby the claimant must be permitted to enter the defendant's premises to inspect, copy or remove any documents belonging to the claimant or relating to his property. It is now called a search order.

Apportionment   To share or divide benefits or monies which more than one person either has the benefit of or must pay.

Attest   To bear witness to or affirm that something is true.

Attestation clause   This is a clause at the end of a document, and usually in a specific form, showing that the signature of a party to the document has been witnessed by another person.

Bench   The judges or magistrates sitting at a court of law.

Bench warrant   An order issued by the court for the immediate arrest of someone.

Beneficiary   A person who is to benefit by receiving something under a will, or for whose benefit property is being held on trust.

Bequeath   To dispose of personal property under a will.

Bequest   Something that is bequeathed.

Breach of contract   The failure by one party to keep to his part of a contract.

Canon law   The ecclesiastical laws governing the Church of England.

Cause list   A list of cases which are to be heard in the Supreme Court.

Caveat   This means 'let him beware'. A *caveat* is a notice often placed with a registry, such as the Probate Registry (see Chapter 11), which prevents any action being taken on the matter without notice first being given to the person lodging the *caveat*.

Certiorari   See under Quashing order.

Chattel   Property other than freehold land (see Chapter 12). There are chattels real which are interests in land and chattels personal, which is other property either tangible or intangible.

Chose in action   Something which can be owned but is intangible, such as the goodwill of a business or a copyright.

Chose in possession   Personal property.

Circumstantial evidence   Evidence which is not actually seen by a witness but strongly suggests that a fact is so because of circumstances.

Codicil   A document which alters or adds to a will and which has been executed in the same manner as a will.

Commissioner for oaths   A person who may administer oaths (see also page 119).

Committal   The sending of a person to prison for a short period or on a temporary basis. Committal for sentence or for trial is the procedure whereby a magistrates' court sends a person to the Crown Court for sentence or for trial (see also page 196).

Compos mentis   Of sound mind.

Conditional fee agreement   See page 34.

Conduct money   Money paid to a witness to cover his expenses in attending court.

Consideration   If someone is making a legal agreement with another, each party must give something to the other. This is known as the 'consideration'. It does not have to be money, it can be action taken, or a promise to pay or act. Consideration cannot be something that has already been done in the past or something that one of the parties to the agreement is already bound to do in any event.

Contributory negligence   Where a person has contributed by their own negligence to, for example, an accident which caused them injury.

Conveyance   A legal document transferring ownership of freehold property when it is sold. It is used only for unregistered land.

Copyright   The exclusive right to publish, perform, etc. the work of someone.

Coram   In the presence of.

Co-Respondent   A third party in divorce proceedings, i.e., where adultery has been alleged in the petition, the co-respondent is the person who might be cited as having committed adultery with the respondent.

Counsel   A barrister.

Counterpart   A document signed by a party to a deed, quite often a lease, which is identical to the original. Each party keeps the copy signed by the other.

Court of Protection   This administers the property of persons suffering from mental disorders.

Covenant   An agreement in a deed whereby one party is obliged to do something which is for the benefit of the other party.

Cross-examination   This is where a person giving evidence in court is examined by the legal representative of another party.

Damages   Money paid by one party to another by way of compensation.

Debenture   A type of charge or mortgage given by a limited company.

Decree absolute   A court order which shows that a divorce is final.

Decree *nisi*   A court order granted mainly in divorce proceedings. It is granted six weeks before the decree absolute. This gives a period of time in which it may be shown that the divorce should not be granted for some reason (see Chapter 5).

Deed   A document which must be prepared for certain transactions, frequently used in conveyancing matters to transfer property. It must comply with certain formalities. (See also page 271.)

De facto   In fact.

De minimis   A small matter.

Demise   To grant land to another, e.g., by way of a lease.

Deponent   A person who gives evidence by deposition.

Deposition   Evidence, either verbal or taken down in writing, given under oath.

Derogate   To detract from, e.g., limit a right.

Devise   To give land under a will.

Dictum   An opinion given by a judge during the hearing of a case.

Disbursement   Out of pocket expenses, e.g., for travel, postage, etc.

Distrain   To seize goods in satisfaction of a debt.

Distress Warrant   A written notice held by the court bailiff authorising him to seize or distrain the goods of a debtor.

Domicile   The country or jurisdiction where a person has his permanent residence.

Dying declaration   A verbal statement made by someone immediately before his death in the knowledge that he is about to die.

E. & O.E.   This means 'errors and omissions excepted'. In effect, this means that no liability is accepted for minor errors, etc.

Easement   An easement is a right enjoyed by an owner of land over another piece of land which he does not own, e.g., rights of way, rights of light, etc.

Empanel   To form a jury.

Encumbrance   A right over land which is held by someone who does not own the land, e.g., a mortgage.

Equity   Very simply, this is a system of rules which when applied by the courts means that fairness will prevail.

Escrow   A document which will come into effect when a certain condition is met.

Estoppel   A rule which provides that a person is barred from denying something which he has previously asserted or which has been decided on by a court case to which he was a party.

Et seq   Abbreviation for *et sequentes* meaning 'and what follows'.

Execution of a document   The proper signing of a document in accordance with legal formalities.

Executor/executrix   A person appointed by a will to deal with the affairs in the will according to the terms of the will. Also known as a personal representative.

Ex gratia   As a favour, not legally obliged.

Ex parte   An application made either by an interested person who is not a party to an action, or by one party in the absence of the other. Since the Civil Procedure Rules came into effect, this is now referred to as 'without notice' (see page 118).

Expert witness   A person who is an expert in a particular field, such as a surgeon or engineer, who is called to give evidence.

Fee simple   This is a term which refers to freehold property (see Chapter 12).

Fiduciary   A relationship involving trust on one person's behalf where the other is legally obliged to act in his best interests.

Fixed charge   A mortgage over a particular property.

Freezing injunction   See under *Mareva* injunction.

Garnishee order   See under Third-party debt order.

General damages   A payment intended to compensate for a wrongful act.

Guardian *ad litem*   Before the Civil Procedure Rules came into effect (see page 58) this was a term applied to a person who defends proceedings in a court action on behalf of another who is unable to do so, such as a child or a person suffering from a mental illness. Such a person is now called a 'litigation friend'.

Hereditament   Land and property which passes on the death of an intestate owner to his heir.

Immemorial   See Time immemorial.

In camera   This means in private, to which the public do not have access.

Incorporation   A process whereby something becomes a legal personality, such as a company being started.

Indemnify   To promise to compensate someone against any loss or damage they may incur.

Indenture   This is a type of deed made between parties.

Injunction   A court order which restrains or compels someone to do a particular act.

In loco parentis   Temporarily in place of a parent.

In personam   An action at court against a person.

In rem   An action against a thing, e.g., a ship or other property. A ship may be arrested through this type of action as security for a claim brought against the owner.

In situ   On the original site.

Insolvency   Being unable to pay debts. An insolvent person may become bankrupt. An insolvent company may go into liquidation or be wound up.

Intellectual property   This relates to intangible property, such as an idea or a design.

Inter alia   Among others.

Interim payment   In a court case where liability has already been determined, the party who is liable makes a payment to the other party before the final amount of damages is calculated.

Interlocutory   A proceeding which is issued before the final case is decided at court.

Interpleader   A process settling a dispute of ownership where one independent person is holding property which is claimed by other parties as being theirs.

Inter vivos   Among living persons.

Intestacy   This occurs where a person dies without having made a valid will. He is said to have died intestate.

Joint and several This is an expression used where two or more people may become liable. They are liable both individually and jointly together.

Judgment The final decision of a court.

Judicial precedent A previous binding decision of a court.

Jurat A memorandum at the end of an affidavit which shows details of how the affidavit was sworn, i.e., before whom, when and where.

Knock for knock agreement An agreement between insurance companies in which each company agrees to pay for the damage to its own insured's vehicles.

Land charges Rights and interests in land which must be registered with the Land Registry if they are to have any legal effect. (See Chapter 12.)

Legacy A gift of personal property under a will.

Legatee A person to whom a legacy is left.

Lessor A person who grants a lease to another. That other person is called the lessee.

Lien A right to hold property until a debt is paid off.

Limitation of actions This is a legal rule whereby different types of actions must be brought before the court within a certain time.

Liquidated damages A fixed sum of damages.

Liquidation This is a process whereby a company is wound up.

Litigation friend This is a term given to a person who conducts proceedings in a court action on behalf of someone who is unable to do so themselves, e.g., a child or someone suffering from mental illness. Before the Civil Procedure Rules came into effect (see page 58), a litigation friend was known as either a 'next friend' or '*guardian ad litem*', depending on the circumstances.

Locus The place.

Locus in quo The place where, i.e., where the accident happened or where the crime was committed.

Locus sigilli The place of the seal. If a document has been sealed by the court and you are sending a copy which does not show the seal you can write on the copy 'L/S' inside a circle and this indicates where the seal is placed on the original document. The date of the seal should also be given under the letters L/S.

Locus standi A right to take part in court proceedings.

Mandamus See under Mandatory order.

Mandatory order An order from the High Court ordering a public duty to be carried out. Used to be known as '*mandamus*'.

Mareva **injunction** Prior to the Civil Procedure Rules (see page 00) this was the name given to a court order which freezes the assets of a person or company so that they cannot dispose of them or take them out of the country. This is now called a freezing injunction.

Mens rea A guilty mind. With the intention of committing a guilty act.

Mesne This means average or intermediate. In landlord and tenant disputes you may find that a landlord claims '*mesne profits*' rather than rent in cases where a tenant remains on the premises after the tenancy has been terminated.

Messuage A dwellinghouse and any buildings or land attached to it.

Mitigation A person whose responsibility or guilt is not disputed may make a plea in mitigation, i.e., a statement which tries to reduce the penalty he must pay. This would normally take the form of a statement showing that he has never done anything like that before and giving reasons as to why this particular offence has occurred.

Mortgage The use of land or other property as security for a loan. The person lending the money is the mortgagee and the person borrowing the money, and thus mortgaging his property, is the mortgagor.

Muniments Title deeds and other documents proving ownership of land.

Next friend   Before the Civil Procedure Rules came into effect, this was a term applied to a person who brings court proceedings on behalf of one who cannot, such as a child. Such a person is now called a 'litigation friend'.

Nisi   This relates to a court order which will become effective at a certain time unless cause is shown within a certain period why it should not become effective.

Nominal damages   These are given where someone wins the case but has not actually suffered any damage. A nominal sum is awarded just to show that the case has actually been won.

Non sequitur   It does not follow.

Notice to admit   A notice by one party to another in civil proceedings that they wish to bring a particular item or document into the evidence without having to prove it.

Notice to quit   A notice given by a landlord to a tenant that the tenancy is to end.

Notice to treat   This is a notice which must be given to a party when it is desired to exercise powers of compulsory purchase over that party's land.

Official Solicitor   An official of the Supreme Court who may, in certain circumstances, be called upon to act in his capacity as a solicitor, e.g., he will quite often act as next friend to a person under a disability.

Office copies   Official copies of a document or record that has been issued by a public office, such as a court. An office copy normally will bear the watermark of the issuing organisation. The Land Registry previously used the term 'office copies' when referring to copies of the register held by it but now refers to these as 'official copies'.

Ombudsman   An official who investigates complaints made against the administrative procedures of government departments and other bodies (see also page 151).

Parcel   A portion or plot of land. Also, a clause in a deed describing the land being sold.

Passing off   One business trying to pass itself off as another, e.g., using a trademark similar to that of a well-known company in the hope that people will believe they are dealing with the well-known company.

Peppercorn rent   A nominal sum stated in a lease for which rent will not actually be collected.

Per se   By itself.

Plaintiff   Before the Civil Procedure Rules came into effect, the person who brought an action in civil court proceedings was called the plaintiff. Such a person is now known as the claimant.

Power of attorney   The giving of authority by one person to another to act on his behalf. It can relate to general matters or a specific matter. Often given if a person is going to be out of the country. It can be revoked at any time. There is also an enduring Power of Attorney which cannot be revoked which has effect when the person giving it is no longer capable of managing their own affairs.

Pre-action protocol   Guidelines for the reasonable conduct of solicitors and clients before certain court proceedings are issued (see page 59).

Prima facie   At first sight, on first impression.

Privilege   The right of a party to refuse to answer a question or to disclose a document on the ground that they have a particular reason for not doing so which is recognised by law.

Product liability   The liability of a manufacturer of goods to the purchaser or consumer of those goods.

Prohibiting order   An order from the High Court directing a lower court or body not to take a particular course of action. Used to be known as prohibition.

Pro rata   In proportion.

Provisional damages   Awarded in personal injury cases if there is a chance that the claimant may, in the future, severely deteriorate due to the injury which caused the condition from which he is suffering and which is the subject of the claim.

Puisne   Junior—in particular, most High Court judges are called puisne judges (but not the head of each division). It also means younger or later, e.g., a second mortgage is a puisne mortgage.

Quantum   Meaning how much, i.e., the amount of damages.

Quarter days   25 March, 24 June, 29 September and 25 December. Often the days on which rent may be due under the terms of a lease.

Quashing order   An order issued by a higher court quashing a decision of an inferior court. Used to be known as '*certiorari*'.

Rack rent   Rent at full market value.

Recitals   Clauses at the beginning of a deed and which usually begin with the word 'WHEREAS' and are descriptive only.

Recognisance   A sum or bond pledged to the court in return for bail being granted.

Res ipsa loquitur   The thing speaks for itself—a term used in negligence actions to state that by the very fact that an accident happened, negligence must have been the cause of it.

Search order   See under Anton Piller Order.

Security for costs   Security deposited with the court in a civil action which guarantees that if that party loses the action there will be money available to pay the costs.

Seisin   Occupation of freehold land.

Service   A procedure governed by the rules of the court to bring documents to the attention of the parties involved.

Sine die   This means without a day. Used in the adjournment of legal proceedings without fixing a date on which the proceedings will be recommenced.

Special damages   A payment which is not intended to compensate for the wrongful act but which is reimbursement for a particular loss such as travel expenses or loss of wages.

Spent conviction   A previous conviction which no longer forms part of a person's criminal record because a certain period of time has elapsed since the time of the conviction.

Stakeholder   An independent person holding deposit money for the purchase of property.

Statutory declaration   A statement solemnly declared before a person empowered to administer oaths.

Stay   A postponement, e.g., of proceedings.

Structured settlement   A way of paying damages to a claimant by way of instalments for the rest of his life.

Subject to contract   A term used mainly in matters relating to the sale/purchase of land and means that anything agreed in such correspondence is not legally binding until the contracts have been signed and exchanged between the parties.

Sub judice   Under trial. If a matter is *sub judice* it may not be publicly discussed.

Tenure   The legally recognised holding of land or of office for a certain period of time or under certain conditions.

Testator/testatrix   A person who makes a Will.

Testimonium   A statement at the end of a deed or Will before the attestation clause that the parties have signed the document. They are effectively acknowledging the contents of the document.

Third-party debt order   When one party has been found to owe another money, a court order may be made so that the person who owes the debtor money pays it to the creditor instead. Used to be known as a 'garnishee order'.

Time immemorial If something is said to have existed since time immemorial, it is taken to have existed as long as anyone can remember, and in fact is presumed to have existed since 1189.

Tort A wrongful act in civil law.

Tortfeasor A person who commits a tort.

Unliquidated damages Damages claimed where the sum is not known and will be determined by the court or by the parties concerned.

Vendor The seller (of property).

Venue The place at which an event, e.g., a trial, is to take place.

Vicarious liability The liability of one person for the act of another, most often the liability of an employer for acts committed by an employee in the course of employment.

Volenti non fit injuria Used as a defence in actions claiming damages for personal injury and means that if a person consents to an act, then no injury is done. For example, in a boxing match one of the boxers cannot claim against the other for punching him on the nose!

Without prejudice A term used when a lawyer is attempting to negotiate a settlement in a claim or dispute. If the settlement proposals are not accepted then anything the lawyer said 'without prejudice' cannot be used in evidence later on. Therefore, when this term is used, it really means that the person using it is protecting his position.

Notes

1

General procedures

Letters and post

Each firm has its own style of setting out letters, e.g., some like typing blocked and some like each paragraph indented. Various firms have their own 'house style' for letters and documents, including using a particular typeface on correspondence and documents.

Always ensure that you have the other person's reference and your own firm's reference on the letter. Usually letters are headed with the name of the matter to which they refer. Most firms keep at least one copy of any letter sent out, but always check in case more are required.

If there are enclosures, ensure you have these clipped to the letter (but see the note about Wills on page 244) and if you do not, it is a good idea to put a note with the letter when it goes to be signed, to show the fee earner there is an enclosure missing. Also ensure that you use the correct size envelope and enclose stamped addressed envelopes where necessary. Before letters are posted they must always be checked and signed by a responsible person.

Letters going to counsels' chambers are usually addressed to the barrister's clerk, e.g., 'Clerk to Mr D. Smith, 25 Brown Buildings, Temple, London EC4 3DA'.

If something is sent out with a 'with compliments' slip only, ensure that references, etc. are on the slip. Also ensure that a copy is kept for the file or a note made on the file of what exactly has been sent out and when it went. This also applies to forms sent out without a covering letter.

You should check with your own firm as to whether post normally goes out first or second class. Post serving documents (see Chapter 3) in civil proceedings must go out first class or by the Document Exchange (see below), where appropriate. 'Service' of a document is the means by which one party formally serves a document on another party and there are certain rules to be complied with regarding service of certain documents (see Chapter 3). You will probably also find in your office that post must be sent out by a certain time and it is wise to check this.

Incoming post is usually dealt with by post clerks or receptionists. However, in smaller firms you may find that one of your duties is to deal with the post. Normal procedures are that ordinary post is date stamped, sorted out and given to those to whom it is addressed with any loose enclosures being clipped to the appropriate letter. If there is post for someone who is away from the office, it should normally be given to another responsible person. In some firms the time of receipt is also stamped on the letters. If post is delivered by hand, again it should be date stamped and also the time of receipt marked on it.

Of course, post is not the only form of written communication—most firms use e-mail or fax. However, procedures should be checked with your own firm.

Using couriers

When post is sent out by hand, most firms have a courier firm they deal with regularly and have their own system for dealing with this. However, it is normal to note on the file in some way details of the despatch including date, time, destination and the courier used. The file reference is normally given to the courier company for use in billing, so that the client can be charged later for the courier fee. It is important also to note these details in case there is a later dispute regarding receipt of the item delivered by the courier.

Postcodes and addresses

You may need to find the postcode of an address or you may have the postcode but not the address. You can find out whichever it is you need to know by:

(a) telephoning Royal Mail Postcodes on 08457 111222; or

(b) visiting the Royal Mail website (details in the Web Addresses section at the back of this book).

Document exchange

Most solicitors' firms are members of the Document Exchange (DX). This is a private postal system used by solicitors, barristers, some building societies and banks, land registries and certain other bodies and companies. The system operates by having a network of local collection and delivery points known as exchanges. If a firm is on this system, they will have on their notepaper their DX number and exchange. When sending mail through the DX system you must always ensure that the recipient's company name, DX number and exchange are clearly printed centrally on the front of all items. You can address a letter being sent via the document exchange system in the following manner:

Messrs Joe Bloggs & Co
DX 123
Weymouth

and put it in your firm's system for handling DX mail. Do not include the recipient's postal address on the envelope and do not put these letters in the ordinary post. The envelope must also show in the top left-hand corner your firm's name, DX number and exchange. This will often be stamped onto the envelope by your firm's post room. A directory of DX numbers is available for firms subscribing to the DX system. This directory gives more detailed information about requirements for using the system. In particular, if you wish to send overseas mail through the system, you will have to refer to the requirements given in the directory.

A service called Address Plus is available to DX members. You will be provided with software to install on to your computer and then when you type in the recipient's postcode, or even their name or DX number, it takes only a few seconds to convert this information into the correct DX address. The DX should be used wherever possible as it is generally cheaper than ordinary post. DX post should reach its destination the next day and can be used for service of certain documents on other solicitors (see page 73). Hays DX, the providers of the document exchange system, offers a number of other services which are outlined on their website (see the Web Address section of this book).

Attendance notes

It is important in many cases for lawyers to record details of conversations they have with clients, other solicitors or barristers, and various other people who may be concerned with a matter the lawyer is dealing with so that an accurate record can be kept. It is also frequently necessary to know how long the lawyer is engaged in a particular conversation relating to his clients so that the time the lawyer spends can be charged and accounted for.

Attendance notes are notes that a fee-earner will write up after he has had a conversation with his client or another firm or any other conversation that he needs to keep a record of. For example, if the lawyer you are working for, Mrs Elizabeth Jones (reference ELJ in the firm), speaks to her client, Mr John O'Groat, who has telephoned the office to discuss the sale of his house, she will more than likely make notes of what they discussed and when they discussed it, recording the time she spent ('time engaged'). She may then ask you to type the attendance note and it might look something like the example below (your firm may have pre-printed forms for you to complete):

Example attendance note

Date	2 August 2005
Time	11.00 a.m.
Initials	ELJ
Client	Mr John O'Groat
Matter	Sale of 54 Duke Street, Warrington
Ref	ELJ/B258

Attending Mr John O'Groat regarding the sale of 54 Duke Street. Mr O'Groat said that he was now including the carpets and curtains in the sale and these would be £500 for the carpets and £250 for the curtains.

I told him that I would write to the buyer's solicitors confirming this and would then include details in the contract.

Time engaged: 20 mins.

Of course, because of house style within a firm, not every attendance note will look like this, but it will be something like this and include all the necessary details. Attendance notes are written not only for telephone conversations, but for many other occasions too, such as the client or other solicitor coming into the office, or a conversation at court before going into a trial.

Taking messages

A message should include similar details to an attendance note: the name of the person you spoke to; whether it was over the telephone or in person (if so, where); the date and time; the main points of what the person said and what they wanted; the person's contact details, such as their telephone number; and if there are any time limits for responding. Also include the client's name and matter reference; your own name, plus any other information that may be relevant. It is also quite usual to note how long you were engaged in taking the message and whether it was an incoming or outgoing telephone call or whether someone called in to the office. If someone is giving you long and complicated instructions, write them down carefully and read your note back to them.

Unless you are specifically authorised, you should not give out information about your clients; you should not agree to do anything on behalf of your firm and you should not give opinions on matters. If in doubt, always ask someone in authority to deal with the matter.

Once you have taken a message, ensure it gets to the person it is meant for straight away. If that person is out of the office and you are unsure as to whether the message is important, give it to some other responsible person. Do not leave it on an empty desk waiting for someone to come back the next day. It is preferable to type messages rather than handwrite them, especially if they are long. Always ensure that you know the name of the caller, their telephone number and the matter to which their call relates.

Forms

You will find that there are quite a lot of forms to be used in a lawyer's office. Many standard pre-printed forms are bought from specialist stationers, some are printed specially for a law firm and some are generated by authorised software on firms' computers. Where a form would normally have information or guidance notes for the person who will be receiving the form, these notes should not be changed in any way. Printed forms can be very helpful because they usually have margin notes or guidance notes which aid in their completion. Some specialist law stationers provide catalogues listing all the forms they print. These catalogues can be quite useful to refer to if you are not sure which form to use. Printed forms should usually be typed or clearly hand-written in black ink. However, with so many forms being provided in electronic format, they can be completed on your PC and saved to the relevant directory.

Precedent forms are also commonly used in lawyers' offices. This is a form or document which has been drafted for use as a guide, e.g., for use as a particular type of agreement. It will have blank spaces in it for names, etc. to be inserted and will give alternative wording that can be used. It is very useful for someone wishing to draft a document because the precedent already contains most of the wording and layout they need.

There are many more forms in use in a legal office than can be shown here and to save space backsheets (see page 69) are not always illustrated. For the same reason, not every page of all forms given in this book are shown. It is always a good idea if, when you complete a form for the first time at work, you keep a spare copy of it so you will know the next time exactly how it should be done. Keep all such copies together and make up your own 'precedent file'.

Printed forms are constantly updated and those used in this book as examples are as up to date as possible at the time of printing.

Copying documents

It is also important, in most offices, to keep a note of how much photocopying you do on a file. This is charged either to the client or sometimes to another firm of solicitors if they have requested copies of documents.

When photocopying, check whether there is something to be copied on both sides of the paper as, if you are in a hurry, this can sometimes be missed. If there is something such as a plan or an amendment to a document which is coloured, ensure you colour it correctly after copying it, or have it colour copied. If something on a plan is referred to as being 'hatched in red' or 'red hatching' it means that it is coloured in by using red parallel lines to do so. If it states 'coloured red' then it is coloured in red and if it is 'edged in red' it is simply that. Copies of plans or part of a plan are often marked at the top right-hand corner with an arrow showing the direction of north.

You may see 'T' marks on a plan showing land. These are sometimes used on plans to indicate ownership of a boundary or liability to maintain and repair it, and the marks would be mentioned in any document relating to the land. If there are any 'T' marks on a plan you are copying, make sure that they are clear on any photocopies.

It may be that a photocopy has to be certified as being a true copy. The following is usually typed or stamped on any such document:

> We certify this to be a true copy of the original.
>
> ....
> Joe Bloggs & Co.
> [*date*]

When something has been photocopied always make sure that the copy is legible before sending it out.

Layout of documents

Most documents and statements are typed on A4 size paper. Although each type of document differs, the layout for those in each section of law is generally the same. You will find in most cases that documents are typed in draft first, i.e., a preliminary first copy which can be amended. Drafts are typed on ordinary A4 paper in double spacing on one side of the paper only. If a document or letter is a draft, it should be marked as such at the top and the pages should be numbered. If the document has a frontsheet or a backsheet (see pages 24 and 69) this should also be marked to show it is a draft.

Where another solicitor is acting for the other party in a matter, two copies of the draft will be sent to that other solicitor for approval and/or amendment. That other solicitor will make any amendments or approve it and send one copy back to the solicitor who originally drafted it, keeping a copy for his own file.

Other draft documents that you may come across are those which might have been amended by another firm and then passed to your firm for agreement on the amendments. Your firm could then make more amendments to the draft before returning it to the other firm or even pass it on to yet another firm that is involved. This type of draft is often referred to as a travelling draft. When a travelling draft is being amended to go to another firm, different colours should be used for each set of amendments. For instance, the first time amendments are made, these would be written in red, the next person making amendments will usually use green, the next blue or violet and so on. When such an amendment is made, it is normal to note this on the top of the first page of the draft document in the same colour as the amendments, e.g., 'Amended in red [*or whatever colour is used*] by John Smith & Co. on [*whatever date the amendments are made*]'. If the draft is being photocopied, make sure it is colour copied or mark the coloured amendments on the copy by hand.

Example frontsheet

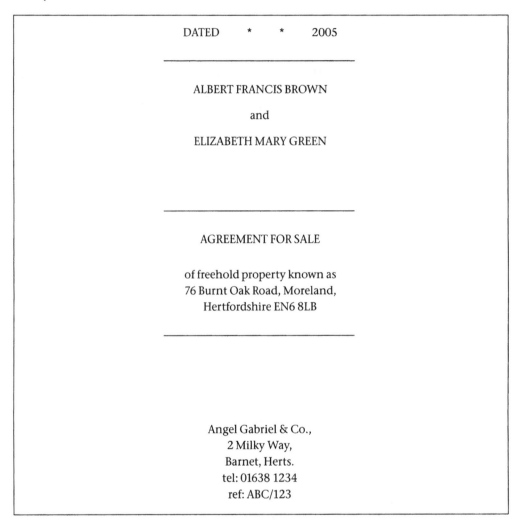

DATED   *   *   2005

ALBERT FRANCIS BROWN

and

ELIZABETH MARY GREEN

AGREEMENT FOR SALE

of freehold property known as
76 Burnt Oak Road, Moreland,
Hertfordshire EN6 8LB

Angel Gabriel & Co.,
2 Milky Way,
Barnet, Herts.
tel: 01638 1234
ref: ABC/123

After a draft document has been approved, it is typed onto good quality paper or 'engrossed'. The engrossment is the final or 'good' copy of a document, which is usually signed by the parties concerned. Important drafts and engrossments which have been re-typed should be proofread, i.e., read over aloud with someone else checking to see if any errors have been made. See the section on Tips for Proofreading. If there are any mistakes or alterations made to a document, you must point these out to the fee earner because, in most cases, where such an alteration is made, the person signing the document must also initial the alteration. If you find a comment in the body of the document, perhaps in brackets such as '[check this]' and it does not make sense, bring it to the notice of the person you are typing for. It may be he has missed something and will not want that actually typed into the final document. You should also check as to whether the engrossment should have its pages numbered.

You may find that you have to type something, very unusually, on 'brief paper'. This is very large paper (A3 size) and if you need to do this you will be specifically asked. In the past, it was customary for brief paper to be used for Instructions and Briefs to Counsel (see page 87) but it is hard to imagine anyone using this now. However, it may still be possible for you to come across this.

Full details on typing Instructions and Briefs to Counsel are given on page 87. Papers going to counsel must always be dated. They are bundled up and tied with pink ribbon before being sent, as shown.

Papers to go to counsel: tying up with pink ribbon

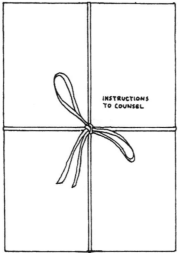

(1) Papers tied up to go to counsel when they are bulky or should not be folded. The name and address of counsel is shown on the outside.

(2) Papers which are not bulky and can be folded in half. (Do not fold photographs.) Again, counsel's name and address are shown on the outside.

You will find that many documents and forms require a backsheet. This is normally typed on the right-hand side of the page only and contains details of what the matter is about, the firm's name, address, reference and telephone number and the date, if appropriate (see the example on page 69). A backsheet to a document has the writing facing outwards like a book cover.

Some firms prefer a frontsheet to be typed for certain agreements. This contains the same type of information as a backsheet but is set out in a different manner (see the example on page 24) and is placed at the beginning of the document.

There are certain rules which must be adhered to with regard to amending court documents and those relating to civil litigation procedures are shown on page 113.

In typing both letters and documents you will sometimes come acrosss a heading, written, for example, as 'Smith –v– Jones' or 'Smith v. Jones'. The 'v' represents the Latin word '*versus*' which means 'against'. The person who commenced the action comes first. However, in correspondence headings some firms like to put the name of their client first even if he is not the person who commenced the action. They may then write 'Jones ats Smith', 'ats' being an abbreviated form of 'at the suit of' meaning Jones is being sued by Smith.

In text, when setting out a case name, the names of the parties to the case should either be in italics or underlined, but not both. Strictly speaking, the 'v' should not be in italics or underlined (except if this is part of a heading such as at the top of a letter), e.g.:

Smith v. *Jones*; or

<u>Smith</u> v. <u>Jones</u>

Whichever style you use, ensure that you use the same style throughout your text—you must always be consistent. The names of the parties in the title of an action on a document are not set out in this manner but should be as shown below. On the heading of court documents the words stating the role or status of the parties, e.g., claimant or defendant, not their names, should normally be underlined, but the house style of individual firms and organisations should be followed.

IN THE HIGH COURT OF JUSTICE	HQ 2005 No. 1234
QUEEN'S BENCH DIVISION	
ROYAL COURTS OF JUSTICE	

BETWEEN:

JOHN GREEN Claimant

–and–

JOHN JONES Defendant

You will see here that the words 'Claimant' and 'Defendant' have been underlined but not their names, which are in capital letters.

A further point—legal documents are quite lengthy and paragraphs often have subdivisions. It is essential that if you are listening to dictation, you are sure of what is being dictated. For example, someone may say 'paragraph 22'. This could mean paragraph 22, or paragraph 20(2), i.e., paragraph 20, sub-paragraph 2. If the person who is dictating does not make this clear then always ask. You can then devise a system between you whereby you will always know exactly what is meant.

There are various requirements for typing different deeds and other documents, and you will need to check with the person you are working for as to what is required in your organisation. Some of these requirements are given below. They apply mainly to conveyancing matters and Wills.

Punctuation

It is not unusual for some legal documents and deeds to have no punctuation in them, especially, for example, in Wills and conveyancing deeds. This is to ensure that there is no ambiguity in the document. If punctuation is not to be used, you would normally include an extra space in the place where you would have typed a full stop or comma:

76 Burnt Oak Road   Moreland   Hertfordshire

Space at the end of a paragraph

At the end of a paragraph, in some documents, if typing does not reach the end of a line, some firms prefer to score through the rest of the line:

everything is left to the Dog's Home --

Dates

Some documents should not be dated with the date you are typing them—they have to be prepared in advance and then dated on a particular day. Therefore, you must leave enough space for the date to be inserted:

this   day of   2005

Dates are sometimes written in words instead of figures, e.g., 10 September 2005 might be written as 'the tenth day of September two thousand and five'.

Sums of money

In many conveyancing documents and Wills, when typing sums of money, the amount should be in words first and then in figures in brackets:

Three hundred and fifty pounds (£350).

Some firms prefer the words to be in capital letters.

Capitals

Words in some clauses are typed in spaced capitals, e.g., 'THIS LEASE', 'IN WITNESS', 'SIGNED by the said ...'. This is more common in older documents but many lawyers still like to use this layout.

In longer documents, each numbered paragraph often has the first word of each paragraph and certain other key words typed in capitals (see example of Lease on page 331). Some firms also like the paragraph number and the first word of the paragraph to be underlined, e.g.,

1. **THE** Lessor hereby demises unto ...

If you are unsure as to what is the correct format or what is preferred in your office, check first before typing the document.

Testimonium and attestation clauses

Certain documents, e.g., Wills and some deeds, will have a clause towards the end, before the attestation clause (see below) called the testimonium. The testimonium states that the parties have signed the document in witness of its contents. Basically, this means that by signing the document, the parties acknowledge the contents of the document. The testimonium will often give the date the document is to take effect but if it does not, then the date is shown at the beginning of the document.

IN WITNESS whereof I have hereunto set my hand this   *   day of   *   2005

or

IN WITNESS whereof I have hereunto set my hand the day and year first before written

This old fashioned wording has now been modernised to a certain extent and the following wording is also acceptable, although you will, no doubt, come across both, and other, formats:

IN WITNESS of which I have hereunto set my hand the first date before written

If the document is a deed (see page 271) these words may include the fact that the document is a deed, e.g.:

IN WITNESS of which this deed has been executed on the first date before written

The attestation clause follows these words, and this gives the names of the parties to the document and details of the witnesses. This is set out as follows. The word 'SIGNED' and the names of the parties are often in capital letters.

```
SIGNED by the said          )
JOHN BLOGGS in the          )
presence of:                )

SIGNED by the said          )
JOSEPH SMITH in the         )
presence of:                )
```

If the document is a deed (see page 271) the attestation clause will be set out in the same manner but the wording usually includes the fact that the document is a deed, e.g.:

```
Signed as a deed by         )
JOHN BLOGGS in the          )
presence of:                )

Signature of witness ...................................................................
Name (in BLOCK CAPITALS) ....................................................
Address .....................................................................................

      .....................................................................................
```

There are different preferences as to whether the attestation clause should be typed in single or double spacing, and which words, if any, will be in capital letters.

The wording of these clauses will differ according to the circumstances, e.g., whether an individual is signing the document or if it is being signed on behalf of a company. The clause is typed only on the left-hand side of the paper in the manner shown above and the person signing will sign on the right-hand side of the page. If possible, these clauses should be on the same page as the last part of the text of the document, i.e., they should not be started on a completely new page. Also, do not split the clause, i.e., do not have 'SIGNED by the said' on the last line of one page and then start the next page 'JOHN BLOGGS in the presence of'. Keep the whole clause together.

When sending documents to people for signature, you should indicate *in pencil* on the document with a 'X' where they should sign. The place where the witness is to sign will usually be indicated on the document (see above) but if this is not done, you can mark *in pencil* where they should sign and indicate *in pencil* that they should also print their name and give their address. Also, documents are often not dated at the same time that they are signed. A document is often signed first and then the solicitor will hold on to it and then date it on the day when the document is to take effect.

Examples of other forms of execution of deeds are:

```
(a)  where a company is using its seal:

The common seal of JOHN SMITH AND         )
COMPANY LIMITED was affixed in the        )
presence of:                              )

.................................
Signature of director

.................................
Signature of secretary
```

The seal of the company would be affixed on the right-hand side of the page alongside the wording.

(b) where a company is not using a seal:		
Signed as a deed by JOHN SMITH	)	
AND COMPANY LIMITED acting	)	Director
by a director and its secretary	)	
		Secretary (or Director)

The signatures might be of a director and company secretary or just two directors, depending on the rules of the company. They would normally sign on the right-hand side of the page next to the wording.

There are provisions for the signing of documents by people who cannot read or understand the document, or who are physically unable to sign.

It is best (and in some cases essential) if witnesses are independent, i.e., they are not related to the person whose signature they are witnessing or to any party to the document, neither should they benefit in any way from the document. They should normally actually witness the signature being signed and sign their own signature in the presence of the person whose signature they have witnessed.

You will also often have to indicate to the person receiving the document that they should not date it. Besides telling them not to do this in a letter the document is generally marked *in pencil* where the space has been left for the date with the words 'Do not date'. This also applies to any space left for a date on a backsheet.

Please remember, it is always important to keep a copy of everything on the file. In most cases originals are kept in the file and copies are sent out (except, of course, when the original has to be sent out for signature). Originals are often eventually formally deposited with, for example, the court, Land Registry, Companies House, etc.

Unwanted copies of documents and letters should be disposed of in a proper manner—some offices have paper shredders or make their own arrangements in this regard.

Tips on proofreading

You may be required to proofread a document before it is sent out. This means checking it over carefully either by yourself or reading it out loud with someone else who also has a copy. You may even sometimes be asked just to look something over for someone. If you are faced with a proofreading job, it is useful to know some of the pitfalls that are easily overlooked, as it is all too easy just to read the body of the text quickly, rather than looking for other smaller, but often important, errors.

Consistency

One of the first things to look out for is consistency throughout the document. Many organisations have their own 'house style' relating not only to the layout of the document, but also to such matters as whether or not a particular word begins with a capital letter. For example, in their documents, some firms like certain words such as Claimant or Defendant to start with a capital letter; others may like certain phrases to be in bold or italic letters. There is often no correct grammatical reason for this: it is just the house style they have adopted. When you are checking a document, you should ensure that the correct house style is adhered to throughout. Inconsistency is especially likely to occur where parts of a particularly large document are being typed by different people who may all type something in a slightly different style; when the variously typed parts are brought together to make one large document, the inconsistencies will be easily spotted. It does not give a very good impression if the style used is inconsistent throughout a document.

Make it easy to read

When checking a document, try to do so from a paper copy, rather than reading it from a computer screen. If the document has particularly small type for some reason, it is helpful to enlarge it by photocopying it so that it is then easier to read.

Easy omissions

(a) Check for mechanical errors, e.g., a margin or tab may not be in the correct place.

(b) If a few words have been typed in bold or italics, make sure that the typing goes back to normal type where it is supposed to.

(c) Numbering: ensure that numbers are in the correct order and correspond to the relevant text. Footnotes, endnotes, etc. should be numbered correctly to correspond with what they relate to in the main text.

(d) Make sure that where brackets or inverted commas have been opened, they are then closed.

(e) Check that any mathematics are correct and that names, addresses and dates are correct. If you are typing large figures with lots of noughts, make sure you have typed in the right number.

(f) Ensure there are no large gaps at the bottom of pages and that you do not have headings at the bottom of a page with no text under them.

Confusing words

(a) There are many words which sound the same but mean something different, e.g., affect/effect; principal/principle.

(b) There are some words which we can never quite get the hang of when it comes to spelling and only one letter makes the difference, e.g., supercede or supersede; defendant or defendent?

If you are proofreading, one of the best things to have at your side is a dictionary. Also, if you are in doubt, you should always ask—it is better to check whether something is correct than to produce a document which is full of avoidable mistakes.

Checking for someone else

If you are checking a document that someone else will be amending, make sure that any alterations you write on to the document are clearly written (perhaps using a red pen) and can be easily seen so that the person who will type them knows straight away to which part of the document your comments refer. You should mark not only the text you wish to be amended, but also indicate in the margin alongside that there is an amendment, for example, by making a tick or a cross in the margin next to the text. If you are writing a comment on the document, rather than an amendment to be typed, it is a good idea to draw a circle around the comment so that the person making the amendment will see that they do not actually have to type the comment. For example, if you want someone to check an address in the document, you might write against the address 'please check'. You would not want them to type that comment, so if you draw a circle around it, they will notice that it is something different from a straightforward amendment.

If amendments you are making are too long to fit in clearly, put them on another sheet of paper (often called a 'rider'). Riders are normally numbered according to the page number to which they refer. If there is more than one rider for a page, the riders should also be given a letter, e.g., two different riders to be inserted on page 6 of a document would be called rider 6A and rider 6B, etc. Ensure that reference to the rider is marked on the main text where it is to be inserted. Do not write too close to the edge of a page, because often when pages are photocopied, writing at the edges will not be clear.

Proofreading websites

Proofreading a website has slightly different requirements from checking hard copy. As well as sticking to the basic rules for hard copy mentioned earlier, it is worth bearing in mind that when people read a web page, they will not read it to the same extent that they will read hard copy. Web users will normally skim over a web page and if they do not find what they are looking for fairly quickly, they will move on to another page. Therefore, there should not be too much text on a web page and what text there is should immediately be of interest. Text should also be broken up as much as possible, such as by using bullet points.

When checking a web page, ensure that all buttons (Home, Back, etc.) and links, including e-mail links, are working correctly. Check that any forms to be completed on-screen work properly. Make sure that any graphics appear correctly on the screen and if there is a graphic, there should be alternate text for it so that if the user chooses not to view graphics on their screen, they will still know what was there by reading the alternate text. Web pages should also have a title at the very top left-hand of the browser and of the page when printed out, even if this is just the name of the firm. Also check that the page downloads reasonably quickly. For further information on the Internet, see Chapter 2.

Sewing up documents

Although it is not required very often these days, some firms still prefer certain types of documents to be sewn with green tape, rather than bound or stapled.

Documents are sewn up as follows (also see the diagrams on page 33):

(a) Neatly clip or pin together the sheets of paper to be sewn together (except when it is a Will—see page 243), so that they do not move around. A backsheet will have the writing facing outwards like a cover.

(b) Make holes in the left-hand margin (Figure 1) of the document about half an inch in from the edge. A bodger or awl (a sharp pointed instrument) is normally used for this. Most people make five holes but some like only three. If making only three holes you would leave out the holes marked (1) and (5) in the diagram and put (2) and (4) slightly further apart. The holes should be evenly spaced with hole No. (3) in the middle.

(c) Measure the amount of green ribbon needed—just over two and a half times the length of the document will be sufficient. Cut this from the roll of ribbon and thread the needle. A special large needle is used for this. Do not double the ribbon over too much.

(d) Starting at the front of the document at hole No. (3) in the diagram (the middle one) insert the needle and pull it through to the other side leaving about two and a half inches of green ribbon loose at the front.

(e) The needle and the rest of the ribbon will now be at the back of the document. Take it back round over the left-hand margin and back again through hole No. (3) (Figure 2). Make sure the needle does not go through the green ribbon already in place and keep the ribbon flat on the document. Do not let it twist or tangle. Keep the ribbon tight and flat but not too tight so as to pull the paper.

(f) The needle will again now be at the back of hole No. (3). Take it up along the back of the document to hole No. (2) (Figure 3). Bring it through hole No. (2) out to the front of the document.

(g) Take the needle over the left-hand margin (as at (e) above), back through the back of hole No. (2) and through to the front of hole No. (2).

(h) Take the needle up to hole No. (1), through to the back, around the left-hand margin and back through hole No. (1)

(i) You will now be at the back of the document. Take the ribbon (now at the back of hole No. (1)) down to hole No. (2) and through to the front.

(j) You will now be at the front of hole No. (2). Take the ribbon down the document and through hole No. (3), to the back. You will now have sewn the top part of the document.

(k) Take the ribbon down to hole No. (4) and through this hole to the front of the document. Take it around the left-hand margin over to the back and then again through hole No. (4).

(l) Take the ribbon down to hole No. (5) and through to the back of the hole. Bring the needle over the margin so that it comes to the front of hole No. (5) again. Take the needle through the hole. You will now be at the back of the document. Go up to hole No. (4) and through the hole to the front of the document.

(m) Now take the needle up to the green ribbon which goes across the margin at hole No. (3). Slide the needle under that ribbon and under the ribbon leading from holes (3) to (2).

(n) Cut the ribbon off now so that the last bit is the same length as the original bit of ribbon left at the front of the document. Tie a firm knot or two with the two ends of ribbon.

Your finished document should be like Figure 4 on both sides and tied off at the front. Remember, while sewing, if you keep the ribbon flat while you work, do not allow it to get twisted, and put the needle cleanly through the holes you should not have too much trouble.

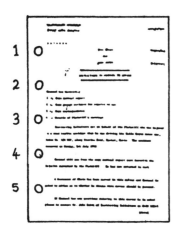

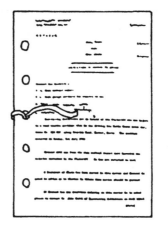

| Figure 1 | Figure 2 | Figure 3 |

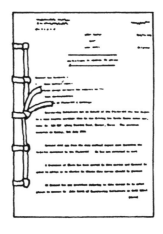

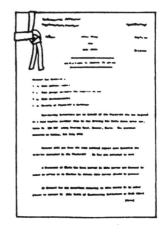

| Figure 4 | Figure 5 |

Sewing up in one corner only

Some documents may be sewn up only in one corner. You will need only about 9 inches of ribbon for this.

Just make one hole where hole No. (1) is shown on the diagrams. Insert the needle from the front through to the back, again leaving about two and a half inches of ribbon loose at the front. Take the needle around the left-hand margin and back through hole No. (1) so that the needle is now at the back of hole No. (1). Then take the needle over the left-hand corner at the top of the page and slide it under the ribbon which is already secure. Then tie off as previously shown. Your document should look like Figure 5. If you are sewing something into the document like a large plan, sew it along the edge in the usual way and then fold it over neatly to fit into the rest of the document.

Financial transactions

Most firms have forms to be completed requisitioning monies, i.e., for petty cash, cheques, etc. A copy is usually given to the accounts department and a copy kept on the file. Solicitors have two basic main accounts—Office Account and Client Account.

Office Account is an account which has money in it used for paying disbursements such as counsel's fees or a court fee, or when a client pays the solicitor's bill that money is paid into Office Account. Client Account holds clients' money, for example, money paid to the solicitor on account of his costs (i.e., an advance payment) when the client first consults him. This is the client's money and can only be transferred to Office Account when the solicitor has either earned the money and submitted a bill to the client, or paid out that amount on behalf of the client, for example, in disbursements. Solicitors must not over-draw on their Client Account or use the money of one client to fund another. If you are completing a form to requisition money always ensure that the money is being taken from the correct account. If money is wrongly taken from a client's account, a solicitor may be disciplined by the Law Society.

Billing and client care

Some large firms have a costs department to prepare their bills of costs. Some employ costs draftsmen who are persons specialising in drafting bills, and deal with other matters for the firm such as drawing bills for assessment of costs (see page 142).

Charges for work carried out by a solicitor are based on the amount of time which he spends on a particular matter. The time of anyone assisting him is also taken into consideration. A solicitor's charges must be fair and reasonable and will also take into account such things as the complexity of the matter and the value of any property or money involved. Everyone concerned with a matter must try to keep a detailed note of meetings, telephone calls and, indeed, time spent on every file. Secretaries, however, do not normally have to note how long they spend typing something except in exceptional circumstances but if you go out, for example, to court, you should make a note of how long you are engaged. In many firms, a formal time recording system is used incorporating either a computer software package or pre-printed time sheets. However, even where there is no such formal system, you must remember the importance of detailed notes.

In some instances, firms may enter into what is known as a conditional fee agreement with their client. Basically, this is an agreement where the firm can charge the client an enhanced fee if they win the case, i.e., a success fee whereby the firm charges a percentage increase on their fee if they win, or no fee if they lose. Firms may enter into a conditional fee agreement in all civil court cases apart from family proceedings. Where such an agreement is entered into, it will often involve insurance policies or other types of funding to cover disbursements (e.g., barristers' fees, experts' fees, etc.) and, potentially, if the case is lost, the costs of the other party. Further information on conditional fee agreements can be obtained from the Law Society.

In many firms you will find that you will have to type the bill (or VAT invoice). Bills should bear the fee earner's reference and the number of the file or matter, the name of the client and a note of which of his matters or files it refers to. They are usually typed in triplicate—the top copy for the client, a copy for the file and one for the accounts department.

You will find that some items bear Value Added Tax ('VAT'—current standard rate $17\frac{1}{2}$%). Solicitors' costs and some expenses or disbursements such as counsels' fees bear VAT. Court fees do not bear VAT. If you are not sure, then you must check with the fee earner. Some bills include VAT charged at zero rate which effectively means that no VAT is charged. This usually applies to persons, businesses and lands outside the United Kingdom.

The Law Society rules state that firms must disclose to the client at the outset, details of billing as well as other client care issues.

Client care effectively means that the solicitor will ensure that the client is dealt with properly and efficiently, and will know what to do if he has a complaint. At the beginning of the solicitor/client relationship, the client is given client care information by the solicitor regarding, as mentioned above, costs relating to the matter and other relevant information, such as who in the firm is responsible for the matter on a day-to-day basis; the partner with overall responsibility for the matter; and details of the firm's complaints handling procedures. A client care letter will normally be sent to the client containing all the relevant information. The Law Society has produced examples of client care letters.

Payment of fees

Throughout this book mention is made of 'fees' to be paid, for example, when issuing certain court proceedings or making enquiries of a local authority. There are many different types of fees payable and these are often amended by the various bodies imposing them. It is therefore not practical to show fees in this book because they could well be amended at any time. Fees like this, which are not part of the solicitor's actual work, are itemised under a separate heading as 'disbursements' when they are included in a solicitor's bill.

Most legal offices keep an up-to-date note of any relevant fees and it is always a good idea to keep a copy of these at your desk. Often books which are relevant to a particular matter will list fees, as do some relevant websites. Many legal diaries also have in them some of the commonly used fees. There are also booklets available listing fees.

If you cannot find out how much a particular fee is, you can always telephone the organisation to whom you will be paying the fee and make a note of it for later use.

Files

All firms have their own system of numbering or labelling files and of storing them when they are finished with. Lots of firms refer to a case or file as a 'matter'.

It is essential in all legal offices to keep filing up to date and neat and tidy. Make sure you always keep a copy of everything sent out on the file and in its correct place.

Some solicitors' offices keep separate files for correspondence and documents. Some also divide the filing into different bundles with correspondence between the solicitor and his client in one bundle, and correspondence between the solicitor and the other party on another bundle. In any event, whichever way the filing is done, it must be kept in date order.

Reminder systems

When working in law, dates are all important. Most documents have to be completed or served at a certain stage during proceedings or within a certain time. Most lawyers therefore keep notes in their diaries for useful time limits and dates of importance and these are usually on the following lines:

(a) The last day on which something has to be done.

(b) A note two or three days before the final date.

(c) A note a week or two before the event, depending on what it is.

You may find that you are frequently asked to make a diary note regarding some event or time limit and mentioned later in various sections are certain time limits that you may wish to make a diary note about. It is this type of diary note which is being referred to. It is best, of course, to check with your fee earner exactly how he wants his diary noted as it is his responsibility to ensure that time limits are adhered to and he should tell you any he wishes to be reminded of.

Some firms have computerised reminder systems which, of course, makes life a lot easier.

Conflict of interest

It sometimes happens that a firm is acting for one party to an action and by coincidence the other party comes along and asks the same firm to act for him. It is not normally permissible for solicitors to act for both sides and this is known as a conflict of interest. Most firms have some system of checking whether they already act for a particular party, and new clients are not taken on normally until this has been cleared.

Conflict of interest can also arise in other ways, e.g., the solicitor being consulted may be a shareholder in a company upon which the client is seeking advice and whereby, depending on the advice given, the company could stand to make a substantial sum of money. In those circumstances, the solicitor would have to inform the client of the potential conflict as soon as he became aware of it himself. He would then ask the client to instruct another firm.

The law library

A great deal of any lawyer's work involves research in textbooks. English law is a 'common law' system where the decision in one case may affect the reasoning of the court in later cases. Decisions of higher courts bind lower courts and law that is built up through decisions made in cases is referred to as 'case law'. A decision made in one court which will have to be followed by another court is referred to as a 'judicial precedent'. A precedent will only be binding on a lower court where the same principles of law are being considered. If a lawyer wishes to quote or 'cite' such a case, he is citing an 'authority'.

There is also a great deal of law made in Parliament, through Acts of Parliament, statutory instruments and regulations (statute law). When typing the word 'Act' in the context of an Act of Parliament, it should begin with a capital 'A'. Similarly, when referring to a Bill that is introduced into Parliament (the Bill will eventually become an Act if it passes successfully through Parliament), a capital 'B' is used. Acts of Parliament are divided into different sections, which in turn may be divided into sub-sections. When referring to a section, you would normally type, e.g., section 2 of the Data Protection Act 1998, although the house style adopted by your firm may differ slightly. An Act of Parliament will usually have a Schedule, which would be referred to as a Schedule 'to' an Act, e.g., Schedule 3 to the Data Protection Act 1998. The books most commonly used to find out about Acts of Parliament are *Halsbury's Laws of England* and *Halsbury's Statutes*.

Halsbury's Laws is set out in alphabetical order and covers practically everything in law, subject by subject. There is an index in each volume and a general index. The first and last subjects in each volume are listed on the spine cover. Regular supplements are published to ensure the information is up to date.

Halsbury's Statutes works in the same way, but contains the text of statutes. There is an alphabetical table of statutes at the beginning of each volume. At the end of each year this book of statutes is produced as a new volume with cross-references to other volumes.

Halsbury's Statutory Instruments contains lists of statutory instruments under subject headings and includes copies of important ones. A statutory instrument is a form of delegated legislation, usually made by a Government minister under powers conferred by an Act of Parliament. A statutory instrument will normally be in the form of Regulations, Rules or Orders and a great number are passed every year. They are numbered throughout each year and are cited by their year and number, e.g., S.I. 2005 No. 123.

Copies of individual Acts of Parliament, statutory instruments, etc. can be obtained from The Stationery Office. Some of these are available on their website (see the section at the end of this book on Useful Web Addresses).

As well as having access to copies of statutes, etc. a solicitor needs to have access to copies of decided cases (law reports) to see what decision was made in a case which may be similar to one he is now dealing with. It is worth noting that cases are not always referred to by the names of the parties involved, e.g., in shipping, you will nearly always find that it is the name of the ship which is referred to, rather than the parties involved.

Certain reference books containing reported cases are widely used by lawyers, e.g., All England Law Reports (All ER), Weekly Law Reports (WLR) and the Law Reports. Law Reports are divided into sub-sections: Appeal Cases (AC), Chancery Division (Ch), Queen's (or King's) Bench Division (QB or KB) and Family Division (Fam). A reference to a case in one of these books would be something like '*Smith* v *Brown* [1976] 1 QB 201'. The case of *Smith* v *Brown* would be found in Queen's Bench series, and would be in volume 1 of those marked 1976, and here the report will be on page 197. 'When quoting a case or 'citing' it, the name of the parties to the case is very often written in italics, e.g., *Smith* v *Brown*, and the reference to that case would be in ordinary type, e.g., [1976] 1 QB 201. There are different law reports covering different aspects of law, for example, 'Tax Cases' or 'Lloyd's Law Reports'. There are many other books which contain case references and details of decided cases but it is not really appropriate to go into further detail here.

You will come across some references to cases which have the year of the case report in square brackets as shown above, and some which have the year of the report inside ordinary round brackets. Square brackets are used when the date is an essential part of the reference and the case cannot be found without knowing the date, e.g., [1976] 1 QB 201. Round brackets are used when the date is not an essential part of the reference, when the case can be found whether or not the date is given (it will usually have a unique volume number) e.g., (1886) 5 App Cas 316.

Most modern law reports will give an example inside their front cover as to how cases from their reports should be cited.

In addition to citing a case with reference to a published law report, neutral citations have been introduced for certain judgments. A neutral citation is a unique reference to the judgment and is allocated by the court. It will be shown as, e.g., Smith v Brown [2005] EWHC 38 (QB). First, this shows the names of the parties and the year of the judgment. EW means England and Wales and HC means the High Court. The number 38 and (QB) show that it is the thirty-eighth numbered judgment of that year given in the Queen's Bench Division of the High Court. Other abbreviations are similar, with each showing in brackets at the end the court where judgment was given. The abbreviations for the House of Lords and the Privy Council are UKHL and UKPC respectively.

There are also books of forms and precedents—*The Encyclopaedia of Forms and Precedents* and *Atkin's Court Forms*, which show how certain documents might be set out. Many books have an annual service system to keep them up to date. When there is a change in the law or procedures, publishers of the relevant books, if they have a service to which the owner of the book has subscribed, will send him new pages to be inserted into the book. These books are in ring binder form and the old page is removed whilst inserting the new one. It is very important that books having this facility are kept up to date and this is often a task given to secretaries.

An increasing number of reference books, e.g., rule books and certain law reports, are available on CD or obtainable by subscription through the Internet. Additionally, the Internet offers a large amount of free information. There are also many computer database systems which lawyers use to gain information.

Going to court

You may find that at some stage you will be asked to go to court, perhaps with a solicitor or with a barrister. If it is a trial at court, you should check beforehand with the clerk to the barrister attending as to which court you will be in and what time the barrister is to be met. You may find that you will have to do this for the fee earner in any event if he is attending court. It is also important that witnesses, etc. are told where to go and what time to be there. The fee earner will normally tell you who to inform.

If you go to court it will be to assist, e.g., ensuring that witnesses are there and letting them know where to go, perhaps making telephone calls and also to take notes of what is happening. If you do not do shorthand (these days a great deal of legal secretaries are audio secretaries and do not do shorthand) then take a note of as much as you can, jotting down important points. You will find with experience that you know what to note and until then, the person you go to court with will tell you what to note. Some of the important points which may be mentioned at court and which must be noted are those relating to liability (whether one party admits or is found to have responsibility in the case), quantum (amounts of money), any time limits imposed, any adjournments made and any orders made or judgment given.

If you are asked how a judge should be addressed during a court hearing, a High Court judge is called 'My Lord' or 'My Lady', a circuit judge is 'Your Honour', and a District judge is 'Sir' or 'Madam'.

Where a hearing takes place in a courtroom, this is called 'open court' and the judge wears robes and a wig. Hearings other than trials may also take place in the judge's room (this used to be referred to as 'in chambers' and you may still hear the expression). A hearing other than a trial could be, for example, an application to a judge to resolve a particular issue in proceedings relating to a forthcoming trial (see page 114 regarding applications). The judge does not wear robes and wig for a hearing in his room.

The cases to be heard in court on a particular day will usually be listed, and the list will normally be displayed in the court building where it can be easily seen. It will tell you which courtroom the case will be heard in. You will find that if you do attend a court hearing or trial, you may well have to wait for some time before your case comes on. The first hearing of the day will normally start at 10.00 a.m.

When going to court, ensure you have with you any documents relating to the matter, names of anyone you have to meet, a notepad, pen or pencil and some change for the telephone. If you have a mobile phone with you, make sure it is switched off in court. Also ensure that you are smartly dressed—remember you are representing your firm when you are out. If you get to court and are not sure about something, you can ask the court usher, if it is appropriate to do so, or telephone back to your office. Always give yourself plenty of time to get where you are going.

It is essential to remember that you must never talk to a witness in the witness box (and this also means if he is out of the witness box but still under oath, e.g., during a break). Similarly, you must never talk to a juror. This is very important and can amount to contempt of court if you do talk to these people. You should also not approach a witness who is to give evidence for the other party in the case.

Always remember that you must never commit your firm to doing or saying anything unless you have been expressly told to do so by a fee earner. If you are not sure about something—ask. It is always best to keep a record of transactions, conversations, etc. If you are taking a message from a client or other solicitor, you should note the time and date of the conversation and what has been said.

Confidentiality

You may find sometimes that the Press will telephone, especially if your firm is dealing with someone famous or a particularly important or newsworthy matter. You should *never*, without a fee earner's permission, give any information whatsoever to the Press or anyone else. Do not even admit that you are acting for a certain client or dealing with a particular matter.

If people from outside the firm have access to your office or you can be overheard on the telephone, you must similarly remember the importance of confidentiality. Do not leave papers lying around on your desk for all to see and be discreet when talking on the telephone. Confidentiality is of the utmost importance. You must *never* discuss anything that you find out at work with anyone outside the office.

Common sense

There are some further useful points to remember.

If the person you are working for leaves something for you to do and goes out and you think you will not finish it by the time he wanted it, or before you go home—never just leave it—always ask a responsible person what should be done.

If someone calls in to the office or is at the other end of the telephone and the person dealing with the matter is not available, do not make decisions yourself about legal matters. You must always refer them to a responsible person in the firm. You must *never* commit the firm to anything.

The golden rule is—if you are in any doubt about anything—ask.

TEST YOURSELF ON CHAPTER 1

Test your knowledge by completing this assignment. If you find that you have difficulty with anything, read the chapter again until you are happy with your answers.

1. What is the DX? How would you find another firm's DX number? How would you address an envelope to a DX address?

2. If you cannot contact someone to find out their postcode and the information is not on the file, how might you be able to obtain this information?

3. What is meant by 'engrossing' a document?

4. If something is referred to on a plan as being 'hatched in red', what does this mean? What are 'T' marks on a plan?

5. If you are certifying a document as being a true copy of an original, what should be written on the copy document?

6. What is the 'testimonium' and an 'attestation clause'? If an individual has to sign a deed, give an example of how you would write the clause where he must place his signature.

7. What is meant by 'client care'?

8. If you are going to court to assist a solicitor or barrister, what sort of things would you take with you?

9. *Ashton* v *Turner* [1980] 3 All ER 870. If you saw this written down, what would it mean to you? If you have access to Law Reports, see if you can find this particular case.

10. Now go through the chapter and if there are any words that are unfamiliar to you or that you cannot spell, write or type them correctly several times until you feel you know them.

2

Quick introduction to the Internet

The Internet is simply a huge, world-wide computer network. Thus, you can be sitting at a computer in your office and you can be looking at information which has come from New York, Tokyo or, in fact, anywhere in the world.

The Internet is accessed either through a telephone line (known as a dial-up connection) or through broadband access. Broadband is a data transmission channel that sends and receives information on a special type of cable which has a wider bandwidth than ordinary telephone lines. This makes it much faster than a dial-up connection.

There are several systems running on the Internet including e-mail, chat rooms and the World Wide Web (or web for short). The web is what most of us utilise when accessing information on the Internet, using Windows and a mouse.

Before you can access the Internet, you must have the right software—browser software and e-mail software. Browser software enables the user to access the information available on the web. You need this software in the same way that you need other software to access material written in that other software. For example, if someone sends you a document written in Word, you will need to have Word installed on your PC to be able to read that document. Similarly, if you want to read a web page, you need to have a web browser. Microsoft's Internet Explorer is pre-installed on all Windows PCs.

You will also need an Internet Service Provider (ISP). This is a company which has set up one or more powerful computers equipped to make a connection to the Internet 'backbone' and which provide the link to the Internet for the users. Well known names here include MSN, AOL, Tiscali and ntl. Most ISPs provide their own browser software to users.

Web pages and addresses

When we access the Internet, we will see one web page. Groups of pages together are referred to as a site or website.

Each website has an address, properly called a Uniform Resource Locator (URL). These are the sets of characters usually starting in http://www (http stands for hypertext transfer protocol and www stands for World Wide Web). The place to type in the address of a website that you are looking for is usually at the top of the screen just below the navigation toolbar (see later)—it will normally be called Address or Location. When typing in a web address, it is not always necessary to type in the http://. Web addresses are not complicated, they just let your browser know where to locate a particular web page.

After these initial sets of letters, you will then see the actual name of the website, e.g., OUP (for The Oxford University Press site), which might end in perhaps, .com; .co.uk; .org.uk; .gov.uk—there are quite a few more. These suffixes simply tell you how that particular organisation has registered itself, for example, .com means that the organisation is an international company, .co.uk means that it is a company in the UK, .org.uk means it is a non-commercial organisation in the UK; .gov.uk is the UK Government, and so on. There are quite a few different suffixes. When saying a web address out loud, a full stop is referred to as 'dot'.

If you know the web address of a particular site that you wish to visit, you can just type the address in the appropriate space on your browser (at the top where it says 'Address' or 'Location') and press the Enter key on your keyboard. Ensure you type the web address correctly, including any full stops, hyphens or underscores, etc., otherwise it will not work.

When a web page is printed, it will usually have its web address in the bottom left-hand corner of the page and the date in the bottom right-hand corner. Therefore, if you have printed a page but have not kept a note of the web address, you will still be able to trace where the page came from by looking at the address at the bottom. You can also 'book-mark' your favourite sites (see page 44).

Web pages are written in a specific format—mainly HTML (hypertext markup language) at the moment. However, if your firm is small and thinking of designing its own website, it is not necessary to know HTML—there are many software packages that will translate your text into HTML for you.

When you look at a page of information on the screen, you may see a number of key-words underlined. Underlining on a web page usually denotes that the underlined word links to something else. Another way of knowing that text or graphics may be linked to another document will be that when you move your mouse pointer over that text or graphic, the mouse pointer will change to a hand symbol. The full name for these links is hyperlinks, and clicking on any of these takes you to the document referred to in the link and brings that up on the screen. That page may well be on a quite different computer in a different country or it may be just down the road.

So that companies and other organisations can have their own specific name for a site or e-mail address, they may register a domain name. This name cannot be used by anyone else and it will stay the same even if the user changes their ISP (see above). For example, if someone currently gets their e-mail through AOL, their e-mail address might be something like smith@aol.com. However, if they register a domain name for themselves called, say, law-firm.co.uk, their web address would be www.lawfirm.co.uk and their e-mail address would then be smith@lawfirm.co.uk, rather than having to have aol.com in their address.

Navigating the Internet

Browsing or 'surfing' is what you do when you use a browser to access the web, follow links and collect information. When you click on a link, your browser is, in effect, sending out a message asking for the page you are hoping to connect to. If the program or computer that looks after that page is running and if it is not excessively busy, it will transmit the document back to your browser and it will be displayed on your screen.

The browser window

The main browser window is the area below the address bar. The browser window displays the information, including text, images and anything else on the web page that you are looking at. If the page is too large to fit in your screen, there will be scroll bars on the right and the bottom of the browser window and these will allow you to move the page so that you can see all the information.

As with other software, users may have different versions of a web browser, and these are continually updated and changed. Most browsers will provide similar facilities enabling the user to carry out functions on the web page and navigate the Internet.

At the top of the browser window below the title of the document is the menu bar. This will usually consist of at least File; Edit; Help and a few others as described below. Some browsers will not have all of these on their menu bar (indeed, some will have more), but if you cannot find the function you want, look in the browser's Help section.

File   As well as a few other things, the file menu allows you to save or print web pages.

Edit   Allows you to copy, paste, select all of a page and find something on a page.

View   You can select which toolbars are displayed (e.g., whether the navigation toolbar and address bar are shown on your screen). You can also change the text size and choose to browse in a screen taking up the whole window—without any toolbars showing.

Favourites   This will show your list of favourite sites. You can add to these here and also organise your sites into different folders.

Tools   Here you can view links that are related to the site you are currently visiting (if any are available) and you can also access Internet options, for example, to change your home page (see under Home below).

If you find that your PC takes a long time to load pages from the Internet, you have the option in your browser to turn off images and sound. Therefore, the web page will download quickly but you will not get any images or sound on the page you look at. If an image is meant to be on the page and it is not there, you will often see an empty box with a cross in the corner. Many sites show text where images are or should be so that even if you do not receive the image, you will know what it is. Also, if you are fed up with waiting for a page to load, you can click on any of the links that have already appeared on that page and your browser will then forget about loading the rest of the page, and will follow the link you have clicked on instead. You can prevent images, etc., from downloading by going into Tools and then Internet Options.

Help   This is your browser's help files.

Go   Not all browsers have this option—it can be used instead of the Enter key to take you to a web page after you have entered a web address in the address bar.

Navigation toolbar

The navigation toolbar consists of 'buttons' at the top of your browser below the menu bar. These buttons are options specific to browser software and will therefore differ according to which browser you have installed on your PC. When it is not possible to use a particular button, it will turn grey.

Back   This button will take you back to the pages you have visited in one session—once you leave the Internet, the button cannot be used to go back to pages visited in other sessions.

Forward   If you have just gone back a page, this button will take you forward again.

Stop   If you are trying to visit a page and it seems to take a long time loading, or you decide that you do not want to go to that page after all, you can use this button to stop the proceedings and then go somewhere else.

Refresh   When you view a web page on your computer, that page is in fact downloaded on to the computer. Therefore if, while you are looking at the page, it is changed in some way by the person who maintains it, you will still be looking at the old page which has been downloaded on to your computer. If you click on Refresh or Reload, you will get a fresh copy of the page. Of course, you do not need to click Refresh or Reload every time you visit any page. Once your computer has left the page and gets it again for you another time, it will give you the newest version.

Home   This will take you right back to the original page you started from. You can change your choice of home page—the page that was opened when you started your browser. Different browsers may have different methods of changing the home page, e.g., in MS Internet Explorer, you can change your choice of home page from the Internet Options under Tools in the menu bar.

Search   This will open a search engine page in the left hand side of your browser. You can fill in a blank space—a search box—with keywords describing what you are looking for and press the Enter key. A list of web pages containing those keywords and with links to those pages will then appear in your browser (see below—Searching the Internet).

Favourites   Here you can bookmark pages you think you will want to return to another time. When you are on a page you like, click on the Favourites button and add the page to your list by choosing the Add option on the menu. You will not then have to remember the web address and you can go straight to it another time if you just click on the name in your Favourites list (which is accessed in the same way).

History   Shows you web addresses that you have visited over a specified time, e.g., over the last week.

Mail   If your PC is set up for e-mail you can read and send e-mail or links by clicking on this button.

Print   You can print a web page by clicking first on the relevant page and then on the Print button. If you use the keyboard shortcut for printing (Ctrl + P) rather than clicking on this print icon, you will bring up a print dialogue box and you can experiment with further print options—you can print documents linked to that page, or a table of the page's links, or print in landscape or portrait, as well as a few other options.

There are many shortcuts for using browsers just as there are shortcuts in other applications, such as Word. Indeed, some of the shortcuts in Explorer are the same as some of the shortcuts for Word, e.g., if you press Ctrl + Find in both Word and Explorer, you will be able to find a word or particular words in a document—the dropdown menus will generally give these. It is well worth discovering the shortcuts that will be most useful to you. Some keyboard shortcuts are given later in this chapter.

Searching the Internet

If you know the address of the site you want, all well and good—you can just type this in the address bar, which is located under the toolbar. If you do not know the address or are just looking for information on a particular subject, then you will have to make a search. There is a Search button on the browser which will take you to a search page. Alternatively, if you know it, you can type in the web address of a particular search engine. Some of the search engines are listed in the Useful Web Addresses section at the end of this book. A search engine will search a whole database of web pages and try to give you results (often far too many) containing the words you searched for.

There are many different search engines and you will get to know which ones you prefer and which are the best for the type of information you are looking for. It is not realistic to go into detail here for each one—ideally, you should experiment with a few—they all have help pages which will tell you how to get the best results.

The Internet contains a huge amount of information but it does not provide all the information that there is on any one subject, so you may still need to use other resources. Once you have found information on the Internet, be aware of a few of the pitfalls in using it.

Although there is a vast amount of well researched, valid information on the Internet, be careful about using information if you do not know its source, especially for legal or financial matters. If someone puts good, sound information on to a website, they will usually say who they are and what the source of their information is. For example, someone may give statistics about certain matters and in that event, you should be sure that the information comes from a reliable source. People and companies may also provide information that is biased in some way, particularly if they are looking at it from a certain country's point of view or because they are carrying adverts on their site.

Not everyone keeps their web pages up to date, so some of the information found could well be old. This may not matter in certain instances, but many times it will be vital to have up-to-date information, so ensure that you are using a reliable site.

Having mentioned some of the drawbacks, there is a huge wealth of excellent information out there and the Internet is an invaluable research tool.

A few general guidelines on searching

Although generally the basic rules apply to searching, different search engines often have their own ways of refining searches and advanced searching. It is therefore well worth getting to grips with one or two search engines and knowing how to search well within those.

Search engines are 'robots' that, once you have typed in the keywords you are looking for, will go out and look for web pages containing these words. They will, very quickly, produce on your screen a list of sites (a 'results' page). This page will normally show the first ten results or 'hits' (listed in an order of priority dictated by the search engine) and the bottom of the page will usually link to other pages with the next ten hits. Some search engines will allow you to change the number of hits shown per page. The results page will show a few lines of text including your keywords and will give a link to the site it has found, so that you can just click on the link and quickly visit that site to see whether it is what you were looking for. If it is not want you want, you can click on the Back button and go back to your results page. Unless you are careful about what you type into the search box, you can receive back thousands of results, many of which are not at all what you are looking for. Therefore, you must learn how to use search engines and define reasonably what it is you are looking for. There are some general tips for searching below, but the various search engines can differ slightly. It is therefore best to get to know a couple of search engines so that they can be used to their best advantage. Each search engine site contains additional help pages and instructions on using it.

On the search page there is a space or box where you will type in the keywords relating to your search. If you have two or more keywords in the box, e.g., "Central Law Training", it is best to type these words in double quotes as shown. This is because if you just type the two words without quotes, the search engine will look for matches on 'Central', 'Law' and 'Training' as separate words and you will get thousands of irrelevant results, but if you put the words in quotes it will treat the words as one item and search only for matches for that item, thereby giving you more relevant results or 'hits'.

If you use all lower case letters, the search is generally not case sensitive, but if you are looking for a proper name and do not want anything else to be brought up, it is best to type it using upper case where appropriate, e.g., "Central Law Training"—that way the search will be limited.

Many search engines have advanced features—you may have to click on their 'advanced search' link to put more detail into your search, although you can still try additional ways of searching from the original search page. You can make a more specific search if, for example, you were looking for information about litigation on the Central Law Training site, you could type in "Central Law Training" +litigation (do not put a space after the plus sign). This should bring up matches for pages that appear to be relevant to litigation as well as to Central Law Training.

We could further broaden the search. For example, we might think that the word 'contentious' might be used as much as 'litigation'. Therefore, our search could be something like "Central Law Training" +litigation OR contentious. In some search engines, extra words may have to be put into brackets.

You may also wish to exclude certain words from your search. For example, we might bring up thousands of hits with a topic in them that we do not want. If we made our search as above and got hits that also related to family law that we did not want, we could include in our search '−family' (not the quotes here, just the minus sign and the word. Do not put a space after the minus sign).

Additionally, you can look at just the title of the document. Most people will give their pages a title name which relates to that page. If you wish to search just through titles and you wanted to find websites where the titles of pages contained the words 'legal secretary', you could put a 't' followed by a colon in front of your keyword(s), thus t: "legal secretary".

You can also use 'wildcards' in many search engines. This is the asterisk symbol (*) and it can be used to represent anything else, for example, if we type in secretar* we will get results for secretary, secretarial, secretaries and anything else that begins with those first eight letters. Similarly, if we type in centrali*e, this would allow for the differences in English and American spelling and we would get results for centralise or centralize. However, some of the search engines do not use wildcards.

Some search engines have simplified search methods and offer boxes on the screen to type in words to be included or excluded from the search, rather than typing 'AND' or 'OR', etc.

To summarise searching

The search engines may vary slightly so get to know how best to search in a few of them. Remember, you may have to select the Advanced Search page from the search engine you are using and get to know the requirements of that particular search engine's advanced search facilities.

"Double quotes" group words together so they are searched together as one keyword.

Use capital letters at the beginning of a proper name, e.g., "Central Law Training".

When searching for more than one term and you want to ensure both terms are found in the result, use one of the following to indicate 'and':

+

AND

&

To get a choice, for example, if one or two terms are similar in documents and you would like to get results showing both, then use OR.

To indicate that you do not want results to show a particular word or phrase, use NOT or the minus sign.

When using AND, OR or NOT (also known as Boolean searching), it is best to put these words into capitals as some search engines will not recognise them otherwise. You can also use other search terms such as NEAR; AND NOT but rather than go into all these here, it is best to check them out for yourself.

Some additional terms will need to be enclosed in brackets in some search engines, e.g., secretary and (legal or law).

Try to use specific terms—if you typed in just 'law', you would get thousands of results—be more specific about what you are looking for.

Check out the different ways of searching offered by various search engines. As well as the individual search engine sites themselves, there are various sites on the web that offer help and advice on searching—a few of these are listed under 'Searching' in the Useful Web Addresses section at the back of this book.

You can limit your search to the UK only or to some other geographical area either by using this facility in the search engine or by visiting a country-specific search engine. Alternatively, when you type into the search box the keywords that you are searching for, you could also try just adding on to the end of your keyword(s) +UK.

There are also directory sites, such as Yahoo! A directory categorises websites by subject matter. You can search a directory or just click on the name of the relevant category on the directory page and this will then give you a sub-category, and so on so that you can 'drill down' until you find what you are looking for.

Web pages can sometimes be very lengthy so it is useful to know that you can use the Find command to locate something on a particular web page once you are on that page. This command works the same way as the Find command on word processing software, usually by going to the Edit menu and then on to Find, or by using a shortcut.

Keeping what you find

Once you have reached information that you would like to keep, you can either save it on to your computer (or a disk), copy it into a document or print it.

To save a web document, you can use the File, Save As command whereby you can save the document as plain text. You can also highlight text you want to copy and then use the Copy command, which will copy the text on to the clipboard. You can then paste this into another application, such as a Word document.

You can save a web address by highlighting it in the address bar and copying it, and then pasting it into a document or an e-mail if you want to send the link to someone else.

Graphics on web pages can be saved by putting your mouse pointer over the graphic and right-clicking on the mouse. A box will appear on the screen giving you the option to save the image and you can then say which directory on your computer you would like to save it in. Be careful of downloading too many graphics because they take up a lot of space on your computer.

Be wary in any event of downloading anything from a site you do not know—there are a lot of viruses around. Also, if you are copying something from a website, whether it is text or an image, remember the copyright issues—work on a website is created by someone else and the copyright will usually belong to them unless they specifically say otherwise. On top of this, the firm you work for will have a policy on downloading material from the Internet, so it is best to check about this before you download or copy anything.

Many sites will give you the option of downloading a document in HTML format, or Word, or .pdf format. If something is in .pdf format, this means that it looks just like the original document, for example, many brochures, publications and forms are put into .pdf format so that they keep the appearance of the printed version, with the same page numbers, layout and graphics, even though they are on a website. If you download something in .pdf format, you will only be able to read it if you have Adobe Acrobat Reader. This can be downloaded from the Adobe site (see section on Useful Web Addresses at the back of this book) and once you have Acrobat Reader on your PC, you will be able to view any documents that are in .pdf format.

Because your computer stores copies of web pages you have visited, you should clear these out from time to time. These files are called temporary Internet files and you can remove them direct from your computer or via your browser.

When browsing on the Internet, you may come across 'cookies'. Cookies are small files passed on to your hard drive by a website that you have visited so that the website will know certain information about you. When a website sends you a cookie, the cookie is stored on the hard drive of your computer. When you then connect back to the same website that sent you the cookie, the information that was stored in the cookie is sent back to that website (or, to be exact, the server where the website is stored). Therefore if, for example, when you originally looked at that website, you entered your name and address for some reason, or you interacted in some other way with that site, the cookie probably stored most of that information. Then, when you next view the site, you would not need to re-enter your name and address or other information you originally gave because the cookie is sent back to that website so that it can retrieve the information you originally gave. Another reason for sending a cookie would be advertising. If you were viewing a shopping website and bought a large amount of dog biscuits and other doggie stuff, a cookie might store that information. Then the next time you viewed that website, there might be information on other dog food and products because the cookie has the information that you are interested in dogs.

You do not have to allow cookies on to your hard disk—most browsers are set up so that you can specify if you want to receive a prompt before a site puts a cookie on to your hard disk and you can make the choice as to whether you want it. Additionally, you can prevent cookies from being accepted altogether. Only the information that you provide, or the choices you make while visiting a website, can be stored in a cookie. For example, the cookie cannot find out your e-mail address unless you have typed it into that particular website. If you do allow a cookie on to your hard drive, it does not give that or any other site access to the rest of your computer. You can delete cookies from your computer but some websites will not then work properly for you or will not remember information you have previously given.

Intranets and extranets

As well as the Internet, there are intranets and extranets.

An intranet is similar to the Internet, but it is normally specific to only one organisation or set of people—it is not on the World Wide Web—and cannot be accessed from outside that organisation. Many firms have their own intranet which provides information about the firm and the people in it, as well as other firm-specific information.

An extranet is similar to an intranet. It gives certain people who are external to the firm access to specific information, usually through a password. Depending on the content of the extranet, everyone within the firm will not necessarily have access to it either. It is often used for clients so that they can access information relating to their matters or information the firm has agreed to provide only to them.

Chat rooms

You can access various discussion forums or newsgroups on the Internet, known as chat rooms. These are places where you can post messages and other people who have accessed the chat room can read the messages and post a reply to them in the chat room. There is probably a chat room for every subject you can imagine. Quite often chat rooms are regulated by the organiser of the chat room, usually called a moderator.

E-mail

Short for electronic mail, e-mails are really just small text files stored on a computer somewhere. An e-mail address is a name, followed by the @ symbol and then the name of the computer that will receive the message. Here is an example of an e-mail address:

bookorders.uk@oup.com

When you have an e-mail address, you have a little piece of disk storage reserved for you on your ISP's computer to receive those e-mails addressed to you.

An e-mail goes virtually instantly and is extremely cheap. You can prepare long and complicated documents off line (i.e., without being online) and then make your connection when you are ready. You will only pay for the few seconds that it takes the computer to send your e-mail—generally at a local rate. This is because you will be dialling in to your ISP on a local rate even if you are sending your e-mail to Hong Kong.

You can attach documents and other files to a simple message and the document can then be read by the software on the PC of the person who is receiving it. This is a major advantage over fax, to add to the advantages of speed and cheapness. However, it is sometimes advisable before sending an attachment to ensure that the recipient has the software to read it and also to ensure that the size of the file you are sending to them is not too large. Be cautious, however, about opening attachments on e-mails from people or organisations you do not know of—many viruses are sent that way.

As with your web browser, you should explore all the options and help facilities available to you in your e-mail so that you can make the most of it. There are many things you can do in e-mail, such as creating address books; sorting by date, subject, sender; creating different folders; and having a personalised signature added to your e-mails. Once you are happy that you no longer need to keep your e-mail, you should delete it or move it to another folder so that you do not clog up your system.

When sending e-mails, although you are not seeing the recipient or writing a formal letter, bear in mind who is receiving it. Do not put anything in an e-mail that you would not actually say to someone. It is quite easy to be very casual when e-mailing, but remember that a real person will be on the receiving end. It is also advisable to remember that an e-mail is as legally binding as a letter. As in a letter, you should also check your spelling and grammar. Most legal offices will have an e-mail policy which should always be adhered to. E-mail guidelines for solicitors are available from The Law Society's website.

Even if you do not have e-mail, but have access to the Internet, you can set up your own e-mail address on the Internet via sites such as Yahoo! or Hotmail. These are free and if you have an e-mail address with any of these, you can access your e-mail at any time from anywhere as long as you have Internet access (although, of course, some organisations do not permit employees access to such sites from within their organisation). However, this sort of e-mail address will include the name of the organisation providing the service, rather than your own company's name, e.g., johnsmith@yahoo.com means that this is an e-mail address provided by Yahoo!.

E-mail etiquette

Although e-mails are informal, there are certain unwritten rules that should be adhered to.

Give your e-mail a suitable heading so that the recipient can see what it is about before it is opened.

Do not type all the text in capital letters—this indicates that you are shouting at the recipient!

Do not send out unwanted messages, such as advertising, to unknown people. When people do this to large groups, it is known as 'spamming'. In the UK, there are now certain legal provisions and restrictions on sending marketing e-mail messages. Unfortunately, there is still a problem because most of the spam sent to the UK originates from another part of the world. However, software is available that can help to filter out unwanted e-mails.

You may also come across acronyms and emoticons. Acronyms and other abbreviations are used to convey a phrase quickly, for example:

BFN—Bye For Now
IMO—In my Opinion
LOL—Lots of laughs
TX—Thanks
Btw—By the way
Msg—message

Emoticons, or 'smileys' are little drawings using the typing keys (turn them on their side and you will see):

:-)
basic smile
,-)
a winking, happy smiley
(:-(
unhappy
:-(
sad

Many people find acronyms and smileys annoying, so use them sparingly unless you know the recipient. It is not advisable to use them in a professional e-mail.

E-commerce

E-commerce is a term used for trading over the Internet. Besides online trading by people like Tesco or Amazon.com, many lawyers have set up e-commerce sites whereby legal services can be bought over the Internet, such as ready-made Wills. There are many trading sites on the Internet, and before you part with your credit card number, ensure that the site you are dealing with is secure. You will usually be able to tell whether a site is secure because it will display a locked padlock icon on the status bar (at the bottom of the page). Double-clicking the icon will show the page's security certificate. It is also wise to know that the company you are dealing with is reputable, either by your previous dealings or someone you know having dealt with the company or by their reputation.

How lawyers might use the Internet

(a) To communicate with clients, official bodies and others in the legal profession.

(b) To keep up to date, on a regular basis, with legal issues, Bills, Acts, Statutory Instruments, cases in progress and judgments. Legal research can be carried out effectively using the Internet, including subscribing to passworded sites with access to online texts that can easily be searched, viewed and printed, rather than having to refer to numerous and lengthy text books.

(c) Many organisations including HM Courts Service, the Land Registry, Companies House, and HM Revenue & Customs offer services that are available online. For example, HM Courts Service offers Money Claim Online (see page 72), as well as the ability to lodge certain documents at certain courts by e-mail. The Land Registry is increasingly developing electronic conveyancing and offers several online facilities. As well as these sort of services, certain sites provide forms online which can be downloaded free of charge. There are indeed many websites that provide information and various other facilities that are extremely useful to lawyers.

(d) It is very useful to be able to access other information sources around the world (not specifically legal), for example, information on medical, scientific, economic, commercial, environmental and social topics, as well as news.

(e) Many areas of law now have a substantial Internet component, for example, electronic commerce, international taxation, defamation, communications, entertainment, liability for content, copyright, trademarks and intellectual property. It would be very difficult to give good advice in any of these areas without understanding a bit about the Internet and how it works.

(f) The Internet can be a medium for attracting new clients, and quite a number of firms are now doing this. Their Internet pages can include articles, publications and other information which attracts their chosen audience and which would be much too expensive to distribute by conventional means.

(g) To provide services to clients. Many law firms provide online advice as well as case management systems (allowing clients to receive reports and to add information relating to their matters) accessed, perhaps, via passworded sites.

It is very important to keep in mind that if you are using your firm's Internet access and e-mail, you must follow any procedures and policies that they have in place.

Some keyboard shortcuts

Instead of pointing and clicking with the mouse, there are many keyboard shortcuts. Just press the relevant key on the keyboard (or if more than one, both together). Depending on your browser, keyboard shortcuts may vary. A few keyboard shortcuts for MS Internet

Explorer 6 are shown below. There are many more for this browser and others. It pays to look at whatever browser you are using to find out the keyboard shortcuts that are handy for you. Most ISPs that have provided browser software will have a list of their keyboard shortcuts in their Help section.

Go back a page	Alt + left arrow
Go forward a page	Alt + right arrow
To find a word or phrase on a page	Ctrl + F
Print	Ctrl + P
Stop a page from downloading	Esc
Help	F1
Refresh	F5
To scroll to the end of a document	Press the down arrow
To scroll to the beginning of a document	Press the up arrow

Some Internet jargon

Address   The unique location of a website, e.g., www.oup.co.uk.

Broadband   The Internet is accessed either through a telephone line (known as a dial-up connection) or through broadband access. Broadband is a data transmission channel that sends and receives information on a special type of cable which has a wider bandwidth than ordinary telephone lines. This makes it much faster than a dial-up connection.

Browser   The software that you need to view pages on the web.

Chat room   A web page where you can send text messages to other people who are visiting that page at the same time as you. There are normally different chat rooms for different subjects.

Cookie   A small file sent to your computer when you visit certain websites and is used by the website to store certain information, such as when you last visited their website and which web pages you have viewed. See also page 48 for further information.

Domain name   Identifies a computer connected to the Internet. Domain names consist of a host name (for Oxford University Press, this is oup) followed by a domain category, such as .com, .co. or .org., and then perhaps a country abbreviation, like .uk. Therefore, the domain name for Oxford University Press is oup.co.uk. This then makes the web address http://www.oup.co.uk. Not everyone has their own domain name and people will often sign up with their ISP to use facilities offered by them, in which case, their web address or e-mail address will normally include the ISP's name too. For example, if someone signed up with AOL, their address could be something like smith@aol.com.

Download   The process of transferring files to your PC from the Internet.

E-mail   Short for electronic mail, it enables you to send messages world-wide across the Internet from one computer to another. You can attach files such as documents and pictures to e-mails. You can also copy an Internet address into an e-mail and send this to someone so that when they receive the e-mail, they can click on the link in their e-mail and that will take them straight to that Internet page (provided of course they are online at the time).

Encryption   If a page is encrypted, this is for security. This is displayed by showing a locked padlock icon on the status bar (at the bottom of the page). Double-clicking the icon will show the page's security certificate.

FAQ (frequently asked questions)   A web page containing a list of commonly asked questions relating to that site, together with the answers.

Gif   This is a suffix after a file name denoting that it is in a particular format—used for certain graphics that can be viewed on web pages.

Home page   The first page you visit when you go to a website.

Html   Hypertext mark-up language. Coding or language used to write web pages.

Http   Hypertext transfer protocol. The system used to transfer web pages over the Internet.

Hyperlink   A link from either text or an image to another part of the same page or another page either within the same website or on a different website. If a link is broken, this means that it is not working properly and access cannot be gained to the linked page or image.

ISP   Internet Service Provider. A company that provides you with Internet access.

Jpeg   This is a suffix after a file name denoting that it is in a particular format—used for certain graphics that can be viewed on web pages.

Link   See hyperlink above.

Modem   Allows two computers to communicate with each other over a telephone line. A modem is normally needed to connect to the Internet.

Offline   You can save or download pages from the Internet and work offline. This means that you can then view these pages when you are not connected to the Internet.

Online   You are online when you are connected to the Internet.

pdf   This is a suffix to a type of file (standing for portable document format). If something is in pdf format, it will normally look just like a printed document (or whatever the original format of the document was). Many online forms are pdf files. You will need software called Acrobat Reader to view a pdf file. This software can be downloaded free of charge from the Adobe site (see Useful Web Addresses section at the back of this book). There is other Adobe software that you can buy which will allow you to create your own pdf files and to work on and save pdf files such as some forms (if the creator of the pdf document or form has made it so that it can be used by others)—Acrobat Reader will allow you to view these files only.

Real time   As something is actually happening, rather than viewing stored information.

Spam   Junk e-mail sent to large groups of people.

Temporary Internet files   Files that you have viewed on the Internet and which are stored on your own PC. They will take up space on your computer and should be periodically deleted. This can usually be done either via your hard drive or your browser.

Thumbnail   A small image used to give a quick preview of a larger image.

URL   Universal Resource Locator. The technical name for the address or location of a website.

Virus   A program designed to infect the files and programs on a computer. It can be passed on in various ways, e.g., downloading from the Internet; sent via e-mail; copied from a floppy disk. You can buy anti-virus software that helps to protect against these.

WAP   Wireless Application Protocol. A system used to access certain websites and e-mail from mobile phones.

Webmaster   The person responsible for maintaining a particular website.

Web Server   A computer which hosts a website or many sites and is permanently online to the Internet. Special software is needed to manage the site, called web server software.

Web space   The space on a ISP's web server which hosts websites. Many ISPs give away free web space so that you can build your own website.

Civil litigation

If you are working in the civil litigation department, you are dealing with matters which involve two or more parties arguing over something which could end up in a court case. This could be a claim for a debt or for damages, e.g., compensation for personal injury resulting from an accident, defamation (slander or libel), breach of contract, or even simply a dispute with a neighbour. Not all such matters end up in court as the great majority are often settled before court proceedings are even started, or during the proceedings. Additionally, alternative methods of resolving disputes, such as through arbitration or mediation, are being encouraged by the courts (see under Alternative Dispute Resolution on page 153).

Proceedings in the courts are known as actions or matters. Generally, an action is a dispute between parties and a matter is a question to be resolved by the court. In the type of actions described in this chapter, the party commencing the action is known as the claimant and the party against whom the action is brought is known as the defendant. The parties are described differently in some other matters and these are dealt with later in their own sections. Most actions or matters have a time limit within which the proceedings may be commenced. For instance, if a person is injured in an accident he must commence court proceedings within three years of the date of the accident, or an action founded on contract must be brought within six years of the date on which the cause of action arose. There is more to this and there are exceptions to these, but the point is that by statute most actions have a set time limit within which proceedings must be brought. This limitation of actions is governed by the Limitation Act 1980.

Once the client consults a solicitor, the solicitor will normally send a 'letter before action' to the other party involved. This contains details of what his client's grievances are and asks the other party to reply within a certain time with his proposals for settlement. In civil litigation, the rules governing court procedures set out guidelines for a letter before action and other matters to be dealt with before court action is commenced. These guidelines are known as pre-action protocols (see page 59). The solicitor must also, where necessary, sort out any funding arrangements such as a conditional fee agreement (see page 34) or legal aid (see Chapter 7). Alternative Dispute Resolution may also be considered. He will also be collecting evidence, having preliminary negotiations with a view to settlement, making enquiries about the other party, etc. and ultimately, if all else fails, he must prepare the matter for trial.

As a result of the Civil Procedure Rules (CPR) that took effect from April 1999, most civil litigation forms and documents are now the same, whether the court involved is the High Court or the county court. Prior to the introduction of the CPR, there were many differences between High Court and county court forms and procedures. Litigation can last a long time and, therefore, because the CPR are relatively new, you may still come across some of the old style forms and documents—some of these are discussed on page 143.

Since the CPR came into effect, court cases are allocated to 'tracks', generally depending on the value of the claim. The tracks are:

(a) the small claims track;

(b) the fast track;

(c) the multi-track.

Further details of these are given on page 95. However, secretaries will not need to worry about which track a case will be allocated to, as this is a decision that will be made by the fee earner in the first instance and, ultimately, by the court.

Throughout this chapter you will see how a fairly typical claim for money progresses. It is fair to say, however, that many cases will be very different, involving injunctions, orders for performance, winding up of companies, arrests of ships and so on. The areas of law you work in will differ greatly because of the particular area of practice of the firm you work for, e.g., personal injury, commercial, entertainment, marine, etc. Each type of specialist litigation has its own special systems and terms, and you can only learn these with experience. Some specialist procedures are still governed by rules which existed before the CPR.

There are many more forms in use than are shown in this book. Even where forms are illustrated, not every page of every form is always given. However, once you are familiar with those shown, others will be easy to complete. Not all firms use all the printed forms—some use their own precedents and in fact if you find you do not have room on a printed form, it can often all be typed onto a plain sheet of A4 paper, but you should always follow the layout of the form and include all the relevant details, including any guidance notes. However, you should check first with the person you are working for that it is permissible not to use the official form. It is worth noting that on HM Courts Service website (http://www.hmcourts-service.gov.uk) there are many forms that can be downloaded to your PC and then completed and printed off, but it is not possible to save the completed form on to your computer without special software. In any event, several companies sell a full range of computerised official forms that can be completed on screen as well as being saved.

Once you have grasped the essentials of an ordinary, straightforward case, you will not go far wrong on other matters.

The Civil Courts

In the structure of the courts, the High Court is a superior court to the county courts. As mentioned on pages 36–37, the English legal system has evolved mainly through case law. This means that inferior courts (county courts, magistrates' courts and certain tribunals) are bound by the decisions made by the High Court. Similarly, the High Court is generally bound by decisions made by the Court of Appeal and the House of Lords. The first time a case is dealt with in court (as opposed to going on to another court by way of appeal) the court is known as the court of first instance.

For a general overview of the structure of the courts in England and Wales, see page 7.

The High Court

The Royal Courts of Justice are based in the Strand in London, with other branches of the High Court, known as District Registries, being in larger towns throughout England and Wales.

The High Court consists of three divisions:

(a) Chancery Division, which deals with matters such as trusts, contentious (i.e., disputed) probate (see Chapter 11), revenue cases and disputes about ownership of land, and also includes the Companies Court and the Patents Court.

(b) Family Division which, as its name implies, deals with family matters such as some defended divorce cases, legitimacy, custody and wardship and adoption (see also Chapter 5). All non-contentious (i.e., undisputed) probate is the responsibility of this division.

(c) The Queen's Bench Division, which is the most used division of the High Court as it deals with all matters which are not specifically allocated to the other divisions (e.g., contract and tort). It also deals with other important matters and includes the Admiralty Court, the Commercial Court and the Technology and Construction Court.

Where the High Court hears a judicial review or case stated (see page 223), this is dealt with by the Administrative and Divisional Court of the High Court.

Generally, appeals against decisions made in the High Court can be made to the Court of Appeal (see Chapter 9).

High Court judges are appointed from the ranks of barristers and solicitors. They hear cases and may be promoted to the Court of Appeal or even to the House of Lords. They also hear some legal matters which may be heard in private and do not have to be heard in open court. These may be heard in a different room within the court or even in a different building. These rooms are known as the judge's room or chambers. As with everything relating to your work, you must not discuss with anyone outside the firm matters which are dealt with in the judge's room.

In the High Court a judge has a clerk to assist him. There is also present during each trial an officer of the court called an associate. The associate records, among other things, any orders made by the judge during the trial, the judgment given and the time occupied by the trial. There are various other court officers but it is not necessary to describe them all in this book.

For the correct ways of referring to judges in a document, see Chapter 13.

In the Royal Courts of Justice in London, interlocutory matters, i.e., those matters which must be dealt with by the court before and after the final trial (but not the trial itself, which is dealt with by a judge), are normally heard by a Master, except where it is requested that a judge be allocated. In the Family Division these matters are dealt with by a District judge of the Principal Registry of the Family Division, and in the Commercial Court, a judge. In District Registries interlocutory matters are dealt with by District judges. All these people have considerable judicial powers.

The county court

There are many county courts throughout England and Wales. Each district has its own county court and a District judge is responsible for his own court. Some of the larger courts in urban areas have more than one District judge, while in some of the smaller areas, courts are grouped together, having just one District judge between them. A District judge is appointed by the Lord Chancellor and is a solicitor or barrister of some years standing. Circuit judges, who travel from one court to another within a particular circuit, also hear cases in the county courts.

The District judge is assisted by clerical staff, who deal with issuing proceedings, keeping the court diaries and records and a whole range of administrative work. The clerical staff come under the supervision of the Court Manager. There is then another department consisting of the court bailiffs who are officers of the court who perform various functions, including personal service of documents and enforcing judgments.

Besides hearing civil litigation cases, some county courts, but not all, may deal with divorce cases, probate, admiralty, bankruptcy and race relations matters. Certain types of proceedings relating to copyright, designs and patents may also be heard in county courts, but an even wider range may be heard in the Patents County Court. Just as a point of interest, in addition to others who have rights of audience at court, registered patent agents have the right to conduct litigation before The Patents County Court. At the Central London County Court, there is also what is known as the Central London County Court Business List. Certain actions may be commenced at that court for inclusion in the business list if they are business actions (there are certain criteria to be fulfilled).

For the correct ways of referring to judges, see Chapter 13.

Sittings, vacations and court office hours

The High Court has four sittings or terms a year. These are known as the Michaelmas, Hilary, Easter and Trinity sittings. When there is no court sitting (except for certain matters) these periods are known as vacations. There is one Long Vacation which lasts from the beginning of August to the end of September. There are shorter vacations—the Christmas, Easter and Whitsun vacations.

Sittings and vacations are as follows:

(a) Michaelmas sitting is from 1 October to 21 December and is followed by the Christmas Vacation.

(b) Hilary sitting is from 11 January to the Wednesday before Easter Sunday and is followed by the Easter Vacation.

(c) Easter sitting is from the second Tuesday after Easter Sunday to the Friday before the Spring Holiday and is followed by the Whitsun Vacation.

(d) Trinity sitting is from the second Tuesday after the Spring Holiday to the end of July and is followed by the Long Vacation.

Some business is carried on in the courts during the vacations but the court office hours are shorter than during sitting or term time. In county courts, business is as usual during vacation times but the court office may close earlier in the afternoons and there will normally be a reduction in numbers of the judiciary (judges, etc.) in attendance.

The courts are normally not open at weekends or bank holidays. Generally, office hours for the courts are 10 a.m. to 4 p.m.

Civil Procedure Rules

The Civil Procedure Rules (CPR) are a relatively recent introduction and it is hoped that they will enable the courts to deal with cases in a more time-saving way and with less expense.

Generally, the CPR apply to all civil litigation proceedings commenced since the Rules came into force on 26 April 1999, except some with their own specialist rules.

The CPR are divided into numbered Parts and are referred to by their relevant number, e.g., CPR Part 6.2(1), which would mean we are referring to subsection (1) of section 2 of Part 6. Nearly all the Parts are supplemented by Practice Directions which bear the same number as the Part to which they refer, so Part 6 would have a corresponding Practice Direction 6. A Practice Direction will give further information on its corresponding Rule.

Amendments to the CPR are made fairly often and all amendments can be found on the website of the Department for Constitutional Affairs (formerly the Lord Chancellor's Department) where, in fact, the CPR may be found in their entirety. Of course, the rules are also published as hard copy.

Before commencing court proceedings

When solicitors are first consulted in a potential litigation case, they will try to resolve the matter without having to go to court. The solicitor acting for the aggrieved party will write to the other party or his solicitor, and they will then try to reach an amicable settlement. The aggrieved party's solicitor will write first, setting out what it is that his client is claiming, and will say in the letter that if no satisfactory reply is received within a certain time, he will commence court proceedings. This type of letter is referred to as a 'letter before action'. There may be a specific pre-action protocol (see below) that deals with the information a letter before action must contain, as well as timescales to be adhered to before proceedings are issued.

Pre-action protocols

For some types of proceedings, there are specific guidelines that apply to letters before action and the preliminary information to be exchanged between solicitors. These guidelines are known as pre-action protocols. The protocols are set out in the CPR and contain specimen letters and details of what should be done at what stage by the solicitors before any court proceedings are issued. The objectives of pre-action protocols are to encourage the early exchange of all information; to enable the parties to try to reach a settlement before court proceedings are started and, if court proceedings cannot be avoided, to ensure that the proceedings are managed efficiently. If a pre-action protocol is relevant to any potential court proceedings and a party does not comply with that protocol, they may be penalised by the court.

The pre-action protocols currently approved are those relating to personal injury; clinical disputes; construction and engineering disputes; defamation; professional negligence; judicial review; disease and illness claims; and housing disrepair cases. It is envisaged that there will be further protocols relating to other areas in due course. Where there is no approved protocol, the rules set out in quite a lot of detail how the parties are expected to act. This includes reasonable behaviour in the exchange of information and documents and generally trying to avoid the issue of proceedings.

Settling a case without going to court

Over the last few years, methods of settling disputes without going to court have been actively encouraged. Since the introduction of the CPR, in many cases, there is provision that the parties must try to settle before issuing court proceedings, court being a last resort. The court will allow time for attempts to be made to settle the case. See Chapter 4 for information on Alternative Dispute Resolution.

Commencing proceedings

High Court proceedings will be issued, i.e., the action will be commenced, in either the Central Office of the Royal Courts of Justice in London or in one of the District Registries of the High Court in England and Wales. Because procedures can vary in the High Court depending on which Division the proceedings are commenced in, where this chapter mentions High Court procedures, it will refer to an ordinary action for a claim for damages in the Queen's Bench Division unless otherwise stated.

The courts which are designated to hear multi-track trials and some fast track trials are known as Civil Trial Centres. There are over 50 civil trial centres throughout the country and a case which has not been started in one of them, or has been started in the Royal Courts of Justice in London, will normally be transferred to a civil trial centre if it is appropriate to do so.

County court proceedings are usually commenced in the court most convenient to the claimant or his solicitors, but may be transferred at a later stage to the defendant's home court (see page 79).

The Civil Procedure Rules are the rules now governing most claims in the High Court and the county court. However, certain procedures will still be governed by old rules, namely the Rules of the Supreme Court for some High Court procedures and the County Court Rules for some county court procedures. The Rules of the Supreme Court are often referred to and abbreviated as 'RSC'. You may come across a reference such as 'RSC O. 14 r.1' which means 'Rules of the Supreme Court, Order 14, rule 1'. County Court Rules are usually abbreviated to 'CCR'. The Civil Procedure Rules are abbreviated to 'CPR', e.g., 'Part 20 CPR'. The books containing the Rules of the Supreme Court and the County Court Rules are *The Supreme Court Practice* known as the 'White Book', and *The Civil Court Practice* known as the 'Green Book' because of the colour of their covers. Both books contain or have supplements referring to the Civil Procedure Rules, which are also published separately in various formats. The CPR do not generally apply to matters such as insolvency proceedings, some probate, family proceedings and certain other matters which have their own rules and regulations. In any event, the rule books will not be something that you, as a secretary, will particularly need to worry about.

If the solicitor has written his letter before action and no satisfactory reply has been received, or it has not been possible to settle the case, then it is time to commence proceedings. The first step is to complete a Claim Form (see below).

Regarding financial value, currently, a claim may be started in the High Court where:

(a) The claimant expects to recover more than £15,000 (or, for a personal injury claim, he must expect to recover more than £50,000 in respect of pain, suffering and loss of amenity).

(b) It is a specific type of claim governed by a statute which states that claims of that type must be commenced in the High Court.

(c) It is a claim which needs to be in a specialist High Court list.

Claims must be started in a county court if the claimant expects to receive:

(a) not more than £15,000 or;

(b) less than £50,000 in respect of pain, suffering and loss of amenity in a personal injury claim.

Where a claim has no financial value, it will be allocated to the track (see page 95) which the court considers to be the most appropriate for it, taking into consideration such factors as the nature of the remedy sought and the complexity of the case.

We are going to deal here mainly with an action for a claim for money. For example purposes, most of the completed forms and documents shown here are for a claim in the county court but High Court forms and documents are in the same format.

Payment of court fees

Fees are payable to the court at various stages of the proceedings when certain forms are to be issued by the court. Your office will undoubtedly have a list of these fees but if you are not sure, you can telephone the relevant court to confirm whether a fee is payable and how much it is. There are different fees for different court procedures and for different types of proceedings, such as family proceedings.

Cheques for court fees should normally be made payable to HM Courts Service (HMCS). When posting a document to the court to be issued, you should include a stamped, addressed envelope so that the court can return the relevant papers. However, if you are on the DX (see page 20), this may not be necessary as the court will usually return anything to your firm through the DX.

The Claim Form and Particulars of Claim

To issue court proceedings for a claim for money or damages, a Claim Form (Form N1) must be completed.

The Claim Form should be typed, but if it is being completed by hand, it should be in black ink and written in capital letters. With the claim form there are notes for the defendant on replying to the claim form. Once the Claim Form is complete, you should photocopy it, together with the notes for the defendant. The number of copies required are one copy for your firm's file, one copy for the court and one copy for each defendant. The forms will then be sent or taken to the court office, together with the appropriate fee. One Claim Form may be used to start more than one claim, if it is appropriate to do so. Correspondence to a court should be addressed to the Court Manager.

The Claim Form must include concise details of the claim (called the Particulars of Claim—see below). The Particulars of Claim will either be typed on to the Claim Form itself or attached to it, or may even follow later on (within a specified time limit).

As a general guide, the Claim Form will normally expire after four months, i.e., it must be served (see page 73) within four months of being issued by the court, or six months where it is to be served outside England and Wales—otherwise it may become invalid. There are exceptions to this and extensions of time may be applied for but it is not necessary to go into detail here.

The Claim Form must contain the following information:

The heading

The heading of the Claim Form must give the name of the court in which the claim is to be started and, if the claim is to be in the High Court, the division or district registry (see page 57 for information on the divisions of the High Court). This information will be inserted into the box at the top right-hand corner of the front page of the claim form and will be in one of the following formats:

(a) For a claim in a county court:

'In the *Southtown* County Court'. (You must insert the correct name of the court.)

(b) For a claim in a District registry of the High Court:

'In the High Court of Justice *Queen's Bench* Division' (inserting the correct division of the court) and directly beneath that:

'*Southtown* District Registry' (inserting the name of the District Registry)

(c) For a claim in the Royal Courts of Justice in London:

'In the High Court of Justice *Queen's Bench* Division' (insert the correct division of the court) and directly beneath that:

'Royal Courts of Justice'.

See also the example forms and documents in this book for layout.

Where an action has been included in a specialist court, e.g., Central London County Court Business List, Patents Court, etc., all documents relating to the action must be marked at the top (right-hand corner on court forms) beneath the name of the court, with words indicating the specialist court, e.g., 'Business List'; 'Patents Court'. Where a claim relates to Chancery business and it is issued in the High Court, it should be marked in the appropriate place, as shown above, 'Chancery Division' and if it is issued in the county court, it should be marked 'Chancery Business'.

The court will allocate a number to the claim after they have received the Claim Form. The claim number will be something like HQ 2005 No.1234. The 'H' is for High Court, and the 'Q' shows that it has been issued in the Queen's Bench Division. A claim issued in the Chancery Division will commence 'HC'. This will be followed by the year of issue and then the actual number allocated by the court. Numbering in the county court may vary according to which county court issues the claim.

All this information, i.e., the court or division where the action is proceeding; the claim number (once a number has been allocated by the court); the name of each party and the status of each party, e.g., claimant or defendant, is known as the 'title' of the action and all court documents should include this information at the top of the document.

There are special procedures for some other types of claim, but these need not be dealt with here.

Claimant and defendant details

Where a party to an action is an individual, all known forenames and surname must be included, stating whether Mr, Mrs, Miss, Ms, or any other title, such as Dr. The residential address must be given, including postcode.

Other information describing parties to the proceedings must be included on the Claim Form, where appropriate. When completing the form with any of the details given below, you should type the relevant party's name where italics are shown here, but do not type in italics.

A party may be trading under a name that is not his own, e.g., he may be the proprietor of a small business. Add after his name the words 'trading as', e.g., '*Mr Bill Green* trading as *Green's Grocers*'. The address for service (see page 75) should be either the residential address of the party or the principal or last known place of business.

Where one of the parties is a firm, the name of the firm should be stated, followed by the words 'a firm', e.g., '*Smith and Associates*—a firm'. The address for service should be either the residential address of a partner in the firm or the principal or last known place of business.

Where a party is suing or being sued in the name of a club or other unincorporated association use: '*Joe Bloggs* suing [or sued on behalf of] *The Local Tennis Club*'.

Where a party is a company registered in England and Wales (see Chapter 10 on companies and businesses), the name of the company must be given, e.g., '*ABC Limited*'. The address must be either the company's registered office (see page 229) or any place of business that has a real, or the most, connection with the claim, e.g., the branch or office of the company that the claimant has been dealing with.

A corporation (other than a company): the name of the corporation must be stated, e.g., '*The Utopia Urban District Council*'. The address must be either the corporation's principal office or any other place where the corporation carries on activities and which has a real connection with the claim.

Where the party is an overseas company, give the name of the company. The address will be either that which is registered under the Companies Act 1985 or the address of the place of business having a real, or the most, connection with the claim.

Where a party is suing or being sued in a representative capacity, use the form of words: '*Mrs Jane Bloggs* as the representative of *Mr Joe Bloggs* (deceased)'.

If either party is under 18 years of age (unless exception is granted by the court) or is a patient within the meaning of the Mental Health Act 1983, they must conduct proceedings through an adult, who is called a litigation friend, and this must be shown on the Claim Form. The person who is the litigation friend used to be called 'next friend' or 'guardian *ad litem*' and you may still come across these terms. The description for such a party in this instance could be:

> Under 18 years old: after the child's name type, e.g., 'a child by *Mr John Smith* his litigation friend'.
>
> A child conducting his own proceedings: type after his name 'a child'.
>
> A patient within the meaning of the Mental Health Act as mentioned above. Type after his name, e.g., 'by *Mr John Smith* his litigation friend'.

You will not need to worry about most of these details, such as whether a company is registered overseas or in England and Wales—the fee earner will know this. However, it will be useful for you to know how the names and details should be set out. Full details are also set out in the court form, Notes for Claimant (Form N1A).

Where there is more than one claimant or more than one defendant, they should be numbered in the title, e.g:

1. John Bloggs

2. Peter Brown

3. Annabel Green   Claimants [Defendants]
                                                    (*whichever is applicable*)

Brief details of claim

This must contain a concise statement setting out the nature of the claim and state the remedy sought, e.g., payment of money; damages for personal injury; return of goods. The full details of the claim should be set out in a Particulars of Claim (see below), which is a statement of case (see page 85).

Value

This will assist the court in deciding which track (see page 95) the case will be allocated to.

If the claim is for a known, specified amount of money, type that sum in the box next to 'Amount claimed' in the box at the bottom right-hand corner of the front page.

If the value of the claim is not known, type in the space under 'Value':

'The Claimant expects to recover' (followed by whichever of the following applies to the claim):

> 'not more than £5,000', or
>
> 'more than £5,000 but not more than £15,000', or
>
> 'more than £15,000' (or 'more than £50,000' if it is a claim for personal injuries to be issued in the High Court).

If the claim includes a personal injury claim for 'not more than £5,000', the form must also state here:

> 'The Claimant's claim includes a claim for personal injuries and the amount he expects to recover as damages for pain, suffering and loss of amenity is'. These words are then followed by either:

> 'not more than £1,000'; or
>
> 'more than £1,000'.

If the claim is for housing disrepair relating to residential premises, similar details concerning the value of the claim must be inserted. The wording can be found on the court form Notes for Claimant on completing a claim form (N1A).

If it is not possible to put a value on the claim, this must be stated on the Claim Form by typing in 'The Claimant cannot say how much he expects to recover'.

Proceedings may be issued in the High Court only if they fulfil specified criteria. If the claim is one that may be started in the High Court, this must be stated on the Claim Form, e.g., 'The Claimant wishes to issue his claim in the High Court because he expects to recover more than £15,000', or whichever reason applies for issuing in the High Court.

Defendant's name and address

The box at the bottom left-hand corner of the first page of the Claim Form must be completed, giving the full name and address of the defendant who is receiving the Claim Form. If there is more than one defendant, a separate Claim Form should be completed for each individual defendant, giving that defendant's details in the box on the relevant Claim Form. If it is anticipated that the proceedings will be served on the defendant outside England and Wales, it may be necessary to obtain the court's permission, but this is something that the fee earner will deal with.

Until you become used to dealing with court forms, read any printed notes for guidance that are with the form. These will nearly always tell you where something has to be inserted or deleted on the form and will usually tell you exactly the sort of information needed to complete it.

Does the claim include any issues under the Human Rights Act 1998?

This box at the top of the second page on Form N1 should be ticked if the claim is being made under the Human Rights Act (which came into force in October 2000). Ticking the box is required for statistical purposes. Generally, the majority of ordinary claims will not be affected by the Human Rights Act. Some of the issues brought about by the Act that you may come across could, for example, relate to disciplinary procedures or privacy rights at a place of employment. Various areas of law may be affected by this Act, but it is not appropriate to go into those issues here.

Particulars of claim

This sets out full details of the claim. If there is room, details should be typed on to the Claim Form but if not, they may be typed on to separate sheets of paper and attached to the Claim Form or sent separately later (see below). Where the Particulars of Claim are on a separate sheet of paper, they should include details of the court where the proceedings are being issued; the claim number, where this has been allocated; the title, i.e., the names of the parties, stating who they are, i.e., claimant or defendant; and should have a heading stating 'Particulars of Claim'. The address for service (usually the solicitor's office) must also be included, as well as a Statement of Truth (see below).

Where a party to the proceedings has a lengthy name, it must appear correctly in the title, but any further reference to that person in that document may be abbreviated, such as by initials or an identified shortened name.

Where the full Particulars of Claim are not served with the Claim Form, the Claim Form must state that Particulars of Claim will follow.

The fee earner will deal with the details in the Particulars of Claim which must include a concise statement of the facts relied upon; details of any interest that is being claimed; and any other matters that may be relevant.

The Particulars will usually state at the end exactly what it is that the claimant claims, e.g., damages and interest. Where interest is being sought by the claimant, the Particulars of Claim must state the grounds on which interest is being claimed, e.g., whether it is under the terms of a contract; or under an enactment, such as under section 69 of the County Courts Act 1984; or whether it is on some other basis. The rate of interest and the dates it is calculated from and to must also be given. If the Particulars have been settled by counsel, i.e., drawn up by a barrister, the document must give his name. The document will also show the date it has been served, the name of the solicitors serving it and stating for which party they act. In personal injury claims, as mentioned above, a copy of any medical report to be relied on, together with a note of special damages claimed, should be included. 'Special damages' is the amount being claimed for particular losses such as repairs to a car, loss of wages, etc. The term 'general damages' refers to the claim for damages for compensation, e.g., compensation for injuries.

There are various other matters to be included in certain types of claim and the fee earner will provide you with the information whenever this is necessary.

The Particulars of Claim may be served separately on the defendant up to 14 days after the date on which the Claim Form is served on him. If this is done, the forms for the defendant to reply to the claim (see below) must be served with the Particulars of Claim (rather than with a Claim Form on its own not accompanied by the Particulars of Claim). When the Particulars of Claim document has been served separately, it must be filed with the court within seven days of it being served on the defendant, together with a Certificate of Service (see page 75).

When a Particulars of Claim is served, whether or not it is included in the Claim Form, it must be accompanied by the Response Pack (Form N9) (see page 77). This includes:

(a) a form for defending the claim and/or making a counterclaim (see page 83),

(b) a form for admitting the claim (see page 81),

(c) a form for acknowledging service (see page 80), and

(d) notes for the defendant on replying to the Claim Form.

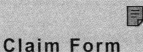

In the	
SOUTHTOWN COUNTY COURT	

	for court use only
Claim No.	
Issue date	

Claimant

Mr Paul Xavier
4 Millionaire's Row
Southtown
Herts
ES3 4PL

SEAL

Defendant(s)

Mr John Jones
1 Breakneck Drive
Southtown
Herts
EN7 6LP

Brief details of claim

Payment of money as reimbursement for damage caused to the Claimant's Rolls Royce motor car, registration No.123 ABC, arising out of a road traffic accident on 5 July 2004 which was due to the negligent driving of the Defendant.

Value

[Note: see the main text of this book for information on when to include something under this heading]

Defendant's name and address		£	
Mr John Jones 1 Breakneck Drive Southtown Herts EN7 6LP	Amount claimed	7000.00
	Court fee	*
	Solicitor's costs	*
	Total amount	*

The court office at

is open between 10 am and 4 pm Monday to Friday. When corresponding with the court, please address forms or letters to the Court Manager and quote the claim number.

N1 Claim form (CPR Part 7) (01.02)   *Printed on behalf of The Court Service*

	Claim No.	

Does, or will, your claim include any issues under the Human Rights Act 1998?   ☐ Yes   ☑ No

Particulars of Claim (~~attached~~)(to follow)

Statement of Truth
*(I believe)(~~The Claimant believes~~) that the facts stated in these particulars of claim are true.
* ~~I am duly authorised by the claimant to sign this statement~~

Full name   Paul Xaviar

Name of claimant's solicitor's firm   John Smith & Co

signed _____   position or office held _____
*(Claimant)(~~Litigation friend~~)(~~Claimant's solicitor~~)   (if signing on behalf of firm or company)

*delete as appropriate

John Smith & Co (ref: XAV/789)
2 Bank Chambers
High Road
Southtown
EN5 6AX

DX 1234 Southtown
Claimant's solicitors

Claimant's or claimant's solicitor's address to which documents or payments should be sent if different from overleaf including (if appropriate) details of DX, fax or e-mail.

There are some exceptions to this under Part 8 CPR, when only the Acknowledgment of Service has to be served with the Claim Form, but this procedure will not be dealt with here.

The Particulars of Claim is a statement of case (see page 85). As with the Claim Form, the appropriate number of copies must be made. There will always be at least three copies required: one for the file, one for the court; and one for each defendant. Whether or not the Particulars are included in the Claim Form, they must be verified by a Statement of Truth.

An example Particulars of Claim is shown below. Most statements of case will follow a similar format. However, regarding layout of documents, the house style of your own organisation should be borne in mind—the layout of a document may differ from that shown but the sort of information given will be the same.

The spaces at the bottom of the document where the date should be are often left blank at the time of typing and will be dated the day it is actually served on or posted to the other party. The date can be either typed or handwritten and must be inserted before the document is served. The original is served and a dated copy must be kept in the file. A backsheet will normally also be typed as shown on the example Particulars Claim.

Example Particulars of Claim (as a separate document from the Claim Form)

IN THE SOUTHTOWN COUNTY COURT   Claim No. 05.12345

BETWEEN:

PAUL XAVIER   Claimant

and

JOHN JONES   Defendant

PARTICULARS OF CLAIM

1. The Claimant was the owner and driver of a Rolls Royce motor car, registration number 123 ABC.
2. On 5th July 2004 the Claimant was driving his said motor car along Mulberry Close, New Barnet, Hertfordshire.
3. The Defendant failed to keep any or any proper lookout and drove his car across the road and into the Claimant's car, causing £7,000 worth of damage to the car as shown in the attached schedule.

The Claimant therefore claims:

(i) damages in the sum of £7,000;
(ii) interest thereon pursuant to section 69 of the County Courts Act 1984
[N.B. *The rate of interest and the dates it is calculated from and to must also be given.*]

ROB ROY

Statement of Truth

The Claimant believes that the facts stated in these Particulars of Claim are true. I am duly authorised by the Claimant to sign this statement.

Full name: John Smith
Name of Claimant's solicitor's firm: John Smith & Co.
Signed
(Claimant's solicitor)

DATED this   *   day of   *   2005 by John Smith and Co., of 2 Bank Chambers, High Road, Southtown, Herts. EN5 6AX. Solicitors for the Claimant.

Example backsheet for Particulars of Claim (or other statement of case) where required

Claim No. 05.12345

IN THE SOUTHTOWN
COUNTY COURT

BETWEEN:

PAUL XAVIER   Claimant

and

JOHN JONES   Defendant

PARTICULARS OF CLAIM

John Smith & Co.,
2 Bank Chambers,
High Road,
Southtown,
Herts. EN5 6AX

tel: 01438 12345

ref: XAV/789

Solicitors for the Claimant

Statement of Truth

A Statement of Truth must be included in the Claim Form as well as certain other documents. It is, in fact, already printed at the end of the Claim Form. It must be included in the Particulars of Claim if they are served separately from the Claim Form. The format for a Statement of Truth in a Claim Form and/or Particulars of Claim is shown below but this will obviously be changed accordingly for other documents.

[I believe] [*or the party on whose behalf the document is being signed believes*] that the facts stated in this [Claim Form] [*or whatever document the statement of truth relates to*] are true.

A Statement of Truth may sometimes be in a separate document, which must contain the heading and title of the action and the claim number, and must identify the document being verified, e.g., '. . . the facts stated in the Claim Form issued on [*date*] are true'; or '. . . the facts stated in the [*Particulars of Claim*] served on the [*Defendant*] on [*date*] are true'.

A Statement of Truth must be signed by either the relevant party, his litigation friend or the solicitor acting for that party on his authority. If the party is a company or other corporation or a partnership, there are formalities regarding who should sign on behalf of the company or other organisation. A legal representative signing on behalf of a party must state that he is authorised by that party to sign the statement and must also state the capacity in which he signs and the name of his firm, if appropriate. As a secretary, you should not sign the Statement of Truth yourself.

Address for documents

The box at the bottom left-hand corner of the second page should be completed to show the postal address of the claimant or the claimant's solicitor to which documents and/or payments should be sent, if it is different from the address already given under the heading 'Claimant'. If your firm is prepared to accept service (see page 73) by DX (see page 20), fax or e-mail, the relevant details should also be included here.

Getting the Claim Form issued by the court

Once the Claim Form has been completed and signed either by the claimant or by the solicitor acting for him, it should be taken or sent, together with the Particulars of Claim, if appropriate, to the court so that it can be issued by the court. It must be accompanied by the correct number of copies (one for your file, one for the court and one for each defendant), plus a stamped and addressed envelope if sent by post. The appropriate number of copies of the Notes for the Defendant (N1C) must also go with the Claim Form. The fee for issuing the proceedings will also have to be paid to the court. Fees to issue a claim are determined according to the value of the claim and you can obtain this information from the court. In reality, your office will no doubt have an up-to-date list of court fees showing when fees are payable and how much they are. Cheques should be made payable to HM Courts Service (HMCS). Any other documents which need to be filed with the court at this time should also accompany the Claim Form. Such other documents might be, e.g., a Notice of Funding (see below) or, if the claimant is receiving funding from the Legal Services Commission (formerly the Legal Aid Board), a copy of the funding certificate and a notice of issue of the certificate. Correspondence to the court should be addressed to the Court Manager.

Many firms have an outdoor clerk, who deals with, amongst other things, taking documents to court. If your firm has such a person, the signed Claim Form and any other relevant documents, together with the correct number of copies and the fee, should be passed to him.

Once the court is satisfied that the Claim Form and any other documents are in order, they will complete their own paperwork to issue the proceedings. They will stamp all the documents to show that they have been issued by the court and give the claim a Claim Number. The court may serve the Claim Form or the claimant's solicitors can request to serve it. If the claimant's solicitors are going to serve it, the court will return to them a sealed copy of the Claim Form for service. The court 'seals' a document by imprinting on it an official stamp which shows that the court has issued that document.

When the court has allocated a claim number, this should always be included on any documents relevant to the proceedings, as well as the court details and the names and status of the parties (see also page 61 regarding title of the action).

Notice of Funding of Case or Claim

Where one of the parties to a claim enters into a funding arrangement, he should inform all the other parties involved in that case. This will usually be done by completing a Notice of Funding of Case or Claim (Form N251). For these purposes, a funding arrangement means a conditional fee agreement (see page 34) or funding by means of an insurance policy or through an agreement with a membership organisation to meet the legal costs.

The Notice of Funding must be completed by the party being funded and should be sent to the court and all other parties to the case. It should be sent either at the commencement of the proceedings; or on the filing of a first document such as an acknowledgment of service or defence (see later) or, if the funding arrangement is entered into or changed at a later stage, the Notice of Funding should be served at that time.

Notice of funding of case or claim

Notice of funding by means of a conditional fee agreement, insurance policy or undertaking given by a prescribed body should be given to the court and all other parties to the case:
- on commencement of proceedings
- on filing an acknowledgment of service, defence or other first document; and
- at any later time that such an arrangement is entered into, changed or terminated.

In the	
SOUTHTOWN COUNTY COURT	

The court office is open between 10 am and 4 pm Monday to Friday. When writing to the court, please address forms or letters to the Court Manager and quote the claim number.

Claim No.	05.12345
Claimant (include Ref.)	PAUL XAVIER (XAV/789)
Defendant (include Ref.)	JOHN JONES (JON/cd)

Take notice that in respect of

☐ all claims herein

☐ the following claims

☐ the case of *(specify name of party)*

[is now][was] being funded by:

(Please tick those boxes which apply)

☐ a conditional fee agreement
⌐Dated⌐

which provides for a success fee

☐ an insurance policy issued on
⌐Date⌐   ⌐Policy no.⌐

⌐Name and address of insurer⌐

☐ an undertaking given on
⌐Date⌐

by
⌐Name of prescribed body⌐

in the following terms

The funding of the case has now changed:

☐ the above funding has now ceased

☐ the conditional fee agreement has been terminated

☐ a conditional fee agreement
⌐Dated⌐

which provides for a success fee has been entered into;

☐ an insurance policy
⌐Date⌐

has been cancelled

☐ an insurance policy has been issued on
⌐Date⌐   ⌐Policy no.⌐

⌐Name and address of insurer⌐

☐ an undertaking given on
⌐Date⌐

has been terminated

☐ an undertaking has been given on
⌐Date⌐

⌐Name of prescribed body⌐

in the following terms

⌐Signed⌐

Solicitor for the (claimant) (defendant) (Part 20 defendant) (respondent) (appellant)

⌐Dated⌐

N251 Notice of funding of case or claim (06.04)

The Court Service Publications Branch

Filing documents with the court by fax and e-mail

It is possible to file certain documents with the court by fax, although if the document is delivered by fax after 4.00 p.m. it will be treated as filed on the next day the court office is open. Before sending any document by fax to the court, you should be sure of the correct fax number to send it to as often a court will allocate a particular fax number to different types of proceedings. Where a document is filed by fax, an additional hard copy must not be sent to the court.

Faxes should not be used to send routine or non-urgent letters or documents. Certain documents should not be filed by fax at all unless it is an unavoidable emergency and if that situation arises, an explanation may be required by the court. If the fax relates to a hearing, the date and time of the hearing should be prominently displayed.

It is also now possible to communicate and file certain documents with the court by e-mail. However, at the moment, this is applicable only in specified courts and these are named on the HM Courts Service website, together with other necessary details.

Where a document is filed by e-mail and received after 4.00 p.m., it will be treated as being filed on the next day after the court office is open. If a document is filed by e-mail, a hard copy must not be sent to the court.

Further information on filing documents with the court is provided in the Civil Procedure Rules.

Issuing in bulk

Where straightforward county court claims for fixed amounts of money are to be issued in bulk, e.g., in their hundreds or thousands, usually by organisations such as debt collection agencies or mail order companies, this would put a great strain on the local court. Therefore, provided certain criteria are fulfilled, application may be made to commence proceedings through the Claim Production Centre in Northampton (the full address is given in the address section at the back of this book). The Claim Production Centre will prepare and issue the claim forms from information in a particular format which has been provided by the organisation wishing to issue the claims. The documents are sent direct to the defendants by the Centre in Northampton whether or not the claims are to be treated as issued in the Northampton County Court.

It is also possible to have further steps in the proceedings dealt with at the Claim Production Centre if the Claim Forms are issued in the name of the Northampton County Court.

Money Claim Online

HM Courts Service now provides a facility on their website whereby civil claims meeting certain criteria may be issued online. This service is called Money Claim Online (MCOL). Claims started using MCOL will be issued by the Northampton County Court and will proceed in that court unless they are transferred to another court.

Service

'Service' is a term used to express the fact that a document has been delivered to another party in accordance with any specific rules that must be adhered to, e.g., the rules of the court. Generally, a document may be served only within the court's jurisdiction, i.e., within England and Wales, but permission may be granted by the court for service outside the jurisdiction.

Once the Claim Form and any other relevant documents have been issued by the court, the documents must be served on the defendant. There are several ways in which service may be effected and this may sometimes depend on exactly which document is going to be served.

Postal

Postal service should be by first class post. Registered post or recorded delivery should not be used for normal postal service of documents in civil litigation matters. Information on permitted addresses for service is given on Form N1A, Notes for Claimant (see under claimant and defendant details on page 62 and also address for service on page 75). Once the Claim Form has been posted by first class post, it is deemed by the court to have been served the second day after it was posted.

As mentioned on page 35 with regard to diary notes, you may be asked to make a diary note for 14 days after deemed service of the Claim Form and/or Particulars of Claim. This will be the date by which the court should have heard from the defendant regarding how he intends to proceed with the claim, often by receiving back from the defendant a completed Acknowledgment of Service (see page 79). If the defendant has done nothing by this time, it may be possible to enter judgment against the defendant (see page 85).

Service using the DX

The Document Exchange (see page 20) may be used for serving documents only if:

(a) the party's address for service includes a DX number; or

(b) the notepaper of the party who is to be served or the notepaper of his solicitor who is authorised to accept service includes a DX number.

As well as one of the two above conditions being satisfied, the party who is to be served or his solicitor must not have indicated in writing that they are unwilling to accept service by DX.

Service by DX is deemed to be effected the second day after it was left at the Document Exchange.

Service by fax, e-mail or other electronic means

Before a document may be served electronically, the party who is to be served or his legal representative must previously have expressly indicated in writing to the party serving the document that he is willing to accept service by electronic means. He must also have provided the fax number, e-mail address or electronic identification to which the document should be sent. Sufficient written indication for these purposes is if there is a fax number on the notepaper of the legal representative of the party who is to be served or if the party to be served has provided a fax number, e-mail address or electronic identification on a statement of case or a response to a claim filed with the court.

Where a party wishes to serve a document by electronic means, he should first clarify with the other party whether that other party is limited in any way in being able to receive the document electronically, e.g., as to the format in which any document can be received and the maximum file size that can be received.

If a document is served by fax and is transmitted on a business day before 4.00 p.m., it is deemed to have been served on that day. Otherwise, it is deemed to have been served on the business day after the day on which it was transmitted.

Where a document is served by any other electronic method, it is deemed to have been served on the second day after the day on which it was transmitted.

Leaving a document at an address

Service may also be effected by delivering a document or leaving it at a permitted address as laid down by the rules of the court. In these circumstances, it is deemed to have been served the day after it is delivered to or left at the permitted address.

Personal service

This is where the documents are simply handed to the defendant personally. (There are specific rules to deal with service in this manner upon a company or partnership.) It is highly unlikely that a secretary will be asked to do this but if you are, make sure that you note the date, time and method of service, i.e., exactly how you handed over the documents, when and where. There are various rules relating to personal service and these should be checked beforehand if the need arises. However, personal service is normally effected by enquiry agents or process servers. If a document is served personally after 5.00 p.m. on a business day or at any time on a Saturday, Sunday or a bank holiday, service will be deemed to be on the next business day.

Delivering or leaving the document at an address

If the document is left at a permitted address (see Address for Service, below), it is deemed to have been served the day after it was delivered to or left at that address.

Other methods of service

Where it is desired to effect service in another way, e.g., by placing advertisements in newspapers, an application must be made to the court. Similarly, the court has power to dispense with service of a document.

If a document is to be served on a child or patient within the meaning of the Mental Health Act 1983, service will usually be on a parent or guardian or a litigation friend. However, there are various rules to be followed in these cases.

There are also steps to be taken if serving a document on a member of HM Forces or on a member of the US Air Force. Details are given in the CPR, including addresses to write to for making enquiries as to the address of that person.

Calculating days for deemed service

When calculating the days for deemed service, a Saturday, Sunday, Bank Holiday, Christmas Day or Good Friday should be excluded. (This applies to all calculations of periods of five days or less.) For information on calculating time for matters not related to service, see page 142.

Address for service

The address to which a document may be delivered, i.e., the address for service, must be in England and Wales but, as stated previously, there are exceptions to this. The address for service is normally somewhere where it is logical to assume that the defendant will receive the documents, such as a usual or last known residence or place of business. The court rules specify which sort of places are permitted, e.g., home address, business address of a firm, registered office of a company. Where someone has instructed a solicitor, the solicitor's business address is usually his client's address for service (but see below regarding service of the Claim Form).

Who may serve the documents

If the document is one which has been issued or prepared by the court, it may be served by the court. However, there are exceptions to this, one of these being where the solicitors notify the court that they wish to serve the document themselves.

A Claim Form may only be served on the defendant's solicitors if the defendant has in fact authorised those solicitors to accept service of documents on his behalf and, in that case, all documents should normally then be served on the solicitors.

Service of the Claim Form

Generally, the Claim Form must be served on the defendant within four months after it has been issued by the court.

If the court is to serve the Claim Form, the form must always include the defendant's address for service and this may be the defendant's solicitors only if they are authorised by the defendant to accept service on his behalf. When the Claim Form is served by the court, the court will send a notice to the claimant informing him of the date when the Claim Form is deemed to have been served.

Where the claimant or his solicitors are serving the Claim Form themselves and they are serving the Particulars of Claim at the same time, they must include the Response Pack (Form N9) which includes an Acknowledgment of Service and the forms for defence and/or counterclaim and admission forms (see page 77). A Certificate of Service (see below) must then be filed with the court.

In certain circumstances, a Claim Form may be served in a manner which has been specified in a contract, e.g., a contract may state how any disputes relating to it are dealt with. The Claim Form may also be served, with the permission of the court, on an agent of someone who is overseas.

Certificate of Service

Some documents, such as the Claim Form, require a Certificate of Service (Form N215) to be completed and filed with the court, giving details of the date of service (and the time if service is by fax), together with details of how service was effected, e.g., whether it was by post and, if so, the date of posting; if it was by using the DX, the date of delivery to the document exchange. A statement of truth must also be completed on the Certificate of Service.

Certificate of service

Name of court	Claim No.
SOUTHTOWN COUNTY COURT	05.12345

Name of Claimant
PAUL XAVIER

Name of Defendant
JOHN JONES

On the ....*...*(insert date)*

the ....Claim Form... *(insert title or description of documents served)*

a copy of which is attached to this notice was served on *(insert name of person served, including position i.e. partner, director if appropriate)*

John Jones ....

Tick as appropriate

[✓] by first class post   [ ] by Document Exchange

[ ] by delivering to or leaving at a   [ ] by personally handing it to or leaving it with
    permitted place *(see notes overleaf)*   *(please specify)* [   ]

[ ] by fax machine (.................time sent) [ ] by other electronic means
    (you may want to enclose a copy of the   *(please specify)* [   ]
    transmission sheet)

[ ] by other means permitted by the court
    (please specify) [   ]

at *(insert address where service effected, include fax or DX number, e-mail address or other electronic identification)*

> 1 Breakneck Drive
> Southtown
> Herts
> EN7 6LP

being the   [ ] claimant's   [✓] defendant's   [ ] solicitor's   [ ] litigation friend:

[✓] usual residence   [ ] principal office of the corportion

[ ] last known residence   [ ] principal office of the company

[ ] place of business   [ ] other *(please specify)* [   ]

[ ] principal place of business

[ ] last known place of business

The date of service is therefore deemed to be .... *(insert date - see overleaf for guidance)*

I believe that the facts stated in this Certificate are true.	
Full name	
Signed [ ]	**Position or office held** [ ]
(Claimant)(~~Defendant~~)('s solicitor)(~~'s litigation friend~~)	*(if signing on behalf of firm or company)*
Date [ ]	

N215 Certificate of service (06.04)   *Printed on behalf on The Court Service*

Notice of Non-service

If a document was going to be served by the court and the court was unable to serve it, the court will complete a Notice of Non-service stating how they attempted to effect service and send this to the party who requested service. The court is then no longer under any further duty to try to effect service—it is up to the party wishing to serve the document.

Defendant's Response to the Claim Form

When the defendant receives the Claim Form and/or Particulars of Claim, he will receive other documents too.

Notes for defendant on replying to the Claim Form

These Notes (Form NIC) accompany the Claim Form. When you are making copies of the Claim Form for service on each defendant, you should ensure that every defendant has a copy of these Notes. They set out the choices open to the defendant which are to:

(a) pay the amount claimed; or

(b) admit that he owes all or part of the claim and ask for time to pay; or

(c) dispute the claim or part of it.

If the Particulars of Claim were received by the defendant at the same time as the Claim Form, he must reply within 14 days of the date it was served on him. If the Claim Form states that the Particulars of Claim will follow, he should not reply until he has received the Particulars of Claim (which should arrive no more than 14 days after he receives the Claim Form).

If the defendant simply does not reply at all, judgment may be entered against him (see page 85).

The Notes will then set out how the defendant should pay if he wishes to do so, and also tell him what he should do if he wishes to admit or dispute the claim. At the same time that he is sent the Particulars of Claim, he must also be sent a Response Pack (see below) which includes the forms he will need to complete, depending on what he decides to do.

Response Pack

The Response Pack (Form N9) includes forms on which the defendant may:

(a) admit all or part of the claim where the claim is for a specified amount (Form N9A);

(b) admit all or part of the claim where the claim is for an unspecified amount of money or is not a claim for money (Form N9C);

(c) submit a Defence and/or Counterclaim where the claim is for a specified amount (Form N9B);

(d) submit a Defence and/or Counterclaim where the claim is for an unspecified amount or is not a claim for money (Form N9D).

The Response Pack Form also comprises an Acknowledgment of Service form which will be completed, signed and returned to the court by the defendant or his solicitors, if necessary (see page 79).

The defendant has a specified time within which to file his Admission form or Defence and Counterclaim Form.

Admitting all or part of the claim

If the defendant admits the claim in full and it is for a specified amount of money, he should take or send the money, together with any interest and costs claimed, to the claimant at the address given for payment on the Claim Form. He must do this within 14 days. When making the payment, the defendant should ensure that he quotes the Claim Number and obtains a receipt. Payment in this instance will not be accepted by the court.

If the defendant admits the claim in full and it is for a specified amount, but he wants time to pay the money, he must complete Form N9A and send it to the claimant at the address given for payment on the Claim Form within 14 days. The claimant will decide whether or not to accept the proposal for payment. If he accepts, he may ask the court to enter judgment (see page 85) against the defendant and the court will then send the defendant a court order telling him how the payments should be made. If the proposal is not accepted, the court will decide on the rate of payment to be made.

Where the claim is for an unspecified amount and the defendant admits that he is liable for the whole claim, he may make an offer to the claimant to settle the claim. He must do this by completing Form N9C and sending it to the court within 14 days. The court will send a copy to the claimant, who will then tell the court whether the offer is acceptable. The claimant must send his reply to the court, sending a copy of his reply to the defendant, within 14 days. If the claimant does not reply in this way, the claim will be stayed, i.e., it will not proceed any further. Once the claimant accepts the defendant's offer, the claimant may request the court to enter judgment against the defendant for the amount due or whatever other remedy is being sought. The request for judgment will be made on the appropriate form.

If an offer made by the defendant is not acceptable to the claimant, the claimant may request the court to enter judgment against the defendant for an amount or remedy that will be decided on by the court, together with any costs. The court will enter judgment and refer its file to a judge for directions for management of the case. The claimant and the defendant will be sent a copy of the order made by the court.

Where the defendant admits that he is liable for the claim but does not make any offer to settle, he should complete Form N9C and send it to the court within 14 days. The court will send a copy to the claimant who may request the court to enter judgment against the defendant for an amount which will be decided by the court, together with costs. The court will then enter judgment and the file will be sent to a judge for directions for management of the case. Both the claimant and the defendant will be sent a copy of the order made by the court.

If the defendant admits part of the claim, but not all of it, he should complete both a form for admission and a form for defence and send them to the court within 14 days. The claimant will then decide whether to accept this part admission. If he does accept, he may request the court to enter judgment against the defendant and the court will then send a court order to the defendant telling him to pay. If the claimant does not accept the part admission, the case will proceed as a defended claim (see below).

When your firm is acting for any party and you are completing the forms, always ensure that you have kept a copy on the file, and remember that a copy of the forms must be served on all parties to the claim.

Disputing/defending the claim

If the claim is for a specified amount of money and the defendant is an individual, i.e., not a company or some other organisation, and he wishes to dispute or defend the claim, the claim may be transferred to the defendant's home court, which means the court for the district in which the defendant resides or carries on business. If the case is a county court case, this will be the local county court for the defendant and if it is a High Court case, it will be the local district registry for the defendant. If it is a High Court case and there is no local district registry, it will be the Royal Courts of Justice.

If the defendant needs more than 14 days to reply to the claim, he must complete the Acknowledgment of Service and send it to the court within 14 days (see below).

The defendant must also complete the appropriate form for admitting/defending the claim, depending on whether the claim is for a specified amount or for an unspecified amount or non-money claim and depending on what it is exactly that he wishes to do regarding the claim. He could:

(a) dispute all of the claim (this might be because he has already paid it or that he simply disagrees with the claim);

(b) admit part of the claim and dispute part of it;

(c) make a claim of his own against the claimant (a counterclaim) or bring someone else into the proceedings (see page 91 regarding Part 20 claims).

In the Defence, the defendant must reply specifically to the allegations contained in the Particulars of Claim, e.g., he must state which allegations he denies, giving his reasons; which he admits, as well as other detailed information regarding the claim.

A Statement of Truth should also be signed by the defendant as for the Claim Form (see above). If the Defence is a separate document, it will have the same type of layout as the Particulars of Claim.

All the forms are very clear and have notes on them to help in their completion. There are boxes on the forms which should either be filled in or ticked.

Acknowledgment of Service

This is on Form N9 (Response Pack). Where the defendant intends to defend the claim and he needs more time to file his Defence or if he is disputing the court's jurisdiction, he should complete the Acknowledgment of Service and return it to the court. It should be filed with the court within 14 days of service of the Particulars of Claim. The court will inform the claimant in writing that the defendant has lodged the Acknowledgment of Service. He is then allowed 28 days from the date of service of the Particulars of Claim to file his Defence (or to make an application to the court if he disputes the fact that the court has jurisdiction to try the claim). The parties may agree to extend this period of time for up to a further 28 days (making a total of 56 days).

Where the defendant has instructed a solicitor, the solicitor's address will usually be inserted in the box where it asks for the address to which documents about the claim should be sent. Do not forget to include your firm's correct reference. The form will now be signed by the solicitor acting for the defendant, or by the defendant himself.

If the defendant has been named incorrectly or not in full on the Claim Form, his correct name should be inserted on the Acknowledgment of Service in the appropriate box. The correct name should be followed by the words 'described as' and then the incorrect name.

Response Pack

You should read the 'notes for defendant' attached to the claim form which will tell you when and where to send the forms

Included in this pack are:

- either **Admission Form N9A**
  (if the claim is for a specified amount)
  or **Admission Form N9C**
  (if the claim is for an unspecified amount
  or is not a claim for money)

- either **Defence and Counterclaim Form N9B** (if the claim is for a specified amount)
  or **Defence and Counterclaim Form N9D**
  (if the claim is for an unspecified amount
  or is not a claim for money)

- **Acknowledgment of service**
  (see below)

Complete

If you admit the claim or the amount claimed and/or you want time to pay ▶	the admission form
If you admit part of the claim ▶	the admission form and the defence form
If you dispute the whole claim or wish to make a claim (a counterclaim) against the claimant ▶	the defence form
If you need 28 days (rather than 14) from the date of service to prepare your defence, or wish to contest the court's jurisdiction ▶	the acknowledgment of service
If you do nothing, judgment may be entered against you	

Acknowledgment of Service

Defendant's full name if different from the name given on the claim form

In the	SOUTHTOWN COUNTY COURT
Claim No.	05.12345
Claimant (including ref.)	PAUL XAVIER (ref: XAV/789)
Defendant	JOHN JONES

Address to which documents about this claim should be sent (including reference if appropriate)

		if applicable
Joe Bloggs & Co 1 Broad Walk Southtown Herts	fax no.	020 8444 2323
	DX no.	DX 56 Southtown
	Ref. no.	
Tel. no. 020 8444 7777 Postcode **EN4 9PP**	e-mail	

Tick the appropriate box

1. I intend to defend all of this claim ☐

2. I intend to defend part of this claim ☑

3. I intend to contest jurisdiction ☐

If you file an acknowledgment of service but do not file a defence within 28 days of the date of service of the claim form, or particulars of claim if served separately, judgment may be entered against you.

If you do not file an application within 28 days of the date of service of the claim form, or particulars of claim if served separately, it will be assumed that you accept the court's jurisdiction and judgment may be entered against you.

Signed _____

(Defendant)(Defendant's solicitor)
(Litigation friend)

Position or office held
(if signing on behalf of firm or company) _____

Date _____

The court office at

is open between 10 am and 4 pm Monday to Friday. When corresponding with the court, please address forms or letters to the Court Manager and quote the claim number.

N9 Response Pack (5.02)

Printed on behalf of The Court Service

Admission (specified amount)

- You have a limited number of days to complete and return this form
- Before completing this form, please read the notes for guidance attached to the claim form

When to fill in this form

Only fill in this form if:

- you are admitting all of the claim **and** you are asking for time to pay; or
- you are admitting part of the claim. (You should also complete form N9B)

How to fill in this form

- Tick the correct boxes and give as much information as you can. **Then sign and date the form.** If necessary provide details on a separate sheet, add the claim number and attach it to this form.
- Make your offer of payment in box 11 on the back of this form. **If you make no offer the claimant will decide how much and when you should pay.**
- If you are not an individual, you should ensure that you provide sufficient details about the assets and liabilities of your firm, company or corporation to support any offer of payment made in box 11.
- You can get help to complete this form at **any** county court office or Citizens Advice Bureau.

Where to send this form

- **If you admit the claim in full**
  Send the completed form to the address shown on the claim form as one to which documents should be sent.
- **If you admit only part of the claim**
  Send the form **to the court** at the address given on the claim form, together with the defence form (N9B).

How much of the claim do you admit?

☐ I admit the full amount claimed as shown on the claim form **or**

☐ I admit the amount of £ _____

In the	SOUTHTOWN COUNTY COURT
Claim No.	05.12345
Claimant (including ref.)	PAUL XAVIER (XAV/789)
Defendant	JOHN JONES

2 Dependants *(people you look after financially)*

Number of children in each age group

under 11 ☐　　11-15 ☐　　16-17 ☐　　18 & over ☐

Other dependants *(give details)* _____

3 Employment

☐ **I am employed as a** _____
My employer is _____

Jobs other than main job *(give details)* _____

☐ **I am self employed as a** _____

Annual turnover is .... £ _____

☐ **I am not** in arrears with my national insurance contributions, income tax and VAT

☐ **I am in arrears** and I owe........... £ _____

Give details of:
(a) contracts and other work in hand _____
(b) any sums due for work done _____

☐ **I have been unemployed for** _____ years _____ months

☐ **I am a pensioner**

4 Bank account and savings

☐ **I have a bank account**
　☐ The account is in credit by........ £ _____
　☐ The account is overdrawn by.... £ _____

☐ **I have a savings or building society account**
　The amount in the account is.......... £ _____

5 Residence

I live in ☐ my own house　　☐ lodgings
　☐ my jointly owned house　☐ council accommodation
　☐ rented accommodation

1 Personal details

Surname	JONES
Forename	JOHN

☐ Mr　☐ Mrs　☐ Miss　☐ Ms

☐ Married　☐ Single　☐ Other *(specify)* _____

Age 36

Address
1 Breakneck Drive
Southtown
Herts

Postcode EN7 6LP

Tel. no. 020 8222 8888

N9A Form of admission (specified amount) (11.01)

Printed on behalf of The Court Service

6 Income

My usual take home pay *(including overtime, commission, bonuses etc)*	£	per
Income support	£	per
Child benefit(s)	£	per
Other state benefit(s)	£	per
My pension(s)	£	per
Others living in my home give me	£	per
Other income *(give details below)*		
	£	per
	£	per
	£	per
Total income	**£**	**per**

8 Priority debts

(This section is for arrears only. Do not include regular expenses listed in box 7.)

Rent arrears	£	per
Mortgage arrears	£	per
Council tax/Community Charge arrears	£	per
Water charges arrears	£	per
Fuel debts: Gas	£	per
Electricity	£	per
Other	£	per
Maintenance arrears	£	per
Others *(give details below)*		
	£	per
	£	per
Total priority debts	**£**	**per**

7 Expenses

(Do not include any payments made by other members of the household out of their own income)

I have regular expenses as follows:

Mortgage *(including second mortgage)*	£	per
Rent	£	per
Council tax	£	per
Gas	£	per
Electricity	£	per
Water charges	£	per
TV rental and licence	£	per
HP repayments	£	per
Mail order	£	per
Housekeeping, food, school meals	£	per
Travelling expenses	£	per
Children's clothing	£	per
Maintenance payments	£	per
Others *(not court orders or credit debts listed in boxes 9 and 10)*		
	£	per
	£	per
	£	per
Total expenses	**£**	**per**

9 Court orders

Court	Claim No.	£	per

Total court order instalments	**£**	**per**

Of the payments above, I am behind with payments to *(please list)*

10 Credit debts

Loans and credit card debts *(please list)*

	£	per
	£	per
	£	per

Of the payments above, I am behind with payments to *(please list)*

11 Offer of payment

☐ I can pay the amount admitted on

or

☐ I can pay by monthly instalments of £

If you cannot pay immediately, please give brief reasons below

12 Declaration

I declare that the details I have given above are true to the best of my knowledge

Signed

Date

Position or office held *(if signing on behalf of firm or company)*

Defence and Counterclaim (specified amount)

In the

SOUTHTOWN COUNTY COURT

Claim No.	05.12345
Claimant (including ref.)	PAUL XAVIER (ref: XAV/789)
Defendant	JOHN JONES

- Fill in this form if you wish to dispute all or part of the claim and/or make a claim against the claimant (counterclaim).
- You have a limited number of days to complete and return this form to the court.
- Before completing this form, please read the notes for guidance attached to the claim form.
- Please ensure that all boxes at the top right of this form are completed. You can obtain the correct names and number from the claim form. The court cannot trace your case without this information.

How to fill in this form
- Complete sections 1 and 2. Tick the correct boxes and give the other details asked for.
- Set out your defence in section 3. If necessary continue on a separate piece of paper making sure that the claim number is clearly shown on it. In your defence you must state which allegations in the particulars of claim you deny and your reasons for doing so. **If you fail to deny an allegation it may be taken that you admit it.**
- If you dispute only some of the allegations you must
  - specify which you admit and which you deny; and
  - give your own version of events if different from the claimant's.

- If you wish to make a claim against the claimant (a counterclaim) complete section 4.
- Complete and sign section 5 before sending this form to the court. Keep a copy of the claim form and this form.

Community Legal Service Fund (CLSF)

You may qualify for assistance from the CLSF (this used to be called 'legal aid') to meet some or all of your legal costs. Ask about the CLSF at any county court office or any information or help point which displays this logo.

Community Legal Service

1. How much of the claim do you dispute?

☐ I dispute the full amount claimed as shown on the claim form

or

☐ I admit the amount of £ [ ]

If you dispute only part of the claim you must **either**:

- pay the amount admitted to the person named at the address for payment on the claim form (see How to Pay in the notes on the back of, or attached to, the claim form). Then send this defence to the court

or

- complete the admission form **and** this defence form and send them to the court.

☐ I paid the amount admitted on (*date*) [ ]

or

☐ I enclose the completed form of admission
(go to section 2)

2. Do you dispute this claim because you have already paid it? *Tick whichever applies*

☐ **No** (*go to section 3*)

☐ **Yes** I paid £ [ ] to the claimant

on [ ] *(before the claim form was issued)*

Give details of where and how you paid it in the box below *(then go to section 5)*

3. Defence

Defence (continued)

Claim No. [   ]

4. If you wish to make a claim against the claimant (a counterclaim)

If your claim is for a specific sum of money, how much are you claiming? £ [   ]

I enclose the counterclaim fee of £ [   ]

My claim is for *(please specify nature of claim)*

[   ]

- To start your counterclaim, you will have to pay a fee. Court staff can tell you how much you have to pay.

- You may not be able to make a counterclaim where the claimant is the Crown (e.g. a Government Department). Ask at your local county court office for further information.

What are your reasons for making the counterclaim?
If you need to continue on a separate sheet put the claim number in the top right hand corner

[   ]

5. Signed
(To be signed by you or by your solicitor or litigation friend)

*(I believe)(The defendant believes) that the facts stated in this form are true. *I am duly authorised by the defendant to sign this statement

delete as appropriate

Position or office held (if signing on behalf of firm or company)

[   ]

Date [*   ]

Give an address to which notices about this case can be sent to you

Joe Bloggs & Co
1 Broad Walk
Southtown
Herts

Postcode **EN4 9PP**

Tel. no. **020 8444 7777**

	if applicable
fax no.	020 8444 2323
DX no.	DX 56 Southtown
e-mail	

Where the defendant does not file either an Acknowledgment of Service or a Defence (or an Admission) within the specified time, judgment in default of filing one of these documents may be entered against him for the full amount of the claim (called 'default judgment').

Always remember to keep a copy of the Acknowledgment of Service for your file.

Entering default judgment

In most cases, if the defendant fails to file the Acknowledgment of Service or Defence or Admission within the specified time, judgment in default of doing so may be entered against him. This means that the claimant may file a request with the court for an order stating that the defendant must comply with whatever the claimant sought in his Claim Form, for example, pay the money claimed plus any interest accrued, plus costs. A form for Request for Judgment will be completed: which form to be used depends on what type of claim it is and whether the court will decide on the amount to be paid. In some cases, an application (see page 114) will have to be made to the court to allow judgment to be entered. Even when judgment has been entered, the defendant may, under certain circumstances, ask for it to be set aside, i.e., made ineffective, or to be varied.

A Request for Judgment and Reply to Admission form will be completed if the defendant admits the claim but asks for time to pay.

Statements of case

As you have seen, there are many forms to complete. However, they do not all need to be completed at the same time nor, indeed, is every single form needed for every case. These forms are necessary so that everyone knows exactly what the other parties involved are saying and so that everyone knows what the next step is that they should take, and when they should take it. Besides completing forms, documents such as the Particulars of Claim and Defence will often need to be drawn up. These documents, and others, the purpose of which is to set out the facts relied upon in the action, are called statements of case. Before the introduction of the Civil Procedure Rules, these documents were known as pleadings.

The first statement of case is the Claim Form and/or Particulars of Claim (if not included in the Claim Form); followed by the Defence and/or Counterclaim and, perhaps, relevant documents under a Part 20 claim (see page 91). The claimant may serve a Reply to the Defence and/or Defence to the Counterclaim. Permission must be obtained from the court before any other statement of case may be served.

When typing a statement of case, always remember to include the title of the action, i.e., the court or division in which the action is proceeding; the claim number; the names and status of the parties; and also state which document it is that is being typed, e.g. Particulars of Claim or Defence. The words stating what the document is, e.g., Particulars of Claim, will usually be typed in capital letters and centred and then perhaps either underlined (see the example Particulars of Claim) or this heading will be between two parallel lines (see heading for Brief to Counsel below). Your organisation will have its own style. Whatever format is used should be followed through to the backsheet (see page 69), if there is one.

Request for judgment and reply to admission (specified amount)

- Tick box A or B. If you tick box B you must complete the details in that part and in part C. Make sure that all the case details are given. Remember to sign and date the form. Your signature certifies that the information you have given is correct.

- If the defendant has given an address on the form of admission to which correspondence should be sent, which is different from the address shown on the claim form, you must tell the court.

- Return the completed form to the court.

In the	
SOUTHTOWN COUNTY COURT	
Claim No.	05.12345
Claimant (including ref)	PAUL XAVIER (XAV/789)
Defendant (including ref)	JOHN JONES (JON/cd)

A ☑ **The defendant has not filed an admission or defence to my claim**

Complete all the judgment details at C. Decide how and when you want the defendant to pay. You can ask for the judgment to be paid by instalments or in one payment.

B ☐ **The defendant admits that all the money is owed**

Tick only **one** box below and complete all the judgment details at C.

☐ **I accept the defendant's proposal for payment**

Say how the defendant intends to pay. The court will send the defendant an order to pay. You will also be sent a copy.

☐ **The defendant has not made any proposal for payment**

Say how you want the defendant to pay. You can ask for the judgment to be paid by instalments or in one payment. The court will send the defendant an order to pay. You will also be sent a copy.

☐ **I do NOT accept the defendant's proposal for payment**

Say how you want the defendant to pay. Give your reasons for objecting to the defendant's offer of payment in the space opposite. (Continue on the back of this form if necessary.) Send this form to the court **with defendant's admission N9A**. The court will fix a rate of payment and send the defendant an order to pay. You will also be sent a copy.

C Judgment details

I would like the judgment to be paid

☑ (immediately)

☐ (by instalments of £ [   ] per month)

☐ (in full by [   ])

Amount of claim as admitted (including interest at date of issue)	
Interest since date of claim (if any)	
Period from . . . . . . to	
Rate . . %	
Court fees shown on claim	
Solicitor's costs (if any) on issuing claim	
Sub Total	
Solicitor's costs (if any) on entering judgment	
Sub Total	
Deduct amount (if any) paid since issue	
Amount payable by defendant	

I certify that the information given is correct

Signed [   ]

(Claimant)(Claimant's solicitor)(Litigation friend)

Date [   ]

Position or office held [   ]

(if signing on behalf of firm or company)

The court office at

is open between 10 am and 4 pm Monday to Friday. When corresponding with the court, please address forms and letters to the Court Manager and quote the Claim number

Generally, all statements of case should have the pages numbered and each paragraph in the body of the document numbered. They must be verified by a Statement of Truth (see page 69). If the document has been settled by counsel (see below), it must bear his name. A statement of case must show the date it has been served, the name of the solicitors serving it and the party for whom they act. The date of service will often be left blank when you type it so that this can be written in later. A backsheet will usually be typed. Remember to proofread documents (see page 29) that have been copy typed and also to keep a dated copy on your file. (For an example layout of these documents, see the example Particulars of Claim on page 68.)

If a statement of case exceeds 25 pages (excluding schedules), a short summary must also be filed and served.

Instructing counsel

Barristers (called 'counsel') are often asked to give advice on a particular matter or to draft a statement of case. When a solicitor wishes to ask counsel to draft a statement of case, or to advise in writing or in a conference, he has to set out exactly what he requires counsel to do. He should state the relevant details of his case and instruct counsel, for example, to settle a Particulars of Claim, or to advise on liability, etc. These instructions being sent to the barrister are called Instructions to Counsel. Incidentally, a meeting with junior counsel is called a conference and a meeting with a QC is called a consultation.

If the solicitor wishes counsel to appear at a trial or hearing of some sort, counsel is instructed in exactly the same way and is briefed to appear at the hearing. Instructions asking counsel to appear in this manner are called Brief to Counsel.

Instructions and Briefs to Counsel are typed on A4 size paper. At one time, they were typed on A3 size paper (brief paper), but it is highly unlikely that you will encounter this any more.

Instructions and Briefs to Counsel start off with the heading and title of the action, including the claim number, if known (same format as statements of case). Of course, if proceedings have not been issued, it will not yet have a claim number. After the title is a description of what is required of counsel, e.g., Instructions to Counsel to Settle Particulars of Claim, and this is typed at the top, after the names of the parties, in the centre of the page. This is usually typed in capital letters and may be underlined or between two parallel lines (as shown), but your own organisation will more than likely have its own style:

BRIEF TO COUNSEL TO APPEAR ON BEHALF OF
THE CLAIMANT AT SOUTHTOWN COUNTY
COURT ON TUESDAY, 13th DECEMBER 2005 at 2.00 P.M.

The fee earner will then list any enclosures with the Instructions or Brief and set out details of the case.

When the Instructions are completed, a backsheet should also be typed. Backsheets are typed on the right-hand side of the page as shown on page 69 because the Instructions are folded over that way. The backsheet must contain the heading and title of the action, as well as any claim number, what the Instructions are about (centred as above, if appropriate), the name, address, reference and telephone number of the instructing solicitors and the date the Instructions are sent. If the matter is urgent, the backsheet should be marked accordingly.

You must always keep a copy of the Instructions or Brief in the file. If Instructions in the same matter are being sent to more than one counsel, a separate backsheet is typed for each of them. In this event, where counsel's name appears on the backsheet, the name and address of the barrister to whom that particular set of papers is being sent must be put first. If this is junior counsel appearing with leading counsel (a QC), then after junior counsel's name type 'you with' and then put the name of leading counsel.

Where the set of papers is going to leading counsel, put his name and address first on the backsheet. Under that type 'with you' and then put the name of junior counsel. See the example backsheet for Instructions to Counsel. Do not forget to include your firm's name, address and reference, and the date. Instructions are normally typed on one side of the paper only, i.e., not back to back.

There are often enclosures, e.g., copies of relevant documents, to go with Instructions to Counsel, and these should either be indexed in a ring binder or, if they are not going into a ring binder, there should be a frontsheet (see page 90) for each enclosure, in which case each frontsheet would be numbered to correspond with the number the enclosure is given in the Instructions.

Once the fee earner is happy that everything is in order, any enclosures to go with the Instructions or Brief are put with it and they are all tied together in a bundle with pink tape showing the backsheet only. If the bundle is thin enough to be folded over showing only the typed part of the backsheet, then this is the preferred method (see page 25). Do not fold X-rays or photographs.

The Instructions are then either taken down by hand to the barrister's chambers if they are near enough or are sent in the post or through the DX. If you are asked to write a letter sending Instructions, you would address it to the barrister's clerk, e.g., Clerk to Mr Rob Roy, then his address, and simply say 'We enclose Instructions to Counsel, which kindly place before Mr Roy.' If the matter is urgent, this should be mentioned in the letter. In some cases, it is also wise to telephone the barrister's clerk and advise him of the urgency of the papers.

You may have to find the barrister's full address or telephone number. Addresses and telephone numbers of barristers and solicitors can be found in a law directory. Most legal offices will have a law directory but there are also quite a few to be found on the Internet.

When the barrister has drafted a document or 'settled' it, it is returned in draft form to the instructing solicitor. When it has been approved by the solicitor (or other fee earner), it must be typed on to good quality A4 size paper and typed in the correct layout, with a backsheet if appropriate. If a barrister has settled a statement of case or other document, the document must bear the barrister's name. If there is anything in a draft document which does not seem to make sense or you are not sure about, then clarify it with the fee earner before typing it, or type it but make a note about it for the fee earner on a separate piece of paper. See also the section 'Layout of Documents' in Chapter 1.

Example Instructions to Counsel

IN THE SOUTHTOWN COUNTY COURT   Claim No. 05.12345

BETWEEN:

PAUL XAVIER   Claimant

and

JOHN JONES   Defendant

INSTRUCTIONS TO COUNSEL TO ADVISE

Counsel has herewith:

1. Copy garage estimate for repairs to car.

2. Copy correspondence.

Instructing Solicitors act on behalf of the Claimant who was involved in a road traffic accident when he was driving his Rolls Royce motor car, index No. 123 DEF, along Station Road, Barnet, Herts. The accident occurred on Monday, 5th July 2004.

Counsel will see from the copy of the garage estimate enclosed the extent of the damage to the Claimant's car.

Particulars of Claim have been served in this matter and Counsel is asked to advise as to whether he thinks this matter should be pursued.

If Counsel has any queries relating to this matter, he is asked please to contact Mr. John Smith of Instructing Solicitors on 01438 12345.

[*date*]

Example backsheet for Instructions to Counsel

Claim No. 05.12345

IN THE SOUTHTOWN
COUNTY COURT

BETWEEN:

PAUL XAVIER   Claimant

and

JOHN JONES   Defendant

INSTRUCTIONS TO COUNSEL TO
ADVISE

Mr John Bloggs, QC,
1 Smith Street,
London EC4

with you

Mr Rob Roy,
2 Smith Street,
London EC4

John Smith & Co.,
2 Bank Chambers,
High Road,
Southtown,
Herts. EN5 6AX

tel: 01438 12345

ref: AB/cd/123
Solicitors for the Claimant
[*date*]

Example frontsheet for an enclosure

IN THE SOUTHTOWN COUNTY COURT   Claim No. 05.12345

BETWEEN:

PAUL XAVIER   Claimant

and

JOHN JONES   Defendant

Bundle 1—Copy Garage Estimate

Defence

When the defendant has received the Claim Form and Particulars of Claim, one of the courses of action open to him is to file a Defence. He may also wish to file a Counterclaim against the claimant and/or some other person (see Part 20 Claims below). A Counterclaim is a claim by the defendant made in response to the claimant's claim and which is included in the same proceedings, for example, if the claimant states that there was a car accident and the defendant damaged his car, the defendant might want to make a counterclaim against the claimant for damage to his own car.

The Defence should be made on the correct form, depending on whether the claim is for a specified amount (Form N9B) or an unspecified amount or non-money claim (Form N9D). If there is not enough room on the form, the Defence should be continued on separate sheets of paper. Each paragraph of the Defence should be numbered and each page numbered, and if the Defence is settled by counsel, his name should appear at the end. Remember to include the details in the box at the top right-hand of the form, i.e., the name of the court, the claim number and names of the claimant and defendant. This information should always be included on any separate sheets of paper.

If the defendant wishes to make a counterclaim against the claimant at the same time as filing his Defence, he may include this on the form for Defence and Counterclaim.

Where a Counterclaim is being served at the same time as the Defence, the Defence and Counterclaim should form one document, with the Defence first, followed by the Counterclaim.

If the claimant serves a Reply and a Defence to the Counterclaim, the Reply and Defence to Counterclaim should form one document, with the Reply going first, followed by the Defence to Counterclaim.

The Defence and/or Counterclaim must contain a Statement of Truth (see page 69) which will be signed by the defendant or his solicitors. Do not, as a secretary, sign this yourself. You should type on the form your firm's name, address and other details, including your reference. Keep a copy of the completed Defence on your file.

If the court is going to serve the Defence, it should be filed at court within 14 days after service of the Particulars of Claim. If the defendant has filed an Acknowledgment of Service, more time may be allowed for him to serve his Defence. The defendant and claimant can agree that the time limit for filing the Defence may be further extended. If they do agree to such an extension of time, the defendant must notify the court in writing. As well as there being a copy for the court, there should be a copy for the claimant and for every other party that is involved in the action.

If the solicitors are serving the Defence, they must file a copy with the court, and serve a copy on all other parties to the proceedings within the specified time limit. Always keep a copy of the Defence on your file.

If a period of six months has expired since the end of the time for filing a Defence and the defendant has not filed an admission, defence or counterclaim, or if he has admitted the claim and the claimant has not applied to enter judgment in that time, the claim will be stayed, i.e., nothing further will happen unless one of the parties applies for the stay to be lifted.

Part 20/Additional claims

On receiving the Claim Form and Particulars of Claim, the defendant may wish to make a claim of his own against the claimant or against someone who is not already a party to the proceedings. These claims are dealt with under Part 20 CPR although the defendant can, in any event, bring a counterclaim against the claimant at the same time as entering his defence. Sometimes, permission is needed from the court to file a Part 20 claim.

A fee is payable to the court on filing a Part 20 Claim Form (Form N211). As with the ordinary Claim Form (N1) discussed on page 61, the Part 20 Claim Form has with it explanatory notes for the Part 20 claimant (Form N211A) and notes for the Part 20 defendant (Form N211C).

If the defendant makes a Part 20 claim, the title to the action (see also page 61) must show clearly that the parties are now involved in a Part 20 claim. (See the form on page 92.)

The example Part 20 Claim Form shows that Paul Xavier is the original claimant, having made a claim against John Jones. This made John Jones the defendant in the original action. John Jones, the defendant, then decided that he would issue a Part 20 claim against Ann Bloggs, making John Jones a Part 20 claimant as well as a defendant to Paul Xavier's action. Because John Jones has now issued his Part 20 claim against Ann Bloggs, she is now a Part 20 defendant.

There can be more than one Part 20 claim, in which case, the parties to the first Part 20 claim would be described as, e.g., 'Part 20 claimant (1st claim)'; the parties to the second Part 20 claim would be described as 'Part 20 claimant (2nd claim)', and so on. However, rather than referring to parties like this throughout a document, as long as the parties are referred to in full in the title of the document, they may thereafter be referred to by name.

Where the Part 20 Claim is served on someone who is not already a party to the proceedings, it must be accompanied by a form for defending the claim; a form for admitting the claim; an Acknowledgment of Service form; together with a copy of every Statement of Case which has already been served in the proceedings and any other document the court may direct that they should have. A copy of the Part 20 Claim Form must be served on everyone that is already a party to the proceedings.

Reply

Having received the Defence, the claimant may reply to it. A Reply will be set out in the same manner as the Particulars of Claim and must include the heading, the claim number and the names and status of the parties to the claim. If the claimant is serving a Reply and

Claim Form
(Additional claims-CPR Part 20)

In the	
SOUTHTOWN COUNTY COURT	
Claim No.	05.12345

Claimant(s)   PAUL XAVIER

Defendant(s)   JOHN JONES

SEAL

Part 20 Claimant(s)   JOHN JONES

Part 20 Defendant(s)   ANN BLOGGS

Brief details of claim

Value

Defendant's name and address

	£
Amount claimed	
Court fee	
Solicitors costs	
Total amount	
Issue date	

The court office at

is open between 10 am and 4 pm Monday to Friday. When corresponding with the court, please address forms or letters to the Court Manager and quote the claim number.

N211 - w3 Claim Form (CPR Part 20 - additional claims)(4.99)   *Printed on behalf of The Court Service*

Claim No.	

Particulars of Claim (attached)

Statement of Truth
*(I believe)(The Part 20 Claimant believes) that the facts stated in these particulars of claim are true.
* I am duly authorised by the Part 20 claimant to sign this statement

Full name _____

Name of Part 20 claimant's solicitor's firm _____

signed _____ position or office held_____
*(Part 20 Claimant)('s solicitor)(Litigation friend)   (if signing on behalf of firm or company)

*delete as appropriate

Part 20 Claimant ('s solicitor's) address to which documents or payments should be sent if different from overleaf. If you are prepared to accept service by DX, fax or e-mail, please add details.

Defence to Counterclaim, these should normally be together in one document, with the Reply going first, followed by the Defence to Counterclaim. It will also contain a Statement of Truth.

A Reply to a Defence will normally be filed with the court when the claimant files his Allocation Questionnaire (see below). At the same time, all parties to the claim must be served with a copy of the Reply and, of course, you must keep a copy on your file.

Where the claim is for a sum of money and the Defence is simply that the money has been paid, the court will send a notice to the claimant asking him to state in writing whether he wants the claim to continue. If the claimant does wish the case to continue, he must serve a copy of his response on the defendant.

Allocation Questionnaire

Once a Defence has been filed, the court will serve an Allocation Questionnaire (Form N150) on each party. The details given on the Questionnaire will assist the court in deciding how the case will be managed and which track it will be allocated to (see below). Each party must complete the Allocation Questionnaire and file it with the court no later than the date specified on it by the court. However, the parties concerned should consult each other when completing the Questionnaire so that they can provide the court with mutually agreed information wherever possible.

If any party wishes to make an application to the court relating to the claim, for example, they may wish to apply for summary judgment (see page 100) or for some special directions regarding the claim, they should send their application to the court at the same time as they file the Allocation Questionnaire. A fee may be payable to the court for certain applications.

Where a party wishes any documents to be taken into account by the judge, he should also file these documents with the court at the same time as the completed Allocation Questionnaire, confirming that the other parties have been sent these documents and stating when they would have received them, and whether any other party has agreed the contents of the documents.

The sections of the Allocation Questionnaire are dealt with as follows.

Settlement

If any party to the claim wishes to have the court proceedings stayed because they think there is a chance that the claim could be settled, they can include this on the Allocation Questionnaire. If a settlement is reached, the claimant must notify the court.

Location of trial

This part of the Questionnaire asks for any reasons why a case may need to be heard at a particular court. The trial will normally take place at the court where the case is being managed, if appropriate, but it is possible for it to be transferred to another court for hearing if there is sufficient reason for this.

Pre-action protocols

These are mentioned on page 59. If a protocol applies to the claim, Part 1 of this section should be completed. If a protocol does not apply to the claim, Part 2 should be completed.

Case management information

This section requires details of any applications that have been made to the court (see page 114). Details of witnesses, including expert witnesses, must also be given. An expert could be someone like a doctor giving evidence in a personal injury claim, or a surveyor giving evidence about the value of property, etc. Any party wishing to call an expert to give evidence or put forward an expert's report as evidence must first obtain the court's permission. Normally, expert evidence will be given as a written report unless the court has directed otherwise. See also page 105 regarding expert evidence.

Finally, this section deals with the track to which the claim will be allocated. Claims are allocated to tracks, depending on the value of the claim and certain other factors such as the nature of the claim, the complexity of the case, the importance of the claim, the amount of oral evidence that may be required or the number of parties involved. Allocating a case to a particular track will determine the way in which the case will be managed. The tracks are:

(a) *The small claims track.*   This is the normal track for a claim which has a financial value of not more than £5,000. However, there are exceptions to this amount where the claim is for damages for personal injuries or the claim is by a tenant of residential premises claiming against his landlord to carry out repairs to the premises. See also page 101.

(b) *The fast track.*   This is the normal track for claims where the value of the claim is not more than £15,000 and where the claim is not one which would be dealt with in the small claims track. Again, exceptions may be made in allocating a case to this track. See also page 102.

(c) *The multi-track.*   This is the normal track for any claim which does not come into the small claims or fast track categories. See also page 105.

Trial or final hearing

To assist the court, an estimate of the length of the trial or final hearing will be given here. Details should also be included of dates when the party completing the form and any of his witnesses would not be able to attend court because of holidays or other commitments.

Proposed directions

A list of any directions that the party thinks are appropriate for the management of the claim should be attached to the form. Directions tell the parties what they must do to prepare the case and also give a timetable within which those steps must be taken. There are standard directions which are laid down by the rules of the court, and there are also special directions that are further directions that the judge might say must be complied with. Parties to a case may also apply to the court for further directions.

Costs

This part of the Questionnaire relates to costs incurred by legal representatives and requires that for certain claims (not those on the small claims track) an estimate of costs should be filed with the court. Any costs estimate should also be served on other parties to the case as well as given to the solicitor's own client.

Other information

The questions in this section should be answered and any other information relevant to the management of the claim should be given.

Allocation questionnaire

To be completed by, or on behalf of,

<table>
<tr><td></td></tr>
</table>

who is [1st][2nd][3rd][   ][Claimant][Defendant]
[Part 20 claimant] in this claim

<table>
<tr><td colspan="2">In the

SOUTHTOWN COUNTY COURT</td></tr>
<tr><td>Claim No.</td><td>05.12345</td></tr>
<tr><td>Last date for filing
with court office</td><td></td></tr>
</table>

Please read the notes on page five before completing the questionnaire.

You should note the date by which it must be returned and the name of the court it should be returned to since this may be different from the court where the proceedings were issued.

If you have settled this claim (or if you settle it on a future date) and do not need to have it heard or tried, you must let the court know immediately.

Have you sent a copy of this completed form to the other party(ies)?   ☐ Yes   ☐ No

A   Settlement

Do you wish there to be a one month stay to attempt to settle the claim, either by informal discussion or by alternative dispute resolution?   ☐ Yes   ☐ No

B   Location of trial

Is there any reason why your claim needs to be heard at a particular court?   ☐ Yes   ☐ No

If Yes, say which court and why?

C   Pre-action protocols

If an approved pre-action protocol applies to this claim, complete **Part 1** only. If not, complete **Part 2** only. If you answer 'No' to the question in either Part 1 or 2, please explain the reasons why on a separate sheet and attach it to this questionnaire.

Part 1	The* [ ] protocol applies to this claim.
*please say which protocol	Have you complied with it? ☐ Yes ☐ No

Part 2	No pre-action protocol applies to this claim.
	Have you exchanged information and/or documents (evidence) with the other party in order to assist in settling the claim? ☐ Yes ☐ No

D Case management information

What amount of the claim is in dispute?   £ [   ]

Applications

Have you made any application(s) in this claim?   ☐ Yes   ☐ No

If Yes, what for? [   ]   For hearing on [   ]
(e.g. summary judgment,
add another party)

Witnesses

So far as you know at this stage, what witnesses of fact do you intend to call at the trial or final hearing including, if appropriate, yourself?

Witness name	Witness to which facts

Experts

Do you wish to use expert evidence at the trial or final hearing?   ☐ Yes   ☐ No

Have you already copied any experts' report(s) to the other party(ies)?   ☐ None yet obtained   ☐ Yes   ☐ No

Do you consider the case suitable for a single joint expert in any field?   ☐ Yes   ☐ No

Please list any single joint experts you propose to use and any other experts you wish to rely on. Identify single joint experts with the initials 'SJ' after their name(s).

Expert's name	Field of expertise (eg. orthopaedic surgeon, surveyor, engineer)

Do you want your expert(s) to give evidence orally at the trial or final hearing?   ☐ Yes   ☐ No

If Yes, give the reasons why you think oral evidence is necessary:

[   ]

continue over ▐▐▐➡

Track

Which track do you consider is most suitable for your claim? Tick one box   ☐ small claims track   ☐ fast track   ☐ multi-track

If you have indicated a track which would not be the normal track for the claim, please give brief reasons for your choice

```
┌─────────────────────────────────────────────────────────────┐
│                                                               │
│                                                               │
│                                                               │
│                                                               │
│                                                               │
│                                                               │
│                                                               │
└─────────────────────────────────────────────────────────────┘
```

E Trial or final hearing

How long do you estimate the trial or final hearing will take?   ____days ____hours ____minutes

Are there any days when you, an expert or an essential witness will not be able to attend court for the trial or final hearing?   ☐ Yes   ☐ No

If Yes, please give details

Name	Dates not available

F Proposed directions *(Parties should agree directions wherever possible)*

Have you attached a list of the directions you think appropriate for the management of the claim?   ☐ Yes   ☐ No

If Yes, have they been agreed with the other party(ies)?   ☐ Yes   ☐ No

G Costs

*Do **not** complete this section if you have suggested your case is suitable for the small claims track **or** you have suggested one of the other tracks and you do not have a solicitor acting for you.*

What is your estimate of your costs incurred to date?   £ _____

What do you estimate your overall costs are likely to be?   £ _____

In substantial cases these questions should be answered in compliance with CPR Part 43

3

H Other information

Have you attached documents to this questionnaire? ☐ Yes ☐ No

Have you sent these documents to the other party(ies)? ☐ Yes ☐ No

If Yes, when did they receive them?

Do you intend to make any applications in the immediate future? ☐ Yes ☐ No

If Yes, what for?

In the space below, set out any other information you consider will help the judge to manage the claim.

Signed

[Counsel][Solicitor][for the][1ˢᵗ][2ⁿᵈ][3ʳᵈ][   ]
[Claimant][Defendant][Part 20 claimant]

Date

Please enter your firm's name, reference number and full postal address including (if appropriate) details of DX, fax or e-mail

	if applicable	
	fax no.	
	DX no.	
Tel. no. Postcode	e-mail	
Your reference no.		

4

Once the Questionnaire is complete, it must be signed as appropriate and dated. It should be returned by the specified date to the court named on the form. A fee is normally payable to the court by the claimant on returning the Questionnaire (or, if allocation takes place without a Questionnaire, the fee is payable within 21 days of allocation). Make sure that you note which court it should go to because the case may already have been transferred to another court.

Remember to keep a copy of the Questionnaire for your file, together with a copy of any costs estimate.

Allocation to a track

The court will allocate the claim to a track (see page 95) when it receives all the Allocation Questionnaires or when the period for filing the Questionnaires has expired or, if it has stayed the proceedings, at the end of the period of the stay. The case will be allocated to a procedural judge who will deal with the management of the case and allocate it to a track. Before deciding on the most suitable track for the case, the court may hold an allocation hearing if it is thought necessary.

Once the court has allocated a case to a track, it will serve a Notice of Allocation on every party (a different form will be used by the court for the Notice of Allocation, depending on the track to which the case has been allocated). At the same time, the court will serve on every party a copy of the Allocation Questionnaires completed by the other parties and a copy of any further information provided by another party. Before it allocates a case to a track, the court may order a party to provide further information about his case. Having allocated a case to a particular track, the court may re-allocate a claim to a different track if it considers it appropriate to do so.

Transferring a case to another court

If the claim is for a specified amount of money and the defendant is an individual (not a company or some other organisation), the court may transfer the proceedings to the defendant's 'home court'. This means that if it is a claim in the county court, the defendant's home court is the county court for the district in which the defendant resides or carries on business. If it is a claim in the High Court, the defendant's home court is the District Registry for the district in which the Defendant resides or carries on business or, if there is no such District Registry, the Royal Courts of Justice. This will usually apply unless the case is one which must be heard in a specialist list in the High Court. If the claim is against more than one defendant with different home courts, the proceedings will be transferred to the home court of the defendant who filed his Defence first.

Before allocating a claim to a particular track, the court may, if it feels it appropriate to do so, transfer a case to another court in any event.

Summary judgment

In many cases (but not those in the small claims track) a party may apply to the court to decide the claim or an issue without a trial, by way of summary judgment. The court may also, of its own initiative, give summary judgment, although in this instance, it must give the parties an opportunity to be heard. Summary judgment is a way of deciding a claim without trial and may be given against either party on all or part of the claim if it is considered that either party has no realistic prospect of success.

The small claims track

The small claims track is for straightforward claims which have a financial value of not more than £5,000 (subject to the exceptions relating to claims for damages for personal injuries or housing disrepair). If a claim of a higher value is suitable for the small claims track, it may be allocated to the small claims track if the parties agree. Claims in the small claims track are heard in a county court, usually by a District judge. The small claims track aims to avoid large amounts of work before trial and hearings for cases on this track are more informal than for claims on the other tracks. Some parts of the CPR which apply to fast track and/or multi-track cases do not apply to small claims procedures, e.g., offers and payments under Part 36 CPR (see page 127) are not part of the small claims procedure.

When a case has been allocated to the small claims track, the court will manage the case by setting dates and time limits for various things which must be done by the parties. The court will also encourage the parties to use an alternative dispute resolution procedure (see Chapter 4) where it considers this to be appropriate. It is possible for someone to conduct his own case in the small claims track without instructing a solicitor. See also page 100 regarding the allocation of claims to a track.

Preparing for the hearing

One of the things the court will do is to give 'directions', i.e., instruct the parties on what they should do to prepare their case for a hearing or for trial. Directions will usually have to be carried out within a certain time limit, e.g., each party must, at least 14 days before the date of the final hearing, file and serve on every other party copies of all documents on which he intends to rely at the hearing. The court may give any other directions that may be laid down, and may also give any special or further directions it considers to be appropriate.

The court will fix a date for a preliminary hearing (see below) if it is considered that this will be helpful, otherwise a date may be fixed for the final hearing. The court must normally give the parties at least 21 days' notice of the final hearing date, and inform them how much time will be allowed for the hearing. It may even be considered by the court that a hearing is not necessary at all, in which case, it must ask the parties whether they agree to this. If the judge decides a case without a hearing, he will prepare a note of the reasons for his judgment and the court will send a copy to each party.

Preliminary hearing

The court may hold a preliminary hearing for various reasons. These include:

(a) it feels that special directions are needed to ensure a fair hearing and also thinks that one of the parties should attend court so that they fully understand the special directions that are to be given;

(b) one of the parties may have no real prospect of success at a final hearing and the court may be able to dispose of the claim at a preliminary hearing before anything further is done;

(c) where the court considers that the claim is not suitable for the small claims track.

If the court does decide to hold a preliminary hearing, it must give the parties at least 14 days' notice. If all parties agree, the court may treat the preliminary hearing as the final hearing of the claim.

At or after the preliminary hearing, the court will give any appropriate directions and will fix the date of the final hearing if this has not already been done, also informing the parties of the time allowed for the final hearing.

The final hearing

A small claims hearing is a public hearing before a District judge or Circuit judge. The judge may decide to hold the hearing in private if the parties agree or if there are other reasons which are permitted. The small claims hearing will usually take place in the judge's room but could take place in a courtroom. It will be more informal than trials on the other tracks, e.g., the court may decide that evidence need not be given on oath. A small claims hearing should normally be disposed of within one day.

If one of the parties does not attend the final hearing and has not given the court written notice at least seven days before the hearing date that he will be unable to attend, the court may strike out that party's Claim or Defence and/or Counterclaim. A party may ask the court to decide the case in his absence but this request must be made to the court in the notice informing the court that he will be unable to attend. As with a case decided without a hearing, if it is heard in the absence of a party who has given suitable notice, the court will send to the parties a copy of the judge's notes giving reasons for his judgment.

If the defendant does not attend the final hearing but the claimant does, the court may proceed with the hearing on the basis of the evidence given by the claimant.

The fast track

The fast track is the normal track for claims where the value of the claim is not more than £15,000 and where the claim is not one which would be dealt with in the small claims track. Exceptions may be made in allocating a case to this track.

When a case is allocated to the fast track, the court will give directions for the management of the case by setting dates and time limits for various things which must be done by the parties. The court will either fix the trial date or fix a specific period of time (not covering more than four weeks)—a 'window'—during which the trial will take place. The Notice of Allocation sent by the court to the parties will specify the date of trial or the period of time in which the trial will take place. The CPR provide that the trial should take place in 30 weeks or less from the time that the directions were given. A case in the fast track should not normally last more than one day which, of course, may depend on the number of witnesses to be called, the number of experts that may be required, and the complexity of the issues involved.

The court will send the parties a Listing Questionnaire (Pre-trial checklist) (Form N170) (see page 106) which they must complete and return by the date specified. Once the date for filing this form has passed, the court will fix the date for trial or, if it has already done this, it will confirm the date. On filing the Listing Questionnaire (Pre-trial checklist), a fee must be paid, usually by the claimant. The court will also give any directions for the trial, including a trial timetable and specify any further steps that need to be taken before trial. At least three weeks' notice of the date of trial will usually be given.

The timetable for the trial may be agreed by the parties, subject to approval of the trial judge. The timetable will specify the time allowed for both the claimant and defendant's evidence and the time allowed for the submissions to be made to the court on behalf of each party.

Request for further information

In fast track and multi-track cases (see page 95), if one party wishes to request further information or clarification from another party, he can make a Request for Further Information under Part 18 CPR. The information being sought may relate to a Statement of Case or other matters in the proceedings. However, before making any application to the court, the party requiring the information should first try to obtain this from the other party.

The party seeking further information (the first party) should serve on the party from whom he is seeking the information (the second party) a written Request, giving a reasonable date by which a Response should be served, and stating that the Request is made under Part 18 CPR. If a Request for Information is very brief and it is likely that the response will be brief, this may be done in a letter, otherwise a Request should be in a separate document. If the Request is made in a letter, it must state that it is a Request under Part 18 CPR and the letter should not contain anything other than the Request. Before the CPR came into effect, a Request for Information was known as a Request for Further and Better Particulars.

All requests for further information, whether in a letter or a separate document, should be headed with the title of the action; identify the first and second parties; give the claim number; and state in its heading that it is a Request made under Part 18 CPR, giving the date when the Request is made. The pages and paragraphs should be numbered and where the Request relates to another document, e.g., it may be a request for further information about something mentioned in the Particulars of Claim, that other document must be referred to and the paragraph or words to which the Request relates should be clearly identified (see the example Request for Further Information, over). The date by which the Response is expected must also be given.

If the Request is in document format, rather than a letter, it may have the numbered paragraphs of the Request on the left-hand side of the paper, so that the second party can reply on the same document opposite each numbered paragraph on the right-hand side of the paper. If the Request is prepared in this way, an extra copy should be prepared for the second party to keep.

Subject to other court rules about service, a Request for Further Information may be served by e-mail if this is practicable.

The Response to a Request must be in writing and dated and signed by the responding party or his legal representative. The Response will have the same type of layout as the Request and must state in the heading that it is a response to that Request. If it is in a separate document (and not one where the answers can be given on the right-hand side of the page of the Request), the text of each paragraph of the Request must be set out and then the Response will be given below that (see example). It may also have a backsheet.

A Response should also be verified by a Statement of Truth (see page 69). When one party serves his Response on another party, he must also serve a copy on any other party to the proceedings and file a copy with the court, as well as keeping a copy on his own file.

Example Request for Further Information

IN THE SOUTHTOWN COUNTY COURT   Claim No. 05.12345

BETWEEN:

PAUL XAVIER   Claimant

and

JOHN JONES   Defendant

REQUEST FOR FURTHER INFORMATION
UNDER PART 18 CPR
DATED 8th APRIL 2005

1. Of paragraph 1 in the Particulars of Claim dated ****, 'the claimant was the owner and driver of a Rolls Royce motor car registration number 123 ABC.' State how long he had owned this car.

2. Of paragraph 3 in the Particulars of Claim dated ****, '...failed to keep any or any proper lookout.' State exactly how the defendant failed to keep any or any proper lookout.

JOHN BROWN
[*counsel's name, if appropriate*]

Dated the 8th day of April 2005.

Joe Bloggs & Co., of 1 Broad Walk, Southtown, Herts. EN4 9PP. Solicitors for the Defendant.

[*The Request would also identify the party seeking the information (the first party) and the party who is to provide the information (the second party). Additionally, it must contain a reasonable date specifying by when the first party expects to receive a Response to the Request. As mentioned previously, it may also be set out in a different format with the questions on the left-hand side of the paper, leaving room on the right-hand side for the other party's Response.*]

Example Response to Request for Further Information

IN THE SOUTHTOWN COUNTY COURT   Claim No. 05.12345

BETWEEN:

PAUL XAVIER   Claimant

and

JOHN JONES   Defendant

RESPONSE TO REQUEST FOR FURTHER
INFORMATION UNDER PART 18 CPR
DATED 8th APRIL 2005

1. Of paragraph 1 in the Particulars of Claim dated ****, 'the claimant was the owner and driver of a Rolls Royce motor car registration number 123 ABC.' State how long he had owned this car.

ANSWER

The claimant had owned this car for 2 years.

2. Of paragraph 3 in the Particulars of Claim dated ****, '...failed to keep any or any proper lookout.' State exactly how the defendant failed to keep any or any proper lookout.

ANSWER

The defendant failed to keep any or any proper lookout because he had his eyes closed at the time.

I believe that the facts stated in this Response to Request for Further Information are true. [*Note: the wording of this Statement of Truth will vary according to who is signing it*]

Signed ....

[*The status of the person signing the Statement of Truth will be inserted, e.g., claimant, claimant's solicitors, and if the solicitors are signing it they will also state that they are authorised by their client to do so*]

DATED this 18th day of April 2005.

John Smith & Co., of 2 Bank Chambers, High Road, Southtown, Herts. Solicitors for the Claimant.

Disclosure and inspection of documents

One of the directions given for fast track and multi-track cases may be about disclosure and inspection of documents. This is described on page 110.

Expert evidence

The parties may obtain reports from experts, for example, medical reports in a claim for personal injuries, or surveyors' reports in cases relating to property, or any other type of expert evidence that may be appropriate for the claim. Often each party will wish to obtain its own expert evidence but it is preferred, where possible, for a single joint expert to be agreed. If a single joint expert cannot be agreed, then expert evidence should be exchanged between the parties. The directions will specify the time by which any such reports must be served on or exchanged with the other parties involved.

The parties should also try to agree their reports if possible, usually no later than 14 days after they have been served on the other party. If the reports cannot be agreed, the directions may provide for the experts to discuss their reports in an attempt to reach agreement. If the experts cannot reach agreement, they must prepare a statement setting out the issues on which they agree and disagree and their reasons, and this statement must be filed with the court.

If one party wishes to address any questions to the other party's expert, the directions deal with how this will be done. See also page 127 regarding experts' evidence.

Witnesses of fact

In a similar way to experts' reports being exchanged, if any party intends to rely on the statements of any witnesses of fact, he should exchange or serve these on the other parties. The directions deal with the timing of this.

The multi-track

The multi-track is the normal track for any claim which does not come into the small claims or fast track categories. A multi-track claim may often be heard in a Civil Trial Centre or may be heard in the Royal Courts of Justice in London (RCJ), although there are special provisions for RCJ cases. In multi-track cases, the court has more flexibility in managing the case than the courts have in small claims track and fast track cases.

As with cases in the other tracks, when a case is allocated to the multi-track, the court will give directions for the management of the case and set a timetable for the steps to be taken between the giving of directions and the trial. In multi-track cases, the court may also hold case management conferences (see below) and may give any other directions it considers to be appropriate.

Case management conferences and pre-trial review

Once a Defence has been filed, the court may fix a case management conference if the case is allocated to the multi-track. This will usually be conducted by the procedural judge, i.e., the judge allocated to deal with the management of the case prior to trial. The party's legal representative must attend the case management conference. The legal representative must be someone who is fully involved in the case and who can deal with any matters that may arise during the conference. If appropriate, the parties to the claim will attend the conference. The fee earner attending the conference may wish to prepare a case summary to assist the court at the conference. If he does, the case summary will set out brief details of the claim in chronological order, together with the issues of fact which are agreed or in dispute and the evidence needed to decide them. The summary should, if possible, be agreed with the other parties and should not normally be longer than 500 words.

Various matters will be discussed at the case management conference, such as proposals for the management of the proceedings, including a proposed trial date or period in which the trial should take place. The parties will normally have to state whether they have discussed the question of Alternative Dispute Resolution (see Chapter 4) and if not, why not.

The case management conference will review the steps which have been taken by the parties to prepare the case, in particular their compliance with any directions that may have been given by the court. Any further directions that may be necessary to progress the claim may also be decided at the conference, as well as trying to ensure that the parties reach agreement on any matters where at all possible.

The court may hold another case conference or a pre-trial review if it is estimated that the case will last for more than 10 days. A pre-trial review will be held between four and eight weeks before the trial date, after the Listing Questionnaire (Pre-trial checklists) (see below) have been filed with the court. The purpose of the pre-trial review is to decide on a timetable for the trial, and this will include such things as the evidence that will be allowed, an estimate of how long the trial will last, and various other matters. The pre-trial review will normally be conducted by the trial judge and it should be attended by the legal representatives who will be representing the parties at the trial.

Listing Questionnaire (Pre-trial checklist)

In fast track and multi-track cases, the court will send each party a Listing Questionnaire (Pre-trial checklist) (Form N170) which they must complete and return to the court by the date specified. The date specified for filing this form will not be more than eight weeks before the trial date or the beginning of the trial period.

The purpose of this form is to ensure that each party has done all that they should within the timescale so that the trial can proceed efficiently. The form itself is self-explanatory and asks the parties to confirm whether they have complied with any directions; details of witnesses, experts and legal representation, as well as other necessary information. At the end of the form, under section F, there is a checklist for the party completing the form to ensure that they have enclosed other required documentation.

Although it is not necessary for the parties to exchange copies of this form before they are filed with the court, it is desirable that they do so to avoid the court being given conflicting or incomplete information.

The form must be signed and dated, with a copy being kept on the file, and then returned to the court, together with the appropriate fee. If listing for trial takes place without this form, the fee is payable within a specified time after the case is listed. Listing fees are payable by the Claimant unless the claim is proceeding on a counterclaim alone.

Once the date for filing the Form N170 has passed, the court will fix the date for trial or, if a trial date has already been fixed, the court will confirm that date. The court will give the parties at least three weeks' notice of the date of trial except in exceptional circumstances. It will also give any appropriate directions for trial and specify any further steps that need to be taken before trial.

Listing questionnaire
(Pre-trial checklist)

To be completed by, or on behalf of,

In the	SOUTHTOWN COUNTY COURT

Claim No.	05.12345
Last date for filing with court office	
Date(s) fixed for trial or trial period	

who is [1st][2nd][3rd][   ][Claimant][Defendant]
[Part 20 claimant][Part 20 defendant] in this claim

This form must be **completed** and **returned** to the court no later than the date given above. If not, your statement of case may be struck out or some other sanction imposed.

If the claim has settled, or settles before the trial date, you must let the court know immediately.

Legal representatives only: You must **attach** estimates of costs incurred to date, and of your likely overall costs. In substantial cases, these should be provided in compliance with CPR Part 43.

For multi-track claims only, you must also **attach** a proposed timetable for the trial itself.

A Confirmation of compliance with directions

1. I confirm that I have complied with those directions already given which require action by me.

☐Yes ☐No

If you are unable to give confirmation, state which directions you have still to comply with and the date by which this will be done.

Directions	Date

2. I believe that additional directions are necessary before the trial takes place.

☐Yes ☐No

If Yes, you should attach an application and a draft order.

*Include in your application all directions needed to enable the claim **to be tried on the date, or within the trial period, already fixed.** These should include any issues relating to experts and their evidence, and any orders needed in respect of directions still requiring action by any other party.*

3. Have you agreed the additional directions you are seeking with the other party(ies)?

☐Yes ☐No

B Witnesses

1. How many witnesses (including yourself) will be giving evidence on your behalf at the trial? *(Do not include experts - see Section C)*

Continued over ↷

Witnesses continued

2. If the trial date is not yet fixed, are there any days within the trial period you or your witnesses would wish to avoid if possible? *(Do not include experts - see Section C)*

Please give details

Name of witness	Dates to be avoided, if possible	Reason

Please specify any special facilities or arrangements needed at court for the party or any witness (e.g. witness with a disability).

3. Will you be providing an interpreter for any of your witnesses?   ☐Yes ☐No

C Experts

You are reminded that you may not use an expert's report or have your expert give oral evidence unless the court has given permission. If you do not have permission, you must make an application (see section A2 above)

1. Please give the information requested for your expert(s)

Name	Field of expertise	Joint expert?	Is report agreed?	Has permission been given for oral evidence?
		☐Yes ☐No	☐Yes ☐No	☐Yes ☐No
		☐Yes ☐No	☐Yes ☐No	☐Yes ☐No
		☐Yes ☐No	☐Yes ☐No	☐Yes ☐No

2. Has there been discussion between experts?   ☐Yes ☐No

3. Have the experts signed a joint statement?   ☐Yes ☐No

4. If your expert is giving oral evidence and the trial date is not yet fixed, is there any day within the trial period which the expert would wish to avoid, if possible?   ☐Yes ☐No

If Yes, please give details

Name	Dates to be avoided, if possible	Reason

D Legal representation

1. Who will be presenting your case at the trial?   ☐ You ☐ Solicitor ☐ Counsel

2. If the trial date is not yet fixed, is there any day within the trial period that the person presenting your case would wish to avoid, if possible?   ☐ Yes ☐ No

If Yes, please give details

Name	Dates to be avoided, if possible	Reason

E The trial

1. Has the estimate of the time needed for trial changed?   ☐ Yes ☐ No

If Yes, say how long you estimate the whole trial will take, including both parties' cross-examination and closing arguments   ☐ days ☐ hours ☐ minutes

2. If different from original estimate have you agreed with the other party(ies) that this is now the **total** time needed?   ☐ Yes ☐ No

3. Is the timetable for trial you have attached agreed with the other party(ies)?   ☐ Yes ☐ No

Fast track cases only

The court will normally give you 3 weeks notice of the date fixed for a fast track trial unless, in exceptional circumstances, the court directs that shorter notice will be given.

Would you be prepared to accept shorter notice of the date fixed for trial?   ☐ Yes ☐ No

F Document and fee checklist

Tick as appropriate

I attach to this questionnaire -

☐ An application and fee for additional directions   ☐ A proposed timetable for trial

☐ A draft order   ☐ An estimate of costs

☐ Listing fee

Signed
[Counsel][Solicitor][for the][1st][2nd][3rd][   ] [Claimant][Defendant] [Part 20 claimant][Part 20 defendant]
Date

Please enter your [firm's] name, reference number and full postal address including (if appropriate) details of DX, fax or e-mail

Postcode

Tel. no.		DX no.		E-mail	
Fax no.		Ref. no.			

3 of 3

Disclosure and inspection of documents

Where a case is allocated to the fast track or the multi-track, the parties should disclose to the other parties in the case details of all documents relating to the case. This means the documents upon which they rely or which materially undermine their own case or support the other party's case. This is termed as 'standard disclosure'. Any further disclosure will be determined by the procedural judge. Where a party has or knows of documents that he should disclose, he must provide a list of those documents to the other party, unless the parties have agreed that there will be no list (or this has been dispensed with by the court), stating that the document exists or has existed. This is referred to as disclosure of documents. Before the Civil Procedure Rules, this was known as 'discovery'.

Once a document has been disclosed in this way, the party to whom it has been disclosed has a right to inspect it unless the document is no longer in the control of the party who disclosed it or the party disclosing it has a right or duty to withhold inspection of it.

The documents which are to be disclosed should be listed on Form N265. They should be listed in chronological or some other convenient order and should be numbered consecutively. Each document should have a brief description, e.g., letter to Peter Smith & Co., brief to counsel. If there is bulky correspondence between the same people, instead of itemising each letter, they can be listed as a bundle with an appropriate description, e.g., letters between Joe Bloggs and John Smith between 1 November 2000 and 8 July 2005. The list must indicate which documents are no longer in that party's control and state what has happened to them.

The list is divided into sections showing:

(a) documents to which there is no objection to them being inspected or copied;

(b) those where there is an objection to them being inspected (giving reasons);

(c) those which the disclosing party has had, but no longer has.

The list must also include a disclosure statement (unless the parties have agreed that there will be no disclosure statement) which gives details of the extent of any search made to locate relevant documents. The disclosure statement must also certify that the party disclosing understands the duty to disclose documents and that he has carried out that duty to the best of his knowledge. The wording of the disclosure statement is shown on the first page of the list of documents (Form N265).

If, after a list of documents has been served, further documents come to light, a supplemental list of documents must be prepared.

If a party wishes to inspect a document, he must give the disclosing party written notice that he wishes to inspect it and the disclosing party must allow inspection within seven days of receiving that notice. The party inspecting may ask for a copy of the document if he agrees to pay reasonable copying charges. The copy should be supplied within seven days.

If it is desired that a document in the list should not be inspected by the other party, e.g., it may be a privileged document, the disclosure statement must summarise the reasons for this. If a document is privileged, this means that the party whose document it is has a right not to disclose or produce it. Examples of such documents are correspondence between the solicitor and his client, Instructions to Counsel, Counsel's Opinion, and 'without prejudice' documents. 'Without prejudice' may be written on correspondence between solicitors when a settlement of the case is being sought. Such correspondence is not produced at any later court proceedings. If it is considered that disclosure of a document may damage the public interest, the relevant party may apply to the court for permission not to disclose that document.

If disclosure is required by someone who is not a party to the proceedings, application must be made to the court.

List of documents: standard disclosure

In the	
	SOUTHTOWN COUNTY COURT
Claim No.	05.12345
Claimant (including ref)	PAUL XAVIER (XAV/789)
Defendant (including ref)	JOHN JONES (JON/cd)
Date	

Notes:
- The rules relating to standard disclosure are contained in Part 31 of the Civil Procedure Rules.
- Documents to be included under standard disclosure are contained in Rule 31.6
- A document has or will have been in your control if you have or have had possession, or a right of possession, of it **or** a right to inspect or take copies of it.

Disclosure Statement

I state that I have carried out a reasonable and proportionate search to locate all the documents which I am required to disclose under the order made by the court on *(insert date)*

(I did not search for documents -

1. pre-dating

2. located elsewhere than

3. in categories other than

)

I certify that I understand the duty of disclosure and to the best of my knowledge I have carried out that duty. I further certify that the list of documents set out in or attached to this form, is a complete list of all documents which are or have been in my control and which I am obliged under the order to disclose.

I understand that I must inform the court and the other parties immediately if any further document required to be disclosed by Rule 31.6 comes into my control at any time before the conclusion of the case.

(I have not permitted inspection of documents within the category or class of documents (as set out below) required to be disclosed under Rule 31(6)(b)or (c) on the grounds that to do so would be disproportionate to the issues in the case.)

Signed		**Date**	

(Claimant)(Defendant)('s litigation friend)

Position or office held *(if signing on behalf of firm or company)*
Please state why you are the appropriate person to make the disclosure statement.

List of documents:

continued overleaf

N265 - w3 standard disclosure (4.99)

Printed on behalf of The Court Service

List and number here, in a convenient order, the documents (or bundles of documents if of the same nature, e.g. invoices) in your control, which you do not object to being inspected. Give a short description of each document or bundle so that it can be identified, and say if it is kept elsewhere i.e. with a bank or solicitor

I have control of the documents numbered and listed here. I do not object to you inspecting them/producing copies.

1. Estimate - Speed & Co - 20 July 2004
2. Car hire account -
        Smith & Co - 1 August 2004

List and number here, as above, the documents in your control which you object to being inspected. (Rule 31.19)

I have control of the documents numbered and listed here, but I object to you inspecting them:

Say what your objections are

I object to you inspecting these documents because:

List and number here, the documents you once had in your control, but which you no longer have. For each document listed, say when it was last in your control and where it is now.

I have had the documents numbered and listed below, but they are no longer in my control.

Amending a statement of case

A statement of case (formerly known as a pleading) may be amended at any time before it is served on another party. If it has already been served, it may be amended only with the written consent of all the other parties involved or with the permission of the court.

If making an application to the court to amend a statement of case, a copy of the statement of case showing the proposed amendments should be filed with the application. Once permission to amend has been given, the amended statement of case should be filed with the court, usually within 14 days. A copy of the amended statement of case should be served on all parties to the proceedings. Where a statement of case is amended, the amendments must be verified by a Statement of Truth unless the court orders otherwise.

An amended statement of case and the court copy of it, if permission was needed from the court, should include the following endorsement:

> Amended [Particulars of Claim *or whatever is the document*] by Order of [Master *Bloggs*] [District Judge *Bloggs*] (*or whoever made the Order*) dated ....

If the court's permission was not required to make the amendment, the statement of case should be endorsed as follows:

> Amended [Particulars of Claim *or whatever is the document*] under CPR [17.1(1)] [17.1(2)(a)] dated ....

Rule 17.1(1) would be inserted in the endorsement above if the statement of case has not yet been served on another party. Rule 17.1(2)(a) applies where the written consent of all the other parties has been obtained.

The amended statement of case does not have to show the original text (which may have been deleted) unless the court thinks this is necessary. Where this is the case both the original text and the amendments would have to be shown. This may be done in one of two ways.

(a) by coloured amendments, either made by hand or computer generated; or

(b) by numbering the amendments in superscript (this may only be done in a computer generated document—the numbers should not be inserted by hand—and colours should not be used in this instance). Where this method is adopted, insertions should be underlined and numbered; and deletions should be struck through and numbered.

Where colour is used to make the amendments, the text to be deleted is struck through in colour and any text replacing it or additional text should be written in the same colour, or written in black and underlined in that colour. Red should be used the first time that any document is amended. If, however, at another time, it is desired to amend the already amended statement of case, a different colour must be used for the amendments to show that it is an entirely different set of amendments. This time, the colour should be green. After green, the next colour is violet and then yellow. It is not, however, very common to go past the green amendment stage.

In the example below showing how coloured amendments would be made, the line striking through the text would be in red and where the text is underlined, either the text would be in red or it would be underlined in red. Therefore, all amendments would be clearly shown in red. Thus:

1. The claimant was the owner and driver of a Rolls Royce motor car, registration number 123 ~~ABC~~ DEF.

2. On 5 July 2001 the claimant was driving his said motor car along Station Road, ~~Mulberry Close~~, Barnet, Hertfordshire.

If the amendments are made by numbering them, you would strike through text to be deleted in black, following this with the appropriate number in superscript, e.g., ~~the car veered off the road~~[1]. Text to be added will be typed in black and underlined, with the superscript number next to it, e.g., <u>the car veered off the road</u>[1].

The number will relate to the stage the amendments have reached, i.e., the first time amendments are made, all the amendments made at that time will be numbered 1 (in relation to the scheme using colours, this would be the red amendment stage); on the next occasion when amendments are made to the document (the green amendment stage if using colours), all the amendments at that stage will be numbered 2, and so on.

If the amendments to the statement of case have been settled by counsel, then as with other documents settled by counsel, it must show his name. If the amended document is one where both the amendments and the original text have to be shown, counsel's name will be typed at the end either in the appropriate colour or with the appropriate numbering. This will be typed beneath where counsel's name is shown on the original text, if applicable. In a similar manner, where amendments have to be shown, if the document had been previously served on another party, once it has been amended, it will have to be re-served on the other party and this will have to be shown on the new document as an amendment.

Thus, if the document has to show all the amendments made, it will contain details of both the date of service of the original document and details of service of the amended document. Remember to amend the backsheet as well to show that the new document is an amended one. For example, if the old document was a Particulars of Claim, you would add in red the word 'Amended' before 'Particulars of Claim' (which would stay in black).

Photocopies of documents which have to show the amendments that have been made must also be clear. Therefore, if colour has been used for making the amendments, this must be shown on the copy, either by colour copying or by underlining and/or striking through the amendments in the appropriate colour so that the copy is the same as the original. However, as stated earlier, not all amended statements of case will require the amendments to be shown.

Applications for court orders

A court order may be required by a party either before issuing proceedings or at some time before the trial date. To obtain a court order, an application must be made to the court by way of an Application Notice. Before the CPR, an application to the court for an order was made by way of summons (indeed, some still are). An application made to the court after proceedings have been issued, but before the trial date, may be termed an 'interlocutory' application. There are many reasons for making an application to the court, such as asking for more time to file a statement of case or perhaps one party will not comply with the request of another and the only way to resolve this would be for the court to make a decision on the matter.

The person making the application is called the Applicant and the person against whom the order is sought is the Respondent. If proceedings have already been started or have been transferred to another court, the application must be made to the court where the proceedings are being dealt with. If the claim has already been listed for trial, the application must be made to the court where the trial will take place. If proceedings have not yet been started, an application must be made to the court where proceedings would normally be started.

Applications to the court must normally be made by filing with the court an Application Notice (Form N244). It must state what order is being sought by the Applicant and why he is seeking the order. As well as all the usual details, such as name of the court, claim number, names of the parties to the action, the Notice must also include:

(a) a request for a hearing or telephone conference, giving an estimate of the time this will take; or a request that the application is dealt with without a hearing;

(b) the full name of the Applicant or his solicitor;

(c) details of the order sought (sometimes a draft order should be attached);

(d) the reasons for making the application;

(e) if the Applicant is not already a party to the proceedings, his address for service;

(f) in some cases, the Application Notice will have to be verified by a Statement of Truth (see below and also see page 69);

(g) it must be signed by the Applicant or his solicitor.

If the application is being verified by a Statement of Truth, it would state 'I believe [*or the Applicant believes*] that the facts stated in this application notice are true.' If the Statement of Truth is in a separate document, it would say 'I believe [*or the Applicant believes*] that the facts stated in the application notice issued on [*date*] for [*whatever remedy is being sought*] are true.' Do not, as a secretary, sign the Statement of Truth yourself.

If an application is supported by a witness statement or some other document, a copy of any such document should be included for service on the Respondent. Similarly, if the application is asking that the Respondent provides further information relating to a statement of case, a copy of the Request for Further Information should be attached to the application.

Two copies of the Application Notice must be prepared, and should then be given to whoever in your firm will go to court to have it issued (the outdoor clerk, or it can be sent to the court by post or DX). There is a box on the form to complete giving an estimate of how long the hearing or telephone conference will take (the fee earner will deal with this aspect). The appropriate fee must be paid to the court to issue the Application Notice. The court will notify the Applicant of the date and time of the hearing (known as the 'return date'). The fee earner may ask you to note in his diary the date and time of the application and inform whoever will be attending.

The court may serve (see page 73) the Application Notice on the Respondent, or the Applicant's solicitors may wish to serve it. The original sealed Application Notice should be kept in the file and a copy will be served on the other party. It must be served at least three days before the date when the court will be dealing with it. Copies of any witness statements in support of the application must be served at the same time. If there is not enough time to serve the Application Notice, e.g., the matter may be extremely urgent, informal notification must be given to the other parties unless it is a case where the application is being made without notice (see below).

If you are asked to write a letter serving an Application Notice, it will be on the following lines:

Dear Sirs,

Xavier v Jones

We enclose, by way of service, Application Notice returnable before Master Bloggs at 11 a.m. on Tuesday, 9th February, 2006. Kindly acknowledge receipt.

Yours faithfully,

Application Notice

You should provide this information for listing the application	

1. How do you wish to have your application dealt with

    a) at a hearing? ☐

    b) at a telephone conference? ☐ } *complete all questions below*

    c) without a hearing? ☐   *complete Qs 5 and 6 below*

2. Give a time estimate for the hearing/conference

    _____(hours)_____(mins)

3. Is this agreed by all parties? ☐ Yes ☐ No

4. Give dates of any trial period or fixed trial date _____

5. Level of judge _____

6. Parties to be served _____

In the	
SOUTHTOWN COUNTY COURT	
Claim no.	05.12345
Warrant no. (If applicable)	
Claimant (including ref.)	PAUL XAVIER (XAV/789)
Defendant(s) (including ref.)	JOHN JONES (JON/cd)
Date	

Note You must complete Parts A **and** B, **and** Part C if applicable. Send any relevant fee and the completed application to the court with any draft order, witness statement or other evidence; and sufficient copies for service on each respondent.

Part A

1. Enter your full name, or name of solicitor   I (We)[1]   **John Smith & Co**   (on behalf of)(the claimant)(the defendant)

2. State clearly what order you are seeking and if possible attach a draft   intend to apply for an order (a draft of which is attached) that[2]

3. Briefly set out why you are seeking the order. Include the material facts on which you rely, identifying any rule or statutory provision   because[3]

Part B

I (We) wish to rely on: *tick one box*

     the attached (witness statement)(affidavit) ☐   my statement of case ☐

4. If you are not already a party to the proceedings, you must provide an address for service of documents   evidence in Part C in support of my application ☐

Signed _____   **Position or office held** _____

(Applicant)('s Solicitor)('s litigation friend)   (if signing on behalf of firm or company)

Address to which documents about this claim should be sent (including reference if appropriate)[4]

		if applicable
	fax no.	
	DX no.	
Tel. no. Postcode	e-mail	

The court office at

is open from 10am to 4pm Monday to Friday. When corresponding with the court please address forms or letters to the Court Manager and quote the claim number.

N244 Application Notice (4.00)   *Printed on behalf of The Court Service*

Part C

Claim No.

I (We) wish to rely on the following evidence in support of this application:

Statement of Truth

*(I believe) *(The applicant believes) that the facts stated in Part C are true

delete as appropriate

Signed

(Applicant)('s Solicitor)('s litigation friend)

Position or office held

(if signing on behalf of firm or company)

Date

Once the Respondent has received the notification of the hearing time and date, he or his solicitors will be able to arrange to attend court and make representations. However, in some instances, applications may be made to the court without giving notice to the Respondent. Before the CPR came into effect, this type of application was known as an *ex parte* application. Without notice applications may also be made by an interested person who is not a party to the action. The rules of the court set out which applications may be heard with or without notice. In practice, most are with notice.

An application will be heard by a Master (at the Royal Courts of Justice in London), or a judge, usually in the rooms of the Master or judge, rather than in a courtroom. If something is heard in the rooms of the Master or judge, it may be referred to as being heard 'in chambers' although this term is not used now under the new Civil Procedure Rules. Alternatively, the court may, if it considers it appropriate, conduct an application hearing over the telephone and, in this event, certain rules and procedures apply. Where it is possible to do so, all applications relating to a particular case should be dealt with by the same Master or judge.

Normally, the Applicant's solicitors should take with them to any hearing a draft of the order they are seeking. If the case is one that is being heard in the Royal Courts of Justice in London and the order sought is particularly long or complicated, the solicitors should also provide the draft of the order to the court on disk in a specified word processing format.

An application may be dealt with by the court without a hearing if the parties agree to the terms of the order sought, or the parties agree that the court should dispose of the application without a hearing, or the court does not consider that a hearing will be appropriate.

The court may issue an Application Notice of its own motion, for example, if it is felt that some issue needs to be resolved between the parties. If a hearing date for an application has been arranged and is then cancelled, this is known as 'vacating' it.

Orders

After the application has been heard, an order is made by the court, i.e., a decision on that particular matter, and this must be adhered to by the parties unless a successful appeal is made against the decision. The order will normally be drawn up and served either by the court or by one of the parties' solicitors with the court's permission. Alternatively, the court may dispense with the need to draw up an order.

If the terms of the application have been agreed by the parties and there is no need for a hearing, the order must be drawn up in the agreed terms and it must state on it that it is 'By Consent'. This can only be done where the parties are legally represented. The consent order must be signed by the solicitors or counsel for all relevant parties. It must be taken or sent to the court office to be sealed and a copy lodged with the court.

An order must normally state on it the name and judicial title of the person who made it, e.g., 'District Judge Bloggs' (the exceptions to this are stated in the Rules). If the hearing was in private, when the order is drawn up, the fact that it was heard in private must be clearly marked in the title, e.g., 'Before [*title and name of judge*] sitting in private.' The order must be dated the date the order was actually made (not necessarily the date it is typed) and must be sealed by the court.

The layout of an order is fairly simple. It is headed, as are all court documents, with the title of the action. The person who made the order, e.g., the judge, will be inserted as mentioned above, and the body of the order will be something like:

Upon hearing solicitors for both parties [*or whoever attended the hearing*]

IT IS ORDERED that [*details of the order are given here*]

And that costs of this application be [*details of how the costs for this application are awarded are inserted here*]

DATED the   *   day of   *   2005

[*The date the order is actually made is inserted here*]

If an order is drawn up by a party to the proceedings but is to be served by the court, that party must provide the court with sufficient copies for a copy to be retained by the court and a copy to be served on him and all the other parties.

If you have to serve an order on another party, you would send a copy of the sealed order (not the original) and your letter would be along the following lines:

Dear Sirs

Xavier v Jones

We enclose, by way of service, copy order in this matter. Kindly acknowledge receipt.

Yours faithfully,

Notice to Admit Facts/Documents

A party may serve a notice on another party requiring him to admit certain facts which he specifies in the notice. This Notice to Admit Facts must be served no later than 21 days before the trial.

Similarly, where a document has been disclosed (see page 110) to a party, he may serve notice on the disclosing party requiring him to prove at trial the authenticity of any document that he specifies in the notice. A notice to prove documents must be served no later than seven days before the trial, or by the latest date for serving witness statements (see page 124).

Affidavits

An affidavit is a written statement of evidence sworn on oath or affirmed to be true. In some proceedings, an affidavit is used as evidence instead of witness statements (see page 124) or statements of case. The person who makes the affidavit and signs it is called the deponent.

An affidavit may be sworn in the presence of a practising solicitor, a Commissioner for Oaths, and certain other people, e.g., a Circuit judge, District judge, Justice of the Peace, or an authorised officer of the court and when they do this, it is known as administering an oath. A fee is normally payable for swearing an affidavit, as well as a smaller fee for each exhibit sworn, to the person who administers the oath, with the exception, at the moment, of an officer authorised by the court. An affidavit relating to a particular matter cannot be sworn before a solicitor whose firm is involved in that matter and must be before someone who is independent of the person swearing it or any of the parties' solicitors. There are rules to be followed where a person making an affidavit cannot read or sign it.

An outline of the procedures involved in the actual swearing of the oath is that the person swearing the affidavit (the deponent) will sign the affidavit and any exhibit sheets (see below for information on exhibits). The person who is administering the oath will give the deponent to hold in a specific manner the New Testament, the Old Testament or the Koran (or whatever is appropriate to that person's religious beliefs). The person administering the oath will hold the signed affidavit and any exhibits and ask: 'Is this your name and handwriting?'. When the deponent answers that it is, he will be asked to repeat words swearing that the contents of the affidavit are true. The person administering the oath will then complete the jurat (see below). If the deponent is under 17, instead of being asked to say that he 'swears' the oath, he will say 'I promise'.

If the deponent does not wish to swear as above, he will be asked what would be binding on his conscience. If the deponent objects altogether to being sworn, he may affirm that the contents are true. If he is swearing a statutory declaration, he will 'declare' that the contents are true.

The affidavit should be typed on good quality A4 size paper and should have a 3.5 cm margin. The pages must be numbered consecutively. It should give the title of the action, which means the court or division in which the claim is proceeding; the claim number; and the names and status (claimant, defendant, etc.) of the parties or the name of the matter to which it refers. Where there are several parties with the same status, e.g., several claimants or several defendants, etc., the name of one of the parties may be given followed by '(and others)', e.g.,

John Bloggs (and others)   claimants

The following information must be typed on each affidavit and any exhibit to that affidavit in the top right-hand corner before the title of the action:

(a) on which party's behalf the affidavit is sworn;

(b) the initials and surname of the person who has sworn it (the deponent);

(c) the number of that person's affidavit, i.e., if it is his first affidavit in that action, you would write '1st';

(d) if the affidavit refers to any exhibits (see below), the identifying initials and number of all exhibits referred to; and

(e) the date it has been sworn.

This information must also be given on any backsheet (see page 69). All numbers, including dates, should be in figures, e.g., '7th July 2006'. If reference is made in the affidavit to any documents, there should be a note in the margin of the affidavit giving the reference of any such document. The body of the affidavit generally begins with words along the following lines or those shown on the example on page 122.

I, (*name of deponent*) of (*address and occupation of deponent*) state on oath:

The paragraphs are then numbered.

If the affidavit is being given in a business or professional capacity, the address should be that of the deponent's employment, rather than his home address, and it should state the position he holds, together with the name of his employer. It should also be stated whether the deponent is a party to the proceedings.

At the very end, where details are given of the swearing, i.e., where and when sworn and in whose presence, this is called the jurat. The jurat should follow immediately after the end of the text and must not be by itself on a separate page—the text of the affidavit should never end on one page with the jurat following on the next. It is typed on the left-hand side of the page in the following manner, and the signature of the deponent should be written opposite the text.

SWORN at   *   )
in the County of   *   )
this   *   day of   *   )
2005   )

                                    Before me,

                                    <u>A Solicitor</u>
                                    [*or whoever else the affidavit has been sworn before*]

The jurat must be signed by everyone swearing the affidavit. There are provisions in the rules for making affidavits by people who cannot read or are unable to sign. The person before whom an affidavit is sworn must sign it, and his name and qualification must be printed beneath his signature. His address must also be given.

The affidavit should have a backsheet (see example). Any alterations made to an affidavit must be initialled by the person swearing it at the time of swearing. Therefore, if you have made any errors or changes to the affidavit, you must draw these to the attention of the fee earner.

If there is more than one page to the affidavit, it must be bound securely in such a way that it will not hinder the court when they are filing it away. Affidavits are sometimes sewn up (see page 31) with green tape along the left-hand margin but mostly they will be stapled or bound. However, you should check the method used in your own firm. If it is not possible to bind the affidavit, each page should be identified with the case number and the initials of the deponent and of the person before whom it was sworn.

An affidavit may have an exhibit, e.g. a document referred to in the affidavit which is part of the affidavit evidence. An exhibit is not bound in with the affidavit itself, but must be kept separate from it. When an exhibit is referred to in an affidavit, it is normally referred to by the initials of the person swearing the affidavit and includes the number of the exhibit. For example, if the affidavit is sworn by Marmaduke Smith, his first exhibit would be 'MS1', the second would be 'MS2' and so on. (See the example exhibit sheet.) These initials and numbers are also included on the first page and backsheet of the affidavit in the top right-hand corner. Each exhibit should then have a frontsheet which includes everything shown on the front of the affidavit down to and including the names of the parties. It would be set out as shown in the example. The exhibit frontsheet is placed on top of the exhibit and they are bound together. If it is sewn, this is usually done only in the top left-hand corner. The exhibit sheet also has to be sworn. Once sworn, keep the original affidavit and exhibits as these may be filed with the court later, and serve photocopies.

If there are several letters to be referred to as exhibits to an affidavit, they should be put together as a bundle. They should be arranged in chronological order with the earliest on the top and secured firmly. If there is a mix of original and copy letters exhibited as one bundle, the front page of the exhibit should state that the bundle consists of so many original letters and so many copies. Bundles should not be stapled but should be securely fastened in a way that does not interfere with the reading of the documents, e.g., sewn, or whatever method is used in your firm. The pages should be numbered consecutively at the bottom.

If an exhibit contains more than one document, the front page should set out a list of the documents giving the dates of the documents.

If an exhibit is something other than a document, it should be clearly marked with an exhibit number or letter in a way that it cannot become detached from the exhibit. A small item can be placed in a container marked appropriately.

Affirmations/statutory declarations

Instead of making an affidavit in which he swears on oath that what he has said is true, a person may 'affirm' the truth instead. The affirmation takes the same format as an affidavit but, at the beginning, instead of saying 'I ... state on oath', he says 'I ... do solemnly and sincerely affirm ...' and in the jurat the word 'sworn' is replaced by the word 'affirmed'. Similarly, someone may swear a document called a statutory declaration. Again the same rules apply, but he will be asked to 'declare' that the contents of his declaration are true.

Example Affidavit

	Filed on behalf of: Claimant
	Name of deponent: J. Bloggs
	No. of Affidavit: 1st
	[Initials and number of any exhibits]
	Date Affidavit Sworn: ****

IN THE SOUTHTOWN COUNTY COURT   Claim No. 05.12345

BETWEEN:

PAUL XAVIER   Claimant

and

JOHN JONES   Defendant

AFFIDAVIT

I, JOSEPH BLOGGS of 26 Southtown Road, Northtown, Essex, IG5 3TR mechanic, MAKE OATH and say as follows:

1. At 6.35 p.m. on the 5th July 2004, I was walking down Mulberry Close, New Barnet, Hertfordshire when I saw a blue Volvo drive straight into a Rolls Royce. The driver of the Volvo appeared to have his eyes closed instead of looking where he was going.

2. The Rolls Royce had no chance to stop in time to avoid the accident.

SWORN at   *   )

in the County of   *   )

this   *   day of   *   )

2005   )

Before me,

A Solicitor

Example backsheet for Affidavit

Claim No. 05.12345

IN THE SOUTHTOWN
COUNTY COURT

BETWEEN:

Filed on behalf of: Claimant
Name of deponent: J. Bloggs
No. of Affidavit: 1st
[Initials and number of any exhibits]
Date Affidavit Sworn: ****

PAUL XAVIER   Claimant

and

JOHN JONES   Defendant

AFFIDAVIT

of

JOSEPH BLOGGS

John Smith and Co.,
2 Bank Chambers,
High Road,
Southtown,
Herts. EN5 6AX.

tel: 01438 12345

ref: AB/cd/123

Solicitors for the Claimant

Example exhibit sheet

Filed on behalf of: Claimants
Name of deponent: M. Smith
No. of Affidavit: 1st
[Initials and number of any exhibits]
Date Affidavit Sworn: ****

IN THE HIGH COURT OF JUSTICE
QUEEN'S BENCH DIVISION
ROYAL COURTS OF JUSTICE   HQ 2005 1234

BETWEEN:

PETER BROWN (and others)   Claimants

and

BEATRICE GREEN (and others)   Defendants

This is the exhibit referred to in the affidavit of Marmaduke Smith and marked 'MS1'.

SWORN at   *   )
in the County of   *   )
this   *   day of   *   )
2005   )

Before me,

A Solicitor

Witnesses

At trial, a witness must attend court and give his evidence orally in public. However, the party relying on that witness must usually serve on the other party a statement by that witness containing the evidence he will be giving orally. At other hearings, witness evidence may be in statement form. The court may make exceptions to this and may also allow a witness to give evidence through video link or some other means.

Witness statements

A witness statement is the equivalent of the evidence that the witness would or will give if he is called to court to give his evidence verbally. The layout is similar to that of an Affidavit (see above). It should show the title of the action and should contain the same type of details at the top right-hand corner of the first page as are on an Affidavit. Therefore, at the top right-hand corner of the first page, it will state the party on whose behalf it is made, e.g., claimant; the initials and surname of the witness; the number of the statement, e.g., if it is the witness's second statement in this action, you would type '2nd'; the identifying initials and number of any exhibits referred to and the date the statement was made. See the example Affidavit, which is similar. The paragraphs should be numbered, but it does not have the jurat at the end. It should be signed by the person who makes the statement and must be verified by a Statement of Truth (see page 69), the wording of which is as follows:

I believe that the facts stated in this witness statement are true.

It must also be dated.

If the Statement of Truth for the witness statement is in a separate document, that document should contain the title of the action, the claim number and it should identify the document being verified:

I believe that the facts stated in the witness statement filed on [*date*] or served on [*whichever party*] on [*date*] are true.

In civil litigation witness statements are used more often now than affidavits because there is no time wasted in getting it sworn and also no fee to pay to someone to administer the oath. However, there are still certain circumstances where the Rules specify that an affidavit must be used.

Witness statements are exchanged between the parties before trial but if one of the parties is unable to obtain a signed statement from a witness by the time exchange of statements is to take place, he may apply to the court for permission to serve a witness summary instead. This is a summary of the evidence that would have been given in the witness statement.

Witness summons

A witness summons is a document issued by the court requiring a witness to attend court to give evidence and/or to produce documents to the court.

There must be a separate summons for each witness. It will be issued and dated by the court office where the case is proceeding or where a particular hearing will be held. Two copies of the witness summons (Form N20) must be filed with the court, which will keep

Witness Summons

In the	
SOUTHTOWN COUNTY COURT	
Claim No.	05.12345
Claimant (including ref)	PAUL XAVIER (XAV/789)
Defendant (including ref)	JOHN JONES (JON/cd)
Issued on	

To

> Joseph Bloggs
> 26 Southtown Road
> Northtown
> Essex
> IG5 3TR

You are summoned to attend at *(court address)*

on   of   at   (am)(pm)

(and each following day of the hearing until the court tells you that you are no longer required.)

☑ to give evidence in respect of the above claim

☐ to produce the following document(s) *(give details)*

The sum of £   is paid or offered to you with this summons. This is to cover your travelling expenses to and from court and includes an amount by way of compensation for loss of time.

This summons was issued on the application of the claimant (~~defendant~~) or the claimant's (~~defendant's~~) solicitor whose name, address and reference number is: **John Smith & Co, 2 Bank Chambers, High Road, Southtown, Herts EN5 6AX. Ref: XAV/789**

Do not ignore this summons

If you were offered money for travel expenses and compensation for loss of time, at the time it was served on you, you must –

- attend court on the date and time shown and/or produce documents as required by the summons; and

- take an oath or affirm as required for the purposes of answering questions about your evidence or the documents you have been asked to produce.

If you do not comply with this summons you will be liable, in county court proceedings, to a fine. In the High Court, disobedience of a witness summons is a contempt of court and you may be fined or imprisoned for contempt. You may also be liable to pay any wasted costs that arise because of your non-compliance.

If you wish to set aside or vary this witness summons, you may make an application to the court that issued it.

The court office at

is open between 10 am and 4 pm Monday to Friday. When corresponding with the court, please address forms or letters to the Court Manager and quote the claim number.

N20 Witness Summons (09.02)   *Printed on behalf of The Court Service*

one and return a sealed copy to the party applying for the summons, if they wish to serve it themselves. The witness summons will be served by the court unless the party issuing it informs the court at the time of issue that they wish to serve the summons themselves. If the court is serving the summons, they will keep one copy and serve the other by post on the witness. The court will keep a copy of the summons they have served and complete a certificate of service which is on the reverse of the copy summons.

If the court is going to serve the summons, money known as 'conduct money' must be deposited with the court. This money will be offered to the witness and should cover his reasonable travelling expenses to get to and from court and a sum to compensate him for loss of his time. Similarly, if your firm is serving the summons, this money must be offered or paid to the witness.

It is sometimes necessary to obtain permission from the court to issue a witness summons, particularly if it is required to issue the summons less than seven days before the date of trial.

As soon as the court date is known, all witnesses should be informed as they may have made other arrangements. You may find that some witnesses, such as police officers or Armed Forces personnel, have a certain way in which they like a witness summons to be served, e.g., through a senior officer, so it is best to check.

Evidence by deposition

It is possible for a party to a case to apply to the court for an order for someone to be questioned or 'examined' at a hearing to obtain evidence from them. They can also be required to produce any necessary documents. Evidence obtained in this way is known as a deposition. The person to be examined to give evidence is called a deponent. He will be questioned under oath before a judge, an examiner of the court or someone else who has been appointed by the court. As with a witness summons, when the order is served on the deponent, he should be offered or paid money to cover his reasonable travel expenses to and from the place where he is to be examined and a sum for compensation for loss of time.

The deponent's evidence may be electronically recorded by the court, as well as being recorded by the examiner in writing or by a shorthand writer or stenographer, so that the deponent's final written statement (the deposition) is accurate. The deposition must be signed by the examiner, who will also make a note of the time taken for the examination.

Civil Evidence Act notice/hearsay evidence

If a party intends to rely on hearsay evidence at trial, either because a witness is unable to attend court or the evidence is some other form of hearsay evidence, he must, depending on the circumstances, either serve a witness statement or notice complying with the Civil Evidence Act 1995 on the other parties. The other parties must be informed if the witness will not be attending the trial to give oral evidence and must be given the reason why the witness will not be attending.

It may be that the evidence will be in the form of a document, in which case a copy of any such document must be supplied to the other parties. The witness statement or notice must contain specific details regarding the evidence and must be served within the time limits laid down by the court rules. There are further rules for cross-examining or attacking evidence given in this way.

In some circumstances, such as if the evidence relates to a hearing other than a trial, a Civil Evidence Act notice will not be necessary.

Expert evidence

Parties may wish to obtain evidence from experts, e.g., in a personal injury case, it may be desired to obtain evidence from a doctor or specialist or, in a property matter, from someone such as a surveyor. However, expert evidence may only be given or taken into consideration with the permission of the court. There are various rules about what an expert's report must contain.

If two or more parties wish to submit expert evidence on a particular issue, it is preferred that the evidence is dealt with by one single expert only and the court may give directions to this effect. The parties wishing to submit the expert evidence are called 'the instructing parties'. If they cannot agree on who should be the expert, the court may select the expert. When one party is instructing a joint expert, he must send a copy of the instructions to the other instructing parties. If there is more than one expert, the court may direct that they discuss the issues between them and try to reach agreement if possible.

Where one party has provided expert evidence or a joint expert has been appointed by the court, another party may pose to the expert certain written questions. This must be done within a specified time. The expert's answers will be treated as part of his report.

Offer to settle/Part 36 payment

Quite often, if the defendant thinks that the claimant is likely to win all or part of the claim, the defendant will offer to settle the claim or make a payment into court to try to settle the claim. If he makes an offer or payment into court in accordance with Part 36 CPR and the claimant does not accept the offer or payment and the case proceeds to trial, and he is then awarded less by the court than the defendant paid in to court or offered, or fails to achieve from the court what was, in effect, offered by the defendant, the claimant may have to pay the costs that the defendant incurs after the date has passed for accepting the offer or payment, including the costs of the trial. If the claimant accepts the payment into court or offer, then he will be entitled to payment of his costs up to the date of accepting the offer or payment in. (See also page 140 regarding costs.) If the claim is for money, a payment into court, rather than an offer, must be made in order to protect costs in this way.

Offers and payments made in this way are known as Part 36 offers or Part 36 payments and do not apply to cases on the small claims track. Part 36 offers and payments may be increased or improved upon. The offer or payment may be made with regard to part of the claim or all of it. The claimant may also make a Part 36 offer to settle the claim. Indeed, any party may make an offer to settle, but if he does not do it in accordance with the rules, he may not gain the benefits regarding costs.

A Part 36 offer or payment must not be made known to the trial judge until after the case has been decided (there are one or two exceptions). This is extremely important because if the judge knows that an offer or payment into court has been made, he will have to adjourn the trial and the solicitors responsible for letting him know may have to pay for the costs of the adjournment, which can be extremely expensive. Make sure that you *never* include in any trial bundle any notices, forms or other documents relating to such an offer or payment.

Notice of payment into court

If the defendant wishes to make a Part 36 payment or an increased Part 36 payment, he must serve on the claimant a Notice of Payment into Court (Form N242A). He must also file with the court a copy of the Notice, together with a Certificate of Service. Additionally, he must send to the Court Funds Office the payment (cheque payable to Accountant General of the Supreme Court), together with a sealed copy of the Claim Form and a Request for Lodgment (Court Funds Office Form 100). The address of the Court Funds Office is given in the Form 100—Notes for Guidance as well as in the address section of this book.

The Part 36 Notice of Payment into Court must include, together with other information, a statement saying that it is a Part 36 payment. On the back of the form there is a section to be completed where the Social Security (Recovery of Benefits) Act 1997 applies. This relates to claims for personal injury, etc where the claimant is in receipt of benefits because of the injuries he has sustained and which are part of his claim against the defendant. For example, the claimant may have been injured and is now in receipt of benefits to assist with costs of care or loss of earnings. Where someone is making a payment by way of compensation, they are liable to pay the amount of what is known as recoverable benefits, i.e., benefits the claimant receives from the government. Therefore, because the defendant has to repay the claimant's recoverable benefits to the government, he will deduct that amount from the payment he is making into court. However, damages for pain and suffering may not be reduced in this way. In order to calculate the correct amount to pay into court in this type of case, the defendant must obtain from the appropriate government department a Certificate of Total Benefits which will show the amount of recoverable benefits and a copy of this must be sent with the Request for Lodgment.

If the Part 36 payment has been made at least 21 days before the trial date, the claimant may accept the payment without the court's permission. He must, in these circumstances, give written notice of acceptance not later than 21 days after the payment was made. There are other rules regarding the acceptance of Part 36 payments outside this time limit or after the trial has started.

Accepting a Part 36 payment

If a party wishes to accept a Part 36 payment, he must file with the Court Funds Office a Notice of Acceptance and Request for Payment (Form N243A/201). Additionally, he must file a copy with the court where the claim is proceeding (and also a copy to the court where the trial is to take place, if different). He must also send Notice of Acceptance to the party making the payment. This must be done within specified time limits otherwise other procedures may have to be followed. In certain circumstances, the court's permission will be required before the payment in can be accepted.

The Notice of Acceptance must show on it the claim number and the title of the proceedings and must be signed by the person accepting the payment, or, if he is legally represented, a partner in the solicitor's firm must sign the form. If the claimant is not legally represented and the claimant wishes to sign the form himself, his signature must be witnessed in accordance with the rules of the court.

Notice of payment into court
(in settlement - Part 36)

In the	
SOUTHTOWN COUNTY COURT	
Claim No.	05.12345
Claimant (including ref)	PAUL XAVIER (XAV/789)
Defendant (including ref)	JOHN JONES (JON/cd)

To the Claimant ('s Solicitor)

John Smith & Co
2 Bank Chambers
High Road
Southtown
Herts
EN5 6AX

Take notice the defendant ___John Jones___ has paid £ _5000_ (~~a further amount of £_____~~)
into court in settlement of
(tick as appropriate)

[✓] the whole of your claim

[ ] part of your claim *(give details below)*

[ ] a certain issue or issues in your claim *(give details below)*

The (part) (issue or issues) to which it relates is(are):*(give details)*

[ ] It is in addition to the amount of £_____ already paid into court on_____ and the
total amount in court now offered in settlement is £_____ *(give total of all payments in court to date)*

[ ] It is not inclusive of interest and an additional amount of £_____ is offered for interest *(give details of
the rate(s) and period(s) for which the amount of interest is offered.)*

[ ] It takes into account all(part) of the following counterclaim:*(give details of the party and the part of the
counterclaim to which the payment relates)*

[ ] It takes into account the interim payment(s) made in the following amount(s) on the following date(s):
(give details)

**Note: This notice will need to be modified where an offer of provisional damages is made (CPR Part 36.7)
and/or where it is made in relation to a mixed (money and non-money) claim in settlement of the whole
claim (CPR Part 36.4).**

For cases where the Social Security (Recovery of Benefits) Act 1997 applies

The gross amount of the compensation payment is £_____.

The defendant has reduced this sum by £_____ in accordance with section 8 of and Schedule 2 to the Social Security (Recovery of Benefits) Act 1997, which was calculated as follows:

    Type of benefit   Amount

The amount paid into court is the net amount after deduction of the amount of benefit.

Signed _____   Position held _____
      Defendant('s solicitor)   (If signing on behalf of a firm or company)

Date _____

Name of bank _____

Account number _____

Sort code _____

Note: To the Claimant

If you wish to accept the payment made into court without needing the court's permission you should:

- complete N243A/Form201 and send to the Court Funds Office, 22 Kingsway, London, WC2B 6LE. (Copies are available from any court office or from the Court Funds Office or the Court Service website at www.courtservice.gov.uk)

- you must also send copies to the defendant and to the court

Request for Lodgment in the _____ Division of the High Court

Please use BLOCK CAPITALS   District Registry/County Court

Before completing this form, please read the notes overleaf

Full Action Title

Claim Number

Please ensure that you answer the relevant question(s) below otherwise this form may be returned to you.

Has a previous lodgment been made in this action?   Yes ☐   No ☐   *(please tick)*

Has the hearing begun?   Yes ☐   No ☐   *(please tick)*

I ask the Accountant General to receive into Court for lodgment to the above account

£ _____ which is paid in *(complete relevant section below)*

A   on behalf of

     in satisfaction of the claim of

B   on behalf of

     against the claim of with defence setting up tender

C   under Order dated   *(delete as appropriate)* Copy attached/I do not have a copy because

D   for the following reason

Signed _____ Dated _____

Name (or name of solicitor)

Address (and/or DX Code)

I am the (Solicitor for the)

Ref _____

Name and address of other sides('s solicitors)

Ref _____

All payments into Court are made to the Court Funds Office, 22 Kingsway, London, WC2B 6LE, or by DX to DX:149780 Kingsway 5
Cheques must be made payable to the ACCOUNTANT GENERAL OF THE SUPREME COURT

For CFO Use

Date Stamp/Seal   Comments

Location Code

Lodgment approved _____   Checked by

A/C No

Placed   B   now/ · 21 days   Inits

Date Input   Inits

Bank Date/Receipt Number

Form 100 Court Funds Office Form 100 (Court Funds Rules 15 & 16) (10.04)

FORM 100 - Notes for guidance

Completing the form

- At the top of the Form 100, you must give the name of the county court in which the claim is proceeding. If the claim is in the High Court you must give the name of the District Registry and specify the Division of the High Court, i.e Queen's Bench, Chancery, Admiralty or Family in which the claim is proceeding.

- The Full Action Title is the name of the case as it appears on the claim form, or the order for payment into court.

- The Claim Number is the reference number given by the court on the front of the claim form and on any subsequent order.

- You must answer each of the two questions by ticking the appropriate box.

- The form must specify the amount being paid into court. If you are paying in more than one cheque, **please complete a separate form for each payment.**

- You should only complete one of the boxes marked A, B, C and D.

    Box A is used for all payments into court made under Part 36 of the Civil Procedure Rules (in satisfaction). Where there is more than one defendant, the form must state which defendant(s) are making the payment into court. Similarly, if there is more than one claimant, the form must state how the payment made is to be apportioned between the claimants.

    Box B should only be completed if the defendant is paying money into court in support of a defence of tender. A copy of the defence should be submitted with the form.

    Box C must be completed when funds are paid into court pursuant to an order. A sealed copy of the order must be provided with the form.

    Box D should only be completed when none of the other boxes is applicable, such as in the case of a refund of an over-payment.

- Finally, the form must be signed and dated by the person making the payment into court. You must also include your name and address and reference and those of the other side(s) or their solicitor(s) if they have one.

Where to send the payment

The payment, completed form and other documents must be sent to the **COURT FUNDS OFFICE, 22 KINGSWAY, LONDON WC2B 6LE**, or by the DX system to the **COURT FUNDS OFFICE DX149780 KINGSWAY 5.**

DO NOT SEND OR TAKE PAYMENTS TO THE COURT – THEY WILL NOT BE ACCEPTED.

Who cheques are payable to

The '**ACCOUNTANT GENERAL OF THE SUPREME COURT**'

Checklist – have you:

- ☐ enclosed the payment
- ☐ enclosed the completed Form 100 (a separate Form 100 must be completed for each payment) and
- ☐ enclosed a sealed copy of the claim form if payment is made in satisfaction, or
- ☐ enclosed a sealed copy of the order for payment into court, if payment is made under order,
- ☐ served the relevant notices on the other side and the Court (Court staff will be able to tell you what is required.)

Notice of acceptance and request for payment (Part 36)

In the

Claim No.

Claimant
(including ref.)

Defendant
(including ref.)

On _____ I accepted the payment(s) into court totalling £ _____

net of CRU benefits in settlement of (the whole of) (part of) (certain issue(s) in) my

claim as set out in the notice of payment into court received on _____

I declare that:-

☐ the claim has been accepted [within 21 days] [after 21 days but costs have been agreed] [less than 21 days before trial but costs have been agreed]

☐ the payment into court was not made in defence of tender

☐ the offeree is not a child or patient

☐ payment into court was not made under the Fatal Accidents Act 1976 and/or the Law Reform (Miscellaneous Provisions) Act 1934

   (If any of the above declaration have not been made, the money in court can only be paid out by order of the court)

☐ the claimant [is] [is not] a person in receipt of legal aid under section 9 of the Access to Justice Act 1999

☐ a copy of this notice has been served on the defendant('s)(solicitor) named below and the court and I request payment of this money held in court to be made to:

For CFO use

A/c No.

Schedule number

Date received

Withdrawn

Inits   Date

Inits   Date

Write on/off

Date

Inits   Claimant's Cheque

Cheque issued stamps

Inits   Defendant's Cheque

Claimant or Solicitor's full name

Address

Ref. No.

Postcode

Name of bank

Account number

Sort code

Defendant('s)(Solicitor) full name

Address

Ref. No.

Postcode

Name of bank

Account number

Sort code

Signature

Note: Before signing this form please read the notes for guidance overleaf. Incorrectly signed forms may be returned unactioned.

Signed

Date

SOLICITOR'S DETAILS

Partner's name (PLEASE PRINT)

Name of firm

Solicitor for the

WITNESS DETAILS

Witnessed by

Occupation of witness

Date

Solicitor or Witness address

Notes for guidance on completion of N243A/Form 201

This form amalgamates form N243A (Notice of acceptance of payment into court (Part 36)) and the Court Funds Office Form 201 (Request for Payment). In order to request payment out of funds in court, send the N243A/Form 201, signed and completed in accordance with these notes for guidance to the **Court Funds Office, 22 Kingsway, London, WC2B 6LE or DX 149780 Kingsway 5**. A copy of this form should also be sent to the court and to the defendant's solicitors.

- When completing the N243A/F201, please ensure that you tick all of the boxes under the heading: **'I declare that'**. If you do not tick all of the boxes, the Court Funds Office will not be able to process your request for payment and will have to return the form to you.

- In cases, where you are accepting the payment into court, following a top-up payment, the defendant's solicitors' bank details should be completed in the boxes provided, to enable the Court Funds Office to pay the interest due to the defendants. You may find these on the N242A, notice of payment into court, which the defendants sent to you when they lodged the money in court.

- The amount accepted should be net of Compensation Recovery Unit benefits (CRU).

- The form should be signed either by the claimant or, if a solicitor is on record, a partner in the solicitor's firm. Under the Court Funds Rules 1987, the Court Funds Office reserves the right to request a partner's signature on the N243A/Form 201 in accordance with audit recommendations.

- If the claimant signs the form their signature must be witnessed. The witness must know the payee and be a professional person or a person of standing in the community, e.g. Bank or Building Society official, Police Officer, Civil Servant, Minister of Religion, Teacher, Accountant, Solicitor, Doctor etc. It MUST NOT be signed by a relative of the payee.

- The Court Funds Office will only issue payment upon receipt of a properly completed N243A/Form 201 with an original signature. Faxed copies of the form and photocopies of signatures will not be accepted and will be returned to sender.

Interim payments

This is a payment often applied for once liability is no longer an issue. This means that if the defendant does not dispute that he must pay the claimant something, but does not agree on the final sum, then the claimant may, in certain circumstances, ask for some money on account until the final amount is resolved. If the defendant pays this, all well and good, but if he does not, then an application for an interim payment may have to be made to the court. In any event, if it is desired to make a voluntary interim payment regarding a claim by a child or patient under the Mental Health Act, the permission of the court must first be obtained.

Any money paid by way of interim payment will be deducted from the final amount eventually recovered by the claimant. An interim payment has no connection with a Part 36 payment as mentioned above.

Notice of Discontinuance

If, after proceedings have been served, the party instigating those proceediigs wishes to discontinue all or part of his action, he must serve a Notice of Discontinuance (Form N279) on the other parties and file a copy with the court. In some cases, consent of the other party or the court's permission may be required to do this. A Notice of Discontinuance will have on it the title of the action (see page 61). The Notice must state in it that all parties to the action have been served with a Notice of Discontinuance, and if there is more than one defendant to the action, it must specify against which parties the claim is discontinued.

Notice of Change of Solicitor

If, for some reason, a new firm of solicitors is to act for a party to an action, a Notice of Change of Solicitor must be completed by the new solicitor. This also applies if someone has been representing himself (a 'litigant in person') and then instructs a solicitor to act for him or, conversely, if a solicitor has been instructed but the person wishes now to represent himself. The Notice of Change of Solicitor (Form N434) should be filed with the court and sent to every other party to the action as well as to the former solicitor. The Notice must give the new address for service (see page 75).

Approaching trial

There is always a great deal of work to be done before a trial. This can include informing witnesses, and bundling up documents for court and for other parties. Conferences and consultations are arranged with counsel and you may find yourself heavily involved at this stage.

In some cases, prior to trial, skeleton arguments are lodged with the court. A skeleton argument is a brief outline of the relevant issues and facts of law pertaining to the case which the judge can read before the hearing, thus saving time. Skeleton arguments should normally be typed in double spacing on A4 paper. A copy should be served on all other parties to the action.

Notice of discontinuance

Note: Where another party must consent to the proceedings being discontinued, a copy of their consent must be attached to, and served with, this form.

In the	
SOUTHTOWN COUNTY COURT	
Claim No.	05.12345
Claimant (including ref.)	PAUL XAVIER (XAV/789)
Defendant (including ref.)	JOHN JONES (JON/cd)

To the court

The claimant (~~defendant~~)

(tick only one box)

☑ discontinues all of this (claim) (~~counterclaim~~)

☐ discontinues that part of this claim (counterclaim) relating to: *(specify which part)*

against the (defendant) ~~(following defendants) (claimant) (following claimants)~~

(.. *(enter name of Judge)* granted permission for the claimant to

discontinue (all) (part) of this (claim)(counterclaim) by order dated ....)

I certify that I have served a copy of this notice on every other party to the proceedings

Signed		**Position or office held**	
	(Claimant)(~~Defendant~~)('s solicitor)(~~Litigation friend~~)		(if signing on behalf of firm or company)
Date			

The court office at

is open between 10 am and 4 pm Monday to Friday. When corresponding with the court, please address forms or letters to the Court Manager and quote the claim number.
N279 - w3 Notice of discontinuance(6.99)   *Printed on behalf of The Court Service*

Notice of change of solicitor

Note: You should tick either box A **or**
B as appropriate **and** box C.
Complete details as necessary.

In the	
SOUTHTOWN COUNTY COURT	
Claim No.	05.12345
Claimant (including ref.)	PAUL XAVIER (XAV/789)
Defendant	JOHN JONES (JON/cd)

I (We) give notice that

A ☐ my solicitor *(insert name and address)*

has ceased to act for me and I shall now be acting in person.

B ☑ we *(insert name of solicitor)*   Jeffrey Armstrong & Co

have been instructed to act on behalf of the ~~claimant~~ (defendant) in this claim

(in place of *(insert name and address of previous solicitors)* Joe Bloggs & Co, 1 Broad Walk, Southtown, Herts EN4 9PP

)

C ☑ I (we) have served notice of this change on every party to claim (and on the former solicitor).

Address to which documents about this claim should be sent (including any reference)

		if applicable	
Jeffrey Armstrong & Co 635 Poddlebank Road London		fax no.	020 7444 33097
ref: 2397/bn		DX no.	DX 34 Poddlebank
Postcode	W13 7PR	e-mail	

Signed		**Position or office held**	
(~~Claimant~~)(Defendant)('s solicitor)(~~Litigation friend~~)		If signing on behalf of firm or company	
Date			

The court office at

is open between 10 am and 4 pm Monday to Friday. When corresponding with the court, please address forms or letters to the Court Manager and quote the claim number.

N434 - w3 Notice of change of solicitor (6.99)   *Printed on behalf of The Court Service*

The trial bundle

The trial bundle is an indexed bundle of documents contained in a ring binder with each page clearly numbered consecutively. Numbering the pages is called paginating and you must ensure that the pagination in each copy of the bundle is identical. The numbers should be centred at the bottom of each page and all documents should be put in chronological order, with the earliest first and the latest at the back of the bundle, so that it can be read in order of events, like a book. It must be lodged at the court within a specified time before the hearing. The judge will normally read these papers before the trial takes place. The bundle will usually include copies of some or all of the following:

(a) a case summary and/or a chronology, if appropriate. This will assist the judge in reading the papers before trial and, if possible, the parties should try to agree the case summary;

(b) the Claim Form and all statements of case;

(c) any requests for further information and responses to the requests;

(d) any witness statements that it is intended to rely on as evidence;

(e) any witness summaries (see page 124);

(f) any notices of intention to rely on hearsay evidence (see page 126);

(g) any notices of intention to rely on evidence that is not being given verbally at court or is not in a witness statement, affidavit or expert's report, or is not hearsay evidence. This could be something like a plan or a photograph.

(h) medical reports and responses to them;

(i) experts' reports and responses to them;

(j) any order giving directions regarding the way the trial is to be conducted; and

(k) any other documents which are necessary.

Of course, all these documents will not be required at every trial. It will depend on the circumstances of the individual case. The original documents, together with copies of any other court orders, should be available at the trial.

If at all possible, the parties should try to agree the contents of the trial bundle.

If there is more than 100 pages in the bundle, numbered dividers should be placed between different groups of documents. If more than one bundle is going to the court, they should each be distinguished, perhaps by using different colours. The party filing the trial bundle must supply identical bundles to all other parties to the proceedings and for the use of the witnesses.

Counsel will obviously be getting a trial bundle and will require certain additional separate information, such as without prejudice correspondence, which must not to go to the judge or to the other party's solicitors.

Judgment

When the trial judge gives his final decision on the outcome of a case, this is known as the judgment. The judgment must be formally written down or 'drawn up'. This will normally be done by the court or one of the parties' solicitors. If it is drawn up by one of the parties and is to be served by the court, sufficient copies must be filed at the court for each of the parties plus one for the court.

Judgments have to be prepared in a specific layout, e.g., in the High Court, single spacing, paragraph numbering in the margins and no page numbering. This is mainly to facilitate the publication of judgments on to the Internet and also to assist in the searching for judgments stored on electronic databases. For consistency, county court judgments should be prepared in a similar manner. Further information on this may be obtained from the relevant court.

Enforcing judgment

If judgment has been entered against the defendant and he does not pay, it may be necessary to force him to pay, normally after enquiries are made about his means. Some of the procedures in the High Court and county court may differ and may apply only to either the High Court or the county court. They will all involve completing the appropriate form and paying a court fee. Some of those you may encounter are:

(a) Seizing goods. Upon completing the correct form and paying a fee, an officer of the court where the judgment debtor (the person who owes the money) has any goods may seize those goods, sufficient to cover the amount owed, plus any costs. The goods are then sold at public auction. Certain goods are exempt from seizure. If someone else comes forward to say that he owns the goods rather than the debtor, this will be resolved by the court.

(b) Third-party debt order (formerly called a garnishee order). This is a process whereby if someone owes money to the judgment debtor, the court can order the person who owes him money to pay the money to the judgment creditor instead. An example would be money held in a bank account and the bank being ordered to pay the money directly to the judgment creditor.

(c) Charging order. This imposes a charge on any land or interest in land or security owned by the judgment debtor.

(d) Attachment of earnings. The debtor's employer must pay out of the debtor's wages a certain sum each week or month until the debt is cleared.

(e) Committal. This is only appropriate where there is disobedience of a court order. It can only follow a hearing before a judge where the defaulter has an opportunity to explain why he has disobeyed the court order.

There are other methods of enforcing judgment, such as obtaining possession of land or an order for the return of specific goods.

Registration of judgments

Details of county court money judgments are registered on the Register of County Court Judgments. The entry stays on the Register for six years. However, if someone pays money satisfying a judgment within a month from the date of the judgment, he may ask the court to cancel the registration of the judgment. The court will send a certificate of cancellation once they have proof that the payment has been made. If the payment was made more than one month after the day the judgment was made, the court can be asked to mark the judgment as satisfied, but the entry will remain on the Register. The court will send the applicant a certificate of satisfaction. A fee is payable to the court for these services.

Besides county court money judgments, other information kept on the Register includes administration orders and some Child Support Agency liability orders.

The Register can be searched on payment of a fee, and this is particularly useful to organisations such as banks, building societies and credit companies to check whether someone is a good credit risk. The Register is kept by the Registry Trust Ltd, at 173/175 Cleveland Street, London W1P 5PE.

There is no register of High Court judgments.

The Registry Trust also maintains registers for other jurisdictions, including Scotland, Ireland, Northern Ireland, Isle of Man and Jersey.

Costs

There are special rules relating to costs for the different tracks to which a case may be allocated. However, generally, the court can make what is called a summary assessment of costs, which means that it orders payment of a sum of money instead of fixed costs or may make an order for detailed assessment (see below). Fixed costs means that the only costs recoverable are those which are allowed in respect of solicitor's charges as set out in the Civil Procedure Rules.

When the court makes an order for costs and the receiving party has entered into a funding arrangement (see page 70), the costs payable by the paying party will include any additional liability incurred relating to the funding arrangement, e.g., the insurance premium or percentage increase. The term 'base costs' is used to mean costs other than any such additional liability.

The court may also order that one party pays only a part of the other's costs, rather than the whole amount, if it considers that there are valid reasons for making such an order. Costs assessed by the court are awarded on the following bases:

(a) Standard basis. The winner of the case will be allowed a reasonable amount in respect of all costs reasonably incurred. If there is a dispute as to what is reasonable, it is resolved in favour of the party paying the costs.

(b) Indemnity basis. All costs are allowed unless they are unreasonable. If there is a dispute as to what is reasonable, it is resolved in favour of the party receiving the costs.

Besides the court awarding costs at the end of a case, costs relating to a specific application notice may be awarded at the time of the application, rather than having to wait until the whole action is finalised. Some of the terms used by the court when costs are awarded in proceedings before trial are:

'Claimant's (or defendant's) costs' or 'costs in any event': this means that whichever party the court names can recover the costs of that particular application from the other party whatever the final outcome of the action.

'Costs reserved': the party in whose favour an order for costs is made at the end of the trial will be entitled to the costs of the application in question unless the court orders otherwise.

'Costs in the case': the costs of a particular application will be paid by the party who is ordered to pay the costs of the trial.

Notice of commencement of assessment of bill of costs

In the	
SOUTHTOWN COUNTY COURT	
Claim No.	05.12345
Claimant (include Ref.)	PAUL XAVIER (XAV/789)
Defendant (include Ref.)	JOHN JONES (JON/cd)

To the claimant(defendant)

Following an _____ (*insert name of document eg. order, judgment*) dated _____
(copy attached) I have prepared my Bill of Costs for assessment. The Bill totals *£ _____ If you choose to
dispute this bill and your objections are not upheld at the assessment hearing, the full amount payable (including the
assessment fee) will be £ _____ (together with interest (*see note below*)). I shall also seek the costs of the
assessment hearing

Your points of dispute must include

- details of the items in the bill of costs which are disputed

- concise details of the nature and grounds of the dispute for each item and, if you seek a reduction in
  those items, suggest, where practicable, a reduced figure

You must serve your points of dispute by _____ (*insert date 21 days from the date of service
of this notice*) on me at:- *(give full name and address for service including any DX number or reference)*

You must also serve copies of your points of dispute on all other parties to the assessment identified below *(you do not
need to serve your points of dispute on the court).*

I certify that I have also served the following person(s) with a copy of this notice and my Bill of Costs:- *(give details of
persons served)*

If I have not received your points of dispute by the above date, I will ask the court to issue a default costs certificate
for the full amount of my bill *(see above*)* plus fixed costs and court fee in the total amount of £ _____

Signed _____ **Date** _____
(Claimant)(Defendant)('s solicitor)

Note: Interest may be added to all High Court judgments and certain county court judgments of £5,000 or more under the
Judgments Act 1838 and the County Courts Act 1984.

The court office at

is open between 10 am and 4 pm Monday to Friday. When corresponding with the court, please address forms or letters to the Court Manager and quote the claim number.

N252 Notice of commencement of assessment of bill of costs (12.99)   *The Court Service Publications Unit*

'Claimant's (or defendant's) costs in the case': the party named at an application will be entitled to recover the costs of his application provided that judgment is given in his favour at the trial. However, if judgment is not given in his favour at the trial, he will not be liable to pay the costs of the other party for the application.

'Costs thrown away': where proceedings or any part of them have been ineffective or have been subsequently set aside, the party in whose favour the order for costs is made will be entitled to recover the costs of those proceedings.

'No order as to costs': each party must bear his own costs.

Detailed assessment of costs

The court may order a detailed assessment of costs or, if there is a dispute about the costs to be paid, the party which is to receive payment (the receiving party) may apply for a detailed assessment of costs. Before the CPR, this procedure was called 'taxation of costs' or costs would be 'taxed'. If there is to be a detailed assessment of costs, an appointment will be made to go before a costs judge or costs officer, who will make a decision on the costs to be paid. The receiving party must serve on the party who will pay the costs (the paying party) a Notice of Commencement of Assessment of Bill of Costs (Form N252), together with a copy of the bill of costs. Copies must also be served on any other relevant parties.

A bill of costs has to be drawn which itemises in chronological order all the steps taken in the action and all time spent on the case, including details of correspondence, telephone calls, witnesses involved, etc. Drawing this bill is very specialised and is usually done by a costs draftsman. The bill has to be lodged with the court within a specified time, together with the solicitor's file which must include all relevant papers, vouchers and receipts. If the parties agree on the amount of costs, either party may apply for a costs certificate.

Any party to the assessment proceedings may serve on another party Points of Dispute if he wishes to dispute any item in the bill of costs. A copy of the Points of Dispute must be served on all parties to the assessment proceedings. A Reply to the Points of Dispute may be served within a specified time.

If any party is not happy with the result of the assessment, he may appeal against this within a specified time.

Calculating periods of time

Where the court or the court rules specify a period of time within which something must be done (other than regarding service: see page 73), a period of time expressed as a number of days should be clear days. This means that when counting the number of days, do not include the day on which the period begins and, if the end of the period is denoted by the occurrence of a particular event, do not include the day on which the event occurs—the days must be full, clear days. Also, where the period is for five days or less and includes a Saturday, Sunday, Bank Holiday, Christmas Day or Good Friday, any of those days should be excluded from the calculation.

Where any sort of time is calculated by using the word 'month', it means a calendar month.

As mentioned above, this information does not relate to service.

Forms and documents in older proceedings

You will undoubtedly come across some of the older forms and documents which were in use before the CPR came into effect. There were different forms for High Court actions and county court actions.

In the High Court, an originating application such as a Writ of Summons (normally simply referred to as a Writ) would be issued. Instead of a Particulars of Claim, a Statement of Claim would set out the details of the claim if these were not included on the Writ. Once a Writ was served, the defendant had to complete an Acknowledgment of Service.

In the county court, proceedings were commenced by requesting the court to issue a summons. The summons or a request for a summons would be prepared by the claimant's solicitors and this would then be sent to the court for issue. There were two types of summons—a default summons and a fixed date summons. The default summons was used for claiming money, whether or not it was a specific amount, but there were two types of default summons—one for a fixed amount and the other for an unspecified amount of damages. The fixed date summons was used for other types of actions, such as for the recovery of land, for the return of goods or for an injunction.

There were various differences between the procedures in the High Court and the county court, even where the action was for the same type of thing. Some of the previous names and terms have been changed by the CPR and you may still hear them used. A few of these are:

(a) Discovery—now called 'disclosure'.

(b) *Ex parte*—now 'without notice'.

(c) Further and Better Particulars—now 'Further Information'.

(d) *In camera* or in chambers—now 'in private'.

(e) Leave of the court—now 'permission of the court'.

(f) Minor or infant is now simply 'child'.

(g) Next friend or *guardian ad litem*—now called 'litigation friend'.

(h) Payment into court. This procedure is now called a 'Part 36 payment'.

(i) Plaintiff—now 'claimant'.

(j) Pleadings—now 'statements of case'.

(k) Statement of Claim (and Points of Claim). High Court documents which were the equivalent of the Particulars of Claim in the county court. Both the High Court and county court now use only a Particulars of Claim.

(l) Summons—now 'application'.

(m) Subpoena. This is now a witness summons.

(n) Taxation of costs. This referred to a procedure relating to costs (see above). It is now, called 'detailed assessment of costs'.

(o) Taxing Master is now called 'costs judge'.

(p) Third Party proceedings—now 'Part 20 Claim' or 'Additional Claim'.

(q) Writ or county court summons—now a 'Claim Form'.

Children

You may come across cases involving children (persons under 18 years of age) or persons with a mental disability. As these persons cannot normally pursue their own litigation they have to have someone to do it for them. Someone who sues on behalf of such a person is known as a litigation friend. This could perhaps be a relative or a social worker. The claimant in such proceedings would, for example, be shown as 'John Smith (a child) by Mary Jones, his litigation friend'.

When such persons are themselves sued, they must have a responsible person to represent them. This person is also known as a litigation friend.

TEST YOURSELF ON CHAPTER 3

Test your knowledge by completing this assignment. If you find that you have difficulty with anything, read the chapter again until you are happy with your answers. There are some forms for you to complete with this assignment. Use the following information to complete the forms.

James McIntyre lives at 83 Camden Hill, Northtown, Sussex S23 7AL. He is suing Amy Crashing for damage caused to his car when he was involved in a road traffic accident with the car she was driving at 3.00 p.m. on 10 June 2005 at Camden Hill. His car is a green Ford Fiesta, registration number P387 LUR. The damage to Mr McIntyre's car is valued at £4,000. The claim will be issued in the Northtown County Court and the claim number will be 05.3865.

The solicitors for Mr McIntyre are Poddleberry, Catt & Co., of 16 Somerset Row, Northtown, Sussex S31 8PP (tel: 01646 58733; ref: LP/McI/68).

Miss Amy Crashing lives at 48 Avon Hills, Northtown, Sussex, S44 6PQ. Her car is a black Rolls Royce, registration number AC1. Her solicitors are Peters, Gold & Barry of Fox Hill, Northtown, Sussex S27 8L (tel: 01646 643821; ref: LB/Crash/321).

1. You are asked to prepare the Claim Form ready for it to be sent to court to be issued. Do this on the appropriate form: the Particulars of Claim will be served later. Once the Claim Form is ready and has been approved by a fee earner, what else would you do before posting it to the court?

2. Draft as far as you can in the correct format the Particulars of Claim, which are being served separately from the Claim Form (you can follow the example on page 68). Also draft a backsheet for the Particulars of Claim. When serving the Particulars of Claim, are any other forms required to be served at the same time?

3. Complete the Acknowledgment of Service on behalf of Amy Crashing. Why might this be completed?

4. If Amy had decided simply to ignore all the papers served on her, Mr McIntyre's solicitors might have decided to enter judgment by default. What does this mean? Complete the appropriate form.

5. What is meant by a 'Part 20 claim'? If a lady called Jean Armstrong had been brought into the action because Amy Crashing wished to allege that the accident was Jean's fault for some reason, how would the status of the parties be described in the title to the action in the Part 20 claim? (James McIntyre will still be described as the claimant.)

6. What are the following:

   (a) statement of case;

   (b) Allocation Questionnaire;

   (c) Listing Questionnaire (Pre-trial checklist).

7. Write down a list of the documents that might be included in a trial bundle.

8. What is meant by 'disclosure and inspection of documents'? What sort of information will go on to a List of Documents?

9. Write out the jurat for an affidavit that is to be sworn.

10. Now go through the chapter and if there are any words that are unfamiliar to you or that you cannot spell, write or type them correctly several times until you feel you know them.

Claim Form

In the

	for court use only
Claim No.	
Issue date	

SEAL

Claimant

Defendant(s)

Brief details of claim

Value

Defendant's name and address		£	
		Amount claimed	
		Court fee	
		Solicitor's costs	
		Total amount	

The court office at

is open between 10 am and 4 pm Monday to Friday. When corresponding with the court, please address forms or letters to the Court Manager and quote the claim number.

Printed on behalf of The Court Service

N1 Claim form (CPR Part 7) (01.02)

Claim No.	

Does, or will, your claim include any issues under the Human Rights Act 1998?   ☐ Yes   ☐ No

Particulars of Claim (attached)(to follow)

Statement of Truth
*(I believe)(The Claimant believes) that the facts stated in these particulars of claim are true.
* I am duly authorised by the claimant to sign this statement

Full name _____

Name of claimant's solicitor's firm _____

signed _____   position or office held _____
*(Claimant)(Litigation friend)(Claimant's solicitor)   (if signing on behalf of firm or company)

*delete as appropriate

Claimant's or claimant's solicitor's address to which documents or payments should be sent if different from overleaf including (if appropriate) details of DX, fax or e-mail.

Response Pack

You should read the 'notes for defendant' attached to the claim form which will tell you when and where to send the forms

Included in this pack are:

- either **Admission Form N9A**
  (if the claim is for a specified amount)
  or **Admission Form N9C**
  (if the claim is for an unspecified amount
  or is not a claim for money)

- either **Defence and Counterclaim Form
  N9B** (if the claim is for a specified amount)
  or **Defence and Counterclaim Form N9D**
  (if the claim is for an unspecified amount
  or is not a claim for money)

- **Acknowledgment of service**
  (see below)

Complete

If you admit the claim or the amount claimed and/or you want time to pay	the admission form
If you admit part of the claim	the admission form and the defence form
If you dispute the whole claim or wish to make a claim (a counterclaim) against the claimant	the defence form
If you need 28 days (rather than 14) from the date of service to prepare your defence, or wish to contest the court's jurisdiction	the acknowledgment of service
If you do nothing, judgment may be entered against you	

Acknowledgment of Service

Defendant's full name if different from the name given on the claim form

In the

Claim No.

Claimant
(including ref.)

Defendant

Address to which documents about this claim should be sent (including reference if appropriate)

if applicable

fax no.

DX no.

Ref. no.

e-mail

Tel. no.   Postcode

Tick the appropriate box

1. I intend to defend all of this claim ☐

2. I intend to defend part of this claim ☐

3. I intend to contest jurisdiction ☐

If you file an acknowledgment of service but do not file a defence within 28 days of the date of service of the claim form, or particulars of claim if served separately, judgment may be entered against you.

If you do not file an application within 28 days of the date of service of the claim form, or particulars of claim if served separately, it will be assumed that you accept the court's jurisdiction and judgment may be entered against you.

Signed

(Defendant)(Defendant's solicitor)
(Litigation friend)

Position or office held
(if signing on behalf of firm or company)

Date

The court office at

is open between 10 am and 4 pm Monday to Friday. When corresponding with the court, please address forms or letters to the Court Manager and quote the claim number.

N9 Response Pack (5.02)

Printed on behalf of The Court Service

Request for judgment and reply to admission (specified amount)

- Tick box A or B. If you tick box B you must complete the details in that part and in part C. Make sure that all the case details are given. Remember to sign and date the form. Your signature certifies that the information you have given is correct.

- If the defendant has given an address on the form of admission to which correspondence should be sent, which is different from the address shown on the claim form, you must tell the court.

- Return the completed form to the court.

In the	
Claim No.	
Claimant (including ref)	
Defendant (including ref)	

A ☐ **The defendant has not filed an admission or defence to my claim**

Complete all the judgment details at C. Decide how and *when you want the defendant to pay*. You can ask for the judgment to be paid by instalments or in one payment.

B ☐ **The defendant admits that all the money is owed**

Tick only **one** box below and complete all the judgment details at C.

☐ **I accept the defendant's proposal for payment**

Say how the defendant intends to pay. The court will send the defendant an order to pay. You will also be sent a copy.

☐ **The defendant has not made any proposal for payment**

Say how you want the defendant to pay. You can ask for the judgment to be paid by instalments or in one payment. The court will send the defendant an order to pay. You will also be sent a copy.

☐ **I do NOT accept the defendant's proposal for payment**

Say how you want the defendant to pay. Give your reasons for objecting to the defendant's offer of payment in the space opposite. (Continue on the back of this form if necessary.) Send this form to the court **with defendant's admission N9A.** The court will fix a rate of payment and send the defendant an order to pay. You will also be sent a copy.

C Judgment details

I would like the judgment to be paid

☐ (immediately)

☐ (by instalments of £ [   ] per month)

☐ (in full by [   ])

Amount of claim as admitted

(including interest at date of issue) . . . . . .

Interest since date of claim (if any) . . . . . .

Period from . . . . to . . . .

Rate . . %

Court fees shown on claim

Solicitor's costs (if any) on issuing claim

Sub Total

Solicitor's costs (if any) on entering judgment

Sub Total

Deduct amount (if any) paid since issue

Amount payable by defendant

I certify that the information given is correct

Signed		**Position or office held**	
(Claimant)(Claimant's solicitor)(Litigation friend)		(if signing on behalf of firm or company)	
Date			

The court office at

is open between 10 am and 4 pm Monday to Friday. When corresponding with the court, please address forms and letters to the Court Manager and quote the Claim number

Tribunals, other bodies, ADR

There are various tribunals which have legal authority and can make binding decisions, such as the Employment Tribunal, Lands Tribunal, Mental Health Review Tribunal, tribunals relating to social security matters and many others.

Additionally, there are numerous other bodies and organisations with varied powers that may assist in resolving disputes. These can range from regulatory bodies and ombudsmen to organisations like the Criminal Injuries Compensation Authority. Tribunals and other such bodies have their own rules and regulations for making applications and for appeals. They also generally supply their own forms, which are not usually available from stationers.

As well as using specific organisations with their own rules and regulations, there are other methods of dispute resolution, such as arbitration and mediation, known collectively as Alternative Dispute Resolution (ADR). This is explained on page 152. It is not possible in this book to go into detail of all the tribunals, etc. you could encounter, but dealt with below are a few of the most common.

Employment tribunals

There are various centres throughout England and Wales where employment tribunal (previously called industrial tribunal) hearings take place. Applications are dealt with in offices according to the postal code for the place where the applicant worked or the place where the matter complained about took place. If help is needed on this, contact the enquiry line on 0845 795 9775.

Employment tribunals deal with employment related matters, including unfair dismissal, redundancy, equal pay applications, sex discrimination, race relations, maternity rights and discrimination in employment against disabled people.

An application to the employment tribunal is made on Form IT1. Forms may be obtained from Job Centres, law centres and Citizens Advice Bureaux. There are notes on the form to assist with its completion. The completed form should be sent to the appropriate office within a specified time limit (usually three months from the date of the act which gave rise to the complaint).

Once the application is received and checked by the Employment Tribunal office, an acknowledgment will be sent to the applicant and the application will be given a case number. A form IT3 (Notice of Appearance), together with a copy of IT1, is sent to the person against whom the claim is made, usually an employer. (In the proceedings, this person is called the Respondent.) The Respondent must set out on form IT3 his answers to the applicant's claim and send this to the Employment Tribunal Office within a specified time.

When the Employment Tribunal Office receives IT3 from the Respondent, a copy is sent to the applicant. Additionally, a copy of both IT1 and IT3 are sent to the Advisory, Conciliation and Arbitration Service (ACAS), who will try to help the parties to resolve the dispute. If the dispute is settled, form COT3, which records the agreement, is filed and that is the end of the matter.

If no settlement is reached, a date for a hearing before the Employment Tribunal is fixed, giving not less than 14 days' notice to each party. Up to seven days before the hearing, either party may make further written points to the tribunal, and if any party does this, they must send a copy of the further points to the other party. If the hearing goes ahead, a decision on the matter is then reached. The parties may be told of the decision at the time or they may have to wait for several weeks. Hearings are usually held in public and the press may attend.

Besides the final hearing (known as the main or full merits hearing), the tribunal might also hold a directions hearing; a pre-hearing review; a hearing of preliminary issue; or an interim relief hearing. A directions hearing is held if the tribunal wishes to clarify any issues and decide on matters such as documents and witnesses. A pre-hearing review is held if the tribunal thinks that either of the parties has no reasonable prospect of success, and if that party still wishes to proceed, he may be ordered to pay a deposit. If the case goes ahead, it will be heard by a different tribunal. A hearing of preliminary issue may be arranged when the tribunal feels it should decide upon a particular issue before the case is listed for a full hearing, e.g., the application to the tribunal may not have been made within the set time limit and they may wish to make a decision on this point before the matter can proceed any further. An interim relief hearing may also take place where a re-employment order or an order continuing the contract of employment might be made.

If one of the parties is unhappy with the decision reached, then, in certain specific circumstances, the employment tribunal can be asked to review its decision and if it agrees to do this, there will be a re-hearing. An appeal against the employment tribunal's decision may be made to the Employment Appeal Tribunal (EAT) on a point of law only. Appeal may be made from the EAT to the Court of Appeal and then to the House of Lords.

Enforcing the decision of a tribunal

Tribunals cannot enforce decisions (known as awards) they make. If it is necessary for a decision to be enforced, then the party wishing to carry out the enforcement must apply to the civil courts.

ACAS

As mentioned above, when an application has been made to the employment tribunal, the relevant forms are sent to ACAS, which is an independent body whose role is to prevent and resolve employment disputes and to conciliate in complaints to employment tribunals.

ACAS will hold workshops and joint working parties in an attempt to help organisations avoid industrial relations problems. They offer conciliation when disputes occur, where those involved can try to reach agreement through discussion and negotiation. However, ACAS cannot impose or recommend settlements. They may also appoint a mediator to help in disputes if the parties request this. If conciliation does not work, the parties can ask ACAS to act as arbitrator, and then an independent arbitrator or board will be appointed to examine the case and make an award. Before the arbitration is arranged, both parties must agree to accept the arbitrator's decision as binding.

ACAS has many enquiry points throughout the country which give free information and advice on most employment matters.

Other bodies

There are numerous regulatory bodies and offices, e.g., Complaints Adjudicator for Companies House; The Information Commissioner (formerly known as the Data Protection Commissioner) who continues to enforce the Data Protection Act 1998 and is now also responsible for enforcing the Freedom of Information Act; Police Complaints Authority; Financial Services Authority (FSA); The Adjudicator, who investigates complaints about HM Revenue & Customs and the Contributions Agency of the Department of Social Security; Office of Water Services (Ofwat), Office of the Gas and Electricity Markets (Ofgem), Office of Communications (Ofcom), and various Ombudsmen.

Ombudsmen are independent investigators appointed to look into complaints of various bodies when an internal complaints procedure has proved unsatisfactory or unfair. Regulators are independent 'watchdogs' who are appointed to look after the interests of customers of privatised utilities such as gas, water and electricity, as mentioned above. Similar to ombudsmen, they will investigate complaints where internal procedures have failed to satisfy.

The Parliamentary Ombudsman, otherwise known as the Parliamentary Commissioner for Administration, deals with complaints by members of the public about their treatment by Government departments and various other public sector bodies. He can only deal with complaints which have been put to him through a Member of Parliament.

Local Government Ombudsmen, otherwise known as Local Government Commissioners, deal with complaints of maladministration by local authorities and certain other bodies. Members of the public may make a complaint direct to a Local Government Ombudsman.

There are many other Ombudsmen who investigate complaints, e.g., the Banking Ombudsman, Building Societies Ombudsman, Health Service Ombudsman, Insurance Ombudsman, Legal Services Ombudsman, Pensions Ombudsman, Personal Investment Authority Ombudsman. Some of these have power to make binding awards or decisions. There is also an Ombudsman who investigates complaints regarding the administration of the institutions and bodies of the European Community: The European Ombudsman.

An Ombudsman or regulator should be contacted as a last resort, after the particular organisation being complained about has been given every opportunity to resolve the matter.

Criminal Injury Compensation Authority

One organisation which you may come across is the Criminal Injury Compensation Authority (CICA), which administers the Criminal Injuries Compensation Scheme—a scheme to compensate victims of crimes of violence. Until April 1996, this was operated by the Criminal Injuries Compensation Board (CICB), which the CICA has replaced. Rules concerning eligibility under the scheme are laid down by the CICA.

Applications for compensation must be made in writing on a form obtainable from the CICA and must be made within two years of the incident causing the injury. However, this time limit may be waived in certain circumstances.

Applications will be decided by claims officers of the CICA. If an applicant disagrees with a claims officer's decision, he may ask for a review of that decision. Such a review must be requested within 90 days. There is a further right of appeal from a decision made on a review. An appeal will be considered by adjudicators, who are members of the Criminal Injuries Compensation Appeals Panel. There may be an oral hearing on appeal, although there is no right to such a hearing.

The amount of compensation payable will be a standard amount based on a tariff formulated by the CICA according to the nature and severity of the injury. There is a maximum amount of compensation payable. Similarly, there is a minimum amount payable and any injury must be serious enough to qualify for the minimum award.

The costs of legal representation will not be paid for by the CICA.

Motor Insurers' Bureau

The Motor Insurers' Bureau (MIB) is an independent body funded by motor insurance companies to settle claims brought by injured persons where a negligent driver is uninsured or cannot be traced. Claims for damage to property can also be made to the MIB but not if the driver of the vehicle causing the damage is unknown. There are various important procedures to be followed when making a claim to the MIB, one of these being that victims must report the accident to the police.

Motor insurers are permitted to operate as such only if they belong to the MIB and pay towards its costs.

Alternative Dispute Resolution

Alternative Dispute Resolution (ADR) is the name given to various methods of resolving disputes without the necessity of going to court. It is now used as an 'umbrella' term to cover matters such as arbitration, early neutral evaluation, expert determination, mediation, conciliation and a few others. Each of these methods of resolving disputes has its own rules and processes. The courts are increasingly encouraging parties to use an alternative method of resolving disputes, rather than resorting to litigation through the courts.

One of the principal international organisations which can assist in matters relating to the use of ADR in commercial and public sector disputes is the Centre for Dispute Resolution (CEDR), based in London. There are other organisations providing dispute resolution services and some professional bodies, e.g., the Royal Institute of Surveyors, provide services for disputes which involve their own members.

Arbitration

Arbitration is frequently used in specialised and commercial matters. Both sides to a dispute agree to let an arbitrator or panel of arbitrators resolve the dispute. The arbitrator might be a lawyer or perhaps an expert in the particular area of dispute. The arbitrator or panel of arbitrators will reach a decision after hearing the evidence, and will make a decision according to the law. The conduct of an arbitration is governed by the rules of the particular arbitral institution which has been chosen by the parties to the dispute. The arbitrator's decision is called an award which is legally binding on the parties and can be enforced through the courts.

Some of the advantages of arbitration are that it enables the parties to have their dispute resolved by a person or a group of people chosen by the parties themselves; it is quicker than going to court; there is no public hearing and the arbitrator will often have knowledge of the subject being disputed. Many commercial contracts contain an arbitration clause specifying that if a dispute arises, the parties to the contract will go to arbitration to settle the matter. There are various arbitral and trade institutions which provide for the needs of a specific trade or area, e.g., Institute of Civil Engineers; International Chamber of Commerce; Joint Contracts Tribunal; London Maritime Arbitrator's Association; Royal Institution of Chartered Surveyors. Even where a contract does not provide for arbitration, the parties may prefer arbitration.

Documents being used in arbitration proceedings are usually similar in layout to statements of case (see Chapter 3). Appointments for arbitration are arranged between the parties to suit themselves and the arbitrators and it may be a secretary's task to arrange such an appointment.

The Chartered Institute of Arbitrators, which is based in London, organises trade association arbitration schemes. Many businesses and other organisations, including many household names, are members of a trade association arbitration scheme and if someone has a dispute with that organisation, they may make a complaint to the trade association. The trade association will try to help both parties reach an agreement but if they cannot, the association may offer to arbitrate.

Early neutral evaluation

This is a process where a neutral professional person, often a lawyer, will hear a summary of each party's case and give an evaluation of the points raised, which can then be used as a basis for further negotiation. Nothing in this procedure is binding on the parties.

Expert determination

This is where an independent person who is an expert on the subject in dispute is appointed to make a decision in the matter. The parties are bound by the expert's decision.

Mediation and conciliation

In mediation, an independent person called a mediator tries to help both parties come to an agreement which each will find acceptable. If a mediation is successful and an agreement is reached, it will normally be written down to form a legally binding contract unless the parties state otherwise. Conciliation is very similar to mediation but the conciliator (rather than a mediator) suggests possible solutions to the parties to try to help them reach an agreement. The term conciliation is not now used so much in its own right, and generally, the term mediation tends to cover both aspects. Both mediation and conciliation are entirely voluntary and their aim is to try to reach a constructive, non-hostile solution agreeable to both parties which, of course, helps enormously if they wish to preserve any sort of business or other relationship.

An important organisation which provides mediation and conciliation services for employment related matters is ACAS, as mentioned earlier. Also mentioned previously are ombudsmen and regulators who can investigate complaints and get matters put right or give satisfactory answers. NHS patients seeking an explanation or apology, if appropriate, can utilise the NHS Complaints Procedure, which has been implemented for that purpose.

There are many mediation and conciliation services available to commercial organisations. With regard to non-commercial matters, there are various organisations offering these services. For example, Mediation UK, based in Bristol, can provide details of local community mediation schemes for matters such as neighbour disputes, e.g., disputes about noise, children's behaviour, etc., and other community matters, even relating to bullying at school.

Court welfare officers provide a large proportion of the mediation service in family matters where children are involved. There are also mediators who operate independently of the courts, such as National Family Mediation, the Family Mediators Association and the British Association of Lawyer Mediators, who provide a service to couples involved in divorce or separation. This involves experienced mediators, who have had suitable training, trying to help both parties reach agreement regarding the care of children and visiting arrangements, housing, financial matters and any other problems which may arise. Of course, divorcing or separating couples do not have to seek the help of mediators but if agreement can be reached in this way, contested court proceedings can often be avoided, thereby saving a lot of distress and expense.

Neutral fact finding

A neutral expert in the subject—usually complex technical issues—is appointed to investigate the dispute and make an evaluation of the case. This is non-binding but, like early neutral evaluation, can form the basis of a settlement or further negotiation.

Med-arb

Med-arb is a combination of mediation and arbitration. This would be where the parties agree at the outcome that they will use mediation but if that fails, they will refer the dispute to arbitration. In this type of dispute resolution, the person who has been appointed mediator may also act as arbitrator.

Court-based schemes

The courts are increasingly urging lawyers to refer suitable cases for ADR early on in proceedings and at various stages of proceedings. Additionally, some courts have introduced or piloted mediation schemes for specific areas of dispute.

Negotiating forums on the Internet

Online claims settlement and dispute resolution schemes are increasingly coming into being. These generally provide mediation and arbitration online for various areas of disputes. Different organisations offer a variety of services and it is worth having a look at some on the Internet to see what they provide.

TEST YOURSELF ON CHAPTER 4

Test your knowledge by completing this assignment. If you find that you have difficulty with anything, read the chapter again until you are happy with your answers.

1. What sort of employment-related matters might the employment tribunal deal with? If someone is not happy with the decision of an employment tribunal, to whom may an appeal be made?

2. Name half a dozen different regulatory bodies. What are Ombudsmen?

3. If someone is a victim of a crime of violence, to whom might he make a claim for compensation?

4. What is meant by 'Alternative Dispute Resolution' (ADR)? Write a few sentences on some of the different ways of resolving disputes and when they would be used.

5. In certain matters, it is often preferred to go to arbitration rather than issuing court proceedings. What are some of the possible advantages of arbitration?

6. Now go through the chapter and if there are any words that are unfamiliar to you or that you cannot spell, write or type them correctly several times until you feel you know them.

Family law

Family law can include not only divorce, but also nullity, legal separation, matters relating to persons co-habiting and children. Some or all of these matters come under the jurisdiction of the High Court, the county court and the magistrates' court.

The Family Law Protocol

The Family Law Protocol was initiated by the Law Society in 2002 and is a set of guidelines which apply to solicitors practising family law. The Protocol aims, among other things, to make divorce less confrontational and to put the interests of any children first, as well as trying to speed things up and keep costs down. The Protocol also encourages use of mediation wherever possible and keeping the other party properly informed. Solicitors involved in divorce proceedings should adhere to these guidelines and act in the spirit of them.

Commencing proceedings

Divorce proceedings are commenced by petition in either a divorce county court or the Divorce Registry in London which, for this purpose, acts as a county court. However, it is not possible to commence divorce proceedings unless the couple have been married for at least one year, although it is possible, in certain circumstances, to apply to the court for an order for judicial separation.

Divorces and ancillary matters are dealt with by a judge in open court or in the judge's room. A District judge will deal with matters related to divorce proceedings, such as those concerning property or finance. (See also Chapter 3 for further information on judges and District judges in the county courts.)

If a divorce becomes defended, it may be transferred to the Family Division of the High Court. This can, of course, be in London or any of the District Registries. There is no restriction as to which divorce county court a petition can be brought in, so proceedings are usually commenced in the court most convenient to the Petitioner.

The Petitioner is the person who starts the divorce proceedings and the person against whom they are brought is known as the Respondent. If proceedings are brought to include another person in those proceedings, he or she is known as the Co-Respondent although it is not necessary to actually name the Co-Respondent unless it is proposed to claim costs against them. Instructions and Briefs to Counsel are set out in the same manner as shown in Chapter 3.

The sole ground for divorce is that the marriage has irretrievably broken down. However, the Petitioner must satisfy the court that this is so, and must prove that one or more of five facts apply which will indeed show that the marriage has irretrievably broken down. The five facts which evidence irretrievable breakdown are:

(a) The Respondent has committed adultery and the Petitioner finds it intolerable to live with the Respondent.

(b) The Respondent has behaved in such a way that the Petitioner cannot reasonably be expected to live with the Respondent.

(c) The Respondent has deserted the Petitioner for a continuous period of at least two years immediately preceding presentation of the divorce petition (i.e., two years immediately preceding the commencement of the divorce proceedings).

(d) The parties have lived apart for a continuous period of at least two years immediately preceding presentation of the divorce petition and the Respondent consents to a divorce.

(e) The parties have lived apart for a continuous period of at least five years immediately preceding presentation of the divorce petition.

To commence proceedings the following documents must be filed at court:

(a) The marriage certificate (see below).

(b) The petition. When the petition is completed you should make a copy for the file, plus a copy for the court's own records, and a copy for each party the petition is to be served on, i.e., the Respondent and perhaps a Co-Respondent.

(c) A certificate with regard to reconciliation (see page 162).

(d) A statement of arrangements regarding children (if any) with a copy for the Respondent (see page 162).

(e) The court fee or an application for exemption of fees, where appropriate.

The documents, once they are checked and signed by the fee earner, can be posted to the court together with a cheque made payable to HM Courts Service ('HMCS') for the fee and a stamped, self-addressed envelope if you are not on the DX (see page 20). Remember always to keep copies of the documents on the file. Most of these documents have back-sheets (see page 69) although these are not shown in the examples.

The marriage certificate

A photocopy of the marriage certificate is not sufficient. It must be an official copy. If the Petitioner does not have this, a copy may be obtained from the office of the Registrar of Births, Deaths and Marriages for the district in which the couple were married.

Copy certificates may also be requested online from the General Register Office (GRO) or by telephone or fax. Additionally, a personal visit may be made at the Family Records Centre in London. A fee is payable for any certificates provided. The GRO is part of the Office for National Statistics and has responsibility for keeping the registration records relating to Births, Marriages and Deaths throughout England and Wales. There are equivalent offices for Scotland and Northern Ireland. Full information is available on the GRO website.

Petition

This can be a pre-printed form containing blank spaces for completion. Different printed forms are available for the different facts that may be relied upon to prove irretrievable breakdown, or there is also a general printed form of petition which can be used for any of the circumstances; the details just need to be inserted into the appropriate place on the form. Most divorce forms can be obtained from the court or bought from specialist law stationers and some solicitors have many forms readily available on their computers through special software. Most court forms have Notes for Guidance that come with them and the Divorce Petition form is no exception. These Notes contain all the information you need on how to complete the form correctly.

A petition starts off with the heading of the matter (see page 61), i.e., the court where the divorce proceedings have been commenced, and has a place for the number it will be given by the court, and states the names of the parties. The example shown below is Divorce Petition (Separation—2 years). Please note that other forms may differ slightly according to which of the five facts is being relied upon. Other versions of the Petition will follow a similar format.

1. The first paragraph must give the particulars shown in the marriage certificate as to the names of the parties, and the date and place of the marriage.

2. The address at which the Petitioner and Respondent last lived together as husband and wife.

3. This paragraph shows that the court has jurisdiction to deal with the divorce. The Notes for Guidance with the form gives the various grounds to show this. The appropriate paragraph taken from the Notes for Guidance should be typed on to the form, e.g., 'The Petitioner and Respondent are both habitually resident in England and Wales' or 'The Petitioner and the Respondent are both domiciled in England and Wales', or whatever is appropriate to the particular circumstances, and as set out in the Notes for Guidance that are with the petition form.

4. Occupation and current address of the Petitioner and the Respondent.

5. This shows whether there are any children of the family and if so, gives their details.

6. This states whether any other child, now living, has been born to the wife during the marriage.

7. This states whether or not there have been any other relevant court proceedings in England and Wales.

8. This states whether the Child Support Agency (see page 184) has had any involvement.

9. This states whether there are any other proceedings relating to the marriage outside England and Wales.

10. States the marriage has irretrievably broken down.

11. This shows which of the five facts, mentioned at the beginning of this chapter, applies to prove that the marriage has indeed irretrievably broken down. The form shown here is based on two years' separation. Other petition forms may have a different clause here depending on which of the five facts is relied upon or there may be nothing printed here and you will have to type in the appropriate clause. The exact wording for the clause should be as shown in the Notes for Guidance to the form.

12. This will give details of the incidents during the marriage which proves that one of the five facts applies.

The petition then ends with a 'prayer' which simply sets out what the Petitioner is asking the court to do, e.g., that the marriage be dissolved; payment of any costs in the proceedings and any orders for ancillary relief that may be applied for (see page 180 for further information on ancillary relief). It is then signed by the solicitor acting on behalf of the

Divorce Petition (Separation— 2 years)

FAMILY PROCEEDINGS RULES

Rule 2.3
Appendix 2

IN THE ___NORTHTOWN_____ **COUNTY COURT***

~~PRINCIPAL REGISTRY*~~

No. of Matter

The Notes for guidance in drafting the petition are on a separate sheet.

The Petition of   JANE BLOGGS

Shows that

Note 1.

1.   On the   1st   day of   April 1996   the Petitioner

JANE BLOGGS   was lawfully

married to   JOHN BLOGGS

(hereinafter called the Respondent) at St Mary's Church, in the Parish of Northtown in the County of Hertfordshire

Note 2.

2.   The Petitioner and the Respondent last lived together as husband and wife at   64 Rotten Row, Northtown, Herts EG4 6RB

Note 3.

3.   The Court has jurisdiction under Article 2(1) of the Council Regulation on the following ground(s):   The Petitioner and Respondent are both habitually resident in England and Wales.

Note 4.

4.   The Petitioner is by occupation a   clerk   and resides at 28 Sunny Street, Northtown, Herts EG7 8NB

The Respondent is by occupation a   pilot   and resides at 42 Lark Rise, Northtown, Herts EG8 3BX

Note 5.

5.   There is ~~[are]~~   one   children of the family now living namely PETER BLOGGS born on 6 February 1997

Note 6.

6.   No other child now living has been born to the [Petitioner] ~~[Respondent]~~

Note 7.

during the marriage

7.   There are or have been no other proceedings in any court in England and Wales or elsewhere with reference to the marriage [or to any children of the family] or between the Petitioner and the Respondent with reference to any property of either or both of them   Note 8.

8.   There are or have been no proceedings in the Child Support Agency with reference to the maintenance of any child of the family   Note 9.

9.   There are no proceedings continuing in any country outside England and Wales   Note 10. which relate to the marriage or are capable of affecting its validity or subsistence

Note 11.

10.   The said marriage has broken down irretrievably.   Note 12.

11.   The parties to the marriage have lived apart for a continuous period of at least two years immediately preceding the presentation of this Petition and the Respondent consents to a decree being granted.

12.   On or about 2 May 2003, the parties agreed that they would live apart and have not lived   Note 14. together since that date.

Note 15.

Note 16.

Note 17.

The Petitioner therefore prays:–

Note 18.   (1)   That the said marriage may be dissolved;

Note 19.   (2)   That the Respondent   may be

ordered to pay   the costs of this suit;

Note 20.   (3)   That [he][she] may be granted the following ancillary relief:–

(i)   [an order for maintenance pending suit] ⎫

(ii)   [a periodical payments order]   ⎪

(iii) [a secured provision order]   ⎪

(iv)   [a lump sum order]   ⎬ for [himself][herself]

(v)   [a property adjustment order]   ⎪

(vi)   [an order under section 24B, 25B or   ⎪
       25C of the Act of 1973 (Pension   ⎪
       Sharing/Attachment Order)]   ⎭

(vii) [a periodical payments order]   ⎫

(viii) [a secured provision order]   ⎬ for the children
                                                ⎪ of the family
(ix)   [a lump sum order]   ⎪

(x)   [a property adjustment order]   ⎭

Note 21.   (Signed)

Note 22.   The names and addresses of the persons who are to be served with this

Petition are:–   John Bloggs

Note 23.   The Petitioner's address for service is:– John Smith & Co,
                    2 Bank Chambers, High Road, Southtown, Herts. LM4 7XB
                    (tel: 01438 12345. ref: AB/cd/123)

Dated this   *   day of   *   20**
Address all communications for the Court to: The Court Manager, County Court*..
....
(or to the Family Proceedings Department, Principal Registry, First Avenue House, 42-49 High Holborn, London WC1V 6NP).
The Court Office is open from 10 a.m. till 4 p.m. (4.30 p.m. at the Principal Registry) on Mondays to Fridays only.

In the ___NORTHTOWN___   **County Court***

~~Principal Registry*~~

No. of Matter

IN THE MATTER of the Petition of

JANE BLOGGS

Divorce Petition

(Separation — 2 years)

Note 23.

John Smith & Co
2 Bank Chambers
High Road
Southtown
Herts
LM4 7BX

ref: AB/cd/123

tel: 01438 12345

Solicitors for the Petitioner

Divorce 4

Petitioner or the Petitioner herself or, if counsel settled the petition, his name should appear in this place.

Details are then given of the names and addresses of the persons who are to be served with the petition, the Petitioner's address for service (usually the solicitor's address) and the form is dated (normally the date it is filed at court). It also has a backsheet which must be completed in the usual way (see page 69). As mentioned earlier, the pre-printed form of petition has with it comprehensive Notes for Guidance and it is well worth reading these to understand the form properly.

Certificate with regard to reconciliation

This is a certificate signed by the solicitor acting for the Petitioner, stating whether or not he has discussed with the Petitioner the possibility of reconciliation and/or given to the Petitioner the names and addresses of persons qualified to help with reconciliation (e.g., marriage guidance council, known as Relate). The solicitor is not compelled to discuss reconciliation—it may be inappropriate to do so because of the circumstances of the divorce—but he must state whether or not he has done so and whether he has given suitable names to the Petitioner.

If the petitioner is being advised by way of legal help under legal aid funding (see Chapter 7), the Certificate with Regard to Reconciliation is not completed by the solicitor because, in these circumstances, the petitioner is deemed to be acting for herself and receiving assistance only to complete the forms.

Statement of arrangements

This is a form which requires the Petitioner to describe the present and proposed arrangements with regard to children of the family (if any). It is also open to the Respondent to file a Statement of Arrangements with the court if he so wishes.

The Petitioner's Statement of Arrangements may be agreed with the Respondent before proceedings are issued. If this happens, the form will be lodged with the court having been signed by both parties. If the Statement of Arrangements is not agreed between the parties, it will be signed just by the Petitioner and the Respondent will deal with it when it is served on him with the divorce documents.

When children are involved, the District judge will consider the proposed arrangements for them. If he considers that there is no need for him to intervene or make any order about the children, he will issue a certificate which states that there are no children that need to be considered.

If the District judge is not satisfied with the arrangements for children, he may issue directions to the parties, such as requiring further evidence, or a court welfare report to be prepared, or that one or both parties attend before him on a certain date and time. These directions will not normally hold up the divorce itself, although there are circumstances where the judge might decide to hold up the divorce if he thinks it necessary.

If it is considered necessary, the court may make any of the following orders relating to the children of the marriage:

(a) A residence order. This determines the child's living arrangements. It will say where the child is to live and may also give details of periods when the child is to live with each parent.

(b) Contact order. This may order that the person with whom the child is to live must allow the child to visit or stay with the other person named in the order. It may also deal with other communication, such as letters and telephone calls.

Certificate with regard
to Reconciliation
(Form M3, Appendix 1,
FPR 1991)
Rule 2.6(3)

FAMILY PROCEEDINGS RULES

IN THE———NORTHTOWN———— **COUNTY COURT** } *

~~PRINCIPAL REGISTRY~~ } *

*Complete
and/or delete
as appropriate.

No. of Matter

Between . . . . JANE BLOGGS . . . . Petitioner

and . . . . JOHN BLOGGS . . . . Respondent

I,   JOHN SMITH

the Solicitor acting for the Petitioner in the above cause do hereby certify that I have [not] discussed

with the Petitioner the possibility of a reconciliation and that I have [not] given to the Petitioner the

names and addresses of persons qualified to help effect a reconciliation.

Dated this   *   day of ***

(Signed) . . . .

Solicitor for the Petitioner

Address all communications for the Court to: The Court Manager, County Court* . . . .
. . . .
(or to the Principal Registry, First Avenue House, 42-49 High Holborn, London WC1V 6NP).
The Court Office is open from 10 a.m. till 4 p.m. (4.30 p.m. in the Principal Registry) on Mondays to Fridays only.

(c) Prohibited steps order. This stops a parent from doing a something without the court's permission, e.g., taking the child abroad.

(d) Specific issue order. The court will make the decision regarding a specific issue where the parents cannot agree, e.g., which school a child should attend.

These orders are known as Section 8 orders because they come under Section 8 of the Children Act 1989.

Also, with regard to children, you may come across CAFCASS (Children and Family Court Advisory and Support Service). CAFCASS only works in the family courts and advises the court, when requested to do so, on what it considers to be in the child's best interests. When required, a Children and Family Reporter from CAFCASS will make various enquiries relating to a child's circumstances and, where appropriate, will try to help the parents reach a suitable agreement. If an agreement cannot be reached or is not appropriate, the Children and Family Reporter will usually be asked to prepare a report for the court.

CAFCASS may become involved where parents who are divorcing or separating cannot agree on the arrangements for their children, or an application for adoption, and other matters where children are involved in care or supervision proceedings.

Action taken by the court

Once the court receives these documents, it allocates the case a matter number. This begins with the last two digits of the year, followed by D for divorce, and the serial number for each case (e.g., 05 D 1234). The court acknowledges receipt of the documents to the Petitioner's solicitor and posts to the Respondent the petition sealed with the court seal, plus the statement of arrangements, if applicable, together with a form of Acknowledgment of Service. This form differs slightly according to which of the five facts is alleged.

The Acknowledgment of Service form is a form that the Respondent has to complete to confirm that he has received all the documents from the court. It asks the Respondent certain questions such as: has he received the petition? where and when was it received? does he intend to defend the case? and also asks particular questions relating to which of the facts are alleged in order to prove irretrievable breakdown of the marriage. The Respondent should answer the questions and return the completed form to the court within a certain time limit. The court will then send a photocopy of the completed form to the Petitioner's solicitors.

If the Post Office returns the documents to the court as being undelivered, the court will send the Petitioner's solicitors a notice telling them this, which is called a Notice of Non-Service. Another way of effecting service (see below) on the Respondent will then be tried by the Petitioner's solicitors. Similarly, if the Respondent simply does not reply, even though the documents have not been returned to the court by the Post Office, the Petitioner's solicitors must try another way of effecting service on the Respondent.

Service of the petition

Service may be effected in one of the following ways:

(a) In the first instance, by the court by post.

Statement of Arrangements for Children

In the	**NORTHTOWN**	County Court
Petitioner	JANE BLOGGS	
Respondent	JOHN BLOGGS	

	No. of matter *(always quote this)*	05 D 789

To the Petitioner

You must complete this form
If you or the respondent have any children • under 16

or • over 16 but under 18 if they are at school or college or are training for a trade, profession or vocation.

Please use black ink.
Please complete Parts I, II and III.

Before you issue a petition for divorce try to reach agreement with your husband/wife over the proposals for the children's future. There is space for him/her to sign at the end of this form if agreement is reached.

If your husband/wife does not agree with the proposals he/she will have an opportunity at a later stage to state why he/she does not agree and will be able to make his/her own proposals.

You should take or send the completed form, signed by you (and, if agreement is reached, by your husband/wife) together with a copy to the court when you issue your petition.

Please refer to the explanatory notes issued regarding completion of the prayer of the petition if you are asking the court to make any order regarding the children.

The Court will only make an order if it considers that an order will be better for the child(ren) than no order.

If you wish to apply for any of the orders which may be available to you under Part I or II of the Children Act 1989 you are advised to see a solicitor.

You should obtain legal advice from a solicitor or, alternatively, from an advice agency. Addresses of solicitors and advice agencies can be obtained from the Yellow Pages and the Solicitors Regional Directory which can be found at Citizens Advice Bureaux, Law Centres and any local library.

To the Respondent

The petitioner has completed Part I, II and III of this form
which will be sent to the Court at the same time that the divorce petition is filed.

Please read all parts of the form carefully.

If you agree with the arrangements and proposals for the children you should sign Part IV of the form.
Please use black ink. You should return the form to the petitioner, or his/her solicitor.

If you do not agree with all or some of the arrangements of proposals you will be given the opportunity of saying so when the divorce petition is served on you.

D8A - w3 F.P. Rule 2.2(2) (Form M4)(5.95)   1

Part 1 - Details of the children

Please read the instructions for boxes 1, 2 and 3 before you complete this section

---

1. **Children of both parties** *(Give details only of any children born to you and the Respondent or adopted by you both)*

———— Forenames ————————————— Surname ————————————— Date of birth ————

(i)

(ii)

(iii)

(iv)

(v)

---

2. **Other children of the family** *(Give details of any other children treated by both of you as children of the family: for example your own or the Respondent's)*

———— Forenames ————————— Surname ————————— Date of birth ————— Relationship to —————
                                                                                       Yourself   Respondent

(i)

(ii)

(iii)

(iv)

(v)

---

3. **Other children who are not children of the family** *(Give details of any children born to you or the Respondent that have not been treated as children of the family or adopted by you both)*

———— Forenames ————————— Surname ————————————— Date of birth ————

(i)

(ii)

(iii)

(iv)

(v)

2

Part II - Arrangements for the children of the family
This part of the form must be completed. Give details for each child if arrangements are different.
(if necessary, continue on another sheet and attach it to this form)

---

4.   **Home details**   *(please tick the appropriate boxes)*

(a) The addresses at which the children now live

(b) Give details of the number of living rooms, bedrooms, etc. at the addresses in (a)

(c) Is the house rented or owned and by whom?

Is the rent or any mortgage being regularly paid?   ☐ No   ☐ Yes

(d) Give the names of all other persons living with the children including your husband/wife if he/she lives there. State their relationship to the children.

(e) Will there be any change in these arrangements?   ☐ No   ☐ Yes   *(please give details)*

3

| 5. | **Education and training details** | *(please tick the appropriate boxes)* |

(a) Give the names of the school, college or place of training attended by each child.

(b) Do the children have any special educational needs? ☐ No ☐ Yes *(please give details)*

(c) Is the school, college or place of training, fee-paying? ☐ No ☐ Yes *(please give details of how much the fees are per term / year)*

Are fees being regularly paid? ☐ No ☐ Yes *(please give details)*

(d) Will there be any change in these arrangements? ☐ No ☐ Yes *(please give details)*

4

6.   Childcare details   *(please tick the appropriate boxes)*

(a) Which parent looks after the
     children from day to day?
     If responsibility is shared,
     please give details

(b) Does that parent go out to   ☐ No   ☐ Yes   *(please give details of his/her hour of work)*
     work?

(c) Does someone look after the   ☐ No   ☐ Yes   *(please give details)*
     children when the parent is
     not there?

(d) Who looks after the children
     during school holidays?

(e) Will there be any change in   ☐ No   ☐ Yes   *(please give details)*
     these arrangements?

7.   Maintenance   *(please tick the appropriate boxes)*

(a) Does your husband/wife   ☐ No   ☐ Yes   *(please give details of how much)*
     pay towards the upkeep of
     the children?
     If there is another source of
     maintenance, please specify.

(b) Is the payment made under a   ☐ No   ☐ Yes   *(please give details, including the name of the court*
     court order?   *and the case number)*

(c) Is the payment following an   ☐ No   ☐ Yes   *(please give details of how much)*
     assessment by the Child
     Support Agency?

(d) Has maintenance for the   ☐ No   ☐ Yes
     children been agreed?

(e) If not, will you be applying for:
     • a child maintenance order   ☐ No   ☐ Yes
       from the court

     • child support maintenance   ☐ No   ☐ Yes
       through the Child Support
       Agency?

5

8.	**Details for contact with the children**	*(please tick the appropriate boxes)*

(a) Do the children see your husband/wife?

☐ No ☐ Yes *(please give details of how often and where)*

(b) Do the children ever stay with your husband/wife?

☐ No ☐ Yes *(please give details of how much)*

(c) Will there be any change to these arrangements?

☐ No ☐ Yes *(please give details of how much)*

Please give details of the proposed arrangements for contact and residence.

6

9. **Details of health**   *(please tick the appropriate boxes)*

(a) Are the children generally in good health?   ☐ No   ☐ Yes   *(please give details of any serious disability or chronic illness)*

(b) Do the children have any special health needs?   ☐ No   ☐ Yes   *(please give details of the care needed and how it is to be provided)*

10. **Details of Care and other court proceedings**   *(please tick the appropriate boxes)*

(a) Are the children in the care of a local authority, or under the supervision of a social worker or probation officer?   ☐ No   ☐ Yes   *(please give details including any court proceedings)*

(b) Are any of the children on the Child Protection Register?   ☐ No   ☐ Yes   *(please give details of the local authority and the date of registration)*

(c) Are there or have there been any proceedings in any court involving the children, for example adoption, custody/residence, access/contact, wardship, care, supervision or maintenance?   ☐ No   ☐ Yes   *(please give details and send a copy of any order to the court)*

(You need not include any Child Support Agency proceedings here)

Part III   To the Petitioner

Conciliation

If you and your husband/wife do not agree about arrangements for the child(ren), would you agree to discuss the matter with a Conciliator and your husband/wife?

☐ No   ☐ Yes

Declaration

I declare that the information I have given is correct and complete to the best of my knowledge.

Signed .... (Petitioner)

Date: ....

Part IV   To the Respondent

I agree with the arrangements and proposals contained in Part I and II of this form.

Signed .... (Respondent)

Date: ....

8

(b) By the court bailiff. In this case a further copy of the petition and appropriate fee must be filed with the court together with a form for Request for Service by Court Bailiff. A photograph or description of the Respondent should also be supplied for the court bailiff. If the bailiff is successful, he will complete a form certifying that he has effected service.

(c) Personal service by a solicitor or process server. On no account may the Petitioner personally serve the Respondent with these documents. If personal service is effected, an affidavit of service must then be filed with the court.

(d) Substituted service—in certain circumstances, a court order for substituted service may be obtained (e.g., newspaper advertisement).

Additionally, in certain cases, for example, where it simply proves impossible to trace the Respondent, an application may be made to the court for an order for service to be dispensed with. However, extensive enquiries have to be made before the court will make this type of order.

The court can also direct that service is deemed to have been effected where, for example, it is known that the Respondent has been properly served with the documents but nevertheless has not replied.

Answer

If your firm is acting for the Respondent, and he wishes to defend the divorce, he has a specific number of days from the service of the petition to file an Answer. (This is equivalent to a defence in other types of actions: see Chapter 3.) The Answer must be headed with the title of the matter and each paragraph numbered. A backsheet also has to be completed.

The Answer will be sent to the court and the case will proceed to trial either in the county court or may be transferred to the Family Division of the High Court. If it is transferred, it will then be given a new matter number by the High Court. If a Co-Respondent is named in the proceedings, he or she also has a right to file an Answer. Once an Answer is filed, a copy is sent to the Petitioner's solicitors by the court and the case will proceed.

Affidavit in support of petition

Before a divorce can be granted, the court will always want evidence. This will usually be in the form of an affidavit, i.e., a sworn statement by the Petitioner verifying the petition and dealing with certain other matters. The affidavit must contain certain specific information and printed forms are available. The affidavit must be sworn (or affirmed) by the Petitioner in the presence of an authorised person, such as a solicitor or authorised court officer. If it is being sworn before a solicitor, the solicitor administering the oath must be an independent solicitor who is not the solicitor acting in the matter or even a solicitor in the same firm. See also the section on affidavits in Chapter 3. The original affidavit, together with any exhibits, are sent to the court, copies being kept in the file.

The affidavit, once sworn, is sent to the court, together with a form of Application for Directions for Trial. This form asks the District judge for directions for trial of the action by

Affidavit by Petitioner in Support of Petition under Section 1(2)(d) of the Matrimonial Causes Act 1973.

FAMILY PROCEEDINGS
RULES

No. of Matter   05 D 789

Rule 2.24(3); Form M7(d)

*Complete
and/or delete
as appropriate.

IN THE —— NORTHTOWN ———— **COUNTY COURT***

~~**PRINCIPAL REGISTRY**~~ *

OF THE FAMILY DIVISION

Between   JANE BLOGGS   Petitioner

and   JOHN BLOGGS   Respondent

QUESTION	ANSWER
About the Divorce Petition 1. Have you read the petition filed in this case?	Yes
2. Do you wish to alter or to add to any statement in the petition? If so, state the alterations or additions.	No
3. Subject to these alterations or additions (if any), is everything stated **in your petition** true? If any statement is not within your own knowledge, indicate this and say whether it is true to the best of your information and belief.	Yes
4. State the date on which you and the respondent separated.	2 May 2003
5. State briefly the reason or main reason for the separation.	The marriage was unhappy for some time and it was agreed that we should live apart.
6. State the date when and the circumstances in which you came to the conclusion that the marriage was in fact at an end.	2 May 2003

7. State as far as you know the various addresses at which you and the respondent have respectively lived since the last date given in the answer to Question 4, and the periods of residence at each address:

Petitioner's Address		*Respondent's Address*	
From 2.5.03 to present date	28 Sunny Street Northtown, Herts. EG7 8NB	From 2.5.03 to present date	42 Lark Rise Northtown, Herts. EG8 3BX

8. Since the last date given in the answer to Question 4, have you ever lived with the respondent in the same household?

   If so, state the address and the period (or periods), giving dates.

   No

About the children of the family

9. Have you read the Statement of Arrangements filed in this case?

   Yes

10. Do you wish to alter anything in the Statement of Arrangements or add to it?

    If so, state the alterations or additions.

    No

11. Subject to these alterations and additions (if any) is everything stated in the **Statement of Arrangements** true?

    If any statement is not within your own knowledge, indicate this and say whether it is true and correct to the best of your information and belief.

    Yes

2

I,   JANE BLOGGS   *(full name)*

of   28 Sunny Street, Northtown   *(full residential address)*
      Herts. EG7 8NB

      clerk   *(occupation)*

make oath and say as follows: —

(1) Delete if the acknowledgment is signed by a solicitor.

1.   I am the petitioner in this cause.

2.   **The answers to Questions 1 to 11 above are true.**

(2) Insert name of the respondent exactly as it appears on the acknowledgment of service signed by him/her.

3.   (¹) I identify the signature   J. BLOGGS   (²)
     appearing on the copy acknowledgment of service now produced to me and marked "A"
     as the signature of my husband/wife, the respondent in this cause.

4.   I identify the signature   J.BLOGGS   (²)
     appearing at Part IV of the Statement of Arrangements dated
     now produced to me and marked "B" as the signature of the respondent.

(3) Exhibit any medical report or document on which the petitioner wishes to rely.

5.   (³)

(4) If the petitioner seeks a judicial separation, amend accordingly.

(5) Amend or delete as appropriate.

6.   I ask the Court to grant a decree dissolving my marriage with the respondent (⁴)

     on the ground stated in my petition [and to order the respondent to pay

      the costs of this suit]. (⁵)

SWORN at

in the County of

this   day of   , 20

Before me

(5) Delete as the case may be.

A Commissioner for Oaths.
Officer of the Court appointed by
the Judge to take Affidavits(⁵).

Address all communications for the Court to: The Court Manager, County Court*

(or to the Principal Registry, First Avenue House, 42-49 High Holborn, London, WC1V 6NP) quoting the number in the top
right-hand corner of the first page. The Court Office is open from 10 a.m. till 4 p.m. (4.30 p.m. in the Principal Registry) on Mondays
to Fridays only.

3

Application for Directions for Trial (Special Procedure)

FAMILY PROCEEDINGS
                   No. of Matter   05 D 789

RULES (Rule 2.24)   **IN THE**   NORTHTOWN   **COUNTY COURT**

Between   JANE BLOGGS   Petitioner

and   JOHN BLOGGS   Respondent

Application for Directions for Trial (Special Procedure)

The Petitioner   JANE BLOGGS   applies to the District Judge for directions for the trial of this undefended cause by entering it in the Special Procedure List.

The Petitioner's affidavit of evidence is lodged with this application.

Signed   [Solicitor for] the Petitioner

Dated

If you write to the Court please address your letters to "The Court Manager"

and quote the **No. of Matter** at the top of this form.

The Court Office is at

and is open from 10am to 4pm on Monday to Friday.

Divorce 51A

1991 Edition
4.2001 T03693
5046486

Notice of Application for Decree Nisi to be made Absolute.
(Form M8, Appendix 1, F.P.R. 1991)

FAMILY PROCEEDINGS RULES

Rule 2.49(1)

*Complete and/or delete as appropriate. If proceeding in a District Registry, delete both headings and insert "in the High Court of Justice, Family Division, District Registry".

IN THE ——— NORTHTOWN ——— COUNTY COURT*

~~PRINCIPAL REGISTRY~~*

No. of Matter 05 D 789

Between .... JANE BLOGGS .... Petitioner

and .... JOHN BLOGGS .... Respondent

TAKE NOTICE that the Petitioner   JANE BLOGGS

applies for the decree nisi pronounced in his (her) favour on the

day of   **   , to be made absolute.

Dated this   *   day of   ***

Signed ....
Solicitors for Petitioner

of ....

....

Address all communications for the Court to: The Court Manager, County Court* ....

....

(or to the Principal Registry, First Avenue House, 42-49 High Holborn, London WC2V 6NP) quoting the number in the top right-hand corner of this form. The Court Office is open from 10 a.m. till 4 p.m. (4.30 p.m. at the Principal Registry) on Mondays to Fridays only.

entering it into the special procedure list. Special procedure is the name given to a straight-forward undefended divorce case.

In an undefended divorce case, the District judge will consider the contents of the Affidavit by the Petitioner together with all the other papers, and if he is satisfied that everything is in order and that the Petitioner has proved the contents of the divorce petition (by the affidavit), he will issue a Certificate of Entitlement to a Decree. This is a standard court form certifying that the Petitioner is entitled to a decree. This certificate does not end the marriage but it gives notice of the place, time and date for pronounce-ment of the decree nisi (see below) and makes any orders for costs.

The District judge will, at the same time, consider the statement of arrangements regarding any children and may make certain directions regarding any children.

Decree nisi

The Certificate of Entitlement which is issued by the District judge gives the date when a judge will pronounce the decree nisi in open court. The decree nisi does not dissolve the marriage: it is a provisional step towards the divorce. It is an order granted by the judge declaring that the marriage has broken down irretrievably and may be dissolved unless cause can be shown within six weeks from the date it is made to show why the decree should not be made absolute. The form of decree nisi stresses that it is not the final decree and that application for the final decree must be made to the court. It is not necessary to attend court to hear the decree nisi being pronounced. This is a straightforward procedure where, on the date for the decree nisi to be pronounced, the judge goes into court and reads out a list of decree nisi appointments for that day. Unless there are any objections or representations, he formally pronounces a decree nisi in each case.

Once the decree nisi has been pronounced, the court will send a copy of it to both parties (or their solicitors). The solicitor will normally send a copy to his client telling her that she is not yet free to re-marry and that there is the six-week waiting period. The soli-citor will usually ask the client (if it is the Petitioner) to confirm that she wishes him to apply for the final decree at the end of the six weeks. Usually, the decree may be applied for by the Petitioner six weeks and one day after the decree nisi has been pronounced.

During the six-week period an appeal may be lodged or matters dealing with children can be sorted out. If it is a straightforward divorce with nothing to be sorted out, neither party needs to attend court. If, however, the District judge is not satisfied with proposed arrangements for any children, he may direct that one or both of the parties attend before him, or that a welfare report is prepared, or that further evidence, by way of affidavit, is filed. These directions do not normally hold up the divorce proceedings.

Decree absolute

Diary notes should be made for six weeks and one day after the decree nisi, because then, the final divorce decree—the decree absolute—can be applied for. It is this decree which finally dissolves the marriage. This is not pronounced in open court but is applied for through the post on a prescribed form, together with the appropriate fee. All being well, the court will send the parties a sealed form of Decree Absolute and the divorce is final.

If the Petitioner fails to apply for the decree absolute, the Respondent can apply at a later date—after three months have passed from the earliest date when the Petitioner could have applied. If the Respondent applies, he must make an application to the court, rather than just completing a form.

The procedure outlined above for obtaining a divorce is known as the 'special procedure'. However, it is in fact the usual procedure where divorces are straightforward and undefended and there are no children involved. It is also often referred to as a postal divorce because it is practically all dealt with by sending forms through the post.

Applications

As in other court procedures, different applications may be made to the court before the divorce is finalised and sometimes afterwards. The Family Proceedings Rules 1991 specify how each application is to be made, and these can be made either 'on notice' or 'without notice' (see pages 114–18). Applications made without notice normally have to be supported by an affidavit which is filed with the court at the same time as the application. (See Chapter 3 for further information on interlocutory applications and affidavits.)

Applications to the court may relate to procedural matters, such as an application to amend typing errors in a document; or other matters to be resolved such as one party requiring further information from the other who may be reluctant to give it; or it may be an application seeking some sort of relief, such as for an occupation order following domestic violence, which would permit one party to remain in the home and the other made to leave it; or an application for ancillary relief which includes matters relating to the finances or property of the parties (see below).

Once an application is made to the court, the judge will make his decision in the matter and this is called an Order (see page 118). Orders made in matrimonial proceedings are normally drawn up by the court and sent to the parties.

Ancillary relief

Ancillary relief is a term given to matters relating to the finances or property of the parties. The Petitioner will usually state in the prayer of the Petition (at the end of the Divorce Petition form) which order(s) she will be asking the court to make with regard to these matters. In fact, all the options open to the petitioner as shown in the prayer will normally be left in without crossing any out. This is so that when the petitioner is ready to proceed with the application, if any circumstances have changed by then, she will still have all the options open to her and can then decide at the appropriate time which order(s) she will be seeking. If the initial application is being made in the prayer, Form A (see below) will have to be completed when the Petitioner is ready to proceed with the application.

The types of order for ancillary relief that may be applied for are:

(a) Maintenance pending suit. Basically an application for maintenance pending the divorce. It will finish once the divorce is finalised and then a full order may well be made.

(b) Periodical payments order. This is an order whereby one party has to pay a certain amount to the other at certain specified times, e.g., payments of a specified sum every month. This sort of order may be varied by either party applying to the court. For example, if the person making the payments became unemployed, he might ask the court to decrease the amounts or, if he received a salary increase, the recipient might ask the court to make him pay her extra money. The order will normally specify how long it will last and this will usually be until either the marriage of the recipient; the death of one party; or until a further order is made; or the court can impose a time limit on the period during which payments will be made.

(c) Secured provision order. This is useful where the person ordered to pay a periodical payments order is not making or is not likely to make the payments. If it can be shown that the Respondent has relevant assets which could have a charge placed upon them, such as his own business, then a secured provision order may be made. This means that the order would specify that if the payments were not made, then the person's assets specified in the order would be used as security and may even become forfeit if the payments were not made.

(d) Lump sum order. A lump sum payment will be made and cannot be varied later like the periodical payments order. It could be used for example, to compensate one party for allowing the other to keep the home they had shared.

(e) Property adjustment order. This can deal with the way the parties own property, e.g., it could say that the matrimonial home is to be sold and the proceeds of the sale are to be divided into certain proportions, or perhaps that the Petitioner will be allowed to live in the matrimonial home until the youngest child reaches 16 and then the house will be sold with the proceeds being divided equally between the parties. Other property may also be provided for in this type of order.

(f) Pension sharing/attachment order. A pension sharing order divides the value of pension benefits between the spouses, effectively transferring a percentage of a spouse's pension rights to the other spouse. This means that the receiving spouse will then have an independent pension in their own right without having to wait until the other party retires. An attachment order with regard to a pension allows a spouse to take part of the other's spouse's pension income after retirement.

Additionally, certain orders may be applied for on behalf of children, but generally, applications for child maintenance must be made to the Child Support Agency.

Pre-application Protocol

This is a series of guidelines for solicitors and clients which should be followed before application is made to the court for ancillary relief.

The Protocol tries to ensure that the initial letters are not written in a hostile manner and are clear about what is being claimed. Procedures should be followed fairly and without delay, causing minimum distress to the parties, as well as safeguarding the needs of any children. The Protocol also encourages efforts to negotiate and achieve a settlement, if possible, before application is made to the court (as long as this does not delay matters or cause unnecessary expense).

Commencing the proceedings

To proceed with the application for ancillary relief the Petitioner's application is made on a notice of application form called Form A. Form A plus two copies and the fee, where payable, should be filed at court.

When the court receives Form A, they will fix a date for a First Appointment between 12 and 16 weeks after the date of the filing of the notice. The Form A notice will normally be served on the Respondent within the required time by the court, together with a notice of the First Appointment date. The court will also give notice of the First Appointment date to the Petitioner applicant. The date for the First Appointment may not be cancelled or changed without permission of the court and if it is changed, the court must fix another date straight away.

The parties must exchange certain information before the appointment. This is to save time and costs and is designed to facilitate settlement.

No less than 35 days before the date of the First Appointment, the parties must simultaneously exchange with each other and file with the court a statement of property and income, on Form E. The completed form has to be sworn or affirmed. Form E requires a considerable amount of information to be provided by the party completing it such as details of current living arrangements; income; earning capacity; other financial resources; financial needs, etc. It also requires that copies of certain documents are attached, e.g., the last three payslips, mortgage statement, bank statements for the last 12 months, any property valuation obtained in the last six months, etc. The form itself states what is required to be filed with it.

At least 14 days before the First Appointment, each party must serve on the other and file with the court certain other information, such as:

(a) a questionnaire setting out details of any further information and documents they are seeking from the other party;

(b) a concise statement of issues between the parties;

(c) a notice in Form G stating whether that party will be in a position to use the First Appointment as the Financial Dispute Resolution Appointment.

The First Appointment is a hearing where the outstanding issues in the case can be defined at an early stage. Both parties must attend with their lawyers unless the court orders otherwise. At this hearing the District judge will decide the extent to which any questionnaires should be answered and which documents should be provided. He may also give directions on other matters, such as valuations to be carried out or perhaps he might require an expert to give evidence on a particular matter.

The District judge will also direct that the case be referred to a Financial Dispute Resolution Appointment unless he feels that is not appropriate. Alternatively, the court may treat the First Appointment as the Financial Dispute Resolution Appointment (see below), if appropriate.

The Financial Dispute Resolution appointment (FDR)

Not later than seven days before the FDR, the applicant must file details of all offers and proposals made and any responses to them. Again, both parties must attend with their lawyers unless the court orders otherwise. If agreement cannot be reached, the judge will fix a date for a final hearing, which will be heard by a different judge. Anything said at the FDR will not normally be admissible at any subsequent hearing.

The final hearing

Not less than 14 days before the final hearing date, the applicant must file and serve on the other party a statement which sets out the details of the orders which the applicant will be asking the court to make. Not more than seven days after service of this statement, the other party must file and serve on the applicant a similar statement.

Estimate of costs

At every hearing, the parties must provide the court with an up-to-date estimate of costs incurred in the application on Form H.

Notice of [intention to proceed with] an Application for Ancillary Relief

■

Respondents (Solicitor(s))
name and address

In the	
	*[County Court] *[Principal Registry of the Family Division]
Case No. *Always quote this*	
Applicant's Solicitor's reference	
Respondent's Solicitor's reference	

(°delete as appropriate)

```
┌─────────────────────────────────────┐
│                                      │
│                                      │
│                                      │
│                                      │
│                                      │
│             Postcode                 │
│                                      │
└─────────────────────────────────────┘
```

The marriage of   **and**

Take Notice that

the Applicant intends; °**to apply** to the Court for

°delete as
appropriate

°**to proceed** with the application in the [petition][answer] for

°**to apply to vary:**

☐ an order for maintenance pending suit
☐ a secured provision order
☐ a property adjustment order *(please provide address)*

```
┌─────────────────────────────────────┐
│                                      │
│                                      │
│                                      │
│                                      │
└─────────────────────────────────────┘
```

☐ a periodical payments order
☐ a lump sum order
☐ an order under Section 24B, 25B
    or 25C of the Act of 1973

If an application is made for any periodical payments or secured periodical payments for children:

- and there is a written agreement made before 5 April 1993 about maintenance for the benefit of children, **tick this box** ☐
- and there is a written agreement made on or after 5 April 1993 about maintenance for the benefit of children, **tick this box** ☐
- but there is no agreement, tick any of the boxes below to show if you are applying for payment:

☐ for a stepchild or stepchildren
☐ in addition to child support maintenance already paid under a Child Support Agency assessment
☐ to meet expenses arising from a child's disability
☐ to meet expenses incurred by a child in being educated or training for work
☐ when either the child **or** the person with care of the child **or** the absent parent of the child
    is not habitually resident in the United Kingdom
☐ Other *(please state)*

Signed: Dated: ■

[Applicant/Solicitor for the Applicant]

The court office at

is open between 10 am and 4 pm (4.30pm at the Principal Registry of the Family Division) Monday to Friday. When corresponding with the court, please address forms or letters to the Court Manager and quote the case number. If you do not do so, your correspondence may be returned.

Form A Notice of [Intention to proceed with] an Application for Ancillary Relief (12.00)   *Printed on behalf of The Court Service*

Child Support Agency

With regard to child support maintenance, which is money that absent parents pay as a contribution to the upkeep of their children, it is generally no longer possible for people who do not already have a court order or a written maintenance agreement to make arrangements for child maintenance through the courts, except in certain circumstances. Child maintenance has been dealt with by the Child Support Agency (CSA) since 5 April 1993. However, the CSA will accept applications for child maintenance usually only when everyone involved is habitually resident in Great Britain or Northern Ireland. The courts will continue to deal with cases where one of those concerned lives abroad. The CSA investigates the parents' means and assesses how much maintenance should be paid.

The amount of support to be paid is looked at periodically and any reviews are based on the individual circumstances of the case and following significant changes in the circumstances of either parent. The CSA also provides a collection service. It may collect payments from the absent parent and pass them on to the person who is to receive them. If the absent parent falls into arrears with payments, the CSA may take action to enforce payment.

Notice of Change of Solicitor

If any party wishes to change their solicitor after proceedings have been issued the new solicitor must complete a Notice of Change of Solicitor form. A copy must be served on all the parties and lodged with the court. See also Notice of Change of Solicitor on page 135.

Involvement of magistrates' courts

Magistrates courts have various powers in family matters but do not have the power to dissolve a marriage. For the purposes of dealing with family matters, a magistrates' court is known as a family proceedings court.

Part of the business of the family proceedings courts is to make orders for personal protection and exclusion of a spouse from the matrimonial home (usually where violence is involved). They may also make certain orders relating to financial provisions and some contact and residence orders involving children. The family proceedings courts may also deal with adoptions and various other matters involving children, e.g., where an unmarried father wishes to exercise his parental responsibilities, he can apply to the court for an order to be made in this regard. Adoption proceedings are held in private (*in camera*), and the court also has power to exclude various people during certain proceedings.

Mediation in family proceedings

Mediation is not an essential step in divorce proceedings (although it is encouraged) but many couples involved in divorce or separation will seek mediation to try to help them resolve certain practicalities, such as arrangements for children; finance; division of property, etc. The aim of mediation is to try to find a solution that all parties consider to be fair and sensible.

Mediation is private and informal, usually with one or perhaps two mediators present and can be used at any stage when the couple feel it may help, whether they are still living together, separately or divorced. A trained mediator will invite the couple to meet together with him in the hope of identifying any issues they need to sort out and to negotiate to find acceptable solutions.

Mediation usually takes between two and four sessions, each lasting about an hour and a half. At the end, the parties will normally get a written summary about the decisions they have made, but this is not legally binding. They may obtain legal advice from a solicitor before committing themselves to a legal agreement or a court order.

There are many organisations offering mediation and there is no standard fee for mediation—different mediators charge different rates, usually by the hour; some have sliding scales according to how much the parties earn. The parties may be eligible for Community Legal Service Funding (see Chapter 7).

TEST YOURSELF ON CHAPTER 5

Test your knowledge by completing this assignment. If you find that you have difficulty with anything, read the chapter again until you are happy with your answers.

1. One or more of five facts must be proved to show that a marriage has irretrievably broken down. What are these five facts? What is the sole ground for divorce?

2. Which documents should be filed at court in order to commence divorce proceedings?

3. Complete as far as you can the form included with this assignment for a Wife's Petition (Separation—2 years), using the following details.

    Your firm, Peter Wolf & Co., of Red Riding Hood Lane, Northtown, Sussex, S21 4PQ (tel: 01646 58903; ref: PW/Smith/23), is acting for Emma Smith of 35 Strawberry Close, Maintown, Sussex. She has lived there since 5 July 2003, the day she separated from her husband. She married Giles Smith on 1 April 1993 at St. Peter's Church, Maintown, Sussex. The address where they lived together was Flat 4, Brighton Court, Maintown. Emma Smith works as an administrator and her husband is a chef, living at 64 Astronomer's Row, Northtown, Sussex. There is one child of the family, John Smith, born on 8 February 1997. They have lived apart for three years, separating on 5 July 2003 because the marriage had been unhappy for a while and they decided to live apart. The divorce proceedings will be commenced in the Maintown County Court.

4. Complete as far as possible the form for Petitioner's Affidavit in support of Petition, based on the details given above.

5. What is a Statement of Arrangements for Children?

6. Explain the differences between a decree nisi and decree absolute.

7. What information is needed to complete a Notice of Application for Decree Nisi to be made absolute?

8. What is the function of the Child Support Agency?

9. What sort of family matters might the magistrates' court become involved in?

10. Now go through the chapter and if there are any words that are unfamiliar to you or that you cannot spell, write or type them correctly several times until you feel you know them.

Divorce Petition (Separation— 2 years)

**FAMILY PROCEEDINGS
RULES**
Rule 2.3
Appendix 2

IN THE _____   **COUNTY COURT***

PRINCIPAL REGISTRY*

No. of Matter

The Notes for
guidance in
drafting the
petition are on
a separate sheet.

The Petition of

Shows that

Note 1.

1. On the   day of   the Petitioner

was lawfully

married to

(hereinafter called the Respondent) at

Note 2.

2. The Petitioner and the Respondent last lived together as husband and

wife at

Note 3.

3. The Court has jurisdiction under Article 2(1) of the Council Regulation on

the following ground(s):

Note 4.

4. The Petitioner is by occupation a   and resides at

The Respondent is by occupation a   and resides at

Note 5.

5. There is [are]   children of the family now living

Note 6.

6. No other child now living has been born to the [Petitioner] [Respondent]

Note 7.

during the marriage

7.   There are or have been no other proceedings in any court in England and Wales or elsewhere with reference to the marriage [or to any children of the family] or between the Petitioner and the Respondent with reference to any property of either or both of them

Note 8.

8.   There are or have been no proceedings in the Child Support Agency with reference to the maintenance of any child of the family

Note 9.

9.   There are no proceedings continuing in any country outside England and Wales which relate to the marriage or are capable of affecting its validity or subsistence

Note 10.

Note 11.

10. The said marriage has broken down irretrievably.

Note 12.

11. The parties to the marriage have lived apart for a continuous period of at least two years immediately preceding the presentation of this Petition and the Respondent consents to a decree being granted.

12.

Note 14.

Note 15.

Note 16.

Note 17.

The Petitioner therefore prays:–

Note 18.

(1)   That the said marriage may be dissolved;

Note 19.

(2)   That the Respondent   may be

ordered to pay   the costs of this suit;

Note 20.

(3)   That [he][she] may be granted the following ancillary relief:–

(i)   [an order for maintenance pending suit]

(ii)   [a periodical payments order]

(iii)   [a secured provision order]

(iv)   [a lump sum order]   for [himself][herself]

(v)   [a property adjustment order]

(vi)   [an order under section 24B, 25B or
        25C of the Act of 1973 (Pension
        Sharing/Attachment Order)]

(vii)   [a periodical payments order]

(viii) [a secured provision order]   for the children
                                              of the family
(ix)   [a lump sum order]

(x)   [a property adjustment order]

Note 21.   (Signed)

Note 22.   The names and addresses of the persons who are to be served with this

Petition are:–

Note 23.   The Petitioner's address for service is:–

Dated this   day of   20
Address all communications for the Court to: The Court Manager, County Court*...
....
(or to the Family Proceedings Department, Principal Registry, First Avenue House, 42-49 High Holborn, London WC1V 6NP).
The Court Office is open from 10 a.m. till 4 p.m. (4.30 p.m. at the Principal Registry) on Mondays to Fridays only.

In the _____ **County Court***

Principal Registry*

No. of Matter

IN THE MATTER of the Petition of

Divorce Petition

(Separation — 2 years)

Note 23.

2001 Edition
9.2001 T03585
5046006
* * * *

Divorce 4

Affidavit by Petitioner in Support of Petition under Section 1(2)(d) of the Matrimonial Causes Act 1973.

FAMILY PROCEEDINGS
RULES

Rule 2.24(3); **Form M7(d)**

No. of Matter

*Complete
and/or delete
as appropriate.

IN THE ————————————

COUNTY COURT*
PRINCIPAL REGISTRY*
OF THE FAMILY DIVISION

Petitioner

Between

and

Respondent

QUESTION	ANSWER
About the Divorce Petition 1. Have you read the petition filed in this case?	
2. Do you wish to alter or to add to any statement in the petition? If so, state the alterations or additions.	
3. Subject to these alterations or additions (if any), is everything stated **in your petition** true? If any statement is not within your own knowledge, indicate this and say whether it is true to the best of your information and belief.	
4. State the date on which you and the respondent separated.	
5. State briefly the reason or main reason for the separation.	
6. State the date when and the circumstances in which you came to the conclusion that the marriage was in fact at an end.	

7. State as far as you know the various addresses at which you and the respondent have respectively lived since the last date given in the answer to Question 4, and the periods of residence at each address:

Petitioner's Address		*Respondent's Address*	
From		From	
to		to	

8. Since the last date given in the answer to Question 4, have you ever lived with the respondent in the same household?

    If so, state the address and the period (or periods), giving dates.

About the children of the family

9. Have you read the Statement of Arrangements filed in this case?

10. Do you wish to alter anything in the Statement of Arrangements or add to it?

    If so, state the alterations or additions.

11. Subject to these alterations and additions (if any) is everything stated in the **Statement of Arrangements** true?

    If any statement is not within your own knowledge, indicate this and say whether it is true and correct to the best of your information and belief.

2

I,   *(full name)*

of   *(full residential address)*

                                                                                            (occupation)

make oath and say as follows: —

(1) Delete if the acknowledgment is signed by a solicitor.

1. I am the petitioner in this cause.

2. **The answers to Questions 1 to 11 above are true.**

(2) Insert name of the respondent exactly as it appears on the acknowledgment of service signed by him/her.

3. (¹) I identify the signature   (²)
    appearing on the copy acknowledgment of service now produced to me and marked "A"
    as the signature of my husband/wife, the respondent in this cause.

4. I identify the signature   (²)
    appearing at Part IV of the Statement of Arrangements dated
    now produced to me and marked "B" as the signature of the respondent.

(3) Exhibit any medical report or document on which the petitioner wishes to rely.

5. (³)

(4) If the petitioner seeks a judicial separation, amend accordingly.

(5) Amend or delete as appropriate.

6. I ask the Court to grant a decree dissolving my marriage with the respondent (⁴)

    on the ground stated in my petition [and to order the respondent to pay

    the costs of this suit]. (⁵)

SWORN at

in the County of   } . . . .

this   day of   , 20

Before me

(5) Delete as the case may be.

A Commissioner for Oaths.
Officer of the Court appointed by
the Judge to take Affidavits(⁵).

Address all communications for the Court to: The Court Manager, County Court*

(or to the Principal Registry, First Avenue House, 42-49 High Holborn, London, WC1V 6NP) quoting the number in the top right-hand corner of the first page. The Court Office is open from 10 a.m. till 4 p.m. (4.30 p.m. in the Principal Registry) on Mondays to Fridays only.

No. of Matter

IN THE HIGH COURT OF JUSTICE
FAMILY DIVISION
(Divorce)

Between

and

Affidavit

**by Petitioner in Support of Petition under Section
1 (2) (d) of the Matrimonial Causes Act 1973**

Date of swearing:

Oyez 7 Spa Road, London SE16 3QQ.   2003 Edition
12.2003 T04153

5046737
*****

Divorce 89

Criminal law

Criminal law is quite varied and complicated and this chapter tries to give you a broad idea of the sort of things you may encounter.

Once a person has been charged (see page 198) with a criminal offence he will be tried in either a magistrates' court or the Crown Court. The law provides that some offences should be tried in the magistrates' court (summary offences) and other, more serious offences tried in the Crown Court (indictable offences). There are some offences which may be tried in either court and these are either-way offences.

The standard of proof in criminal cases is much higher than that required in civil cases; a criminal case must be proved 'beyond reasonable doubt'. Where a jury is involved, the jurors must endeavour to reach a unanimous verdict. If this is not possible, the judge may indicate that he will accept a majority verdict, i.e., at least 10 out of 12 jurors must agree on the verdict.

The new Criminal Procedure Rules will govern the way criminal trials are managed.

The magistrates' court

A magistrates' court normally consists of not less than two nor more than three Justices of the Peace, who are assisted by a legally qualified clerk, or of one magistrate who is himself legally qualified (formerly called a 'stipendiary' but now 'District judge'). In court the clerk does not actually sit with the magistrates, but apart from them, usually in front of them. He is there to advise on procedural matters and has no say in the outcome of the case. The clerk is also responsible for the administrative side of the court offices and has staff to assist him.

In certain circumstances, a single Justice of the Peace or a justices' clerk may preside over the first appearance of an accused person who has been charged at a police station (see page 198) with an offence. This type of hearing is known as an early administrative hearing. It does not decide whether the accused is guilty or innocent and only certain matters, such as granting of legal aid, bail, etc. may be dealt with at the hearing.

All criminal cases are started in the magistrates' court. Summary offences are tried in the magistrates' court: the magistrates may find a person guilty of a summary offence and decide upon the sentence.

If the offence is an indictable offence, the magistrates' court will hold a preliminary hearing. This covers such things as bail and legal representation of the accused. Once these matters are dealt with, the case is automatically sent to the Crown Court to be dealt with.

If the offence is triable either way, then it could be tried completely in the magistrates' court or be transferred to the Crown Court for trial. In order to make the decision as to where the case will be heard, a mode of trial hearing must be held in the magistrates' court before the trial itself commences. If it is decided that the case should be heard in the Crown Court, the magistrates' court will hold committal proceedings (see below) in order to transfer the case to the Crown Court.

There are two types of committal proceedings: one where only documentary evidence is produced and the other, more common method where no evidence is produced (prosecution statements will have been served on the accused in advance). This latter method is permissible only where the accused is legally represented and where he agrees that there is a case to answer. By accepting that there is a case to answer, the accused is not admitting guilt in any way whatsoever, he is just accepting that the prosecution would appear to have sufficient evidence for a trial to take place.

Magistrates' courts also have jurisdiction with regard to certain family matters and some administrative matters.

The Crown Court

The best known Crown Court, of course, is the Central Criminal Court or the Old Bailey. There are other Crown Courts throughout England and Wales and these are presided over by a judge who may be assisted by a jury. The different kinds of judge who may sit at the Crown Court are the High Court judge, the Circuit judge, Deputy Circuit judge and the Recorder (and Assistant Recorder). A Recorder is a barrister or solicitor in practice, but sits as a judge at the Crown Court for a certain number of days each year. The Crown Courts deal with more serious offences where an accused person has been sent or transferred by a magistrates' court to the Crown Court for trial or sentence as mentioned above, and also deals with the trial of someone accused of an indictable offence. With certain offences there is a right to trial by jury and this must be heard by the Crown Court.

Things you may be doing

As a secretary, you could find yourself working in a lawyer's office dealing with criminal law or working for the police or the Crown Prosecution Service.

As a criminal offence is, strictly speaking, an offence against the Crown, you will often find that a case is headed something like 'R -v- Smith'. 'R' means '*Regina*', the Latin word for Queen. 'R' also stands for '*Rex*' or King, if appropriate. You will find, however, if the name of the case is spoken in court, it will be said as, for example, 'The Queen against Smith'.

Forms relating to legal aid (see Chapter 7) are frequently used in criminal work. Instructions and Briefs to Counsel (see page 87) are also quite common. These documents must contain the name of the court and the number of the charge or the summons (see later), together with any other court reference number.

It is extremely important to proofread (see page 29) documents in criminal cases. It must always be remembered that a person's liberty may be at stake and therefore accuracy is vital. Confidentiality must always be strictly adhered to. There may be instances where certain material must not reach the jury or there may be an express no-publication order. Never give out any information to the Press or to anyone else. Do not even admit that you are acting for a certain person. Any queries from persons outside the firm must be referred to the appropriate person in your firm, such as the responsible partner. If you attend court you must not speak to the jurors or witnesses in the box (see also page 39).

Statements

You may find that you have to type many statements, either of witnesses or of an accused person. These are also known as 'proofs of evidence'.

Witness statements should be typed in double spacing. Only one side of the paper should be used, a space larger than normal should be left at the top of the first page for headings to be entered by the clerk of the court, and each page should have a wide margin on the left.

The person making the statement has to sign a clause at the top of the page declaring that the statement is true—particular wording is used. Each page of the statement is also signed at the bottom by the person making it and his signature is witnessed.

Example witness statement

Statement of witness (CJ Act 1967, s. 9; MC Act 1980, ss. 5A(3)(a) and 5B, MC Rules 1981, r. 70)

STATEMENT OF [*name of witness*]

Age of Witness: (*if over 18 enter 'over 18'*)

Occupation of witness:

This statement [, consisting of   *   pages each signed by me,] is true to the best of my knowledge and belief and I make it knowing that, if it is tendered in evidence, I shall be liable to prosecution if I have wilfully stated in it anything which I know to be false or do not believe to be true.

Dated the   *   day of   *   200*

(Signed).......................

[Additionally, if the person making the statement is unable to read, it would be read to him by someone else who would also sign the statement as follows:

[*Name of person making the statement*] being unable to read the above statement, I [*name and address of person reading the statement to him*], read it to him before he signed it.

Dated the   *   day of   *   200*

(Signed).......................

[*Note*: the content of the statement will be typed in double line spacing.]

How is someone brought to court?

Criminal proceedings are commenced by way of charge, indictment or summons.

Note that there are many strict rules with regard to criminal procedures. Some of these include the fact that the police must caution an accused person at certain times (see below), he has a right to contact a solicitor whilst being questioned, and various other matters.

Most prosecutions are brought by the police through the Crown Prosecution Service which is an independent body that works closely with the police. There have been proposals to change the name of the Crown Prosecution Service to the Public Prosecution Service but, at the time of writing, this has not occurred. Other authorities, such as HM Revenue & Customs, may sometimes bring prosecutions too. A private individual can also bring criminal proceedings in limited circumstances.

Offences are divided into arrestable offences and non-arrestable offences. Arrestable offences include those whose penalty is fixed by law, such as murder, which carries life imprisonment. Other quite serious offences, such as those under the Theft Acts, are also arrestable. In fact, all offences of any seriousness are arrestable. Non-arrestable offences are mainly motoring offences, although under certain circumstances an arrest may be made here. In certain circumstances, an individual other than a police officer may make what is known as a 'citizen's arrest'.

Arrest and charge

If the police wish to question a person at a police station, they must either arrest him or ask him to attend voluntarily. The Police and Criminal Evidence Act 1984 deals with police powers of arrest.

An arrest may be made either with a warrant or without a warrant. A warrant is an authority signed by a magistrate giving a police officer the power to arrest a person. The procedure for arrest with a warrant is usually that the police officer makes a written statement regarding the alleged offence and the warrant is then signed by a magistrate. This is called 'laying an information'. An Information can be laid by someone else who wishes to bring a case before a magistrates' court when an offence has been committed. An Information is basically information put before the court in order to start proceedings. Of course, when an Information is laid, this does not always lead to someone's arrest; a summons may be issued. The most common method of arrest, however, is arrest without a warrant. A police officer may arrest without warrant any person he reasonably suspects of committing, having committed or being about to commit an arrestable offence.

One of the times when a person must be cautioned as to his rights is at the time of his arrest or as soon as practicable thereafter. A caution informs the arrested person that he does not have to say anything unless he wishes to do so, but anything he does say may be given in evidence. The caution also informs the suspect that his defence may be harmed if he does not mention when questioned anything which he is later going to rely upon in court. An accused person used to have the right to maintain silence without any adverse inferences being drawn, but that right to be free from adverse inferences was removed by the Criminal Justice and Public Order Act 1994, and 'proper' inferences may now be drawn against the accused if he remains silent regarding any facts which he should have mentioned in his defence. The caution he is given by the police reflects this and it must be made clear to the accused the risks he incurs if he fails to mention any relevant facts. A person should also be cautioned when he is informed that he will be reported for an offence and told that he may receive a summons to attend court with regard to that offence.

Once a person is arrested and taken to a police station (a 'designated' police station if he is to be detained for more than six hours), he is handed over to an officer who has the rank of sergeant or above, known as the 'custody officer', who will ensure that a custody record is kept of all procedures and events at the police station involving that person. A designated police station is one which has facilities for detaining arrested persons. The custody officer decides if there is sufficient evidence to charge the arrested person. A charge is a way of formally accusing a person of an offence. The accusation on the charge sheet forms an Information.

Eventually, it is hoped that charging a person at a police station by the police will be replaced by the Statutory Charging Scheme. This scheme requires the Crown Prosecution Service, rather than the police, to make the decision about charging someone in all but the most minor or routine cases. At the time of writing, the Scheme has not yet been fully implemented in all areas.

A person may not normally be detained for longer than 24 hours unless he is charged, although in certain circumstances and if certain conditions are met, he may be detained for a longer period. Once a person is charged, he may be detained in custody until he first appears before a court. He must be brought before a court as soon as practicable and this should not be later than the first time the court sits after he has been charged with the offence. This is usually the same day that he is charged or perhaps the next day.

If a person is not detained in custody pending his court appearance, he may be released on bail.

Bail

Bail is the release of the defendant from a police station or court subject to his surrendering himself into custody at a later date. A person commits a further offence and can be arrested if he is granted bail and fails to surrender to his bail. Bail is sometimes conditional on a surety, i.e., someone must guarantee that the defendant will turn up on the appointed date. If the person on bail does not turn up on the appointed date the surety may have to pay a sum of money, known as a 'recognisance'. There are often certain other conditions to be complied with before bail will be granted.

Indictment

An indictment is a written accusation of a crime which is triable only by the Crown Court, e.g., very serious offences such as murder, rape and robbery. An indictment is the basis for the trial of an accused person who has been committed for trial at the Crown Court. It states where the trial will take place and gives details of the charges made against him. Each offence that the person is accused of is set out in a separate paragraph, known as a 'count'.

Once an indictable offence goes to the Crown Court, there is a preliminary hearing in the Crown Court where various matters are dealt with and a date for a Plea and Case Management Hearing will be set (except in cases of serious fraud).

The Plea and Case Management Hearing is to ensure that all the necessary procedures relating to the trial have been complied with and that the court has sufficient information to fix a date for the trial. The Defendant will be asked at the Plea and Case Management Hearing to plead guilty or not guilty. If he pleads guilty, the judge will, if possible, proceed to sentence. If the Defendant pleads not guilty, the court must be provided with information relating to the trial, e.g., the number of witnesses that will be called, the estimated length of trial, etc.

Summons

A person may also appear at court by way of summons. The summons will have on it the date the accused person must appear at court and will give details of the offence for which he is being summoned. It is not necessary for separate summonses to be issued against a person for each separate offence where there is more than one offence (although, in practice, separate summonses are commonly issued for separate offences). However, if different offences are specified in one summons, each offence must be stated separately.

A summons relating to criminal matters is issued by the court and service on a person (not a corporation) may be effected by:

(a) delivering it to the person to whom it is addressed; or

(b) by leaving it for him with someone at his last known or usual place of abode; or

(c) by sending it by post in a letter addressed to him at his last known or usual place of abode. However, service by post is not allowed if the summons requires the attendance of a witness to give evidence or to produce a document or thing.

Service of a summons on a corporation may be effected by delivering the summons at, or sending it by post to, the registered office (see Chapter 10) of the corporation if that office is in the United Kingdom, or, if there is no registered office in the United Kingdom, any place in the United Kingdom where the corporation trades or conducts its business.

Mitigation

If someone is convicted of a crime, the defence may submit to the court a plea in mitigation, putting forward reasons for the sentence to be made less severe than it might otherwise be. This will usually include details of any circumstances which may have led to the offender committing the offence and any other information which may be helpful to the court when considering sentence, for example, the offender may have been under some pressure at home or at work which caused him to commit the offence and if the court knows of this, it may be more lenient when sentencing him.

Offender's past history

Once a person has been convicted of an offence and before he is sentenced, the court is told of that person's previous criminal record, if any. However, fairly recent legislation has made it permissible in certain cases, under certain circumstances, for an accused person's previous convictions to be disclosed to the court as part of the prosecution case.

The court is also informed of the offender's personal circumstances, such as his salary, savings, whether he has any family, etc. This can assist the court if, for example, a fine is to be imposed. This information is called the offender's 'antecedents'.

Taking offences into consideration

An offender can also have other offences taken into consideration. He may ask for other offences he has committed, e.g., a series of burglaries, to be taken into consideration when sentence is passed. If someone does have other offences taken into consideration, this effectively means he cannot be tried for those other offences at another time.

Formal cautions

The practice of issuing a formal caution to an offender, rather than prosecuting him at court, was developed some time ago for juveniles (see below) although for juveniles cautions have now been replaced with a final warning scheme, which includes police reprimands and warnings. However, cautioning is now used quite extensively for adults. Under certain circumstances, the police have discretion to issue a formal caution to an adult offender and if a caution is issued, it is not counted as a conviction, although a record of cautions is kept (normally for at least five years).

If an adult is to be cautioned, he must first sign a form acknowledging that he agrees to the caution and admitting the offence. There are other factors to be taken into consideration before a caution can be administered.

Besides a straightforward caution, conditional cautioning is being introduced for adults. A conditional caution is a caution with conditions imposed and if the offender fails to comply with any condition, he may be prosecuted for the original offence. As with an ordinary caution mentioned above, certain criteria must be met, including the fact that the offender must have admitted the offence. He must also consent to the conditions imposed.

Youth courts

Where the magistrates' court deals with young offenders under the age of 18 (juveniles), the court is known as a youth court. There are special rules to be adhered to when it comes to dealing with children and young persons, one being that they must normally have a parent or guardian with them when they are being dealt with under the process of the law. A 'child' is a person under the age of 14 years and a 'young person' is a person who has attained the age of 14 years but is under 18. In pre-trial procedures, e.g., the investigation of an offence or remand proceedings, juveniles who have attained the age of 17 are treated in the same manner as adults. No child under the age of 10 years can be guilty of a criminal offence.

It is extremely important to remember that juveniles must not be identified to the public in any way, and you must always bear in mind that confidentiality is of the utmost importance. Any newspaper reports of proceedings in a youth court must not reveal the name, address or any other identifying detail of any juvenile (even those who are witnesses) who is involved in the proceedings unless the court specifically permits this.

Youth courts not only deal with offences committed by children and young persons, but also matters relating to their care and treatment. A youth court is always heard in private (*in camera*) and members of the public are not allowed in.

It is also possible, under certain circumstances, for a juvenile who has committed an offence to receive a police reprimand or warning, rather than having to go to court. This means that the juvenile offender attends with his parent or guardian at the relevant police station at an appointed time before a senior officer. The juvenile may receive a reprimand or final warning, depending on the crime. Additionally, other methods have been introduced in an effort to prevent a child or young person who has committed an offence from having to go to court.

Driving offences

In driving offences, apart from any other punishment the court can impose, it may order the offender's licence to be endorsed. According to what the court decides, a number of penalty points varying from 1–11 are noted on the licence. If the number of penalty points reaches 12 or more within three years, the court will normally disqualify that person from driving for at least six months. Additionally, if six or more penalty points are acquired by a new driver within two years of passing his driving test, he will have his licence revoked and will have to take a fresh driving test if he wishes to regain a full driving licence. Certain offences require disqualification to be ordered automatically.

In some cases (often less serious driving offences), and under certain circumstances, the defendant may be permitted to plead guilty by post instead of having to attend court.

Dealing with offenders

Generally, magistrates' courts may fine offenders—the maximum fine is set by law. They may also send an offender to prison for up to six months (sometimes up to 12 months for two or more offences, depending on the type of offence). With certain exceptions, there is no statutory limit on the amount of the fine that the Crown Court may impose. With regard to sentencing, the Crown Court's powers are limited only by the maximum sentence prescribed for the offence in question. Some of the other methods of dealing with offenders are:

(a) Absolute discharge. The person has been convicted of an offence but is released immediately without any punishment. This usually happens in trivial or technical cases.

(b) Conditional discharge. The offender may be discharged on condition that, for a specified period of up to three years, he does not commit another offence. If he does commit another offence, then he will be sentenced for that and for the original offence.

(c) Community order. This is where the offender will have to serve his sentence in the community rather than being placed in custody. The court may place certain requirements upon the offender. These could include electronic tagging, curfew, unpaid work, living at a specified address, drug or alcohol treatment and testing, attending certain behaviour programmes, or doing or refraining from doing certain things or going to certain places.

Additionally, the court may defer sentencing for a period of up to six months. This means that they would not pass sentence until the end of the specified period. The reason for this is that the defendant may request the court to defer sentencing him so that after the specified period has elapsed, he will appear before the court again, and hopefully be able to show that he has reformed (perhaps by having taken steps to show that he has changed, e.g., having obtained employment), in which case the court may be more lenient with him when passing sentence.

Besides sentencing, there are other orders that the court may make, such as compensation orders where an offender must pay compensation to a victim; forfeiture orders where, for example, if the offender used property, perhaps certain tools, to commit an offence, he might be ordered to forfeit those tools; deportation orders where the offender is not a UK citizen; or confiscation orders when the proceeds of the crime might be confiscated.

Criminal Cases Review Commission

This is an independent body set up under the Criminal Appeal Act 1995 and was formally established at the beginning of 1997. It investigates suspected miscarriages of criminal justice in England, Wales and Northern Ireland. However, the Commission can normally only review a case if the original case was appealed against or the person was refused permission to appeal.

Although the Commission cannot overturn a conviction or change a sentence, it can refer cases which meet specified criteria to the Court of Appeal, the Crown Court or the relevant court in Northern Ireland. The court will treat a case referred to it by the Commission as an appeal against the original conviction and it is the court that will decide whether to alter the conviction or sentence. In some cases, legal aid (see Chapter 7) is available to apply to the Commission.

Prisoners

It may be helpful to know that prisoners whose whereabouts you do not know can be traced through the Prisoner Location Service, PO Box 2152, Birmingham, B15 1SD; fax: 0121 626 3474.

Solicitors acting on behalf of clients must fax their enquiry on headed paper, providing full name, date of birth, sentence details (if known), and confirming that the person is their client.

Solicitors who are not acting on behalf of the prisoner but have papers sealed by the court must also fax their enquiry with the top copy of the sealed document.

All other enquiries should be in writing giving full details as above and the reason for the enquiry. The prisoner's consent is obtained before disclosure in accordance with the Data Protection Act 1998.

Further information on prisoners and the prison service can be found on the HM Prison Service website.

TEST YOURSELF ON CHAPTER 6

Test your knowledge by completing this assignment. If you find that you have difficulty with anything, read the chapter again until you are happy with your answers.

1. At which courts may a person be tried for a criminal offence?
2. What are committal proceedings?
3. Write out the layout for a witness statement.
4. Explain the meaning of bail.
5. What is the role of the Crown Prosecution Service?
6. Name four ways offenders may be dealt with upon conviction.

7. With relation to driving offences, what are penalty points?

8. What must be remembered when dealing with juveniles in relation to publicity about them?

9. Explain what is meant by someone having other offences 'taken into consideration'.

10. Now go through the chapter and if there are any words that are unfamiliar to you or that you cannot spell, write or type them correctly several times until you feel you know them.

7

Legal aid

Legal aid is available to people who need legal assistance but cannot afford to pay for it. The Legal Services Commission (LSC) has overall responsibility for the management of legal aid through the Community Legal Service (CLS) fund for civil matters and the Criminal Defence Service (CDS) for criminal matters. The LSC has its head office in London with area offices in England and Wales.

Solicitors wishing to provide legal aid services do so through a quality control scheme and the use of LSC logos. For the funding of civil matters through the CLS, the CLS Quality Mark has been introduced and this logo is displayed by firms who are approved by the CLS. For criminal matters, a similar scheme has been introduced using the CDS Quality Mark. Solicitors who work in these areas will have a contract with the LSC to provide legal services in a defined or specified area of work.

With both the CLS and CDS, there are certain levels of funding for legal services and some of these require the applicant to be means tested before his application is accepted. This means that before someone can receive legal aid, they may have to show that they are eligible. If means testing is appropriate, this is done by assessing whether they meet certain criteria regarding their financial circumstances and their capital and income will be assessed. Additionally, consideration may be given to whether there will be sufficient benefit to the applicant to justify providing the service.

Applications for legal aid must be made for a defined level of service, e.g., for Legal Help or perhaps Legal Representation (see below). If it is later considered necessary to provide further services for a higher level of funding, a further application for that level of service will normally have to be made to the LSC. Applications are made on forms provided by the LSC. It is also possible in some circumstances to make emergency applications for legal aid.

Civil matters

Certain legal services are not eligible for legal aid. Some of those are:

(a) most personal injury cases (other than clinical negligence);

(b) conveyancing;

(c) making a Will; and

(d) various matters relating to companies and businesses.

There are exceptions to these, depending on the circumstances.

Legal Help

This provides initial advice and assistance with any legal problem. Funding will be provided for matters such as general advice, writing letters, preparing documents and negotiating on the client's behalf. Legal Help does not cover court proceedings although the solicitor may assist a client in the completion of application forms for Legal Representation (see below). For Legal Help, the solicitor will assess the client and will be able to tell him straight away whether he is eligible to receive funding.

Help at Court

This will pay for a solicitor (or other legal representative) to speak on behalf of a client at certain court hearings without actually officially acting for the client throughout the whole proceedings. This could be perhaps where the client needs specific help in asking the court for something in relation to particular proceedings.

Approved Family Help

This will provide funding for help regarding a family dispute. It includes services provided by Legal Help but also includes issuing proceedings and representation on certain matters. It is available in two forms:

(a) Help with Mediation. This provides legal advice and assistance for those who are attending family mediation.

(b) General Family Help. This gives legal advice and assistance on family matters for those who are not attending family mediation.

Family Mediation

This provides funding for mediation in a family dispute. It will also cover finding out if mediation would be appropriate.

Legal Representation

This level provides legal representation in court and is available in two forms:

(a) Investigative Help. This is funding to investigate how strong the claim is.

(b) Full Representation. Provides full funding for representation throughout legal proceedings.

Support Funding

This is partial funding for very expensive cases which will not be covered by legal aid but where a client enters into a conditional fee agreement (see page 34) with a solicitor. Support Funding is available in two forms:

(a) Investigative Support. Funding will be provided to investigate the strength of the claim. If it is then considered appropriate, the client will continue the claim through a conditional fee agreement.

(b) Litigation Support. This gives partial funding of expensive court proceedings under a conditional fee agreement.

The statutory charge

Normally, if someone wins a civil case, the other party (the losing party) will have to pay the costs of the case. However, in some instances, the losing party may not have to pay all the costs. In these circumstances, if the successful party received legal aid from the CLS for their case and they have obtained or kept money or property as a result of that funded case, they may have to repay to the CLS all or some of their legal costs from the recovered money or property. This payment is called the statutory charge and, once it has been paid, then the legally aided person will be able to keep what is left over. Certain matters, such as maintenance payments and various other exemptions are not subject to this payment. A legally aided person may have to pay contributions towards his case whilst it is ongoing, but he will be told of this at the outset.

Criminal matters

Criminal matters are funded through the CDS. As well as certain solicitors in private practice having a contract to carry out this work, the LSC has also directly employed criminal defence lawyers, called public defenders, who may be consulted, rather than a private solicitor. At the moment, there are eight public defender offices throughout England and Wales.

Advice and Assistance

This provides eligible clients with assistance once they consult their solicitor. It does not cover representation in court, but allows the solicitor to give advice and assistance to the client, such as general advice, assistance regarding interviews, writing letters, preparing a written case, etc.

Advice and Assistance can also be given at a police station (or elsewhere) when someone is being questioned about an offence, whether or not they have been arrested.

Advocacy Assistance

This provides funding for the solicitor to prepare the case and initial representation, but only for certain proceedings.

Representation

This is where the client needs to be represented fully throughout a criminal court case. Application in this instance is made to the court, not the LSC. The application may be made orally to the court or in writing on a specified form.

Duty Solicitor Scheme

If someone is at a police station, either because they have been arrested or have attended voluntarily, they are entitled to free legal advice from a solicitor whose firm has a contract with the LSC. This could be the client's own solicitor or a solicitor who is part of the Duty Solicitor Scheme.

The Duty Solicitor Scheme provides for solicitors from approved and contracted firms who have joined a rota scheme to be available within a certain area to go to a police station and give advice or they may give advice by telephone.

Similarly, the Duty Solicitor Scheme covers advice and assistance given to a defendant before he actually appears before a magistrates' court for the first hearing and also covers representation in various matters that will be dealt with before that first hearing. This can include advice about such things as to whether or not to plead guilty, making an application for bail and other such matters. There will usually be a duty solicitor available at most magistrates' courts or on call (they can be contacted by court staff), although, of course, it is best if the defendant obtains legal advice before attending court.

TEST YOURSELF ON CHAPTER 7

Test your knowledge by completing this assignment. If you find that you have difficulty with anything, read the chapter again until you are happy with your answers.

1. What is the Community Legal Service and what is the Criminal Defence Service?

2. What is meant by the statutory charge?

3. Name two areas in civil law that are excluded from legal aid.

4. When might someone make use of the services of a duty solicitor?

5. Now go through the chapter and if there are any words that are unfamiliar to you or that you cannot spell, write or type them correctly several times until you feel you know them.

*Community
Legal Service*

Legal Help and
Help at Court

Please complete in Block Capitals

Equal Opportunities Monitoring

➤ *Completion of this section is voluntary. This will be treated in the strictest confidence and will
be used purely for statistical monitoring and research.*

Please tick the boxes which your client would describe themselves as being:

Ethnic Monitoring

White	**Mixed**	**Asian or Asian British**
☐ (a) British	☐ (a) White and Black Caribbean	☐ (a) Indian
☐ (b) Irish	☐ (b) White and Black African	☐ (b) Pakistani
☐ (c) White Other	☐ (c) White and Asian	☐ (c) Bangladeshi
Black or Black British	☐ (d) Mixed Other	☐ (d) Asian Other
☐ (a) Black Caribbean		
☐ (b) Black African	☐ **Chinese**	☐ **Other**
☐ (c) Black Other		

Disability Monitoring

The Disability Discrimination Act defines disability as: a physical or mental impairment with
long term, substantial effects on a person's ability to perform day-to-day activities.
Does your client consider himself or herself to have a disability?   ☐ Yes   ☐ No

Your client's details

Title: _____   Initials: _____

Surname: _____

First name: _____

Surname at birth: _____
(if different)

Unique Client Number: _____
(immigration cases only)

Date of birth: ____ / ____ / ____   National Insurance no: | | | | | | | | |

Sex: ☐ Male   ☐ Female

Marital status: ☐ Single   ☐ Married/Cohabiting   ☐ Married but separated
☐ Divorced   ☐ Widowed

Place of birth: _____   Job: _____
(town)

Current address: _____

Town: _____

County: _____   Postcode: _____

Supplier's Details

(Only complete when submitting a copy of this page with an application for extension of a Cost Limit)

Please complete in Block Capitals

Name of supplier: _____

Address of supplier: _____

Town: _____

County: _____   Postcode: _____

DX (with exchange): _____

Telephone number: _____

Contract number: _____

Financial Eligibility

The client is directly or indirectly in receipt of Income Support, Income Based Jobseeker's Allowance or Guarantee State Pension Credit.

Yes ☐   No ☐

Part A should be completed in all cases where the client is applying for Legal Help or Help at Court.

Part B need not be completed if the client receives Income Support, Income Based Jobseeker's Allowance or Guarantee State Pension Credit.

Does the client have a partner whose means are to be aggregated?

☐ Yes   Please complete PARTS A and/or B as applicable providing details of both client's and partner's means.

☐ No   Please complete PARTS A and/or B as applicable providing details of client's means only.

Part A   Capital

Capital includes:

		Client	Partner
➤ Equity in home above £100,000 *(after allowing up to £100,000 for mortgage(s) outstanding)*		£ _____	£ _____
➤ Savings *(bank, building society, etc)*		£ _____	£ _____
➤ Investments *(including shares and insurance policies)*		£ _____	£ _____
➤ Valuable items *(eg boat, caravan, jewellery, etc)*		£ _____	£ _____
➤ Other capital *(including money due to the client)*		£ _____	£ _____
TOTAL CAPITAL		£ _____	£ _____

Capital excludes:

➤ Subject matter of dispute
➤ Household furniture and effects (unless exceptional value)
➤ Clothes, Tools of trade

TOTAL CAPITAL (Client and Partner)   £ _____

Part B   Income

➤ *Use monthly figures*
(if paid weekly, multiply by 52 & divide by 12)
(if paid four weekly, multiply by 13 & divide by 12)

Income includes:

	Client	Partner
➤ Gross monthly earnings	£ _____	£ _____
➤ Other income *(including child benefit, pensions, maintenance, dividends, etc)*	£ _____	£ _____
TOTAL GROSS INCOME	£ _____	£ _____

TOTAL GROSS INCOME (Client and Partner)   £ _____

	Client	Partner
TOTAL GROSS INCOME (brought forward)	£ _____	£ _____

Less monthly allowances:

➤ Housing costs, including:
   Mortgage instalment* (capped if client has no dependants)   £ _____   £ _____

   Rent* (capped if client has no dependants)   £ _____   £ _____
   *amounts should be net of housing benefit

➤ Dependants' allowances:
   Partner   £ _____

   Dependants   Aged 15 and under   £ _____

   Aged 16 or over   £ _____

➤ Tax and National Insurance   £ _____   £ _____

➤ Standard allowance for employment expenses   £ _____   £ _____

➤ Maintenance payments actually being made   £ _____   £ _____
   (eg for children and/or a former/separated spouse)

➤ Childcare costs because of work   £ _____

TOTAL ALLOWANCES   £ _____   £ _____

TOTAL MONTHLY DISPOSABLE INCOME   £ _____   £ _____

TOTAL MONTHLY DISPOSABLE INCOME (Client and Partner)   £ _____

Evidence

Evidence given in support of means   Yes ☐   No ☐

If no please record justification or exceptional circumstance.

Client's Certification

Please tick the box below which applies to you:-

☐   I have not already received Legal Help from a solicitor or contracted supplier on this matter.

☐   I have already received Legal Help from a solicitor or contracted supplier on this matter. If so, please state when

I agree to my solicitor or contracted supplier having a first charge on any money or property (including costs) which I recover or preserve in or in relation to the matter for which I am being advised. (Personal injury, clinical negligence and family matters only).

As far as I know all the information I have given is true including information as to my means and I have not withheld any relevant information.

I understand that if I give false information the services provided to me may be cancelled and I may be prosecuted.

Signed: _____   **Date:** _____

Data Protection Act - access to personal data

The personal data provided by you will be processed in accordance with the principles of the Data Protection Act 1998 and for the purposes of the Legal Services Commission's functions under the Access to Justice Act 1999. You have the right to make a formal request in writing for access to personal data held about you to inspect it and have it corrected if it is wrong. The Legal Services Commission may receive information about you from certain third parties, or give information to them; these third parties include some government departments. However, we will not disclose information about you unless the law permits us to.

Legal Help and Help at Court

Tick the relevant box below if you have:

Travelled out of the office to visit the client, other than at court. ☐

Accepted an application from a child or patient or someone on their behalf. ☐

Provided Legal Help to a client who has already received it on the same matter within the last 6 months. ☐

Given telephone advice before the signature of the form. ☐

Claimed for outward travel before the signature of the form. ☐

Accepted a postal application. ☐

If you have ticked any of the above boxes, please provide the circumstances justifying this in accordance with the relevant Rule in the Specification.

Was an application for Legal Representation made in this matter?

☐ Yes   ☐ No

Time spent and costs

(This section should be completed by suppliers with a solicitors contract.)

Item	Time Spent
1. Attendance	_____
2. Preparation	_____
3. Help at Court	_____
4. Travel and Waiting	_____
Total:	_____

Item	Number
1. Letters written	_____
2. Phone calls	_____

Total Profit Costs £ _____   **Vat £** _____

Value or amount of contractual or statutory charge **£** _____

Disbursements	Amount	Vat
Mileage	£ : _____	£ : _____
Other disbursements	£ : _____	£ : _____
Total	£ : _____	£ : _____
Counsel's fees	£ : _____	£ : _____

Dated _____

Note: When calculating profit costs, the time spent on each activity and the letters and telephone calls must be separated out according to the remuneration rate which applied at the time the work was carried out. Annex A to your Contract Schedule sets the rates for Contract Work and specifies when franchised or non franchised rates must be charged. See also Part E of Volume I of the LSC Manual.

Remember that you may not charge separately for letters in.

The totals for profit costs, disbursements and counsel's fees from this form and the Controlled Legal Representation Form (if applicable) should be the same (after adding VAT and net of the amount of the statutory charge and any payment on account), as those reported by you in relation to the matter on the Consolidated Matter Report Form. Where a staged bill has been submitted in an Immigration matter a separate copy of this page should be completed for each stage reported on the CMRF.

8

Licensing

The Licensing Act 2003 will completely change the way that various types of licence are applied for. At the time of writing, the new Act has not yet been fully implemented, but it is anticipated that the new procedures will take effect from November 2005.

Currently, under transitional arrangements, the licensing authorities under the new Act are processing applications for conversion to the new types of licence and also various applications for new licences and certificates. When the new licensing regime takes effect, the new licences will be given effect and the old licensing regime will end.

Set out below is a brief explanation of the old regime and of the new regime.

Prior to the Licensing Act 2003 becoming effective

Under the old licensing regime, applications for a liquor licence, i.e., applications to sell alcoholic drinks, would be made to licensing justices who sit at magistrates' courts during licensing sessions, which were held at certain times of the year. A liquor licence could authorise the sale of all types of intoxicating liquor or put a limit on the type of liquor that was sold, e.g., wine only. Some of the different types of liquor licence that could be applied for are:

    (a) An on-licence which normally allowed intoxicating liquor to be consumed both on and off the premises.

    (b) An occasional licence authorising the holder of an on-licence to sell intoxicating liquor at a place other than his ordinary licensed premises.

    (c) An off-licence allowing consumption off the premises only.

    (d) Restaurant licence which allows the sale of liquor with meals.

    (e) Residential licences granted to places such as boarding houses.

    (f) Club licence.

Under this regime, a licence was generally granted for three years and then had to be renewed. An appeal from a decision of licensing justices could be made to the Crown Court.

To apply for a liquor licence, various procedures were undertaken, and these included giving a copy of the Notice of Application for Grant of a Licence to certain people, including the clerk to the licensing justices, the Chief Officer of Police, the local authority, and the local fire authority. The Notice of Application had to be displayed near the premises in a public place for a specified period and also had to be advertised in a local newspaper.

The Licensing Act 2003

Rather than applying for a licence to licensing justices sitting at magistrates' courts, providers of services will generally need to apply to their local authority which, for these purposes, is known as the licensing authority. In future, as far as licensing is concerned, magistrates' courts will be used only in appeal proceedings and certain other specified matters. Additionally, instead of applying for different types of liquor licences, businesses will be able to apply for a premises licence (see below) to cover all the licensable activities they wish to carry on.

Licensable activities are:

(a) The sale by retail of alcohol.

(b) The supply of alcohol by or on behalf of a club to, or to the order of, a member of the club.

(c) The provision of regulated entertainment.

(d) The provision of late night refreshment.

There will no longer be fixed permitted hours or closing times for licensed premises. This will therefore provide for more flexible opening times and, in some instances, 24-hour opening could be possible.

The licensing objectives

Under the new laws, local authorities, licensees and others must promote the licensing objectives which are:

(a) Prevention of crime and disorder.

(b) Prevention of public nuisance.

(c) Public safety.

(d) Prevention of harm to children.

Personal licence

A personal licence is necessary for the supervision of the sale of alcohol in any premises. This includes public houses, off-licences, restaurants, hotels and private members clubs. Application may be made to the licensing authority for the area in which the applicant lives. That licensing authority will then remain responsible for continuing to licence that person even if they move away from the area.

A personal licence is valid for ten years. The holder must comply with any terms of the licence. If they are convicted of any relevant offences, their licence can be taken away by the court. The police also have a right to object to a licensee on the ground of crime prevention.

Before being allowed to apply for a personal licence, the applicant must:

(a) Be over 18.

(b) Not have any relevant criminal convictions. These are detailed in the Licensing Act 2003.

(c) Possess an approved licensing qualification.

(d) Pay the required fee.

Grandfather rights

People who already hold a Justices' Licence or Club Registration Certificate under the previous licensing laws may transfer to a new personal licence. This is known as 'grandfather rights'.

Premises licence

A premises licence can be granted for a business supplying alcohol or entertainment or late night food (on or off the premises). Unlike the old licensing regime, there will not be a hearing when an application is made for a licence as hearings will only take place when representations are made from interested parties. Also, a premises licence does not have a time limit on it unless particularly requested, neither does it have to be renewed every three years.

An applicant for a premises licence must submit to the licensing authority the following:

(a) A completed application form.

(b) A plan of the premises.

(c) An operating schedule. This is a description of how the premises will be operated, including the relevant licensable activities, e.g., the sale of alcohol; the times during which the activities will take place; whether the supply of alcohol will be for on or off the premises; a statement of how the applicant proposes to promote the licensing objectives (see above), and various other information.

(d) If the application is for authorisation to sell alcohol, a form containing the consent of the proposed designated premises supervisor (see below) must also be included. This is the person who will manage the premises and authorise the sale of alcohol. This person must hold a personal licence (see above). If they leave or move from those particular premises, then a new designated premises supervisor must be notified to the licensing authority.

(e) The fee. Certain premises, e.g., community centres, are exempt from payment of fees.

When a licence is first applied for, copies of the application must also be sent to the responsible authorities. These include the police, the fire authority, the local environmental health department, and the local planning department. Each of these may make representations about the application and this could lead to the licence being refused or conditions being imposed on the granting of the licence. Interested parties, such as local residents, may also make representations to the licensing authority regarding the application. Additionally, the applicant must advertise his application within a certain prescribed period and in a particular way.

If no representations are made, the licensing authority has to grant a licence unless it conflicts with one of the four licensing objectives mentioned above. Conditions, e.g., noise control measures, can also be imposed. If representations are made, the licensing authority must hold a hearing to decide what will happen unless everyone concerned considers that this is not necessary.

Once a premises licence has been granted, it will incorporate the operating schedule mentioned above and will specify the permitted activities together with any limitations. The holder of a premises licence may apply to the licensing authority to vary the licence, e.g., perhaps to change the opening times of the premises, or anything else that they may wish to change.

An appeal against a licensing authority's decision regarding the granting of a premises licence is made to the magistrates' court in the area that covers the licensing authority that made the decision.

Provisional statements

If someone intends to open premises that will be used for any licensable activity, they may want some assurance before spending money on the premises that when the work has been done, they will be able to obtain a premises licence. Therefore, they may apply for a provisional statement. Once the provisional statement is issued, they can then be sure that a full licence will be granted later, provided that the premises are built according to the original operating schedule and the plans that were submitted to the licensing authority.

Designated premises supervisor

As mentioned above, premises where alcohol is supplied under a premises licence must have a designated premises supervisor and that person will be named on the premises licence. Although the designated premises supervisor must hold a personal licence, it is not necessary for him to be the holder of the premises licence. He will be the contact person should any problems arise relating to the premises.

If the designated premises supervisor leaves the premises or moves away, he must inform the licensing authority. He must also, within a specified period, give to the holder of the premises licence a copy of the notice he has sent to the licensing authority. He must also send a notice to the holder of the premises licence informing them that they must send their premises licence to the licensing authority. The premises licence holder must do this within 14 days of receiving the notice and if they are unable to do so, they must inform the licensing authority what their reasons are for failing to do this.

Temporary and occasional events

If someone organising an event where less than 500 people will be at any one time and the event is one where licensable activities will be carried on, an event organiser, known as the premises user, can give a temporary event notice to the licensing authority, with a copy to the police. The temporary event notice must be sent in duplicate no later than ten working days before the day on which the event is due to start. The police may object to it on grounds of crime and disorder.

Anyone over 18 who does not hold a personal licence can give a maximum of five temporary event notices a year. If someone holds a personal licence, they may give up to 50 temporary event notices a year at other premises that are not licensed.

Where events are covered by temporary event notices there are other criteria to be met, such as how long the event can last.

Club premises certificates

Certain types of clubs, such as social clubs, are known as qualifying clubs and, although they provide alcohol to their members (but not to the general public), are not treated in the same way as for premises licences. Rather than applying for a member or employee of the club to hold a personal licence, such a club would apply to the licensing authority for a club premises certificate. Additionally, such a club will not need to have a designated premises supervisor.

Applications for a club premises certificate will contain the completed application form; a plan of the premises; a copy of the club rules and an operating schedule that specifies the activities that the club requires to carry on. Applications will also have to be advertised in a prescribed way.

Clubs that do not fall into the qualifying clubs category must apply for a premises licence.

Regulated entertainment

Generally, if it is desired to provide entertainment at licensed premises, authorisation to provide such entertainment will be applied for at the same time as making the application for a premises licence or club premises certificate, and this will be incorporated into that licence. There are certain exemptions from having to have a premises licence or club premises certificate when entertainment is being provided although, if alcohol is being sold, a licence will still be required for that.

Regulated entertainment is described in the Licensing Act 2003 and includes the performance of a play; showing a film; an indoor sporting event, a live music performance; playing recorded music; a dance performance; and a few other events. For regulated entertainment to be considered as such, it must take place in the presence of an audience and be provided for a purpose including the entertainment of that audience.

Security Industry Authority (SIA)

Door supervisor licences and badges are gradually being changed by the new laws. The previous system of licences and badges being issued by the local authority is being phased out. The SIA has been set up to issue licences. When someone is issued a licence by the SIA they will need only one licence to work anywhere within England and Wales.

A licence will be granted by the SIA only to those have had correct training and who can pass a criminal background check.

Gaming licences, permits and registrations

Depending upon the activity that it is intended to carry on, there are different criteria for different gaming activities. For example, certain applications, e.g., for gaming machines, are made to the licensing authority. Other types of applications, e.g., to operate as a casino, must be made to the Gaming Board of Great Britain. At the time of writing, legislation regarding gambling is being reviewed. It is proposed that the new legislation will establish a new regulator, the Gambling Commission, and the Gaming Board for Great Britain will become a new body with wider functions.

TEST YOURSELF ON CHAPTER 8

Test your knowledge by completing this assignment. If you find that you have difficulty with anything, read the chapter again until you are happy with your answers.

1. Who may apply for a personal licence?

2. When might a premises licence be required?

3. What is an operating schedule?

4. What is the sort of thing that a designated premises supervisor might do?

5. If someone wishes to become a door supervisor, who should they apply to for a licence?

6. Now go through the chapter and if there are any words that are unfamiliar to you or that you cannot spell, write or type them correctly several times until you feel you know them.

9

Appeals, judicial review, case stated

You will understand this chapter better if you read it in conjunction with other relevant chapters in this book so that you are familiar with the terms used. It is not appropriate, in a book of this nature, to deal too deeply with appeals, and this chapter is meant to give you only a brief insight into the subject. The appeals mentioned in this chapter are a broad outline only and procedures can vary according to the type of matter being dealt with. Further information on appeals may be obtained from the relevant rules.

If someone is not happy with the decision of a court they may, in certain circumstances, appeal against it to a higher court. The original court from which the appeal is made is known as the court of first instance. The party who appeals is the appellant and the other party is the respondent. Where an appeal is made and the decision on the appeal has been reached, the appeal is said to be either dismissed or allowed. If it is allowed, then the decision of the lower court is reversed or varied. In criminal cases when an appeal against a conviction is successful, the conviction is quashed. The Court of Appeal may also order a new trial to take place.

Civil matters

Permission to appeal

It is usually necessary to obtain the court's permission before an appeal can be pursued. Generally, where permission is needed to bring an appeal, application for permission may be made either to the court at the hearing at which the decision to be appealed was made or to the court where it is intended to bring the appeal.

Generally, where an appeal is going to be made, the decision of:

(a) a District judge of a county court is appealed to a Circuit judge;

(b) a Master or District Judge of the High Court is appealed to a High Court judge;

(c) a Circuit judge is appealed to a High Court judge; and

(d) a High Court judge is appealed to the Court of Appeal.

Of course, these are all subject to any permission which may be necessary. There are also other criteria for certain matters specified in the court rules.

Where it is desired to make an application to a higer court for an appeal, the appellant must complete a form called Appellant's Notice (Form N161). As with most court forms, there are Guidance Notes to assist with the completion of this form. When filing the Appellant's Notice with the court to which it is intended to bring the appeal, a copy must also be served on each respondent and at the same time, other documents must be filed and served. Amongst the other documents to be filed with the court at this time is a skeleton argument (see below). The Appellant's Notice must be filed with the court within a specified time limit.

Skeleton arguments

The Appellant's Notice must normally be accompanied by a skeleton argument. This outlines and summarises the points to be relied upon at certain hearings.

Skeleton arguments going to the court to which an appeal is being made should contain certain information, including a time estimate for the complete hearing and a numbered list of the points that it is intended to argue. These should be stated in no more than a few sentences. Each point should refer to any documentation on which the appellant intends to rely.

The appellant should also provide any other relevant information that the court may need, such as a chronology of events outlining significant dates; or perhaps an explanation of technical terms used in the papers.

Copies should be made of all documents going to the court so that there is the required number of copies for the court, a copy for every respondent and a copy for your own firm.

House of Lords

Appeals to the House of Lords are rare. It is unlikely in any event that you will type the final documents for the appeal as they have to be set out in a certain way and these are often sent to specialists to be typed or printed. However, an appeal may be made from the Court of Appeal to the House of Lords. Permission to appeal must be obtained from either the Court of Appeal or the House of Lords. If permission from the House of Lords is sought, the petition and a copy of the order appealed against must be lodged with the House of Lords within one month. In some circumstances, an appeal may be made direct from the High Court to the House of Lords.

Appeals from a licensing authority

Appeals against decisions of a licensing authority may be made to a magistrates' court.

Family proceedings from magistrates' courts

In the majority of cases, appeal is made to a High Court judge of the Family Division.

Criminal matters

Appeal to the Crown Court

An appeal may be made to the Crown Court against the decision of a magistrates' court either against sentence if the appellant pleaded guilty at the magistrates' court, or against sentence or conviction if he pleaded not guilty. The notice of appeal must be given within 21 days of the decision appealed against and must be served on the clerk to the magistrates and on the prosecution. An appeal may also be made to the Crown Court against a magistrates' court's binding over or contempt of court order.

Court of Appeal

An appeal may be made in certain cases to the Court of Appeal (Criminal Division) by a person who has been convicted and/or sentenced by the Crown Court. Permission to appeal must sometimes be obtained from the Court of Appeal before the appeal can proceed. Notice of appeal, or application for permission to appeal, must be given within the specified time from the date of conviction or sentence and must be served on the Registrar of Criminal Appeals.

House of Lords

Before an appeal can be made to the House of Lords, permission is required. Either the convicted person or the prosecutor may apply and is only granted permission if the court from which the appeal is made certifies that a point of law of general public importance is involved and that the court thinks the House of Lords should consider the point. Application to the lower court for permission to appeal to the House of Lords must be made within a specified time limit. If permission is refused, application to appeal may be made by petition to the House of Lords.

Judicial review and case stated

In certain circumstances, in both civil and criminal matters, decisions of courts, tribunals and certain other bodies may be questioned by application to the Administrative and Divisional Court (which is part of the High Court) for judicial review or by way of case stated. Certain matters in this court may be dealt with by a single judge and other matters are dealt with by Divisional Courts, which consist of at least two judges.

A claim for a judicial review means that the claimant is applying to the court to review the lawfulness of a particular act or decision, or an action or failure regarding a public function, e.g., perhaps where someone needs to have a decision reviewed that has been made by a Government Minister and where all other avenues of appeal have been explored. It is not a process that is used for ordinary appeal procedures.

Before a claim for judicial review is lodged, parties must, where appropriate, comply with the pre-action protocol for judicial review. The purpose of the protocol is to try to avoid unnecessary litigation and it sets out what the parties should do before a claim is made. For example, the protocol states that before making a claim, the claimant should send a letter to the defendant setting out the issues and try to establish whether litigation can be avoided. Further information on the protocol can be found in the Civil Procedure Rules.

A Claim Form (Form N461) for judicial review must be filed with the Administrative and Divisional Court. This will either be in London or in Cardiff. The claimant must also file and serve a skeleton argument (see above) containing particular information within a specified time, together with a paginated and indexed bundle of relevant documents. Similarly, the defendant and any other party wishing to make representations at the hearing of the judicial review must file and serve a skeleton argument.

Some of the orders the court may make are as follows:

(a) Mandatory order (formerly known as *mandamus*): to compel a tribunal, court or public body to perform a certain duty.

(b) Quashing order (formerly known as *certiorari*): to quash a decision where an error of law has been made or where an order, conviction, etc., has been made without jurisdiction, or where the rules of natural justice have not been observed.

(c) Prohibiting order (formerly known as prohibition): to prevent an unlawful decision from taking effect.

The claimant may also use the judicial review procedure where he is asking for a particular type of injunction or declaration allowed by the rules, and the claim may include a claim for damages.

An appeal by way of case stated may be made from certain decisions of magistrates' courts or the Crown Court to the Administrative and Divisional Court. If a party to proceedings wishes to appeal by way of case stated, they may apply to the court which made the decision to state a case for the opinion of the High Court. A magistrates' court will prepare a statement of the matters which are relevant to the point being appealed. Where the Crown Court is asked to state a case, the appellant drafts a case which is put before the judge who presided over the relevant proceedings. The respondent may also draft a case and submit it to the Crown Court judge for consideration. The judge will read the draft(s) and then state and sign a case. If the application to state a case is refused, the refusing court will provide the applicant with a certificate stating that the application has been refused. The applicant may then apply to the Administrative and Divisional Court for a mandatory order compelling the court to state a case.

The matter will usually be heard by a Divisional Court who may confirm, reverse or vary the decision which is the subject of the case stated. The usual procedure, where appropriate, will be that the Divisional Court will then send the case back to the original court, together with any appropriate opinion or directions.

Appeals from tribunals and arbitrations

Depending on the type of tribunal, etc., an appeal may be made in certain circumstances either to the courts or to another specific body, e.g., Employment Appeal Tribunal. The right of appeal from a tribunal decision is specified in the statute or regulation which set up that particular tribunal. The appellant has a specified time limit after the date of the order, decision or award against which he is appealing to file a request for the entry of the appeal, together with the appropriate number of copies, plus a copy of the order, decision or award he is appealing against.

Appeal from an employment tribunal may be made as follows:

(a) In certain specified circumstances, application for a review of the case may be made by either party at the hearing or within 14 days. If the application is granted, there is a re-hearing.

(b) On a point of law, appeal may be made within a certain time limit to the Employment Appeal Tribunal. This is presided over by a High Court judge with two lay members assisting him.

Appeal on a point of law from the Employment Appeal Tribunal may be made, with permission, to the Court of Appeal and then on to the House of Lords.

There is only a limited right of appeal with regard to arbitration, and this is on a question of law, to the High Court. Further appeal is allowed to the Court of Appeal only if there are special grounds and the court grants permission. This is usually given only if the matter is of general public importance.

TEST YOURSELF ON CHAPTER 9

Test your knowledge by completing this assignment. If you find that you have difficulty with anything, read the chapter again until you are happy with your answers.

1. Explain what is meant by allowing or dismissing an appeal.

2. What is the 'court of first instance'?

3. What is meant by judicial review and case stated?

4. When may an appeal be made against the decision of an employment tribunal?

5. Now go through the chapter and if there are any words that are unfamiliar to you or that you cannot spell, write or type them correctly several times until you feel you know them.

Companies and businesses

There are several ways to carry on a business or trade:

(a) A sole trader, or sole proprietor, being a person carrying on business on his own. Although being a sole trader is possibly the simplest way for a person to set up in business on his own account, the law does require him to comply with certain requirements, e.g., keeping employment documents, and certain other obligations. The sole trader will be entirely liable for any debts he may incur in his business and he can be sued personally for his business debts.

(b) A partnership, where two or more persons carry on business together, with a view to profit. There does not have to be a written formal agreement between partners but a great deal of partnerships do in fact have formal partnership agreements. Partners are liable personally for debts incurred by the partnership. Limited liability partnerships have also been introduced, which enables the business to bear any legal liability rather than the individual partners of the business. The liability of the partners in the business is limited to the amount of capital they have invested in the business, similar to a limited company (see below). A limited liability partnership must be registered with the Registrar of Companies (see below) and its trading name should incorporate 'Limited Liability Partnership' (LLP).

(c) A company. Basically, companies fall into one of four categories: a public limited company (plc); a private company limited by shares; a private company limited by guarantee and a private unlimited company. The first two are the most common. If a company is limited, it means that the liability of the members of the company is limited to the amount, if any, unpaid on the shares they hold or the amount they have already undertaken to contribute if the company is wound up. Companies are regulated by several Companies Acts. A company is a 'legal person'. This means that all transactions are carried out in the name of the company and not in that of its shareholders. The company itself owns property and is sued for any debt incurred. Once a company is 'born' or comes into existence it is 'incorporated'.

Information about companies

Companies are registered (details of the company are lodged) with the Registrar of Companies at Companies House and are given a registered number. As well as lodging registration documents with Companies House, there are legal requirements to lodge various other documents. The original documents are kept by Companies House who capture them electronically. Because Companies House produces electronic images of documents for their records, the documents submitted to them must be easy to scan. They can, in fact, reject documents if they cannot copy them clearly.

Companies House requires documents to show in a prominent position the registered number of the company. This should be on the first page of any document and preferably at the top right corner. Documents should be on plain white, A4 size paper and the text should be in black and legible. Carbon copies should not be used and it should be borne in mind that even photocopies can be dark and, therefore, unsuitable. Paper with a matt finish, rather than glossy, should be used. In addition, pages must have a good margin all round. Companies House will accept documents in other formats and for guidance, telephone Companies House Contact Centre at 0870 3333636.

Companies House has Information Centres in Cardiff, London and Edinburgh, where a personal visit may be made. The Contact Centre (mentioned above) deals with telephone queries and takes orders for copies of company documents. When ordering over the telephone, payment must be made either by credit card or through an account with Companies House. Where payments are made by credit card or account, it is possible to have copies of documents sent by fax or e-mail. When ordering by post, payments may be made by cheque and the copy documents requested will be delivered by post.

It is also possible to obtain information about a company by subscribing to Companies House on-line service called Companies House Direct. Information can be viewed and downloaded on your firm's PC.

A considerable amount of information is available on-line via the Companies House website (see section on Web Addresses at the back of this book). This information may be obtained simply by using a credit card and it is not necessary to have any sort of account with Companies House. There is also a certain amount of free information that can be obtained on the website.

Companies House Monitor is a service for anyone wishing to monitor a company and wishes to receive particular documentation about that company as soon as it is registered at Companies House. The documents specified will be sent to you by fax. It is necessary to have an account with Companies House to take advantage of this service.

Another service offered is the Companies House CD Directory which contains basic information on all live companies. It is updated monthly and the customer has the choice of buying just one disk or 12 for the year. Additionally, there is a Change of Name and Dissolved Companies Index on CD, providing basic information on companies that have changed their name or been dissolved in the last 20 years. This is produced annually.

Many firms requiring information on companies employ agencies who specialise in company searches.

Starting a company

Some specialist firms will sell 'off the shelf' ready-made companies with appropriate documents already drawn up. However, your firm may have to draw up the documents themselves and some of these are briefly explained below.

Memorandum of Association

A limited company must have a Memorandum of Association. You may come across the term 'Table B' when reference is made to a Memorandum of Association. This is a form of Memorandum set out in Table B of Companies (Tables A to F) Regulations 1985 (as amended). Any Memorandum of Association must comply as nearly as possible with the form set out in Table B.

A Memorandum of Association must contain the following:

(a) The name of the company

(b) Whether the registered office of the company is in England and Wales, or in Scotland. The registered office is the address where it is known that communications will be received by the company, e.g., where documents can be served on the company. This address is lodged with the Companies Registrar at Companies House on Companies Form 10. A change of address of registered office must be notified to Companies House within 14 days and this is done on Companies Form 287. The registered office does not have to be the address from which the company carries on business. Quite a few solicitors' offices are registered offices for companies. Court proceedings relating to companies should normally be served at their registered office unless, of course, a solicitor has been instructed to accept service on behalf of that company. (See Chapter 3 for further information regarding 'service'.)

(c) An Objects Clause. This is a statement of the company's objects and powers. It will usually include what a company may wish to do in the future as well as at the present, e.g., it may state that the object of the company is to carry on business as a general commercial company. The Objects Clause can be changed by a special resolution being passed by the members of the company.

(d) A clause stating that the company has limited liability.

(e) A statement showing the amount of nominal capital held by the company and declaring how it is divided into shares.

(f) The subscribers sign the Memorandum stating they wish to form a company and the number of shares they will have. This is known as the Association Clause.

Articles of Association

This states the rules governing the internal management of the company. When reference is being made to the Articles of Association you may come across the term 'Table A'. This is a standard form of Articles of Association set out in Table A of Companies (Tables A to F) Regulations 1985. By statute, if no other articles apply, then Table A is adopted.

Other documents

(a) Declaration of Compliance on Application for Registration (Companies Form 12). This is a declaration made by either a solicitor engaged in the formation of the company or a secretary or director named on Form 10 (see below) stating that the Companies Acts have been complied with. It must be witnessed independently by someone who has the power to administer oaths (see page 119).

(b) First Directors and Secretary and Intended Situation of Registered Office (Companies Form 10). This gives details of the first directors and secretary and also states where it is intended that the registered office should be situated. It must be signed by those who signed the Memorandum of Association.

These forms are all sent to the appropriate Companies House together with the registration fee. As with other areas, nearly all the forms have extremely helpful guidance notes and it is worth taking the time to read them.

One additional document must be filed if the company being formed is going to be a public limited company. This is Companies Form 117: application by a public company for certificate to commence business.

Please complete in typescript, or in bold black capitals.

CHFP041

10

First directors and secretary and intended situation of registered office

Notes on completion appear on final page

Company Name in full

BLOGGS AND BLACK LIMITED

Proposed Registered Office
(PO Box numbers only, are not acceptable)

2 MILKY WAY

Post town
BARNET

County / Region
HERTS

Postcode
EN4 6PP

If the memorandum is delivered by an agent for the subscriber(s) of the memorandum mark the box opposite and give the agent's name and address.

X

Agent's Name
ANGEL, GABRIEL & CO

Address
2 MILKY WAY

Post town
BARNET

County / Region
HERTS

Postcode
EN4 6PP

Number of continuation sheets attached

You do not have to give any contact information in the box opposite but if you do, it will help Companies House to contact you if there is a query on the form. The contact information that you give will be visible to searchers of the public record.

MR A STAR (ref: AS/468)

ANGEL, GABRIEL & CO, 2 MILKY WAY,

BARNET, HERTS.   Tel   01638 1234

DX number   123   DX exchange   BARNET

Companies House receipt date barcode

When you have completed and signed the form please send it to the Registrar of Companies at:
Companies House, Crown Way, Cardiff, CF14 3UZ   DX 33050 Cardiff
for companies registered in England and Wales
or
Companies House, 37 Castle Terrace, Edinburgh, EH1 2EB
for companies registered in Scotland   **DX 235 Edinburgh**

Form revised April 2002

Company Secretary (see notes 1-5)

Company name	BLOGGS AND BLACK LIMITED	

NAME *Style / Title

*Honours etc.

*Voluntary details

Forename(s) JOHN

Surname BLACK

Previous forename(s)

Previous surname(s)

†† Tick this box if the address shown is a service address for the beneficiary of a Confidentiality Order granted under section 723B of the Companies Act 1985 otherwise, give your usual residential address. In the case of a corporation or Scottish firm, give the registered or principal office address.

Address ††

34 NORTH STREET

Post town SOUTHTOWN

County / Region HERTFORDSHIRE   Postcode EN5 2PP

Country ENGLAND

I consent to act as secretary of the company named on page 1

Consent signature   Date

Directors (see notes 1-5)

Please list directors in alphabetical order

NAME *Style / Title

*Honours etc.

Forename(s) JOHN

Surname BLACK

Previous forename(s)

Previous surname(s)

†† Tick this box if the address shown is a service address for the beneficiary of a Confidentiality Order granted under section 723B of the Companies Act 1985 otherwise, give your usual residential address. In the case of a corporation or Scottish firm, give the registered or principal office address.

Address ††

34 NORTH STREET

Post town SOUTHTOWN

County / Region HERTFORDSHIRE   Postcode EN5 2PP

Country ENGLAND

	Day	Month	Year		
Date of birth	0 7	0 7	1 9 4 9	**Nationality**	BRITISH

Business occupation SALESMAN

Other directorships NONE

I consent to act as director of the company named on page 1

Consent signature   Date

Directors (continued) (see notes 1-5)

Please list directors in alphabetical order

NAME   *Style / Title   *Honours etc.

*Voluntary details

Forename(s): PETER

Surname: BLOGGS

Previous forename(s):

Previous surname(s):

† Tick this box if the address shown is a service address for the beneficiary of a Confidentiality Order granted under section 723B of the Companies Act 1985 otherwise, give your usual residential address. In the case of a corporation or Scottish firm, give the registered or principal office address.

Address † : 81 GREEN STREET

Post town: SOUTHTOWN

County / Region: HERTFORDSHIRE   Postcode: EN3 6PP

Country: ENGLAND

Date of birth: Day 2 9 Month 1 2 Year 1 9 4 7   Nationality: BRITISH

Business occupation: SALESMAN

Other directorships: NONE

I consent to act as director of the company named on page 1

Consent signature   Date

This section must be signed by

Either

an agent on behalf of all subscribers   Signed   Date

Or the subscribers

(i.e those who signed as members on the memorandum of association).

Signed   Date

Signed   Date

Signed   Date

Signed   Date

Signed   Date

Signed   Date

Notes

1. Show for an individual the full forename(s) NOT INITIALS and surname together with any previous forename(s) or surname(s).

    If the director or secretary is a corporation or Scottish firm - show the corporate or firm name on the surname line.

    Give previous forename(s) or surname(s) except that:

    - for a married woman, the name by which she was known before marriage need not be given,

    - names not used since the age of 18 or for at least 20 years need not be given.

    A peer, or an individual known by a title, may state the title instead of or in addition to the forename(s) and surname and need not give the name by which that person was known before he or she adopted the title or succeeded to it.

    Address:

    Give the usual residential address.

    In the case of a corporation or Scottish firm give the registered or principal office.

    Subscribers:
    The form must be signed personally either by the subscriber(s) or by a person or persons authorised to sign on behalf of the subscriber(s).

2. Directors known by another description:

    - A director includes any person who occupies that position even if called by a different name, for example, governor, member of council.

3. Directors details:

    - Show for each individual director the director's date of birth, business occupation and nationality. **The date of birth must be given for every individual director.**

4. Other directorships:

    - Give the name of every company of which the person concerned is a director or has been a director at any time in the past 5 years. You may exclude a company which either **is** or at **all times during the past 5 years,** when the person was a director, **was:**

    - dormant,

    - a parent company which wholly owned the company making the return,

    - a wholly owned subsidiary of the company making the return, or

    - another wholly owned subsidiary of the same parent company.

    If there is insufficient space on the form for other directorships you may use a separate sheet of paper, which should include the company's number and the full name of the director.

5. Use Form 10 continuation sheets or photocopies of page 2 to provide details of joint secretaries or additional directors.

The Registrar of Companies issues a Certificate of Incorporation, all being well, and issues a plc with a Certificate of Compliance (also called a Trading Certificate) as well as the Certificate of Incorporation.

Many other forms may need to be completed and sent to the Registrar of Companies. Most of them have a large number on them at the top as can be seen from the example Form 10, and consist mainly of completing appropriate boxes.

Once a company has been incorporated it may have a 'company seal'. A company seal is the 'mark' of the company, in other words, a type of signature. It is a circular impression or stamp showing the name of the company and is often used when a company signs a document which binds the company. It is usually stamped over a red wafer seal, i.e., a thin red circular 'star' about an inch or so in diameter. (This replaces the old usage of red wax for seals.) The seal on a document is usually accompanied by a signature of one or more officers of the company, e.g., a director and/or secretary of the company.

There is generally no longer a legal requirement for a company to have a seal although, for various reasons, many companies will still have one and use it. (See also page 271 on deeds.) It should be borne in mind that certain corporations which have not been incorporated under the Companies Acts still generally have to execute deeds under seal.

Members and officers of a company

The members of a company are those who own the shares in the company. The profits of the company are distributed amongst the members according to how many shares they hold. This distribution is done by paying a dividend. The officers of a company are the directors and the company secretary (they can also be members). The company secretary can also be a director. Company secretary in this context does not mean a secretary such as yourself: it means an officer of the company with certain duties and powers within that company. In the case of a public company, the company secretary must have formal company secretary qualifications.

The directors have the power to manage the business of the company within the constraints of the Memorandum and Articles of Association (see above) as well as any further powers given to them by members. However, the directors are appointed by the members and the members can vote to remove a director. One of the directors will usually be appointed managing director and he will normally be given certain authority and power by the other directors. If officers of a company do not comply with legal requirements relating to companies, they may sometimes incur personal liability, for example, if an officer of a company signs a cheque on behalf of the company and the name of the company is not on the cheque, then the officer signing may find that he will be personally liable to pay the amount of the cheque. Non-compliance with company law by officers of the company may sometimes even be a criminal offence.

Certain people are barred from becoming company directors, e.g., an undischarged bankrupt or someone who has been disqualified by the court from holding a company directorship, unless they are given permission by the court to act in respect of a particular company. With regard to a plc or its subsidiaries, a person aged 70 or over cannot be a director unless specially appointed. However, there is no minimum age restriction on becoming a company director, except that the person must be able to consent to being a director.

Auditors to the company must also be appointed. An auditor to a company must be a professionally qualified person.

Keeping company records

The law requires companies to keep certain records, including a register of members; a register of directors and of company secretaries; minutes of company meetings, as well as other important information. These records will normally be kept at the company's registered office (see above).

Every company has a file at Companies House and this file is open to public inspection. A copy of the company's records are kept in the file and must be kept up to date. Therefore, each time particular events occur within a company, e.g., a change of registered office, the company must notify Companies House. Every company must also file its annual accounts (see later) with Companies House.

Besides keeping records, some of the legal requirements to be met by a company include the fact that the name of the company must appear on all business letters, notices, etc., as well as cheques, order forms, receipts and various other documents. Sometimes, additional information must also be included, such as where the company is registered; the company number; the address of the registered office; and certain other information. The company must display its name outside every place it carries on business.

Shares and capital

The Memorandum of Association will state the maximum amount of capital to be held by a company and will declare how that amount is divided into shares. The shares will be of a stated value, quite often £1. For example, a company might have a share capital of £1,000 divided into 1,000 ordinary shares of £1 each. The shares in a company will normally be of equal value. However, the company does not have to issue all of the share capital and sometimes only a few shares are issued, especially in the first stages of formation of a company.

A company must have funds in order to carry on business and money will generally be obtained either by borrowing money or by issuing shares to people who will become members (or shareholders) and will pay the company for those shares. Once the company is established, it will hopefully make a profit and its shareholders will usually receive their share of the profit by a payment called a dividend. There are different classes of shares:

(a) Ordinary shares: often also called equity shares. Persons who own ordinary shares normally take the most risk in the business but also normally receive most of the profit. These shares usually carry full voting rights.

(b) Preference shares: these give preference in some stated way over other shares, e.g., holders of preference shares may receive their dividend payments first.

(c) Deferred shares: usually, other shares take priority over these. They are often held by first members who originally formed the company, in order to give confidence to other new members.

Fixed and floating charges

A charge is a way of borrowing money against assets, so that if the borrower cannot repay the money, the assets can be taken by the lender and sold so that the lender can recover his money. A fixed charge is a way of borrowing money using specific property as security for the loan.

A floating charge is where a company can use all its assets as security, e.g., it can borrow money and no specific property is held as security but if the loan has to be called in, the charge is 'crystallised', which means that it will cover all the company's existing assets over which the charge was granted, rather than just one specific item. Therefore, the floating charge is a charge that 'floats' over the assets of the company. The document that grants a floating charge is normally called a debenture.

Meetings

The annual general meeting (AGM)

These are held each calendar year and must not be more than 15 months apart. A newly incorporated company must hold its first AGM within 18 months of incorporation. When an AGM is called, the notification of it to members of the company must specify that it is the AGM and not any other meeting.

Extra-ordinary general meeting

This is a specially called meeting of the members of the company and may be called by shareholders holding a certain amount of shares in the company. All members of the company are entitled to attend these meetings unless they are specifically excluded by the company's Articles of Association.

There are certain other meetings which may be held by members of a company. If a member of the company wishes to vote on a matter being discussed at a meeting of the company and he cannot attend, he can give someone else his right to vote. This is known as his 'proxy'.

Decisions made at general meetings of a company are known as resolutions. There are certain formalities relating to resolutions. Rules governing company meetings are laid down in the Companies Acts.

Annual return and accounts

Every year a company must deliver its Annual Return to the Registrar of Companies. This is done by updating the previous year's Annual Return and must be made up to the date which is the company's 'return date', which is either the anniversary of the company's incorporation or, if the company's last return was delivered on a different date in accordance with the Companies Acts, the anniversary of that date. This must be filed with the Registrar within 28 days after the date to which it is made up. The Annual Return must state the date to which it is made up and must contain certain information relating to the company including, among other things, the address of its registered office, details of directors and secretary, the address where the register of members of the company is kept, principal business activities and details of issued share capital to the return date. The annual return is made on Form 363a and must be sent to Companies House, together with a fee.

Companies must also prepare annual accounts and submit these to the Registrar of Companies. Annual accounts report on the company's financial activities during the previous year, and this period of accounting is called the financial year. The financial year starts on the day after the previous financial year ends or, if it is a new company, it starts on the day the company was incorporated. The day on which a company's financial year ends is its accounting reference date and there are certain rules which apply to this.

Companies House will accept a company's accounts drawn up in the euro if the directors and auditors of the company consider that by using that currency a true and fair view of the company's affairs will be given.

Dissolution of a company

When a company is no longer going to exist it is 'wound up' or 'goes into liquidation'. This can be voluntary or it can be compulsory. The court may order a company to be wound up under certain circumstances when it is petitioned to do so by creditors of the company. When a company is wound up, a liquidator may be appointed to sort out the company's financial affairs. Sometimes the Official Receiver is appointed as liquidator. If a company cannot pay its debts it is said to be 'insolvent'.

Other matters involving companies and businesses

Companies and businesses can, of course, just like individuals, become involved in a variety of court actions. One type of court action is a 'passing off' action which occurs where one company or business tries to pass off its product as though it has been manufactured by another company, usually a larger, better known company.

You may come across the term 'intellectual property' or 'industrial property'. This type of property refers to rights over such things as patents, copyright, trade marks, designs and goodwill. Such property can be transferred from one person to another in the same manner as other property.

You may encounter references to the Director General of Fair Trading, who performs the functions assigned to him by the Fair Trading Act 1973. The Director General is appointed by the Secretary of State and is head of the Office of Fair Trading. He has responsibilities regarding consumer protection and competition law enforcement. Competition law is the law that governs the processes of competitiveness in trade.

You may also hear of the Competition Commission (called the Monopolies and Mergers Commission until April 1999). This body will continue to deal with aspects of the work carried out by the Monopolies and Mergers Commission regarding monopolies and mergers. It will also be the body to whom appeals may be made against decisions of the Director General under the Competition Act.

As with all matters relating to a lawyer's office, confidentiality is of the utmost importance. It must also be remembered that information gained inside the lawyer's office cannot be used for other purposes, for example, you may have access to information not known to the public which could assist someone in deciding to buy or sell certain shares in a particular company. This information must not be divulged or used in any way. If it is so used, this could amount to a criminal offence being committed, known as 'insider dealing'.

The law relating to companies and businesses is extensive and it is inappropriate to go any further into this subject in this type of book.

TEST YOURSELF ON CHAPTER 10

Test your knowledge by completing this assignment. If you find that you have difficulty with anything, read the chapter again until you are happy with your answers.

1. A company is a 'legal person'. What does this mean?

2. What is the registered office of a company?

3. How might you obtain information about a limited company registered at Companies House?

4. What sort of information does a Memorandum of Association contain?

5. What are Articles of Association?

6. Complete as far, as possible the Form 10 included with this assignment, using the following information:

   You are employed by a firm called John Smith & Co., of 2 Bank Chambers, High Road, Westbourne, Suffolk (tel: 01876 9342; ref: JL/Orange/43), and you are working for Jane Lawman, a solicitor in that firm. Jane is acting for Peter Green and Ann Brown who wish to form a limited company called The Orange Company Limited. The registered office will be at 64 Hillside View, Westbourne, Suffolk WA3 2AB. Peter Green lives at 87 Summer Road, Westbourne, Suffolk WA3 8LB; his date of birth is 11.3.1970; his occupation is landscape gardener. Ann Brown lives at 69 Spring Hill, Westbourne, Suffolk, WA3 4PQ; her date of birth is 15.8.1965 and she is also a landscape gardener. They are both British. Peter Green will also be the company secretary.

7. Explain the difference between an Annual General Meeting and an Extra-Ordinary General Meeting.

8. What is meant by a company's 'financial year'?

9. Explain the term 'intellectual property'.

10. Now go through the chapter and if there are any words that are unfamiliar to you or that you cannot spell, write or type them correctly several times until you feel you know them.

Please complete in typescript, or in bold black capitals.

CHFP041

First directors and secretary and intended situation of registered office

10

Notes on completion appear on final page

Company Name in full

Proposed Registered Office
(PO Box numbers only, are not acceptable)

Post town

County / Region   Postcode

If the memorandum is delivered by an agent for the subscriber(s) of the memorandum mark the box opposite and give the agent's name and address.

Agent's Name

Address

Post town

County / Region   Postcode

Number of continuation sheets attached

You do not have to give any contact information in the box opposite but if you do, it will help Companies House to contact you if there is a query on the form. The contact information that you give will be visible to searchers of the public record.

Tel

DX number   DX exchange

Companies House receipt date barcode

When you have completed and signed the form please send it to the Registrar of Companies at:
Companies House, Crown Way, Cardiff, CF14 3UZ   DX 33050 Cardiff
for companies registered in England and Wales
or
Companies House, 37 Castle Terrace, Edinburgh, EH1 2EB
for companies registered in Scotland   **DX 235 Edinburgh**

Form revised April 2002

Company Secretary (see notes 1-5)

Company name

NAME   *Style / Title

*Honours etc.

*Voluntary details

Forename(s)

Surname

Previous forename(s)

Previous surname(s)

†† Tick this box if the address shown is a service address for the beneficiary of a Confidentiality Order granted under section 723B of the Companies Act 1985 otherwise, give your usual residential address. In the case of a corporation or Scottish firm, give the registered or principal office address.

Address ††

Post town

County / Region

Postcode

Country

I consent to act as secretary of the company named on page 1

Consent signature

Date

Directors (see notes 1-5)

Please list directors in alphabetical order

NAME   *Style / Title

*Honours etc.

Forename(s)

Surname

Previous forename(s)

Previous surname(s)

†† Tick this box if the address shown is a service address for the beneficiary of a Confidentiality Order granted under section 723B of the Companies Act 1985 otherwise, give your usual residential address. In the case of a corporation or Scottish firm, give the registered or principal office address.

Address ††

Post town

County / Region

Postcode

Country

Day   Month   Year

Date of birth

Nationality

Business occupation

Other directorships

I consent to act as director of the company named on page 1

Consent signature

Date

Directors (continued) (see notes 1-5)

Please list directors in alphabetical order

NAME *Style / Title* | *Honours etc.*

Voluntary details

Forename(s)

Surname

Previous forename(s)

Previous surname(s)

† Tick this box if the address shown is a service address for the beneficiary of a Confidentiality Order granted under section 723B of the Companies Act 1985 otherwise, give your usual residential address. In the case of a corporation or Scottish firm, give the registered or principal office address.

Address †

Post town

County / Region   Postcode

Country

Day Month Year

Date of birth   Nationality

Business occupation

Other directorships

I consent to act as director of the company named on page 1

Consent signature   Date

This section must be signed by

Either

an agent on behalf of all subscribers   Signed   Date

Or **the subscribers**   Signed   Date

(i.e those who signed as members on the memorandum of association).   Signed   Date

Signed   Date

Signed   Date

Signed   Date

Signed   Date

Notes

1. Show for an individual the full forename(s) NOT INITIALS and surname together with any previous forename(s) or surname(s).

   If the director or secretary is a corporation or Scottish firm - show the corporate or firm name on the surname line.

   Give previous forename(s) or surname(s) except that:

   - for a married woman, the name by which she was known before marriage need not be given,

   - names not used since the age of 18 or for at least 20 years need not be given.

   A peer, or an individual known by a title, may state the title instead of or in addition to the forename(s) and surname and need not give the name by which that person was known before he or she adopted the title or succeeded to it.

   Address:

   Give the usual residential address.

   In the case of a corporation or Scottish firm give the registered or principal office.

   Subscribers:
   The form must be signed personally either by the subscriber(s) or by a person or persons authorised to sign on behalf of the subscriber(s).

2. Directors known by another description:

   - A director includes any person who occupies that position even if called by a different name, for example, governor, member of council.

3. Directors details:

   - Show for each individual director the director's date of birth, business occupation and nationality. **The date of birth must be given for every individual director.**

4. Other directorships:

   - Give the name of every company of which the person concerned is a director or has been a director at any time in the past 5 years. You may exclude a company which either **is** or at **all times during the past 5 years,** when the person was a director, **was:**

   - dormant,

   - a parent company which wholly owned the company making the return,

   - a wholly owned subsidiary of the company making the return, or

   - another wholly owned subsidiary of the same parent company.

   If there is insufficient space on the form for other directorships you may use a separate sheet of paper, which should include the company's number and the full name of the director.

5. Use Form 10 continuation sheets or photocopies of page 2 to provide details of joint secretaries or additional directors.

11

Wills and probate

The department in a firm that deals with matters relating to Wills and probate is often called the Private Client department, or sometimes the Probate department. This department will normally also give advice to clients on inheritance tax, as well as advising where someone has died without making a Will, and various other related matters.

Wills

A Will is a document which states the wishes of a person as to how he or she would like their property dealt with after their death. If a person dies without making a Will (or a valid will), he dies 'intestate', in which case, the law states how his property will be dealt with. There are certain legal conditions to be met before a Will can be made. These are not all dealt with here because it is the responsibility of the fee earner to ensure these conditions are met.

A Will must normally be in writing, be signed by the testator (the person making it), or by someone else in his presence and at his direction, e.g., where the testator is unable for some reason to sign it himself. At the signing of a Will it is dated and the signature must be written or acknowledged in the presence of two or more witnesses who must both be present at the same time. The normal procedure for witnesses is that they also sign the Will, or acknowledge their signatures, in the presence of each other and in the presence of the testator, all being present at the same time. At the end of the Will, there will be the clauses called the testimonium and the attestation clause (see pages 27–29). The attestation clause shows that the Will has been correctly signed and witnessed. Additionally, if, for example, the testator is unable to read his Will, perhaps because he is blind or illiterate, the Will must be read over to him before he signs it and the wording of the attestation clause will reflect that this has been done. It may be that as a secretary you will often be asked to witness a Will. If you are lucky enough to be a beneficiary of a Will, you should not witness it, as this may bar you from obtaining your inheritance!

Normally, the client will call in to the office to sign his Will but it may be that it is posted to him for signature. If it is posted, he will be sent instructions on how the Will must be signed—your firm may have a pro forma containing all the instructions and this will be sent to the client with the Will. The pro forma will also include guidance about not damaging or marking the Will (see page 244).

The basic contents of a Will can be explained as follows:

(a) The name, address and, perhaps, occupation of the testator, followed by a declaration that this is his last Will.

(b) A revocation clause, which revokes any Wills or codicils (see below) that may have been made previously.

(c) The appointment of executors (also known as personal representatives). Broadly speaking, an executor (a female executor is called an executrix) is someone who will ensure that the wishes of the person who made the Will are carried out. Executors are sometimes beneficiaries under the Will and/or often professional people, such as bank managers and solicitors. If an executor is a professional person there is usually a clause in the Will stating that such a person may charge a fee for his service.

(d) The main body of the Will then contains details of any gifts or legacies and powers and obligations of the trustees in the Will.

(e) A survivorship clause will normally be included in the Will. This is a clause that states that a particular beneficiary (often husband or wife) will not inherit unless they survive the deceased by, say, 30 days. The purpose of this is so that if the beneficiary does not survive the testator for the specified number of days, then both parties' estates will be dealt with separately for inheritance tax purposes, which may have the effect of lessening the burden of inheritance tax for other beneficiaries.

(f) There is usually a receipt clause, which provides that the proper person, e.g., an officer of a charity, a parent or guardian, etc. can give a valid receipt to the personal representatives or trustee, so that the personal representative or trustee can hand over money to that proper person and they can obtain a receipt from him which will then absolve the personal representative or trustee of any further responsibility with regard to the money.

There are many other clauses that may be included in a Will, depending on what is required.

Once the Will has been approved by the client, it is executed, i.e., signed and dated by him and the witnesses, as explained above. It should also have a typed backsheet (see page 245) which should also be dated.

Any new Will cancels out (revokes) a previous Will. Similarly, if the testator deliberately destroys the Will, e.g., by burning it or tearing it up, then the Will is revoked. A Will is also revoked through the marriage of the testator unless the Will is made in anticipation of the marriage and specifically states this. A Will is affected by divorce, in that it treats the spouse as though they had died. If minor amendments are to be made to an existing Will, a Codicil (see page 246) should be drawn up.

The Will should be typed on good quality paper. It should not have any unnecessary spaces or blank pages in it and should be typed on both sides of the paper. There should not be any alterations or erasures to a Will but if any are made you must bring these to the attention of the fee earner before the Will is signed. If the alterations are acceptable, they must be initialled by both the testator and the witnesses, otherwise the Will must be re-typed. If there are any figures showing sums of money in the Will these are often typed both in words and then in figures in brackets, e.g., ONE HUNDRED POUNDS (£100).

Paragraphs in the Will should be numbered and, as you will see from the example, the first word at the beginning of each paragraph and certain other words are usually typed in capitals and underlined. (This layout is not essential—it is simply traditional.)

On no account should you staple or attach anything by paperclips, etc. to a Will. This is because at some later stage, if the Will is in dispute and it bears a mark of something having been attached to it, then those disputing it may argue that part of the Will is missing. If a Will consists of more than one sheet of paper, it may sometimes be sewn together in the top left-hand corner (see page 31) but remember, do not hold the sheets of paper together with a paperclip. However, most firms these days will generally bind the pages of a Will together using a binding machine—find out what your own firm does.

Clients sometimes retain their Will or ask the firm of solicitors to keep it for them. In any event, it is normal to keep a photocopy of it in the file. If the original is kept by the firm it must be kept in the firm's safe.

Example Will

I JANE BLOGGS of 123 North Road Southtown Essex Waitress <u>HEREBY REVOKE</u> all Wills and testamentary dispositions heretofore made by me and declare this to be my last Will

1. <u>I APPOINT</u> my sister <u>DOREEN BLOGGS</u> of 234 South Road Northtown Esssex to be the Executor and Trustee of this my Will or any Codicil hereto (hereinafter called 'my Trustee')

2. <u>I DIRECT</u> that all my just debts funeral and testamentary expenses shall be paid as soon as possible after my death

3. <u>I GIVE</u> the sum of <u>ONE THOUSAND POUNDS</u> (£1000) to <u>SOUTHTOWN DOGS HOME</u> of 4 Barking Road Southtown aforesaid and <u>I DECLARE</u> that the receipt of the proper officer for the time being of the said charity shall be sufficient discharge to my Trustee

4. <u>I DEVISE AND BEQUEATH</u> the residue of my estate both real and personal to my said sister <u>DOREEN BLOGGS</u>

IN WITNESS whereof I have hereunto set my hand this   *   day of   *   2005

SIGNED by the said JANE BLOGGS   )
as her last Will in the presence   )
of us both present at the same   )
time and who in her presence and   )
in the presence of each other have   )
hereunto subscribed our names as   )
witnesses   )

[or perhaps, more simply:]

SIGNED by the testator   )
JANE BLOGGS in our joint presence   )
and then by us in hers   )

DATED   2005

_____

WILL

of

JANE BLOGGS

Angel Gabriel & Co.,
2 Milky Way,
Barnet,
Herts.

tel: 01638 1234
ref: ABC/123

Gifts and legacies

Where a gift or legacy is given under a Will, you will normally see a clause saying something like 'I give devise and bequeath'. Devise means giving land, bequeath is giving other property. A gift or legacy is either specific or general.

A specific legacy is a clearly identifiable object, e.g., 'my gold necklace with the rubies and diamonds, given to me by my husband on my 10th wedding anniversary'. If that specific gift is no longer part of the estate (it may have been lost or sold), then the beneficiary will not get anything else instead, because that specific gift is no longer there to be given. This is known as ademption. However, this can be got round by giving a substitutional gift: if the necklace is no longer there, the Will may provide that the beneficiary will be given a substitution.

A general gift is non-specific, e.g., 'I leave £2,000 to Uncle Fred and a watch to my niece Sarah Brown'. This does not say a particular £2,000 from a certain bank account; neither does it refer to a particular watch—any watch will do. A general gift of money is called a pecuniary legacy.

Besides general and specific gifts, there are additional ways of leaving gifts under a Will, either to overcome a particular problem or to make things easier for beneficiaries and executors.

Gifts made during a lifetime

If someone makes a gift during their lifetime to someone else, this is called a lifetime gift or a lifetime transfer. Everyone is allowed to give away so much to someone else without any inheritance tax being payable on the gift, e.g., a specific amount each year may be given away (an annual allowance); maintenance payments to a spouse; wedding gifts up to a certain amount for each child and various other gifts. These gifts (or transfers), because they are exempt from inheritance tax, are called exempt transfers.

However, if a gift other than an exempt transfer is given away and the person making the gift dies within 7 years of making the gift, inheritance tax may be payable on the value of the gift. Depending on how long after the gift is given the person giving it dies, the inheritance tax payable goes down on a sliding (or tapering) scale: this is called taper relief. Therefore, because this sort of gift might become exempt at some stage, depending on how long the person giving it survives after giving it, the gifts or transfers are potentially exempt from inheritance tax and are known as potentially exempt transfers (PETs).

There is also a category of gift called chargeable lifetime transfers. These do not fall into either of the above two categories and the most common are a type of trust called a discretionary trust, or gifts made to companies. If a gift falls within this category and depending upon the amount of money involved, a certain amount of inheritance tax may be payable at the time the gift is made and then if the person making the gift dies within 7 years, the full amount of inheritance tax becomes payable (the amount paid at the time of giving will be deducted).

Codicils

You may also be asked to type a codicil to a Will. This is a document making minor alterations to a Will and is set out in the same manner as a Will but states that it is a codicil to a Will dated whatever, by whoever. It has to be executed in the same manner as a Will. As with Wills, nothing should be stapled or attached to a codicil. If major changes are required to be made to the Will, a new Will should be drawn up, rather than a codicil.

Obtaining probate

After someone has died, the estate needs to be dealt with, e.g., collect money in from banks, sell property and pay out accordingly, as well as ensuring beneficiaries receive any gifts, etc. Therefore, the people (the personal representatives) who are going to deal with this process, known as administering the estate, will usually have to apply to the court for a Grant of Representation. The Grant will prove that they have authority to deal with the estate so that they can, for example, produce the Grant to say, a bank holding money in an account in the deceased's name, and the bank will be satisfied on production of the Grant that the personal representative has authority to withdraw that money.

There are two types of personal representative: executors and administrators, but both come under the general term of personal representative. The difference between the two is that an executor is appointed under a Will and an administrator is not appointed under a Will. For example, if someone is named in a valid Will as an executor of that Will, they are appointed under the Will. If there is no Will, or the Will is invalid, the person who will deal with the estate is called an administrator and any potential administrator must apply to the court for authority to act. Similarly, if there is a valid Will but the testator has not appointed an executor or an executor has been appointed but for some reason cannot or does not wish to act, then a person who wishes to be an administrator may apply for a Grant. There are rules regarding who may be appointed as an administrator.

There may be more than one personal representative and their job is basically to collect in the assets of the estate; to pay off any debts and to pass the net available amount to the beneficiaries. Before any debts and liabilities are paid, the value of the estate is known as the gross value. The net value is the value of what is left after debts and so on have been paid, e.g., credit card bills, funeral expenses, tax incurred by the deceased before he died, etc. Also, inheritance tax may be payable—this is tax payable once the value of the estate exceeds a certain amount (known as the tax threshold). Inheritance tax is not payable on the entire estate but only on the amount that exceeds the tax threshold. Therefore, if the value of the estate is less than the tax threshold, no inheritance tax will be payable. Whether or not tax is payable also depends on the rules and regulations relating to exemptions.

Applications for a Grant are made to the Family Division of the High Court, either to a district probate registry or to the Principal Registry of the Family Division in London. In some cases, where the value of the estate is small, it is not necessary to obtain a Grant but this depends on the circumstances.

When applying for a Grant, the Oath for Executors or an Oath for Administrators must be completed. This is an affidavit (see page 119) containing evidence which establishes the executor's right to administer the estate. It must also give details of the value of the estate and say whether an Inland Revenue Account is required to be delivered (see below under Inheritance Tax). As with other affidavits, the oath must not be sworn before a solicitor whose firm is dealing with the matter. A pre-printed form is available and it must be typed carefully. It there are any alterations or erasures, they must be initialled by the solicitor administering the oath, as well as by the person swearing it. There are usually notes in the margin of the form or at the end to help with its completion.

Grant of Probate

This is granted where the validity of the Will has been proved. The Grant is issued to the executors of the Will. To obtain the Grant of Probate, the following must be lodged with the Probate Registry:

(a) Oath for Executors.

(b) Original Will and any Codicils. These are signed by the executors and by the person administering the oath. The Will is then said to be 'marked'. Typed copies or drafts may be accepted if the original is lost. You should always keep a copy of any documents before sending them anywhere.

(c) Any other relevant affidavit evidence.

(d) A form relating to inheritance tax. The necessary form would be IHT205 (or IHT207 where the deceased was domiciled abroad) for excepted estates; or a D18 in all other cases. See below under Inheritance Tax for more detailed information.

(e) The appropriate fee, if any.

If the Probate Registry is satisfied that everything is in order, they will issue the Grant. They will send to the solicitor the original Grant which will be bound to a copy of the Will, and any office copies required, i.e., further copies of the grant bearing the seal of the court, will be provided but without a further copy of the Will.

Letters of Administration

There are two types of Letters of Administration:

(a) A Grant of Letters of Administration (with Will annexed), which is issued to a person, other than an executor, for various reasons, e.g., there is no executor appointed by the Will or where the appointed executor has died without proving the Will.

(b) A Grant of Letters of Administration, which is issued where a person has died intestate and the Grant is necessary to administer the estate.

Applications for Grants of Letters of Administration may be made to the appropriate probate registry and must be supported by:

(a) An Oath for Administrators.

(b) Items (d) and (e) above, where appropriate.

If the court is satisfied, they will send the solicitor the Grant of Letters of Administration together with any office copies requested.

Other grants

The grants discussed above are known as general grants and are the most common. However, there are other grants that may be applied for to cover specific circumstances, e.g., limited grants to cover a certain period of time whilst a legal dispute is being settled regarding the Will, or a grant applying only to particular assets forming part of the estate, such as perishable goods that may need to be disposed of quickly.

On receipt of the grant

The Grant of Probate or Grant of Letters of Administration is proof that the executor (or administrator) is entitled to act in the matter. Office copies of the Grant may have to be

Oath for Executors

IN THE HIGH COURT OF JUSTICE

Extracting Solicitor   Angel Gabriel & Co
Address   2 Milky Way, Barnet, Herts AB1 2XL
                       (ref: ABC/123)

Family Division   DX

*"Principal" or "District
Probate". If "District Probate"
add "at..........................".

The*   District Probate   **Registry** at Southtown

† If necessary to include alias of
deceased in grant add "otherwise
(alias name)" and state below
which is true name and reason
for requiring alias.

IN the Estate of †   JANE BLOGGS

                                                        deceased.

(1) "I" or "We". Insert the full
name, place of residence and
occupation or, if none, description
of the deponent(s). State the
postcode of the deponent(s) and
deceased's place of residence, if
known.

(1)   I, DOREEN BLOGGS of 234 South Road, Northtown, Essex
      ES8 9OB   School Teacher

(2) Or "do solemnly and sincerely
affirm".
(3) Each testamentary paper must
be marked by each deponent, and
by the person administering the
oath.

make Oath and say,(2)   that
(1)   I   believe the paper writing   now produced to and marked by (3) me

to contain the true and original last Will and Testament (4)
of † JANE BLOGGS

(4) "with one, two (or more)
Codicils", as the case may be.

of 123 North Road, Southtown, Essex ER5 7AV

                                                        deceased,

(5) This should be the date of
birth as shown in the Register
of Deaths.
(6) If exact age is unknown, give
best estimate.
(7) Where there are separate legal
divisions in one country, the state,
province, etc., should be
specified.
(8) Delete "no", if there was land
vested in deceased which
remained settled land
notwithstanding his or her death.
(9) Include the names of the
executors who have renounced.

who was born on the (4)   1st   day of   June 1903
and who died on the   2nd   day of   July 2005
aged   102   years (6) domiciled in (7) England
and that to the best of   my   knowledge, information and belief there was (8) [no] land
vested in the said deceased which was settled previously to her death (and not by her Will
(4)   )
and which remained settled land notwithstanding her   death

~~And (1)   further make oath and say (2)~~
~~that (9)~~

~~executor(s) named in the said Will (4)~~
~~have renounced probate thereof~~
~~Notice of this application has been given to~~

~~the executor(s) to whom power is to be reserved, [save~~

(10) Delete or amend as appropriate. Notice of this application
must be served on all executors to
whom power is to be reserved
unless dispensed with by a
Registrar under Rule 27 (3), or
unless Rule 27(1A) applies.

                                                        ](10)

(11) "I am" or "we are". Insert
relationship of the executors to
the deceased only if necessary
to establish title or identification.

And (1)   I   further make Oath and say (2)
that (11) (12)   I am the sole
                                                        Executrix

(12) "The sole", or "the
surviving", or "one of the", or
"are the", or "two of the", etc.

named in the said   Will

                                                        [P.T.O.
                                                        PRO4/1

(13) If there was settled land
the grant should exclude it.
Insert "save and except
settled land".

and that (1) I   will (i) collect, get in and administer according to law the real and
personal estate (13)
of the said deceased; (ii) when required to do so by the Court, exhibit in the Court a full
inventory of the said estate (13)
and when so required render an account thereof to the Court; and (iii) when required to
do so by the High Court, deliver up the grant of probate to that Court; and that to the best
of my   knowledge, information and belief

(14) Complete this paragraph only
if the deceased died on or after
1 April 1981 and an Inland
Revenue Account is not required;
the next paragraphs should be
deleted.

(15) The amount to be inserted here
should be in accordance with the
relevant figure shown in paragraph 1
of the PEP List.

(16) The amount to be inserted here
should be the net value of the estate,
rounded up to the next whole
thousand.

(17) Complete this paragraph only
if an Inland Revenue Account is
required and delete the previous
and following paragraph.

(18) Complete this paragraph only
if the estate qualifies under
paragraph 2 of the PEP list and
delete the previous two paragraphs.

(19) The amount to be inserted
here is the exact amount of the
gross estate.

(20) The amount to be inserted
here is the exact amount of the
net estate.

N.B. The names of all
executors to whom power is to
be reserved must be included
in the Oath.

(14) [the gross estate passing under the grant does not exceed (15) £
and the net estate does not exceed (16) £   and that this is not
a case in which an Inland Revenue Account is required to be delivered]

(17) [the gross estate passing under the grant amounts to £ 285,000
and the net estate amounts to £ 279,000   ].
†

(18) [the gross estate passing under the grant amounts to (19) £   and
the net estate amounts to (20) £   and that this is not a case in
which an Inland Revenue Account is required to be delivered]

SWORN by   DOREEN BOGGS   ⎞
                                                                 ⎟
the above-named Deponent   ⎟
at   ⎟
                                                                 ⎬
                                                                 ⎟
this   day of   ⎟
                                                                 ⎟
Before me,   ⎠
                              A Commissioner for Oaths/Solicitor.

SWORN by   ⎞
                                                                 ⎟
the above-named Deponent   ⎟
at   ⎟
                                                                 ⎬
                                                                 ⎟
this   day of   ⎟
                                                                 ⎟
Before me,   ⎠
                              A Commissioner for Oaths/Solicitor.

SWORN by   ⎞
                                                                 ⎟
the above-named Deponent   ⎟
at   ⎟
                                                                 ⎬
                                                                 ⎟
this   day of   ⎟
                                                                 ⎟
Before me,   ⎠
                              A Commissioner for Oaths/Solicitor.

sent to certain persons to enable the executor (or administrator) to gather in all the money belonging to the estate (i.e., the property of the deceased person). This could be, for example, sending a copy of the Grant to a building society where the deceased person had a savings account. On receipt of the Grant, the building society would close the account and send the money to the executor (or administrator) or his solicitors so that it could be dealt with properly. All this administration of the deceased person's property (known as his 'estate') is called 'winding-up the estate'.

Death verification form

Where a death certificate is required by banks, building societies or insurance companies, it is now possible to send a death verification form to that organisation rather than a death certificate. The death verification form must be signed by a partner of the firm and guarantees that the firm has inspected an original death certificate and has this in its possession.

This procedure has been agreed by the Law Society with the British Bankers Association, the Building Societies Association and the Association of British Insurers. Further details together with a protocol letter and the form can be obtained from the practice advice service at the Law Society.

Copies of Wills and Grants

If a copy of a Will or Grant is required and it is known when and where the grant issued, copies of the Will or Grant may be ordered by post or in person from the Principal Registry of the Family Division in London or from any District Probate Registry. The information required to order should include the full name of the deceased, the date of the grant and where it issued, how many copies are required and the appropriate fee should be paid.

If you need to know whether a grant has issued, a search of the Probate Calendar may be made. Details of where a personal search may be made and where postal applications should be sent are available on HM Courts Service website.

Inheritance tax

Depending on the value of the estate and various other factors, inheritance tax may be payable. It is paid to the Inland Revenue (now known as HM Revenue & Customs) and becomes due six months after the end of the month in which the death occurred. If it is not paid within this time, interest may be charged. The branch of HM Revenue & Customs that deals with inheritance tax is called IR Capital Taxes. Inheritance tax is payable on the net value of the estate which exceeds the tax threshold and will normally have to be paid before a Grant of Representation can be obtained. The tax threshold is a specified amount where, if the net value of the estate exceeds that amount, then inheritance tax may be payable. The tax will not be payable on the entire estate, just the amount which exceeds the tax threshold. This figure is often changed each year at the time of the Budget.

The net value of the estate is calculated by deducting debts and liabilities that the estate has to pay out. Exemptions and reliefs are then deducted. An example of an exemption is property passing to a husband or wife (known as spouse exemption). Other exemptions might be property left to a charity and various other qualifying bodies.

Some inheritance tax may be paid by instalments, e.g., tax on land and buildings and certain other assets. However, interest may be payable if payment is made by instalments.

If help is required on inheritance tax matters, there are various booklets available from HM Revenue & Customs (also on their website). There is also the Probate and Inheritance Tax Helpline (0845 3020900), which is open from 9.00 a.m. to 5.00 p.m., Monday to Friday. This service is managed and staffed by HM Revenue & Customs.

Excepted estates

Where inheritance tax is not payable, this may mean that the estate is an 'excepted estate'. The rules defining exactly what is an excepted estate can be obtained from HM Revenue & Customs, or found on their website. However, generally, an estate is treated as an excepted estate if the gross value of the estate plus the chargeable value of any transfers made in the seven years prior to death does not exceed the inheritance tax threshold; or where these values do not exceed £1 million but because of spouse and/or charity exemption, the net chargeable estate is less than the inheritance tax threshold and therefore there is no inheritance tax to pay.

Form IHT205

Where an application for a Grant of Representation is being made and there is no tax to pay because the estate comes within the excepted estates regulations, the application must be accompanied by Form IHT205 (or IHT207 where the deceased was domiciled abroad).

Form IHT205 gives brief details of the deceased and of the estate. If there is tax to pay, or under certain other circumstances, Form IHT200 (see later), which is a more formal Inland Revenue Account, will have to be completed and sent to IR Capital Taxes.

Before completion of IHT205, enquiries will have to be made to find out all the necessary information, including a valuation of assets. The assets belonging to the estate are valued at the open market value. This means that they are valued as if sold on the open market on the date of the deceased's death.

When completing IHT205, pence should not be included and figures should be rounded down to the next pound. To assist with completing the IHT205, HM Revenue & Customs produce a booklet IHT206.

IHT205 is sent direct to the Probate Registry when making the application for a grant, together with other relevant documents. However, as with all this type of documentation, always remember to keep a copy on your file.

Form IHT200

IHT200 is a more formal account, known as an Inland Revenue account. It must be completed if inheritance tax is payable and also under certain other conditions. When IHT200 is completed, Form D18 (see below) must also be completed. These two forms must be sent to IR Capital Taxes.

Before IHT200 can be completed, the personal representative or his solicitor will arrange for the necessary valuation of any property, shares, furniture, etc., so that the value of these items can be entered on the form.

IHT200 has various supplementary pages. However, each supplementary page only needs to be completed if the main part of the form refers to something that one of the

Return of estate information

Probate and inheritance tax Helpline 0845 30 20 900

*Fill in this form where the person who has died ("the deceased") had their permanent home in the United Kingdom at the date of death and the **gross value of the estate for inheritance tax***

*   *is less than the excepted estate limit, **or***
*   *is less than £1,000,000 **and** there is no inheritance tax to pay because of spouse or charity exemption **only**.*

"✓"
☐
☐

About the person who has died

Title 1.1	Surname 1.2	
	Other name(s) 1.3	
Date of death 1.4 / /	Marital status 1.5	
Occupation 1.6	National Insurance number 1.7	

Surviving relatives "✓"

Husband/Wife 1.8   Brother(s)/Sister(s) 1.9 "✓"   Parent(s) 1.10 "✓"

Number of children 1.11   Number of grandchildren 1.12

You should read the notes about each question in booklet IHT206 as you fill in this form. Everyone must answer questions 2 - 8.

About the estate

No   Yes

2. Within seven years of death did the deceased

   a. make any gifts or other transfers totalling more than £3,000 per year, other than normal birthday, festive or wedding gifts, **or**   ☐ ☐

   b. give up the right to benefit from any assets held in trust.   ☐ ☐

   *If you answer 'Yes' to either part of question 2, include the chargeable value of the gifts in box 12.1. But if this value is more than £100,000 or the assets do not qualify as 'specified transfers' (see IHT206) **stop filling in this form, you will need to fill in form IHT200 instead.***

3. On or after 18 March 1986, did the deceased make a gift where

   a. they continued to benefit from, or had some right to benefit from, or use all or part of the asset, **or**   ☐ ☐

   b. the person receiving the gift did not take full possession of it?   ☐ ☐

   *If you answer 'Yes' to either part of question 3, **stop filling in this form, you will need to fill in form IHT200 instead.***

4. Did the deceased have the right to receive the benefit from any assets held in a trust?   ☐ ☐

   If you answer 'Yes' to question 4 and the deceased
   *   *was entitled to benefit from a single trust, and*
   *   *the value of the assets in that trust was less than £100,000,*
   *include the value of the trust assets in box 12.2. But if the value is more than £100,000, or there is more than one trust, **stop filling in this form, you will need to fill in form IHT200 instead.***

5. Did the deceased own or benefit from any assets outside the UK?   ☐ ☐

   *If you answer 'Yes' to question 5 include the value of the overseas assets in box 12.5. But if the value of the overseas assets is more than £75,000, **stop filling in this form, you will need to fill in form IHT200 instead.***

6. Did the deceased pay premiums on any life insurance policies that were not for the deceased's own benefit or did not pay out to the estate?   ☐ ☐

   If you answer 'Yes' to question 6, you must also answer question 9.

IHT205

	No	Yes

7. Was the deceased a member of a pension scheme or did they have a personal pension policy from which they had not taken their full retirement benefits before the date of death? ☐ ☐

   If you answer 'Yes' to question 7, you must also answer question 10.

8. a. Was the deceased entitled to receive payments from a pension which continued to be paid after they had died (other than arrears of pension)? ☐ ☐

   b. Was a lump sum payable under a pension scheme or pension policy as a result of the death? ☐ ☐

   If you answer 'Yes' to question 8, see IHT206 to find out how to include the asset in section 11.

Do not answer questions 9 or 10 unless you answered 'Yes' to questions 6 or 7.

9. Within seven years of the death, did the deceased

   a. pay any premium on a life insurance policy under which the benefit is payable other than to the estate, or to the spouse of the deceased, *and if so* ☐ ☐

   b. did they buy an annuity at any time? ☐ ☐

   If you answer 'Yes' to question 9(a), see IHT206 to find out how to include the premiums paid on this form. If you answer 'Yes' to both question 9(a) & 9(b), stop filling in this form, you will need to fill in form IHT200 instead.

10. At a time when they were in poor health or terminally ill, did the deceased change their pension scheme or personal pension policy so as to

    a. dispose of any of the benefits payable, or ☐ ☐

    b. make any change to the benefits to which they were entitled? ☐ ☐

    If you answer 'Yes' to question 10(a) or 10(b), stop filling in this form, you will need to fill in form IHT200 instead.

---

11.   Deceased's own assets (including joint assets NOT passing by survivorship - see IHT206)

- *You must include the gross value for each item below, before deduction of any exemption or relief.*
- *You must include all the assets that were part of the deceased's estate as at the date of death, ignoring any changes that may take place through an Instrument of Variation made after the death.*
- *You must make full enquiries so that you can show that the figures that you give in this form are right. If you cannot find out the value for an item, you may include your best estimate.*   Tick the box to show estimates "✓"

11.1 Cash, including money in banks, building societies and National Savings	11.1 £	☐
11.2 Household and personal goods	11.2 £	☐
11.3 Stocks and shares quoted on the Stock Exchange	11.3 £	☐
11.4 Stocks and shares not quoted on the Stock Exchange	11.4 £	☐
11.5 Insurance policies, including bonuses and mortgage protection policies	11.5 £	☐
11.6 Money owed to the person who has died	11.6 £	☐
11.7 Partnership and business interests	11.7 £	☐
11.8 Freehold/leasehold residence of the person who has died	11.8 £	☐

Address (including postcode)

11.9 Other freehold/leasehold residential property	11.9 £	☐

Address (including postcode)

11.10 Other land and buildings	11.10 £	☐

Address/location

11.11 Any other assets not included above	11.11 £	☐

Total estate for which a grant is required (sum of boxes 11.1 to 11.11) | A £ |

2

12.   Other assets forming part of the estate   *Tick the box to show estimates "✓ "*

12.1   Gifts and other lifetime transfers (after deduction of exemptions) | 12.1 £ | | |

Details of gifts

12.2   Assets held in trust for the benefit of the deceased | 12.2 £ | | |

Details of trust

12.3   Share of joint assets passing automatically to the surviving joint owner | 12.3 £ | | |

Details of joint assets

12.4   Nominated assets | 12.4 £ | | |

12.5   Assets outside the United Kingdom (value in £ sterling) | 12.5 £ | | |

Total (sum of boxes 12.1 to 12.5) | B £ |

Gross estate for inheritance tax (A + B) | C |

13.   Debts of the estate

13.1   Funeral expenses | 13.1 £ | | |

13.2   Mortgage on a property in the sole name of the deceased | 13.2 £ | | |

13.3   Other debts owed by the deceased in the UK | 13.3 £ | | |

Total debts owing in the UK (sum of boxes 13.1 to 13.3) | D |

13.4   Debts payable out of trust assets | 13.4 £ | | |

13.5   Share of mortgage on a property owned in joint names | 13.5 £ | | |

13.6   Share of other debts payable out of joint assets | 13.6 £ | | |

13.7   Debts owing to persons outside the UK | 13.7 £ | | |

Total of other debts (sum of boxes 13.4 to 13.7) | E £ |

Total debts (D + E) | F £ |

Net estate for inheritance tax (C - F) | G £ |

14. | *Use this space to provide any other information we have asked for or you would like taken into account.* |
|---|

3

Carried Foward   **G** £

15.   Exemptions (you should read IHT206 before filling in this section)

In the box below, deduct any exemption for assets passing on death to
- *the spouse of the deceased, or*
- *a UK charity or for national purposes*

Describe the extent of the exemption deducted. If for charities, etc give the name of the charity(s) or other organisation(s) benefiting. Where exemptions are deducted for particular assets, list those assets and show the amount deducted.

15.1

H £

Net qualifying value for excepted estates (G - H)   **J** £

15.2   Tax district and/or income tax reference number   **15.2**

If the value in box J is more than the excepted estate limit, you must fill in form IHT200.

If you find something has been left out, or if any of the figures you have given in this form change later on, you only need to tell us if, taking all the omissions and changes into account,
- the figure at box G is now higher than the inheritance tax threshold, **and**
- there are no exemptions to deduct which keep the value at box J below the inheritance tax threshold.

If, at any time, the value at box J is more than the inheritance tax threshold, you must list any new items and the items that have changed in a Corrective Account (form C4) and send it to us with a copy of this form along with a cheque for the tax that has become payable.

The issue of the grant does not mean that there is no inheritance tax due on this estate.

To the best of my/our knowledge and belief, the information I/we have given in this form is correct and complete. I/We have read and understand the statements above.

I/We understand that I/we may have to pay financial penalties if the answers to the questions or figures that I/we give in this form are wrong because of my/our fraud or negligence, OR if the estate fails to qualify as an excepted estate and I/we do not deliver a corrective account within 6 months of the failure coming to my/our notice.

	Name Address	
	Signature & Date	
	Name Address	
	Signature & Date	

Summary

Gross estate in the United Kingdom passing under Will or by intestacy		**A** £
Debts in the United Kingdom owed by the deceased alone		**D** £
Net estate in the United Kingdom	(A - D)	**K** £

Probate and inheritance tax Helpline 0845 30 20 900

4

supplementary pages deals with. IHT200 deals with all the matters relevant to the assets and liabilities of the estate, and provides all the information required by IR Capital Taxes relating to the person who died, including where they lived, whether they left a Will, what they owned, any debts they might have had, as well as details of any exemptions and reliefs being claimed by the estate. It also gives details of the intending personal representatives of the estate.

When completing the IHT200, you should answer all the questions and if something does not apply, you would normally put either a dash or 0 in the appropriate box. The first eight pages are always completed when an Inland Revenue Account is required, together with any supplementary pages.

Page 1 gives formal details about the person who has died; the surviving relatives; and your own firm's details.

Page 2 is completed to identify which supplementary pages have to be completed. Each supplementary page refers to a specific aspect of the estate and is only completed where that aspect is relevant to that estate. The page lists a number of questions and a tick box is completed for each question. If the answer given is 'yes', then the relevant supplementary page must be completed. For example, half-way down the page, there is a question asking whether the deceased owned any stocks or shares. If the answer is 'yes', supplementary page D7 must be completed. All these questions relate to property the deceased held in his own name: property that was owned jointly will be listed on supplementary page D4.

Page 3 gives details of the value of property owned by the deceased where tax may not be paid by instalments.

Page 4 shows liabilities, funeral expenses, exemptions and reliefs.

Page 5 itemises the value of assets in the UK where tax may be paid by instalments.

Page 6 will be completed once any tax due has been worked out. The figures on this page will be taken from the Worksheet IHT (WS). The fee earner will work out how much tax is to be paid and to help him with that, there is another form—a worksheet IHT(WS), so that he can take all the figures from IHT200 and any supplementary pages and fill in the relevant boxes on the worksheet, which will then tell him how to arrive at the correct IHT figure to be paid. The worksheet should not be sent to IR Capital Taxes.

Page 7 shows the final figures for tax to be paid—once this page is completed, the tax liability will have been calculated. At the bottom of this page there is a box for authority for repayment of Inheritance Tax. This box will be completed with the name of any person to whom a cheque should be made payable in the event that there has been an overpayment of tax. If the box is not completed, any cheque will be made payable to all those who sign the form.

Page 8 is a declaration by the personal representative(s) that the information given is true to the best of their knowledge. The form is signed at the bottom by everyone who will be named on the Grant.

If any additional information is to be given regarding IHT200, this should be given on Form D17—Continuation Sheet for Additional Information.

To assist with the completion of IHT200, HM Revenue & Customs produce a booklet IHT210 (How to Fill in Form IHT200). Your firm will probably already have a copy of this but if not, it can be obtained from HM Revenue & Customs. The booklet also contains the address and telephone numbers of IR Capital Taxes either for sending correspondence and forms, as well as their Helpline if you need any advice.

Probate Summary: Form D18

Form D18 (Probate Summary) will be submitted to IR Capital Taxes at the same time as IHT 200. The information given in the D18 will be taken from the IHT200. If tax is payable, a cheque is sent with the D18 to IR Capital Taxes. Even if no tax is payable but an IHT200 has to be submitted, D18 must also be submitted to IR Capital Taxes who will stamp the D18 with their authorisation and return it. The D18 will then be sent to the Probate Registry when applying for the Grant of Representation. D18 is not completed where Form IHT205 is used: IHT205 is sent direct to the Probate Registry and does not need to be sent to IR Capital Taxes.

Payment of inheritance tax

Inheritance tax can be paid either by cheque, electronic transfer, Bank Giro credit, or by using National Savings investments owned by the deceased.

Make cheques payable to 'Inland Revenue only' (although the Inland Revenue has changed its name, at the time of writing, cheques should still be made payable as shown) and:

(a) put a line through any space left on the 'Pay' line;

(b) cross the cheque 'A/c payee';

(c) write the full name of the deceased and the date of death on the back of the cheque.

The cheque with all relevant papers should be sent to the appropriate branch of IR Capital Taxes.

Methods of payment are outlined in the booklet IHT 213: How to Fill in Form IHT(WS).

As previously mentioned, inheritance tax must usually be paid before a Grant of Representation can be obtained. However, HM Revenue & Customs have a scheme called the Inheritance Tax Direct Payment Scheme, which allows payment of inheritance tax directly from money in the deceased's bank or building society (if in his sole name) before probate is granted. Not all banks and building societies operate the scheme so it is advisable to check first and, at the same time, check to see what proof they will need from the personal representatives to show that they are entitled to do this. It is also advisable to check whether the bank or building society will make a charge.

Form D21, which is effectively a request to HM Revenue & Customs for a reference number, must be completed and sent to IR Capital Taxes at least two weeks before submission of the IHT200. IR Capital Taxes will then provide you with a reference number. When the completed IHT200 and D18 are then sent to IR Capital Taxes, form D20 must be completed and sent to the relevant bank or building society that holds the deceased's account(s) from which the inheritance tax is to be paid. The D20 will provide the bank or building society with the IR Capital Taxes reference number and will instruct them to make the payment from the deceased's account. The bank or building society will then pay the inheritance tax direct to IR Capital Taxes who will then complete D18 and send it to your firm.

Additionally, if the estate includes certain qualifying investments such as National Savings investments, the personal representatives can apply to transfer these funds to HM Revenue & Customs to pay the inheritance tax. Also, if the estate includes certain national heritage property, it may be possible to transfer this to the Crown by way of payment in lieu of inheritance tax. Further information on these matters can be obtained from HM Revenue & Customs.

Cheques for court fees

Make cheques payable to 'HM Courts Service' and write the name of the deceased on the reverse of the cheque.

Inland Revenue Account for Inheritance Tax

Fill in this account for the estate of a person who died on or after 18 March 1986.
You should read the related guidance note(s) before filling in any particular box(es).
The notes follow the same numbering as this form, so section headings are shown
by capital letters and the items in each section are on a dark background.

A Probate Registry, Commissary Court or Sheriff Court District

Name A1 SOUTHTOWN DISTRICT REGISTRY   Date of Grant [   ]

B About the person who has died

Title B1 MRS   Surname B2 BLOGGS

First name(s) B3 JANE

Date of birth B4 1 / 6 / 1903   Date of death B5 2 / 7 / 2005

Marital status B6 WIDOW

Last known usual address

B7 123 North Road
Southtown
Essex

Postcode ER5 7AV

Surviving relatives

Husband/Wife B8

Brother(s)/Sister(s) B9

Parent(s) B10

Number of

Children B11 1

Grandchildren B12

Is B7 a Nursing /
Residential home B13

Domicile B14 England & Wales

Occupation B15 Artist

National Insurance number B16 Y M 1 2 3 4 5 6 X

Income tax district B17 SOUTHTOWN 6

Income tax reference or self assessment reference B18 89764321

Did the deceased grant a Power of Attorney? B19

C Solicitor or other person to contact

Name and address of firm or person
dealing with the estate

C1 Angel Gabriel & Co
2 Milky Way
Barnet
Herts

Postcode AB1 2XL

DX number and town

C2 DX 82   Southtown

Contact name and reference

C3 Miss A Star

Telephone number

C4 01638 1234

Fax number

C5 01638 5678

For IR CT use

IHT 200

R2H4154 IRCT 10/03

(D) Supplementary pages

You must answer all of the questions in this section. You should read the notes starting at page 10 of form IHT 210 before answering the questions.

If you answer "Yes" to a question you will need to fill in the supplementary page shown. If you do not have all the supplementary pages you need you can download them from the internet (www.inlandrevenue.gov.uk/cto) or request them from the orderline: e-mail (ir.purchasing@gtnet.gov.uk) or telephone 0845 2341000.

		No	Yes	Page
● The Will	Did the deceased leave a Will?	☐	☐	)))➤ D1
● Domicile outside the United Kingdom	Was the deceased domiciled outside the UK at the date of death?	☐	☐	D2
● Gifts and other transfers of value	Did the deceased make any gift or any other transfer of value on or after 18 March 1986?	☐	☐	)))➤ D3
● Joint assets	Did the deceased hold any asset(s) in joint names with another person?	☐	☐	)))➤ D4
● Nominated assets	Did the deceased, at any time during their lifetime, give written instructions (usually called a "nomination") that any asset was to pass to a particular person on their death?	☐	☐	)))➤ D4
● Assets held in trust	Did the deceased have any right to any benefit from any assets held in trust or in a settlement at the date of death?	☐	☐	D5
● Pensions	Did the deceased have provision for a pension from employers, a personal pension policy or other provisions made for retirement other than the State Pension?	☐	☐	)))➤ D6
● Stocks and shares	Did the deceased own any stocks or shares?	☐	☐	D7
● Debts due to the estate	Did the deceased lend any money, either on mortgage or by personal loan, that had not been repaid by the date of death?	☐	☐	)))➤ D8
● Life insurance and annuities	Did the deceased pay any premiums on any life insurance policies or annuities which are payable to either the estate or to someone else or which continue after death?	☐	☐	)))➤ D9
● Household and personal goods	Did the deceased own any household goods or other personal possessions?	☐	☐	)))➤ ▮
● Interest in another estate	Did the deceased have a right to a legacy or a share of an estate of someone who died before them, but which they had not received before they died?	☐	☐	)))➤ D11
● Land, buildings and interests in land	Did the deceased own any land or buildings in the UK?	☐	☐	D12
● Agricultural relief	Are you deducting agricultural relief?	☐	☐	D13
● Business interests	Did the deceased own all or part of a business or were they a partner in a business?	☐	☐	)))➤ D14
● Business relief	Are you deducting business relief?	☐	☐	)))➤ D14
● Foreign assets	Did the deceased own any assets outside the UK?	☐	☐	D15
● Debts owed by the estate	Are you claiming a deduction against the estate for any money that the deceased had borrowed from relatives, close friends, or trustees, or other loans, overdrafts or guarantee debts?	☐	☐	)))➤ D16

2

E Domicile in Scotland - entitlement to claim legal rights

- Scottish legal rights entitlement (jus relicti/æ and or legitim) is relevant to this estate? No ☐ Yes ☐

- How many children are under 18 ☐ or 18 and over ☐

F Estate in the UK where tax may not be paid by instalments

• Quoted stocks, shares and investments *(box SS1, form D7)*	F1 £
• UK Government and municipal securities *(box SS2, form D7)*	F2 £
• Unquoted stocks, shares and investments	F3 £
• Traded unquoted stocks and shares	F4 £
• Dividends or interest	F5 £
• Premium Bonds	F6 £
• National Savings investments *(show details on form D17)*	F7 £
• Bank and building society accounts *(show details on form D17)*	F8 £
• Cash	F9 £
• Debts due to the deceased and secured by mortgage *(box DD1, form D8)*	F10 £
• Other debts due to the deceased *(box DD1, form D8)*	F11 £
• Rents due to the deceased	F12 £
• Accrued income	F13 £
• Apportioned income	F14 £
• Other income due to the deceased *(box IP4, form D9, box PA1 form D6)*	F15 £
• Life insurance policies *(box IP3, form D9)*	F16 £
• Private health schemes	F17 £
• Income tax or capital gains tax repayment	F18 £
• Household and personal goods *(sold, box HG1, form D10)*	F19 £
• Household and personal goods *(unsold, box HG2, form D10)*	F20 £
• Interest in another estate *(box UE1, form D11)*	F21 £
• Interest in expectancy (reversionary interest)	F22 £
• Other personal assets in the UK *(show details on form D17)*	F23 £
Total assets *(sum of boxes F1 to F23)*	F24 £

3

Liabilities, funeral expenses, exemptions and reliefs

● Liabilities

Name	Description of liability	

	Total liabilities	F25	£

● Funeral expenses

Total of funeral expenses	F26	£
Total liabilities and funeral expenses *(box F25 plus box F26)*	F27	£
Net total of assets less liabilities *(box F24 less box F27)*	F28	£

● Exemptions and reliefs

Total exemptions and reliefs	F29	£
Chargeable value of assets in the UK where tax may not be paid by instalments *(box F28 less box F29)*	F30	£

4

G **Estate in the UK where tax may be paid by instalments**

Do you wish to pay the tax on these assets by instalments? No [ ] Yes [ ]

- Deceased's residence | G1 £
- Other residential property | G2 £
- Farms | G3 £
- Business property | G4 £
- Timber and woodland | G5 £
- Other land and buildings | G6 £

	Interest in a business	Interest in a partnership	
• Farming business	G7.1 £	G7.2 £	G7 £

	Interest in a business	Interest in a partnership	
• Other business interests	G8.1 £	G8.2 £	G8 £

	Farm trade assets	Other business assets	
• Business assets	G9.1 £	G9.2 £	G9 £

- Quoted shares and securities, control holding only | G10 £

	Control holding	Non-control holding	
• Unquoted shares	G11.1 £	G11.2 £	G11 £

	Control holding	Non-control holding	
• Traded unquoted shares	G12.1 £	G12.2 £	G12 £

Total assets *(sum of boxes G1 to G12)* G13 £

Liabilities, exemptions and reliefs

- Name and address of mortgagee

G14 £

- Other liabilities

Total of other liabilities G15 £

Net total of assets less liabilities *(box G13 less boxes G14 and G15)* G16 £

- Exemptions and reliefs

Total exemptions and reliefs G17 £

Chargeable value of assets in the UK where tax may be paid by instalments *(box G16 less box G17)* G18 £

5

H   ## Summary of the chargeable estate

You should fill in form IHT200(WS) so that you can copy the figures to this section and to section J.
If you are applying for a grant without the help of a solicitor or other agent and you do not wish to work out the tax yourself, leave this section and section J blank. Go on to section K.

Assets where tax may not be paid by instalments

- Estate in the UK *(box WS1)*   H1 £
- Joint property *(box WS2)*   H2 £
- Foreign property *(box WS3)*   H3 £
- Settled property on which the trustees would like to pay tax now *(box WS4)*   H4 £

  Total of assets where tax may not be paid by instalments *(box WS5)*   H5 £

Assets where tax may be paid by instalments

- Estate in the UK *(box WS6)*   H6 £
- Joint property *(box WS7)*   H7 £
- Foreign property *(box WS8)*   H8 £
- Settled property on which the trustees would like to pay tax now *(box WS9)*   H9 £

  Total of assets where tax may be paid by instalments *(box WS10)*   H10 £

Other property taken into account to calculate the total tax

- Settled property *(box WS11)*   H11 £
- Gift with reservation *(box WS12)*   H12 £

  Chargeable estate *(box WS13)*   H13 £

  Cumulative total of lifetime transfers *(box WS14)*   H14 £

  Aggregate chargeable transfer *(box WS15)*   H15 £

6

J Calculating the tax liability

Calculating the total tax that is payable

- Aggregate chargeable transfer *(box WS16)* J1 £ _____
- Tax threshold *(box WS17)* J2 £ _____
- Value chargeable to tax *(box WS18)* J3 £ _____

Tax payable *(box WS19)* J4 £ _____

- Tax (if any) payable on lifetime transfers *(box WS20)* J5 £ _____
- Relief for successive charges *(box WS21)* J6 £ _____

Tax payable on total of assets liable to tax *(box WS22)* J7 £ _____

Calculating the tax payable on delivery of this account

- Tax which may not be paid by instalments *(box TX4)* J8 £ _____
- Double taxation relief *(box TX5)* J9 £ _____
- Interest to be added *(box TX7)* J10 £ _____

Tax and interest being paid now which may not be paid by instalments *(box TX8)* J11 £ _____

- Tax which may be paid by instalments *(box TX12)* J12 £ _____
- Double taxation relief *(box TX13)* J13 £ _____
- Number of instalments being paid now J14 _____ / 10 *(box TX15)*
- Tax now payable *(box TX16)* J15 £ _____
- Interest on instalments to be added *(box TX17)* J16 £ _____
- Additional interest to be added *(box TX18)* J17 £ _____

Tax and interest being paid now which may be paid by instalments *(box TX19)* J18 £ _____

Total tax and interest being paid now on this account *(box TX20)* J19 £ _____

K Authority for repayment of inheritance tax

In the event of any inheritance tax being overpaid the payable order for overpaid tax and interest in connection with this estate should be made out to

_____

7

Declaration

I/We wish to apply for a **L1** Grant of Probate

To the best of my/our knowledge and belief, the information I/we have given and the statements I/we have made in this account and in supplementary pages **L2** D1, D6, D7, D10, D12 attached (together called "this account") are correct and complete.

I/We have made the fullest enquiries that are reasonably practicable in the circumstances to find out the open market value of all the items shown in this account. The value of items in box(es)

L3 _____ are provisional

estimates which are based an all the information available to me/us at this time. I/We will tell IR Capital Taxes the exact value(s) as soon as I/we know it and I/we will pay any additional tax and interest that may be due.

I/We understand that I/we may be liable to prosecution if I/we deliberately conceal any information that affects the liability to inheritance tax arising on the deceased's death, OR if I/we deliberately include information in this account which I/we know to be false.

I/We understand that I/we may have to pay financial penalties if this account is incorrect by reason of my/our fraud or negligence, OR if I/we fail to remedy anything in this account which is incorrect in any material respect within a reasonable time of it coming to my/our notice.

I/We understand that the issue of the grant does not mean that

- I/we have paid all the inheritance tax and interest that may be due on the estate, or
- the statements made and the values included in this account are accepted by IR Capital Taxes.

I/We understand that IR Capital Taxes

- will only look at this account in detail after the grant has been issued
- may need to ask further questions and discuss the value of items shown in this account
- may make further calculations of tax and interest payable to help the persons liable for the tax make provision to meet the tax liability.

I/We understand that where we have elected to pay tax by instalments that I/we may have to pay interest on any unpaid tax according to the law.

Each person delivering this account, whether as executor, intending administrator or otherwise must sign below to indicate that they have read and agreed the statements above.

| Full name and address

Doreen Bloggs
234 South Road
Northtown
Essex
ES8 9OB

Signature   Date | Full name and address

Signature   Date |
| Full name and address

Signature   Date | Full name and address

Signature   Date |

8

Inland
Revenue
Capital Taxes

Probate summary

Fill in this form to give details of the estate that becomes the property of the personal representatives of the deceased. It is this property for which the grant of representation is to be made. You should read form D18(Notes) before filling in this form.

A	Name and address

Angel Gabriel & Co
2 Milky Way
Barnet
Herts
AB1 2XL   (ref: ABC/123)

Probate registry

SOUTHTOWN

Date of grant
(for probate registry use)

B	About the person who has died

Title   MRS

Surname   BLOGGS

First name(s)   JANE

Date of death   2 / 7 / 2005

Domicile

Last known usual address

123 North Road
Southtown
Essex

Postcode   ER5 7AV

C	Summary from IHT200		

Add the value of any general power property on form D5 to boxes PS1-PS5

Gross assets, section F, box 24	PS1	£
Gross assets, section G, box 13	PS2	£
Gross value to be carried to Probate papers *(box PS1 plus box PS2)*	PS3	£
Liabilities, section F, box F27	PS4	£
Liabilities, section G, boxes G14 plus G15	PS5	£
Net value to be carried to Probate papers *(box PS3 less box PS4 less box PS5)*	PS6	£
Tax and interest paid on this account, section J, box J19	PS7	£

	Miss A Star	/ /
Signature of person or firm calculating the amount due	Contact name and /or reference	Date

(For IR CT use only)

IR CT reference

EDP

Cashier's reference

IR CT Cashiers

| D18 | (PDF) Version 2.0.0.2 |

R0G4138 IRCT7/01

Post-grant procedures

Once the Grant of Representation is received from the court, the fee earner will check that the correct number of office copies have been sent to him and that all the details in the Grant are correct. Office copies of the Grant will be sent to each institution holding money belonging to the estate, asking them to record that they have seen the Grant and asking them to release the amounts held plus any interest.

Some assets, e.g., property, shares, etc. may have to be sold in order to satisfy legacies given under the Will. Additionally, the personal representatives may have had to take out a bank loan in order to pay Inheritance Tax and, if so, this loan will have to be repaid from the monies belonging to the estate.

Before the personal representatives dispose of the property comprising the estate, they may advertise in various newspapers giving at least two months' notice of the distribution of the estate, so that any unknown creditors or would-be claimants can come forward. These advertisements are known as statutory advertisements and protect the personal representatives against liability if an unknown claimant comes forward later. The advertisements give notice of intention to distribute the assets of the estate, requiring any person interested as a beneficiary or creditor to send particulars to them within a stated time limit (a minimum of two months from date of notice). The notice is given by placing an advertisement in the London Gazette; advertising in a newspaper local to the district in which any land to be distributed is situated; and advertising in any local or national papers which might be appropriate in the circumstances, e.g., if the deceased had business in a different district, it would be appropriate to advertise in the local paper in case creditors are in that area. Once the time limit has expired, the personal representatives may distribute the estate.

If the personal representatives are executors—appointed under the Will, they may have taken out these advertisements at the outset before waiting for the Grant as their authority comes from the Will itself. However, if the personal representatives are administrators, they might wait until they receive the Grant of Letters of Administration from the court as their authority is derived from the court, rather than through a Will.

Separate steps are taken where the personal representatives are aware of a beneficiary but cannot find him.

A record will be kept of any money brought in and this money will be held on deposit in a designated account. After any debts and liabilities of the estate have been paid, any legacies will be paid and when money is sent to a beneficiary, a receipt for that person's signature should also be enclosed with any payment.

Final estate accounts must be drawn up, showing how the assets and liabilities have been dealt with. These accounts will normally be signed by the personal representatives to indicate their approval. The accounts are then submitted to the beneficiaries who should also sign an endorsement agreeing to them.

Possible disputes

If anyone is disputing a Will or wishes something to do with it to be decided at court, such proceedings are usually commenced in the Chancery Division of the High Court. Some county courts have jurisdiction provided the net estate does not exceed a certain amount.

Caveats

A *caveat* is a written notice given by someone to (in this instance) the Principal Registry or a district registry not to issue a Grant without first giving notice to that person. A fee is payable to the court when entering a *caveat*. These are sometimes entered by a person who, for various reasons, has an interest in the estate of a deceased person. Where a *caveat* has been entered and an application is subsequently made for a Grant, various procedures must be followed. A *caveat* is effective only for six months, although extensions may be applied for. An application may be made to find out whether there is a *caveat* against the issue of a Grant. Such application may be made to any registry, as they all hold a computerised index.

Standing search

If someone simply wants to know whether a Grant has been issued, they may make an application to the Principal Registry or to a district probate registry accompanied by the appropriate fee. They will be sent an office copy of any Grant made within 12 months before, or six months after, receipt of the application. The application can be renewed at the end of six months.

Other deeds and documents

During the course of working in a probate department, you will come across deeds (see page 271) of trust and of gift, among many other things. If these are not typed onto a printed form they are typed in the same way as other deeds, i.e., usually no blank pages and with a backsheet.

Deed of variation

This is a document that allows the beneficiaries of a deceased's estate to alter the way that some or all of the assets are distributed. It is entered into by the beneficiaries, the personal representatives and any trustees, and must normally be done within 2 years of the person's death. A deed of variation might be entered into perhaps because one or more of the beneficiaries wishes to redirect whatever they have inherited to someone else, so that person can benefit straight away. Making changes in this way may also be beneficial for various tax purposes, including inheritance tax.

A deed of variation is also sometimes known as a deed of family arrangement, a deed of assignment, a deed of surrender, or a deed of release.

Living Will

Living Wills are now becoming quite common. These are made by people who wish a certain course of action to be taken if they become extremely ill and are unlikely to recover. The document will normally be set out in the same way as an ordinary Will and will commence with words along the lines of 'I hereby revoke all former Living Wills made by me and declare this to be my last Living Will'. It will go on to say that if that person at any time suffers from certain medical conditions (probably listed in a schedule at the end of the document) and they have been examined by independent doctors and are unlikely to recover, then in those circumstances, they will want certain things to happen, such as there being no medical intervention to prolong or sustain their life, or they are not to be force-fed, etc. The document will go on to absolve doctors from any liability in the matter and will appoint someone to ensure their wishes are carried out. It will then be signed and witnessed in same way as a Will. However, at the time of writing, Living Wills are not always upheld by the courts.

Power of Attorney

A Power of Attorney is a deed which gives someone else the power to act in the name of the person making the Power of Attorney with regard to any property they own. The person who is giving the authority is called the donor and the person to whom the authority is given is known as an attorney. The document must state how the power is given, e.g., it could be in general terms dealing with all the donor's financial affairs, or perhaps in specific terms, such as being limited to the sale of particular property. There are legal restrictions on what an attorney can do, e.g., he cannot use it to benefit himself (unless the donor would normally have been expected to provide for him in any event).

An Enduring Power of Attorney

This is another type of Power of Attorney that someone might sign so that in the event that they become unable to deal with their own affairs, the Enduring Power of Attorney gives someone else power to deal with their property in their name once certain conditions have been met, e.g., if they become ill to a certain specified extent (which would be set out in the document). The power to act can be given to more than one person and, like an ordinary Power of Attorney, can be in general or specific terms. Once the Donor becomes mentally incapacitated, the Attorney must register the Enduring Power of Attorney with the Court of Protection as soon as possible. The Court of Protection looks after the interests of people who cannot look after their own affairs.

TEST YOURSELF ON CHAPTER 11

Test your knowledge by completing this assignments. If you find that you have difficulty with anything, read the chapter again until you are happy with your answers.

1. Explain the basic contents of a Will.

2. Type out a draft Will basing the clauses and layout on the example given in this chapter. Use the following information to do this. The Will is for Valerie Simmons of 19 Astronomer's Row, Northtown, Sussex SE4 2LQ. She has appointed her son, Andrew Simmons of the same address to be the executor. She wishes to include suitable clauses stating that: any debts should be paid off; she is leaving £750 to a cats' home called Pussies Galore of Cat Hill, Felixstowe, Suffolk FG3 5PQ; the remainder of her estate will be left to her son, Andrew.

3. What sort of information must be included in an Oath for Executors?

4. What is inheritance tax?

5. What is the purpose of applying for a Grant to a deceased person's estate? Explain the procedures involved.

6. Explain the following terms:

   (a) codicil;

   (b) caveat.

7. How might you obtain a copy of a Will or Grant?

8. How would you find out whether a Grant had already been issued to someone?

9. Now go through the chapter and if there are any words that are unfamiliar to you or that you cannot spell, write or type them correctly several times until you feel you know them.

12

Conveyancing

Conveyancing includes matters relating to the transfer of ownership of land, rights and usage over land and buildings on that land. Such property is either 'freehold' or 'leasehold' (see below). The person selling property is called the 'Vendor' or 'Seller' and the person buying it is the 'Purchaser' or 'Buyer'.

It is also helpful to know the distinction between real property and personal property. Real property is freehold property such as land, houses, etc., and personal property is other property such as a necklace or a car.

Freehold

Freehold land can be inherited without restriction after the owner dies, is owned immediately the transaction transferring possession of it has taken place and is free from conditions, e.g., it is not held for a specified period of time. You may come across the term 'fee simple absolute in possession' which basically means that the property is freehold. You will find that most houses are freehold.

Leasehold

A lease gives exclusive possession to the person holding the lease. It sets out the rights and obligations of the landlord and tenant to each other, states the rent payable and the period of time the lease is to be held for. Leasehold property is owned for a definite period of time, e.g., 99 years. You may come across the term 'term of years absolute' which means that the property is leasehold. Most flats are leasehold as, indeed, are most commercial premises (which often have fairly short leases). See also page 330 regarding leases.

A deed

Most transactions involving leasehold and freehold property must be made by deed, except in cases involving leasehold property where the term does not exceed three years, although in those cases, there are certain conditions to be fulfilled. A deed is a document which passes something, for example, property, a right or an obligation, from one person to another. A deed must be in writing but, with proposals for moves towards full electronic conveyancing, it will be possible for deeds to be in electronic format with electronic signatures. It must also be clear from the deed that it is intended to be a deed by the person making it. This can be done either by describing itself as a deed or expressing itself to be executed or signed as a deed. You will see in old documents that a deed bore the words at the end 'SIGNED, SEALED and DELIVERED by . . . in the presence of' and it was signed by the parties to the deed. Alongside their signatures was a little red wafer seal (a red circular 'star' about half an inch in diameter). There is no longer a requirement for an individual to seal a deed or for all companies to have a seal, and you will now encounter words at the end such as 'SIGNED and DELIVERED as a deed by . . . in the presence of or 'SIGNED as a deed by . . . in the presence of'. (See also Chapter 10 regarding company seals and page 27 regarding attestation clauses and general information regarding deeds and other documents.) This signing of a deed is known as 'executing' it and it must be done in the correct manner. How this is done varies as to whether it is to be executed by an individual or a company or some other organisation. Before a deed becomes effective, it has to be 'delivered'. 'Delivery' occurs when the person executing the deed (or someone authorised to act on his behalf) does something to show that he intends the deed to be effective, e.g., handing over the deed to the other party; or confirming that it has been sent through the post.

Registration of land

A great deal of land in England and Wales is registered with the Land Registry. The purpose of registration is to enable a record of ownership and any mortgages (see page 333) and certain other interests in that land to be recorded, which greatly simplifies transactions involving that land. Additionally, if land is registered, the Land Registry guarantees that if someone is shown on the register as the owner of land, a potential buyer can rely on that as being proof of ownership. Also, when property is registered, transactions can be carried out using simple forms rather than long documents. All freehold property and leasehold property where the lease is for over 7 years is now subject to compulsory registration. The rules governing land registration state that when certain transactions regarding land take place, registration will be 'triggered' and where this happens, if the land is currently unregistered, it must be registered with the Land Registry once the transaction has taken place. An example of this would be if unregistered land were sold, once the sale is complete, the new owner must register the land with the Land Registry. The Land Registry has local district registries to cover particular areas (not always the one nearest the property) and it is important that all applications to the Land Registry are made to the correct district registry.

Registered property is given a Title Number. This is the number given to it by the Land Registry and is shown on all documents relating to that land. All correspondence and forms sent to the Land Registry should bear the Title Number. The Title Number has letters first and then a figure, e.g., HD 123456. The letters show the area in which the land was registered.

The owner of registered property is called the 'registered proprietor' by the Land Registry.

Addresses and details of the relevant District Land Registry relating to a particular area can be obtained from any district land registry or from the *Directory of Local Authorities* (Sweet & Maxwell). Land Registry addresses are also included at the back of this book. All cheques for the Land Registry should be made payable to 'Land Registry'.

Where land is unregistered, the process of buying and selling varies slightly, and this is dealt with briefly on page 317.

The Register held by the Land Registry

The Land Registry holds a register on all properties that have been registered in England and Wales. A copy of the register relating to a particular property will show the title number of the property and will be divided into three sections to include the following information.

(a) The Property Register. This describes the land, i.e., gives the address or location of the property and refers to a filed plan (or 'title plan') showing the boundaries of the property. It will state whether the property is freehold or leasehold. If the registered property is leasehold, it gives brief details of the lease, such as terms of the lease and rent payable. This part of the register may also give details of any rights that are of benefit to the land, e.g., a right of way over someone else's land.

(b) The Proprietorship Register gives details of the registered proprietor or owner. It also states the quality of the title to the property, for example, where the Land Registry is completely satisfied about the ownership of the property, they will give absolute title. Depending upon the circumstances, other different classes of title may be given.

Since April 2000, the Proprietorship Register will now give the price paid or value of the property unless the Land Registry decides that there are particular circumstances where this is not appropriate.

(c) The Charges Register consists of entries adverse to the land, for example, a mortgage (see page 333), and may also give notice of rights and interests to which the property may be subject, for example, a right of way over the property.

When someone wishes to see a copy of the register relating to a particular property, they apply to the Land Registry for official copies of the register (see page 277). Until fairly recently, these were referred to as Office Copy Entries.

Until October 2003, when someone purchased property, the Land Registry would issue an official legal document proving ownership of the property. This would be in the form of either a Land Certificate or a Charge Certificate. A Land Certificate shows details of the property which are registered at the Land Registry and which are contained on the register, together with a plan of the property. A Charge Certificate is similar to a Land Certificate but, where the property is mortgaged, also contains a copy of the mortgage deed. However, Land and Charges Certificates are no longer issued by the Land Registry. Anyone now purchasing property will have a Title Information Document issued to them. This is simply an official copy of the register together with, where appropriate, a plan. A plan will be issued only where a previous plan has been amended or a new plan is drawn up for the first time. The Title Information Document is not a legal document of title but is for information only. Title Information Documents and old Land or Charge Certificates should not be lodged with the Land Registry.

These changes are part of the Land Registry's move towards electronic conveyancing.

Sale/Purchase of a freehold property which has been registered

Usually the first steps in the sale and/or purchase of a house are done through an estate agent. In any event, the parties to the transaction agree to sell or buy the house at a certain price 'subject to contract' (see page 274). This means that the terms they have agreed between them are not legally binding until contracts are exchanged (see page 290). Quite often the property will include the sale of curtains, carpets, etc. at an agreed price for these items. The steps to be taken shown here may be varied at certain stages and some of the forms used may differ slighty with regard to domestic conveyancing if the firm you are working for is implementing the National Conveyancing Protocol (see page 336).

The solicitor acting on behalf of the person selling the house ('the Vendor') will prepare documentation for the Purchaser's solicitor. Also, if the property is mortgaged, the lender must be notified.

The Vendor's solicitors may obtain a Land Certificate from the owner of the property or, if the property is mortgaged, they may obtain a Charge Certificate which might be held by the lender. However, as mentioned above, these documents are no longer issued or required by the Land Registry and, if referred to, would be used for information purposes only. The Vendor's solicitor will, however, obtain from the Land Registry official copies of the entries on the register (see page 277). If the property is unregistered, the Vendor's solicitor will obtain the title deeds.

If the Vendor's solicitor has adopted the National Conveyancing Protocol for the transaction, he will put together a pack of information relating to the property (see page 336).

Home Information Pack

At the time of writing, it is envisaged that Home Information Packs will be introduced in early 2007 for most residential properties. This will be a pack of information supplied at an early stage by the Vendor and it is thought that it will include details of the terms of the sale; proof of title to the property; a list of fixtures and fittings; standard searches; any planning consents, etc; any warranties or guarantees; an energy efficiency assessment; the Seller's Property Information form (see page 287); and a Home Condition Report (HCR). The HCR will be produced by accredited home inspectors and will be in a certain format. It will not be a valuation of the property: it will be a report on the condition of the property. The HCR will show the date of inspection of the property and it is envisaged that it will have a limited lifespan, requiring a further report once that period of time expires.

If the property to be sold is leasehold, the Home Information Pack will also contain a copy of the lease; details of service charges on the property plus details of building insurance; the landlord or management company's memorandum and articles of association (see page 228), together with details of any company regulations; and details of any current or future works to the property.

Subject to contract

The Purchaser's solicitor will write to the solicitor acting for the Vendor to confirm that he is acting in the matter. Correspondence between the parties up to exchange of contracts is often headed 'Subject to Contract' or it is stated in the correspondence that everything is subject to contract. This confirms that anything agreed at this stage is not legally binding until signed contracts have been exchanged. However, although this is the usual procedure, it is unlikely that a contract would be entered into just because 'subject to contract' was omitted from the correspondence. An example of this type of letter is shown below.

Dear Sirs,

re: Green from Brown   SUBJECT TO CONTRACT
76 Burnt Oak Road, Moreland, EN6 8LB

We are acting on behalf of Miss Elizabeth Mary Green who, we understand, has agreed to purchase the above property from your client, Mr Albert Francis Brown, at the price of £96,000, subject to contract.

We look forward to receiving the draft contract from you as soon as possible.

Yours faithfully,

Enquiries of the local authority

Before contracts can be exchanged, certain enquiries have to be made by the Purchaser's solicitors of the local authority where the property is situated. The enquiries are made by requesting the local authority to carry out searches relating to the property in question. The procedure is known as 'making local searches'. These searches are made to ensure that there are no adverse entries in the register of charges kept by the local authority which might affect the land, e.g., there could be some financial charge or restriction on the property, and also to ascertain whether there is anything else affecting the property that the local authority may know about. The searches are made irrespective of whether or not the land is registered.

Addresses of local authorities can be found in the *Directory of Local Authorities* (Sweet & Maxwell). This directory lists the local authorities in England, Wales and Scotland and also contains information relating to conveyancing and land registration fees and charges. To find details relating to a particular authority, if the district is known, it can be looked up under its name, but if the district is not known, the relevant authority can be found by looking up the place name in another part of the book which lists by name thousands of towns, cities, villages, etc. The *Directory* also contains names and addresses of other useful organisations. You may find the *Directory* useful when you have to provide details of the administrative area of a property. This information is often required to be entered on Land Registry forms. An administrative area is the county, county and district, county borough or London borough. If you are not sure whether you should enter two area names, e.g., the county and the district, then enter both. If you are dealing with registered property, you should find the administrative area on any title information documents.

Local searches can be made electronically (see the section below on National Land Information Service). However, printed forms may be completed and submitted to the local authority. One of the forms is Requisition for Search in the Register of Local Land Charges (Form LLC1). Local authorities have to keep a register of certain matters affecting properties in their area and this register is called the Register of Local Land Charges. It contains details of certain types of financial burdens and other restrictions affecting properties within their area. The Register is in 12 parts and what is contained in each part can be seen on the reverse of the form (see page 279). A search can be made in just one of these parts of the Register or all of it. In most conveyancing matters, a search would be made in all of the Register. Form LLC1 asks the local authority to search their register and to certify either that there are no entries affecting that property, or to give details of any entries. The form must be completed in duplicate and, where it is a pre-printed form purchased from legal stationers, it will have a copy attached for this purpose. However, it is not self-carbonating and therefore you will have to use carbon paper with this form. Most firms complete forms on-screen nowadays and these will obviously not require any carbon copies as a duplicate will usually be printed where necessary. However, a copy should also be kept on the file or the file noted to show that the search form has been sent. Most firms will have their own system for this.

The other form, Form Con 29 (2002), which accompanies LLC1, comes in two parts. Part I is called Con 29 Part I Standard Enquiries of Local Authority (2002) and Part II is called Con 29 Part II Optional Enquiries of Local Authority (2002). Each part should be completed in duplicate. Part I will be completed in all instances and Part II will be completed where any of the Optional Enquiries listed on that form are required. If Optional Enquiries are required, the box on the front of Part II indicating which enquiries are required must be completed and the form should be attached to Part I. A fee is payable for all local authority enquiries. Fees may vary depending on which local authority you are sending the enquiries to.

Form Con 29 enquires about matters which are not on the Register of Local Land Charges, but over which the local authority has control, e.g., planning and building regulations, compulsory purchase orders, etc. The actual enquiries are listed on each Part of the Con 29.

Any further additional enquiries which are not dealt with by form Con 29 must be attached on a separate sheet of paper in duplicate, and an additional fee will be charged for any query that the local authority is willing to answer. Where optional or additional enquiries are required to be answered, this should be indicated in the appropriate box on Part 1 of the form.

When submitting Con 29 (2002), a plan in duplicate identifying the property must be attached to the form(s).

The searches will reveal only matters relevant to the particular property in question and not to any neighbouring property, even if something on neighbouring property could affect the property being searched, e.g., planning permission may have been granted to build on adjoining land, but this will not be revealed on the search—a search would also have to be made relating to the adjoining land.

If a search is urgent, you should write clearly, in red, on the forms 'Urgent: please expedite'. You should also telephone the local authority to see if they can do the search quickly. However, they are not obliged to do your search any quicker than anyone else's.

The forms are signed and dated and then sent off to the local authority where the land is situated with the cheque for the fee. The cheque should be made payable to the authority. A covering letter is not required. The fee would be for a single parcel of land if it is just one property that is concerned, plus the fee for any Part II and additional enquiries. Property is often referred to as a 'parcel of land'. Simply, a parcel is one particular property or piece of land and has one Title Number (see page 272). The fees payable for these searches may vary with each local authority so you should check with them by telephone as to what their fees are before sending the forms to them. A note should be made on the file that the search has been sent off (or a copy of the search kept on the file), the date it was sent, and how much the fee was.

If local searches have been made and would be more than three months old before contracts are exchanged (see later) or more than six months old at completion, fresh searches will normally be carried out so that the information is up to date.

Plans identifying the property are usually required by most local authorities before they will carry out these searches.

Unique Property Reference Number (UPRN)

You will notice in box B on Form Con 29 that there is a space for NLPG UPRN. NLPG stands for National Land and Property Gazetteer. Although not yet widely used, the NLPG has given reference numbers to properties in England and Wales and these are called unique property reference numbers (UPRNs). UPRNs will be a means by which government departments, e.g., local authorities, HM Revenue & Customs, etc can quickly and easily identify properties. If the UPRN is known, it should be inserted, although at the time of writing, it is not essential to include this. UPRNs can be obtained from the providers of NLIS services (see below).

Other searches

As well as the local searches mentioned above, a separate search (Con 29DW) must normally be made with the water authority in order to obtain information about the water and drainage to the property.

Additionally, there are other searches you will encounter from time to time, such as a Coal Mining Search (Con 29M), which is used to ascertain whether a property is or may be affected by any previous, current or proposed coal mining activity in a particular area. A Coal Mining Search would be sent to The Coal Authority. Another search that you may occasionally make is a Commons Registration Search (CR Form 21) which is made to find out whether land is registered as a village green or common land, which would give members of the public certain rights over it, e.g., such as allowing animals to graze on it. This type of search would usually be carried out where a building company is buying undeveloped land to build on, especially if the land is already near a village green.

In addition to these, many other specialist searches may be required, e.g., for properties in particular areas affected by local regulations or perhaps mineral extractions, polluting processes or properties near to tube lines or other tunnels or to find the location of sewers, cables, electricity and gas pipes, etc.

National Land Information Service (NLIS)

NLIS is a service providing information about land and property, enabling such information to be provided in a faster and more efficient way. It promotes electronic delivery of that information and part of the service has been to develop the way searches are carried out. There are three private organisations that are licensed to operate the NLIS services via the internet. When someone subscribes to one of these providers, they can obtain information online about a particular property. Currently, information can be obtained from local authorities, the Land Registry and the Coal Authority, as well as various other searches and information. Therefore, rather than doing local searches and certain other searches individually and posting them, a subscriber can go online, input details of the property and can receive back search results electronically. Subscribers will be billed directly by the service provider.

As mentioned above, NLIS providers can identify and match properties against the UPRN and if a UPRN is required for other purposes, an NLIS provider can supply this.

The organisations operating NLIS services are NLIS Searchflow; TM Search; and Transaction Online. Their web addresses are given in the appropriate section at the back of this book.

Official copies

The Vendor's solicitor will obtain as soon as possible, from the appropriate district registry of the Land Registry, official copies of any entries in the register (see page 273) at the Land Registry and a copy of the filed plan. These are copies of the entries in the register and are marked with the date of issue so that anyone looking at them may know how up to date they are. Official copies will quote a time as well as a date. This is because it is possible for the Land Registry to complete applications throughout the day and all applications will take priority from the time that they are entered on the Land Registry's day list. Therefore, it will be possible, if there is more than one application made in the same day relating to one property, for different versions of the register to exist during a particular day.

Once the official copies are received, they are sent to the Purchaser's solicitors, a copy having been kept for your file. The Purchaser's solicitors will also later apply for up-to-date official copies. One of the reasons for obtaining official copies is to find out whether there is anything registered against the land, such as a mortgage that must be repaid before the property is sold, or whether someone has registered some other sort of interest or right over the land. Application for official copies may be made on Form OC1, together with the

Form LLC1. *(Local Land Charges Rules 1977 Schedule 1, Form C)*

Official Number _____
(To be completed by the registering authority)

The duplicate of this form must also be completed: a carbon copy will suffice

For directions, notes and fees see overleaf.

Insert name and address of registering authority in space below

> Land Charges Department
> Moreland District Council
> 56 Green Street
> Moreland
> Herts
> EN3 2NL

Register of local land charges

Requisition for search

and official certificate

of search

fold

Requisition for search
(A separate requisition must be made in respect of each parcel of land except as explained overleaf)

An official search is required in *Part(s)* _____ *of*
the register of local land charges kept by the above-named registering authority for subsisting registrations against the land [defined in the attached plan and]² described below.

Description of land sufficient to enable it to be identified

> 76 Burnt Oak Road, Moreland
> EN7 8CB

Name and address to which certificate is to be sent

> Peter Wolf & Co
> Red Riding Hood Lane
> Northtown
> Essex
> 1CD 3LA

Signature of applicant *(or his solicitor)*

Date
> 1 June 2005

Telephone number
> 01234 5678

Reference
> PW/74

Enclosure
Cheque/~~Money Order/Postal Order/Giro~~

Official certificate of search

It is hereby certified that the search requested above reveals no subsisting registrations³

or the _____ registrations described in the Schedule hereto³ up to and including the date of this certificate.

Signed..

On behalf of ....⁴
Date

To be completed by authorised officer

1 Delete if inappropriate. Otherwise insert Part(s) in which search is required.

2 Delete if inappropriate. (A plan should be furnished in duplicate if it is desired that a copy should be returned.)

3 Delete inapplicable words. (The Parts of the Schedule should be securely attached to the certificate and the number of registrations disclosed should be inserted in the space provided. Only Parts which disclose subsisting registrations should be sent.)

4 Insert name of registering authority.

Directions and notes

1 This form and the duplicate should be completed and sent by post to or left at the office of the registering authority.

2 A separate requisition for search should be made in respect of each parcel of land in respect of which a search is required except where, for the purpose of a single transaction, a certificate is required in respect of two or more parcels of land which have a common boundary or are separated only by a road, railway, river, stream or canal.

3 'Parcel of land' means land (including a building or part of a building) which is separately occupied or separately rated or, if not occupied or rated, in separate ownership. For the purpose of this definition an owner is the person who (in his own right or as trustee for any other person) is entitled to receive the rack rent of land, or, where the land is not let at a rack rent, would be so entitled if it were so let.

4 The certificate of the result of an official search of the register refers to any subsisting registrations, recorded against the land defined in the application for search, in the Parts of the register in respect of which the search is requested. The Parts of the register record:

Part 1	General financial charges.
Part 2	Specific financial charges.
Part 3	Planning charges.
Part 4	Miscellaneous charges.
Part 5	Fenland ways maintenance charges.
Part 6	Land compensation charges.
Part 7	New towns charges.
Part 8	Civil aviation charges.
Part 9	Opencast coal charges.
Part 10	Listed buildings charges.
Part 11	Light obstruction notices.
Part 12	Drainage scheme charges.

5 An office copy of any entry in the register can be obtained on written request and on payment of the prescribed fee.

Fees

Official search (including issue of official certificate of search) in respect of one parcel of land —

in any one part of the register £2.00

in the whole of the register

(i) where the requisition is made by electronic means in accordance with rule 16 . . . . £4.00

(ii) in any other case £6.00

and in addition, but subject to a maximum fee of £16.00, in respect of each additional parcel of land, where more than one parcel is included in the same requisition (see notes 2 and 3 above) whether the requisition is for a search in the whole or any part of the register £1.00

Office copy of any entry in the register (not including a copy or extract of any plan or document filed pursuant to these Rules) £1.50

Office copy of any plan or other document filed pursuant to these Rules . . . . Such fee as may be reasonable according to the time and work involved.

All fees must be prepaid

Oyez   7 Spa Road, London SE16 3QQ   *2003 Edition*
11.2003 F41828

LLC1   5063019
                                                                               ★ ★ ★

CON 29 Part I STANDARD ENQUIRIES of Local Authority (2002 Edition)
This form and a plan must be submitted in duplicate.

The Law Society

Please type or use BLOCK LETTERS

A.

> **To [Local Authority address]**
>
> LAND CHARGES DEPARTMENT
> MORELAND DISTRICT COUNCIL
> 56 GREEN STREET
> MORELAND
> HERTS
> EN3 2NL

For Local Authority Completion only

> Search No. ....
>
> The replies are attached
>
> Signed: ....
>
> Proper Officer
>
> Dated: ....

B.

> **Enter address of the land/property**
>
> NLPG UPRN:
>
> Address 1:
>
> Address 2:
>
> Street: 76 BURNT OAK ROAD
>
> Locality:
>
> Town/Village: MORELAND
>
> County: HERTFORDSHIRE
>
> Post Code: EN7 8CB

C.

> **Other roadways, footways and footpaths**

D.

> **Attachments**
>
> **A plan in duplicate must be attached. This form may be returned if the land/property cannot be easily identified.**
>
> Optional Enquiries to be answered: YES/~~NO~~
> *(if so, please attach Con 29 Part II Optional Enquiries of Local Authority form)*
>
> Are any additional enquiries attached?   ~~YES~~/NO
> *(If so, please attach on a separate sheet in duplicate)*

E.

> **Fees**
>
> £   **   is enclosed/NLIS transfer (delete as applicable).
>
> Signed:
>
> Dated: 1 June 2005
>
> Reference: PW/74
>
> Tel No: 01234 5678
>
> Fax No: 01234 5679
>
> E-mail Contact:

Notes.

> A. Enter name and address of Council for the area to which this form has been officially submitted. If the property is near a local authority boundary, consider raising certain enquiries (e.g. road schemes) with the adjoining Council.
> B. Enter address and description of the property, add the NLPG UPRN (Unique Property Reference Number) where known.
> C. Enter name and/or mark on plan any other roadways, footpaths and footways abutting the property (in addition to those entered in Box B) to which a reply to enquiry 2 and 3.6 is required.
> D. A duplicate plan is required for all searches. If required, the Optional Enquiries form, ticked where necessary, should be attached along with the relevant fee. Additional enquiries must be attached on a separate sheet in duplicate. An additional fee will be charged for any that the Council is willing to answer.
> E. Details of fees can be obtained from the Council or your chosen NLIS Channel.
> F. Enter the name and address/DX address of the person or company lodging this form.

F.

> **Please reply to**
>
> PETER WOLF & CO
> RED RIDING HOOD LANE
> NORTHTOWN
> ESSEX
> 1CD 3LA
>
> DX Address

Conveyancing 29 Part I STANDARD ENQUIRIES

CON 29 Part I STANDARD Enquiries of Local Authority (2002 Edition)

PLANNING AND BUILDING REGULATIONS

1.1. Decisions and Pending Applications
What applications for any of the following (if applicable) have been granted, refused or are now pending?
- (a) planning permissions
- (b) listed building consents
- (c) conservation area consents
- (d) certificates of lawfulness of use or development
- (e) building regulation approvals
- (f) building regulation completion certificates
- (g) certificate of compliance of a replacement window, rooflight, roof window or glazed door.

How can copies of any of the above be obtained?

1.2. Planning Designations and Proposals
What designations of land use for the property or the area, and what specific proposals for the property, are contained in any current adopted or proposed development plan?

ROADS

2. Which of the roads, footways and footpaths mentioned in boxes B and C are:
- (a) highways maintainable at public expense;
- (b) subject to a current legal agreement for adoption and, if so, is the agreement supported by a bond or other financial security;
- (c) to be made up at the cost of the frontagers under a current Council resolution;
- (d) to be adopted without cost to the frontagers under a current Council resolution.

OTHER MATTERS

Apart from matters entered on the registers of local land charges, do any of the following matters apply to the property? How can copies of relevant documents be obtained?

3.1. Land required for Public Purposes
Inclusion of the property in a category of land required for public purposes within Schedule 13 paras 5 & 6 of the Town & Country Planning Act 1990.

3.2. Land to be acquired for Road Works
Inclusion of the property in land to be acquired for an approved scheme of highway construction or improvement.

3.3. Drainage Agreements and Consents
- (a) An agreement under the Building Act 1984, s.22 for drainage of any part of the property in combination with another building through a private sewer?
- (b) Statutory agreement or consent for a building or extension to a building on the property to be constructed over or in the vicinity of a drain, sewer or disposal main.

  Note: The sewerage undertaker for the area should also be asked about 3(b) and drainage generally.

3.4. Nearby Road Schemes
Location of any part of the property within 200 metres of:
- (a) the centre line of a new trunk road or special road specified in an order, draft order or scheme notified to the Council by the appropriate Secretary of State; or
- (b) the centre line of a proposed alteration or improvement to an existing road, notified to the Council by the appropriate Secretary of State, involving the construction of a subway, underpass, flyover, footbridge, elevated road or dual carriageway (whether or not within existing highway limits); or
- (c) the limits of construction of a proposed alteration or improvement to an existing road, notified to the Council by the appropriate Secretary of State, involving the construction of a roundabout (other than a mini-roundabout) or widening by the construction of one or more additional traffic lanes; or
- (d) the limits of construction of an approved new road to be constructed by the Council or an approved alteration or improvement by the Council to an existing road involving the construction of a subway, underpass, flyover, footbridge, elevated road or dual carriageway (whether or not within existing highway limits) or the construction of a roundabout (other than a mini-roundabout) or widening by the construction of one or more additional traffic lanes; or
- (e) the centre line of the possible route of a new road under proposals published for public consultation by the Council or by the appropriate Secretary of State; or
- (f) the limits of construction of a possible alteration or improvement to an existing road involving the construction of a subway, underpass, flyover, footbridge, elevated road or dual carriageway (whether or not within existing highway limits) or the construction of a roundabout (other than a mini-roundabout) or widening by the construction of one or more additional traffic lanes, under proposals published for public consultation by the Council or by the appropriate Secretary of State.

  Note: A mini-roundabout is a roundabout having a one-way circulatory carriageway around a flush or slightly raised circular marking less than 4 metres in diameter and with or without flared approaches.

3.5. Nearby Railway Schemes
Location of any part of the property within 200 metres of the centre line of a proposed railway, tramway, light railway or monorail.

3.6. Traffic Schemes
Approval by the Council of any of the following, not yet implemented, in respect of such of the roads, footways and footpaths mentioned in Box B (and, if applicable, Box C) which abut the boundaries of the property:
- (a) permanent stopping up or diversion
- (b) waiting or loading restrictions
- (c) one way driving
- (d) prohibition of driving
- (e) pedestrianisation
- (f) vehicle width or weight restriction
- (g) traffic calming works e.g. road humps
- (h) residents parking controls
- (i) minor road widening or improvement
- (j) pedestrian crossings
- (k) cycle tracks
- (l) bridge construction.

3.7. Outstanding Notices
Current statutory notices relating to the property under legislation relating to building works, environment, health and safety at work, housing, highways or public health, other than those falling elsewhere within 3.1 to 3.13.

3.8. Infringement of Building Regulations
Proceedings authorised by the Council for infringement of the Building Regulations in respect of the property.

3.9. Notices, Orders, Directions and Proceedings under Planning Acts
Subsisting notices, orders, directions, or proceedings, or those which the Council has decided to issue, serve, make or commence in the following categories (other than those which are shown in the Official Certificate of Search or which have been withdrawn or quashed) relating to the property:
- (a) enforcement notice
- (b) stop notice
- (c) listed building enforcement notice
- (d) breach of condition notice
- (e) planning contravention notice
- (f) other notice relating to breach of planning control
- (g) listed building repairs notice
- (h) order for compulsory acquisition of a listed building with a minimum compensation provision
- (i) building preservation notice
- (j) direction restricting permitted development
- (k) order revoking or modifying a planning permission or discontinuing an existing planning use
- (l) tree preservation order
- (m) proceedings for breach of a statutory planning agreement.

3.10. Conservation Area
Creation of the area before 31st August 1974 as a Conservation Area or a subsisting resolution to designate the area as a Conservation Area.

3.11. Compulsory Purchase
Inclusion of the property in land which is subject to an enforceable order or resolution for compulsory purchase.

3.12. Contaminated Land
- (a) Entry relating to the property in the register maintained under s.78R(1) of the Environmental Protection Act 1990.
- (b) Notice relating to the property served or resolved to be served under s.78B(3).
- (c) Consultation with the owner or occupier of the property having taken place, or being resolved to take place under s.78G(3) in relation to anything to be done on the property as a result of adjoining or adjacent land being contaminated land.
- (d) Entry in the register, or notice served or resolved to be served under s.78B(3) in relation to any adjoining or adjacent land, which has been identified as contaminated land because it is in such a condition that harm or pollution of controlled waters might be caused on the property.

3.13. Radon Gas
Location of the property in a Radon Affected Area.

NOTES:
This form must be submitted in duplicate and should be read in conjunction with the guidance notes available separately.
(1) *Unless otherwise indicated, matters will be disclosed only if they apply directly to the property described in Box B.*
(2) *"Area" means any area in which the property is located.*
(3) *References to "the Council" include any predecessor Council and also any council committee, sub-committee or other body or person exercising powers delegated by the Council and their "approval" includes their decision to proceed. The replies given to certain enquiries cover knowledge and actions of both the District Council and County Council.*
(4) *References to the provisions of particular Acts of Parliament or Regulations include any provisions which they have replaced and also include existing or future amendments or re-enactments.*
(5) *The replies will be given in the belief that they are in accordance with information presently available to the officers of the replying Council, but none of the Councils or their officers accept legal responsibility for an incorrect reply, except for negligence. Any liability for negligence will extend to the person who raised the enquiries and the person on whose behalf they were raised. It will also extend to any other person who has knowledge (personally or through an agent) of the replies before the time when he purchases, takes a tenancy of, or lends money on the security of the property or (if earlier) the time when he becomes contractually bound to do so.*

appropriate fee. However, applications may be made by other means (see below). No covering letter is required, but the file should be marked or a copy of the form kept to indicate when the application was sent.

If the title number of the property is unknown, the application on Form OC1 can still be made and the words 'Please supply the title number' should be printed in bold lettering at the top of the form.

Completion of Form OC1 is fairly straightforward. Panel 7 should be completed if the title number is not quoted in Panel 2 and it is the fee earner's responsibility to provide this information. However, a brief explanation of the terms in that panel is as follows. Freehold and leasehold have been mentioned on page 271, and a caution against first registration is mentioned on page 319 in the section relating to the Index Map. A rentcharge is not very common: it is a type of periodic payment of money relating to land but is not rent from a lease or tenancy. A franchise does not refer to a commercial franchise, but is a right or privilege granted by the Crown, e.g., to operate a toll or hold a fair on a piece of land. Profit a prendre in gross is the right to take something from someone else's land, e.g., the right to hunt or fish on that land or take something like gravel or turf. Manor refers to lordship titles, i.e., how the lord of the manor is known even though they might not own any land or rights. It is no longer possible to register new lordship titles but those already previously registered can be searched.

See also below regarding applications to the Land Registry by fax, telephone and direct computer access, and key numbers.

Key numbers and credit accounts

When completing Land Registry forms, you will see there is a place for a 'key number'. This is the firm's account number with the Land Registry and is a means by which the Land Registry can identify a firm. It should be quoted on all forms, etc. Some firms have a rubber stamp bearing their key number to avoid mistakes being made. If your firm has a credit account with the Land Registry a cheque does not have to be sent immediately for the fee, if one is payable—the firm will be billed later.

A great advantage of having a credit account with the Land Registry is that many applications and searches may be made by telephone, fax, and direct computer access by those with a credit account. Of course, where telephone applications are made, there is no need even to complete a form. However, these methods are acceptable only where the firm concerned has a credit account. Further information may be obtained from the Land Registry. If it is desired to make payment through a credit account, then you must place a 'X' in the appropriate box on the form. Cheques must be made payable to 'Land Registry'. Land Registry forms do not require a covering letter to go with them but the file must be noted to show that the form has been sent or a copy of the form retained on the file. See also page 326 dealing with Land Charges searches.

Land Registry application by telephone

Credit account holders may make various applications to the Land Registry by telephoning Telephone Services, without the necessity of completing any forms. There are two telephone numbers; one is for registered land in England and the other, which is for registered land in Wales, also provides a Welsh language service.

For England, the telephone number is 0845 308 4545. The line is open from 8.30 a.m. to 6.30 p.m. Monday to Friday (excluding public holidays) and from 8.30 a.m. to 1.00 p.m. on Saturdays (excluding Christmas Day if it is a Saturday).

**Application for official
copies of register/plan or
certificate in Form CI**

Land Registry **OC1**

Land Registry _STEVENAGE_ Office

BRICKDALE HOUSE
SWINGATE
STEVENAGE
HERTS
SG1 1XG

Use one form per title. If you need more room than is provided for in a panel, use continuation sheet CS and attach to this form.

1. **Administrative area** if known	MORELAND, HERTFORDSHIRE

2. **Title number** if known	HD12345

3. Property

Postal number or description	76
Name of road	BURNT OAK ROAD
Name of locality	
Town	MORELAND
Postcode	EN7 8CB
Ordnance Survey map reference (if known)	

4. Payment of fee _Place "X" in the appropriate box._

☐ The Land Registry fee of £ [   ] accompanies this application.

☐ Debit the Credit Account mentioned in panel 5 with the appropriate fee payable under the current Land Registration Fee Order.

For official use only

Impression of fees

5. The application has been lodged by:

Land Registry Key No. (if appropriate) 8964117

Name   PETER WOLF & CO
Address/DX No.   RED RIDING HOOD LANE
             NORTHTOWN
             ESSEX 1CD 3LA

Reference PW/74
E-mail

Telephone No. 01234 5678	Fax No. 01234 6789

6. If the official copies are to be sent to anyone other than the applicant in panel 5, please supply the name and address of the person to whom they should be sent.

Reference

7. Where the title number is **not** quoted in panel 2, place "X" in the appropriate box(es).
   As regards this property, my application relates to:

   ☐ freehold estate   ☐ caution against first registration   ☐ franchise   ☐ manor
   ☐ leasehold estate   ☐ rentcharge   ☐ profit a prendre in gross

8. In case there is an application for registration pending against the title, place "X" in the appropriate box:

   ☐ I require an official copy back-dated to the day prior to the receipt of that application   **or**
   ☐ I require an official copy on completion of that application

9. **I apply for:** *Place "X" in the appropriate boxes) and indicate how many copies are required.*

   ☐ ____ official copy(ies) of the **register** of the above mentioned property
   ☐ ____ official copy(ies) of the **title plan or caution plan** of the above mentioned property

   ☐ ____ a certificate in Form CI, in which case **either**:

   ☐ an estate plan has been approved and the plot number is _____

   or

   ☐ no estate plan has been approved and a certificate is to be issued in respect of the land
   shown _____ on the attached plan and copy

10. **Signature of applicant** _____   **Date** _____

© Crown copyright (ref: LR/HQ/Internet) 10/03

For Wales, the telephone number is 0845 307 4535. The line is open from 9.00 a.m. to 5.00 p.m. Monday to Friday (excluding public holidays). Only requests for certain applications can be made to these numbers: they should not be used for general enquiries to the Land Registry, when the relevant District Land Registry should be contacted.

Before making an application by telephone to Telephone Services, in all cases, you should have the following information:

(a) your organisation's credit account key number;

(b) your organisation's name, address and DX number, as well as a contact name, reference and telephone number;

(c) if the Land Registry is to deliver the result to anyone other than your own organisation, you should have the name and address, plus other contact details of that other person or organisation.

Depending on the type of application being made, other information will need to be provided to Telephone Services before they can process the application. The information required for each type of application is given in the Land Registry's Practice Guide 61 which may obtained from the Land Registry or printed off their website (see the section on Useful Web Addresses).

Where appropriate, applicants may be given the results of a telephone search immediately. Following a telephone search, a guaranteed paper result will normally be sent to the applicant by post or by DX, usually on the same or next working day.

Land Registry application by fax

Certain applications may be made to the Land Registry by fax by credit account holders only. Although the application may be made by fax, the Land Registry will not, at present, return information by fax. Any official copies or search results will be sent by post or through the DX to the applicant. Several types of application may be made by fax and these must be made to specific fax numbers at the relevant Land Registry. Details of such applications and the fax numbers are available from the Land Registry. Fax applications should be completed in black ink or black type.

The fax facility may also be used for general correspondence to the Land Registry, provided there is no accompanying documentation.

Computerised searches

Land Registry credit account customers are able to conduct searches via their own computer provided, of course, that they are registered to do so with the Land Registry. As long as the user has the title number or postal address, they can gain access to a computerised register of a particular property. Hard copies for internal office use can be printed out from the screen. The user may order official copies directly through the computer and these will normally be posted on the same day by the Land Registry. In some cases, where requested, an official search certificate may be issued in .pdf format. Further information on these services may be obtained from the Land Registry.

Draft contract

The Vendor/Seller's solicitor prepares a draft contract for sale. This will be prepared in duplicate and once it is approved, each party will sign a copy which will later be exchanged with the other party so that each party will hold a copy signed by the other. It will be when contracts are exchanged (see later) that the whole transaction becomes legally binding. The contract may be typed on A4 size paper but often a standard printed form is used. For domestic conveyancing, this is the Law Society's Contract (Incorporating the Standard Conditions of Sale (Fourth Edition)) and only the outer pages are to be completed. The inner pages contain general conditions of sale which apply to all contracts drawn up on that form unless expressly varied or excluded. The printed conditions must not be actually physically amended. Any alteration to the conditions must be by a Special Condition on the back of the form. There is a similar form for commercial premises.

The contract must incorporate all the terms which have been expressly agreed by the parties and includes the following information.

Agreement date.   At the drafting stage of the contract, this date will be left blank. It will not be dated until contracts are going to be exchanged (see later). If you are posting the contract to a client for signature, it is normal to write in pencil in the space for the date 'do not date'.

Seller and buyer details.   These include the full names and addresses (including postcode) of the Buyer and the Seller.

Property.   Under the word 'property', freehold or leasehold should be deleted accordingly. A description and/or address of the property (including postcode) will be given in this section.

Root of title/title number.   One of these will be deleted as appropriate, depending on whether the property is registered or not. If it is unregistered property, details of the root of title will be given (see page 317) and if the property is registered with the Land Registry, it will have a Title Number, as discussed earlier.

Incumbrances on the property.   This section will give details of any burdens, etc. on the property. It may say there are no incumbrances or may refer to any charges on the register (held by the Land Registry) or give other relevant details.

Title guarantee.   Below these words, either full or limited will be deleted and details will be given in the space provided. The most usual will be full title which basically means that the property is the seller's to dispose of free of any charges or burdens. A limited guarantee is similar but does not guarantee that the person transferring the property knows of all charges and burdens that may affect the property, perhaps, for example, when the property is being sold by executors or trustees of a Will.

Completion date.   This is the date when the property will actually be transferred over to the new owner. Again, this space will normally be left blank at the drafting stage.

Contract rate.   This states the rate of interest that will be payable if the terms of the contract are not adhered to once contacts have been exchanged. This will often state an interest rate above a certain bank's lending rate, or often will refer to a rate set by the Law Society (especially where the National Conveyancing Protocol is being used).

Purchase price.   This is the price agreed for the property itself.

Deposit.   The amount of any deposit agreed to be paid on exchange of contacts will be inserted here. The most common deposit would be 10 per cent of the purchase price and this would be payable on exchange of contracts.

Amount payable for chattels.   This means any additional items that are being sold separately at the same time as the property. If other items are included, they should be listed on a separate sheet and a copy attached to each part of the contract. Where the National Conveyancing Protocol is being used, any such items will be listed on Form Prop 6 (Fixtures, Fittings and Contents Form) which must be attached to each part of the contract.

Balance. This is the balance of purchase monies that will be payable by the Purchaser on completion day. It is the price of the property itself less any deposit that will have been paid by then, plus any additional amount for separately sold chattels.

There is a box at the bottom right-hand corner of the page and each contract will be signed by either the Seller or the Buyer. When exchange takes place (see later), the contracts will be exchanged so that each party will then hold the copy signed by the other.

On the reverse of the form, there are some Special Conditions which will normally apply. Condition No. 4 contains two clauses, one of which will be deleted according to whether the property will be empty on completion or whether it is being sold subject to any lease or tenancy, and if that is the case, details will be given.

Any further conditions may be typed on the reverse of the form.

At the bottom of the reverse of the form, there is a space for details of the parties' solicitors. These details should include the firm's name, address, telephone number and the reference of the person dealing with the matter. A firm's e-mail address may also be included if they are willing to accept service of certain documents by e-mail.

The conditions on the inner pages of the contract must not be altered or deleted in any way. If it is agreed that a particular condition will be varied or will not apply, rather than changing the printed condition, a clause must be inserted on the reverse of the form.

The contract may refer to an attached plan, in which case, you must ensure that the plan is correctly coloured and marked (see page 23). Each copy of the contract would have a copy of any plan securely attached to it. Once the draft contract is agreed by the parties, final copies or 'engrossments' can be prepared for signature.

Enquiries before contract/Seller's Property Information Form

Before the Purchaser's solicitors can approve any contract, they must have all details of the registered title and of any unregistered rights or obligations affecting the property. They will also want any other relevant information, such as guarantees for any work done to the property; details of any disputes with neighbours, etc. They will ask certain questions of the Vendor's solicitor in a form of preliminary enquiries or Enquiries Before Contract (Conveyancing 29). There is a printed form available with standard enquiries on it or the solicitor can prepare his own form. This form is typed and sent out in duplicate so that when the other solicitors answer the queries, they can keep a copy of the questions and answers.

The questions are posed on the left-hand side of the page, so that the answers can be given alongside the questions. Extra questions may be added if this is desired. When the Vendor's solicitors receive these enquiries, a copy is sent to the Vendor for him to answer as best he can. When they receive his replies back they complete the form in duplicate, with the answers on the right-hand side of the page and return one copy to the Purchaser's solicitors. The form should be signed and dated before it is sent out.

Where the Conveyancing Protocol (see later in this chapter) is adopted for a transaction, the Seller's Property Information Form (Prop 1) would be used instead of the Enquiries before Contract Form. The Seller's Property Information Form has two sections to it. Part I contains a lot of the same sort of information as Form Con 29, but more detailed, and it is completed by the Seller himself. Part II of the Seller's Information Form should be completed by the Seller's solicitor (who should check the information given in Part I with other information he has, such as what is shown in the deeds, etc). Once both sections are complete, the form will be sent to the Buyer's solicitors with a copy of the

CONTRACT
Incorporating the Standard Conditions of Sale (Fourth Edition)

Date	:	
Seller	:	ALBERT FRANCIS BROWN of 76 BURNT OAK ROAD MORELAND HERTS EN7 8CB
Buyer	:	ELIZABETH MARY GREEN of 46 OLD ROAD NORTHTOWN HERTS EN4 7AB
Property (freehold/~~leasehold~~)	:	76 BURNT OAK ROAD, MORELAND HERTFORDSHIRE registered at HM Land Registry under Title No. HD 12345.
Title number/~~root of title~~	:	The Seller's title is registered with absolute title under Title No. HD 12345 at the Stevenage District Land Registry
Specified incumbrances	:	None
Title guarantee (full/~~limited~~)	:	Full title guarantee
Completion date	:	
Contract rate	:	4% per annum above the base rate from time to time of the Greenback Bank plc.
Purchase price	:	£96,000
Deposit	:	£9,600
Chattels price (if separate)	:	
Balance	:	£86,400

The seller will sell and the buyer will buy the property for the purchase price.

WARNING This is a formal document, designed to create legal rights and legal obligations. Take advice before using it.	**Signed** Seller/Buyer

SPECIAL CONDITIONS

1. (a) This contract incorporates the Standard Conditions of Sale (Fourth Edition).

    (b) The terms used in this contract have the same meaning when used in the Conditions.

2. Subject to the terms of this contract and to the Standard Conditions of Sale, the seller is to transfer the property with either full title guarantee or limited title guarantee, as specified on the front page.

3. The chattels which are on the property and are set out on any attached list are included in the sale and the buyer is to pay the chattels price for them.

4. The property is sold with vacant possession.

(or) 4. The property is sold subject to the following leases or tenancies:

Seller's conveyancers*:   Angel Gabriel & Co, 2 Milky Way,
                                  Barnet, Herts. EN5 6AX

                                  Ref: ABC/612   Tel: 01638 1234

Buyer's conveyancers*:   Peter Wolf & Co, Red Riding Hood Lane,
                                  Northtown, Essex 1CD 3LA

                                  Ref: PW/74   Tel: 01234 5678

*Adding an e-mail address authorises service by e-mail: see condition 1.3.3(b)

Fixtures, Fittings and Contents Form (which will, as mentioned earlier, eventually be attached to the contact), plus copies of any guarantees, etc. Copies of all forms must be kept in the file.

Where the National Conveyancing Protocol is being used, the Seller's Property Information Form will be completed at the outset, so that it is ready to be sent immediately to any Buyer's solicitor as soon as a Buyer has been found. The form will be part of a contract package sent out at this early stage in order to assist speeding up the conveyancing process. See page 336 for further information on the Protocol. See also page 274 regarding Home Information Packs.

Any relevant documents, such as guarantees, etc., should be kept in the file or with the deeds and copies only should be sent to the other party.

Exchanging contracts

Once the Purchaser's solicitor receives the replies to Enquiries Before Contract, the searches back from the local authority, the official copies from the Land Registry and is satisfied that all is clear, he can go ahead and approve the draft contract.

The parties will agree on a completion date, i.e., the day the purchase money is handed over in exchange for the property and other formalities are completed to finalise the transaction. This completion date will be inserted into the contract.

If the draft contract is unaltered it can be used for signature, otherwise a fresh one may need to be re-typed. A copy has to be sent to the other solicitor for his client's signature. Clients either call in to the office to sign their contract or do this through the post. The contract must not yet be dated at this stage. It will be dated the day it is exchanged and once exchange has taken place, the parties are legally bound by the terms of the contract.

The contracts signed by all parties are exchanged between solicitors so that each party holds the copy of the contract signed by the other. Even if it has been signed, it is not yet binding until it has been exchanged. It is normal for solicitors to agree by telephone that contracts are exchanged at a certain day and time and then put them in the post to the other solicitors. In this event, as soon as exchange is agreed on the telephone, the contracts become legally binding. This telephone agreement assists greatly especially where there is a 'chain' of Purchasers and Vendors. *Never* agree to exchange contracts without first having explicit permission from a fee earner. When contracts are exchanged you may hear of reference being made to Formula A, B or C. These are procedures for exchange of contracts laid down by the Law Society and are the responsibility of the fee earner. Once contracts have been exchanged, the Purchaser normally insures the property and this is something his solicitor may help him with.

Once contracts are exchanged, a deposit may be paid by the Purchaser to the Vendor. This is normally 10 per cent of the purchase price and the sum paid will be deducted from the final price at completion. If the Purchaser does not complete the purchase, the Vendor can keep the deposit, unless there is a very good reason for not proceeding.

A deposit will often be held by the Vendor's solicitor either as stakeholder or as agent for the Vendor. Broadly, this means that if it is held as stakeholder, the money must not be used or parted with in any way by the stakeholder until completion takes place. If the deposit is held as agent for the Vendor, this means that the Vendor can use the deposit in a related purchase, e.g., to fund the deposit for the property he himself is buying.

In some cases, instead of paying a deposit, the Purchaser may take out an insurance policy whereby the insurance company will pay the money if he does not proceed with the

Short description
of the property   re   **76 BURNT OAK ROAD, MORELAND**

Parties   **A. F. BROWN**

to   **E. M. GREEN**

— Oyez —

ENQUIRIES

BEFORE CONTRACT

**These enquiries are copyright
and may not be reproduced**

**Please strike out enquiries
which are not applicable**

Replies are requested to the following enquiries.

The replies are as follows.

Proposed Buyer's solicitors.

Proposed Seller's solicitors.

Date...

Date...

ENQUIRIES

REPLIES

These replies, except in the case of any enquiry expressly requiring a reply
from the Seller's solicitors, are given on behalf of the proposed Seller and
without responsibility on the part of his solicitors, their partners or
employees. They are believed to be correct but the accuracy is not
guaranteed and they do not obviate the need to make appropriate
searches, enquiries and inspections.

1. Boundaries

(A) To whom do all the boundary walls, fences, hedges and ditches belong?

(B) If no definite indications exist, which has the Seller maintained or regarded as his responsibility?

(C) Is the Seller aware of any divergence between the physical boundaries and the boundaries shown on the title deeds?

1. All fences belong to the property.

2. Disputes

Is the Seller aware of any past or current disputes regarding boundaries or other matters relating to the property or its use, or relating to any neighbouring property?

2. None so far as the vendor is aware.

3. Notices

Please give particulars of all notices relating to the property, or to matters likely to affect its use or enjoyment, that the Seller (or, to his knowledge, any predecessor) has given or received.

3. None so far as the vendor is aware.

4. Guarantees etc.

(A) Please supply a copy of any of the following of which the Buyer is to have the benefit:

agreement, covenant, guarantee, warranty, bond, certificate, indemnity and insurance policy,

relating to any of the following matters, and affecting the property, any part of it, or any building of which it forms part:

construction, repair, replacement, treatment or improvement of the fabric; any contamination which was, is or may be at or under the property; maintenance of any accessway; construction costs of any road (including lighting, drainage and crossovers) to which the property fronts, and adoption charges for such a road; defective title; breach of restrictive covenant.

(B) What has become apparent, which might give rise to a claim under any document mentioned in (A), and what claims have third parties made, and has notice of such a claim been given?

(C) Has any document relating to the property been the subject of any application for designation as an exempt information document by you or, to your knowledge, by anyone else?

4.

(A) ~~There are none with the title deeds and~~ The vendor believes there are none.

(B) Nothing so far as the vendor is aware. The purchaser must rely on inspection and survey.

5. Services and Facilities

(A) Does the property have drainage, water, electricity and gas services and are they all connected to the mains?

(B) Are any of the following facilities either shared, or enjoyed by exercising rights over other property?

access for light and air; access for pedestrians and vehicles; emergency escape routes; access and facilities for repair, maintenance and replacement; pipes and wires for services not mentioned in (A).

5.

(A) Yes

(B) No

If so, please give particulars (including copies of relevant documents; liabilities for carrying out work and for making payment; work proposed, in hand, and completed but not paid for).

6. Adverse Rights

(A) Please give details of any rights or facilities over the property to which anyone other than the owner is entitled, or which any such person currently enjoys.

(B) (i) Please give the full names, and ages if under 18, of all persons in actual occupation of the property.

(ii) What legal or equitable interest in the property has each of those persons?

(C) Is the Seller aware of any other interests as defined in Schedules 1, 3 and 12 of the Land Registration Act 2002?

7. Restrictions

Have all restrictions affecting the property or its use been observed up to the date hereof? If not, please give details.

8. Planning etc.

(A) When did the present use of the property commence?

(B) Please supply a copy of any planning permission authorising or imposing conditions upon this use, and authorising the erection or retention of the buildings now on the property.

(C) Please supply a copy of any bye-law approval or building regulations consent relating to the buildings now on the property.

(D) Has any window, roof light, roof window or glazed door been installed at the property since 31st March 2002? If it has, was the work carried out in accordance with the Building Regulations in force at the relevant time?

9. Fixtures, Fittings etc.

(A) Does the sale include all of the following items now on the property, and attached to or growing in it?

Trees, shrubs, plants, flowers, and garden produce. Greenhouses, garden sheds and garden ornaments. Aerials and satellite reception dishes. Fitted furniture and shelves. Electric switches, points and wall and ceiling fittings.

(B) What fixtures to the property are not included in the sale?

(C) If any central heating or other oil is to be sold to the Buyer, what arrangements are proposed?

10. Outgoings

What other periodic charges affect the property or its occupier, apart from council tax and water services charge?

11. Completion

(A) How long after exchange of contracts will the Seller be able to give vacant possession of the whole of the property?

(B) The Buyer's solicitors wish to complete by adopting the Law Society's Code for Completion by Post (1984 edition). Do the Seller's solicitors agree?

12. Environment

(A) Is the Seller aware of:

(i) the presence of dangerous or polluting substances or materials in any soil, groundwater or body of water at or under the property, or at or under any adjoining or neighbouring land?

(ii) any previous use or activities, or any current use or activities, involving dangerous or polluting substances or materials, at the property or at any adjoining or neighbouring land?

or

(iii) a landfill site, whether closed or in operation, at, or within 250 metres of, the property?

If the answer to any of the above questions is "Yes", please give details.

© 1998, 2001, 2002, 2003 Oyez 7 Spa Road, London SE16 3QQ

11.2003 F41922
5033028
★ ★ ★

Conveyancing 29 (Short)

purchase after exchange of contracts. This type of insurance is known as a deposit guarantee scheme.

The Purchaser's solicitor also has to ensure that the balance of the purchase money—'completion monies'—will be available. This usually entails correspondence with the Purchaser's building society. (See the section on Mortgages below.)

Requisitions on Title

The Purchaser's solicitor puts final questions to the Vendor's solicitors to ensure nothing has altered since the Enquiries before Contract were answered and also puts any additional queries he may have. These are called Requisitions on Title. There are a couple of different types of this Form; Conveyancing 28B is shown here. They are typed and sent out in duplicate in the same format as Enquiries Before Contract. The printed forms available can be for either freehold or leasehold property, or both. Requisitions are signed and dated by each party's solicitors as they are sent out and returned. The answers to the requisitions include details about water rates, service charges, etc. If these have been paid in advance, they will have to be apportioned, i.e., the Purchaser will have to pay for the share for the period of time the Vendor has already paid in advance, for example, the Vendor has paid a charge up to August but the completion date is in the middle of June. The Purchaser will get the benefit from the date of completion to August so he must pay to the Vendor the amount of that charge from completion date to August.

Where the National Conveyancing Protocol (see later) has been adopted, Form Prop 7, Completion Information and Requisitions on Title, will be used instead of the Requisitions on Title form.

Transfer

The document which actually transfers ownership of freehold registered land is a deed called a Transfer. This is prepared by the Purchaser's solicitors on a TR or TP form. Here we are using Form TR1 (transfer of whole). A different form is used for certain other matters, such as where the property is part of a larger registered title, e.g., a new house on an estate which is registered under one title number and it has been divided into plots. The cost of the property (the consideration) is shown on the form and this is given in both words and figures. The Transfer form has numbered panels. Do not alter these numbers even if there is nothing to go in a particular numbered panel. The form is completed as follows.

Panel 1
Before December 2003, where stamp duty was payable and after completion had taken place, the first paragraph of Panel 1 would be stamped by the Inland Revenue Stamp Office to show that the appropriate stamp duty had been paid. (Please note: the Inland Revenue has recently changed to become HM Revenue & Customs.) However, since December 2003, stamp duty (now called stamp duty land tax (SDLT)) is payable on the transaction, rather than the document. This means that the Stamp Office will no longer stamp a document to show that SDLT has been paid: instead, on payment of the SDLT, a certificate is issued to say that the correct amount has been paid. Therefore, the space on this part of the form will now be left blank as, indeed, can the whole of Panel 1. Before December 2003, the other part of Panel 1 was completed to show that the correct stamp duty had been paid. Eventually, no doubt, new forms will be printed to take this into account. See page 302 for further information on SDLT.

These requisitions are copyright and may not be reproduced

Short
description
of the
property   *re*...... 76 Burnt Oak Road, Moreland ....

Parties
A. F. Brown
....

E. M. Green
to,...

═══════ Oyez ═══════

REQUISITIONS

ON TITLE

*(For use where Enquiries before Contract have
already been answered)*

Please strike out any requisitions which are not applicable.

---

1. PREVIOUS ENQUIRIES

If the enquiries before contract replied to on behalf of the Seller were repeated here, would the replies now be the same as those previously given? If not, please give full particulars of any variation.

1. These are confirmed unless varied by correspondence.

---

2. OUTGOINGS AND APPORTIONMENTS

(A) On completion the Seller must produce receipts for the last payments of outgoings, of which either he claims reimbursement of an advance payment or arrears could be recovered from the Buyer.

(B) (i) In the case of a leasehold property or property subject to a legal rentcharge, the receipt for rent due on the last rent day before the day of completion, as well as the receipt for the last fire insurance premium, must be produced on completion.

(ii) Does the former receipt contain any reference to a breach of any of the covenants and conditions contained in the lease or grant?

(C) Please send a completion statement.

2.
(A) Confirmed

(B) N/A

(C) Herewith.

---

3. TITLE DEEDS

A. *Unregistered land*

(i) Which abstracted documents of title will be delivered to the Buyer on completion?

(ii) Who will give to the Buyer the statutory acknowledgment and undertaking for the production and safe custody of those not handed over?

(iii) Why will any documents not handed over be retained?

B. *Registered land*

If the Land Registry has approved an estate lay-out plan for use with official searches of part of the land in the title, on what date was it approved?

3.
(A) N/A

(B) N/A

---

4. MORTGAGES

(A) Please specify those mortgages or charges which will be discharged on or before completion.

(B) In respect of each subsisting mortgage or charge:

(i) Will a vacating receipt, discharge of registered charge or consent to dealing, entitling the Buyer to take the property freed from it, be handed over on completion?

(ii) If not, will the Seller's solicitor give a written undertaking on completion to hand one over later?

(iii) If an undertaking is proposed, what are the suggested terms of it?

4.
(A) Mortgage dated 7 July 1994 between Givemore Building Society and Albert Francis Brown.

(B) Yes.

5. POSSESSION

(A) (i) Vacant possession of the whole of the property must be given on completion.

(ii) Has every person in occupation of all or part of the property agreed to vacate on or before completion?

(iii) What arrangements will be made to deliver the keys to the Buyer?

Or

(B) The Seller must on completion hand over written authorities for future rents to be paid to the Buyer or his agents.

5.

(A) (i) Confirmed
   (ii) Yes

(iii) The vendor and purchaser have made their own arrangements.

6. NOTICES

Please give the name and address of any solicitor, residential tenant or other person to whom notice of any dealing with the property must be given.

6. None that the vendor knows of.

7. COMPLETION ARRANGEMENTS

Please answer any of the following requisitions against which X has been placed in the box.

[ ] (A) Where will completion take place?

[X] (B) We should like to remit the completion monies direct to your bank account. If you agree, please give the name and branch of your bank, its sort code, and the title and number of the account to be credited.

[ ] (C) In whose favour and for what amounts will banker's drafts be required on completion?

[ ] (D) Please confirm that you will comply with the Law Society's Code for Completion by Post (1998 edition).

7.

(B) Greenback Bank plc
62 Southside Avenue, Moreland, Herts. SG4 2AP

Sort code: 46 00 21

Account: Angel Gabriel & Co
(No.1 A/c) No. 1234560000.

The right is reserved to make further requisitions which may arise on the replies to the above, the usual searches and enquiries before completion, or otherwise.

Note. — Requisitions founded on the title or contract must be added to the above.

DATED   DATED

Buyer's Solicitor.   *Seller's Solicitor.*

Panel 2

This will show the Title Number of the property or, if the property is not yet registered with the Land Registry, it will be left blank.

Panel 3

A full description and/or address of the property, including the postcode.

Panel 4

The completion date. This will be left blank until completion is to take place and if the Transfer is being sent to the client for signature, it would be normal to write in pencil here 'do not date'.

Panel 5

The Transferor is the person who has the authority (generally the owner) to transfer the property over to someone else.

Panel 6

The Transferee is the person who will be receiving the property.

Panel 7

The Transferee's intended address will, in most domestic conveyancing transactions, be the address of the property being bought as most people will buy the property to live in it. However, the Transferee's address may be a different one, e.g., where someone is buying the property to let it out, or various other circumstances where the owner of the property will not actually be occupying it.

Panel 8

The clause simply states that the Transferor is transferring the property to the Transferee, so that once the Transfer is properly executed and any money is paid, together with any other conditions that may apply, the property will belong to the Transferee.

Panel 9

Consideration. This is what is being given in return for the property—in most cases, this will be money: the purchase price, but it could be something other than money. The appropriate box should be ticked.

Panel 10

The box should be ticked here to show whether the title being transferred is full title or limited title. This information can normally be found in the contract (see page 286).

Panel 11

Declaration of trust. One of these boxes should be ticked to indicate how the property is to be owned where it is being bought by joint purchasers. For example, if the Transferees are going to hold the property on trust for themselves as joint tenants, this means that they will own the property jointly and if one of them dies, the property will automatically pass to the other. However, if it is going to be held by them as joint tenants in common in equal shares, if one of them dies, their share will form part of their estate (see Chapter 11 on Probate). This means that whoever is left that person's property under a Will, or if there is no Will, whoever is legally entitled to their estate on their death, will be entitled to that share in the property, rather than it automatically going to the other joint owner of the property.

If the property is to be held jointly in a different way from the two mentioned above, then the third box would be ticked and details given.

Panel 12

This panel can be completed with any additional information as necessary. If there is insufficient room here, Form CS (see below) should be used.

Panel 13

The Transfer is a deed (see page 271) and must be executed accordingly (see also page 28). Only the Vendor has to sign the Transfer unless it contains any covenants by the Purchaser, in which case it must then be signed by all parties. However, in practice, it is common for all parties to sign in any event.

If there is not enough room on the printed Transfer form, a continuation sheet in Land Registry Form CS must be used and then stapled to the form of which it has become a continuation. Form CS is for use with several Land Registry forms where the panel on a form does not allow enough room for the information to be provided. Form CS is self-explanatory, asking you to type on it the number of the form which you are continuing from, e.g., TR1. Also to be included are the title number of the property, the panel number to be continued, i.e., if you need to expand on the information for panel number 12, you would state this on the Form CS. Finally, Form CS asks you to provide the sheet number you are now working on and the total number of sheets.

Once the draft Transfer form is approved by the Vendor's solicitors, the top copy is returned to the Purchaser's solicitors. If necessary, a fresh copy will be typed or 'engrossed' for signature but if no amendments have been made, it is quite usual to use the draft. Do not type a date on to the Transfer. This must be done only when completion of the transaction is to take place and must be authorised by the person who is dealing with the matter.

A Transfer on the printed form will not require a backsheet or a frontsheet but other longer deeds, such as a Conveyance (see section on Unregistered Land) or Lease (see later), do usually need one or the other. The backsheet shows the date of the document, the parties, the address of the property and describes what the document is, e.g., 'Lease', and it gives the details of the firm of solicitors preparing the document.

If you have to type a sum of money, it is normal to set this out in words first and then in figures in brackets, e.g., TWENTY THOUSAND POUNDS (£20,000). Some firms like this written in capitals as shown. Dates are also sometimes written in words instead of figures, e.g., 10 September 2002 might be written as 'the tenth day of September Two thousand and two'. In longer documents (see example of Lease) each numbered paragraph often has the first word of each paragraph and certain other key words, typed in capitals and perhaps underlined. For further information on preparation and presentation of documents, see Chapter 1. Drafts of these documents (not the printed forms) are normally typed on one side of the paper only in one and a half or double line spacing, and the pages should be numbered.

Remember, when you have engrossed a document which has involved any re-typing, such as amendments being made to the draft, you should proofread it, i.e., read it out aloud with someone else checking the draft. This helps to eliminate any typing errors. Engrossments may be bound by machine, stapled or sewn up with green tape, depending on what your organisation prefers. (See the sections in Chapter 1 on Tips on Proofreading and Sewing up Documents.)

Completion statement

The Purchaser's solicitors prepare a completion statement (see example) for their client, to show exactly what money will be needed for completion day. This usually includes the firm's bill.

**Transfer of whole
of registered title(s)**

Land Registry

If you need more room than is provided for in a panel, use continuation sheet CS and attach to this form.

1.	**Stamp Duty**

Place "X" in the appropriate box or boxes and complete the appropriate certificate.

☐ It is certified that this instrument falls within category ☐ in the Schedule to the Stamp Duty (Exempt Instruments) Regulations 1987

☐ It is certified that the transaction effected does not form part of a larger transaction or of a series of transactions in respect of which the amount or value or the aggregate amount or value of the consideration exceeds the sum of £

☐ It is certified that this is an instrument on which stamp duty is not chargeable by virtue of the provisions of section 92 of the Finance Act 2001

2. Title Number(s) of the Property *Leave blank if not yet registered.*

HD 12345

3. Property 76 Burnt Oak Road, Moreland, Herts EN7 8CB

4. Date

5. Transferor *Give full names and company's registered number if any.*

ALBERT FRANCIS BROWN

6. Transferee **for entry on the register** *Give full name(s) and company's registered number, if any. For Scottish companies use an SC prefix and for limited liability partnerships use an OC prefix before the registered number, if any. For foreign companies give territory in which incorporated.*

ELIZABETH MARY GREEN

Unless otherwise arranged with Land Registry headquarters, a certified copy of the Transferee's constitution (in English or Welsh) will be required if it is a body corporate but is not a company registered in England and Wales or Scotland under the Companies Acts.

7. Transferee's intended **address(es) for service (including postcode) for entry on the register** *You may give up to three addresses for service one of which must be a postal address but does not have to be within the UK. The other addresses can be any combination of a postal address, a box number at a UK document exchange or an electronic address.*

76 Burnt Oak Road, Moreland, Herts EN7 8CB

8. The Transferor transfers the Property to the Transferee

9. Consideration *Place "X" in the appropriate box. State clearly the currency unit if other than sterling. If none of the boxes applies, insert an appropriate memorandum in the additional provisions panel.*

☒ The Transferor has received from the Transferee for the Property the sum of *In words and figures.*
NINETY-SIX THOUSAND POUNDS (£96,000)

☐ *Insert other receipt as appropriate.*

☐ The transfer is not for money or anything which has a monetary value

10. The Transferor transfers with *Place "X" in the appropriate box and add any modifications.*

    ☒ full title guarantee   ☐ limited title guarantee

11. Declaration of trust *Where there is more than one Transferee, place "X" in the appropriate box.*

    ☐ The Transferees are to hold the Property on trust for themselves as joint tenants

    ☐ The Transferees are to hold the Property on trust for themselves as tenants in common in equal shares

    ☐ The Transferees are to hold the Property *Complete as necessary.*

12. Additional provisions *Insert here any required or permitted statements, certificates or applications and any agreed covenants, declarations, etc.*

13. Execution *The Transferor must execute this transfer as a deed using the space below. If there is more than one Transferor, all must execute. Forms of execution are given in Schedule 9 to the Land Registration Rules 2003. If the transfer contains Transferee's covenants or declarations or contains an application by the Transferee (e.g. for a restriction), it must also be executed by the Transferee (all of them, if there is more than one).*

Signed as a deed by
ALBERT FRANCIS BROWN
in the presence of:

Signature of witness...
Name (in BLOCK CAPITALS) ....
Address...

Signed as a deed by
ELIZABETH MARY GREEN
in the presence of:

Signature of witness...
Name (in BLOCK CAPITALS)...
Address...

**Continuation sheet
for use with
application and
disposition forms**

Land Registry

CS

1. Continued from Form	Title number(s)

2. *Before each continuation, state panel to be continued, e.g. "Panel 12 continued".*

Continuation sheet **of**
*Insert sheet number and total number of
continuation sheets e.g. "sheet 1 of 3".*
© Crown copyright (ref: LR/HQ/CD-ROM) 6/03

Example

```
                        COMPLETION STATEMENT
     Sale of 2 Railway Cuttings
     Sale price                                                  £65,000.00
     Less:     Mortgage redemption                30,000.00
               Mortgage redemption fee                10.00
               Legal fees, etc. (as per attached bill)   250.00      30,260.00

               Due to you:                                       34,740.00


     Purchase of 76 Burnt Oak Road
     Purchase price                                              £96,000.00

     Less:     Mortgage                           35,000.00
               Sale proceeds from 2 Railway Cuttings  34,740.00
               Bank loan                            2,000.00      71,740.00

                                                                 24,260.00
     Plus:     Chattels                              500.00
               Search fees, etc.                      40.00
               Apportionment of outgoings            200.00
               Legal fees, etc.                      750.00       1,490.00

               Balance due to complete                          £25,750.00

                                                                 E. & O.E.
```

Land Registry search with 'priority'

About ten days before completion, the Purchaser's solicitors will make an application for an official search with priority (Form OS1) to the Land Registry either by first class post or by another permitted method. Form OS2 (search of part) is used where the property is part of a larger property registered under one title number. The official search will ascertain whether any further entries have been registered with the Land Registry since the date on the official copies in the Purchaser's solicitor's possession. See page 282 regarding searches made by telephone, fax and computerised on-line access. The certificate received back from the Land Registry shows the 'priority date', i.e., the date by which the Purchaser must lodge at the Land Registry the Transfer and any supporting papers for registration as the new owner. The priority date gives a period of 30 working days. Up until this date the Land Registry guarantees that no other entries will be registered ahead of the new owner. The relevant documents must be lodged with the Land Registry by 9.30 a.m. on the date given as the priority date.

During the priority period, the new owner is protected so that they have plenty of time to give the Land Registry all the necessary information to show themselves as new owner on the Register held by the Land Registry, as well as details of any new mortgages, etc. Therefore, the purpose of this search is twofold. First, it protects an intending Purchaser before completion takes place, ensuring that no-one else can register anything against the property during the priority period. Then, secondly, once completion takes place, the Purchaser (now the new owner) will again be protected during the priority period until they are registered with the Land Registry as the new owner.

If the property is to be mortgaged by the Purchaser, the search will generally be made in the name of the lender rather than in the name of the Purchaser. This is because if the search is in the name of the lender, they too will be protected by the priority period as well as the Purchaser. However, if it is made in the Purchaser's name, only the Purchaser has protection. If it is being made in the lender's name, the appropriate box in Panel 9 should be ticked, e.g., here it would be 'C' because the applicant (the lender) would be intending to take a registered charge on the property. Otherwise, whichever box applies should be ticked.

Completion

Completion monies (the balance due to complete the purchase) are usually paid by way of electronic transfer by the Purchaser's solicitors' bank to the Vendor's solicitors' bank account. The other formalities then normally take place through the post or DX in accordance with the code laid down by the Law Society. However, completion can be carried out personally by the Purchaser's solicitor attending at the offices of the Vendor's solicitors although this is not very common these days, especially with property that is registered with the Land Registry. Arrangements are made for the collection of the keys to the property once completion has taken place The keys are often held by estate agents and are handed over by the estate agent to the Purchaser once it has been confirmed that completion has taken place.

Stamp duty land tax (SDLT)

SDLT is payable to the Inland Revenue (now called HM Revenue & Customs) on most property transactions, including those where the value of the property exceeds a certain amount, or where the transaction is part of a larger transaction where the total value exceeds that amount. This tax is calculated according to which band the value of the property falls into, i.e., if the value of the property is under a certain amount, then no SDLT is payable; if it falls into the next category, SDLT is payable at a certain percentage of the purchase price; the next category incurs a higher percentage and the next is higher still. For example, in a domestic freehold transaction, if the property has been sold for £185,000, this falls within the current band having a value of between £120,000 and £250,000.

Since December 2003, documents themselves are no longer sent to be stamped but instead, a Land Transaction Return must be submitted to HM Revenue & Customs within 30 days of the date of the transaction. There are comprehensive Guidance Notes (SDLT6) which should be referred to when completing the Land Transaction Return as these notes give various codes and other information that must be used. However, HM Revenue & Customs has produced a CD which enables completion of the SDLT forms without the guidance notes. The CD includes interactive help and drop-down menus. There are specific instructions about the submission of forms produced using the CD.

The main Land Transaction Return is form SDLT1 which must be completed for all transactions except those that are specifically exempt. A list of exempt transactions may be obtained from HM Revenue & Customs. All transactions that are not exempt are notifiable, and a Land Transaction Return will need to be completed for the majority of transactions. However, where no Land Transaction Return is required, a self-certificate must be sent to the Land Registry. In these cases, the self-certificate (Certification that no Land Transaction Return is required for a Land Transaction) (SDLT60) is completed and sent direct to the Land Registry at the time of registration of the property, without having to go to HM Revenue & Customs first. The appropriate box on the SDLT60 must be ticked to show the reason why no Land Transaction Return is required.

Application by purchaser⁽ᵃ⁾ for official search with priority of the whole of the land in a registered title or a pending first registration application

Land Registry

OS1

Land Registry ___STEVENAGE___ Office

BRICKDALE HOUSE
SWINGATE
STEVENAGE
HERTS
SG1 1XG

Use one form per title. If you need more room than is provided for in a panel, use continuation sheet CS and attach to this form.

1. Administrative area and postcode if known   MORELAND, HERTFORDSHIRE   EN7 8CB

2. Title number *Enter the title number of the registered estate or that allotted to the pending first registration.*
HD 12345

3. Payment of fee ⁽ᵇ⁾ *Place "X" in the appropriate box.*

	For official use only
☐ The Land Registry fee of £ [____] accompanies this application.	Impression of fees
☐ Debit the Credit Account mentioned in panel 4 with the appropriate fee payable under the current Land Registration Fee Order.	

4. The application has been lodged by:⁽ᶜ⁾
Land Registry Key No. (if appropriate)   8964117
Name   PETER WOLF & CO
Address/DX No.   RED RIDING HOOD LANE
NORTHTOWN
ESSEX
1CD 3LA
Reference⁽ᵈ⁾ PW/74
E-mail

Telephone No. 01234 5678	Fax No. 01234 6789

5. If the result of search is to be sent to anyone other than the applicant in panel 4, please supply the name and address of the person to whom it should be sent.

Reference⁽ᵈ⁾

6. Registered proprietor/Applicant for first registration *Enter FULL name(s) of the registered proprietor(s) of the registered estate in the above mentioned title or of the person(s) applying for first registration of the property specified in panel 10.*

SURNAME/COMPANY NAME: BROWN
FORENAME(S):   ALBERT FRANCIS
SURNAME/COMPANY NAME:
FORENAME(S):

7. Search from date *For a search of a* **registered title** *enter in the box a date falling within the definition of search from date in rule 131 of the Land Registration Rules 2003.*[c] *If the date entered is not such a date the application may be rejected. In the case of a* **pending first registration** *search, enter the letters 'FR'.*

> **

8. Applicant *Enter FULL name of each purchaser* **or** *lessee* **or** *chargee.*

ELIZABETH MARY GREEN

9. Reason for application I certify that the applicant intends to: *Place "X" in the appropriate box.*

[X] [P] purchase   [ ] [C] take a registered charge

[ ] [L] take a lease

10. Property details *Address or short description of the property.*

76 BURNT OAK ROAD, MORELAND, EN7 8CB

11. Type of search *Place "X" in the appropriate box.*

[X] **Registered land search**
Application is made to ascertain whether any adverse entry has been made in the register or day list since the date shown in panel 7.

[ ] **Pending first registration search**
Application is made to ascertain whether any adverse entry has been made in the day list since the date of the pending first registration application referred to above.

12. Signature of applicant
or their conveyancer _____ **Date** _____

Explanatory notes

(a) "Purchaser" is defined in Land Registration Rules 2003, r.131. In essence, it is a person who has entered, or intends to enter, into a disposition for valuable consideration as disponee where: (i) the disposition is a registrable disposition (see Land Registration Act 2002, s.27), or (ii) there is a person subject to a duty under the Land Registration Act 2002, s.6, to apply for registration, the application is pending and the disposition would have been a registrable disposition had the estate been registered.
An official search in respect of registered land made by a person other than a "purchaser" should be made in Form OS3.

(b) Cheques are payable to 'Land Registry'. If you hold a credit account but do not indicate that it should be debited, and do not enclose a cheque, the registrar may still debit your account.

(c) If you hold a credit account and want the official search certificate sent to an address different from that associated with your key number, enter your key number, reference and telephone number but otherwise leave panel 4 blank. Complete panel 5 instead.

(d) Enter a maximum of 25 characters including stops, strokes, punctuation etc.

(e) Enter the date shown as the subsisting entries date on an official copy of the register or given as the subsisting entries date at the time of an access by remote terminal.

Practice Guide 12 'Official Searches and Outline Applications' contains further information.

Photocopies of SDLT1 are not acceptable as each Land Transaction Return has a unique reference number printed on it, which is for the use of HM Revenue & Customs.

The Land Transaction Return should be completed in capital letters, in black ink, unfolded and sent to HM Revenue & Customs at the address on the form. Only this particular office will be able to deal with the Land Transaction Return as the data is read by a special computer that other offices do not have. No other documentation or letter should be sent with the form except where a plan may be required. Plans are sometimes required to identify the property but domestic property will not generally need a plan. If a mistake is made on the form, do not use correcting fluid. Check the Guidance Notes (SDLT6) on what to do if an error is made and for full requirements on completion of the form. If using the CD to produce forms, the instructions relating to the CD must be followed.

The completed Land Transaction Return must be signed by the Purchaser. If there is more than one Purchaser it must be signed by all of them. The sections to be completed are as follows (but note that if using the CD mentioned above, some aspects may differ slightly and any specific requirements must be adhered to).

About the transaction

The information in this section gives details about the property, e.g., whether it is residential or not, whether it is freehold or leasehold and the date from which it is to be effective (usually completion date). Most of the boxes to be completed require codes to be inserted which are obtained from SDLT6 (or, as mentioned above, the CD (or other approved software) to complete the forms may be used).

About the tax calculation

This part of the form shows how much was paid for the property, whether in money or money's worth. Whatever is given for the property is called the consideration. This is usually money but, of course, could be something else. This section also deals with other monetary aspects of the transaction, e.g., whether the transaction is linked to another. For example, if someone were selling their house and garden as two separate pieces of land to the same buyer, this would be considered a linked transaction and, therefore, the SDLT payable would be on the total amount, rather than the two individual pieces of land. For complete information, read this section and the whole of the form in conjunction with SDLT6.

About new leases

This will be completed if a new lease is being created.

About the land

Again, for full information, read SDLT6. You will see in this section a reference to NLPG UPRN. This is explained on page 276. This number can be obtained from the NLIS providers mentioned on page 277, even by non-subscribers.

About the Vendor

This gives information about the seller of the property. The agent's details will be whoever is acting for the Vendor, e.g., their solicitor.

Additional Vendor

This part will be completed if the property is being sold jointly and details of the other Vendor will be given here. If there are three or more Vendors, then a supplementary form (SDLT2) must be completed.

About the Purchaser

Details to be given here of the Purchaser or first Purchaser, if there is more than one. The first Purchaser's National Insurance number, if they have one, must be included. The agent will usually be the solicitor acting for the Purchaser.

Additional Purchaser

Details of any second joint Purchaser will be shown here. If there are more than two Purchasers, an additional supplementary form (SDLT2) must be completed.

Additional Supplementary Returns

This part will be completed where applicable, showing which additional forms have been completed and how many of each.

Declaration

This must be signed by the Purchaser(s).

Payment of the SDLT must be made at the same time as sending the form. Payment may be made by cheque enclosed with the return; or various other methods of payment may be used and details of these can be obtained from HM Revenue & Customs website. Once the Land Transaction Return has been submitted with the correct information being provided, and the payment made, HM Revenue & Customs will verify the calculation of SDLT and will issue a certificate. This certificate replaces the impressed stamp on a document and provides proof that SDLT has been paid. The certificate must be sent to the Land Registry when applying for registration of title.

In some instances, where more information is required, supplementary forms may need to be completed in addition to SDLT1. SDLT2 should be completed where there are more than two sellers and/or Purchasers. SDLT3 is completed where additional information is required to identify the property or the transaction involves more than one property. SDLT4 should be completed where additional information is required about the transaction, e.g., where the Purchaser is a company. SDLT60 is a certificate that no Land Transaction Return is required. This is the self-certificate required by the Land Registry mentioned above. Ensure a copy of any of these forms and the SLDT1 are kept on the file.

There is also a scheme whereby residential property purchased in certain specified areas for up to a certain value may be exempt from paying all or some SDLT, although such transactions are still notifiable. These areas are known as disadvantaged areas and further information may be found on HM Revenue & Customs website.

Registering the new owner

After completion, the documents have to be submitted promptly to the Land Registry so that the Register may be updated. The documents must be sent by the new owner's solicitor to the Land Registry with a Land Registry form called Application to Change the Register (Form AP1). At the same time, the Land Transaction Return or a self-certificate, where appropriate, must also be sent to the Land Registry.

The documents being sent to the Land Registry will be listed on the AP1. Besides sending original documents, it is sometimes a requirement that certified copies (see below) must be sent as well. If a copy is sent, this must be listed separately as such on the form. Indeed, the Land Registry stipulates on the form that if it is required to return certain documents, a certified copy must be supplied. The documents that will be sent to the Land Registry are documents such as the Transfer; the new mortgage (or 'charge') and a copy of the charge; and

 **Revenue**

Land Transaction Return

For official use only

Your transaction return

How to fill in this return

The guidance notes that come with this return will help you answer the questions.

- Write inside the boxes. Use black ink and CAPITAL letters.
- If you make a mistake, please cross it out and write the correct information underneath.
- **Leave blank any boxes that don't apply to you** — please don't strike through anything irrelevant.
- Show amounts in whole pounds only, rounded down to the nearest pound. Ignore the pence.

- Fill out the payslip on page 7.
- Do not fold the return. Send it back to us unfolded in the envelope provided.
- **Photocopies are not acceptable.**

If you need help with any part of this return or with anything in the guidance notes, please phone the Stamp Taxes enquiry line on **0845 603 0135**, open 8:30am to 5:00pm Monday to Friday, except Bank Holidays. Calls are charged at local rates. You can get further copies of this return and any supplementary returns from the Orderline on **0845 302 1472**.

Starting your return

ABOUT THE TRANSACTION

sample

1 **Type of property**

Enter code from the guidance notes

2 **Description of transaction**

Enter code from the guidance notes

3 **Interest transferred or created**

Enter code from the guidance notes

4 **Effective date of transaction**

5 **Any restrictions, covenants or conditions affecting the value of the interest transferred or granted?** Put 'X' in one box

☐ Yes   ☐ No

If 'yes' please provide details

6 **Date of contract or conclusion of missives**

7 **Is any land exchanged or part-exchanged?** Put 'X' in one box

☐ Yes   ☐ No

If 'yes' please complete address of location
Postcode

House or building number

Rest of address, including house name, building name or flat number

8 **Is the transaction pursuant to a previous option agreement?** Put 'X' in one box

☐ Yes   ☐ No

SDLT 1   PG 1   BS09/03

+

ABOUT THE TAX CALCULATION

9 Are you claiming relief? Put 'X' in one box

☐ Yes   ☐ No

If 'yes' please show the reason

☐ Enter code from the guidance notes

Enter the charity's registered number, if available, or the company's CIS number

For relief claimed on part of the property only, please enter the amount remaining chargeable

£ [   ] . 0 0

10 What is the total consideration in money or money's worth, including any VAT actually payable for the transaction notified?

£ [   ] . 0 0

11 If the total consideration for the transaction includes VAT, please state the amount

£ [   ] . 0 0

12 What form does the consideration take?
Enter the relevant codes from the guidance notes

13 Is this transaction linked to any other(s)?
Put 'X' in one box

☐ Yes   ☐ No

Total consideration or value in money or money's worth, including VAT paid for all of the linked transactions

£ [   ] . 0 0

14 Total amount of tax due for this transaction

£ [   ] . 0 0

15 Total amount paid or enclosed with this notification

£ [   ] . 0 0

Does the amount paid include payment of any penalties and any interest due? Put 'X' in one box

☐ Yes   ☐ No

ABOUT NEW LEASES

If this doesn't apply, go straight to box 26 on page 3.

16 Type of lease

☐ Enter code from the guidance notes

17 Start date as specified in lease

D D M M Y Y Y Y

18 End date as specified in lease

D D M M Y Y Y Y

19 Rent-free period
Number of months

20 Annual starting rent inclusive of VAT (actually) payable

£ [   ] . 0 0

End date for starting rent

D D M M Y Y Y Y

Later rent known? Put 'X' in one box

☐ Yes   ☐ No

21 What is the amount of VAT, if any?

£ [   ] . 0 0

22 Total premium payable

£ [   ] . 0 0

23 Net present value upon which tax is calculated

£ [   ] . 0 0

24 Total amount of tax due – premium

£ [   ] . 0 0

25 Total amount of tax due – NPV

£ [   ] . 0 0

Check the guidance notes to see if you will need to complete supplementary return 'Additional details about the transaction, including leases', SDLT4.

SDLT 1   PG 2

ABOUT THE LAND including buildings

Where more than one piece of land is being sold or you cannot complete the address field in the space provided, please complete the supplementary return 'Additional details about the land', SDLT3.

26 Number of properties included

27 Where more than one property is involved, do you want a certificate for each property? Put 'X' in one box

   Yes   No

28 Address or situation of land
Postcode

House or building number

Rest of address, including house name, building name or flat number

Is the rest of the address on the supplementary return 'Additional details about the land', SDLT3?
Put 'X' in one box

   Yes   No

29 Local authority number

30 Title number, if any

31 NLPG UPRN

32 If agricultural or development land, what is the area (if known)? Put 'X' in one box

   Hectares   Square metres
Area

33 Is a plan attached? Please note that the form reference number should be written/displayed on map. Put 'X' in one box

   Yes   No

ABOUT THE VENDOR including transferor, lessor

34 Number of vendors included (Note: if more than one vendor, complete boxes 45 to 48)

35 Title Enter MR, MRS, MISS, MS or other title
Note: only complete for an individual

36 Vendor (1) surname or company name

37 Vendor (1) first name(s) Note: only complete for an individual

38 Vendor (1) address
Postcode

House or building number

Rest of address, including house name, building name or flat number

SDLT 1   PG 3

ABOUT THE VENDOR CONTINUED

39 Agent's name

40 Agent's address
    Postcode

    Building number

    Rest of address, including building name

41 Agent's DX number

42 Agent's e-mail address

43 Agent's reference

44 Agent's telephone number

ADDITIONAL VENDOR

Details of other people involved (including transferor, lessor), other than vendor (1). If more than one additional vendor please complete supplementary return 'Land Transaction Return – Additional vendor/purchaser details', SDLT2.

45 Title Enter MR, MRS, MISS, MS or other title
    Note: only complete for an individual

46 Vendor (2) surname or company name

47 Vendor (2) first name(s)
    Note: only complete for an individual

48 Vendor (2) address

    Put 'X' in this box if the same as box 38.

    If not, please give address below
    Postcode

    House or building number

    Rest of address, including house name, building name
    or flat number

SDLT 1   PG 4

+

ABOUT THE PURCHASER including transferee, lessee

49 **Number of purchasers included** (Note: if more than one purchaser is involved, complete boxes 65 to 69)

50 **National Insurance number (purchaser 1), if you have one.** Note: only complete for an individual

51 **Title** Enter MR, MRS, MISS, MS or other title
Note: only complete for an individual

52 **Purchaser (1) surname or company name**

53 **Purchaser (1) first name(s)**
Note: only complete for an individual

54 **Purchaser (1) address**

Put 'X' in this box if the same address as box 28.

If not, please give address below
Postcode

House or building number

Rest of address, including house name, building name or flat number

55 **Is the purchaser acting as a trustee?** Put 'X' in one box

Yes   No

56 **Please give a daytime telephone number – this will help us if we need to contact you about your return**

57 **Are the purchaser and vendor connected?**
Put 'X' in one box

Yes   No

58 **To which address shall we send the certificate?**
Put 'X' in one box

Property (box 28)   Purchaser's (box 54)

Agent's (box 61)

59 **I authorise my agent to handle correspondence on my behalf.** Put 'X' in one box

Yes   No

60 **Agent's name**

61 **Agent's address**
Postcode

Building number

+

Rest of address, including building name

62 **Agent's DX number**

63 **Agent's reference**

64 **Agent's telephone number**

SDLT 1   PG 5

+

ADDITIONAL PURCHASER

Details of other people involved (including transferee, lessee), other than purchaser (1). If more than one additional purchaser, please complete supplementary return 'Land Transaction Return – Additional vendor/purchaser details', SDLT2.

65 **Title** Enter MR, MRS, MISS, MS or other title
Note: only complete for an individual

66 **Purchaser (2) surname or company name**

67 **Purchaser (2) first name(s)**
Note: only complete for an individual

68 **Purchaser (2) address**

Put 'X' in this box if the same as purchaser (1) (box 54).

If not, please give address below
Postcode

House or building number

Rest of address, including house name, building name or flat number

69 **Is the purchaser acting as a trustee?** Put 'X' in one box

Yes   No

+ ## ADDITIONAL SUPPLEMENTARY RETURNS

70 **How many supplementary returns have you enclosed with this return?** Write the number in each box. If none, please put '0'.

Additional vendor/purchaser details, SDLT2

Additional details about the land, SDLT3

Additional details about the transaction, including leases, SDLT4

DECLARATION

71 The purchaser(s) **must sign this return.** Read the notes in Section 1 of the guidance notes, SDLT6, 'Who should complete the Land Transaction Return?'.

If you give false information, you may face financial penalties and prosecution.
The information I have given on this return is correct and complete to the best of my knowledge and belief.

Signature of purchaser 1   Signature of purchaser 2

Please keep a copy of this return and a note of the unique transaction reference number, which is in the 'Reference' box on the payslip.

Finally, please send your completed return to:
Inland Revenue, Stamp Taxes/SDLT, Comben House, Farriers Way, NETHERTON, Merseyside, Great Britain, L30 4RN, or the DX address is: Rapid Data Capture Centre, DX725593, Bootle 9

Please don't fold it – keep it flat and use the envelope provided. Fill out the payslip on the next page and pay in accordance with the 'How to pay' instructions.

SDLT 1   PG 6

How to pay

 Please allow enough time for payment to reach us by the due date. We suggest you allow at least 3 working days for this.

MOST SECURE AND EFFICIENT

We recommend the following payment methods. These are the most secure and efficient.

 Direct Payment
Use the Internet, telephone, BACS Direct Credit or CHAPS to make payment. Provide your bank or building society with the following information
- payment account
- sort code 10-50-41
- account number 23456000
- your reference as shown on the payslip.

 At your bank
Take this form with payment to **your** bank and where possible to **your own** branch. Other banks may refuse to accept payment. If paying by cheque, please make your cheque payable to 'INLAND REVENUE ONLY'.

 At a Post Office
Take this form with your payment to any Post Office. If paying by cheque, please make your cheque payable to 'POST OFFICE LTD'.

Alliance Leicester If you have an Alliance & Leicester account send the completed payslip direct to Bootle.

OTHER PAYMENT METHODS

By post
If you use this method
- Make your cheque payable to 'INLAND REVENUE ONLY'.
- Write your payslip reference after 'INLAND REVENUE ONLY'.
- Send the payslip and your cheque, **both unfolded**, in the envelope provided to
Inland Revenue SDLT
Netherton
Merseyside
L30 4RN

By DX
As above, but send to
Rapid Data Capture Centre
DX725593
Bootle 9

FURTHER PAYMENT INFORMATION

You can find further payment information at
www.inlandrevenue.gov.uk/howtopay

or telephone
01274 530750

▽ Please do not write or mark below this perforation ▽

Alliance & Leicester *Trans cash* **Payslip** **Revenue**   sample   **bank giro credit**

COMMERCIAL BANK
Bootle Merseyside GIR 0AA

Reference 159 209 24

Credit account number 610 5041 £

By transfer from Alliance & Leicester account number

Amount due
(no fee payable at PO counter)
CHEQUE ACCEPTABLE

Name _____
Signature _____ Date _____

Cashier's stamp and initials

For official use only
CASH
CHEQUE

BANK OF ENGLAND
HEAD OFFICE COLLECTION A/C
INLAND REVENUE   £

10-50-41

SDLT1/P

Please do not fold this payslip or write or mark below this line

the form of discharge of the Vendor's mortgage (Form DS1). This form of discharge will not be required where the lender has notified the Land Registry by electronic means that the mortgage has been repaid. This system of Electronic Notification of Discharge of a mortgage is abbreviated to END and if this applies, on Panel 6 of Form AP1, rather than stating that Form DS1 is being lodged with the Land Registry, you would refer to the fact that the END system had been used instead, by typing in, for example, 'Discharge by END' or just 'END'. There has also been the introduction of electronic discharges (EDs) where the lender's computer directly notifies the Land Registry's computer that a mortgage has been repaid. See page 334 for further information on ENDs and EDs.

A fee is payable to the Land Registry for this application. The fee will normally be based upon the value of the transaction. Reference cards to assist in the calculation of fees are obtainable from district land registries. Cheques should be made payable to Land Registry and you should write the title number or address of the property on the reverse of the cheque. Credit accounts cannot be used for making this application although a direct debit payment can be made with agreement of the Land Registry.

Form AP1, together with the relevant documents, must be lodged with the Land Registry within a certain time limit (the time when the 'priority' period expires—see above). If the END or ED system of repaying the Vendor's mortgage (see above) has not been used and Form DS1 is to be submitted to the Land Registry, it sometimes happens that the DS1 has not been received by the new owner's solicitor before the expiry of the priority period. In this case, the Vendor's solicitors will supply an undertaking to the Purchaser's solicitors that they will forward to them the signed DS1 as soon as they receive it. A certified copy of this undertaking will be sent to the Land Registry and DS1 will be sent on to them when it becomes available. However, it is preferable for the DS1, when it is used, to be sent wherever possible with the other documents, so as to save time and expense, and there is usually plenty of time within which to do this. See also page 334 on Paying off the mortgage.

A certified copy is a photocopy of the original document, marked and signed to the effect that it is a true copy. You should ensure that all copies are legible and any plans, etc. are coloured and marked the same as the original. See page 22 regarding copying documents. On the copy of the document, usually at the top, words in the following format are typed certifying the document as a true copy:

We hereby certify this to be a true copy of the original.
Dated this   *   day of   *   2005

This is signed by the solicitor dealing with the matter and the firm's name and address are also given. Many firms in fact have a rubber stamp to certify documents, rather than having to type the wording every time.

Registration can take some time, depending on how busy the Land Registry is. Once the registration is complete, the Land Registry will issue a Title Information Document which contains a copy of the register relating to that property, together with a plan if this is appropriate. A plan will be issued only where changes have been made to any plan previously held by the Land Registry or if a new plan is issued for the first time.

Outline Applications

Although not part of the usual conveyancing process, it is worth mentioning Outline Applications. This type of application enables an interest in land to be registered with the Land Registry where that interest cannot be protected by a priority official search. An

Application to change the register

Land Registry

If you need more room than is provided for in a panel, use continuation sheet CS and attach to this form.

1.	**Administrative area and postcode** if known Moreland - Hertfordshire EN3 2NL
2.	**Title number(s)** HD 12345
3.	If you have already made this application by **outline application**, insert reference number:

4. **This application affects** *Place "X" in the appropriate box.*

☒ the **whole** of the title(s) *Go to panel 5.*

☐ **part** of the title(s) *Give a brief description of the property affected.*

5. **Application, priority and fees** *A fee calculator for all types of applications can be found on Land Registry's website at www.landregistry.gov.uk/fees*

Nature of applications numbered   Value £   Fees paid £
in priority order
1. Discharge
2. Transfer   96,000   **
3. Charge   35,000
                          TOTAL £

Fee payment method: *Place "X" in the appropriate box.*
I wish to pay the appropriate fee payable under the current Land Registration Fee Order:

☐ by cheque or postal order, amount £   made payable to "Land Registry".

☐ by Direct Debit under an authorised agreement with Land Registry.

FOR OFFICIAL USE ONLY
Record of fees paid

Particulars of under/over payments

Fees debited £

Reference number

6. **Documents lodged with this form** *Number the documents in sequence; copies should also be numbered and listed as separate documents. Alternatively you may prefer to use Form DL. If you supply the original document and a certified copy, we shall assume that you request the return of the original; if a certified copy is not supplied, we may retain the original document and it may be destroyed.*

1. Form DS1   2. Transfer   3. Copy Transfer   4. Charge   5. Copy Charge

7. **The applicant is:** *Please provide the full name(s) of the person(s) applying to change the register.*
ELIZABETH MARY GREEN
The application has been lodged by: Peter Wolf & Co
Land Registry Key No. (if appropriate) 8964117
Name (if different from the applicant)
~~Address~~/DX No.   7749 NORTHTOWN

Reference PW/74
E-mail

Telephone No. 01234 5678	Fax No. 01234 8904

FOR OFFICIAL USE ONLY
Codes
Dealing

Status

8.   Where you would like us to deal with someone else *We shall deal only with the applicant, or the person lodging the application if different, unless you place "X" against one or more of the statements below and give the necessary details.*

☐ Send title information document to the person shown below

☐ Raise any requisitions or queries with the person shown below

☐ Return original documents lodged with this form (see note in panel 6) to the person shown below
   If this applies only to certain documents, please specify.

Name
Address/DX No.

Reference
E-mail

Telephone No.	Fax No.

9.   Address(es) for service of the proprietor(s) of the registered estate(s). The address(es) will be entered in the register and used for correspondence and the service of notice. *Place "X" in the appropriate box(es). You may give up to three addresses for service **one** of which **must** be a postal address but does not have to be within the UK. The other addresses can be any combination of a postal address, a box number at a UK document exchange or an electronic address.*

☐ Enter the address(es) from the transfer/assent/lease

☐ Enter the address(es), including postcode, as follows:

☐ Retain the address(es) currently in the register for the title(s)

10. Disclosable overriding interests *Place "X" in the appropriate box.*

☐ This is not an application to register a registrable disposition or it is but no disclosable overriding interests affect the registered estate(s) *Section 27 of the Land Registration Act 2002 lists the registrable dispositions. Rule 57 of the Land Registration Rules 2003 sets out the disclosable overriding interests. Use Form DI to tell us about any disclosable overriding interests that affect the registered estate(s) identified in panel 2.*

☐ Form DI accompanies this application

The registrar may enter a notice of a disclosed interest in the register of title.

11. Information in respect of any new charge *Do not give this information if a Land Registry MD reference is printed on the charge, unless the charge has been transferred.*
Full name and address (including postcode) for service of notices and correspondence of the person to be registered as proprietor of each charge. *You may give up to three addresses for service **one** of which **must** be a postal address but does not have to be within the UK. The other addresses can be any combination of a postal address, a box number at a UK document exchange or an electronic address. For a company include company's registered number, if any. For Scottish companies use an SC prefix and for limited liability partnerships use an OC prefix before the registered number, if any. For foreign companies give territory in which incorporated.*

Unless otherwise arranged with Land Registry headquarters, we require a certified copy of the chargee's constitution (in English or Welsh) if it is a body corporate but is not a company registered in England and Wales or Scotland under the Companies Acts.

**12. Signature of applicant
 or their conveyancer** _____   **Date** _____

Outline Application can be lodged if someone is applying to protect an interest with the whole of the land in a title, but this can only be made if the application cannot be protected by an official search. Outline Applications cannot be made for first registration applications or for matters affecting only part of the land in a title.

For example, an Outline Application cannot be made instead of using Form OS1 but it could be made where a charging order is obtained from the court against a particular property and it is desired to register a notice straight away with the Land Registry.

The Outline Application is made over the telephone using Telephone Services, or by using Land Registry Direct (the computer link with the Land Registry), or by attending in person at a Land Registry, and papers supporting the application must be lodged with the correct Land Registry by noon on the fourth working day (including the day on which the outline application was lodged). There is no form to complete for an Outline Application but specific information has to be given. To assist with the information that will be required, the Land Registry provides desk aid information sheets so that these can be referred to before contacting the Land Registry with the Outline Application.

When the supporting papers are lodged with the Land Registry, an application form must be completed and must quote the Outline Application reference that was given by the Land Registry at the time the Outline Application was made. As long as the papers are correctly lodged within the specified time, the Land Registry will effect registration of the application from the date and time that the Outline Application was received.

Effectively, therefore, an Outline Application is simply a way of quickly lodging certain types of application with the Land Registry, which must be followed up later by lodging supporting papers within a specified time. This can be helpful where it is important to lodge certain notices, etc., with the Land Registry straight away.

Unregistered land

Land in all areas is now subject to compulsory registration (see page 272) and where the property has not been previously registered there are some additional procedures to be dealt with.

Proof of title to unregistered land

Because transactions relating to unregistered land have not been registered with the Land Registry, the person owning the land must be able to produce all old deeds and documents to prove he has good title (or ownership) to that land. Usually, he has to be able to prove good title back through the last 15 years. This is done by showing continuity of title throughout that time, e.g., by choosing a transaction, for example, the sale of the property from one person to another at least 15 years ago. The document used might be an older document called a Conveyance. That document would show that Mr A sold the property to Mr B and then, to show continuity through to the present day, the next document showing Mr B sold the property to Mr C would be produced, and then the next, showing Mr C selling to Mr D—until the current owner, say, Mr E, produces the document showing the sale of the property to him from Mr D. The transaction chosen to begin proving title is known as the 'root of title'.

Abstract of Title

It is sometimes necessary to refer to an earlier deed which may be mentioned in the documents and this document may be 'abstracted'. Abstracting is a very specialised procedure and would normally be done by a fee earner, although it is not really done at all these days. It used to be prepared on brief paper (A3 size). It is headed 'Abstract of Title' and gives the address of the property and the names of the parties to each document. If you see an Abstract you will notice that everything is written in the past tense and is in an abbreviated form, e.g., 'Witnessed in the presence of' becomes 'Witned in psce of', 'The Vendor hereby acknowledges' becomes 'Vdr thby acknd', and so on. In the margin it shows the date of the original document and states that it has been examined with the original, e.g., '1 May 2002. exd. with orig. at the offices of Smith & Jones, 1 High Street, Barnet'. It will also show details of stamp duty that was paid on the original deed. Stamp duty on documents has now been superseded by stamp duty land tax (see page 302). Where stamp duty has been paid on an older document, the abstract would show this, e.g., 'Stp. £10'. Thus, an Abstract is an abbreviated form of an original document. If you do speedwriting you will get the idea very fast!

When an Abstract of Title was done, all deeds and documents that were required to prove title were abstracted into one document so that anyone looking at the abstract could easily see how title to the property had passed from one person to another.

Epitome of title

Alternatively, and this is the usual method these days, photocopies of all deeds and documents constituting proof of title are provided, together with a schedule listing the deeds of which copies are supplied. This is known as an epitome of title.

The schedule will show the year that it is being prepared, with details of the property concerned. The name and date of each document will be typed in date order, with the oldest first and the most recent last, also giving the names of the parties to the document (if any), such as the names of any Purchaser and Vendor. Each document should be numbered consecutively in the schedule. It should also state whether the original document or a photocopy will accompany the schedule. The schedule may even include details of documents that are not deeds, such as death and marriage certificates, because they may show that ownership in the property has passed to someone else.

[Insert the year of typing the epitome]

Epitome of Title

Relating to freehold/leasehold property [*delete as appropriate*]

Known as: [insert the description (address) of the property]

Date of document	Number of document	Details of document	Parties	Whether photocopy or abstract	Whether original to be handed over

The typed schedule should be attached securely to the documents, sometimes by sewing them together in the top left-hand corner (see page 31), or by using some other form of fastening, such as a treasury tag. Before land was registered, the document most commonly used to transfer the land was called a Conveyance. It is the equivalent of a Transfer (see above) but is a longer document. A Conveyance may still be used for the transfer of unregistered land only, although a Transfer may be used instead. Remember, when photocopying deeds, check that the copies are legible and if there is a plan in the original document, you must colour the photocopy to look the same as the original (see Chapter 1 regarding deeds and documents).

Search of the Index Map

The Index Map is a computerised map system based on the Ordnance Survey map. It is an index of registered titles and pending applications for first registration of land.

A search of the Index Map will usually be made where property is unregistered. An application for a search of the Index Map may be made on Land Registry form SIM. The search might be made to ascertain whether land is registered or to find out an unknown title number. (However, if the unknown title number to be found is part of an application for official copies on Form OC1 where it is known that the title is registered, the request can be made on Form OC1 by writing in bold at the top 'Please supply the title number'. In these circumstances, a separate search of the Index Map on form SIM does not need to be made). An Index Map search will also reveal whether there is a pending application to register land for the first time or whether there is a caution against first registration of the land. A caution against first registration would be registered perhaps by someone to protect some sort of right or claim they may have over someone else's as yet unregistered property. The person registering the caution would be notified by the Land Registry when an application is made to register the property.

The application will often be accompanied by a plan showing the property boundaries. There are certain requirements regarding plans submitted with applications, including that they must be based on the latest edition of the large scale Ordnance Survey map.

The Index Map does not contain information on relating franchises or manors. See page 282 for information on franchises and manors. A relating franchise is similar to a franchise as described but instead of being a right over a particular piece of land, it is a right granted within an administrative area. For example, rather than having the right to hold a fair on an identified property, someone might have the right to hold a fair in a certain administrative area. An index is kept of relating franchises and manors, and if it is desired to make a search of this, a separate application should be made on Form SIF.

Further information on these searches may be obtained from the Land Registry.

Registration

After completion of the purchase of unregistered freehold land, the solicitor for the Purchaser has two months in which to lodge the deeds with the Land Registry, together with the application for first registration on Form FR1. This form must be accompanied by the deeds and certain other documents listed on form DL (in duplicate). Where you have to send a copy of a deed, rather than an original, you must indicate this on the form by typing, e.g., 'Copy Conveyance' or 'Certified copy Conveyance', whatever is appropriate. Before sending the deeds to the Land Registry, ensure that you have kept photocopies on the file. The appropriate fee must also be sent to the Land Registry. In due course, the Land Registry will issue the Title Information Document.

The Form FR1 is very similar to the AP1 submitted with regard to registered land. However, there are two additional points on FR1 that are worth mentioning: in Panel 5, a box should be ticked according to the title applied for. Most commonly, absolute title will be applied for, which means that it is only subject to the entries on the Register held by the Land Registry.

Also, the box in Panel 14 will normally be left blank unless you are told to tick it. This is a statement by the person signing the form that they have investigated the title to the property on their client's behalf.

**Application for an
official search
of the index map**

Land Registry

SIM

Land Registry ___STEVENAGE___ Office

BRICKDALE HOUSE
SWINGATE
STEVENAGE
HERTS
SG1 1XG

If you need more room than is provided for in a panel, use continuation sheet CS and attach to this form.

1. Administrative area	MORELAND, HERTFORDSHIRE
2. Property to be searched Postal number or description	76
Name of road	BURNT OAK ROAD
Name of locality	
Town	MORELAND
Postcode	EN7 8CB
Ordnance Survey map reference (if known)	
Known title number(s)	

3. Payment of fee *Place "X" in the appropriate box.*

☐ The Land Registry fee of £ [＿＿＿] accompanies this application.

☐ Debit the Credit Account mentioned in panel 4 with the appropriate fee payable under the current Land Registration Fee Order.

For official use only

Impression of fees

4. The application has been lodged by:

Land Registry Key No. (if appropriate) 8964117
Name   PETER WOLF & CO
Address/DX No.   RED RIDING HOOD LANE
           NORTHTOWN
           ESSEX
           1CD 3LA
Reference PW/74
E-mail

Telephone No. 01234 5678   Fax No.   01234 6789

Material produced by Land Registry
© Crown copyright material is reproduced with the permission of Land Registry

5. If the result of search is to be sent to anyone other than the applicant in panel 4, please supply the name and address of the person to whom it should be sent.

Reference

6. **I apply for an official search of the index map in respect of the land referred to in panel 2 above and shown** _____ **on the attached plan.**

Any attached plan must contain sufficient details of the surrounding roads and other features to enable the land to be identified satisfactorily on the Ordnance Survey map. A plan may be unnecessary if the land can be identified by postal description.

7. **Signature of applicant** _____ **Date** _____

Explanatory notes

1. The purpose and scope of Official Searches of the Index Map are described in Practice Guide 10 'Official searches of the Index Map' obtainable from any Land Registry office. It can also be viewed online at www.landregistry.gov.uk.

2. Please send this application to the appropriate Land Registry office. This information is contained in Practice Guide 51 'Areas served by Land Registry offices'.

3. Please ensure that the appropriate fee payable under the current Land Registration Fee Order accompanies your application. If paying fees by cheque or postal order, these should be crossed and payable to "Land Registry". Where you have requested that the fee be paid by Credit Account, receipt of the certificate of result is confirmation that the appropriate fee has been debited.

© Crown copyright (ref: LR/HQ/Internet) 10/03

First registration application

Land Registry

If you need more room than is provided for in a panel, use continuation sheet CS and attach to this form.

1.	**Administrative area and postcode** *if known* MORELAND, HERTFORDSHIRE EN7 8CB

2. **Address or other description of the estate to be registered**
76 BURNT OAK ROAD, MORELAND, HERTFORDSHIRE EN7 8CB

On registering a rentcharge, profit a prendre in gross, or franchise, show the address as follows:- "Rentcharge, franchise etc, over 2 The Grove, Anytown, Northshire NE2 9OO".

3. **Extent to be registered** *Place "X" in the appropriate box and complete as necessary.*

☒ The land is clearly identified on the plan to the   Conveyance 27.4.1999
Enter nature and date of deed.

☐ The land is clearly identified on the attached plan and shown _____
Enter reference e.g. "edged red".

☐ The description in panel 2 is sufficient to enable the land to be clearly identified on the Ordnance Survey map

When registering a rentcharge, profit a prendre in gross or franchise, the land to be identified is the land affected by that estate, or to which it relates.

4. **Application, priority and fees** *A fee calculator for all types of applications can be found on Land Registry's website at www.landregistry.gov.uk/fees*

Nature of applications
in priority order   Value/premium £   Fees paid £
1. **First registration of the estate** 96,000   *
2. Charge
3.
4.

                                                 TOTAL £ *

Fee payment method: *Place "X" in the appropriate box.*
I wish to pay the appropriate fee payable under the current Land Registration Fee Order:

☐ by cheque or postal order, amount £ _____ made payable to "Land Registry".

☐ by Direct Debit under an authorised agreement with Land Registry.

FOR OFFICIAL USE ONLY
Record of fees paid
Particulars of under/over payments
Fees debited £
Reference number

5. **The title applied for is** *Place "X" in the appropriate box.*

☒ absolute freehold   ☐ absolute leasehold   ☐ good leasehold   ☐ possessory freehold
☐ possessory leasehold

6. **Documents lodged with this form** *List the documents on Form DL. We shall assume that you request the return of these documents. But we shall only assume that you request the return of a statutory declaration, subsisting lease, subsisting charge or the latest document of title (for example, any conveyance to the applicant) if you supply a certified copy of the document. If certified copies of such documents are not supplied, we may retain the originals of such documents and they may be destroyed.*

7. **The applicant is:** *Please provide the full name of the person applying to be registered as the proprietor.*
ELIZABETH MARY GREEN
Application lodged by: PETER WOLF & CO
Land Registry Key No.(if appropriate) 8964117
Name (if different from the applicant)
Address/DX No.   RED RIDING HOOD LANE
                        NORTHTOWN
Reference PW/74   ESSEX. ICD 3LA
E-mail

FOR OFFICIAL USE ONLY Status codes

Telephone No. 01234 5678   Fax No. 01234 6789

8. Where you would like us to deal with someone else *We shall deal only with the applicant, or the person lodging the application if different, unless you place "X" against one or more of the statements below and give the necessary details.*

    ☐ Send title information document to the person shown below

    ☐ Raise any requisitions or queries with the person shown below

    ☐ Return original documents lodged with this form (see note in panel 6) to the person shown below
      If this applies only to certain documents, please specify.

Name
Address/DX No.

Reference
E-mail

Telephone No.	Fax No.

9. Address(es) for service of every owner of the estate. The address(es) will be entered in the register and used for correspondence and the service of notice. *In this and panel 10, you may give up to three addresses for service* **one** *of which* **must** *be a postal address but does not have to be within the UK. The other addresses can be any combination of a postal address, a box number at a UK document exchange or an electronic address. For a company include the company's registered number, if any. For Scottish companies, use an SC prefix, and for limited liability partnerships, use an OC prefix before the registered number if any. For foreign companies give territory in which incorporated.*

76 BURNT OAK ROAD
MORELAND
HERTS
EN7 8CB

Unless otherwise arranged with Land Registry headquarters, we require a certified copy of the owner's constitution (in English or Welsh) if it is a body corporate but is not a company registered in England or Wales or Scotland under the Companies Acts.

10. Information in respect of a chargee or mortgagee *Do not give this information if a Land Registry MD reference is printed on the charge, unless the charge has been transferred.*
Full name and address (including postcode) for service of notices and correspondence of the person entitled to be registered as proprietor of each charge. *You may give up to three addresses for service; see panel 9 as to the details you should include.*

Unless otherwise arranged with Land Registry headquarters, we require a certified copy of the chargee's constitution (in English or Welsh) if it is a body corporate but is not a company registered in England and Wales or Scotland under the Companies Acts.

11. Where the applicants are joint proprietors *Place "X" in the appropriate box*

    ☐ The applicants are holding the property on trust for themselves as joint tenants

    ☐ The applicants are holding the property on trust for themselves as tenants in common in equal shares

    ☐ The applicants are holding the property *(complete as necessary)*

12. Disclosable overriding interests *Place "X" in the appropriate box.*

    ☒ No disclosable overriding interests affect the estate

    ☐ Form DI accompanies this application

Rule 28 of the Land Registration Rules 2003 sets out the disclosable overriding interests that you must tell us about. You must use Form DI to tell us about any disclosable overriding interests that affect the estate.

The registrar may enter a notice of a disclosed interest in the register of title.

13. The title is based on the title documents listed in Form DL which are all those that are in the possession or control of the applicant.

Place "X" in the appropriate box. If applicable complete the second statement; include any interests disclosed only by searches other than local land charges. Any interests disclosed by searches which do not affect the estate being registered should be certified.

☐ All rights, interests and claims affecting the estate known to the applicant are disclosed in the title documents and Form DI if accompanying this application. There is no-one in adverse possession of the property or any part of it.

☐ In addition to the rights, interests and claims affecting the estate disclosed in the title documents or Form DI if accompanying this application, the applicant only knows of the following:

14. *Place "X" in this box if you are NOT able to give this certificate.* ☐

We have fully examined the applicant's title to the estate, including any appurtenant rights, or are satisfied that it has been fully examined by a conveyancer in the usual way prior to this application.

15. We have authority to lodge this application and request the registrar to complete the registration.

16. **Signature of applicant
or their conveyancer** _____ **Date** _____

Note: Failure to complete the form with proper care may deprive the applicant of protection under the Land Registration Act if, as a result, a mistake is made in the register.

© Crown copyright (ref: LR/HQ/CD-ROM) 6/03

List of documents

Please complete in duplicate.

Land Registry

DL

---

1. Property

76 Burnt Oak Road, Moreland, Herts EN7 8CB

---

2. Documents lodged

Notes (a) *The first column is for official use only. If the Registry places an asterisk "*" in this column, it shows that we have kept that document.*

(b) *Number the documents in sequence; copies should also be numbered and listed as separate documents.*

(c) *If you supply the original document and a certified copy, we shall assume that you request the return of the original; if a certified copy is not supplied, we may retain the original document and it may be destroyed. For first registration applications, see the note in panel 6 of Form FR1.*

OFFICIAL USE ONLY (a)	Item No. (b)	Date	Document (c)	Parties
	1	1988	Abstract of Title	
	2	27.4.99	Conveyance	(1) Peter Wiseman (2) Albert Francis Brown
	3	27.4.99	Copy conveyance	(1) Peter Wiseman (2) Albert Francis Brown
	4	2.8.2005	Transfer	(1) Albert Francis Brown (2) Elizabeth Mary Green
	5	2.8.2005	Copy Transfer	(1) Albert Francis Brown (2) Elizabeth Mary Green
	6	2.8.2005	Charge	(1) Elizabeth Mary Green (2) Givemore Building Society
	7	2.8.2005	Copy Charge	(1) Elizabeth Mary Green (2) Givemore Building Society

Land Charges searches

It is essential to carry out a search of the Land Charges Register at Plymouth if land is not registered with the Land Registry. The Land Charges Register is computerised and has records of charges and interests which may be registered against a particular owner of land. Additionally, a solicitor acting for a building society or other lender must carry out a bankruptcy only search in the Land Charges Register to check that the purchaser is solvent, whether the land is registered or not.

Form K15 is completed to make a full search. The form must specify the precise name of the person being searched against, the district and the period of years to be covered. Where the form mentions 'former county', this is to be completed if the name of the county has been changed, or if the property is now in a different county, e.g., where county boundaries may have been changed. The fee earner will provide you with any necessary information. A search is usually made against present owners and sometimes previous owners. Make sure you enter the names to be searched against exactly as requested on the form, taking care that the surname is entered on the correct line of the form. This is extremely important. You should use the names as shown on the title documents or however the fee earner specifies, always ensuring that they are correctly typed: the name entered on the form is the name that will be searched against. If there is any doubt about how a person's name is set out, for example, whether double barrelled or not, then an extra search should be applied for, covering each possibility. This applies to all variations of names, such as abbreviations or change of name. Each name must be entered separately on the form and should be in capital letters. If a person is titled, or the name being searched against is a company or other organisation, the form must be completed in accordance with the instructions laid down by the Land Registry. These instructions can be found in a booklet which is available from the Land Charges Department, and gives full instructions on all aspects of completing the form.

Search forms may be sent through the post and do not need an accompanying covering letter, but a note must be made on the file to show that the search has been done. It is best to keep a photocopy on your file. See below for information on making Land Charges searches in person or by fax or telephone. A fee per name searched against is payable. Postal or hand delivered searches may be paid for by cheque (payable to Land Registry), postal order, money order or credit account. See also page 282 regarding key numbers and credit accounts.

If the result of a search shows an entry, the Purchaser's solicitor will send it to the Vendor's solicitor, asking if the entry does in fact relate to their client. Often it will not, and the Vendor's solicitor will certify on the search result form that the entries do not relate to their client. If further information is required relating to an entry which has been revealed, an application may be made on Form K19.

Bankruptcy only searches

Whether or not property is registered, a solicitor acting for a building society or other lender may carry out a bankruptcy only search in the Land Charges Register to check that the potential borrower is solvent. This application is made on Form K16 and is similar to K15, except that it requires only the names to be searched to be inserted on the form.

The Land Charges Department will return the result of the search on a form which will reveal any subsisting entries or will state that there are none.

Form K15   **Land Charges Act 1972** | Payment of fee |

APPLICATION FOR AN OFFICIAL SEARCH

NOT APPLICABLE TO REGISTERED LAND

Application is hereby made for an official search in the index to the registers kept pursuant to
the Land Charges Act 1972 for any subsisting entries in respect of the undermentioned particulars.

Insert a cross (X) in this box if the fee is to be paid through a credit account (see Note 3 overleaf).   **X**

IMPORTANT: Please read the notes overleaf before completing this form.

For Official Use Only		NAMES TO BE SEARCHED (Please use BLOCK LETTERS and see Note 4 overleaf)		PERIOD OF YEARS (see Note 5 overleaf)	
STX				From	To
	Forename(s)	ALBERT FRANCIS		2000	2005
	SURNAME	BROWN			
	Forename(s)				
	SURNAME				
	Forename(s)				
	SURNAME				
	Forename(s)				
	SURNAME				
	Forename(s)				
	SURNAME				
	Forename(s)				
	SURNAME				

COUNTY (see Note 6 overleaf)	HERTFORDSHIRE
FORMER COUNTY	
DESCRIPTION OF LAND (see Note 7 overleaf)	76 BURNT OAK ROAD MORELAND EN7 8CB
FORMER DESCRIPTION	

Particulars of Applicant (see Notes 8, 9 and 10 overleaf)		Name and address (including postcode) for despatch of certificate (Leave blank if certificate is to be returned to applicant's address)
KEY NUMBER	Name and address (including postcode)	
8964117	PETER WOLF & CO RED RIDING HOOD LANE NORTHTOWN ESSEX ICD 3LA	

Applicant's reference	Date	FOR OFFICIAL USE ONLY
PW/74	**	

Material produced by Land Registry
© Crown copyright material is reproduced with the permission of Land Registry

NOTES FOR GUIDANCE OF APPLICANTS

The following notes are supplied for assistance in making the application overleaf. Detailed information for the making of all kinds of applications to the Land Charges Department is contained in a booklet entitled "Computerised Land Charges Department: a practical guide for solicitors" which is obtainable on application at the address shown below.

1. **Effect of search.** The official certificate of the result of this search will have no statutory effect in relation to registered land (see Land Registration Act 1925, s.59 and Land Charges Act 1972, s.14).

2. **Bankruptcy only searches.** Form K16 should be used for Bankruptcy only searches.

3. **Fees.** These must be paid by credit account or by cheque or postal order made payable to "HM Land Registry" (see the guide referred to above).

4. **Names to be searched.** The forename(s) and surname of each individual must be entered on the appropriate line of the form. The name of a company or other body should commence on the forename line and may continue on the surname line (the words "Forename(s)" and "Surname" should be crossed through). If you are searching more than 6 names, use a second form.

5. **Period of years to be searched.** The inclusive period to be covered by a search should be entered in complete years, e.g. 1968-1975.

6. **County names.** This must be the appropriate name as set out in the Appendix to Land Charges Practice Leaflet No. 3. Searches affecting land within the Greater London area should state "GREATER LONDON" as the county name. ANY RELEVANT FORMER COUNTY SHOULD ALWAYS BE STATED (see the Appendix to Land Charges Practice Leaflet No. 3 which lists county names).

7. **Land description.** It is not essential to provide a land description but, if one is given, any relevant former description should also be given (see the guide referred to above).

8. **Key Number.** If you have been allocated a key number, please take care to enter this in the space provided overleaf, whether or not you are paying fees through your credit account.

9. **Applicant's name and address.** This need not be supplied if the applicant's key number is correctly entered in the space provided overleaf.

10. **Applicant's reference.** Any reference must be limited to 25 characters, including any oblique strokes and punctuation.

11. **Despatch of this form.** When completed, send this application to the address shown below, which is printed in a position so as to fit within a standard window envelope.

┌ **The Superintendent** ┐
Land Charges Department   (see Note 11 above)
Search Section
Plumer House, Tailyour Road,
Crownhill, PLYMOUTH PL6 5HY
└ **DX 8249 PLYMOUTH (3)** ┘

Crown Copyright (ref: LR/HQ) 11/01

Land Charges searches in person

Personal applications for full searches may be made to the Land Charges Department during the hours of 10.00 a.m. to 5.00 p.m. Monday to Friday. The applicant will be able to see the result of the search on the Land Charges operator's computer terminal screen, up to a maximum of 25 entries against one name. However, if a personal application is made, no certificate is issued by the Land Charges Registry at the time of the search—it will be posted in Form K17 or K18 to the address supplied by the applicant. Personal applications must be paid for by cash or credit account.

Telephone, telex and fax searches can only be made where solicitors have a credit account with the Land Charges Registry. The solicitor has a reference number to quote, known as a 'key number' (see page 282). If you make a search other than by post, do *not* write to confirm it.

The Land Charges Department is at Plumer House, Tailyour Road, Crownhill, Plymouth, Devon, PL6 5HY (General enquiries, tel: (01752) 636666).

Land Charges searches by fax

Certain applications may be made by fax and these are as follows:

(a) Application for a full or bankruptcy only search on Form K15 or K16.

(b) Application for an office copy of an entry in a register on Form K19.

The result of the search or office copy will be sent to the applicant by post. This service is available only to those with a credit account.

Land Charges searches by telephone

Telephone applications for full searches or bankruptcy only searches may be made from 9 a.m. to 5 p.m. on normal working days. Applications for office copies may only be made by telephone if it transpires that there is an entry whilst a search is being conducted by telephone. The procedure is as follows:

(a) Dial the correct number.

(b) When the operator answers, give your key number, together with the name and address of the firm.

(c) Give your firm's reference—the maximum number of digits allowed is 10, including punctuation. This will be printed on the certificate.

(d) The operator will ask if you require a full search or a bankruptcy only search.

If a full search is required, give particulars of the first search to be done, in the following order:

(a) County (and any former county).

(b) Name to be searched—forename and then surname.

(c) Period in whole years to be covered by the search.

If a bankruptcy only search is required, the only particulars needed are the names to be searched.

If there are 10 or less entries, the operator will read them out over the telephone. If there are more than 10, the operator will state this but will not read them out. If there are more than 100 entries the operator will ask for a short description of the land (and any former description). If an entry is disclosed you can ask for an office copy of that entry.

The Land Charges Registry will post the certificate (on Form K17 or K18). This will be sent only to the firm making the application. Form K17 shows that there is no entry on the Register. Form K18 shows details of any entry.

Applications may also be made by telex but for the exact layout and further details on all Land Charges Department searches, you should consult their booklet called 'Computerised Land Charges Department—A Practical Guide'.

Leases

For secretarial purposes, if the property to be sold is leasehold, most of the enquiries and forms are as described earlier for freehold property. Where the lease is for more than 7 years, the details have to be registered with the Land Registry, just as they are for freehold property. Additionally, where a lease is concerned, you may have to type a new lease setting out all the terms agreed between the parties.

A Lease grants occupancy of property for a specified time in exchange for a sum of money and/or rent. The rent payable under a Lease can vary greatly, for example, where someone buys the lease of domestic property for, say, a 99-year period, they will pay a large sum of money similar to what they would pay if the property were freehold, and they will probably pay what is known as a 'peppercorn' rent which is a rent of nominal value only. However, especially where commercial premises are leased, the rent will usually be at a high commercial rate. Where rent is payable at the full market value for the property, this is known as a rack rent.

Payment of rent under a lease is normally made on the 'usual quarter days'. These are 25 March, 24 June, 29 September and 25 December.

The owner of the property is the Landlord or Lessor, and the person to whom he grants the occupancy of the property is the Tenant or the Lessee. A person holding a Lease may wish to sell his rights in it to another person. This is called 'assigning the lease' and the document is called an Assignment. The original landlord is then called Head Lessor or Superior Landlord and the document he holds is the Head Lease or Superior Lease. The person who is assigning the Lease is the Assignor, Vendor or Seller, and the person taking it is the Assignee or Purchaser.

There is some protection in law for leaseholders where the lease does not have long to run. If someone owns a leasehold house, they may, under certain circumstances, buy the freehold of that property. This is called enfranchisement.

Where someone owns a leasehold flat, they may apply (certain criteria must be met) to buy a new long lease. Alternatively, if all the leaseholders in a block of flats were willing and conditions were met, they could all join in the purchase of the freehold of the building, which is known as collective enfranchisement. However, this would require all the leaseholders wanting to do this at the same time.

A Lease will be engrossed in duplicate, so that when the transaction has been completed, each party holds a copy executed by the other—an 'original' (signed by the Lessor) and 'counterpart' (signed by the Lessee). It is usually a much longer document than the example given here. You will see each paragraph is numbered and normally the first word of each paragraph, along with certain other keywords, are typed in capital letters and perhaps underlined, but this layout is traditional only and you must follow your organisation's own house style. For further information on the layout of documents and attestation clauses, see Chapter 1.

Example lease

THIS LEASE is made the   day of   2005 BETWEEN JOSEPH BLOGGS of 123 North Road Southtown in the County of Essex Salesman (hereinafter called the 'Lessor' which expression where the context so admits includes the owner or owners for the time being of the reversion immediately expectant on the term hereby granted) of the one part and JEAN SMITH of 234 South Road Northtown in the County of Essex Waitress (hereinafter called the 'Lessee' which expression shall where the context so admits include her successors in title) of the other part NOW THIS DEED WITNESSES as follows:

1. THE Lessor hereby demises unto the Lessee ALL THAT ground floor flat known as 22A Seventeen Street Northtown aforesaid (hereinafter called the 'property') TO HOLD the same unto the Lessee for the term of eighteen years from the   day of   2005 YIELDING AND PAYING therefor during the said term the yearly rent of FIVE THOUSAND THREE HUNDRED POUNDS (£5,300) free of all deductions by equal quarterly payments on the usual quarter days in every year the first of such payments to be made on the   day of   2005

2. THE Lessee hereby covenants with the Lessor as follows

(1) TO PAY the said rent free of all deductions at the times and in the manner aforesaid

(2) TO PAY all rates taxes assessments charges and outgoings which are now or shall during the said term become payable in respect of the property

Signed as a deed by   )
JOSEPH BLOGGS in the   )
presence of:)

Signature of witness ....
Name (in BLOCK CAPITALS) ....
Address ....
....

Signed as a deed by   )
JEAN SMITH in the   )
presence of:)

Signature of witness...
Name (in BLOCK CAPITALS) ....
Address ....
....

DATED   2005

JOSEPH BLOGGS

to

JEAN SMITH

LEASE

of

Flat 22A Seventeen Street
Northtown Essex

Peter Wolf & Co.,
Red Riding Hood Lane,
Northtown,
Essex

tel: 01234 5678
ref: PW/89

Commonhold

It is appropriate, whilst mentioning leases, to explain about commonhold, which has been recently introduced. Although it is not leasehold, commonhold is an alternative to creating long leases and will, perhaps, better serve the requirements of owners of flats and other properties where there are communal areas. It is not a replacement for leases, but simply another way of dealing with ownership of property that has been divided up into, say, flats or offices.

Commonhold properties are known as units and the owners will be unit holders. The unit holder will own the freehold of his individual property but with some restrictions. A Commonhold Association will be formed to deal with the provision of services and upkeep to the areas of property that are common to all the unit holders. A Commonhold Association is effectively a private company and will be registered at Companies House. The Land Registry will also register the association on presentation of the memorandum and articles of association (see page 228).

There are various criteria to be met before commonhold property can be created and it is unlikely that many existing leasehold properties will be able to be converted to commonhold as all the existing leaseholders in a property (as well as the owner of the freehold) would have to give their consent. It will more than likely be used, where required, for new developments and renovations of blocks of flats or offices which have not yet been occupied.

NHBC agreement

This is another document you may come across in a conveyancing transaction. A body called the National House Building Council (NHBC) was set up some years ago to protect house Purchasers from, among other things, bad workmanship of house builders who subsequently became insolvent. Most reputable building firms are now registered members of the NHBC and in fact lenders will not normally lend money on a new property unless the builder is registered as a member of the NHBC.

The NHBC Scheme gives a ten-year warranty to Purchasers of new homes and the current scheme is called Buildmark Cover. If the first Purchaser sells his property, then subsequent Purchasers are still covered by the scheme until its cover ends. Any documents relating to the NHBC should be kept safely and with any other deeds or documents relating to the property.

Public sector housing

You may also meet the expression 'public sector housing'. This relates to housing where, for example, the landlord is a local authority, a housing corporation or certain other specified public body. Under certain circumstances, persons renting such housing have the right to buy their house or flat at a discounted price.

Business premises

Leasing of business premises varies in some instances from the way in which matters relating to dwellinghouses are dealt with.

Business leases, i.e., for factories, shops, offices, etc., are usually for relatively short terms. There is often no purchase price as the property is let out at a full market rent for a set period of years. Where the period of time is very short, there is often no contract. The parties agree on the rent and terms of the tenancy—known as 'heads of agreement'. If the tenant has to carry out all the maintenance on the property, this is known as a 'full repairing lease'.

Mortgages

Most people buying property take out a loan or 'mortgage' with a building society, bank or other financial institution. In some cases, a local authority will lend money, especially if the property in question belongs to the council and is being sold to the tenant. A mortgage is a type of 'legal charge'.

There are several types of mortgage available, e.g., repayment mortgage, endowment mortgage, pension mortgage, and often the terms of individual mortgages will vary depending on any special incentives offered by the lender or other factors taken into consideration.

Building society's panel of solicitors

Solicitors acting for a Purchaser will also often act for the building society or other lender who is providing the mortgage. The solicitor must normally be on the building society's 'panel'. This means that the building society has approved that firm of solicitors to act for it in dealing with mortgages. Most firms dealing in conveyancing are on most national building societies' panels.

Offer of advance

The building society will usually carry out its own survey on the property to be purchased. Once the building society (the 'mortgagee') is happy that the property is suitable to lend money on, and its enquiries about the person to whom it is lending money (the 'mortgagor') are satisfactory, it will make an 'offer of advance' to the mortgagor, i.e., an offer to lend him an amount of money using the property in question as security. This offer of advance is sent to the mortgagor and to his solicitors.

Once contracts have been exchanged, the building societies (both those of the Vendor and the Purchaser) are informed by their respective solicitors of the completion date.

Building society forms

After exchange of contracts, the Vendor's solicitors will request a redemption statement from the building society, i.e., a statement showing how much money is required to pay off the outstanding mortgage on the completion date. Then when the completion monies are received from the Purchaser's solicitors, the Vendor can account to the building society for outstanding monies and thus redeem his mortgage. The building society's redemption statement will also show the daily rate of interest due in case there is a delay in completion. Also, after exchange of contracts, the Purchaser's solicitors report to the building society on a form provided by the building society, known as the Report on Title. This is to assure the building society that title to the property is satisfactory and that there are no adverse obligations or covenants affecting the property.

The building society reference relating to the mortgage is also called a roll number and must be quoted in all correspondence with the building society. The mortgage deed also has to be completed and signed by the mortgagor.

Bankruptcy search

Where solicitors are acting for a lender, they will make a bankruptcy search against the potential borrower (see page 326). Many solicitors, when acting for a Purchaser who is taking out a mortgage, will also act for the lender. Therefore, in these circumstances, they will be making the search in their capacity as acting for the lender and they will be making the search against the Purchaser who may also be their client. The bankruptcy search will be made whether the property being mortgaged is registered or unregistered.

Paying off the mortgage

When someone wishes to sell his property, he must pay off any mortgage or 'redeem' or 'discharge' it. The solicitors acting for the borrower will complete the appropriate form, usually Land Registry Form DS1, and send it, together with the cheque if the money has not already been remitted, to the lender to sign or seal the form by way of receipt. You should ensure that a copy is kept on the file before it is posted. The form will then be returned to the borrower's solicitors and this is proof that the mortgage has in fact been settled. However, the form cannot be signed by the lender until it knows that the money has been paid (usually this will be when the sale has been completed). Therefore, the Vendor's solicitors will undertake to the Purchaser's solicitors to obtain this form duly executed (signed and/or sealed) from the lender and then forward it on to the Purchaser's solicitors.

Getting the completed Form DS1 to the Land Registry can be a rather convoluted process and the Land Registry will accept an electronic message from authorised lenders as evidence that the mortgage has been discharged, rather than having to use Form DS1. This Electronic Notification of Discharge system (ENDs) may be used by authorised lenders when any residential charge is repaid through a conveyancer.

Where the ENDs is being used and the borrower wishes to repay his mortgage, the lender will provide the borrower's solicitor with a Form END1. This form is for electronic use only and not in paper format. It should be completed and returned to the lender instead of sending Form DS1. As soon as the lender receives payment, it will transmit by a secure electronic link, the END to the Land Registry. Many lenders are now using ENDs and a list of ENDs users can be found on the Land Registry's website.

Where any forms are being sent to the Land Registry which would otherwise have mentioned Form DS1 as being submitted, they will instead refer to the use of the END system, e.g., by stating 'Discharge by END' or just 'END'.

More recently, electronic discharges (EDs) have been introduced. This is a system that allows mortgage lenders to electronically discharge a mortgage direct with the Land Registry. When a mortgage is redeemed, the lender's computer system will send a message to the Land Registry's computer system via a secure network. The Land Registry's computer system will automatically make certain checks and if everything is in order, the details of the mortgage on the register will be automatically cancelled. This will generally happen immediately and the entire process will normally take a few seconds. An ED can be sent only for the discharge of whole. At the time of writing, not all lenders have the facility to use this method of discharge.

Where the only transaction taking place is the paying off of a mortgage, and there is no sale or purchase to consider nor anything else that would normally be required to be

**Cancellation of entries
relating to a
registered charge**

Land Registry

DS1

This form should be accompanied by either Form AP1 or Form DS2.
If you need more room than is provided for in a panel, use continuation sheet CS and attach to this form.

1. Title Number(s) of the Property	HD 12345
2. Property	76 Burnt Oak Road, Moreland, Hertfordshire EN7 8CB
3. Date	
4. Date of charge	2 August 2005
5. Lender	Givemore Building Society of Peartree House, 1 Little Road, Southtown, Herts EN3 8LX

6. The Lender acknowledges that the property is no longer charged as security for the payment of sums due under the charge

7. Date of Land Registry facility letter, if any

8. *To be executed as a deed by the lender or in accordance with the above facility letter.*

[The appropriate attestation clause will be inserted here]

© Crown copyright (ref: LR/HQ/CD-ROM) 6/03

registered with the Land Registry, Form DS2 (application to cancel entries relating to a registered charge) may be completed and sent to the Land Registry.

Second mortgage

You may often come across people taking out a second mortgage on their property. This is to obtain a further loan since taking out the first mortgage.

Insurance policies

Insurance policies are often taken out at the same time as a mortgage. This is to protect the building society or other lender (the 'mortgagee') in case the mortgagor dies before the mortgage has been repaid. If this unfortunate event does not occur and once the mortgage is finally repaid, the insurance policy will often provide for a lump sum to be paid to the insured person. This type of insurance policy is different from the insurance policies taken out to cover the property itself.

National Conveyancing Protocol

This is a scheme which may be used on a voluntary basis by solicitors when dealing with domestic conveyancing matters. It is designed to speed up conveyancing procedures and make those procedures easier for clients to understand. Although the scheme, which is known as TransAction, is not compulsory, most solicitors are registered with the Law Society as potential users of it. The scheme uses the terms 'Buyer' and 'Seller', rather than 'Purchaser' and 'Vendor'.

Solicitors involved in domestic conveyancing must notify the solicitors acting for the other party whether they will be using the Protocol and, if so, whether the whole transaction will be carried out under the Protocol, or just part of it. Once the Protocol is in use for a particular transaction, any departure from it must be notified in writing to the other party.

For those firms who are users of the scheme, some of the forms and documents used are different from those mentioned earlier and where this occurs, the text in this chapter indicates which is the alternative National Conveyancing Protocol form to be used. The idea of TransAction is to do away with lengthy questions and answers between the Buyer and Seller—this system uses questionnaires and information forms where, in many cases, all that is required is the ticking of a box. The first two pages of the Seller's Property Information Form are shown here to give you an idea as to what the TransAction forms look like. Additionally, National Conveyancing Protocol forms will often contain more information and detail than the other forms they replace so that the Purchaser will not have to keep coming back to the Seller to ask lots of further questions (the information will have been provided in advance), thus saving time.

Briefly, if the Protocol is to be adopted, the Seller's solicitor puts together as much information about the property as possible so that as soon as a buyer is found, the solicitor can send a prepared package of information to the Buyer's solicitor. This package will contain such documents as a draft contract, official copies of the register, the Seller's Property Information Form together with copies of any planning permissions, guarantees, etc., the completed Fixtures, Fittings and Contents form and, if the property concerned is leasehold, a copy of the lease, together with details of insurance, maintenance charges, etc.

SELLER'S PROPERTY INFORMATION FORM (4th edition)

Address of the Property:

IMPORTANT NOTE TO SELLERS – PLEASE READ THIS FIRST

* Please complete this form carefully. If you are unsure how to answer the questions, ask your solicitor before doing so.

* This form in due course will be sent to the buyer's solicitor and will be seen by the buyer who is entitled to rely on the information.

* For many of the questions you need only tick the correct answer. Where necessary, please give more detailed answers on a separate sheet of paper. Then send all the replies to your solicitor. This form will be passed to the buyer's solicitor.

* The answers should be those of the person whose name is on the deeds. If there is more than one of you, you should prepare the answers together.

* It is very important that your answers are correct because the buyer is entitled to rely on them in deciding whether to go ahead. Incorrect or incomplete information given to the buyer direct through your solicitor or selling agent or even mentioned to the buyer in conversation between you, may mean that the buyer can claim compensation from you or even refuse to complete the purchase.

* If you do not know the answer to any question you must say so.

* The buyer takes the property in its present physical condition and should, if necessary, seek independent advice, e.g. instruct a surveyor. You should not give the buyer your views on the condition of the property.

* If anything changes after you fill in this questionnaire but before the sale is completed, tell your solicitor immediately. THIS IS AS IMPORTANT AS GIVING THE RIGHT ANSWERS IN THE FIRST PLACE.

* Please pass to your solicitor immediately any notices you have received which affect the property, including any notices which arrive at any time before completion of your sale.

* If you have a tenant, tell your solicitor immediately if there is any change in the arrangement but do nothing without asking your solicitor first.

* You should let your solicitor have any letters, agreements or other documents which help answer the questions. If you know of any which you are not supplying with these answers, please tell your solicitor about them.

* Please complete and return the separate Fixtures, Fittings and Contents Form. It is an important document which will form part of the contract between you and the buyer. Unless you mark clearly on it the items which you wish to remove, they will be included in the sale and you will not be able to take them with you when you move.

* You may wish to delay the completion of the Fixtures, Fittings and Contents Form until you have a prospective buyer and have agreed the price.

Prop 1/1

Part I – to be completed by the seller

Information in the seller's possession or knowledge

1   Boundaries

"Boundaries" mean any fence, wall, hedge or ditch which marks the edge of your property.

1.1   Looking towards the house from the road, who either owns or accepts responsibility for the boundary:

Please mark the appropriate box

(a) on the left?

WE DO	NEXT DOOR	SHARED	NOT KNOWN

(b) on the right?

WE DO	NEXT DOOR	SHARED	NOT KNOWN

(c) across the back?

WE DO	NEXT DOOR	SHARED	NOT KNOWN

1.2   If you have answered "not known", which boundaries have you actually repaired or maintained?

(Please give details)

_____

_____

_____

1.3   Do you know of any boundary being moved in the last 20 years?

(Please give details)

_____

_____

_____

2   Disputes and complaints

2.1   Do you know of any disputes or anything which might lead to a dispute about this or any neighbouring property?

NO	YES: (PLEASE GIVE DETAILS)

_____

_____

_____

Prop 1/2

Notification should also be given of the Seller's anticipated date for completion. The Seller's solicitor should also supply details about the Seller's own sale, provided he has consent to divulge this information. At the same time, the Buyer's solicitor should be asked whether the Buyer will be paying a 10 per cent deposit. The sale will continue to completion using, where appropriate, the TransAction forms.

If you do find you are working under this scheme, you will easily get used to a few things being done at different stages and the different forms being used. Forms for local searches, etc. are still the same.

Further information on the Protocol scheme is available from the Law Society.

Forms

Forms are often sent without a covering letter. In these cases, you must note your file in some way to show exactly what form went out and when, together with a note of any fee paid. Some people make a note on the file and others keep a photocopy of the form. It is worth remembering that the Land Registry uses the DX system (see page 20) and therefore if your firm is on the DX you should give your DX number in the address box on the Land Registry forms. It is essential that forms go to the correct district Land Registry.

Many forms are now electronically produced within firms either by using software they have purchased or their own forms which have been approved by the Land Registry, rather than completing forms which have been individually purchased. A considerable number of forms are used in conveyancing—more than can be mentioned here—but once you have the ability to complete those which have been mentioned here and you have grasped conveyancing terminology, you have more than won the battle. Also, there are often helpful notes on forms to assist with their completion.

Cheques for the Land Registry

When cheques are sent to the Land Registry, it is helpful if, where there is a title number involved, it is written on the reverse of the cheque or, in the case of one cheque covering several title numbers, all the relevant title numbers are written on the reverse of the cheque. Cheques should also be stapled to the application form.

Electronic conveyancing

There have been several fairly recent initiatives to introduce the concept of electronic conveyancing. It is envisaged that in the relatively near future, it should be possible to conduct most conveyancing transactions electronically, even including electronic deeds with secure electronic signatures.

It has been possible for some time to access the Land Registry via a computer based terminal to obtain certain information (Land Registry Direct). Land Registry Direct works with services provided by the National Land Information Service (NLIS). NLIS aims to provide comprehensive online search facilities to its users, which will link together through the Internet, local authorities, the Land Registry and other service providers such as the Coal Authority. Currently, there are three licensed providers for this service. These are NLIS Searchflow; TM Search; and Transaction Online. Their web addresses are given in the appropriate section at the back of this book. Subscribers to these services are able to make various searches through one online source and receive results electronically, with direct billing by the service operators.

As well as ongoing plans to introduce other electronic services, some of those currently offered by the Land Registry include the END system and Electronic Discharges (see page 334) and the use of e-mail, where appropriate, to raise queries that arise during registration. Further information on the various aspects of electronic conveyancing can be obtained from the Land Registry's website.

TEST YOURSELF ON CHAPTER 12

Test your knowledge by completing this assignment. If you find that you have difficulty with anything, read the chapter again until you are happy with your answers. There are several forms for you to complete with this assignment. Use the following information to complete the forms.

Assume that the land is registered freehold property unless otherwise stated. If a date is required on a form and you would normally insert the date before posting it, insert the date you are actually completing the form.

Michael Peterson lives at 77 Copenhagen Hill, Ashton, Hertfordshire P38 6PQ. He is selling this house to Miss Joanne Howard. His solicitors are: Ryan Loganberry & Co., of 13 High Road, Ashton, Hertfordshire (tel: 01834 5863; ref: RL/MP/266). Their DX number is 3821 Ashton. The property is mortgaged to the Greenback Building Society, Moneypenny Road, Farthingdale, Suffolk FG4 38H, the roll number with the building society being 27/3864-474. The Title Number of the property is LB 1234. It has been agreed that the purchase price of the property will be £190,000. Additionally, carpets and curtains will be sold for a total of £500.

The local authority is the Ashton District Council. Their DX number is 434 Ashton.

Miss Joanne Howard is buying Mr Peterson's house. She lives at 54 Leamington Road, Ashton, Hertfordshire, AH3 5PQ. Her solicitors are: Greg Pottersbury & Co., of 15 Sticklepath Row, Ashton, Hertfordshire, AH5 6PQ (tel: 01834 555789; ref: GP/JH). Their DX number is 5986 Ashton and their key number for their credit account with the Land Registry is 67417.

1. The first pages only of the forms necessary for making local searches are reproduced here. Complete these using the details given above. Why would you be making local searches?

2. What information is contained in a Title Information Document?

3. Prepare, as far as you are able, the draft contract for this transaction.

4. Complete as far as possible the form TR1, including the attestation clause.

5. Complete form OS1 (making sure you know why you are doing it).

6. What is stamp duty land tax?

7. When might you make a search of the Index Map?

8. What is a bankruptcy only search?

9. Explain what is the National Conveyancing Protocol.

10. Now go through the chapter and if there are any words that are unfamiliar to you or that you cannot spell, write or type them correctly several times until you feel you know them.

Form LLC1. *(Local Land Charges Rules 1977 Schedule 1, Form C)*

Official Number _____
(To be completed by the registering authority)

The duplicate of this form must also be completed: a carbon copy will suffice

For directions, notes and fees see overleaf.

Insert name and address of registering authority in space below

┌   ┐

└   ┘

Register of local land charges
Requisition for search
and official certificate
of search

fold

Requisition for search
(A separate requisition must be made in respect of each parcel of land except as explained overleaf)

An official search is required in *Part(s)*_____*of* [1]
the register of local land charges kept by the above-named registering authority for subsisting registrations against the land [defined in the attached plan and][2] described below.

Description of land sufficient to enable it to be identified

Name and address to which certificate is to be sent

┌   ┐

└   ┘

Signature of applicant *(or his solicitor)*
_____

Date
_____

Telephone number
_____

Reference
_____

Enclosure
Cheque/Money Order/Postal Order/Giro

Official certificate of search

To be completed by authorised officer

It is hereby certified that the search requested above reveals no subsisting registrations[3]

*or the*_____ registrations described in the Schedule hereto[3] up to and including the date of this certificate.

Signed...

On behalf of ....[4]
Date

1 Delete if inappropriate. Otherwise insert Part(s) in which search is required.

2 Delete if inappropriate. (A plan should be furnished in duplicate if it is desired that a copy should be returned.)

3 Delete inapplicable words. (The Parts of the Schedule should be securely attached to the certificate and the number of registrations disclosed should be inserted in the space provided. Only Parts which disclose subsisting registrations should be sent.)

4 Insert name of registering authority.

CON 29 Part I STANDARD ENQUIRIES of Local Authority (2002 Edition)

This form and a plan must be submitted in duplicate.

The Law Society

Please type or use BLOCK LETTERS

A.

To [Local Authority address]

For Local Authority Completion only

Search No. ....

The replies are attached

Signed: ....

Proper Officer

Dated: ....

B.

Enter address of the land/property

NLPG UPRN:

Address 1:

Address 2:

Street:

Locality:

Town/Village:

County:

Post Code:

C.

Other roadways, footways and footpaths

D.

Attachments

A plan in duplicate must be attached. This form may be returned if the land/property cannot be easily identified.

Optional Enquiries to be answered: YES/NO
(if so, please attach Con 29 Part II Optional Enquiries of Local Authority form)

Are any additional enquiries attached?   YES/NO
(If so, please attach on a separate sheet in duplicate)

E.

Fees

£   is enclosed/NLIS transfer (delete as applicable).

Signed:

Dated:

Reference:

Tel No:

Fax No:

E-mail Contact:

Notes.

A. Enter name and address of Council for the area to which this form has been officially submitted. If the property is near a local authority boundary, consider raising certain enquiries (e.g. road schemes) with the adjoining Council.
B. Enter address and description of the property, add the NLPG UPRN (Unique Property Reference Number) where known.
C. Enter name and/or mark on plan any other roadways, footpaths and footways abutting the property (in addition to those entered in Box B) to which a reply to enquiry 2 and 3.6 is required.
D. A duplicate plan is required for all searches. If required, the Optional Enquiries form, ticked where necessary, should be attached along with the relevant fee. Additional enquiries must be attached on a separate sheet in duplicate. An additional fee will be charged for any that the Council is willing to answer.
E. Details of fees can be obtained from the Council or your chosen NLIS Channel.
F. Enter the name and address/DX address of the person or company lodging this form.

F.

Please reply to

DX Address

CONTRACT
Incorporating the Standard Conditions of Sale (Fourth Edition)

Date   :

Seller   :

Buyer   :

Property   :
(freehold/~~leasehold~~)

Title number/~~root of title~~ :

Specified incumbrances   :

Title guarantee   :
(full/~~limited~~)

Completion date   :

Contract rate   :

Purchase price   :

Deposit   :

Chattels price   :
(if separate)

Balance   :

The seller will sell and the buyer will buy the property for the purchase price.

WARNING	Signed
This is a formal document, designed to create legal rights and legal obligations. Take advice before using it.	Seller/Buyer

SPECIAL CONDITIONS

1. (a) This contract incorporates the Standard Conditions of Sale (Fourth Edition).

    (b) The terms used in this contract have the same meaning when used in the Conditions.

2. Subject to the terms of this contract and to the Standard Conditions of Sale, the seller is to transfer the property with either full title guarantee or limited title guarantee, as specified on the front page.

3. The chattels which are on the property and are set out on any attached list are included in the sale and the buyer is to pay the chattels price for them.

4. The property is sold with vacant possession.

(or) 4. The property is sold subject to the following leases or tenancies:

Seller's conveyancers*:

Buyer's conveyancers*:

*Adding an e-mail address authorises service by e-mail: see condition 1.3.3(b)

**Transfer of whole
of registered title(s)**

Land Registry

If you need more room than is provided for in a panel, use continuation sheet CS and attach to this form.

1.	**Stamp Duty**

Place "X" in the appropriate box or boxes and complete the appropriate certificate.

☐ It is certified that this instrument falls within category ☐ in the Schedule to the Stamp Duty (Exempt Instruments) Regulations 1987

☐ It is certified that the transaction effected does not form part of a larger transaction or of a series of transactions in respect of which the amount or value or the aggregate amount or value of the consideration exceeds the sum of   £ ☐

☐ It is certified that this is an instrument on which stamp duty is not chargeable by virtue of the provisions of section 92 of the Finance Act 2001

2. Title Number(s) of the Property *Leave blank if not yet registered.*

3. Property

4. Date

5. Transferor *Give full names and company's registered number if any.*

6. Transferee **for entry on the register** *Give full name(s) and company's registered number, if any. For Scottish companies use an SC prefix and for limited liability partnerships use an OC prefix before the registered number, if any. For foreign companies give territory in which incorporated.*

Unless otherwise arranged with Land Registry headquarters, a certified copy of the Transferee's constitution (in English or Welsh) will be required if it is a body corporate but is not a company registered in England and Wales or Scotland under the Companies Acts.

7. Transferee's intended **address(es) for service (including postcode) for entry on the register** *You may give up to three addresses for service **one** of which **must** be a postal address but does not have to be within the UK. The other addresses can be any combination of a postal address, a box number at a UK document exchange or an electronic address.*

8.   **The Transferor transfers the Property to the Transferee**

9. Consideration *Place "X" in the appropriate box. State clearly the currency unit if other than sterling. If none of the boxes applies, insert an appropriate memorandum in the additional provisions panel.*

☐ The Transferor has received from the Transferee for the Property the sum of *In words and figures.*

☐ *Insert other receipt as appropriate.*

☐ The transfer is not for money or anything which has a monetary value

10. The Transferor transfers with *Place "X" in the appropriate box and add any modifications.*

☐ full title guarantee   ☐ limited title guarantee

11. Declaration of trust *Where there is more than one Transferee, place "X" in the appropriate box.*

☐ The Transferees are to hold the Property on trust for themselves as joint tenants

☐ The Transferees are to hold the Property on trust for themselves as tenants in common in equal shares

☐ The Transferees are to hold the Property *Complete as necessary.*

12. Additional provisions *Insert here any required or permitted statements, certificates or applications and any agreed covenants, declarations, etc.*

13. Execution *The Transferor must execute this transfer as a deed using the space below. If there is more than one Transferor, all must execute. Forms of execution are given in Schedule 9 to the Land Registration Rules 2003. If the transfer contains Transferee's covenants or declarations or contains an application by the Transferee (e.g. for a restriction), it must also be executed by the Transferee (all of them, if there is more than one).*

Application by purchaser[(a)] **for official search with priority of the whole of the land in a registered title or a pending first registration application**

Land Registry   # OS1

Land Registry _____ Office

Use one form per title. If you need more room than is provided for in a panel, use continuation sheet CS and attach to this form.

1. Administrative area and postcode if known

2. Title number *Enter the title number of the registered estate or that allotted to the pending first registration.*

3. Payment of fee [(b)] *Place "X" in the appropriate box.*

☐   The Land Registry fee of £ [_____] accompanies this application.

☐   Debit the Credit Account mentioned in panel 4 with the appropriate fee payable under the current Land Registration Fee Order.

For official use only

Impression of fees

4. The application has been lodged by:[(c)]
Land Registry Key No. (if appropriate)
Name
Address/DX No.

Reference[(d)]
E-mail

Telephone No.	Fax No.

5. If the result of search is to be sent to anyone other than the applicant in panel 4, please supply the name and address of the person to whom it should be sent.

Reference[(d)]

6. Registered proprietor/Applicant for first registration *Enter FULL name(s) of the registered proprietor(s) of the registered estate in the above mentioned title or of the person(s) applying for first registration of the property specified in panel 10.*

SURNAME/COMPANY NAME:

FORENAME(S):

SURNAME/COMPANY NAME:

FORENAME(S):

7. Search from date *For a search of a* ***registered title*** *enter in the box a date falling within the definition of search from date in rule 131 of the Land Registration Rules 2003.*[c] *If the date entered is not such a date the application may be rejected. In the case of a* ***pending first registration*** *search, enter the letters 'FR'.*

8. Applicant *Enter FULL name of each purchaser* ***or*** *lessee* ***or*** *chargee.*

9. Reason for application I certify that the applicant intends to: *Place "X" in the appropriate box.*

☐ | P | purchase   ☐ | C | take a registered charge

☐ | L | take a lease

10. Property details *Address or short description of the property.*

11. Type of search *Place "X" in the appropriate box.*

☐ **Registered land search**
Application is made to ascertain whether any adverse entry has been made in the register or day list since the date shown in panel 7.

☐ **Pending first registration search**
Application is made to ascertain whether any adverse entry has been made in the day list since the date of the pending first registration application referred to above.

12. Signature of applicant or their conveyancer _____ **Date** _____

Explanatory notes

(a) "Purchaser" is defined in Land Registration Rules 2003, r.131. In essence, it is a person who has entered, or intends to enter, into a disposition for valuable consideration as disponee where: (i) the disposition is a registrable disposition (see Land Registration Act 2002, s.27), or (ii) there is a person subject to a duty under the Land Registration Act 2002, s.6, to apply for registration, the application is pending and the disposition would have been a registrable disposition had the estate been registered.
An official search in respect of registered land made by a person other than a "purchaser" should be made in Form OS3.

(b) Cheques are payable to 'Land Registry'. If you hold a credit account but do not indicate that it should be debited, and do not enclose a cheque, the registrar may still debit your account.

(c) If you hold a credit account and want the official search certificate sent to an address different from that associated with your key number, enter your key number, reference and telephone number but otherwise leave panel 4 blank. Complete panel 5 instead.

(d) Enter a maximum of 25 characters including stops, strokes, punctuation etc.

(e) Enter the date shown as the subsisting entries date on an official copy of the register or given as the subsisting entries date at the time of an access by remote terminal.

Practice Guide 12 'Official Searches and Outline Applications' contains further information.

© Crown copyright (ref: LR/HQ/Internet) 10/03

13

Forms of address for the judiciary

Secretaries may have to write letters to people of title or rank and this chapter deals with forms of address for members of the judiciary, e.g., a High Court judge. Everyone mentioned in this chapter is not necessarily mentioned otherwise in the book. For more information and other forms of address there are a number of books on etiquette.

How to end a letter is not shown below because nowadays the form of 'Yours faithfully' or 'Yours sincerely' is nearly always used for those mentioned here, according to whether it is a formal or social matter and this is perfectly acceptable. However, for those wishing to stick to the older rules of etiquette for peers, etc., there are other ways of ending a letter to such persons but these are not gone into here as it is not essential. When addressing correspondence to a peer it is best to check whether he is, for example, 'Lord Bloggs' or 'Lord Bloggs of Northshire'. His correct title should be used and if you are not sure about this, a glance in *Who's Who* should help you. If there is further doubt about this or any other matter relating to the form of address to be used, you should telephone the appropriate clerk or secretary, usually to be found at the Royal Courts of Justice in London when it concerns a member of the judiciary. Further information on the judiciary may also be found on the Department for Constitutional Affairs' website.

Lord Chancellor

His proper title is the Lord High Chancellor of Great Britain and he is the chief judicial officer.

Address the envelope to: The Rt. Hon. the Lord Chancellor

Letter:
Salutation (instead of
'Dear Sir'):

	Formal matters:	My Lord
	Social matters:	Dear Lord Chancellor

If he holds a different rank in the peerage, he will be addressed accordingly. Do not put the letters QC after his name. The Lord Chancellor's Department is now known as the Department for Constitutional Affairs.

Lord Chief Justice of England

He is head of the judges in the Queen's Bench Division and also presides over the Court of Appeal (Criminal Division).

Address the envelope to: The Rt. Hon. the Lord Chief Justice of England

Letter:

    Salutation: Formal matters: My Lord

                       Social matters: Dear Lord Chief Justice

If he holds a different rank in the peerage, he will be addressed accordingly. Do not put the letters QC after his name.

Master of the Rolls

He presides over the Court of Appeal (Civil Division). As with some other appointments (President of the Family Division and Vice-Chancellor; see below), he is usually a knight on appointment and is often created a peer after appointment. He should be addressed according to his rank. If you are not sure about this, telephone the Royal Courts of Justice in London who should be able to assist.

President of the Family Division

He presides over the Family Division of the High Court. See under 'Master of the Rolls' above for further information.

Vice-Chancellor

He presides over the Chancery Division of the High Court. See under 'Master of the Rolls' above for further information.

Lords of Appeal in Ordinary

They preside over appeals relating to judicial matters in the House of Lords. They are created peers for life. Do not use the letters QC after their name.

Lords Justice of the Court of Appeal

They sit in the Court of Appeal with the Master of the Rolls. Do not put the letters QC after their name.

Address the envelope to: The Rt. Hon. Lord Justice Bloggs

Salutation: Formal matters: My Lord

                 Social matters: Dear Lord Justice

A retired Lord Justice is addressed as, for example, 'The Rt. Hon. Sir John Bloggs'.

High Court judge

Address the envelope to:	Formal and judicial matters:	The Hon. Mr Justice Bloggs
	Social matters:	Sir John Bloggs
Salutation:	Formal matters:	Dear Sir, or Sir
	Judicial matters:	My Lord
	Social matters:	Dear Judge (do not use his name)

Do not use the letters QC after his name.

Female High Court judge

Address the envelope to:	Formal matters:	The Hon. Mrs Justice Bloggs
	Social matters:	Dame Jane Bloggs
Salutation:	Formal matters:	Dear Madam, or Madam
	Social matters:	Dear Dame Jane

Do not use the letters QC after her name.

Retired High Court judge

Address the envelope to:	All matters:	Sir John Bloggs
Salutation:	Formal matters:	Dear Sir, or Sir
	Social matters:	Dear Judge (do not use his name)
	If slightly acquainted:	Dear Sir John Bloggs

Circuit judge

In this instance the letters QC should be used after the name in correspondence, if appropriate.

Address the envelope:	All matters:	His (or Her) Honour Judge Bloggs

If there is more than one Circuit judge of the same name at the same address, the forename may be added in brackets.

If he has been knighted

Address the envelope to:	Formal matters:	His Honour Judge Sir John Bloggs
	Social matters:	Sir John Bloggs
Salutation:	Formal matters:	Dear Sir, or Sir or Dear Madam, or Madam
	Social matters:	Dear Judge

Retired circuit judge

Address the envelope:	All matters:	His Honour John Bloggs, or Her Honour Jane Bloggs
If knighted:		His Honour Sir John Bloggs
Salutation:	Formal matters:	Dear Sir, Sir, or Madam
	Social matters:	Dear Mr Bloggs or Dear Mrs Bloggs or Dear Judge

Recorders

Address the envelope:	All matters:	J. Bloggs, Esq.
Salutation:	Formal matters:	Dear Sir, or Sir
	Official matters:	Dear Mr Recorder
	Social:	Ordinary form of address or according to his rank.

Senior District judge of the Principal Registry of the Family Division

Address the envelope:	Senior District Judge, Principal Registry of the Family Division
Salutation:	Dear Judge

District judge

Address the envelope:	District Judge Bloggs
Salutation:	Dear Judge

Barristers

If a barrister is a QC, the letters QC are placed after his name whilst he is still at the Bar. A barrister is no longer referred to as a 'barrister-at-law' but simply a 'barrister'. See also page 87 as to instructing barristers.

Other

Most other legal persons, such as magistrates and coroners, are addressed in the ordinary way. A Justice of the Peace may have the letters 'JP' after his name.

References to judges

The correct way of referring to a judge in a document intended to be read by lawyers is shown in the following examples:

(a) The Lord Chancellor	Lord Falconer of Thoroton LC
(b) The Lord Chief Justice	Lord Woolf CJ
(c) The Master of the Rolls	Lord Phillips of Worth Matravers MR
(d) The President of the Family Division	Sir Mark Howard Potter P
(e) The Vice-Chancellor	Sir Robert Andrew Morritt CVO V-C
(f) Two or more Court of Appeal judges	Bloggs and Jones LJJ
(g) Court of Appeal judge	Bloggs LJ
(h) Two or more High Court judges	Bloggs and Jones JJ
(i) High Court Judge (i.e., those from the Queen's Bench, Chancery and Family Divisions)	Bloggs J
(j) Circuit and County Court judge	Judge Bloggs

When two or more judges have the same surname, they should be referred to by their first name and their surname, e.g., Joseph Bloggs LJ, Peter Bloggs LJ. If a Deputy Judge is being referred to, the name and position held are used, e.g., Mr Joseph Bloggs QC (sitting as a Deputy High Court Judge). A retired Court of Appeal judge is referred to by name, e.g., Sir Joseph Bloggs. If the judge is a peer, he is referred to as such, e.g., Lord Woolf.

When judges are referred to in a document drafted for non-lawyers to read, abbreviations of position should not be used; the document should say, e.g., Mr Justice Bloggs.

With regard to members of the House of Lords, if the member is, for example, Lord Bloggs of Northshire, this is his correct name and he should (at least the first time he is mentioned) be referred to as such, and not just as Lord Bloggs.

See also page 38 on addressing judges in court.

Legal documents

When a person of a certain rank is a party to a legal document he or she should be described in the document in such a way as to show his or her rank or title, e.g., 'The Most Noble John Joseph Duke of. .'. At the end of the document where their name is typed for signature, their rank or title should also be shown. *Butterworth's Encyclopaedia of Forms and Precedents* is very helpful in this and it sets out how certain ranks and titles should be described in legal documents. Similarly, *Atkin's Court Forms* gives the correct titles of parties to an action, i.e., the correct way to describe certain parties when they become involved in a court action, e.g., Bank of England, a building society, local authority, peers of the realm, police forces and many more. Both of these publications consist of several volumes and to find which volume contains a particular topic, look in the Index volume under, e.g., 'PARTY', 'PARTIES' or 'PARTY TO ACTION'. This will then refer you to the appropriate part of the volume you need.

Finding the right job

This chapter has been written by Zarak Legal, the leading supplier of permanent and temporary legal support in London. They source legal secretaries, personal assistants, WP operators, accounts staff, paralegals, receptionists, IT specialists and general support staff for law firms and in-house legal departments. Zarak Legal is the founding division of the Zarak Group, a specialist recruitment consultancy based in the City of London. Established in 1984, Zarak Legal has built an outstanding reputation for supplying quality staff by thoroughly assessing candidates to pinpoint the right person for the job.

The role of the legal secretary

For the last few years, we have been hearing about the demise of the traditional legal secretary within law firms. Voice recognition systems, improved partner usage of word-processing software, e-mails and the Internet, appear to be squeezing out the demand for the girl-with-the-shorthand-notepad.

The reality is that whilst traditional elements of their job brief may have become defunct, today's secretaries are still a vital part of the office support system—it is just their role within it which is changing. Increasingly, firms expect their secretarial support staff to have additional skills: to act as an 'intelligent buffer' between the fee earner and the client and to be capable of liaising with the client on the firm's behalf in a much more client-service type role.

As law firms follow the lead shown by other professional service firms, what were once purely internal administrative roles are becoming increasingly client-focused. Many of Zarak Legal's clients see this evolution as vital with these roles becoming more important commercially. In addition, a secretary can shield a fee earner from unnecessary interruption whilst maintaining the relationship with the client.

So, is there still a place for the secretary who enjoys typing and wants to pursue this new route? Different law firms deploy their support staff in diverse ways. Some already operate administrator/customer service teams, which are based in lower-rental out-of-town areas. These support large numbers of fee earners via telephone and e-mail, efficiently and cost effectively.

But does the 'traditional' legal secretarial role still exist in the City? And, who is doing the filing? Zarak Legal believes that the changes within administrative support will happen slowly and that they cannot be translated easily into all areas of law. Advances in technology may have reduced the need for endless copy typing, and the use of e-mail has made information almost instantaneous but there are many areas of law that still need people who are willing and able to deal with large volumes of typing and who can produce complex transactional documentation.

Many companies are enhancing the role of legal secretaries, freeing them from a purely WP-bashing role to dealing with the administrative side of legal casework and, in some cases, encouraging them to take on paralegal duties. Many of Zarak Legal's clients, who range from some of the biggest firms in the country to specialist niche practices, demonstrate a real willingness to look at ways of encouraging secretarial career development. Apart from providing ongoing training for existing staff, they are also interested in bringing in non-legal secretaries from other business areas because they may have skill sets and experiences which could prove useful to law firms.

The future is still rosy for legal secretaries because there will be a continuous need for the traditional skills of fast typing and an eye for detail, as well as an increased demand for legal secretaries who want more involvement, responsibility and opportunities to build careers as true legal PAs.

The marketplace

The secretarial marketplace has always provided a stable, secure platform for those wanting to pursue a varied, interesting and fulfilling career within the support function of any industry.

Over the last few years, however, there has been a radical change in the attitude of both candidates and employers alike. More and more secretaries are reviewing their career options on a far more regular basis, aiming either to progress up the secretarial career ladder or to try different professional areas, e.g., from an accountancy practice into the specialist area of law or from law into management consultancy.

Employers, on the other hand, are becoming much more selective in the recruitment process and increasingly seek new strengths in addition to pure technical ability in order to develop their support teams.

The days of 'just being a good typist' are long gone. Competition for the top secretarial jobs is fiercely competitive and to gain the important edge necessary to secure the best career opportunity, you will need so much more than a good typing speed and a smile!

Try to obtain as many skills as you can, for example:

(a) A good standard of education. A minimum of five GCSE passes (C and above), preferably including English and Mathematics.

(b) A recognised secretarial qualification, e.g., RSA (or equivalent) and/or having completed a secretarial course.

(c) Effective communication skills: the ability to liaise clearly and concisely at all levels, both externally and internally.

(d) Team-building skills. Adding value to the workplace by developing an awareness of the role of your colleagues, lending necessary support where required, which will automatically enhance your own job satisfaction and security.

(e) Organisational skills. Adding value to your employer's role by providing an efficient administrative support system, thereby increasing productivity.

(f) Technical skills. Excellent keyboard skills (particularly in terms of speed and accuracy), an extensive knowledge of word processing systems and an exposure to spreadsheet or presentation packages, e.g., Excel; or PowerPoint.

Getting experience and training

So, how do you get started? We are very familiar with the age old conundrum of 'you can't get a job without experience'—but how do you get experience in the first place?

Firstly, if you are already a secretary but wanting to 'get into legal', not all law firms require legal experience. Many of them are prepared to 'buy in' the skills that you already have and assist you in picking up the legal jargon once you get there. Secretaries with transferable skills and knowledge of industries which translate well into law are sought after. Knowledge gained within a property company often translates well across into conveyancing work within a law firm, for example, and another popular 'get into legal' area is corporate law, due to its relatively straightforward nature. Litigation, however, is an area which demands prior legal experience or training.

Secondly, if you are still looking for your first secretarial role as a college leaver, you will find many college leaver secretaries are taken on by the larger firms via work experience schemes organised between the firms and local secretarial colleges. It can be difficult finding college leaver positions without going through this route. It can also be difficult if you do not have a legal secretarial qualification at college leaver level. Older secretaries with practical work experience are often able to get into legal by virtue of the fact that they have gained skills in a workplace which law firms may be interested in. If you cannot get into legal work straight from college, try looking for a job in a professional services company or 'City' type businesses such as Accountants, Banks, Finance Houses, Insurance Companies or Management Consultants. These are often excellent stepping stones into legal work once you have acquired some decent experience and become a 'second jobber' and are no longer a college leaver as, by this time, you will have faster typing speeds and better technical knowledge of various software packages and the useful, practical work experience that is of more value to busy law firms.

There are also various commercially run courses for secretaries who want to learn about a particular legal area.

Job applications

General points

E-mail is playing an increasing role in the sending of covering letters and CVs. If you do chose to send your information like this, ensure that you think about how it will be read at the other end.

Attach your covering letter and CV as separate files using a common software package like Word. The recipient will not have the patience to scroll down through a long e-mail containing vast tracts of text which may well have reformatted itself during sending! Make sure that your 'subject' is something along the lines of 'Job Application from Mary Smith'.

The covering letter

(a) Should cover no more than one side of A4.

(b) Where possible, ensure that you have the proper contact name for the position required. 'Dear Sir/ Madam' or even worse 'To Whom It May Concern' looks awful, and shows that you did not make enough effort to find this information out.

(c) If possible, use the reference number quoted in the advertisement and also refer to the job title and publication (where relevant): it makes it so much easier for the person who has to deal with your CV.

(d) Your covering letter should relate to the job described in the advertisement/job description by linking the skills required with those that you possess. For example, 'I believe that I would be suitable for this position because...'.

(e) Do not duplicate your CV, but use this letter to highlight your achievements without 'waffling'.

(f) Remember the basics. If you do know the addressee's name, your 'close' must be 'Yours sincerely'. If you have had to use 'Dear Sir or Madam', then it must be 'Yours faithfully'.

CV layout and presentation

Your CV is the first point on which an employer judges you and is therefore an essential component in the job seeking process. It should immediately create sufficient impact with a potential employer to invite you for interview and needs to:

(a) reflect qualifications and experience, in reverse chronological order;

(b) highlight your skills and achievements to date, again most recent first;

(c) differentiate you from other candidates;

(d) package, present and sell you in the strongest possible way.

Your CV should fall into two distinct sections: personal details; career details and qualifications/education. It is recommended that your CV does not exceed three pages, although two pages is preferable. Zarak Legal has the expertise to draft your CV and are happy to help. *Do:*

- Keep the layout straightforward.
- Remember that the person reading your CV may be reading dozens at a time. Keep your wording simple and the content relevant.
- Always check your CV for accuracy: mistakes immediately turn a prospective employer off and can undo all of your fantastic experience and achievements.

Don't:

- Lie. You will often be found out!
- Leave gaps in your work history. Even if you were not working for a period of time, identify something achieved during this 'gap' as otherwise it looks as if you have something to hide.
- Use 'novelty' paper, envelopes or fonts. You want to project a professional image and this should be done on either white or cream A4 sized paper, where possible, in a straightforward font like Times.
- Use poor photocopies of your CV—it looks shoddy.

Interview technique: hints and tips

Presentation and preparation are the key. Having created a strong first impression with your CV, the interview is your chance to build on this and convince the interviewer that you are the right person for the job.

Remember, an interview is a two-way process. Whilst the interviewer is vetting you as a potential employee, it is also your opportunity to decide whether firstly, the firm or company is right for you and beyond that, the suitability of the role which is being discussed.

Before the interview

Find out as much as possible about the firm/company; ask for as many details as are available from your consultant in terms of firm/company profile, job description, location, company benefits and long-term career prospects.

Check the name and position of the person(s) who will be conducting the interview. Where possible, ascertain the specific recruitment style that your interviewer normally adopts.

If you have friends or contacts with any knowledge of the firm or company, speak to them to gain as much 'inside info' to help you in the decision-making process.

Review and familiarise yourself with your CV. If your consultant has prepared the CV which was forwarded to the interviewer, ask for a copy well in advance and check any alterations or additions which may have been made including, for example, reasons for leaving previous jobs. Make sure you have a spare copy with you.

Make a mental note of the specific questions you would like answered.

Make a list of all the positive points you would want to put across about yourself, e.g., education and qualifications, communication and organisational skills, technical and team-building abilities, not forgetting, of course, previous relevant experience.

Identify your areas of weakness as well as your strengths. Consider how best to address these points: you are likely to be asked.

Check the time of your interview and the location. Leave yourself plenty of time to make your journey so that you arrive as relaxed as possible and with at least five or ten minutes to spare.

If you have not been interviewed for some time, your consultant should be happy to conduct a 'mock interview' and give you hints on how to get through the interview process.

Don't forget: first impressions are vital. The majority of interviewers make a judgement within the first five minutes. Your presentation is a vital part of the interview process, therefore:

- Dress for success! Suits which are conservative in style are the ideal choice if you want to make an impression, remembering also to co-ordinate accessories effectively;
- Make sure that you are well presented.

Suggested questions that may be asked during the interview

1. Why are you interested in this job?
2. Why does this firm/company interest you?
3. What added value could you bring to the role on offer?
4. What are your short/long-term career objectives?
5. Why are you particularly suited to this role?
6. Why do want to leave your present job?
7. Why did you leave your last job?
8. What do you consider your strengths and weaknesses?
9. What do you enjoy most about your career?
10. If offered the position, would you accept?

The interview

A well prepared interview will normally have five stages:

1. Introductions.
2. Questions from the interviewer.
3. Expansion on the job description and responsibilities.

4. Questions from the candidate.

5. Conclusion of Interview.

Hints and tips during the interview

You will normally be received in the reception area of the firm by the interviewer. Remember to stand up (if sitting), smile and shake hands firmly. Look enthusiastic.

Having prepared responses to general questions which may be asked, do not be put off guard by any difficult questions. Often, the interviewer is merely interested in how you present a response, rather than the response itself.

Reserve asking questions on salary and benefits until the second interview stage.

Remember: posture and composure are important elements of an interview. Try not to fidget; and make continuous eye contact (if you find this difficult, focus at eyebrow level!).

If you are being interviewed by more than one person, you must address your responses to all parties.

Listen carefully

- Do not interrupt the interviewer: wait for an appropriate pause before asking questions.

- If you are unsure of the question, ask for further clarification before responding.

- Pause before responding, as this will give the impression that you have given thought to the question.

- Remember that if you look interested and react positively to what is being said throughout the interview, you will be giving the right impression.

- Don't forget to smile!

At the end of the interview, remember to thank the interviewer for their time, taking the opportunity to reiterate your interest in both the firm/company and the position on offer.

Make notes afterwards about the interview, the people you met and your own thoughts.

Further advice

The advice and guidance offered by experienced consultants guarantee legal secretarial, receptionists, accounts staff, clerks, office juniors and more, both temporary and permanent, a much brighter future.

Zarak Legal, for instance, will work on interview techniques, a vital part of the process and confirmation of their belief that preparation is everything. As a result, they will also recommend training and cross-training courses aimed at broadening your skills base, along with assessment days designed to keep you fully up to date with the latest systems. They will also prepare your CV, putting your personality, experience and abilities in the most positive light. They will provide a comprehensive pre-interview briefing, including a detailed information pack, full job specification and application form, and even a brief summary of the style of interview clients prefer.

If you would like to talk about any aspect of your career, feel free to contact Zarak Legal or visit their website. Full contact details are given in the address and web address sections of this book.

Addresses and telephone numbers

ACAS (Advisory Conciliation and Arbitration Service).
There are various local and regional offices where telephone numbers can be found in
local telephone directories.

British Association of Lawyer Mediators,
30 Church Street,
Godalming,
Surrey GU17 1EP   01483-417121

Centre for Effective Dispute Resolution,
International Dispute Resolution Centre,
70 Fleet Street,
London EC4Y 1EU   020-7536 6000

Charity Commission Helpline   0870-3330123

Chartered Institute of Arbitrators,
International Arbitration Centre,
12 Bloomsbury Square
London WC1A 2LP   020-7421 7444

Child Support Agency,
(There are various offices throughout
the country.)   08457-133 133 (National Enquiry Line)

Claim Production Centre,
St Katherine's House,
21/27 St Katharine's Street,
Northampton NN1 2LH
DX 702885 Northampton 7   01604-609517

Companies House Contact Centre   0870-3333636
Competition Commission,
Victoria House,
Southampton Row,
London WC1B 4AD   020-7271 0100

Court Funds Office,
22 Kingsway,
London
WC2B 6LE
DX 149780 Kingsway 5   020-7947 7648

Court of Protection Enquiry Line   0845-330 2900

Criminal Cases Review Commission,
Alpha Tower,
Suffolk Street Queensway,
Birmingham,
West Midlands B1 1TT   0121-633 1800

Criminal Injury Compensation Authority,
Tay House,
300 Bath Street,
Glasgow G2 4LN
DX CICAGW 379 Glasgow   0141-331 2726

Criminal Injuries Compensation Authority,
Morley House,
26–30 Holborn Viaduct,
London EC1A 2JQ   020-7842 6800

Crown Prosecution Service,
50 Ludgate Hill,
London EC4M 7EX   020-7796 8000

Department for Constitutional Affairs,
Selbourne House,
54 Victoria Street,
London
SW1E 6QW
DX 117000 Selbourne House   020-7210 8614

DVLA,
Customer Enquiries (Drivers) Group,
Sandringham Park,
Swansea
SA7 0EE   0870-240 0009

DVLA
Customer Enquiries (Vehicles) Unit,
Sandringham Park,
Swansea
SA7 0EE   0870-240 0010

Employment Appeal Tribunal,
Audit House,
58 Victoria Embankment,
London EC4Y 0DS   020-7273 1040

Employment Tribunals
There are various regional offices
throughout the country.
Enquiry line: 0845-7959775

Equal Opportunities Commission   0845-601 5901 (General enquiries)

Fair Trading, Office of
Fleetbank House,
2-6 Salisbury Square,
London EC4Y 8JX   020-7211 8000

Family Records Centre
Births, marriages, deaths, adoptions, overseas
enquiries, and general enquiries about certificates   0845-603 7788

Financial Services Authority,
25 The North Colonnade, Canary Wharf,
London E14 5HS   020-7066 1000

General Register Office,
PO Box 2,
Southport
PR8 2JD   0845-603 7788

Home Office,
50 Queen Anne's Gate,
Direct Communications Unit, 7th Floor,
London SW1H 9AT   0870-0001585 (General enquiries)

Inland Revenue (now called HM Revenue & Customs)
There are offices throughout the country.
Specific telephone numbers are available in
local telephone directories or from the
HM Revenue & Customs website.

Insolvency Service
Central Public Enquiry Line   020-7291 6895

Land Charges Department,
Plumer House,
Tailyour Road,
Crownhill,
Plymouth PL6 5HY   01752-636666
DX 8249 Plymouth 3

District Land Registries

Birkenhead (Rosebrae) District Land Registry,
Rosebrae Court,
Woodside Ferry Approach,
Birkenhead,
Merseyside CH41 6DU
DX 24270 Birkenhead 4   0151-472 6666

Birkenhead (Old Market) District Land Registry,
Old Market House,
Hamilton Street,
Birkenhead,
Merseyside CH41 5FL
DX 14300 Birkenhead 3   0151-473 1110

Coventry District Land Registry,
Leigh Court,
Torrington Avenue, Tile Hill,
Coventry CV4 9XZ
DX 18900 Coventry 3   024-7686 0860

Croydon District Land Registry
Sunley House,
Bedford Park,
Croydon CR9 3LE
DX 2699 Croydon 3   020-8781 9103

Durham (Boldon House) District Land Registry,
Boldon House,
Wheatlands Way,
Pity Me,
Durham DH1 5GJ
DX 60860 Durham 6   0191-301 2345

Durham (Southfield House) District Land Registry,
Southfield House,
Southfield Way,
Durham DH1 5TR
DX 60200 Durham 3   0191-301 3500

Gloucester District Land Registry,
Twyver House,
Bruton Way,
Gloucester GL1 1DQ
DX 7599 Gloucester 3   01452-511111

Harrow District Land Registry,
Lyon House,
Lyon Road,
Harrow,
Middx. HA1 2EU
DX 4299 Harrow 4   020-8235 1181

Kingston-upon-Hull District Land Registry,
Earle House,
Colonial Street,
Hull HU2 8JN
DX 26700 Hull 4   01482-223244

Lancashire District Land Registry,
Wrea Brook Court
Lytham Road,
Warton, Lancs. PR4 1TE
DX 721560 Lytham St Annes 6   01772-836838

Leicester District Land Registry,
Westbridge Place,
Leicester LE3 5DR
DX 11900 Leicester 5   0116-265 4000

Lytham District Land Registry,
Birkenhead House,
East Beach,
Lytham St Annes,
Lancs. FY8 5AB
DX 14500 Lytham St Annes 3   01253-849849

Nottingham (East) District Land Registry,
Robins Wood Road,
Nottingham NG8 3RQ
DX 716126 Nottingham 26   0115-906 5353

Nottingham (West) District Land Registry,
Chalfont Drive,
Nottingham NG8 3RN
DX 10298 Nottingham 3   0115-935 1166

Peterborough District Land Registry,
Touthill Close,
City Road,
Peterborough PE1 1XN
DX 12598 Peterborough 4   01733-288288

Plymouth District Land Registry,
Plumer House,
Tailyour Road,
Crownhill,
Plymouth PL6 5HY
DX 8299 Plymouth 4   01752-636000

Portsmouth District Land Registry,
St Andrew's Court,
St Michael's Road,
Portsmouth,
Hants. PO1 2JH
DX 83550 Portsmouth 2   023-9276 8888

Stevenage District Land Registry,
Brickdale House,
Swingate,
Stevenage,
Herts. SG1 1XG
DX 6099 Stevenage 2   01438-788889

Swansea District Land Registry,
Tŷ Bryn Glas,
High Street,
Swansea SA1 1PW
DX 33700 Swansea 2   01792-458877

Telford District Land Registry,
Parkside Court
Hall Park Way,
Telford TF3 4LR
DX 28100 Telford 2   01952-290355

Tunbridge Wells District Land Registry,
Forest Court,
Forest Road,
Tunbridge Wells,
Kent TN2 5AQ
DX 3999 Tunbridge Wells 2   01892-510015

Wales The District Land Registry for Wales,
Tŷ Cwm Tawe,
Phoenix Way,
Llansamlet,
Swansea SA7 9FQ
DX 82800 Swansea 2   01792-355000

Weymouth District Land Registry,
Melcombe Court,
1 Cumberland Drive,
Weymouth,
Dorset DT4 9TT
DX 8799 Weymouth 2   01305-363636

York District Land Registry,
James House,
James Street,
York YO10 3YZ
DX 61599 York 2   01904-450000

Land Registry Headquarters
Land Registry,
32 Lincoln's Inn Fields,
London WC2A 3PH
DX 1098 London/Chancery Lane   020-7917 8888

The Law Society's Hall,
113 Chancery Lane,
London WC2A 1PL
DX London/Chancery Lane   020-7242 1222

Legal Services Commission Offices

Head Office,
85 Gray's Inn Road,
London WC1X 8TX
DX 328 LON/CH'RY LN WC 2   020-7759 0000

London Regional Office
29-37 Red Lion Street,
London WC1R 4PP
DX 170 LON/CH'RY LN WC2   020-7759 1966

South East Regional Offices
80 Kings Road,
Reading RG1 3BJ
DX 4016 Reading   0118 955 8600

3rd & 4th Floors,
Invicta House, Trafalgar Place,
Brighton BN1 4FR
DX 2752 Brighton 1   01273-878800

North East Regional Office
Eagle Star House, Fenkle Street,
Newcastle-upon-Tyne NE1 5RU
DX 61005 Newcastle-u-Tyne 1   0191-244 5800

Yorkshire and Humberside Regional Office
Harcourt House,
Chancellor Court,
21 The Calls
Leeds LS2 7EH
DX 12068 Leeds 1   0113-390 7300

North Western Regional Office
2nd Floor, Lee House,
90 Great Bridgewater Street,
Manchester M1 5JW
DX 14343 Manchester 1   0161-244 5000

Chester Office
2nd Floor, Pepper House,
Pepper Row,
Chester CH1 1DW
DX 19981 Chester   01244-404500

Merseyside Regional Office
Cavern Walks,
8 Mathew Street,
Liverpool L2 6RE
DX 14208 Liverpool 1   0151-242 5200

West Midlands Regional Office
Centre City Podium,
5 Hill Street, Birmingham B5 4UD
DX 13041 Birmingham 1   0121-665 4700

East Midlands Regional Office
2nd Floor,
Fothergill House,
16 King Street,
Nottingham NG1 2AS
DX 10035 Nottingham 1   0115-908 4200

Eastern Regional Office
62–68 Hills Road,
Cambridge CB2 1LA
DX 5803 Cambridge 1   01223-417800

South Western Regional Office
33-35 Queen Square,
Bristol BS1 4LU
DX 7852 Bristol 1   0117-302 3000

Wales Office
Marland House,
Central Square
Cardiff CF10 1PF
DX 33006 Cardiff 1   02920-647100

Lloyd's of London,
One Lime Street,
London EC3M 7HA   020-7327 1000

London Stock Exchange 10 Paternoster Square, London EC4M 7LS	020-7797 3322
Mediation UK, Alexander House, Telephone Avenue, Bristol BS1 4BS	0117-904 6661
Metropolitan Police Office, New Scotland Yard, Broadway, London SW1H 0BG	020-7230 1212
Motor Insurers' Bureau, Linford Wood House, 6–12 Capital Drive, Linford Wood, Milton Keynes MK14 6XT DX 142620 Milton Keynes 10	01908-240000
The National Archives, Kew, Richmond, Surrey TW9 4DU	020-8876 3444
Official Solicitor and Public Trustee, 81 Chancery Lane, London WC2A 1DD DX 0012 Lon/Ch'ry Ln WC2	020-7911 7127
Office for National Statistics National Statistics Customer Enquiry Service	0845-601 3034
Oxford University Press, Great Clarendon Street, Oxford OX2 6DP	01865-556767
Principal Registry of the Family Division, First Avenue House, 42–49 High Holborn, London WC1V 6NP	020-7947 6000
Racial Equality, Commission for, St Dunstan's House, 201–211 Borough High Street London SE1 1GZ	020-7939 0000
Registry Trust Ltd, 173/175 Cleveland Street, London W1T 6QR	020-7380 0133
Royal Courts of Justice, Strand, London WC2A 2LL	020-7947 6000
Treasury Solicitor, Queen Anne's Chambers, 28 Broadway, London SW1H 9JX DX 123242 St James Park	020-7210 3000
Zarak Legal, 4 Crown Place, London EC2 4BT e-mail: legal.secguide@zarakgroup.com	020-7539 0010

Useful web addresses

ACAS
http://www.acas.org.uk

Adobe
http://www.adobe.com
You can download Acrobat
Reader from here (see page 53).

**Arbitrators, Chartered
Institute of**
http://www.arbitrators.org

Bank of England
http://www.bankofengland.co.uk

Bar Council
http://www.barcouncil.org.uk

BBC News
http://news.bbc.co.uk

**British Association of Lawyer
Mediators**
http://www.lawwise.co.uk/balm.html

Central Law Training
http://www.clt.co.uk
Offers a large variety of legal training
courses, including courses for secretaries
run by the author.

**Centre for Effective Dispute
Resolution (CEDR)**
http://www.cedr.co.uk

Chamber of Commerce, International
http://www.iccwbo.org

Charity Commission
http://www.charity-commission.gov.uk

Chartered Institute of Arbitrators
http://www.arbitrators.org

Child Support Agency
http://www.csa.gov.uk

The Coal Authority
http://www.coal.gov.uk

Companies House
http://www.companieshouse.gov.uk

Competition Commission
http://www.competition-commission.org.uk

Court Service
http://www.hmcourts-service.gov.uk
Recently changed to Her Majesty's Courts
Service in order to amalgamate the
Magistrates' Courts Service and Court
Service. Administers the civil, family and
criminal courts in England and Wales.

Criminal Cases Review Commission
http://www.ccrc.gov.uk

Crown Prosecution Service
http://www.cps.gov.uk

Currency Converter
http://www.oanda.com/converter/classic

Department for Constitutional Affairs
(Formerly the Lord Chancellor's
Department). As well as other
information, you can download the
CPR (see Chapter 3).
http://www.dca.gov.uk

Department for Work and Pensions
http://www.dwp.gov.uk/

Driver and Vehicle
Licensing Agency (DVLA)   http://www.dvla.gov.uk
Employment Appeal Tribunal   http://www.employmentappeals.gov.uk
Encyclopaedia Britannica   http://www.britannica.com
Environment Agency   http://www.environment-agency.gov.uk/
Equal Opportunities Commission   http://www.eoc.org.uk
Euro   http://www.euro.gov.uk
This is an official UK Government site
containing information for
businesses about the euro.

Europa   http://www.europa.eu.int
Provides information and links on
European institutions.

European Court of Human Rights   http://www.echr.coe.int
European Court of Justice   http://curia.eu.int
Financial Services Authority   http://www.fsa.gov.uk
Financial Times   http://www.ft.com
General Register Office   http://www.gro.gov.uk
Government Information
Services Online   http://www.direct.gov.uk
A good starting-point for anything
Government-related. Numerous links
through the indexes maintained on
this site.

Greenwich Mean Time (GMT):
World Time   http://wwp.greenwichmeantime.com
Hays DX   http://www.haysdx.co.uk
Health & Safety Executive   http://www.hse.gov.uk
Practical advice for
employers on safety at work.

Hemmington Scott   http://www.hemscott.net
This site provides corporate and
company information and
share price information.

HM Stationery Office (HMSO)   http://www.hmso.gov.uk
Home Office   http://www.homeoffice.gov.uk
Information Commissioner   http://www.informationcommissioner.gov.uk
Responsible for the Data Protection
and Freedom of Information Acts.

Inland Revenue   http://www.hmrc.gov.uk
Recently changed to HM Revenue &
Customs, amalgamating the Inland
Revenue and HM Customs & Excise.

Insolvency Service   http://www.insolvency.gov.uk
International Court of Justice   http://www.icj.law.gla.ac.uk
International Criminal Court   http://www.icc-cpi.int
ITN   http://www.itn.co.uk
News, weather, etc.

Land Registry   http://www.landregistry.gov.uk

Land Registry Direct   http://www.landregistry.gov.uk/direct
Information about this Land
Registry service (registration
required to use the service).
Law Society   http://www.lawsociety.org.uk
Legal Services Commission   http://www.legalservices.gov.uk
Licensed Conveyancers
(Council for)   http://www.theclc.gov.uk
Lloyd's of London   http://www.lloyds.com
Local Governments   http://www.gwydir.demon.co.uk/uklocalgov
                                        http://www.oultwood.com (includes some over-
                                        seas local government sites)

Maps and Directions   http://www.multimap.co.uk
Mediation UK   http://www.mediationuk.org.uk
Metropolitan Police   http://www.met.police.uk
Motor Insurers Bureau   http://www.mib.org.uk
The National Archives   http://www.nationalarchives.gov.uk
NLIS (National Land
Information Service)   http://www.nlis.org.uk/
NLIS providers
NLIS Searchflow   http://www.searchflow.co.uk
TM Search   http://www.tmproperty.co.uk
Transaction Online   http://www.transaction-online.co.uk
National Rail   http://www.nationalrail.co.uk
Travel information on the trains.
Office for National Statistics   http://www.statistics.gov.uk
Office of Fair Trading   http://www.oft.gov.uk
Official Solicitor   http://www.offsol.demon.co.uk
Ombudsman (British & Irish
Ombudsman Association)   http://www.bioa.org.uk
Information and directory.
Oxford University Press   http://www.oup.com
(Legal publishers and publishers
of this book)
Oyez Straker   http://www.oyezstraker.co.uk
Legal forms suppliers, business
services, office supplies.
Parliament   http://www.parliament.uk
Patent Office   http://www.patent.gov.uk
HM Prison Service   http://www.hmprisonservice.gov.uk
Privy Council   http://www.privy-council.org.uk
Public Guardianship Office   http://www.guardianship.gov.uk
RAC   http://www.rac.co.uk
Provides the latest travel news, has a
route planner, plus lots of other
interesting information.
Racial Equality,
Commission for   http://www.cre.gov.uk
Registry Trust Limited   http://www.registry-trust.org.uk

Royal Mail	http://www.royalmail.com
Search engines	
A selection of search engines to	http://www.excite.com
help you find things on the	http://www.google.com
Internet.	http://www.lycos.com
	http://www.ukplus.com
	http://www.yahoo.com
Security Industry Authority	http://www.the-sia.org.uk
Solicitors' Family Law	
Association	http://www.sfla.co.uk
Stock Exchange, London	http://www.londonstockexchange.com
Ticketmaster UK Ltd	http://www.ticketmaster.co.uk
Book tickets, search for events.	
The Times	http://www.timesonline.co.uk
Translator	http://world.altavista.com
Translation site for getting	
the gist of a document or web	
page in a selection of languages.	
Transport for London	http://www.tfl.gov.uk/tfl
Treasury, HM	http://www.hm-treasury.gov.uk
The Treasury Solicitor	http://www.treasury-solicitor.gov.uk
United Nations	http://www.un.org
US House of Representatives	http://www.house.gov
Venue Directory	http://www.venuedirectory.com
Handy if you are looking for	
somewhere to hold a	
conference or event (worldwide).	
Weather	http://www.metoffice.com
The latest weather	
from the Met Office.	
World Trade Organisation	http://www.wto.org
Zarak Legal	http://www.zarakgroup.com
Recruitment consultancy who	
have written Chapter 14 of	
this book.	

national
STATISTICS

Deborah Lader
Howard Meltzer

A report on research
using the ONS Omnibus
Survey produced by
the Office for National
Statistics on behalf of
the Department of
Health

Smoking Related Behaviour and Attitudes, 2002

London: Office for National Statistics

This report has been produced in accordance with the National
Statistics Code of Practice.

ISBN **0 11 705608 1**

Applications for reproduction should be submitted to HMSO
under HMSO's Class Licence:
www.clickanduse.hmso.gov.uk

Alternatively applications can be made in writing to:

HMSO
Licensing Division
St Clement's House
2–16 Colegate
Norwich
NR3 1BQ

Contact point
For enquiries about this publication, contact
Howard Meltzer
Tel: **0207 533 5391**
E-mail: **howard.meltzer@ons.gov.uk**

For general enquires, contact the National Statistics Customer
Enquiry Centre on **0845 601 3034**
(minicom: 01633 812399)
E-mail: info@statistics.gov.uk
Fax: 01633 652747
Letters: Room D.115, Givernment Buildings,
         Cardiff Road, Newport NP10 8XG

You can also find National Statistics on the Internet –
at **www.statistics.gov.uk**

About the Office for National Statistics
The Office for National Statistics (ONS) is the government
agency responsible for Compiling, analysing and disseminating
many of the United Kingdom's economic, social and
demographic statistics, including the retail prices index, trade
figures and labour market data, as well as the periodic census of
the population and health statistics. The Director of ONS is also
the National Statistician and the Registrar General for England
and Wales, and the agency that administers the registration of
births, marriages and deaths there.

Contents

List of tables and figures

Page

List of Tables

Chapter 2

Chapter 3

List of figures

Notes to tables

1. Very small bases have been avoided wherever possible because of the relatively high sampling errors that attach to small numbers. In general, percentage distribution is shown if the base is 30 or more. Where the base is smaller than this, actual numbers are shown within square brackets.

2. A percentage may be quoted in the text for a single category that is identifiable in the tables only by summing two or more component percentages. In order to avoid rounding errors, the percentage has been recalculated for the single category and therefore may differ by one percentage point from the sum of the percentages derived from the tables.

3. The row or column percentages may add to 99% or 101% because of rounding.

4. Unless otherwise stated, changes and differences mentioned in the text have been found to be statistically significant at the 95% level.

Summary

This report presents the results of a survey on smoking behaviour and attitudes carried out in 2002. The survey is the latest in a series of surveys carried out as part of the ONS Omnibus Survey for the Department of Health. The surveys in the series were designed to explore views on passive smoking, smoking restrictions and giving up smoking.

The key findings are outlined below.

Giving up smoking *(Chapter 3)*

- The percentage of current smokers who said they would like to give up smoking was not significantly different to the 2001 figure (70% in 2002, 72% in 2001, 71% in 2000 and 72% in 1999).

- Nearly nine out of ten smokers who wanted to give up mentioned at least one health-related reason for wanting to give up smoking. For example, 68% said they wanted to stop smoking because it would be better for their health. A further 28% said they wanted to give up smoking because they could not afford to smoke or considered smoking a waste of money.

- Just over half (51%) of smokers said that they intended to give up smoking within the next 12 months – this was not significantly different to the figures of 51% in 2001 and 48% in 2000. These smokers tended to be younger, light smokers, smokers of packeted cigarettes, and aware of the effect of passive smoking.

- Nearly four-fifths (79%) of current smokers had tried to give up smoking in the past, and over a half (53%) of current smokers had made a serious attempt in the past 5 years. The corresponding figures for 2001 were 79% and 54% respectively. A quarter (24%) of ex-smokers had given up within the past 5 years.

Seeking advice and help for quitting smoking *(section 4.2.1)*

- Overall, 36% of current smokers and 55% of those who had given up smoking in the past year had sought some kind of help or advice for stopping smoking. This was similar to the 2001 and 2000 figures for current smokers (38% and 37% respectively) but lower than in 1999 when 44% of smokers said they had sought some help or advice.

Knowledge and views about passive smoking *(section 5.2)*

- People had a high level of knowledge about the effect of passive smoking. 90% of respondents thought that a child's risk of getting chest infections was increased by passive smoking and over 80% thought that passive smoking would increase a non-smoking adult's risk of lung cancer, bronchitis and asthma. The percentages were similar to those found in 2001.

Non-smokers' attitudes towards people smoking near them *(section 6.1)*

- Over half (55% – 51% of men and 58% of women) who did not smoke said they would mind if other people smoked near them. This was similar to the percentages found in 2001 (55%), 2000 (55%), 1999 (54%) and 1997 (56%).

Smokers' behaviour in the company of non-smokers *(section 6.2)*

- 66% of smokers said they do not smoke at all when they are in a room with a child (63% in 2001) and 21% said they would smoke fewer cigarettes in the presence of a child (26% in 2001).

- Smokers said they would modify their smoking in the company of adult non-smokers – 52% would not smoke at all and 30% would smoke fewer cigarettes. This was similar to the percentages found in 2001 (48% and 34% respectively).

Views on smoking restrictions *(sections 6.3 and 6.4)*

- Half of respondents (50%) who were in work said that smoking was not allowed at all on the premises where they worked – this was similar to the 47% reported in 2001, 44% in 2000, 48% in 1999, 42% in 1997 and 40% in 1996.

- Over four-fifths agreed that there should be restrictions on smoking at work (86%), in restaurants (88%) and in other public places such as banks and post offices (87%). A smaller percentage of respondents, 54%, thought that smoking should be restricted in pubs.

- The support for smoking restrictions has been increasing since 1996. The percentage in favour of restrictions at work rose from 81% in 1996 to 86% in 2002, in restaurants, from 85% to 88%, in pubs, from 48% to 54%, and in other public places from 82% to 87%.

- 43% of people considered whether or not a place has a non-smoking area as an important factor when deciding where to go for a meal. This was similar to those found in previous years (42% in 2001, 45% in 2000 and 41% in 1999).

- 19% said they would take account of whether a place has a non-smoking area when selecting a place to go for a drink (19% in 2001, 22% in 2000, 18% in 1999 and 19% in 1997).

1 Introduction

This report presents the results of a survey on smoking behaviour and attitudes. This survey was the seventh in a series of studies carried out for the Department of Health and was conducted in October and November 2002 as part of the ONS Omnibus Survey. Earlier surveys were carried out in November and December 1995,[1] 1996[1] and 1997[2] and October and November 1999,[3] 2000,[4] and 2001.[5]

The first three surveys in the series were designed to monitor smoking behaviour, people's awareness of the effect of smoking and passive smoking and attitudes towards smoking, tobacco advertising and smoking restrictions.

In December 1998, the Department of Health released *Smoking Kills – a White Paper on tobacco*[6] which set out practical measures to reduce smoking. The success of the White Paper will be judged by measuring its performance alongside three key targets for reducing the prevalence of cigarette smoking among adults, children and pregnant women.

The *NHS Cancer Plan*[7] released in September 2000 builds on the 1998 White Paper and has a target 'to reduce smoking rates among manual groups from 32% in 1998 to 26% by 2010'. These targets are backed by new programmes of targeted action, building on new and effective interventions to help people who want to stop smoking.

The Department of Health document *Priorities and Planning Framework 2003–2006*[8] set out the national requirements for local planning in order to meet the target of reducing the rate of smoking in manual groups. It also set the target of 800,000 smokers from all groups successfully quitting at the four week stage by 2006.

One of the measures proposed in the 1998 White Paper was to end tobacco advertising and tobacco sponsorship and promotion (it was banned in February 2003[9]), and so the questions on people's knowledge of restrictions on tobacco advertising and their attitudes towards tobacco advertising and sponsorship were dropped in the 1999 survey. In their place, an expanded section on giving up smoking was included. This was repeated in 2000, 2001 and 2002. In 2002 two new questions were added to look at difficulties respondents have when trying to give up smoking.

In addition to examining trends, the analysis also explores the relationship between various smoking-related attitudes and behaviour. The key topics examined and presented in this report include:

- smoking behaviour and habits (Chapter 2);
- views about giving up smoking (Chapter 3);
- attempts to stop smoking (Chapter 4);
- perceptions and awareness of issues related to smoking (Chapter 5);
- attitudes related to smoking (Chapter 6); and
- smokers' response to their attitudes (Chapter 6).

Notes and references

1. Dawe F and Goddard E (1997) *Smoking related behaviour and attitude*, TSO: London.

2. Freeth S (1998) *Smoking related behaviour and attitudes, 1997*, The Office for National Statistics: London.

3. Lader D and Meltzer H (2000) *Smoking related behaviour and attitudes, 1999*, The Office for National Statistics: London.

4. Lader D and Meltzer H (2001) *Smoking related behaviour and attitudes, 2000*, The Office for National Statistics: London.

5. Lader D and Meltzer H (2002) *Smoking related behaviour and attitudes, 2001*, The Office for National Statistics: London.

6. Department of Health (1998) *Smoking Kills. A White Paper on Tobacco*, TSO: London.

7. Department of Health (2000) *The NHS Cancer Plan - a plan for investment, a plan for reform*. See http://www.doh.gov.uk/cancer/cancerplan.htm

8. Department of Health (2002) *Improvement, Expansion and reform: The Next 3 Years Priorities and Planning Framework 2003-2006*. See http://www.doh.gov.uk/planning2003-2006/index.htm

9. See the Tobacco Advertising and Promotion Act 2002 which can be accessed at http://www.legislation.hmso.gov.uk/acts/acts2002/20020036.htm

2 Smoking behaviour and habits

The key source of data for monitoring changes in the prevalence of cigarette smoking in the adult population is the General Household Survey (GHS). The relevant GHS questions were included in the Omnibus Survey to help interpret the other data related to smoking.[1]

About a quarter of respondents on the Omnibus survey (26% of men and 24% of women) smoked cigarettes at the time of the interview while two-fifths of the men (44%) and over half (54%) the women had never or only occasionally smoked cigarettes. Men aged 25–44 and women aged 16–34 have the highest prevalence of smoking.

Overall, the prevalence of cigarette smoking as measured on the 2002 Omnibus Survey was slightly but not statistically significantly higher than that measured in 2001.

From April 2001 the National Statistics Social-economic Classification (NS-SEC) was used on the Omnibus to replace Socio-economic group (SEG) and social class.[2] Prevalence of smoking by NS-SEC is shown in Table 2.3 for 2001 and 2002 only.

The Omnibus data on the prevalence of cigarette smoking by social-economic classification showed that people in non-manual occupations were less likely to smoke than those in manual occupations (17% of men and 16% of women in managerial and professional occupations compared with 34% of men and 30% of women in routine and manual occupations). The percentages were not significantly different to those found in 2001.

About a third of male and a quarter of female smokers smoked 20 cigarettes or more a day (35% men and 26% women). Twenty four per cent of male smokers and 32% of female smokers smoked fewer than 10 a day. **Table 2.4**

Overall, 18% of people smoked hand-rolled cigarettes and a further 9% smoked both packeted and hand-rolled cigarettes. Men were much more likely than women to smoke hand-rolled cigarettes or to smoke both packeted and hand-rolled cigarettes. **Table 2.5**

Only a handful of women smoked cigars or a pipe, but 4% of men smoked at least one cigar a month and 1% smoked a pipe. **Table 2.6**

In 2002, similar to previous years, 12% of smokers said that they smoked their first cigarette within five minutes of waking up in the morning. Heavy smokers (those who smoked 20 or more cigarettes a day) were much more likely than light smokers to do this; over a quarter (24%) of heavy smokers smoked their first cigarette within five minutes of waking compared with only 3% of those who smoked fewer than 10 cigarettes a day. **Table 2.7**

Notes and references

1. Office for National Statistics (2001) *Living in Britain*. Results from the 2000 General Household Survey, TSO: London. Also available on-line at http://www.statistics.gov.uk/lib

2. See Appendix A for more information on the transition from SEG to NS-SEC.

Table 2.1 **Cigarette smoking status by sex, 1996–2002**

All respondents

Cigarette smoking status	2002	2001	2000	1999	1997	1996
	%	%	%	%	%	%
Men						
Current cigarette smoker	26	26	26	27	26	28
Ex-regular cigarette smoker	30	32	34	34	32	32
Never or only occasionally smoked cigarettes	44	43	40	39	41	39
Base=100%	*1747*	*1547*	*1594*	*1644*	*1711*	*1787*
Women						
Current cigarette smoker	24	23	26	26	27	28
Ex-regular cigarette smoker	23	21	22	22	23	19
Never or only occasionally smoked cigarettes	54	56	51	52	50	52
Base=100%	*2074*	*1946*	*1734*	*1916*	*2006*	*1911*
All						
Current cigarette smoker	25	24	26	27	26	28
Ex-regular cigarette smoker	26	25	28	28	27	26
Never or only occasionally smoked cigarettes	49	50	46	46	46	46
Base=100%	*3821*	*3495*	*3328*	*3560*	*3717*	*3698*

Table 2.2 Prevalence of cigarette smoking, by sex and age: 1996–2002

All respondents

Age	2002	2001	2000	1999	1997	1996
	Percentage smoking cigarettes					
Men						
16–24	27	30	38	39	31	39
25–34	35	40	35	33	35	39
35–44	33	28	28	31	27	29
45–54	24	31	24	30	26	26
55–64	29	20	24	22	26	23
65-74	14	14	16	17	18	15
75 and over	8	7	13	9	8	10
Total	26	26	26	27	26	28
Bases=100%						
16–24	*225*	*199*	*189*	*204*	*223*	*218*
25–34	*256*	*225*	*232*	*259*	*283*	*364*
35–44	*322*	*287*	*296*	*299*	*326*	*332*
45–54	*323*	*267*	*307*	*297*	*331*	*301*
55–64	*256*	*247*	*220*	*262*	*254*	*265*
65–74	*237*	*191*	*231*	*190*	*189*	*190*
75 and over	*129*	*134*	*119*	*133*	*105*	*115*
Total	*1748*	*1550*	*1594*	*1644*	*1711*	*1787*
	Percentage smoking cigarettes					
Women						
16-24	32	26	35	33	26	36
25-34	30	35	34	36	35	34
35-44	26	29	28	28	31	32
45-54	23	23	26	27	28	27
55-64	23	16	26	21	23	27
65-74	16	12	19	17	23	22
75 and over	10	10	6	10	8	10
Total	24	23	26	26	27	28
Bases=100%						
16-24	*256*	*261*	*199*	*248*	*254*	*218*
25-34	*328*	*310*	*286*	*361*	*368*	*385*
35-44	*375*	*364*	*352*	*382*	*371*	*354*
45-54	*364*	*337*	*305*	*301*	*386*	*324*
55-64	*326*	*243*	*232*	*244*	*254*	*266*
65-74	*210*	*243*	*203*	*220*	*196*	*216*
75 and over	*213*	*187*	*156*	*159*	*178*	*149*
Total	*2072*	*1945*	*1733*	*1916*	*2007*	*1911*

Table 2.3 **Prevalence of cigarette smoking, by sex and social-economic classification, 2001 and 2002**

All respondents

Social-economic Classification	2002	2001	Bases=100% 2002	2001
	Percentage smoking cigarettes			
Men				
Managerial and professional occupations	17	17	*647*	*586*
Intermediate occupations	31	26	*290*	*244*
Routine and manual occupations	34	33	*675*	*651*
Never worked and long-term unemployed	22	26	*135*	*68*
Total	26	26	*1747*	*1549*
Women				
Managerial and professional occupations	16	20	*574*	*544*
Intermediate occupations	22	22	*499*	*467*
Routine and manual occupations	30	27	*799*	*802*
Never worked and long-term unemployed	24	14	*203*	*131*
Total	24	23	*2075*	*1944*
All				
Managerial and professional occupations	16	18	*1221*	*1132*
Intermediate occupations	25	24	*790*	*711*
Routine and manual occupations	32	30	*1474*	*1452*
Never worked and long-term unemployed	23	19	*338*	*199*
Total	25	24	*3823*	*3494*

Table 2.4 Daily cigarette consumption by sex, 1996–2002

Current cigarette smokers

Number of cigarettes smoked per day	2002	2001	2000	1999	1997	1996
	%	%	%	%	%	%
Men						
20 and over a day	35	37	34	36	32	38
10–19 a day	41	40	39	38	43	37
Fewer than 10 a day	24	23	27	25	25	25
Base=100%	*456*	*396*	*414*	*446*	*448*	*506*
Women						
20 and over a day	26	25	32	24	29	28
10–19 a day	42	41	37	47	42	41
Fewer than 10 a day	32	34	31	29	29	31
Base=100%	*488*	*448*	*452*	*502*	*536*	*539*

Table 2.5 Type of cigarette smoked by sex, 1996–2002

Current cigarette smokers

Type of cigarette	2002	2001	2000	1999	1997	1996
	%	%	%	%	%	%
Men						
Packeted	59	59	60	62	66	68
Hand-rolled	28	25	27	22	22	21
Both types	12	16	13	17	12	11
Base=100%	*457*	*397*	*415*	*446*	*449*	*507*
Women						
Packeted	86	80	79	85	92	92
Hand-rolled	9	12	12	7	5	3
Both types	5	8	9	8	4	5
Base=100%	*488*	*449*	*456*	*503*	*536*	*539*
All						
Packeted	73	70	70	74	80	80
Hand-rolled	18	18	19	14	12	12
Both types	9	12	11	12	7	8
Base=100%	*945*	*846*	*871*	*950*	*985*	*1046*

Table 2.6 **Prevalence of cigar and pipe smoking among men, by age, 1996–2002**

All male respondents

Age	Cigar smoking*						Pipe smoking						Bases=100%					
	2002	2001	2000	1999	1997	1996	2002	2001	2000	1999	1997	1996	2002	2001	2000	1999	1997	1996
16-24	2	2	8	3	5	3	1	-	-	0	-	0	225	199	189	203	223	218
25-34	4	2	4	4	6	5	-	0	0	0	1	1	256	225	232	260	283	364
35-44	7	6	6	6	6	8	1	0	1	-	1	2	322	286	296	298	326	332
45-54	4	7	6	7	8	7	2	1	1	1	4	2	323	267	308	298	331	297
55-64	3	8	10	5	6	5	2	4	4	2	5	2	255	248	220	262	254	264
65-74	4	5	4	4	5	3	2	2	1	3	2	4	237	190	230	190	188	188
75 and over	1	2	2	4	7	5	3	6	2	6	6	7	129	133	119	132	105	115
Total	4	5	6	5	6	5	1	2	1	2	2	2	1747	1548	1594	1643	1710	1778

* Smoke at least one cigar per month.

Table 2.7 Time between waking and the first cigarette, by sex, 1996–2002

Current cigarette smokers

Time between waking and the first cigarette	2002	2001	2000	1999	1997	1996
	%	%	%	%	%	%
Men						
Less than 5 minutes	14	12	14	15	14	13
5–14 minutes	14	17	17	14	15	16
15–29 minutes	16	15	15	16	12	17
30 mins but less than 1 hour	21	22	19	17	18	19
1 hour but less than 2 hours	16	13	14	16	14	13
2 hours and over	19	21	23	22	26	22
Base=100%	*458*	*397*	*416*	*443*	*449*	*505*
Women						
Less than 5 minutes	10	14	12	11	12	12
5–14 minutes	15	14	15	12	16	15
15–29 minutes	12	12	14	14	12	15
30 mins but less than 1 hour	20	16	20	19	19	17
1 hour but less than 2 hours	15	16	14	16	16	14
2 hours and over	28	28	25	29	26	26
Base=100%	*484*	*447*	*455*	*504*	*536*	*538*
All						
Less than 5 minutes	12	13	13	13	13	13
5–14 minutes	14	15	16	13	15	15
15–29 minutes	14	14	14	15	12	16
30 mins but less than 1 hour	20	19	19	18	19	18
1 hour but less than 2 hours	16	15	14	16	15	14
2 hours and over	24	25	24	26	26	24
Base=100%	*942*	*845*	*867*	*949*	*983*	*1043*

Table 2.8 **Time between waking and the first cigarette, by sex and number of cigarettes smoked per day, 2002**

Current cigarette smokers

Time between waking and the first cigarette	Number of cigarettes a day			2002 Total
	20 and over	10–19	0–9	
	%	%	%	%
Men				
Less than 5 minutes	25	11	6	14
5–14 minutes	23	11	4	14
15–29 minutes	20	19	4	16
30 mins but less than 1 hour	23	26	9	21
1 hour but less than 2 hours	7	20	24	16
2 hours and over	2	13	52	19
Base=100%	*158*	*188*	*112*	*458*
Women				
Less than 5 minutes	22	9	1	10
5–14 minutes	31	13	4	15
15–29 minutes	13	16	5	12
30 mins but less than 1 hour	17	28	10	20
1 hour but less than 2 hours	12	17	16	15
2 hours and over	5	17	63	28
Base=100%	*127*	*203*	*154*	*484*
All				
Less than 5 minutes	24	10	3	12
5–14 minutes	27	12	5	14
15–29 minutes	17	18	5	14
30 mins but less than 1 hour	20	27	10	20
1 hour but less than 2 hours	9	18	19	16
2 hours and over	3	15	58	24
Base=100%	*284*	*392*	*266*	*942*

3 Giving up smoking

3.1 Models of health behaviour change

The design and analysis of the questions included on the Omnibus Survey have been informed by two models which explore the relationships between attitudes, knowledge and behaviour. The two models represent two different types of theoretical approach to explaining health behaviour change – continuum models and stage models.

Ajzen's Theory of Planned Behaviour[1] argues that a person's intention to, for example, stop smoking, is a function of their attitude towards stopping smoking, subjective norms of smoking and the amount of control they perceive they have over their smoking. Each of these components is a function of beliefs which need to change in order to change the behaviour.

Prochaska and DiClemente's[2] Stages of Change Model maps the five stages of change people pass through: precontemplation (not seriously thinking about change); contemplation (seriously thinking about change); preparation (ready to change); action (attempting to change); and maintenance (change achieved). Successful change involves progressing through the stages and progress is often in a cyclical manner with relapse the rule rather than the exception. Most individuals do not give up after relapsing, but cycle back into the precontemplation stage.

Marsh and Matheson[3] conclude that smoking is a behavioural choice and that there are three measures of behaviour: desire, resolve and confidence. They also show a relationship between the resolve to give up smoking and success in doing so.

3.2 Wanting to give up smoking

Clearly, in order to meet the targets on prevalence of cigarette smoking set in the White Paper, people have to be discouraged from starting to smoke and current smokers have to be encouraged to stop.

3.2.1 Smokers who want to give up

The first stage to giving up is to want to give up, which equates to Marsh and Matheson's *desire* component.

Seventy per cent of current smokers said that they wanted to give up smoking. Twenty six per cent of smokers said that they very much wanted to stop smoking, and a further fifth (23%) said they wanted to stop "quite a lot". This was not significantly different to previous years (for example, 72% of smokers wanted to give up in 2001 and 71% in 2000).

As in previous years, there was no difference in the percentage of men and women smokers who wanted to stop.

Older smokers were the least likely to want to stop smoking (43% of those aged 65 and over, compared with 68% or more of the younger age groups). As smoking prevalence is lower among older age groups (see Table 2.2), this suggests that smokers in the older age cohorts who may have wanted to give up smoking are likely to have already given up by the age of 65, or to have died.

As in 2001 and 1999 (but not 2000), smokers with children under 16 years of age present in the household were more likely to want to quit smoking than those without children (76% and 67% respectively). There was no significant difference in wanting to give up between those in different social-economic classification categories.

There was some difference in the percentage of smokers wanting to give up by level of cigarette consumption: those who smoked fewer than 10 cigarettes a day were the least likely to want to give up (65% compared with 75% of those who smoked 10-19 cigarettes a day). Although it appeared that those who smoked hand rolled cigarettes were less likely to want to give up smoking, the differences were not statistically significant.

Prochaska and DiClemente's Stages of Change Model suggests that people move cyclically through the five stages, and individuals do not abandon their attempts to quit smoking after relapsing but cycle back into the precontemplation stage. This is shown in Table 3.6 where those who had made a serious attempt to give up in the last 5 years were more likely to say that they wanted to give up very much compared with those who had not tried (35% and 15% respectively). Similarly, those who had tried to give up twice or more in the last year appeared to feel more strongly about giving up than those who had tried less often (but due to small bases the differences were not statistically significant).   **Figure 3.1, Tables 3.1–3.7**

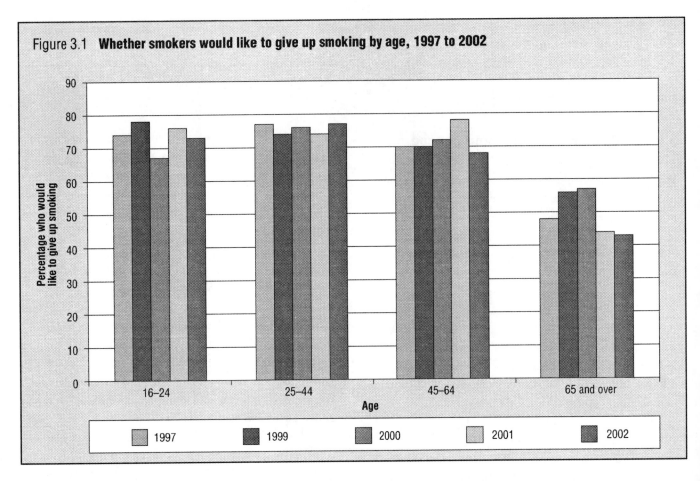

Figure 3.1 **Whether smokers would like to give up smoking by age, 1997 to 2002**

Legend: 1997 | 1999 | 2000 | 2001 | 2002

The characteristics discussed above may themselves be inter-related – for example, the presence of children under 16 in the household is probably confounded by the age of the smokers (that is, older people are less likely than younger people to live in the same household as children under 16). A statistical procedure, logistic regression, was therefore used in the analysis to identify the influences that are independently associated with wanting to give up smoking.[4] Overall, smokers who were most likely to want to give up smoking were:

- younger (those aged 16–64 were two or three times as likely as those aged 75 and over to want to give up smoking);
- aware of the effect of passive smoking on chest infections among children; and
- aware of the effect of passive smoking on heart disease among adults.

3.2.2 Reasons for wanting to give up smoking

Those who wanted to give up smoking were asked why they wanted to do so and up to three answers were recorded. Just under nine out of ten (86%) smokers who wanted to quit mentioned at least one health reason as their reason for wanting to give up smoking:

- 68% of those who wanted to give up said it was because it would be better for their health in general;
- 30% said that giving up smoking would reduce their risk of getting a smoking related illness; and
- 16% because of health problems they had at present.

After health reasons, the next most common reason given for wanting to give up was a financial one – 28% could not afford to smoke or considered smoking as a waste of money. Sixteen per cent said they wanted to give up because of family pressure and 13% because of the effect of smoking on children.

Men were more likely than women to say they want to give up smoking because it is better for their health in general (72% and 63% respectively). Conversely, women were more likely to be worried about the effect smoking has on children (16% of women and 10% of men cited this as a reason for wanting to quit smoking).

There was an increase in the percentage of smokers wanting to give up smoking for financial reasons between 2000 and 2002.

Overall, health was equally likely to be given as a reason regardless of how much respondents smoked – indicating that the health education message that all smoking, rather than just heavy smoking, is bad for you, is being accepted.

Smokers who said they wanted to stop very much were slightly more likely than other smokers to cite health-related reasons (91% compared with 74% of those who only want to give up smoking a little). They were also more likely to give more than one reason (61% compared with only 35% of those who want to give up smoking a little).   **Tables 3.8–3.10**

3.3 Intending to give up smoking

In 1999, a new set of questions was included asking if smokers intended to give up smoking, and if so when. These questions were repeated in 2000, 2001 and 2002.

Seventy per cent of smokers said they intended to give up smoking, similar to previous years. There were no significant differences between men and women.

Only 30% of smokers said that they did not intend to give up, a percentage that rose sharply with age from 17% among those aged 16–24 to 65% among those aged 65 or more. The gap between younger and older smokers was more marked in 2001 and 2002 than in 2000.

The youngest smokers were more likely to say they would give up in the next six months (36%) compared with about a quarter (24%) of those aged 45–64. Younger and older people may have opposing reasons for continuing to smoke in the short term: older people may think it is too late to give up, whereas younger people may think they have plenty of time to give up in the future before the health risks of smoking become apparent.

Smokers who have children under 16 present in the household were also more likely to intend to stop smoking than those who do not have children in the household. Unlike in 2001, smokers in managerial and professional occupations were more likely than others to intend to give up smoking (77% compared with 65% of smokers in routine and manual occupations). Those who had never worked or were long term unemployed were the most likely to intend to give up smoking (80%).   **Table 3.13**

Fifty-one per cent of smokers said they intended to give up in the next 12 months. Heavy smokers were less likely to intend to give up than light smokers: 40% of those smoking 20 or more a day intended to give up within a year, compared with 54% of those

smoking fewer than 10. Unlike 2001 when there was no significant difference, smokers who smoked packeted cigarettes were more likely to intend to give up smoking than those who smoked hand-rolled cigarettes (74% and 62% respectively).   **Tables 3.14 and 3.15**

It is possible that age, the presence of children in the household and cigarette consumption all have an independent effect on the intention to stop smoking, but the bases would be too small to enable further investigation. Logistic regression was therefore used in the analysis to identify the influences that are independently associated with intentions to give up smoking. It was found that people who intended to give up smoking in the next year were:

• younger;
• aware of the effect of passive smoking on chest infections among children;
• aware of the effect of passive smoking on lung cancer among adults;
• light smokers; and
• smokers of packeted cigarettes;

As with desire to give up smoking, those smokers who had made a serious attempt to give up in the past 5 years were more likely to intend to give up (85%) than those who had not tried to stop smoking (55%). Over two-fifths (43%) of smokers who had tried to stop in the past 5 years intended to try again within the next 6 months. Among those who had tried to give up in the past year, 53% intended to try again in the next 6 months, and only 9% said they no longer intended to give up smoking.   **Tables 3.16 and 3.17**

As a measure of how successful respondents thought they would be at giving up smoking, they were asked how likely it was that they would still be smoking in 12 months time.

Current smokers appeared to be fairly pessimistic about their chances of success in giving up smoking – half of all smokers (50%) said they would probably or definitely be smoking in 12 months, and only 24% thought they would probably or definitely not be smoking. There was no significant change since 1999. Among ex-regular smokers, a small percentage (2%) said they thought they would have started smoking again in 12 months time.   **Table 3.18**

As expected, the majority (94%) of smokers who did not intend to give up smoking said they would probably or definitely be smoking in 12 months, compared with only 18% of those intending to give up within a year. Tables 3.20 to 3.25 therefore, show the respondents' expectations of their smoking in 12 months only for those who said that they intended to give up smoking in the next year. It should be noted, of course, that not all smokers are correct in their prediction of their future smoking status.

There were no significant differences in expectations between men and women, but younger smokers were less confident about their ability to give up than older smokers: 31% of those aged 16–24 thought they would probably or definitely be smoking in 12 months, compared with only 15% of older age groups.

Light smokers appeared the most optimistic about their smoking status in 12 months (only 13% thought they would probably or definitely be smoking, compared with 17–21% of heavier smokers). There were no differences between smokers of packeted and hand-rolled cigarettes.   **Tables 3.22 and 3.23**

Smokers who had attempted to give up in the last 5 years and those who had made 2 or more attempts in the past year were as likely as others to say they would have stopped smoking in 12 months time. This suggests that they have not been completely disillusioned by their previous attempts and are still moving through the different stages of giving up.   **Tables 3.24 and 3.25**

3.4 The relationship between wanting to and intending to give up smoking

Two dimensions to stopping smoking were presented above – wanting to stop (or desire) and intending to stop (or resolve). These are two separate concepts and a smoker can legitimately give any combination of yes and no to the two questions. Not surprisingly, smokers who said they did *not want* to give up were also more likely to say they did *not intend* to give up (77% compared with only 9% of those who did want to give up). This confirms Marsh and Matheson's[3] suggestion that *desire* may only reflect the tendency of those who intend to give up smoking to confirm that that is what they want to do. Overall, 91% of smokers who wanted to give up, intended to give up smoking.

However, 23% of smokers who had said they did *not want* to give up smoking, went on to say that they *intended* to give up at some time.   **Table 3.26**

Tables 3.27 to 3.31 present the information about desire and resolve together for different sub-groups. There were no significant differences between men and women. Younger smokers were the most likely to say that they intended to give up smoking even though they did not want to quit (12% of those aged 16–24). In contrast, the older smokers were more likely to want to give up but

not intend to (10% of those aged 45 and above compared with 2% of those aged 16–24). Older smokers were also more likely to neither want to give up nor intend to give up smoking (53% of those aged 65 or over compared with 15% of those aged 16–24).

As in 2001 (but unlike 2000), smokers with no children in the household were more likely than those with children to neither want to give up nor intend to do so (26% and 18% respectively). There were very few differences between smokers from different social-economic classificatory groups.   **Table 3.29**

Light smokers were the most likely group to both want to and intend to give up smoking in the next 6 months (16%, compared with only 6% of heavy smokers). Although it appeared that those who smoke hand-rolled cigarettes were more likely to neither want nor intend to give up smoking, the differences were not statistically significant.   **Tables 3.30 and 3.31**

Notes and references

1. Ajzen I (1991) The theory of planned behaviour. *Organisational Behaviour and Human Decision Processes* **50**, 179–211.

2. Prochaska J O (1994) Strong and weak principles for progressing from precontemplation to action on the basis of twelve problem behaviours. *Health Psychology* **12**, 46–51.

3. Marsh A and Matheson J (1983) *Smoking attitudes and behaviour*, HMSO: London.

4. Logistic regression is explained in detail in Appendix C and the factors included in the analysis are listed in Tables C3.1 and C3.2 in Appendix C.

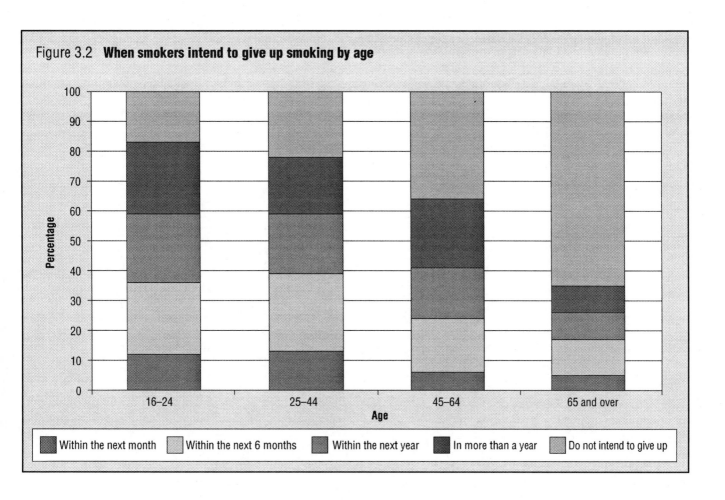

Figure 3.2 **When smokers intend to give up smoking by age**

Table 3.1 Views on giving up smoking by sex, 1997–2002

All smokers

Views on giving up smoking	2002	2001	2000	1999	1997
	%	%	%	%	%
Men					
Would like to give up:					
Very much indeed	26	29	29	29	..
Quite a lot	24	18	20	20	..
A fair amount	13	17	16	16	..
A little	8	8	6	6	..
Total would like to give up	71	72	71	72	68
Would not like to give up	29	28	29	28	32
Base=100%	*454*	*390*	*414*	*447*	*449*
Women					
Would like to give up:					
Very much indeed	26	27	32	30	..
Quite a lot	22	26	20	22	..
A fair amount	15	14	15	12	..
A little	7	7	5	8	..
Total would like to give up	70	73	71	72	74
Would not like to give up	30	27	29	28	26
Base=100%	*482*	*446*	*454*	*503*	*536*
All					
Would like to give up:					
Very much indeed	26	28	30	30	..
Quite a lot	23	22	20	21	..
A fair amount	14	15	16	14	..
A little	8	7	6	7	..
Total would like to give up	70	72	71	72	71
Would not like to give up	30	28	29	28	29
Base=100%	*936*	*836*	*868*	*950*	*987*

.. Data not available.

Table 3.2 **Views on giving up smoking by age, 1997–2002**

All smokers

Views on giving up smoking	Age 16–24	25–44	45–64	65 and over	Total
	%	%	%	%	%
2002					
Would like to give up:					
Very much indeed	26	27	27	17	26
Quite a lot	20	25	23	14	23
A fair amount	17	19	10	5	14
A little	10	6	8	6	8
Total would like to give up	73	77	68	43	70
Would not like to give up	27	23	32	57	30
Base=100%	*142*	*389*	*304*	*98*	*936*
2001					
Would like to give up:					
Very much indeed	16	29	35	16	28
Quite a lot	25	24	22	11	22
A fair amount	20	14	14	12	15
A little	13	6	7	5	7
Total would like to give up	76	74	78	44	72
Would not like to give up	24	26	22	56	28
Base=100%	*127*	*380*	*247*	*81*	*836*
2000					
Would like to give up:					
Very much indeed	20	34	33	22	30
Quite a lot	16	20	23	15	20
A fair amount	20	17	13	12	16
A little	11	5	3	8	6
Total would like to give up	67	76	72	57	71
Would not like to give up	33	24	28	43	29
Base=100%	*141*	*363*	*265*	*100*	*868*
1999					
Would like to give up:					
Very much indeed	26	30	33	26	30
Quite a lot	27	24	15	19	21
A fair amount	19	14	14	8	14
A little	6	7	8	4	7
Total would like to give up	78	74	70	56	72
Would not like to give up	22	26	30	44	28
Base=100%	*160*	*412*	*279*	*98*	*950*
1997					
Would like to give up	74	77	70	48	71
Would not like to give up	26	23	30	52	29
Base=100%	*136*	*431*	*318*	*102*	*987*

Table 3.3 **Views on giving up smoking, by social-economic classification and by presence of children in the household, 2002**

All smokers

Views on giving up smoking	Social-economic classification Managerial and professional occupations	Intermediate occupations	Routine and manual occupations	Never worked and long-term unemployed	Children under 16 in household	No children in household	2002 Total
	%	%	%	%	%	%	%
Would like to give up:							
Very much indeed	25	26	25	30	29	24	26
Quite a lot	28	18	23	21	24	22	23
A fair amount	12	20	13	10	14	14	14
A little	8	8	6	14	9	7	8
Total would like to give up	71	73	68	76	76	67	70
Would not like to give up	29	27	32	24	24	33	30
Base=100%	*199*	*196*	*464*	*76*	*329*	*605*	*936*

Table 3.4 **Views on giving up smoking, by number of cigarettes smoked per day and sex, 2002**

All smokers

Views on giving up smoking	Number of cigarettes per day 20 and over	10–19	0–9	2002 Total
	%	%	%	%
Men				
Would like to give up:				
Very much indeed	24	31	20	26
Quite a lot	24	19	29	24
A fair amount	14	17	7	13
A little	10	6	6	8
Total would like to give up	73	74	62	71
Would not like to give up	27	26	38	29
Base=100%	*155*	*186*	*111*	*454*
Women				
Would like to give up:				
Very much indeed	21	27	27	26
Quite a lot	21	28	15	22
A fair amount	10	16	17	15
A little	10	5	8	7
Total would like to give up	63	76	67	70
Would not like to give up	37	24	33	30
Base=100%	*126*	*202*	*154*	*482*
All				
Would like to give up:				
Very much indeed	23	29	24	26
Quite a lot	23	24	21	23
A fair amount	12	16	13	14
A little	10	6	7	8
Total would like to give up	68	75	65	70
Would not like to give up	32	25	35	30
Base=100%	*280*	*387*	*265*	*936*

Table 3.5 **Views on giving up smoking, by type of cigarette smoked and sex, 2002**

All smokers

Views on giving up smoking	Men Type of cigarette smoked			Women Type of cigarette smoked		
	Packeted	Hand-rolled	Both types	Packeted	Hand-rolled	Both types
	%	%	%	%	%	%
Would like to give up:						
Very much indeed	26	24	32	25	30	[6]
Quite a lot	23	26	21	22	18	[5]
A fair amount	14	13	7	15	11	[4]
A little	8	5	12	7	7	[2]
Total would like to give up	71	68	73	70	66	[17]
Would not like to give up	29	32	27	30	34	[8]
Base=100%	269	129	56	413	44	25

Table 3.6 **Views on giving up smoking, by whether attempted to give up smoking in the last five years, 2002**

All smokers

Views on giving up smoking	Attempted to give up in last 5 years	Not attempted to give up in last 5 years	2002 Total
	%	%	%
Would like to give up:			
Very much indeed	35	15	26
Quite a lot	29	16	23
A fair amount	14	14	14
A little	5	10	8
Total would like to give up	84	55	70
Would not like to give up	16	45	30
Base=100%	496	438	936

Table 3.7   **Views on giving up smoking, by number of attempts to give up smoking in the last year, 2002**

Smokers who have tried to give up in last year

Views on giving up smoking	Number of attempts in the last year			2002 Total
	1	2	3 or more	
	%	%	%	%
Would like to give up:				
Very much indeed	36	48	58	42
Quite a lot	33	26	21	29
A fair amount	17	11	9	14
A little	4	2	-	3
Total would like to give up	90	87	88	88
Would not like to give up	11	13	12	12
Base=100%	*129*	*54*	*33*	*216*

Table 3.8 **Main reasons for wanting to stop smoking by sex, 1996–2002**

Smokers who want to stop

Reasons for wanting to stop	2002	2001	2000	1999	1997	1996
	%	%	%	%	%	%
Men						
Better for health in general	72	75	76	75	72	64
Less risk of getting smoking related illness	30	34	38	33	36	32
Present health problems	18	14	15	13	16	17
At least one health reason	**89**	**90**	**91**	**89**	**88**	**83**
Financial reasons	25	28	38	35	40	34
Family pressure	13	20	22	18	11	15
Harms children	10	10	10	12	16	14
Doctor's advice	4	7	6	7	3	7
Pregnancy	0	0	-	1	1	1
Other	3	2	4	4	3	4
Gave more than one reason	**52**	**62**	**73**	**66**	**63**	**59**
Base=100%	*321*	*279*	*292*	*319*	*305*	*351*
Women						
Better for health in general	63	63	73	68	68	65
Less risk of getting smoking related illness	30	28	40	29	33	26
Present health problems	14	17	17	13	17	16
At least one health reason	**89**	**84**	**90**	**84**	**88**	**83**
Financial reasons	30	32	44	36	39	37
Family pressure	19	19	18	21	16	14
Harms children	16	20	18	24	24	22
Doctor's advice	4	7	6	7	8	9
Pregnancy	2	3	5	4	3	2
Other	4	5	3	3	4	2
Gave more than one reason	**56**	**63**	**79**	**67**	**73**	**60**
Base=100%	*336*	*327*	*322*	*362*	*398*	*361*
All						
Better for health in general	68	68	75	71	70	65
Less risk of getting smoking related illness	30	31	39	31	34	29
Present health problems	16	16	16	13	16	17
At least one health reason	**86**	**87**	**91**	**87**	**88**	**83**
Financial reasons	28	31	41	35	39	36
Family pressure	16	19	20	19	14	14
Harms children	13	15	14	18	21	18
Doctor's advice	4	7	6	7	6	8
Pregnancy	1	2	3	3	2	1
Other	4	4	4	3	4	3
Gave more than one reason	**54**	**62**	**76**	**66**	**68**	**59**
Base=100%	*657*	*606*	*617*	*681*	*703*	*712*

Percentages sum to more than 100 as respondents could give more than one answer.

Table 3.9 **Main reasons for wanting to stop smoking, by sex and number of cigarettes smoked per day, 2002**

Smokers who want to stop

Reasons for wanting to stop	Number of cigarettes per day			2002 Total
	20 and over	10–19	0–9	
	%	%	%	%
Men				
Better for health in general	67	80	63	72
Less risk of getting smoking related illness	31	30	30	30
Present health problems	21	12	23	18
At least one health reason	**88**	**91**	**88**	**89**
Financial reasons	33	23	15	25
Family pressure	16	12	11	13
Harms children	11	11	7	10
Doctor's advice	4	5	2	4
Pregnancy	1	-	-	0
Other	5	3	2	3
Gave more than one reason	**60**	**54**	**32**	**52**
Base=100%	*114*	*138*	*69*	*321*
Women				
Better for health in general	59	61	70	63
Less risk of getting smoking related illness	30	30	30	30
Present health problems	13	15	13	14
At least one health reason	**81**	**81**	**87**	**83**
Financial reasons	34	36	17	30
Family pressure	23	22	11	19
Harms children	15	11	25	16
Doctor's advice	4	7	2	4
Pregnancy	0	2	4	2
Other	6	4	3	4
Gave more than one reason	**58**	**59**	**52**	**56**
Base=100%	*79*	*154*	*103*	*336*
All				
Better for health in general	64	70	67	68
Less risk of getting smoking related illness	31	30	30	30
Present health problems	18	14	17	16
At least one health reason	**85**	**86**	**88**	**86**
Financial reasons	33	30	16	28
Family pressure	19	17	11	16
Harms children	13	11	18	13
Doctor's advice	4	6	2	4
Pregnancy	1	1	2	1
Other	5	3	2	4
Gave more than one reason	**59**	**57**	**44**	**54**
Base=100%	*193*	*293*	*172*	*657*

Percentages sum to more than 100 as respondents could give more than one answer.

Table 3.10 **Main reasons for wanting to stop smoking, by sex and how much would like to give up, 2002**

Smokers who want to stop

| Reasons for wanting to stop | How much would like to give up | | | | 2002 Total |
	Very much	Quite a lot	A fair amount	A little	
	%	%	%	%	%
Men					
Better for health in general	73	71	79	60	72
Less risk of getting smoking related illness	33	31	34	13	30
Present health problems	25	16	10	10	18
At least one health reason	**96**	**87**	**90**	**71**	**89**
Financial reasons	24	28	19	30	25
Family pressure	9	8	27	15	13
Harms children	9	12	9	9	10
Doctor's advice	7	3	1	2	4
Pregnancy	1	-	-	-	0
Other	3	4	-	7	3
Gave more than one reason	**56**	**48**	**59**	**37**	**52**
Base=100%	*118*	*107*	*61*	*35*	*321*
Women					
Better for health in general	65	66	61	53	63
Less risk of getting smoking related illness	37	26	29	18	30
Present health problems	17	16	8	9	14
At least one health reason	**87**	**82**	**82**	**77**	**89**
Financial reasons	31	28	35	20	30
Family pressure	21	24	12	9	19
Harms children	14	17	16	18	16
Doctor's advice	5	6	4	2	4
Pregnancy	3	2	2	3	2
Other	7	2	-	5	4
Gave more than one reason	**65**	**61**	**47**	**31**	**56**
Base=100%	*123*	*106*	*72*	*35*	*336*
All					
Better for health in general	69	68	69	56	68
Less risk of getting smoking related illness	35	28	31	16	30
Present health problems	21	16	9	10	16
At least one health reason	**91**	**84**	**86**	**74**	**86**
Financial reasons	28	28	28	25	28
Family pressure	16	16	19	12	16
Harms children	12	15	13	14	13
Doctor's advice	6	4	2	2	4
Pregnancy	2	1	1	2	1
Other	5	4	-	6	4
Gave more than one reason	**61**	**54**	**53**	**35**	**54**
Base=100%	*241*	*213*	*132*	*70*	*657*

Percentages sum to more than 100 as respondents could give more than one answer.

Table 3.11 **When smokers intend to give up smoking by sex, 1999–2002**

All smokers

When smokers intend to give up smoking	2002	2001	2000	1999
	%	%	%	%
Men				
Within the next month	10	7	12	12
Within the next 6 months	21	21	17	21
Within the next year	16	18	17	16
In more than a year	21	27	21	20
Total intend to give up	69	72	68	69
Do not intend to give up	31	28	32	31
Base=100%	*449*	*393*	*413*	*435*
Women				
Within the next month	9	12	10	12
Within the next 6 months	22	24	20	22
Within the next year	20	22	20	19
In more than a year	20	19	23	17
Total intend to give up	72	77	73	71
Do not intend to give up	28	23	27	29
Base=100%	*483*	*444*	*446*	*496*
All				
Within the next month	10	9	11	12
Within the next 6 months	22	22	18	22
Within the next year	19	20	19	18
In more than a year	20	23	22	18
Total intend to give up	70	75	71	70
Do not intend to give up	30	25	29	30
Base=100%	*932*	*837*	*859*	*931*

Table 3.12 When smokers intend to give up smoking by age, 1999–2002

All smokers

When smokers intend to give up smoking	Age 16–24	25–44	45–64	65 and over	Total
	%	%	%	%	%
2002					
Within the next month	12	13	6	5	10
Within the next 6 months	24	26	18	12	22
Within the next year	23	20	17	9	19
In more than a year	24	19	23	9	20
Total intend to give up	83	79	64	35	70
Do not intend to give up	17	21	36	65	30
Base=100%	*143*	*387*	*304*	*96*	*932*
2001					
Within the next month	6	11	8	9	9
Within the next 6 months	35	22	21	7	22
Within the next year	25	21	22	6	20
In more than a year	25	23	24	14	23
Total intend to give up	91	77	75	36	75
Do not intend to give up	9	23	25	64	25
Base=100%	*128*	*381*	*247*	*81*	*837*
2000					
Within the next month	11	14	10	6	11
Within the next 6 months	19	21	17	10	18
Within the next year	16	21	19	11	19
In more than a year	30	22	20	19	22
Total intend to give up	76	78	66	46	71
Do not intend to give up	24	22	34	54	29
Base=100%	*141*	*361*	*261*	*97*	*859*
1999					
Within the next month	14	12	12	8	12
Within the next 6 months	25	24	20	9	22
Within the next year	23	22	12	9	18
In more than a year	26	18	17	12	18
Total intend to give up	88	76	61	27	70
Do not intend to give up	12	24	39	63	30
Base=100%	*159*	*403*	*274*	*93*	*931*

Table 3.13 **When smokers intend to give up smoking, by presence of children in the household and by social-economic classification, 2002**

All smokers

When smokers intend to give up smoking	Social-economic classification Managerial and professional occupations	Intermediate occupations	Routine and manual occupations	Never worked and long-term unemployed	Children under 16 in household	No children in household	2002 Total
	%	%	%	%	%	%	%
Within the next month	11	8	9	17	15	7	10
Within the next 6 months	28	24	18	23	25	20	22
Within the next year	19	18	18	20	18	19	19
In more than a year	18	22	20	21	20	20	20
Total intend to give up	77	72	65	80	78	66	70
Do not intend to give up	23	28	35	20	22	34	30
Base=100%	*197*	*196*	*462*	*77*	*328*	*604*	*932*

Table 3.14 **When smokers intend to give up smoking, by number of cigarettes smoked per day, 2002**

All smokers

When smokers intend to give up smoking	Number of cigarettes per day 20 and over	10–19	0–9	2002 Total
	%	%	%	%
Within the next month	6	8	16	10
Within the next 6 months	14	25	25	22
Within the next year	20	22	13	19
In more than a year	24	20	17	20
Total intend to give up	63	76	71	70
Do not intend to give up	37	24	29	30
Base=100%	*280*	*386*	*262*	*932*

Table 3.15 **When smokers intend to give up smoking, by type of cigarette smoked, 2002**

All smokers

When smokers intend to give up smoking	Type of cigarette smoked			2002 Total
	Packeted	Hand-rolled	Both types	
	%	%	%	%
Within the next month	11	5	12	10
Within the next 6 months	23	20	12	22
Within the next year	19	16	21	19
In more than a year	21	21	15	20
Total intend to give up	74	62	60	70
Do not intend to give up	26	38	40	30
Base=100%	*680*	*170*	*81*	*932*

Table 3.16 **When smokers intend to give up smoking, by whether they have attempted to give up smoking in the last 5 years, 2002**

All smokers

When smokers intend to give up smoking	Attempted to give up in last 5 years	Not attempted to give up in last 5 years	2002 Total
	%	%	%
Within the next month	15	4	10
Within the next 6 months	28	14	22
Within the next year	23	13	19
In more than a year	18	23	20
Total intend to give up	85	55	70
Do not intend to give up	15	45	30
Base=100%	*492*	*440*	*932*

Table 3.17 **When smokers intend to give up smoking, by number of attempts to give up smoking in the last year, 2002**

Smokers who have tried to give up in last year

When smokers intend to give up smoking	Made one attempt to give up in last year	Made two or more attempts to give up in last year	2002 Total
	%	%	%
Within the next month	16	26	20
Within the next 6 months	33	33	33
Within the next year	20	15	18
In more than a year	22	16	20
Total intend to give up	91	90	91
Do not intend to give up	9	10	9
Base=100%	*127*	*88*	*215*

Table 3.18 **Whether respondents will be smoking in 12 months, by smoking status, 1999–2002**

All respondents

Whether respondents will be smoking in 12 months	Smoking status Current smokers	Ex-regular smokers	Never smoked regularly	Total
	%	%	%	%
2002				
Definitely will be smoking	21	1	1	6
Probably will be smoking	29	1	0	7
Might or might not be smoking	26	2	0	7
Probably will not be smoking	17	4	2	6
Definitely will not be smoking	7	92	97	74
Base=100%	*934*	*998*	*1878*	*3810*
2001				
Definitely will be smoking	18	2	1	5
Probably will be smoking	27	1	1	7
Might or might not be smoking	29	3	0	8
Probably will not be smoking	17	4	3	7
Definitely will not be smoking	9	90	96	73
Base=100%	*842*	*887*	*1761*	*3490*
2000				
Definitely will be smoking	20	2	1	6
Probably will be smoking	32	1	0	9
Might or might not be smoking	26	2	0	8
Probably will not be smoking	16	6	2	7
Definitely will not be smoking	5	89	96	70
Base=100%	*865*	*921*	*1535*	*3321*
1999				
Definitely will be smoking	19	2	1	6
Probably will be smoking	29	2	0	8
Might or might not be smoking	23	1	0	7
Probably will not be smoking	18	6	2	7
Definitely will not be smoking	11	88	96	71
Base=100%	*942*	*977*	*1629*	*3548*

Table 3.19 **Whether respondents will be smoking in 12 months, by whether intend to give up smoking, 2002**

All smokers

Whether respondents will be smoking in 12 months	Intend to give up smoking: within the next 12 months	in more than a year	Do not intend to give up	2002 Total
	%	%	%	%
Definitely will be smoking	1	13	62	21
Probably will be smoking	17	54	32	29
Might or might not be smoking	35	28	7	25
Probably will not be smoking	33	4	-	18
Definitely will not be smoking	15	-	0	8
Base=100%	*464*	*188*	*270*	*922*

Table 3.20 **Whether respondents will be smoking in 12 months by sex, 2002**

Current smokers who intend to give up smoking within the next year

Whether respondents will be smoking in 12 months	Sex Men	Women	2002 Total	2001 Total	2000 Total	1999 Total
	%	%	%	%	%	%
Definitely will be smoking	1	1	1	0	2	3
Probably will be smoking	14	18	17	13	16	19
Might or might not be smoking	35	35	35	39	40	33
Probably will not be smoking	34	32	33	32	31	30
Definitely will not be smoking	16	13	15	16	10	15
Base=100%	*214*	*249*	*463*	*433*	*412*	*478*

Table 3.21 **Whether respondents will be smoking in 12 months by age, 2002**

Current smokers who intend to give up smoking within the next year

Whether respondents will be smoking in 12 months	Age 16–24	25–44	45–64	65 and over	2002 Total
	%	%	%	%	%
Definitely will be smoking	2	1	1	[0]	1
Probably will be smoking	29	14	14	[2]	17
Might or might not be smoking	37	34	37	[5]	35
Probably will not be smoking	25	34	34	[11	33
Definitely will not be smoking	7	17	14	[5]	15
Base=100%	*85*	*232*	*124*	*23*	*463*

Table 3.22 **Whether smokers will be smoking in 12 months, by number of cigarettes smoked per day, 2002**

Current smokers who intend to give up smoking within the next year

Whether respondents will be smoking in 12 months	Number of cigarettes per day			2002 Total
	20 and over	10–19	0–9	
	%	%	%	%
Definitely will be smoking	1	2	1	1
Probably will be smoking	16	19	12	17
Might or might not be smoking	38	38	27	35
Probably will not be smoking	29	28	43	33
Definitely will not be smoking	16	12	17	15
Base=100%	*110*	*212*	*141*	*463*

Table 3.23 **Whether smokers will be smoking in 12 months, by type of cigarette smoked, 2002**

Current smokers who intend to give up smoking within the next year

Whether respondents will be smoking in 12 months	Type of cigarette			2002 Total
	Packeted	Hand-rolled	Both types	
	%	%	%	%
Definitely will be smoking	1	1	-	1
Probably will be smoking	17	16	18	17
Might or might not be smoking	33	34	50	35
Probably will not be smoking	33	31	29	33
Definitely will not be smoking	15	17	3	15
Base=100%	*356*	*70*	*38*	*463*

Table 3.24 **Whether smokers will be smoking in 12 months, by whether attempted to give up smoking in the last 5 years, 2002**

Current smokers who intend to give up smoking within the next year

Whether respondents will be smoking in 12 months	Attempted to give up in last 5 years	Not attempted to give up in last 5 years	2002 Total
	%	%	%
Definitely will be smoking	1	1	1
Probably will be smoking	16	18	17
Might or might not be smoking	36	33	35
Probably will not be smoking	33	32	33
Definitely will not be smoking	14	16	15
Base=100%	*323*	*139*	*463*

Table 3.25 **Whether smokers will be smoking in 12 months, by number of attempts to give up smoking in the last year, 2002**

Smokers who have tried to give up in last year and who intend to stop within next year

Whether respondents will be smoking in 12 months	Made one attempt to give up in last year	Made two or more attempts to give up in last year	2002 Total
	%	%	%
Definitely will be smoking	1	2	1
Probably will be smoking	10	11	10
Might or might not be smoking	34	36	35
Probably will not be smoking	40	35	38
Definitely will not be smoking	14	17	15
Base=100%	*87*	*66*	*153*

Table 3.26 **When smokers intend to give up smoking, by whether they want to give up smoking, 1999–2002**

All smokers

When smokers intend to give up smoking	Views on giving up smoking: Would like to give up	Would not like to give up	Total
	%	%	%
2002			
Within the next month	14	1	10
Within the next 6 months	30	2	22
Within the next year	24	5	19
In more than a year	23	14	20
Do not intend to give up	9	77	29
Base=100%	*649*	*276*	*925*
2001			
Within the next month	13	0	9
Within the next 6 months	31	2	23
Within the next year	26	6	20
In more than a year	23	21	23
Do not intend to give up	8	70	25
Base=100%	*596*	*231*	*827*
2000			
Within the next month	16	-	11
Within the next 6 months	26	1	18
Within the next year	25	3	19
In more than a year	25	15	22
Do not intend to give up	8	81	30
Base=100%	*606*	*249*	*855*
1999			
Within the next month	17	0	12
Within the next 6 months	29	3	22
Within the next year	24	2	18
In more than a year	19	17	18
Do not intend to give up	11	78	30
Base=100%	*669*	*259*	*928*

Table 3.27 **Whether respondents want to and intend to give up smoking by sex, 2002**

All smokers

Whether smokers want or intend to stop	Sex Men	Women	2002 Total	2001 Total	2000 Total	1999 Total
	%	%	%	%	%	%
Want to give up and intend to in next 6 months	10	9	10	9	11	12
Want to give up and intend to in more than 6 months	53	55	54	57	54	52
Want to give up but do not intend to	8	5	6	5	6	8
Do not want to give up but intend to	6	8	7	8	6	6
Do not want to give up and do not intend to	23	23	23	20	24	22
Base=100%	*448*	*478*	*926*	*827*	*855*	*927*

Table 3.28 **Whether respondents want to and intend to give up smoking by age, 2002**

All smokers

Whether smokers want or intend to stop	Age 16–24	25–44	45–64	65 and over	2002 Total
	%	%	%	%	%
Want to give up and intend to in next 6 months	12	13	6	5	10
Want to give up and intend to in more than 6 months	59	61	52	25	54
Want to give up but do not intend to	2	4	10	12	6
Do not want to give up but intend to	12	6	7	4	7
Do not want to give up and do not intend to	15	17	25	53	23
Base=100%	*143*	*386*	*301*	*96*	*926*

Table 3.29 **Whether smokers want to and intend to give up smoking by social-economic classification and by presence of children in the household, 2002**

All smokers

| Whether smokers want or intend to stop | Social-economic classification | | | | Children under 16 in household | No children in household | 2002 Total |
	Managerial and professional occupations	Intermediate occupations	Routine and manual occupations	Never worked and long-term unemployed			
	%	%	%	%	%	%	%
Want to give up and intend to in next 6 months	11	8	9	17	14	7	10
Want to give up and intend to in more than 6 months	56	57	51	56	58	52	54
Want to give up but do not intend to	4	8	7	4	4	8	6
Do not want to give up but intend to	9	8	5	8	7	7	7
Do not want to give up and do not intend to	20	19	27	16	18	26	23
Base=100%	*195*	*194*	*459*	*77*	*326*	*598*	*926*

Table 3.30 **Whether respondents want to and intend to give up smoking by number of cigarettes smoked a day, 2002**

All smokers

| Whether smokers want or intend to stop | Number of cigarettes per day | | | 2002 Total |
	20 and over	10–19	0–9	
	%	%	%	%
Want to give up and intend to in next 6 months	6	8	16	10
Want to give up and intend to in more than 6 months	53	60	47	54
Want to give up but do not intend to	9	6	3	6
Do not want to give up but intend to	5	8	8	7
Do not want to give up and do not intend to	27	18	27	23
Base=100%	*278*	*383*	*261*	*926*

Table 3.31 **Whether respondents want to and intend to give up smoking by type of cigarette smoked, 2002**

All smokers

Whether smokers want or intend to stop	Type of cigarettes Packeted	Hand-rolled	Both types	2002 Total
	%	%	%	%
Want to give up and intend to in next 6 months	10	5	12	10
Want to give up and intend to in more than 6 months	55	54	46	54
Want to give up but do not intend to	5	10	12	6
Do not want to give up but intend to	8	5	2	7
Do not want to give up and do not intend to	22	27	26	23
Base=100%	*675*	*170*	*80*	*926*

4 Attempting to give up smoking

4.1 Previous attempts to give up smoking

4.1.1 Current smokers

Nearly four-fifths (79%) of current smokers had tried to give up smoking in the past, and over a half (53%) had made a serious attempt in the past 5 years. This compares with 79% and 54% respectively in 2001.

These percentages did not vary significantly between men and women. Smokers aged 25–64 were the most likely to have ever tried to give up: over 80% had tried, compared with 64% of those aged 65 or more. There were also no significant differences in the percentage of smokers in different social-economic classificatory groups who had ever tried to give up smoking. Smokers with children under 16 in the household were more likely to have ever tried to give up smoking (83% compared with 76% of those without children in the household).

Heavy smokers were the most likely to have tried to give up: 85% had ever tried compared with 72% of those who smoked fewer than 10 cigarettes a day. **Tables 4.1–4.4**

Smokers were also asked if they had made a serious attempt to give up smoking in the past five years, and there were no statistically significant differences among men and women, nor among heavy, moderate and light smokers. **Table 4.5**

Smokers who had tried to give up in the past year were asked how many attempts they had made and Table 4.6 shows that, as predicted by the Stages of Change Model, smokers keep on trying to give up – 15% had made 3 or more attempts in the past year. Heavy smokers were the most likely to have made only one attempt to stop smoking (73% compared with 48% of moderate smokers). **Tables 4.6–4.8**

Current smokers who had previously tried to give up were asked how long it was for, the last time. DiClemente *et al* (1985)[1] found that the temptation to smoke did not level off until about three years after quitting, and Table 4.9 shows that only 10% of smokers had previously given up for two years or more. Those who have

successfully given up for more than 2 years are more likely to stay quit (without relapsing).

Nearly a quarter (24%) had only given up for a week, and just under two thirds (65%) had given up for less than six months. Just over half (55%) had given up for more than 4 weeks. There was little difference between men and women in the time they had stopped smoking. Younger smokers tended to have given up for less time than older smokers: 94% of those aged 16–24 had lasted less than a year, compared with 74% of those aged 65 or more. However, it should be noted that younger smokers are likely to have had shorter smoking careers in which to attempt to quit.

Heavy smokers were also less likely than others to have given up for 6 months or more (28% compared with 48% of those smoking fewer than ten a day). **Tables 4.10 and 4.11**

Two new questions were added in 2002. Smokers who had stopped smoking for more than a day in the last 12 months, were asked why they had started to smoke again. Smokers who wanted to give up smoking were asked why they had never tried to stop or why they had not succeeded in stopping for more than a day.

A third (34%) of smokers who had given up for more than a day in the past year, said they had started again because they found life too stressful. About a sixth mentioned missing the habit (17%), liking smoking (16%) or that their friends smoke (14%). A further 12% said they couldn't cope with the cravings. Only 16% gave more than one reason.[2] There were no significant differences between men and women.

Heavy smokers were nearly twice as likely to say that they found life too stressful (48% of those who smoke 20 and over a day compared with 26% of those who smoked fewer than 10). Heavy smokers were also more likely to say they couldn't cope with the cravings. Conversely, light smokers were more likely to say they started again because they like smoking (23% compared with only 9% of heavy smokers). **Tables 4.12 and 4.13**

Similar reasons were given for not trying to stop or for not succeeding in stopping. Nearly three-tenths (29%) of smokers who want to give up smoking but have not tried or have not succeeded for more than one day said that they found life too stressful, and a further 29% said that they had a lack of commitment to quitting. A substantial minority (15%) mentioned liking smoking and not being able to cope with the cravings. About a fifth (21%) gave more than one reason.[2] The only significant difference between men and women was that women were more likely to say they were worried about putting on weight if they stopped smoking (8% of women compared with 1% of men). There were no significant differences between heavy and light smokers.   **Tables 4.14 and 4.15**

As a measure of support in giving up smoking, all smokers were asked if anyone had been trying to get them to quit smoking in the last year, and if so, who. Just under half (48%) said someone had been trying to get them to stop smoking, and this tended to be a partner, or a son or daughter or parent. Women smokers were more likely than men smokers to say that their children were trying to get them to stop smoking (20% and 9% respectively), possibly because they tend to have more contact with children than their male counterparts. Young smokers aged 16–24 were no more likely than older smokers to say that someone was trying to get them to quit smoking. Not surprisingly, the youngest smokers were the most likely to say that it was a parent who was trying to get them to stop (33% compared with 15% or fewer of older smokers).

Unlike 2001, light smokers were no less likely than heavy smokers to say that other people were trying to get them to stop smoking.
                    Tables 4.16–4.18

4.1.2   Ex-regular cigarette smokers

Those people who said they used to smoke regularly but no longer did so were asked how long ago they stopped smoking. Three quarters (76%) had stopped smoking for five years or more, and men tended to have stopped for longer than women. As would be expected, older smokers had stopped for longer than younger smokers. Those who used to smoke less than ten cigarettes a day tended to have given up longer ago than heavier smokers.

To allow the factors related to someone successfully giving up to be examined, all the surveys in this series have asked ex-regular smokers about their reasons for giving up smoking.

In 2002, as in previous years, ex-smokers were more likely than current smokers to give reasons for stopping that did not fall into the pre-coded categories. In some cases this was because ex-smokers had given up a long time ago and had forgotten if there was a

specific reason why. Other reasons included 'other people's health problems' and 'not enjoying smoking any longer'.

Ex-smokers who had given up smoking 20 or more years ago were least likely to give a health-related reason or to give more than one reason. They were also less likely to cite the effect smoking has on children. This probably reflects the recent increased public awareness of the health risk of smoking by smokers as well as the effects on their families.   **Tables 4.19–4.25**

4.2   Help giving up smoking

4.2.1   Seeking advice and help for quitting smoking

The 1999 Omnibus Survey included a new section of questions about the sources of help and advice sought by smokers in the past year. In 2000, 2001 and 2002, the questions covering nicotine replacement therapy (NRT gums, patches or inhalers) were amended to allow respondents to distinguish between prescription and non-prescription NRT as well as whether they paid for it. The questions were asked of both smokers and those who had given up in the past year.

Table 4.26 shows the sources of help and advice used by both current smokers (that is those that have failed to give up smoking) and those who have succeeded in giving up smoking in the past year. Not surprisingly, those who have successfully given up smoking in the past year were more likely to have sought help and advice (55% compared with 36% of those who were still smoking). Although it appeared that successful quitters were more likely to have read leaflets and/or booklets on how to stop and to have used NRT products than those who were currently smoking, the differences were not statistically significant.

Tables 4.27 to 4.30 present the sources of help and advice for current smokers only. Overall, 36% of smokers had sought some kind of help or advice for stopping smoking. This was similar to the 2001 and 2000 figures (38% and 37% respectively) but lower than in 1999 when 44% of smokers said they had sought some help or advice. Nearly three tenths (28%) of smokers said they had read leaflets and/or booklets on how to stop smoking. A small percentage had asked a doctor or other health professional for help (10%), rung a smokers telephone helpline (3%) or been referred to a stop smoking group (4%).

About a tenth (11%) had bought some type of nicotine replacement therapy (NRT gums, patches or inhalers), but, only 4% had been given free NRT.

Unlike previous years, women were no more likely than men to have read leaflets about quitting, to have asked a doctor or other health professional for help or to have used NRT products. Older smokers were least likely to have read leaflets, whereas those in the middle age groups (25–64) were the most likely to have used NRT products.

Smokers in managerial and professional occupations and routine and manual occupations were more likely than their counterparts engaged in intermediate occupations to have read leaflets/booklets on how to stop. There was no difference in use of NRT products between different social economic groups.

Although it appeared that (as in previous years) heavy smokers were more likely than light smokers to say that they had used NRT, the difference was not statistically significant. Moderate smokers were the most likely to have read booklets or leaflets on how to stop smoking.

4.2.2 Advice from health professionals

Respondents were also asked whether they had been given advice on smoking by members of the medical profession in the *five* years before their interview. Forty-two per cent of all current smokers said that they had – the percentage was similar to that in previous surveys. The most common source of advice was the respondent's own GP (35%) and someone else at the GP surgery (14%). Eight per cent mentioned a variety of other medical personnel (consultants, specialists, other hospital doctors and nurses) as having advised them on smoking. Only 2% had been given advice on smoking by a pharmacist.

Women smokers were more likely than men smokers to have been given advice (46% of women had been given advice compared with 38% of men). Older smokers were also more likely to have been given advice than their younger counterparts.

Unsurprisingly, heavy smokers (both men and women) were more likely than light smokers to say they had been given advice on smoking by the medical profession.

In the majority of cases (86%) the advice was in the form of discussion about smoking (with or without literature to read), with 14% of smokers being given printed literature only.

Just over half the people (52%) said that they had found the advice helpful – those who discussed smoking as well as been given literature were more likely to have found the advice helpful (54%

compared with only 42% of smokers who had only been given literature to look at). **Tables 4.31–4.35**

Overall, 35% of people who had stopped smoking in the past five years said they had received advice in the past five years. Compared with current smokers, ex-regular smokers who had been given advice on smoking in the five years before the interview were more likely to say that the advice, in particular discussion about smoking, was helpful (76%, table not shown, compared with 52% of current smokers). However, this result should be interpreted with caution because it may be related to the fact that the respondent had successfully given up smoking. **Table 4.36**

Notes and references

1. DiClemente C *et al* (1985) Self-efficacy and the stages of self-change of smoking. *Cognitive therapy and research* **9**, 181–200.

2. Respondents could give up to eight reasons.

Table 4.1 **Ever tried to give up smoking by sex, 1999–2002**

All smokers

Attempts at giving up smoking	Sex Men	Women	2002 Total	2001 Total	2000 Total	1999 Total
	%	%	%	%	%	%
Has ever tried to give up	78	80	79	79	78	77
Has not ever tried to give up	22	20	21	21	22	23
Base=100%	*456*	*489*	*945*	*846*	*871*	*950*

Table 4.2 **Ever tried to give up smoking, by age, 2002**

All smokers

Attempts at giving up smoking	Age 16–24	25–44	45–64	65 and over	Total
	%	%	%	%	%
Has ever tried to give up	71	82	83	64	79
Has not ever tried to give up	29	18	17	36	21
Base=100%	*143*	*393*	*310*	*99*	*945*

Table 4.3 **Ever tried to give up smoking, by social-economic classification and by presence of children in the household, 2002**

All smokers

Attempts at giving up smoking	Social-economic classification Managerial and professional occupations	Intermediate occupations	Routine and manual occupations	Never worked and long-term unemployed	Children under 16 in household	No children in household	2002 Total
	%	%	%	%	%	%	%
Has ever tried to give up	82	78	79	68	83	76	79
Has not ever tried to give up	18	22	21	32	17	24	21
Base=100%	*201*	*199*	*468*	*77*	*331*	*614*	*945*

Table 4.4 **Ever tried to give up smoking, by number of cigarettes smoked per day, 2002**

All smokers

Attempts at giving up smoking	Number of cigarettes per day			2002 Total
	20 and over	10–19	0–9	
	%	%	%	%
Has ever tried to give up	85	79	72	79
Has not ever tried to give up	15	21	27	21
Base=100%	*284*	*392*	*268*	*945*

Table 4.5 **Attempts to give up smoking in past 5 years, by number of cigarettes smoked per day and sex, 1999–2002**

All smokers

Made a serious attempt in past 5 years	Number of cigarettes per day			2002 Total	2001 Total	2000 Total	1999 Total
	20 and over	10–19	0–9				
	Percentage who have made a serious attempt to stop smoking in past 5 years						
Men	47	48	54	49	51	50	48
Women	52	58	60	57	57	49	55
All	49	53	57	53	54	50	52
Base=100%							
Men	*158*	*187*	*111*	*456*	*396*	*415*	*445*
Women	*126*	*205*	*156*	*487*	*447*	*452*	*503*
All	*284*	*391*	*267*	*942*	*846*	*867*	*948*

Table 4.6 **Number of attempts to give up smoking in the last year by sex, 1999–2002**

Smokers who have tried to give up in past year

Number of attempts at giving up smoking	Sex		2002 Total	2001 Total	2000 Total	1999 Total
	Men	Women				
	%	%	%	%	%	%
One	60	60	60	58	58	44
Two	25	26	25	20	18	28
Three or more	16	15	15	22	24	28
Base=100%	*89*	*129*	*218*	*203*	*193*	*244*

Table 4.7 **Number of attempts to give up smoking in the last year by age, 2002**

Smokers who have tried to give up in past year

Number of attempts at giving up smoking	Age 16–24	25–44	45–64	65 and over	2002 Total
	%	%	%	%	%
One	51	64	62	[7]	60
Two	30	23	23	[4]	25
Three or more	19	13	15	[3]	15
Base=100%	*57*	*95*	*53*	*14*	*218*

Table 4.8 **Number of attempts to give up smoking in the last year, by number of cigarettes smoked per day, 2002**

Smokers who have tried to give up in past year

Number of attempts at giving up smoking	Number of cigarettes per day 20 and over	10–19	0–9	2002 Total
	%	%	%	%
One	73	48	66	60
Two	14	32	24	25
Three or more	14	20	11	15
Base=100%	*44*	*90*	*84*	*218*

Table 4.9 **Length of time gave up for the last time stopped smoking, by sex, 1999–2002**

Smokers who have tried to give up

Length of time gave up smoking	Sex Men	Women	2002 Total	2001 Total	2000 Total	1999 Total
	%	%	%	%	%	%
A week	23	24	24	20	23	23
2 weeks	10	10	10	9	10	10
3–4 weeks	10	11	11	13	11	11
5–9 weeks	10	9	10	12	11	10
10–25 weeks	11	12	12	14	14	13
6–12 months	19 ⎫	20 ⎫	19 ⎫	18 ⎫	17 ⎫	16 ⎫
More than 1 year, but less than 2	7 ⎬ 36	5 ⎬ 34	6 ⎬ 35	5 ⎬ 32	5 ⎬ 30	8 ⎬ 33
2 years or more	10 ⎭	9 ⎭	10 ⎭	9 ⎭	8 ⎭	9 ⎭
Base=100%	*354*	*389*	*743*	*666*	*667*	*723*

Table 4.10   **Length of time gave up for the last time stopped smoking by age, 2002**

Smokers who have tried to give up

Length of time gave up smoking	Age 16–24	25–44	45–64	65 and over	2002 Total
	%	%	%	%	%
A week	26	21	24	29	24
2 weeks	22	9	8	5	10
3–4 weeks	17	12	8	8	11
5–9 weeks	13	8	11	6	10
10–25 weeks	4	13	12	18	12
6–12 months	14 ⎫	23 ⎫	19 ⎫	10 ⎫	19 ⎫
More than 1 year, but less than 2	2 ⎬ 20	6 ⎬ 37	7 ⎬ 37	8 ⎬ 35	6 ⎬ 35
2 years or more	4 ⎭	8 ⎭	11 ⎭	18 ⎭	10 ⎭
Base=100%	*102*	*321*	*257*	*63*	*743*

Table 4.11   **Length of time gave up for the last time stopped smoking, by number of cigarettes smoked per day, 2002**

Smokers who have tried to give up

Length of time gave up smoking	Number of cigarettes per day 20 and over	10–19	0–9	2002 Total
	%	%	%	%
A week	26	26	17	24
2 weeks	12	10	6	10
3–4 weeks	12	10	9	11
5–9 weeks	12	9	8	10
10–25 weeks	10	12	14	12
6–12 months	13 ⎫	19 ⎫	28 ⎫	19 ⎫
More than 1 year, but less than 2	6 ⎬ 28	5 ⎬ 32	7 ⎬ 48	6 ⎬ 35
2 years or more	8 ⎭	8 ⎭	13 ⎭	10 ⎭
Base=100%	*242*	*307*	*193*	*743*

Table 4.12 Main reasons for starting smoking again by sex, 2002

Smokers who gave up for at least one day in past year

Reasons for starting smoking again	Men	Women	Total
Life too stressful/just not a good time	33	36	34
Missed the habit/something to do with my hands	17	17	17
I like smoking	15	17	16
My friends smoke	16	13	14
Couldn't cope with the cravings	12	12	12
Put on weight	1	4	3
My spouse/partner smokes	2	6	4
Other	21	19	20
Gave more than one reason	**13**	**19**	**16**
Base=100%	*210*	*223*	*433*

Percentages sum to more than 100 as respondents could give more than one answer.

Table 4.13 Main reasons for starting smoking again by number of cigarettes smoked per day, 2002

Smokers who gave up for at least one day in past year

| Reasons for starting smoking again | Number of cigarettes per day | | | Total |
	20 and over	10–19	0–9	
Life too stressful/just not a good time	48	37	26	34
Missed the habit/something to do with my hands	21	16	16	17
I like smoking	9	13	23	16
My friends smoke	7	18	15	14
Couldn't cope with the cravings	17	15	6	12
Put on weight	5	2	3	3
My spouse/partner smokes	3	3	6	4
Other	19	17	23	20
Gave more than one reason	**19**	**16**	**15**	**16**
Base=100%	*79*	*184*	*170*	*433*

Percentages sum to more than 100 as respondents could give more than one answer.

Table 4.14 **Main reasons for not trying to give up smoking by sex, 2002**

Smokers who want to give up but who have not succeeded for more than one day

Reasons for not trying to stop smoking	Men	Women	Total
Life too stressful/just not a good time	27	32	29
Lack of commitment to quitting	26	32	29
I like smoking	18	12	15
Couldn't cope with the cravings	13	17	15
Would miss the habit/something to do with my hands	12	14	13
My friends smoke	6	6	6
Worried about putting on weight	1	8	5
My spouse/partner smokes	4	5	5
Other	16	15	16
Gave more than one reason	**15**	**26**	**21**
Base=100%	*145*	*156*	*300*

Percentages sum to more than 100 as respondents could give more than one answer.

Table 4.15 **Main reasons for not trying to give up smoking by number of cigarettes smoked per day, 2002**

Smokers who want to give up but who have not succeeded for more than one day

Reasons for not trying to stop smoking	Number of cigarettes per day			Total
	20 and over	10–19	0–9	
Life too stressful/just not a good time	27	27	40	29
Lack of commitment to quitting	27	33	25	29
I like smoking	14	13	21	15
Couldn't cope with the cravings	14	18	10	15
Would miss the habit/something to do with my hands	15	14	5	13
My friends smoke	6	3	12	6
Worried about putting on weight	5	3	7	5
My spouse/partner smokes	6	3	6	5
Other	21	15	4	16
Gave more than one reason	**25**	**19**	**16**	**21**
Base=100%	*117*	*132*	*51*	*300*

Percentages sum to more than 100 as respondents could give more than one answer.

Table 4.16   **Influence of others in encouraging smokers to quit by sex, 1999–2002**

All smokers

Who has tried to get you to quit smoking in last year?	Sex Men	Women	2002 Total	2001 Total	2000 Total	1999 Total
Partner/spouse	22%	16%	19%	20%	21%	22%
Children	9%	20%	15%	15%	19%	18%
Parents	9%	15%	12%	12%	12%	15%
Friend	5%	6%	6%	8%	9%	10%
Sibling	1%	3%	2%	3%	3%	5%
Workmate	3%	1%	2%	2%	2%	3%
Other	5%	4%	5%	4%	5%	6%
Someone	44%	51%	48%	49%	52%	55%
No one	56%	49%	52%	51%	48%	45%
Base=100%	*457*	*489*	*946*	*845*	*871*	*950*

Percentages sum to more than 100 as respondents could give more than one answer.

Table 4.17   **Influence of others in encouraging smokers to quit by age, 2002**

All smokers

Who has tried to get you to quit smoking in last year?	Age 16–24	25–44	45–64	65 and over	2002 Total
Partner/spouse	8%	22%	20%	17%	19%
Children	-	14%	22%	17%	15%
Parents	33%	15%	2%	-	12%
Friend	10%	4%	6%	5%	6%
Sibling	3%	2%	2%	-	2%
Workmate	2%	3%	1%	-	2%
Other	3%	4%	5%	9%	5%
Someone	51%	50%	46%	40%	48%
No one	49%	50%	54%	60%	52%
Base=100%	*142*	*393*	*310*	*99*	*946*

Percentages sum to more than 100 as respondents could give more than one answer.

Table 4.18   **Influence of others in encouraging smokers to quit, by number of cigarettes smoked per day, 2002**

All smokers

Who has tried to get you to quit smoking in last year?	Number of cigarettes per day 20 and over	10–19	0–9	2002 Total
Partner/spouse	17%	18%	21%	19%
Children	19%	14%	13%	15%
Parents	10%	16%	9%	12%
Friend	6%	7%	3%	6%
Sibling	3%	2%	0%	2%
Workmate	3%	2%	1%	2%
Other	5%	6%	2%	5%
Someone	47%	51%	43%	48%
No one	53%	49%	57%	52%
Base=100%	*285*	*392*	*268*	*946*

Percentages sum to more than 100 as respondents could give more than one answer.

Table 4.19 **Length of time since stopped smoking, by sex, 1999–2002**

Ex-smokers

Length of time since stopped smoking	2002	2001	2000	1999
	%	%	%	%
Men				
Less than a year	6	4	7	4
1–4 years	14	13	14	12
5–9 years	10	11	13	14
10–14 years	14	12	11	14
15–19 years	12	11	10	12
20–24 years	14	16	15	12
25 years or more	32	33	31	31
Base=100%	*528*	*487*	*533*	*557*
Women				
Less than a year	10	7	6	9
1–4 years	19	20	14	13
5–9 years	11	15	11	15
10–14 years	11	13	15	15
15–19 years	9	9	12	13
20–24 years	11	14	14	14
25 years or more	28	22	28	22
Base=100%	*472*	*400*	*390*	*419*
All				
Less than a year	8	6	6	6
1–4 years	16	16	14	13
5–9 years	10	13	12	14
10–14 years	12	13	13	14
15–19 years	10	10	11	12
20–24 years	13	15	14	13
25 years or more	30	28	30	27
Base=100%	*1000*	*887*	*923*	*976*

Table 4.20 **Length of time since stopped smoking, by age and sex, 2002**

Ex-smokers

Length of time since stopped smoking	Age 16–24	25–44	45–64	65 and over	2002 Total
	%	%	%	%	%
Men					
Less than a year	[4]	14	6	0	6
1–4 years	[12]	30	10	4	14
5–9 years	[4]	22	8	4	10
10–14 years	[0]	16	15	12	14
15–19 years	[0]	16	14	9	12
20–24 years	[0]	3	20	15	14
25 years or more	[0]	1	28	55	32
Base=100%	*20*	*110*	*195*	*203*	*528*
Women					
Less than a year	[14]	18	5	3	10
1–4 years	[13]	28	15	10	19
5–9 years	[0]	17	11	9	11
10–14 years	[0]	17	12	8	11
15–19 years	[0]	11	9	9	9
20–24 years	[0]	5	14	15	11
25 years or more	[0]	3	35	46	28
Base=100%	*27*	*115*	*196*	*136*	*472*
All					
Less than a year	39	16	5	1	8
1–4 years	52	29	12	7	16
5–9 years	9	20	10	6	10
10–14 years	-	16	14	11	12
15–19 years	-	14	12	9	10
20–24 years	-	4	17	15	13
25 years or more	-	2	31	51	30
Base=100%	*46*	*223*	*391*	*339*	*1,000*

Table 4.21   Length of time since stopped smoking, by number of cigarettes smoked per day and sex, 2002

Ex-smokers

Length of time since stopped smoking	Number of cigarettes per day			2002 Total
	20 and over	10–19	0–9	
	%	%	%	%
Men				
Less than a year	5	6	8	6
1–4 years	10	20	19	14
5–9 years	10	9	8	10
10–14 years	16	8	19	14
15–19 years	11	13	9	12
20–24 years	17	12	-	14
25 years or more	30	32	38	32
Base=100%	*304*	*169*	*53*	*528*
Women				
Less than a year	10	8	13	10
1–4 years	16	26	13	19
5–9 years	13	13	8	11
10–14 years	14	11	9	11
15–19 years	9	8	10	9
20–24 years	10	13	11	11
25 years or more	28	22	36	28
Base=100%	*173*	*166*	*132*	*472*
All				
Less than a year	7	7	11	8
1–4 years	12	23	15	16
5–9 years	11	11	8	10
10–14 years	15	10	12	12
15–19 years	11	10	10	10
20–24 years	15	12	8	13
25 years or more	29	27	36	30
Base=100%	*478*	*334*	*186*	*1,000*

Table 4.22 **Main reasons for having stopped smoking, by sex, 1996–2002**

Ex-regular cigarette smokers

Reasons for having stopped	Men	Women	2002 Total	2001 Total	2000 Total	1999 Total	1997 Total	1996 Total
	%	%	%	%	%	%	%	%
Better for health in general	55	50	53	50	55	53	50	48
Less risk of getting smoking related illness	13	15	14	15	18	18	15	12
Present health problems	16	15	15	12	13	13	14	15
At least one health reason	**71**	**64**	**68**	**64**	**67**	**67**	**65**	**64**
Financial reasons	19	20	19	20	24	25	22	24
Family pressure	16	12	14	11	15	12	14	13
Harms children	8	8	8	8	9	8	10	8
Doctor's advice	6	4	5	8	6	7	6	5
Pregnancy	2	13	7	5	6	6	8	6
Other	11	11	11	19	17	14	17	12
Gave more than one reason	**35**	**37**	**36**	**36**	**44**	**41**	**42**	**32**
Base=100%	*527*	*472*	*999*	*884*	*919*	*975*	*1018*	*944*

Percentages sum to more than 100 as respondents could give more than one answer.

Table 4.23 **Main reasons for having stopped smoking by age, 2002**

Ex-regular cigarette smokers

Reasons for having stopped	Age 16–24	25–44	45–64	65 and over	2002 Total
	%	%	%	%	%
Better for health in general	72	59	53	46	53
Less risk of getting smoking related illness	18	15	15	11	14
Present health problems	8	8	16	21	15
At least one health reason	**72**	**67**	**68**	**67**	**68**
Financial reasons	21	14	17	25	19
Family pressure	26	18	15	10	14
Harms children	1	15	9	4	8
Doctor's advice	0	5	3	8	5
Pregnancy	10	15	7	1	7
Other	3	10	11	13	11
Gave more than one reason	**45**	**44**	**34**	**31**	**36**
Base=100%	*47*	*223*	*391*	*338*	*999*

Percentages sum to more than 100 as respondents could give more than one answer.

Table 4.24 **Main reasons for having stopped smoking, by number of cigarettes smoked per day and sex, 2002**

Ex-regular cigarette smokers

Reasons for having stopped	Number of cigarettes per day 20 and over	10–19	0–9	2002 Total
	%	%	%	%
Men				
Better for health in general	55	54	58	55
Less risk of getting smoking related illness	12	15	9	13
Present health problems	20	13	3	16
At least one health reason	**74**	**70**	**65**	**71**
Financial reasons	19	21	9	19
Family pressure	16	17	19	16
Harms children	8	10	7	8
Doctor's advice	7	6	1	6
Pregnancy	2	1	2	2
Other	10	11	17	11
Gave more than one reason	**36**	**38**	**19**	**35**
Base=100%	*304*	*168*	*53*	*527*
Women				
Better for health in general	52	48	50	50
Less risk of getting smoking related illness	15	17	13	15
Present health problems	17	13	14	15
At least one health reason	**65**	**62**	**64**	**64**
Financial reasons	23	18	18	20
Family pressure	12	14	11	12
Harms children	13	5	7	8
Doctor's advice	4	4	3	4
Pregnancy	16	16	7	13
Other	7	13	14	11
Gave more than one reason	**45**	**36**	**27**	**37**
Base=100%	*173*	*165*	*133*	*472*
All				
Better for health in general	54	51	52	53
Less risk of getting smoking related illness	13	16	12	14
Present health problems	19	13	11	15
At least one health reason	**71**	**66**	**64**	**68**
Financial reasons	20	19	15	19
Family pressure	14	16	13	14
Harms children	10	7	7	8
Doctor's advice	6	5	2	5
Pregnancy	7	8	6	7
Other	9	12	15	11
Gave more than one reason	**39**	**37**	**25**	**36**
Base=100%	*477*	*333*	*185*	*999*

Percentages sum to more than 100 as respondents could give more than one answer.

Table 4.25 **Main reasons for having stopped smoking, by length of time since stopped, 2002**

Ex-regular cigarette smokers

Reasons for having stopped	Length of time since stopped			2002 Total
	Less than 5 years	5–19 years	20 years and over	
	%	%	%	%
Better for health in general	60	52	49	53
Less risk of getting smoking related illness	20	12	12	14
Present health problems	19	17	12	15
At least one health reason	**76**	**68**	**63**	**68**
Financial reasons	17	16	23	19
Family pressure	20	14	12	14
Harms children	13	7	7	8
Doctor's advice	5	7	3	5
Pregnancy	8	8	7	7
Other	7	12	13	11
Gave more than one reason	**49**	**35**	**29**	**36**
Base=100%	*238*	*334*	*426*	*999*

Percentages sum to more than 100 as respondents could give more than one answer.

Table 4.26 **Sources of help and advice used in the last year by smoking status, 2002**

Current smokers and those who have given up smoking in past year

Percentage who have:	Current smokers	Gave up smoking in past year
Read leaflets/booklets on how to stop	28%	40%
Asked doctor or other health prof for help	10%	14%
Called a smokers' telephone helpline	3%	3%
Been referred/self-referred to stop smoking group	4%	12%
Bought non-prescription NRT	8%	14%
Paid for prescription NRT	2%	4%
Free prescription NRT	4%	4%
Free non-prescription NRT	0%	-
Prescribed other 'stop smoking' drugs	1%	5%
Had any NRT/other prescribed drugs to help stop smoking	14%	24%
Sought any help or advice	36%	55%
Did not seek help or advice	64%	45%
Base=100%	*944*	*78*

Table 4.27 **Sources of help and advice used in the last year by sex, 1999–2002**

All smokers

Percentage who have:	Sex Men	Women	Total
2002			
Read leaflets/booklets on how to stop	25%	30%	28%
Asked doctor or other health prof for help	10%	11%	10%
Called a smokers' telephone helpline	4%	3%	3%
Been referred/self-referred to stop smoking group	4%	4%	4%
Bought non-prescription NRT*	8%	8%	8%
Paid for prescription NRT*	2%	1%	2%
Free prescription NRT*	3%	4%	4%
Free non-prescription NRT *	-	0%	0%
Prescribed other 'stop smoking' drugs*	2%	0%	1%
Had any NRT/other prescribed drugs to help stop smoking	14%	14%	14%
Sought any help or advice	33%	39%	36%
Did not seek help or advice	67%	61%	64%
Base=100%	*456*	*488*	*944*
2001			
Read leaflets/booklets on how to stop	23%	37%	30%
Asked doctor or other health prof for help	7%	12%	10%
Called a smokers' telephone helpline	2%	6%	4%
Been referred/self-referred to stop smoking group	2%	4%	3%
Bought non-prescription NRT*	8%	11%	10%
Paid for prescription NRT*	0%	1%	0%
Free prescription NRT*	1%	3%	2%
Free non-prescription NRT *	0%	0%	0%
Prescribed other 'stop smoking' drugs*	2%	2%	2%
Had any NRT/other prescribed drugs to help stop smoking	11%	16%	13%
Sought any help or advice	32%	44%	38%
Did not seek help or advice	68%	56%	62%
Base=100%	*397*	*448*	*846*
2000			
Read leaflets/booklets on how to stop	26%	35%	31%
Asked doctor or other health prof for help	5%	10%	7%
Called a smokers' telephone helpline	2%	3%	3%
Been referred/self-referred to stop smoking group	2%	2%	2%
Bought non-prescription NRT*	10%	10%	10%
Paid for prescription NRT*	1%	1%	1%
Free prescription NRT*	-	1%	0%
Free non-prescription NRT *	0%	0%	0%
Prescribed other 'stop smoking' drugs*	1%	1%	1%
Had any NRT/other prescribed drugs to help stop smoking	12%	13%	12%
Sought any help or advice	32%	41%	37%
Did not seek help or advice	68%	59%	63%
Base=100%	*416*	*456*	*872*
1999			
Read leaflets/booklets on how to stop	34%	40%	38%
Asked doctor or other health prof for help	4%	6%	5%
Called a smokers' telephone helpline	2%	4%	3%
Been referred/self-referred to stop smoking group	2%	1%	1%
Bought NRT (gums, patches, inhalators)*	12%	20%	16%
Been given free NRT*	0%	2%	1%
Sought help or advice	40%	48%	44%
Did not seek help or advice	60%	52%	56%
Base=100%	*447*	*503*	*950*

* Question changed between 1999 and 2000.

Table 4.28 **Sources of help and advice used in the last year by age, 1999–2002**

All smokers

Percentage who have:	Age 16–24	25–44	45–64	65 and over	Total
2002					
Read leaflets/booklets on how to stop	40%	26%	25%	25%	28%
Asked doctor or other health prof for help	8%	9%	13%	8%	10%
Called a smokers' telephone helpline	5%	4%	2%	1%	3%
Been referred/self-referred to stop smoking group	4%	3%	5%	3%	4%
Bought non-prescription NRT*	8%	8%	9%	2%	8%
Paid for prescription NRT*	-	2%	2%	0%	2%
Free prescription NRT*	0%	4%	5%	3%	4%
Free non-prescription NRT*	0%	0%	0%	-	0%
Prescribed other 'stop smoking' drugs*	-	1%	1%	3%	1%
Had any NRT/other prescribed drugs to help stop smoking	9%	15%	17%	8%	14%
Sought any help or advice	47%	35%	35%	31%	36%
Did not seek help or advice	53%	65%	65%	69%	64%
Base=100%	*143*	*393*	*310*	*100*	*944*
2001					
Read leaflets/booklets on how to stop	27%	34%	30%	17%	30%
Asked doctor or other health prof for help	2%	13%	10%	6%	10%
Called a smokers' telephone helpline	5%	4%	4%	1%	4%
Been referred/self-referred to stop smoking group	-	3%	4%	2%	3%
Bought non-prescription NRT*	9%	10%	11%	5%	10%
Paid for prescription NRT*	-	1%	1%	-	0%
Free prescription NRT*	0%	3%	1%	3%	2%
Free non-prescription NRT*	-	0%	0%	-	0%
Prescribed other 'stop smoking' drugs*	-	3%	3%	-	2%
Had any NRT/other prescribed drugs to help stop smoking	9%	15%	15%	7%	13%
Sought any help or advice	35%	43%	39%	22%	38%
Did not seek help or advice	65%	57%	61%	78%	62%
Base=100%	*127*	*385*	*251*	*83*	*846*
2000					
Read leaflets/booklets on how to stop	41%	30%	30%	26%	31%
Asked doctor or other health prof for help	3%	7%	10%	7%	7%
Called a smokers' telephone helpline	1%	3%	3%	4%	3%
Been referred/self-referred to stop smoking group	-	3%	3%	1%	2%
Bought non-prescription NRT*	8%	12%	11%	4%	10%
Paid for prescription NRT*	-	1%	2%	1%	1%
Free prescription NRT*	1%	-	0%	3%	0%
Free non-prescription NRT*	-	0%	1%	-	0%
Prescribed other 'stop smoking' drugs*	0%	1%	2%	2%	1%
Had any NRT/other prescribed drugs to help stop smoking	9%	13%	14%	10%	12%
Sought any help or advice	43%	35%	39%	31%	37%
Did not seek help or advice	57%	65%	61%	69%	63%
Base=100%	*141*	*363*	*267*	*100*	*872*
1999					
Read leaflets/booklets on how to stop	48%	37%	36%	29%	38%
Asked doctor or other health prof for help	3%	7%	4%	2%	5%
Called a smokers' telephone helpline	5%	3%	2%	-	3%
Been referred/self-referred to stop smoking group	1%	1%	1%	1%	1%
Bought NRT (gums, patches, inhalators)*	10%	17%	21%	9%	16%
Been given free NRT*	-	2%	1%	1%	1%
Sought help or advice	52%	43%	45%	33%	44%
Did not seek help or advice	48%	57%	55%	67%	56%
Base=100%	*160*	*412*	*279*	*98*	*950*

* Question changed between 1999 and 2000.

Table 4.29 **Sources of help and advice used in the last year by social-economic classification, 2002**

All smokers

| Percentage who have: | Social-economic classification | | | | 2002 Total |
	Managerial and professional occupations	Intermediate occupations	Routine and manual occupations	Never worked and long-term unemployed	
Read leaflets/booklets on how to stop	29%	22%	29%	36%	28%
Asked doctor or other health prof for help	8%	8%	11%	20%	10%
Called a smokers' telephone helpline	2%	4%	3%	4%	3%
Been referred/self-referred to stop smoking group	3%	4%	3%	12%	4%
Bought non-prescription NRT	10%	8%	7%	6%	8%
Paid for prescription NRT	2%	0%	2%	-	2%
Free prescription NRT	3%	4%	4%	5%	4%
Free non-prescription NRT	-	-	1%	-	0%
Prescribed other 'stop smoking' drugs	1%	2%	1%	1%	1%
Had any NRT/other prescribed drugs to help stop smoking	13%	14%	15%	10%	14%
Sought help or advice	35%	35%	37%	43%	36%
Did not seek help or advice	65%	65%	63%	57%	64%
Base=100%	*201*	*199*	*468*	*77*	*944*

Table 4.30 **Sources of help and advice used in the last year, by number of cigarettes smoked per day, 2002**

All smokers

| Percentage who have: | Number of cigarettes per day | | | 2002 Total |
	20 and over	10–19	0–9	
Read leaflets/booklets on how to stop	28%	32%	23%	28%
Asked doctor or other health prof for help	10%	12%	8%	10%
Called a smokers' telephone helpline	4%	4%	2%	3%
Been referred/self-referred to stop smoking group	2%	6%	4%	4%
Bought non-prescription NRT	10%	8%	6%	8%
Paid for prescription NRT	2%	2%	3%	2%
Free prescription NRT	5%	4%	1%	4%
Free non-prescription NRT	0%	0%	0%	0%
Prescribed other 'stop smoking' drugs	0%	1%	2%	1%
Had any NRT/other prescribed drugs to help stop smoking	16%	15%	10%	14%
Sought help or advice	38%	41%	28%	36%
Did not seek help or advice	62%	59%	72%	64%
Base=100%	*285*	*392*	*268*	*944*

Table 4.31 Source of advice on smoking in the last 5 years by sex, 1996–2002

All smokers

Source of advice	Sex Men	Women	2002 Total	2001 Total	2000 Total	1999 Total	1997 Total	1996 Total
GP	30%	39%	35%	32%	35%	37%	34%	38%
Someone else at the surgery	11%	17%	14%	15%	12%	13%	11%	13%
Pharmacist	3%	2%	2%	5%	4%	3%	2%	2%
Other medical person	8%	8%	8%	9%	9%	12%	10%	11%
Any of the above	38%	46%	42%	42%	44%	45%	43%	46%
Base=100%	*456*	*485*	*941*	*844*	*871*	*950*	*985*	*1047*

Percentages sum to more than the 'Any of the above' total as respondents could give more then one answer.

Table 4.32 Source of advice on smoking in the last 5 years by age, 2002

All smokers

Source of advice	Age 16–24	25–44	45–64	65 and over	2002 Total
GP	29%	32%	39%	39%	35%
Someone else at the surgery	8%	11%	19%	16%	14%
Pharmacist	2%	3%	1%	1%	2%
Other medical person	3%	8%	11%	7%	8%
Any of the above	35%	39%	47%	46%	42%
Base=100%	*139*	*393*	*310*	*99*	*941*

Percentages sum to more than the 'Any of the above' total as respondents could give more then one answer.

Table 4.33 **Source of advice on smoking in the last 5 years by number of cigarettes smoked per day and sex, 2002**

All smokers

Source of advice	Number of cigarettes per day			2002 Total
	20 and over	10–19	0–9	
Men				
GP	39%	24%	29%	30%
Someone else at the surgery	12%	9%	12%	11%
Pharmacist	2%	2%	3%	3%
Other medical person	9%	8%	7%	8%
Any of the above	45%	33%	34%	38%
Base=100%	158	187	111	456
Women				
GP	44%	42%	30%	39%
Someone else at the surgery	21%	17%	13%	17%
Pharmacist	2%	2%	2%	2%
Other medical person	12%	8%	6%	8%
Any of the above	50%	51%	38%	46%
Base=100%	126	201	157	485
All				
GP	41%	33%	30%	35%
Someone else at the surgery	16%	13%	13%	14%
Pharmacist	2%	2%	3%	2%
Other medical person	10%	8%	6%	8%
Any of the above	47%	42%	36%	42%
Base=100%	284	388	268	941

Percentages sum to more than the 'Any of the above' total as respondents could give more then one answer.

Table 4.34 **Type of advice given in the last 5 years, and whether it was helpful or not by sex, 1996–2002**

Current smokers given advice

Nature of advice	2002	2001	2000	1999	1997	1996
	%	%	%	%	%	%
Men						
Type of advice						
Discussion and literature	87	84	82	88	87	86
Literature only	13	16	18	12	13	14
Whether helpful						
Yes	54	58	45	52	52	56
No	46	42	55	48	48	44
Base=100%	*168*	*142*	*166*	*180*	*175*	*252*
Women						
Type of advice						
Discussion and literature	86	86	87	82	85	83
Literature only	14	14	13	18	15	17
Whether helpful						
Yes	50	50	47	45	53	42
No	50	50	53	55	47	58
Base=100%	*223*	*202*	*212*	*248*	*245*	*303*
All						
Type of advice						
Discussion and literature	86	85	85	85	86	85
Literature only	14	15	15	15	14	15
Whether helpful						
Yes	52	53	46	48	52	48
No	48	47	54	52	48	52
Base=100%	*391*	*344*	*378*	*428*	*420*	*555*

Table 4.35 **Type of advice given in the last 5 years by whether it was helpful or not, 2002**

Current smokers given advice

	Nature of advice Discussion and literature	Literature only
	%	%
Whether helpful		
Yes	54	42
No	46	58
Base=100%	*332*	*53*

Table 4.36 **Whether given advice on smoking in the last 5 years by amount smoked, 1999–2002**

Ex-regular smokers

Whether given advice when smoked	Number of cigarettes per day when smoked			2002 Total	2001 Total	2000 Total	1999 Total
	20 and over	10–19	0–9				
Been given advice	46%	34%	19%	35%	36%	48%	35%
Base=100%	*90*	*100*	*48*	*238*	*195*	*183*	*189*

5 Perception and awareness of issues related to smoking

5.1 Perception of relative risk

In order to obtain insights into people's perception of the risk of smoking, respondents were asked which of a list of possible causes they thought was responsible for most deaths before the age of 65 (premature deaths) in the United Kingdom. The question was asked at the beginning of the section on smoking, so that answers would not be influenced by the questions on smoking behaviour and attitudes that followed. Answers to this kind of question should be interpreted with caution because the concept of cause of premature death is a difficult one which is likely to mean different things to different people.

The most frequently mentioned cause of the most premature deaths was smoking – 47% of respondents mentioned it in 2002. The next most common answer was road accidents (35%) followed by illicit drugs (7%). The percentage of people giving each answer were very similar to that found in previous years. Although it is difficult to give an accurate estimate of the actual number of premature deaths attributable to each of the causes covered, public perception of the risks of death due to road accidents compared with those due to smoking are clearly wrong. In the United Kingdom, fewer than 3,000 people under 65 die in road accidents each year compared with an estimate of almost 27,000 from smoking.

Variations in perception about relative risk by sub-groups were similar to those revealed in previous years. Current smokers were just as likely as other people to say that smoking causes the most premature deaths. Men were more likely than women to say that smoking causes the most deaths under the age of 65 (50% compared with 44%). Younger respondents were the least likely to think that smoking was the main cause of premature death (37% of those aged 16-24 compared with 42% or more of older age groups).

Tables 5.1–5.3

5.2 The effect of passive smoking

To evaluate people's awareness of the effect of passive smoking, respondents were asked whether or not they thought that living with a smoker increased the risk of *a child* getting a range of medical conditions known, or thought to be, caused or exacerbated by passive smoking. These conditions included asthma, ear infections, cot death, chest infections, and other infections. Respondents were then asked a similar set of questions about whether or not passive smoking would increase the risk of a *non-smoking adult* getting asthma, lung cancer, heart disease, bronchitis, and coughs and colds. One further health problem was included on both lists – diabetes, the risk of which is not medically proven to be increased by either active or passive smoking. At both questions, one respondent in six said they thought that the risk of becoming diabetic would be increased by passive smoking so the figures for other conditions should generally be taken as reflecting perceptions rather than knowledge.

Of all the health problems covered in the survey, people appeared to be the most aware of the effect of passive smoking on a child's risk of getting chest infections and asthma. Respectively, 90% and 83% of respondents thought that a child's risk of getting chest infections and asthma were increased by passive smoking. These were also the two health problems for which the percentage who did not answer was lowest – 3% and 5% respectively.

People appeared to be the least aware of the effect of passive smoking on a child's risk of cot death and ear infections. About a fifth of respondents were unable to say whether or not the risk of ear infections would be increased by passive smoking and about a sixth did not know whether passive smoking increases a child's risk of cot death.

The percentage of respondents who thought that passive smoking would increase the risk of a child getting the medical conditions was similar to the figures for previous years.

Ex-smokers and those who had never smoked regularly tended to be more aware of the risks of passive smoking. For example, of people who had never smoked, 89% said that passive smoking increased a child's risk of asthma, and 59% said it increased their risk of cot death. This compared with only 58% and 36%

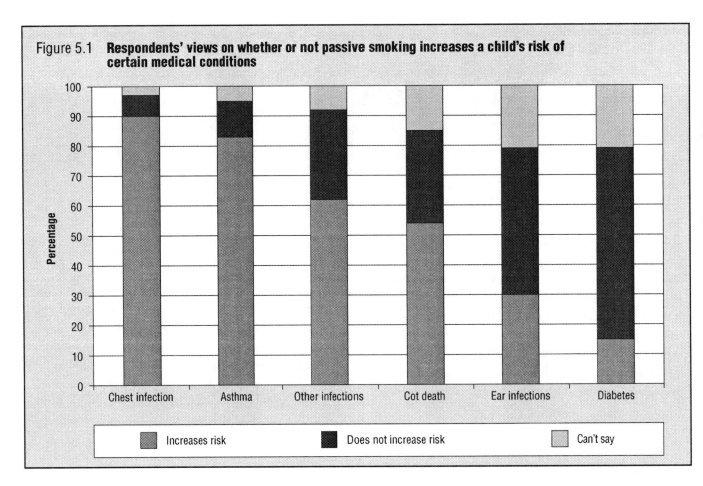

Figure 5.1 **Respondents' views on whether or not passive smoking increases a child's risk of certain medical conditions**

respectively of those who smoked 20 or more cigarettes a day. Women were more aware than men of the link between passive smoking and cot death (61% of women and 45% of men said they thought it increased the risk).

People who were not living in a household containing children were less likely to know whether or not passive smoking increased the risk of cot death or ear infections. Those in manual occupations were less likely to know whether or not passive smoking increased the risk of any of the medical conditions with the exception of diabetes. **Figure 5.1 and Tables 5.4–5.7**

Eighty per cent or more thought that a non-smoking adult's risk of lung cancer, bronchitis and asthma would be increased by passive smoking. Somewhat fewer – 69% – said that passive smoking would increase the risk of heart disease and coughs and colds.

The 2002 percentages who thought passive smoking would increase the risk of a non-smoking adult getting the medical conditions were similar to the levels in 2000 and 2001.

As with knowledge about the effect of passive smoking on children, people who had never or who no longer smoked were more likely

than smokers to be aware of the effect of passive smoking on adults. There were no differences between men and women.
Figure 5.2 and Tables 5.8–5.11

Logistic regression was used in the analysis to assess the influences that are independently associated with knowledge about the effect of passive smoking.[1] Generally, the following groups of people were more likely to know about the effect of passive smoking on both adults and children:

- those in the younger age-groups (under 35); and
- those who had never smoked.

In addition, women and people living with a child under the age of 11 were more likely to know that passive smoking increases the risk of cot death or ear infections in a child.

Note

1. Logistic regression is explained in detail in Appendix C and the factors included in the analysis are listed in Tables C5.1 and C5.2 in Appendix C.

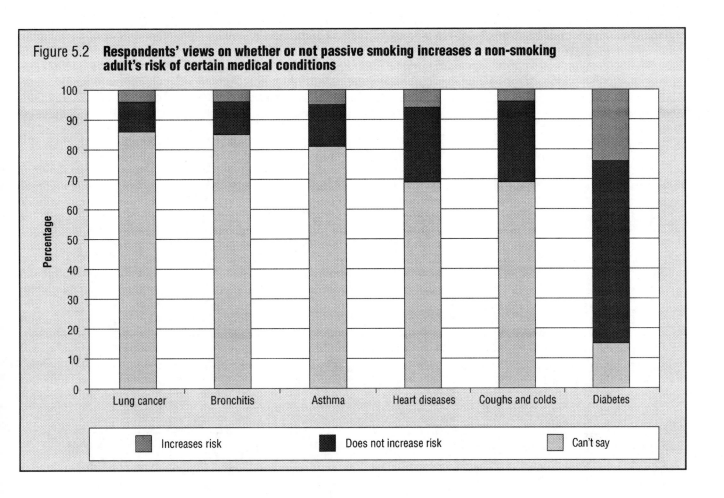

Figure 5.2 **Respondents' views on whether or not passive smoking increases a non-smoking adult's risk of certain medical conditions**

Table 5.1 **What respondents think is the main cause of deaths before the age of 65 in the United Kingdom, 1996–2002**

All respondents

Main cause of death before age 65	2002	2001	2000	1999	1997	1996
	%	%	%	%	%	%
Smoking	47	49	44	46	45	43
Road accidents	35	36	42	39	40	43
Illicit drugs	7	6	6	6	5	6
Alcohol misuse	6	4	4	4	4	4
Accidents at work	2	2	2	2	2	2
AIDS	1	2	1	1	1	1
Murder/manslaughter	1	1	1	1	1	1
Base=100%	*3751*	*3434*	*3305*	*3460*	*3648*	*3624*

Table 5.2 **What respondents think is the main cause of deaths before the age of 65 in the United Kingdom, by smoking status, 2002**

All respondents

Main cause of death before age 65	Heavy smokers*	Light smokers*	All current smokers	Ex-regular smokers	Never smoked regularly	Total
	%	%	%	%	%	%
Smoking	39	44	43	51	47	47
Road accidents	40	33	35	32	37	35
Illicit drugs	8	11	10	6	5	7
Alcohol misuse	8	8	8	6	6	6
Accidents at work	2	2	2	3	2	2
AIDS	1	2	1	2	1	1
Murder/manslaughter	3	1	2	1	1	1
Base=100%	*278*	*649*	*927*	*981*	*1844*	*3751*

* Heavy smokers are those who smoke 20 or more cigarettes a day and light smokers are those who smoke less than 20 cigarettes a day.

Smoking Related Behaviour and Attitudes, 2002 ●

Table 5.3 **What respondents think is the main cause of deaths before the age of 65 in the United Kingdom, by sex and age, 2002**

All respondents

Main cause of death before age 65	Age 16–24	25–44	45–64	65 and over	2002 Total
	%	%	%	%	%
Men					
Smoking	33	51	58	46	50
Road accidents	43	35	30	36	34
Illicit drugs	9	3	4	7	5
Alcohol misuse	4	9	6	5	6
Accidents at work	5	2	2	3	3
AIDS	4	1	1	2	2
Murder/manslaughter	3	0	-	1	1
Base=100%	*217*	*573*	*569*	*354*	*1713*
Women					
Smoking	41	46	47	39	44
Road accidents	37	37	34	37	36
Illicit drugs	7	8	8	12	8
Alcohol misuse	6	6	6	7	6
Accidents at work	1	1	3	3	2
AIDS	1	1	1	2	1
Murder/manslaughter	8	1	1	1	2
Base=100%	*253*	*698*	*681*	*403*	*2035*
All					
Smoking	37	48	52	42	47
Road accidents	40	36	32	36	35
Illicit drugs	8	6	6	10	7
Alcohol misuse	5	7	6	6	6
Accidents at work	2	2	2	3	2
AIDS	2	1	1	2	1
Murder/manslaughter	5	1	1	1	1
Base=100%	*472*	*1273*	*1249*	*757*	*3751*

Table 5.4 **Views on whether or not passive smoking increases a child's risk of certain medical conditions, 1996–2002**

All respondents

Condition	2002	2001	2000	1999	1997	1996
	%	%	%	%	%	%
Chest infection						
Increases risk	90	90	90	89	91	91
Does not increase risk	7	7	8	8	6	7
Can't say	3	3	2	3	3	3
Asthma						
Increases risk	83	82	84	83	85	84
Does not increase risk	12	12	12	12	10	11
Can't say	5	6	4	5	5	6
Other infections						
Increases risk	62	62	64	63	66	66
Does not increase risk	30	29	28	28	22	23
Can't say	8	10	8	9	12	12
Cot death						
Increases risk	54	55	54	53	53	53
Does not increase risk	31	28	31	32	26	28
Can't say	15	16	15	16	21	19
Ear infections						
Increases risk	30	28	31	32	36	29
Does not increase risk	49	50	48	48	36	27
Can't say	22	21	21	21	27	44
Diabetes						
Increases risk	15	15	16	15	19	18
Does not increase risk	64	62	61	62	50	51
Can't say	21	23	23	23	32	32
Base=100%	*3818*	*3493*	*3327*	*3547*	*3718*	*3696*

Table 5.5 **Views on whether or not passive smoking increases a child's risk of certain medical conditions, by smoking status, 2002**

All respondents

Whether increases risk	Heavy smokers*	Light smokers*	All current smokers	Ex-regular smokers	Never smoked regularly	2002 Total
	Percentage saying smoking increased the risk of the complaint					
Chest infections	74	86	83	92	93	90
Asthma	58	78	72	83	89	83
Other infections	42	56	52	60	68	62
Cot death	36	45	42	54	59	54
Ear infections	16	27	24	28	33	30
Diabetes	8	10	9	16	17	15
	Percentage saying smoking did not increase the risk of the complaint					
Chest infection	22	11	14	7	4	7
Asthma	31	18	22	12	7	12
Other infections	48	36	39	31	24	30
Cot death	48	38	41	30	27	31
Ear infections	67	52	56	47	46	49
Diabetes	73	69	70	60	63	64
	Percentage who did not know whether smoking increased the risk of the complaint or not					
Chest infections	4	3	3	2	3	3
Asthma	11	4	6	5	4	5
Other infections	10	8	9	9	8	8
Cot death	16	16	17	17	14	15
Ear infections	16	17	20	25	21	22
Diabetes	19	21	21	24	20	21
Base=100%	*286*	*657*	*943*	*998*	*1877*	*3818*

* Heavy smokers are those who smoke 20 or more cigarettes a day and light smokers are those who smoke less than 20 cigarettes a day.

Table 5.6 **Views on whether or not passive smoking increases a child's risk of certain medical conditions, by sex and by age, 2002**

All respondents

Whether increases risk	Sex Men	Women	Age 16–24	25–44	45–64	65 and over	2002 Total
	Percentage saying smoking increased the risk of the complaint						
Chest infections	90	91	93	93	90	84	90
Asthma	82	84	87	86	82	78	83
Other infections	63	61	70	66	62	50	62
Cot death	45	61	48	66	51	41	54
Ear infections	25	33	22	34	30	26	30
Diabetes	15	15	14	14	14	18	15
	Percentage saying smoking did not increase the risk of the complaint						
Chest infections	7	7	4	6	7	11	7
Asthma	12	12	10	11	12	13	12
Other infections	28	32	23	28	30	36	30
Cot death	36	27	38	25	32	37	31
Ear infections	49	48	57	48	48	47	49
Diabetes	61	66	68	66	64	57	64
	Percentage who did not know whether smoking increased the risk of the complaint or not						
Chest infections	3	2	3	1	3	5	3
Asthma	6	4	3	3	6	9	5
Other infections	9	7	7	6	8	13	8
Cot death	19	12	14	9	18	22	15
Ear infections	26	19	21	19	22	27	22
Diabetes	24	19	18	19	22	25	21
Base=100%	*1746*	*2072*	*480*	*1281*	*1265*	*790*	*3818*

Table 5.7 **Views on whether or not passive smoking increases a child's risk of certain medical conditions, by social-economic classification and by presence of children under 16 in household, 2002**

All respondents

Whether increases risk	Social-economic classification				Children under 16 in household	No children in household	2002 Total
	Managerial and professional occupations	Intermediate occupations	Routine and manual occupations	Never worked and long-term unemployed			
Percentage saying smoking increased the risk of the complaint							
Chest infections	94	90	88	89	91	90	90
Asthma	85	83	81	87	85	83	83
Other infections	65	61	58	68	64	61	62
Cot death	59	58	48	51	65	49	54
Ear infections	34	28	27	29	33	28	30
Diabetes	14	15	14	20	13	16	15
Percentage saying smoking did not increase the risk of the complaint							
Chest infections	4	8	10	5	7	7	7
Asthma	10	12	14	8	12	12	12
Other infections	27	30	33	23	30	30	30
Cot death	25	30	36	36	26	33	31
Ear infections	43	50	52	50	49	48	49
Diabetes	63	64	64	64	68	62	64
Percentage who did not know whether smoking increased the risk of the complaint or not							
Chest infections	2	2	2	6	2	3	3
Asthma	5	5	5	5	3	6	5
Other infections	8	8	9	9	6	9	8
Cot death	16	13	17	13	9	18	15
Ear infections	23	22	21	21	18	23	22
Diabetes	24	21	21	16	19	22	21
Base=100%	*1221*	*789*	*1471*	*338*	*1152*	*2666*	*3818*

Table 5.8 **Views on whether or not passive smoking increases a non-smoking adult's risk of certain medical conditions, 1996–2002**

All respondents

Condition	2002	2001	2000	1999	1997	1996
	%	%	%	%	%	%
Lung cancer						
Increases risk	86	86	85	84	86	83
Does not increase risk	10	10	12	12	11	12
Can't say	4	4	3	4	4	5
Bronchitis						
Increases risk	85	85	86	84	86	84
Does not increase risk	11	11	11	12	10	12
Can't say	4	4	3	4	4	4
Asthma						
Increases risk	81	80	81	80	81	79
Does not increase risk	14	15	15	16	14	14
Can't say	5	5	4	4	6	6
Heart disease						
Increases risk	69	69	70	68	74	68
Does not increase risk	25	24	23	25	19	22
Can't say	7	7	7	7	7	10
Coughs and colds						
Increases risk	69	68	69	67	70	68
Does not increase risk	27	29	28	29	25	27
Can't say	4	3	4	4	5	5
Diabetes						
Increases risk	15	14	16	16	20	17
Does not increase risk	61	62	60	61	48	50
Can't say	23	24	24	24	32	33
Base=100%	*3820*	*3493*	*3328*	*3546*	*3716*	*3696*

Table 5.9 **Views on whether or not passive smoking increases a non-smoking adult's risk of certain medical conditions, by smoking status, 2002**

All respondents

Whether increases risk	Heavy smokers*	Light smokers*	All current smokers	Ex-regular smokers	Never smoked regularly	2002 Total
	Percentage saying smoking increased the risk of the complaint					
Lung cancer	63	76	72	88	92	86
Bronchitis	62	76	72	88	90	85
Asthma	55	72	67	84	86	81
Heart Disease	47	64	59	72	72	69
Coughs and colds	44	62	57	72	73	69
Diabetes	9	13	12	16	17	15
	Percentage saying smoking did not increase the risk of the complaint					
Lung cancer	29	19	22	9	6	10
Bronchitis	30	20	23	9	7	11
Asthma	33	23	26	12	10	14
Heart Disease	42	30	34	22	21	25
Coughs and colds	50	34	39	25	23	27
Diabetes	73	65	67	57	60	61
	Percentage who did not know whether smoking increased the risk of the complaint or not					
Lung cancer	8	5	6	3	2	4
Bronchitis	8	4	5	3	4	4
Asthma	12	5	7	4	4	5
Heart Disease	11	6	8	6	7	7
Coughs and colds	7	4	4	3	4	4
Diabetes	18	23	21	27	23	23
Base=100%	*285*	*656*	*941*	*998*	*1877*	*3817*

* Heavy smokers are those who smoke 20 or more cigarettes a day and light smokers are those who smoke less than 20 cigarettes a day.

Table 5.10 **Views on whether or not passive smoking increases a non-smoking adult's risk of certain medical conditions, by sex and by age, 2002**

All respondents

Whether increases risk	Sex Men	Women	Age 16–24	25–44	45–64	65 and over	2002 Total
	Percentage saying smoking increased the risk of the complaint						
Lung cancer	86	86	89	89	85	81	86
Bronchitis	84	85	82	87	84	84	85
Asthma	81	80	83	82	80	79	81
Heart Disease	72	66	73	70	67	66	69
Coughs & colds	69	69	71	70	67	68	69
Diabetes	17	14	16	14	15	18	15
	Percentage saying smoking did not increase the risk of the complaint						
Lung cancer	10	10	8	9	11	13	10
Bronchitis	11	11	12	10	12	12	11
Asthma	14	15	14	14	15	14	14
Heart Disease	21	28	21	25	25	26	25
Coughs & colds	27	28	25	27	29	27	27
Diabetes	58	64	66	65	60	54	61
	Percentage who did not know whether smoking increased the risk of the complaint or not						
Lung cancer	3	4	3	2	4	6	4
Bronchitis	4	4	6	2	4	4	4
Asthma	5	5	3	4	5	7	5
Heart Disease	7	7	6	5	8	8	7
Coughs & colds	5	3	4	3	5	5	4
Diabetes	25	22	18	20	25	28	23
Base=100%	*1746*	*2072*	*480*	*1282*	*1266*	*790*	*3818*

Table 5.11 **Views on whether or not passive smoking increases a non-smoking adult's risk of certain medical conditions, by social-economic classification and by presence of children under 16 in the household, 2002**

All respondents

Whether increases risk	Social-economic classification				Children under 16 in household	No children in household	2002 Total
	Managerial and professional occupations	Intermediate occupations	Routine and manual occupations	Never worked and long-term unemployed			
	Percentage saying smoking increased the risk of the complaint						
Lung cancer	90	85	83	88	88	85	86
Bronchitis	90	84	82	83	87	84	85
Asthma	84	82	76	84	82	80	81
Heart Disease	70	69	66	74	68	69	69
Coughs and colds	71	69	66	72	69	68	69
Diabetes	15	14	16	17	15	15	15
	Percentage saying smoking did not increase the risk of the complaint						
Lung cancer	7	10	14	9	10	11	10
Bronchitis	8	12	14	10	11	12	11
Asthma	12	13	18	11	15	14	14
Heart Disease	24	25	27	19	25	24	25
Coughs and colds	25	28	30	21	28	27	27
Diabetes	60	63	60	66	65	60	61
	Percentage who did not know whether smoking increased the risk of the complaint or not						
Lung cancer	2	4	4	4	2	4	4
Bronchitis	2	4	4	7	3	4	4
Asthma	4	5	5	5	3	6	5
Heart Disease	6	6	7	7	6	7	7
Coughs and colds	4	3	4	6	3	4	4
Diabetes	25	23	24	18	20	25	23
Base=100%	*1220*	*788*	*1471*	*338*	*1151*	*2666*	*3817*

6 Attitudes related to smoking

6.1 Non-smokers' attitudes towards people smoking near them

Non-smokers (that is, both ex-smokers and those who had never smoked) were asked if they would mind if other people smoked near them and 55% of non-smokers said they would. This was similar to the percentages found in 2001 and 2000 (55%), 1999 (54%) and 1997 (56%). Women non-smokers were more likely to mind people smoking near them (58% compared with 51% of men). People who had never smoked were also more likely to mind smokers smoking near them (60% compared with 46% among ex-regular smokers).

The main reasons why non-smokers said they would mind if people smoked near them were the smell of cigarette smoke (64%) and the health effect of passive smoking (43%). A notable percentage also mentioned the residual smell of smoke on clothing (37%) and that cigarette smoke affects breathing (19%) or makes them cough (15%) and gets into the eyes (15%). As in previous years, the majority of non-smokers in 2002 (67%) gave both health-related and other reasons; 18% cited only health-related reasons.

Figure 6.1 and Tables 6.1–6.3

Non-smokers who were aware of the health effects of passive smoking were also more likely to mind smokers smoking near them. For example, 58% of those who said that passive smoking would increase the risk of asthma would mind if someone smoked near them compared with 32% of those who were not aware of the risk of asthma.

Table 6.4

As the characteristics discussed above may themselves be inter-related, a statistical procedure, logistic regression, was used in the analysis to identify the influences that are independently associated with smoking-related attitudes.[1] Non-smokers who were the most likely to say they would mind if people smoke near them included:

- Women.
- Older people.
- Those who had never smoked.
- Those who were aware of the health effects of passive smoking.

Table C6.1

6.2 Smokers' behaviour in the presence of non-smokers

Smokers were asked if they modified their smoking behaviour when in the presence of non-smoking adults or children.

The majority of smokers (82%) said that they modified their behaviour when in the presence of non-smoking adults: 52% do not smoke at all and 30% smoke fewer cigarettes. This was similar to the percentages found in 2001 (48% and 34% respectively). As would be expected, light smokers (those who smoke fewer than 20 cigarettes a day) were most likely to say that they do not smoke at all (58%) while heavy smokers (those who smoke 20 or more cigarettes a day) were most likely to smoke fewer cigarettes (36%).

Table 6.5 and Figure 6.2

Women were more likely not to smoke at all in the presence of non-smoking adults: 55% of women compared with 48% of men. Of those who carried on smoking, men and women were equally likely to smoke fewer cigarettes. People who knew of the effects of passive smoking on adults were more likely to modify their behaviour than those who did not: for example, 56% of smokers who thought that passive smoking can increase the risk of asthma said they would not smoke at all, compared with 40% of smokers who did not believe that passive smoking could cause asthma.

Smokers tended to impose stricter controls on their smoking in the presence of children than in the company of adult non-smokers. In 2002:

- A larger percentage of smokers said that they would limit their smoking in the company of children than in the presence of adult non-smokers (87% compared with 82%).

- 66% of smokers said they would not smoke at all if they are in the room with children compared with 52% who would not smoke at all in the company of adult non-smokers.

- 75% of light smokers would not smoke at all in front of a child while only 58% would abstain in front of an adult non-smoker. The figures for heavy smokers were 45% and 38% respectively.

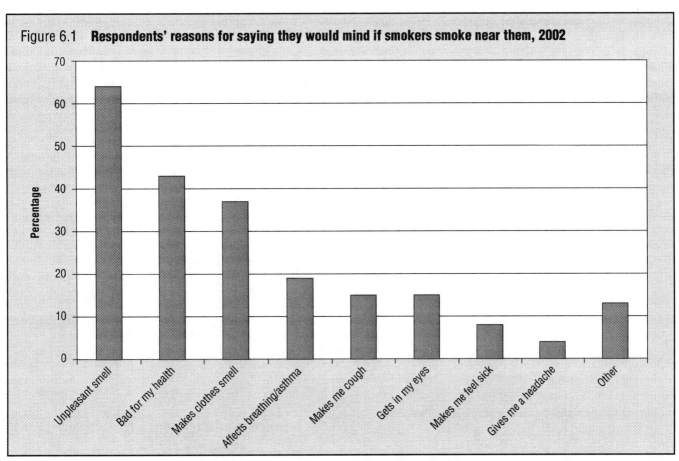

Figure 6.1　Respondents' reasons for saying they would mind if smokers smoke near them, 2002

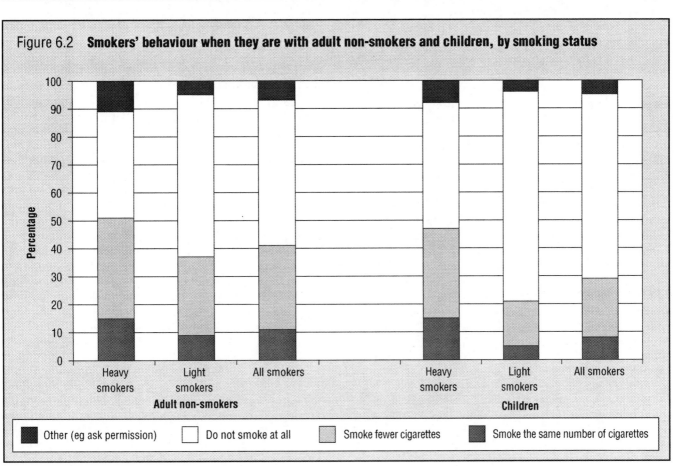

Figure 6.2　Smokers' behaviour when they are with adult non-smokers and children, by smoking status

- A similar percentage of smokers would not smoke at all in front of adults over the survey years (52% in 2002, compared with 48% in 2001).

- A similar percentage of smokers would not smoke at all in front of children in 2002, 2001 and 2000 (66%, 63% and 67% respectively).

Smokers who thought that passive smoking increased the risk of children getting various medical conditions were more likely to not smoke at all when they are in a room with children (70% or more compared with between 45% and 63% among those who were not aware of the effect of passive smoking on the risk of getting various conditions).   **Figure 6.2 and Tables 6.5–6.8**

6.3   Views on smoking restrictions

In December 1998, the Department of Health released *Smoking Kills – a White Paper on tobacco*[2] which set out practical measures to reduce smoking. One of the measures proposed was to produce an Approved Code of Practice on smoking in the workplace. This defined the kind of smoking policies employers need to operate to comply with existing health and safety legislation.

Half of respondents (50%) who were in work said that smoking was not allowed at all on the premises where they worked – similar to the 47% reported in 2001 but a significant increase since 1996 (40%).

A smaller percentage (36%) worked at premises where smoking was allowed only in designated smoking rooms. Men and heavy smokers were the most likely to work at premises that did not restrict smoking.[3]   **Tables 6.9–6.11**

The White Paper also recognised the need for smoking restrictions in public places and proposed a 'Public Places Charter' which set out objectives for providing facilities for non-smokers and the availability of clean air.

Over four-fifths of those interviewed agreed that there should be restrictions on smoking at work (86%), in restaurants (88%) and in other public places such as banks and post offices (87%). A smaller percentage of respondents, 54%, thought that smoking should be restricted in pubs.

As would be expected, non-smokers were more likely to be in favour of restricting smoking than current smokers; 92% of never

smokers and 89% of ex smokers were in favour of smoking restrictions at work (94% and 91% respectively in restaurants) compared with 70% of current smokers (72% in restaurants). People who were the most likely to be in favour of restrictions were:[1]

- People aged over 35.
- Those who have never smoked.
- Those in managerial and professional occupations.
- People who were aware of the effect of passive smoking on the health of children and non-smoking adults.

The extent of the support for smoking restrictions varied between the various types of location. Details are presented in Tables 6.13–6.16.

The support for smoking restrictions has been increasing since 1996. The percentage in favour of restrictions at work rose from 81% in 1996 to 86% in 2002, in restaurants, from 85% to 88%, in pubs, from 48% to 54%, and in other public places from 82% to 87%.   **Table 6.12**

6.4   Actions and response related to views on smoking restrictions

Over four in ten people (43%) considered whether or not a place has a non-smoking area as an important factor when deciding where to go for a meal. Just under a fifth (19%) regarded whether a place has a non-smoking area as an important consideration in their choice of a place to go for a drink. These percentages are similar to those found in previous years.

People who were most likely to take account of the provision of non-smoking areas when they select places to go for a meal were:[3]

- People aged over 45 (just under half compared with a quarter to a third of younger people).

- Non-smokers (about a half compared with 14% of current smokers).

- Those with children under 16 in the household.

- Those who were aware of the effect of passive smoking (46% and over compared with between 19% and 40% among people who were not aware of the effect of passive smoking on the risk of getting various conditions).

- Respondents who support smoking restrictions (between 46% and 57% compared with under a quarter of those who were not in favour of smoking restrictions in various public places).

Non-smokers and those who were aware of the effects of passive smoking were also more likely to take account of whether or not a place has a non-smoking area when deciding where to go for a drink but the percentage doing so was lower than in the case for selecting a place to go for a meal.   **Tables 6.17–6.22 and C6.3**

6.5   Taxation on tobacco

Respondents were asked how they thought tax increases directed at smokers should relate to inflation. In 2002, nearly one half (48%) the respondents said that tax on tobacco should be increased by more than the rate of inflation. This is similar to the percentages in 2001 (47%), 2000 (46%) and 1999 (48%).

As would be expected there was a wide divergence of views on taxation between smokers and non-smokers; only 17% of current smokers said that taxation should be increased by more than the rate of inflation, compared with 62% of those who had never smoked. Nearly three quarters (72%) of heavy smokers said that tobacco tax should not be increased at all, whereas only 13% of those who have never smoked took that view.

There were no marked differences in opinion according to sex or age.   **Tables 6.23–6.25**

Notes and references

1   Logistic regression is explained in detail in Appendix C and the factors included in the analysis are listed in Tables C6.1, C6.2 and C6.3 in Appendix C.

2. Department of Health (1998) *Smoking Kills. A White Paper on Tobacco*, TSO: London.

3. It should be noted that men are more likely than women to work in outdoor jobs (for example, construction or agriculture) where smoking restrictions are less appropriate.

Table 6.1 **Non-smokers' attitude to people smoking near them, 1997–2002**

All non-smokers

Attitude	2002	2001	2000	1999	1997
	%	%	%	%	%
Would mind if people smoke near them	55	55	55	54	56
Would not mind	35	34	34	37	35
It depends	10	11	11	9	9
Base=100%	*2872*	*2645*	*2455*	*2609*	*2730*

Table 6.2 **Non-smokers' attitude to people smoking near them, by sex and by smoking status, 2002**

All non-smokers

Attitude	Men	Women	Smoking status Ex-regular smokers	Never smoked regularly	2002 Total
	%	%	%	%	%
Would mind if people smoke near them	51	58	46	60	55
Would not mind	39	32	45	30	35
It depends	10	10	10	10	10
Base=100%	*1291*	*1580*	*998*	*1874*	*2872*

Table 6.3 **Non-smokers' reasons for saying that they would mind if smokers smoke near them, 1997–2002**

All non-smokers who mind if smokers smoke near them

Reason	2002	2001	2000	1999	1997
			*Percentage giving the reason**		
Health reasons					
Bad for my health	43	43	51	46	45
Affects breathing/asthma	19	21	23	25	21
Makes me cough	15	17	23	21	17
Gets in my eyes	15	17	21	20	18
Makes me feel sick	8	9	9	8	9
Gives me a headache	4	4	7	6	4
Other reasons					
Unpleasant smell	64	61	65	62	61
Makes clothes smell	37	36	40	39	37
Other	13	17	15	13	19
Health reasons alone	**18**	**19**	**18**	**19**	**17**
Health and other reasons	**67**	**67**	**72**	**71**	**72**
Other reasons alone	**15**	**14**	**11**	**10**	**11**
Base = 100%	*1581*	*1462*	*1352*	*1406*	*1529*

* Percentages add up to more than 100% because some respondents gave more than one reason.

Table 6.4 **Non-smokers' attitude to people smoking near them, by views on whether or not passive smoking increases a non-smoking adult's risk of certain medical conditions, 2002**

All non-smokers

Attitude	Passive smoking increases a non-smoking adult's risk of:												2002 Total*
	Lung cancer		Bronchitis		Asthma		Heart disease		Coughs and colds		Diabetes		
	Yes	No	Yes	No	Yes	No	Yes	No	Yes	No	Yes	No	
	%	%	%	%	%	%	%	%	%	%	%	%	%
Would mind if people smoke near them	58	23	58	28	58	32	60	39	59	42	64	50	55
Would not mind	32	68	32	64	31	60	30	50	31	47	28	39	35
It depends	10	10	10	9	10	8	10	11	10	10	9	11	10
Base=100%	*2605*	*190*	*2557*	*217*	*2449*	*307*	*2064*	*625*	*2086*	*679*	*480*	*1701*	*2872*

* Includes people who said they did not know if smoking increases the risk of having a certain condition.

Table 6.5   **Smokers' behaviour in the company of non-smokers, by number of cigarettes smoked per day, 1997–2002**

All smokers

Behaviour in the company of:	Number of cigarettes per day		2002 Total	2001 Total	2000 Total	1999 Total	1997 Total
	20 and over	0–19					
	%	%	%	%	%	%	%
... adult non-smokers							
Smoke the same number of cigarettes	15	9	11	12	11	12	12
Smoke fewer cigarettes	36	28	30	34	34	34	37
Do not smoke at all	38 〉74	58 〉86	52 〉82	48 〉82	50 〉85	49 〉83	45 〉82
Other (eg ask permission)	11	5	7	6	4	5	6
Base=100%	*284*	*658*	*943*	*844*	*867*	*948*	*986*
... children							
Smoke the same number of cigarettes	15	5	8	8	6	8	10
Smoke fewer cigarettes	32	16	21	26	25	30	32
Do not smoke at all	45 〉77	75 〉91	66 〉87	63 〉90	67 〉92	60 〉90	54 〉86
Other (eg ask permission)	8	4	5	3	2	2	3
Base=100%	*283*	*657*	*941*	*843*	*867*	*945*	*985*

Table 6.6   **Smokers' behaviour in the company of non-smokers, by sex, 2002**

All smokers

Behaviour in the company of:	Sex Men	Women	2002 Total
	%	%	%
... adult non-smokers			
Smoke the same number of cigarettes	14	8	11
Smoke fewer cigarettes	30	31	30
Do not smoke at all	48	55	52
Other (eg ask permission)	8	6	7
Base=100%	*455*	*488*	*943*
... children			
Smoke the same number of cigarettes	11	6	8
Smoke fewer cigarettes	20	22	21
Do not smoke at all	64	68	66
Other (eg ask permission)	6	4	5
Base=100%	*451*	*487*	*941*

Table 6.7 **Smokers' behaviour in the company of non-smokers, by views on whether or not passive smoking increases a child's risk of certain medical conditions, 2002**

All smokers

Behaviour in the company of:	Passive smoking increases a child's risk of…													Total*
	Chest infections		Asthma		Other infections		Cot death		Ear infections		Diabetes		
	Yes	No	Yes	No	Yes	No	Yes	No	Yes	No	Yes	No	
	%	%	%	%	%	%	%	%	%	%	%	%	%
… adult non-smokers													
Smoke the same number of cigarettes	9	19	9	15	10	12	7	14	8	12	7	12	11
Smoke fewer cigarettes	31	29	30	34	30	31	28	33	30	32	21	32	30
Do not smoke at all	54	41	56	40	56	46	60	44	60	48	67	48	52
Other (eg ask permission)	6	11	6	11	4	10	5	10	2	9	5	8	7
Base=100%	*776*	*133*	*676*	*208*	*490*	*370*	*401*	*386*	*226*	*532*	*86*	*663*	*943*
… children													
Smoke the same number of cigarettes	6	18	6	13	5	10	4	12	5	9	6	9	8
Smoke fewer cigarettes	20	27	18	31	19	24	20	23	18	24	13	23	21
Do not smoke at all	70	45	73	47	74	58	72	59	76	61	77	63	66
Other (eg ask permission)	4	10	3	8	2	9	4	6	1	6	5	5	5
Base=100%	*777*	*129*	*675*	*205*	*488*	*368*	*400*	*384*	*226*	*530*	*87*	*661*	*941*

* Includes people who said they did not know if smoking increases the risk of having a certain condition.

Table 6.8 **Smokers' behaviour in the company of non-smokers, by views on whether or not passive smoking increases a non-smoking adult's risk of certain medical conditions, 2002**

All smokers

Behaviour in the company of:	Passive smoking increases a non-smoking adult's risk of...												Total*
	Lung cancer		Bronchitis		Asthma		Heart disease		Coughs and colds		Diabetes		
	Yes	No	Yes	No	Yes	No	Yes	No	Yes	No	Yes	No	
	%	%	%	%	%	%	%	%	%	%	%	%	%
... adult non-smokers													
Smoke the same number of cigarettes	10	15	10	13	9	15	10	13	8	14	8	11	11
Smoke fewer cigarettes	30	33	31	30	29	35	30	32	31	31	21	32	30
Do not smoke at all	54	43	53	48	56	41	54	48	56	46	66	49	52
Other (eg ask permission)	6	10	6	9	6	9	6	8	5	10	5	7	7
Base=100%	*680*	*206*	*679*	*217*	*630*	*244*	*556*	*316*	*536*	*365*	*108*	*634*	*943*
... children													
Smoke the same number of cigarettes	6	14	7	10	6	12	6	12	5	12	6	8	8
Smoke fewer cigarettes	19	29	20	26	18	32	20	23	20	23	12	25	21
Do not smoke at all	70	52	70	55	73	49	71	58	72	57	78	62	66
Other (eg ask permission)	4	5	3	8	4	7	3	7	3	8	5	5	5
Base=100%	*680*	*203*	*679*	*215*	*629*	*241*	*554*	*314*	*536*	*363*	*108*	*632*	*941*

* Includes people who said they did not know if smoking increases the risk of having a certain condition.

Table 6.9 **Restrictions on smoking where respondent currently works, 1996–2002**

Those currently working

Level of restriction	2002 Total	2001 Total	2000 Total	1999 Total	1997 Total	1996 Total
	%	%	%	%	%	%
No smoking at all	50	47	44	48	42	40
Designated areas only	36	38	40	37	41	42
No restrictions at all	9	9	11	11	13	13
Don't work with others	5	6	5	4	4	5
Base=100%	*2251*	*2040*	*1883*	*2104*	*2195*	*2154*

Table 6.10 **Restrictions on smoking where respondent currently works, by smoking status, 2002**

Those currently working

Level of restriction	Smoking status Heavy smokers*	Light smokers*	All current smokers	Ex-regular smokers	Never smoked regularly	2002 Total
	%	%	%	%	%	%
No smoking at all	33	43	40	58	51	50
Designated areas only	45	43	43	27	37	36
No restrictions at all	14	10	11	9	7	9
Don't work with others	8	4	5	6	4	5
Base=100%	160	420	583	513	1158	2251

* Heavy smokers are those who smoke 20 or more cigarettes a day and light smokers are those who smoke less than 20 cigarettes a day.

Table 6.11 **Restrictions on smoking where respondent currently works, by sex and by age, 2002**

Those currently working

Level of restriction	Sex Men	Women	Age 16–24	25–44	45 and over	2002 Total
	%	%	%	%	%	%
No smoking at all	42	58	45	50	52	50
Designated areas only	41	32	44	32	31	36
No restrictions at all	10	7	9	11	12	9
Don't work with others	6	3	2	5	6	5
Base=100%	1129	1122	308	856	907	2251

Table 6.12 **Percentage agreeing that smoking should be restricted in certain places, 1996–2002**

All respondents

Smoking should be restricted	2002	2001	2000	1999	1997	1996
	Percentage agreeing smoking should be restricted...					
... at work	86	86	86	85	84	81
... in restaurants	88	87	88	88	85	85
... in pubs	54	50	53	54	51	48
... in other public places	87	85	86	87	85	82
Base=100%	3812	3473	3320	3523	3716	3696

Table 6.13 **Percentage agreeing that smoking should be restricted in certain places, by smoking status, 1996–2002**

All respondents

Smoking should be restricted	Smoking status Heavy smokers*	Light smokers*	All current smokers	Ex-regular smokers	Never smoked regularly	Total
			Percentage agreeing smoking should be restricted...			
... at work						
2002	62	74	70	89	92	86
2001	60	77	72	87	92	86
2000	68	76	73	88	92	86
1999	61	74	71	87	92	85
1997	63	72	69	86	92	84
1996	55	70	65	83	89	81
... in restaurants						
2002	62	77	72	91	94	88
2001	64	74	71	89	94	87
2000	67	77	73	92	94	88
1999	64	75	72	91	94	88
1997	66	71	69	88	93	85
1996	64	73	70	88	92	85
... in pubs						
2002	22	30	28	55	67	54
2001	18	28	25	52	61	50
2000	22	30	28	59	65	53
1999	26	26	26	59	67	54
1997	23	24	24	57	64	51
1996	19	28	25	52	60	48
... in other public places						
2002	79	87	84	87	89	87
2001	71	87	82	83	88	85
2000	73	84	80	86	88	86
1999	76	86	83	85	90	87
1997	73	82	79	86	89	85
1996	74	83	80	82	84	82
Base=100%						
2002	*282*	*653*	*937*	*997*	*1869*	*3812*
2001	*258*	*582*	*841*	*883*	*1748*	*3473*
2000	*286*	*580*	*869*	*919*	*1530*	*3320*
1999	*278*	*662*	*941*	*974*	*1609*	*3523*
1997	*301*	*678*	*981*	*1017*	*1703*	*3716*
1996	*344*	*700*	*1046*	*946*	*1704*	*3696*

* Heavy smokers are those who smoke 20 or more cigarettes a day and light smokers are those who smoke less than 20 cigarettes a day.

Table 6.14 **Percentages agreeing that smoking should be restricted in certain places, by sex, by age and by social-economic classification, 2002**

All respondents

Smoking should be restricted	Sex		Age				Social-economic classification:				2002
	Men	Women	16–24	25–44	45–64	65 and over	Managerial and professional occupations	Intermediate occupations	Routine and manual occupations	Never worked and long-term unemployed	Total
							Percentage agreeing smoking should be restricted				
... at work	84	88	76	88	87	87	94	87	80	81	86
... in restaurants	88	87	81	87	89	91	91	87	86	83	88
... in pubs	54	54	37	52	61	58	65	54	48	46	54
... in other public places	86	88	87	89	88	85	89	89	85	84	87
Base=100%	*1743*	*2060*	*477*	*1280*	*1266*	*779*	*1218*	*789*	*1468*	*327*	*3812*

Table 6.15 **Percentage agreeing that smoking should be restricted in certain places, by views on whether or not passive smoking increases a child's risk of certain medical conditions, 2002**

All respondents

Smoking should be restricted	Passive smoking increases a child's risk of...												2002 Total*
	Chest infections		Asthma		Other infections		Cot death		Ear infections		Diabetes		
	Yes	No	Yes	No	Yes	No	Yes	No	Yes	No	Yes	No	
						Percentage agreeing smoking should be restricted							
... at work	88	64	89	69	90	80	91	78	91	82	91	84	86
... in restaurants	90	69	90	73	91	83	91	83	92	85	93	86	88
... in pubs	56	31	58	31	60	43	61	44	64	47	64	51	54
... in other public places	89	74	89	77	90	93	91	82	92	84	91	87	87
Base=100%	*3436*	*273*	*3170*	*449*	*2361*	*1135*	*2045*	*1188*	*1124*	*1857*	*566*	*2431*	*3812*

* Includes people who said they did not know if smoking increases the risk of having a certain condition.

Table 6.16 **Percentage agreeing that smoking should be restricted in certain places, by views on whether or not passive smoking increases a non-smoking adult's risk of certain medical conditions, 2002**

All respondents

Smoking should be restricted	Passive smoking increases a non-smoking adult's risk of...												2002 Total*
	Lung cancer		Bronchitis		Asthma		Heart disease		Coughs and colds		Diabetes		
	Yes	No	Yes	No	Yes	No	Yes	No	Yes	No	Yes	No	
						Percentage agreeing smoking should be restricted							
... at work	89	64	89	68	90	70	90	78	90	78	89	84	86
... in restaurants	90	70	91	71	90	75	91	79	91	80	92	86	88
... in pubs	58	27	58	31	59	34	60	41	60	40	64	50	54
... in other public places	90	72	90	76	90	77	90	81	90	82	90	86	87
Base=100%	*3281*	*393*	*3232*	*432*	*3073*	*549*	*2615*	*939*	*2616*	*1040*	*587*	*2331*	*3812*

* Includes people who said they did not know if smoking increases the risk of having a certain condition.

Table 6.17 **Percentage who would take the provision of non-smoking areas into account when selecting a place to go for a meal or drink, 1997–2002**

All respondents

Would take the provision of non-smoking areas into account when selecting a place to go for :	2002	2001	2000	1999	1997
	Percentage who would take the provision of non-smoking areas into account				
... a meal	43	42	45	41	42
... a drink	19	19	22	18	19
Base=100%					
... a meal	*3822*	*3495*	*3345*	*3522*	*3716*
... a drink	*3807*	*3479*	*3321*	*3523*	*3716*

Table 6.18 **Percentage who would take the provision of non-smoking areas into account when selecting a place to go for a meal or drink, by smoking status, 2002**

All respondents

Would take the provision of non-smoking areas into account when selecting a place to go for :	Smoking status Heavy smokers*	Light smokers*	All current smokers	Ex-regular smokers	Never smoked regularly	2002 Total
	Percentage who would take the provision of non-smoking areas into account					
... a meal	11	16	14	48	55	43
... a drink	1	3	2	20	26	19
Base=100%						
... a meal	*285*	*660*	*944*	*998*	*1878*	*3822*
... a drink	*282*	*656*	*939*	*996*	*1872*	*3807*

* Heavy smokers are those who smoke 20 or more cigarettes a day and light smokers are those who smoke less than 20 cigarettes a day.

Table 6.19 **Percentage who would take the provision of non-smoking areas into account when selecting a place to go for a meal or drink by sex and by age, 2002**

All respondents

Would take the provision of non-smoking areas into account when selecting a place to go for :	Sex Men	Women	Age 16–24	25–44	45–64	65 and over	2002 Total
	Percentage who would take the provision of non-smoking areas into account						
... a meal	42	44	24	41	48	51	43
... a drink	17	20	8	17	22	21	19
Base=100%							
... a meal	*1748*	*2074*	*480*	*1281*	*1270*	*790*	*3822*
... a drink	*1744*	*2062*	*478*	*1280*	*1265*	*784*	*3807*

Table 6.20 **Percentage who would take the provision of non-smoking areas into account when selecting a place to go for a meal or drink, by views on whether or not passive smoking increases a child's risk of certain medical conditions, 2002**

All respondents

Would take the provision of non-smoking areas into account when selecting a place to go for:	Passive smoking increases a child's risk of... Chest infections Yes	No	Asthma Yes	No	Other infections Yes	No	Cot death Yes	No	Ear infections Yes	No	Diabetes Yes	No	2002 Total*
	Percentage who would take the provision of non-smoking areas into account												
... a meal	46	19	48	19	50	32	50	33	52	37	53	40	43
... a drink	20	6	21	5	22	13	22	12	25	15	28	16	19
Base=100%													
... a meal	*3440*	*274*	*3178*	*450*	*2366*	*1137*	*2047*	*1191*	*1127*	*1860*	*566*	*2436*	*3822*
... a drink	*3436*	*272*	*3172*	*448*	*2362*	*1136*	*2045*	*1189*	*1124*	*1857*	*567*	*2432*	*3807*

* Includes people who said they did not know if smoking increases the risk of having a certain condition.

Table 6.21 **Percentage who would take the provision of non-smoking areas into account when selecting a place to go for a meal or drink, by views on whether or not passive smoking increases a non-smoking adult's risk of certain medical conditions, 2002**

All respondents

Would take the provision of non-smoking areas into account when selecting a place to go for:	Passive smoking increases a non-smoking adult's risk of...												2002 Total*
	Lung cancer		Bronchitis		Asthma		Heart disease		Coughs and colds		Diabetes		
	Yes	No	Yes	No	Yes	No	Yes	No	Yes	No	Yes	No	
	Percentage who would take the provision of non-smoking areas into account												
... a meal	47	20	47	20	48	20	48	31	48	33	52	39	43
... a drink	21	6	21	6	21	7	22	11	22	11	26	16	19
Base=100%													
... a meal	*3287*	*397*	*3238*	*434*	*3080*	*552*	*2622*	*942*	*2623*	*1045*	*588*	*2337*	*3822*
... a drink	*3283*	*395*	*3234*	*433*	*3074*	*551*	*2617*	*942*	*2619*	*1044*	*588*	*2334*	*3807*

* Includes people who said they did not know if smoking increases the risk of having a certain condition.

Table 6.22 **Percentage who would take the provision of non-smoking areas into account when selecting a place to go for a meal or drink, by views on smoking restrictions, 2002**

All respondents

Would take the provision of non-smoking areas into account when selecting a place to go for :	Smoking should be restricted:								2002 Total*
	...at work		...in restaurants		...in pubs		...in other public places		
	Agree	Disagree	Agree	Disagree	Agree	Disagree	Agree	Disagree	
	Percentage who would take the provision of non-smoking areas into account								
... a meal	48	17	48	10	57	21	46	24	43
... a drink	21	7	21	3	28	5	20	8	19
Base=100%									
... a meal	*3270*	*220*	*3340*	*228*	*2062*	*973*	*3319*	*220*	*3822*
... a drink	*3265*	*219*	*3334*	*225*	*2059*	*972*	*3314*	*220*	*3807*

* Includes people who neither agree nor disagree with smoking restrictions

Table 6.23 Views on acceptable amount of tax increase, 1996–2002

All respondents

Acceptable amount of increase	2002	2001	2000	1999	1997	1996
	%	%	%	%	%	%
A lot more than inflation	31	30	32	34	35	36
Just above inflation	16	17	14	14	18	16
In line with inflation	26	26	27	24	28	28
None at all	27	27	27	28	20	21
Base=100%	*3703*	*3385*	*3221*	*3450*	*3626*	*3611*

Table 6.24 Views on acceptable amount of tax increase by smoking status, 2002

All respondents

Acceptable amount of increase	Heavy smokers*	Light smokers*	All current smokers	Ex-regular smokers	Never smoked regularly	2002 Total
	%	%	%	%	%	%
A lot more than inflation	5	12	10	32	40	31
Just above inflation	5	8	7	15	22	16
In line with inflation	18	28	24	28	24	26
None at all	72	52	58	24	13	27
Base=100%	*283*	*639*	*922*	*969*	*1811*	*3703*

* Heavy smokers are those who smoke 20 or more cigarettes a day and light smokers are those who smoke less than 20 cigarettes a day.

Table 6.25 Views on acceptable amount of tax increase by sex and by age, 2002

All respondents

Acceptable amount of increase	Sex Men	Women	Age 16–24	25–44	45–64	65 and over	2002 Total
	%	%	%	%	%	%	%
A lot more than inflation	30	32	29	31	31	31	31
Just above inflation	16	17	18	17	16	16	16
In line with inflation	26	25	25	26	24	26	26
None at all	28	26	28	26	29	27	27
Base=100%	*1701*	*2001*	*458*	*1262*	*1228*	*755*	*3703*

Appendix A The ONS Omnibus Survey

The Omnibus Survey is a multi-purpose survey carried out by the Office for National Statistics for use by Government departments and other public or non-profit making bodies. Interviewing is carried out most months and each month's questionnaire covers a variety of topics, reflecting different user's requirements.

The sample

A random probability sample of 3,000 private households in Great Britain is selected each month using the Postcode Address File as a sampling frame. One hundred new postal sectors are selected and are stratified by region, the proportion of households renting from the local authorities and the proportion in which the head of household is in Socio-Economic Groups 1–5 or 13 (that is a professional employer or manager). The postal sectors are selected with probability proportional to size and within each sector 30 addresses are selected randomly.

At multi-household addresses, interviewers use a standard ONS procedure to select just one household randomly. Within households with more than one adult, one person aged 16 or over is randomly selected for interview. No proxy interviews are taken.

Weighting

Because only one household member is interviewed at each address, people in households containing few adults have a higher probability of selection than those in households with many. Where the unit of analysis is individual adults, as it is for this module, a weighting factor is applied to correct for this unequal probability of selection.

Fieldwork

Interviews are carried out in respondents' homes by interviewers who have been trained to carry out a range of ONS surveys. Advance letters are sent to all addresses giving a brief account of the survey. Interviewers must make at least three to four calls at an address at different times of the day and week.

As with all ONS surveys, a quality check on fieldwork is carried out through recall interviews with a proportion of respondents.

The Omnibus Survey uses computer assisted interviewing which has well documented effects on the quality of the data.

Questions

The module of questions (which are shown in Appendix B) was developed in conjunction with the Department of Health.

Response Rates

The small users' Postal Address File includes some business addresses and other addresses, such as new and empty properties, at which no private households are living. The expected proportion of such addresses, which are classified as ineligible, is about 11–12%. This figure is removed before the response rate is calculated.

The response rate for the October and November 2002 Omnibus surveys was 70%, as shown below:

Set sample	6,000	100%
Ineligible addresses	523	9%
Eligible addresses	5,477	100%
Refusals	1,230	22%
Non-contacts	425	8%
Respondents	3,822	70%

Note on Socio-economic classification

From April 2001 the National Statistics Social-economic Classification (NS-SEC) was used for all official statistics and surveys. It replaced Social Class based on Occupation (SC, formerly Registrar General's Social Class) and Socio-economic Groups (SEG).

In the past, this series of reports has presented information on smoking by grouping Socio-economic group (SEG) into non-manual and manual classes.

The operational categories of the NS-SEC can be aggregated to produce approximated SEG based on Occupation, as shown in the table below. This approximation achieves a continuity level of 87 per cent.

The tables in this report show a three class collapsed version of NS-SEC. More information on the continuity issues and the relationship between the 8, 5 and 3-class versions of NS-SEC is given at

http://www.statistics.gov.uk/methods_quality/ns_sec/downloads/NS-SEC.doc

Categories of the NS-SEC linked to Socio-economic Groups

Socio-economic Group		NS-SEC Categories
1	Employers and managers in central and local government, industry, commerce, etc. – large establishments	
	1.1 Employers in industry, commerce, etc. – large establishments	1
	1.2 Managers in central and local government, industry, commerce, etc. – large establishments	2
2	Employers and managers, industry, commerce, etc. – small establishments	
	2.1 Employers in industry, commerce, etc. – small establishments	8.1
	2.2 Managers in industry, commerce, etc. – small establishments	5
3	Professional workers – self-employed	3.3
4	Professional workers – employees	3.1
5	Intermediate non-manual workers	
	5.1 Ancillary workers and artists	3.2, 3.4, 4.1, 4.3, 7.3
	5.2 Foremen and supervisors non-manual	6
6	Junior non-manual workers	4.2, 7.1, 7.2, 12.1, 12.6,
7	Personal service workers	12.7, 13.1
8	Foremen and supervisors – manual	10
9	Skilled manual workers	7.4, 11.1, 12.3, 13.3
10	Semi-skilled manual workers	11.2, 12.2, 12.4, 13.2
11	Unskilled manual workers	13.4
12	Own account workers (other than professional)	4.4, 9.1
13	Farmers – employers and managers	8.2
14	Farmers – own account	9.2
15	Agricultural workers	12.5, 13.5
16	Members of the armed forces	-
17	Inadequately described and not stated occupations	16

Appendix B The questions

ASK ALWAYS:

M130_1

SHOWCARD C130.1

This next question asks you about causes of death.

[*] Which of these do you think causes the most deaths before the age of 65 in the UK each year?

(1) Road accidents
(2) Accidents at work
(3) AIDS
(4) Smoking
(5) Murder and manslaughter
(6) Illicit drugs
(7) Alcohol misuse

ASK ALWAYS:

M130_2

I'm now going to ask you some questions about smoking.

Do you smoke cigarettes at all nowadays?

(1) Yes
(2) No

ASK IF: Smokes nowadays

M130_3

How many cigarettes a day do you usually smoke at weekends?
0..200

ASK IF: Smokes nowadays

M130_4

How many cigarettes a day do you usually smoke on weekdays?
0..200

ASK IF: Smokes nowadays

M130_5

Do you usually smoke packeted cigarettes, hand-rolled cigarettes or both?

IF RESPONDENT SAYS BOTH – PROMPT 'IS THAT MAINLY PACKETED OR MAINLY HAND-ROLLED CIGARETTES?'

(1) Packeted
(2) Hand-rolled
(3) Both packeted and hand-rolled, but mainly packeted
(4) Both packeted and hand-rolled, but mainly hand-rolled

ASK IF: Does not smoke nowadays

M130_6

Have you ever smoked cigarettes regularly?

(1) Yes
(2) No

ASK IF: Does not smoke nowadays

AND: ever smoked regularly

M130_7

About how many cigarettes a day did you smoke when you smoked regularly?
0..200

ASK ALWAYS:

M130_8

Do you smoke at least one cigar of any kind per month nowadays?

(1) Yes
(2) No

ASK IF: Ask men only

M130_9

Do you smoke a pipe at all nowadays?

(1) Yes
(2) No

ASK IF: Smokes cigarettes nowadays

M130_10

How soon after waking do you smoke your first cigarette of the day?

(1) Less than 5 minutes
(2) 5–14 minutes
(3) 15–29 minutes
(4) 30 minutes but less than 1 hour
(5) 1 hour but less than 2 hours
(6) 2 hours or more

ASK IF: Smokes nowadays – cigarettes, cigars, or pipe

M130_11

Would you like to give up smoking?

(1) Yes
(2) No

ASK IF: Smokes nowadays – cigarettes, cigars, or pipe
AND: like to give up
M130_12

How much would you like to give up smoking, ...

RUNNING PROMPT
(1)   A little,
(2)   a fair amount,
(3)   quite a lot,
(4)   or very much indeed?

ASK IF: Smokes nowadays – cigarettes, cigars, or pipe
AND: like to give up
M130_13
SHOW CARD C130.13

What are your main reasons for wanting to give up?
SET [3] OF
(1)   Because of a health problem I have at present
(2)   Better for my health in general
(3)   Less risk of getting smoking related illnesses
(4)   Doctor said I should stop
(5)   Family/friends wanted me to stop
(6)   Financial reasons (couldn't afford it)
(7)   Pregnancy
(8)   Worried about the effect on my children
(9)   Other (specify)

ASK IF: Smokes nowadays – cigarettes, cigars, or pipe
AND: like to give up
AND: other IN M130_13
spec13
Please specify other reasons

STRING[200]

ASK IF: Smokes nowadays – cigarettes, cigars, or pipe
M130_14
Which of the following statements best describes you....
RUNNING PROMPT
(1)   I intend to give up smoking within the next month
(2)   I intend to give up smoking within the next 6 months
(3)   I intend to give up smoking within the next year
(4)   I intend to give up smoking, but not in the next year?
(5)   I have no intention of giving up smoking

ASK IF: Smokes nowadays – cigarettes, cigars, or pipe
M130_14a
Have you ever tried to give up?
(1)   Yes
(2)   No

ASK IF: Smokes nowadays – cigarettes, cigars, or pipe
AND: Has tried to give up
M130_15
Have you made a serious attempt to give up smoking in the last five years, that is since October 1996?
(1)   Yes
(2)   No

ASK IF: Smokes nowadays – cigarettes, cigars, or pipe
AND: Has tried to give up
AND: Serious attempt to give up in last 5 years
M130_15a
Have you tried to give up in the last 12 months?
(1)   Yes
(2)   No

ASK IF: Smokes nowadays – cigarettes, cigars, or pipe
AND: Has tried to give up
AND: Serious attempt to give up in last 5 years
AND: Tried to give up in last year
M130_15b

How many times have you tried to give up smoking in the last year?
1..50

ASK IF: Smokes nowadays – cigarettes, cigars, or pipe
AND: Has tried to give up
M130_15c
Thinking about last time you attempted to give up, how long did this attempt last?

PLEASE RECORD WHETHER YEARS, MONTHS OR WEEKS and ACTUALLY HOW LONG AT NEXT QUESTION
IF LESS THAN A WEEK RECORD AS ZERO WEEKS
(1)   Years
(2)   Months
(3)   Weeks

ASK IF: Smokes nowadays – cigarettes, cigars, or pipe
AND: Has tried to give up
INT15
How many years/months/weeks was this?
ASK OR CODE THE NUMBER HERE

IF LESS THAN A WEEK RECORD AS ZERO WEEKS
0..99

ASK IF: Smokes nowadays – cigarettes, cigars, or pipe
M130_15d
May I just check, have you succeeded in stopping smoking for more than a day in the last 12 months?
(1)   Yes
(2)   No

ASK IF: (m130_2 = Yes) AND (M130_15d = Yes)
M130_15eM
[*] Why did you start smoking again after the last time you tried to give up? Please give your main reasons.

CODE ALL THAT APPLY
SET [8] OF
(1)   My spouse/partner smokes
(2)   My friends smoke
(3)   Life too stressful/just not a good time
(4)   Couldn't cope with the cravings
(5)   Missed the habit/something to do with my hands
(6)   Put on weight
(7)   I like smoking
(8)   Other (SPECIFY)

ASK IF: (m130_2 = Yes) AND (M130_15d = Yes)
AND: Other IN M130_15eM
SPEC15eM
INTERVIEWER: RECORD OTHER REASON
STRING[255]

ASK IF: ((m130_2 = Yes) AND (m130_11 = Yes)) AND (M130_15d = No)
M130_15fM
[*] Why do you think you haven't succeeded in stopping smoking or why haven't you tried to give up in the last 12 months?

CODE ALL THAT APPLY
SET [9] OF
(1)   My spouse/partner smokes
(2)   My friends smoke
(3)   Life too stressful/just not a good time
(4)   Couldn't cope with the cravings
(5)   Would miss the habit/something to do with my hands
(6)   Worried about putting on weight
(7)   I like smoking too much
(8)   Lack of commitment to quitting
(9)   Other (SPECIFY)

ASK IF: ((m130_2 = Yes) AND (m130_11 = Yes)) AND (M130_15d = No)
AND: Other IN M130_15fM
SPEC15f
INTERVIEWER: RECORD OTHER REASON
STRING[255]

ASK IF: Has given up smoking
M130_18
How long ago is it since you stopped smoking cigarettes?

PLEASE RECORD WHETHER YEARS, MONTHS OR WEEKS AGO and ACTUALLY HOW LONG AT NEXT QUESTION IF LESS THAN A WEEK RECORD AS ZERO WEEKS
(1)   Years
(2)   Months
(3)   Weeks

ASK IF: Has given up smoking
INT18
How many years/months/weeks ago was this?
ASK OR CODE THE NUMBER HERE
0..99

ASK IF: Has given up smoking
M130_21
SHOW CARD C130.13

What were your main reasons for wanting to give up smoking cigarettes? SET [3] OF
(1)   Because of a health problem I have at present
(2)   Better for my health in general
(3)   Less risk of getting smoking related illnesses
(4)   Doctor said I should stop
(5)   Family/friends wanted me to stop
(6)   Financial reasons (couldn't afford it)
(7)   Pregnancy
(8)   Worried about the effect on my children
(9)   Other (specify)

ASK IF: Has given up smoking
AND: q13oth IN M130_21
spec21
Please specify other reasons
STRING[200]

ASK ALWAYS:
M130_21a
A year from now, how likely do you think it is that you will be smoking?
(1)   Definitely will be smoking
(2)   Probably will be smoking
(3)   Might or might not
(4)   Probably will not
(5)   Definitely will not be smoking

ASK IF: Smokes now or if gave up less than 5 years ago
M130_22a
In the last 5 years, have you been given advice on smoking by your GP?
(1)   Yes
(2)   No

ASK IF: Smokes now or if gave up less than 5 years ago
M130_22b
In the last 5 years, have you been given advice on smoking by someone else who works at the surgery or health centre?
(1)   Yes
(2)   No

ASK IF: Smokes now or if gave up less than 5 years ago
M130_22c
In the last 5 years, have you been given advice on smoking by a pharmacist?
(1)   Yes
(2)   No

ASK IF: Smokes now or if gave up less than 5 years ago
M130_22d
In the last 5 years, have you been given advice on smoking by any other health professional?
(1)   Yes
(2)   No

ASK IF: Smokes now or if gave up less than 5 years ago
AND: received advice on smoking from other health professional
SPEC22d
Please specify who the other medical person was
STRING[200]

ASK IF: Smokes now or if gave up less than 5 years ago
AND: any advice given by GP or any other relevant person
M130_23
And may I just check,was the advice you received part of general health advice or was it connected with a particular health problem you were concerned about?
(1)   General advice
(2)   Particular health problem
(3)   Both

ASK IF: Smokes now or if gave up less than 5 years ago
AND: any advice given by GP or any other relevant person
M130_24
(On any of these occasions) Did you have a discussion about giving up smoking, or were you just given something to take away and read?
IF BOTH CODE 1 FOR DISCUSSION
(1)   Discussion
(2)   Literature only

ASK IF: Smokes now or if gave up less than 5 years ago
AND: any advice given by GP or any other relevant person
M130_25
Did you find the advice helpful?
(1)   Yes
(2)   No

ASK IF: Smokes now or gave up in last year
M130_25a
Have you in the past year done any of the following.

Rung the NHS Smoking Helpline, Quitline, or an alternative?
(1)   Yes
(2)   No

ASK IF: Smokes now or gave up in last year
M130_25b
(Have you in the past year....)

Asked the doctor or other health professionals for help to quit?
(1)   Yes
(2)   No

ASK IF: Smokes now or gave up in last year
M130_25c
(Have you in the past year ....)

Been referred/self referred to a stop smoking group/clinic/ service?
(1)   Yes
(2)   No

ASK IF: Smokes now or gave up in last year
M130_25M
SHOWCARD C130.25M
(Have you in the past year.....)

Had any Nicotine Replacement Therapy (NRT), such as gums, patches, inhalator, or other drugs designed to help people quit smoking?

Please choose your answers from the card.
CODE ALL THAT APPLY
SET [5] OF
(1)   I have been prescribed Nicotine Replacement Therapy (NRT) and my prescription was free
(2)   I have been prescribed Nicotine Replacement Therapy (NRT) and paid for my prescription (including by pre-payment certificate)
(3)   I have been given free Nicotine Replacement Therapy (NRT) (i.e. from an NHS smoking cessation clinic), without a prescription
(4)   I have bought Nicotine Replacement Therapy (NRT) over the counter, without a prescription

(5)   I have been prescribed other drugs to help me stop smoking, with or without NRT

(6)   I have not had any NRT, or other prescribed drugs, to help me stop smoking

ASK IF: Smokes now or gave up in last year
AND: Has been prescribed other drugs to help stop smoking
Spec25M
Please specify 'Other prescribed drugs'
STRING[200]

ASK IF: Smokes now or gave up in last year
M130_25f
(Have you in the past year ....)

Read any leaflets/booklets on how to stop smoking?
(1)   Yes
(2)   No

ASK IF: Smokes nowadays
M130_25g
During the last year has anybody been trying to get you to quit smoking?
(1)   Yes
(2)   No

ASK IF: Smokes nowadays
AND: Somebody has been trying to get respondent to give up smoking
M13025hM
Who has been trying to get you to quit smoking?
SET [7] OF
(1)   Partner/spouse
(2)   Parents
(3)   Children
(4)   Sibling
(5)   Friend
(6)   Work mate
(7)   Other

ASK ALWAYS:
M130_31
[*] Do you think the government should increase the tax on cigarettes ...

RUNNING PROMPT
(1)   much more than the rate of inflation,
(2)   just above the rate of inflation,
(3)   only in line with inflation,
(4)   or, not at all?

ASK ALWAYS:
M130_32A
[*] Do you think that living with someone who smokes does, or does not, increase a child's risk of..
asthma?
(1)   Increases risk
(2)   Does not increase risk

ASK ALWAYS:
M130_32b
[*] (Do you think that living with someone who smokes does, or does not, increase a child's risk of..)
ear infections?
(1)   Increases risk
(2)   Does not increase risk

ASK ALWAYS:
M130_32c
[*] (Do you think that living with someone who smokes does, or does not, increase a child's risk of..)
diabetes?
(1)   Increases risk
(2)   Does not increase risk

ASK ALWAYS:
M130_32d
[*] (Do you think that living with someone who smokes does, or does not, increase a child's risk of..)
cot death?
(1)   Increases risk
(2)   Does not increase risk

ASK ALWAYS:
M130_32e
[*] (Do you think that living with someone who smokes does, or does not, increase a child's risk of..)
chest infections?
(1)   Increases risk
(2)   Does not increase risk

ASK ALWAYS:
M130_32f
[*] (Do you think that living with someone who smokes does, or does not, increase a child's risk of..)
other infections?
(1)   Increases risk
(2)   Does not increase risk

ASK ALWAYS:

M130_33a

[*] Do you think that breathing someone else's smoke increases the risk of a non-smoker getting..

asthma?

(1)   Increases risk

(2)   Does not increase risk

ASK ALWAYS:

M130_33b

[*] (Do you think that breathing someone else's smoke increases the risk of a non-smoker getting..)

lung cancer?

(1)   Increases risk

(2)   Does not increase risk

ASK ALWAYS:

M130_33c

[*] (Do you think that breathing someone else's smoke increases the risk of a non-smoker getting..)

diabetes?

(1)   Increases risk

(2)   Does not increase risk

ASK ALWAYS:

M130_33d

[*] (Do you think that breathing someone else's smoke increases the risk of a non-smoker getting..)

heart disease?

(1)   Increases risk

(2)   Does not increase risk

ASK ALWAYS:

M130_33e

[*] (Do you think that breathing someone else's smoke increases the risk of a non-smoker getting..)

bronchitis?

(1)   Increases risk

(2)   Does not increase risk

ASK ALWAYS:

M130_33f

[*] (Do you think that breathing someone else's smoke increases the risk of a non-smoker getting..)

coughs and colds?

(1)   Increases risk

(2)   Does not increase risk

ASK ALWAYS:

M130_34a

SHOWCARD C130.34

[*] How far do you agree or disagree that there should be restrictions on smoking..

at work?

(1)   Agrees strongly

(2)   Agrees

(3)   Neither agrees nor disagrees/doesn't mind

(4)   Disagrees

(5)   Disagrees strongly

ASK ALWAYS:

M130_34b

SHOWCARD C130.34

[*] (How far do you agree or disagree that there should be restrictions on smoking..)

in restaurants?

(1)   Agrees strongly

(2)   Agrees

(3)   Neither agrees nor disagrees/doesn't mind

(4)   Disagrees

(5)   Disagrees strongly

ASK ALWAYS:

M130_34c

SHOWCARD C130.34

[*] (How far do you agree or disagree that there should be restrictions on smoking..)

in pubs?

(1)   Agrees strongly

(2)   Agrees

(3)   Neither agrees nor disagrees/doesn't mind

(4)   Disagrees

(5)   Disagrees strongly

ASK ALWAYS:

M130_34d

SHOWCARD C130.34

[*] (How far do you agree or disagree that there should be restrictions on smoking..)

in public places such as banks and post offices?

(1)   Agrees strongly

(2)   Agrees

(3)   Neither agrees nor disagrees/doesn't mind

(4)   Disagrees

(5)   Disagrees strongly

Ask if: Currently working
M130_35
SHOWCARD C130.35
What sort of restrictions are there on smoking where you work?
(1)   No smoking at all on the premises
(2)   Smoking only allowed in designated smoking rooms or areas
(3)   No restrictions at all.
(4)   Don't work in a building with other people

Ask if: Smoker
M130_36
If you are in a room with adults who don't smoke, do you .....
RUNNING PROMPT
(1)   Smoke the same number of cigarettes as usual
(2)   Smoke fewer cigarettes
(3)   Or do you not smoke at all?
(4)   Other

Ask if: Smoker
And: M130_36 = Other
SPEC36
SPECIFY 'OTHER'
STRING[200]

Ask if: Smoker
M130_37
And if you are in a room with children, do you ......
RUNNING PROMPT
(1)   Smoke the same number of cigarettes as usual
(2)   Smoke fewer cigarettes
(3)   Or do you not smoke at all?
(4)   Other

Ask if: Smoker
And: M130_37 = Other
SPEC37
SPECIFY 'OTHER'
STRING[200]

Ask if: Smokes now or gave up in last year
And: Parent of child
M130_37a
[*] How likely, if at all, do you think it is that your smoking will influence whether or not the children in this household become smokers?
(1)   Very Likely
(2)   Fairly Likely
(3)   Fairly Unlikely
(4)   Very Unlikely

Ask if: Non smoker
M130_38
In general, do you mind if other people smoke near you, or not?
(1)   Yes
(2)   No
(3)   It depends

Ask if: Non smoker
And: M130_38 = It depends
SPEC38
Please specify 'it depends'
STRING[200]

Ask if: Non smoker
And: Minds if others smoke near them
M13039M
Why is that?
CODE ALL THAT APPLY
SET [9] OF
(1)   Affects my breathing/makes my asthma worse
(2)   Makes me cough
(3)   Gives me a headache
(4)   Makes my clothes smell
(5)   Gets in my eyes
(6)   Unpleasant smell
(7)   Makes me feel sick
(8)   Bad for my health
(9)   Other
Ask if: Non smoker
And: Minds if others smoke near them
And: M13039M = Other
SPEC39
Please specify 'other'
STRING[200]

Ask always:
M13040M
SHOW CARD C130.40

[*] If you go out for a meal, which, if any, of the items on the card are important when you are deciding where to go?

CODE ALL THAT APPLY
SET [5] OF
(1)   Location
(2)   Menu
(3)   Price
(4)   Non-smoking area
(5)   Other
(6)   None of these
(7)   Never go out for a meal

ASK IF: M13040M = Other
SPEC40
Please specify 'other'
STRING[200]

ASK ALWAYS:
M13041M
SHOW CARD C130.41

[*] And if you go out for a drink, which, if any, of the items on the
card are important when you are deciding where to go?

CODE ALL THAT APPLY
SET [7] OF
(1)   Quality of the beer etc
(2)   Atmosphere
(3)   Location
(4)   Price of beer etc
(5)   Non-smoking area
(6)   Somewhere you can take children
(7)   Other
(8)   None of these
(9)   Never go out for a drink

ASK IF: M13041M = Other
SPEC41
Please specify 'other'
STRING[200]

Appendix C Logistic regression

Logistic regression was used in the analysis to assess the influence of a number of variables (for example, age, sex, smoking status, social-economic classification and household formation) on people's opinions on smoking. The procedure took account of inter-relationships between the variables to:

- identify the variables that are independently associated with an opinion; and

- quantify the influence of each of the independent variables.

The influence of an independent variable is expressed in terms of odds. The odds of holding a particular opinion are the ratio of the proportion of respondents having the opinion to the proportion not having it. Logistic regression estimates the influence of each category of an independent variable by producing a coefficient which represents the factors by which the odds of having a particular opinion differs from those of a reference group. The reference group has a coefficient of 1.0. The choice of the reference groups is arbitrary and varies from analysis to analysis.

Tables C3.1 to C6.3 present the results of the logistic regression. The variables examined in the analysis are set out in the first column of each table and the factors that measure the relative influence of each category of the independent variables – the odds ratios – are shown in the columns headed 'odds ratios'. The 95% confidence intervals around the odds ratios are shown in the next column. Those variables not selected into the final model are marked as being not significant (NS). The usual conventions are used to show which odds ratios are significantly different from 1.0.

The second column in Table C3.1 shows that people aged 25–34 have a multiplying factors of 4.36 in wanting to give up smoking. This means that, all things being equal, the odds of someone aged 25–34 wanting to give up smoking is over four times those of someone aged 75 and over (the reference group in this case).

Only those variables that were found to be significantly associated with the opinion examined are discussed in the report. The commentary is based on the original (raw) data and relationships are illustrated using two-way tables. Very occasionally, the results of the logistic regression differ slightly from the associations revealed

in the two-way tables. This is because two-way tables consider only the relationship between an opinion and one factor whereas logistic regression takes account of the effect of the other independent factors.

Note

1 The independent variables were identified by developing statistical models. The models were developed using a stepwise procedure starting with the variable that was the most strongly related to the attitude or opinion being studied.

Table C3.1 Odds of wanting to give up smoking

All smokers

Variables in the model	Odds ratios for wanting to give up smoking	95% Confidence Intervals
Sex		
Men	NS	
Women (reference group)		
Age		
16–24	2.97 **	(1.36–6.48)
25–34	4.36 **	(2.08–9.11)
35–44	3.52 **	(1.70–7.28)
45–54	3.34 **	(1.58–7.04)
55–64	2.38 **	(1.14–4.99)
65–74	1.32	(0.60–2.90)
75 and over (reference group)	1	
Smoking status		
Heavy smoker	NS	
Light smoker (reference group)		
Type of cigarette smoked		
Packeted	NS	
Both		
Roll ups (reference group)		
Age of youngest child in household		
Less than 5	NS	
5–10		
11–15		
No children in household (reference group)		
Number of adults in the household	NS	
Social-economic classifiction		
Managerial and professional occupations	NS	
Intermediate occupations		
Routine and non-manual occupations		
Never worked and long-term unemployed (reference group)		
Said smoking did not increase the risk of a child getting: [†]		
Chest infection	0.55 **	(0.38–0.80)
Asthma	NS	
Other infections	NS	
Cot death	NS	
Ear infections	NS	
Said smoking did not increase the risk of a non-smoking adult getting: [†]		
Lung cancer	NS	
Bronchitis	NS	
Asthma	NS	
Heart disease	0.60 **	(0.45–0.82)
Coughs and colds	NS	

$* \ p < 0.05$, $** \ p < 0.01$ NS = the variable did not enter the model

† Reference group is people who said smoking did increase the risk of a child or non-smoking adult getting the medical condition.

Table C3.2 **Odds of intending to give up smoking in the next year**

All smokers

Variables in the model	Odds ratios for intending to give up smoking	95% confidence intervals
Sex		
Men	NS	
Women (reference group)		
Age		
16–24	3.25 **	(1.37-7.70)
25–34	4.53 **	(1.99-10.32)
35–44	4.18 **	(1.84-9.50)
45–54	2.62 *	(1.13-6.08)
55–64	2.15	(0.92-4.99)
65–74	1.25	(0.50-3.15)
75 and over (reference group)	1	
Smoking status		
Heavy smoker	0.62 **	(0.46-0.84)
Light smoker (reference group)	1	
Type of cigarette smoked		
Packeted	1.52 *	(1.07-2.15)
Both	0.97	(0.56-1.69)
Roll ups (reference group)	1	
Age of youngest child in household		
Less than 5	NS	
5–10		
11–15		
No children in household (reference group)		
Number of adults in the household	NS	
Social-economic classifiction		
Managerial and professional occupations	NS	
Intermediate occupations		
Routine and non-manual occupations		
Never worked and long-term unemployed (reference group)		
Said smoking did not increase the risk of a child getting: [†]		
Chest infection	0.46 **	(0.31-0.69)
Asthma	NS	
Other infections	NS	
Cot death	NS	
Ear infections	NS	
Said smoking did not increase the risk of a non-smoking adult getting: [†]		
Lung cancer	0.60 **	(0.43-0.83)
Bronchitis	NS	
Asthma	NS	
Heart disease	NS	
Coughs and colds	NS	

* $p < 0.05$, ** $p < 0.01$ NS = the variable did not enter the model

† reference group is people who said smoking did increase the risk of a child or non-smoking adult getting the medical condition.

Table C5.1 **Odds of saying passive smoking increases the risk of a child getting certain medical conditions**

All respondents

Variables in the model	Chest infections	95% Confidence Intervals	Asthma	95% Confidence Intervals	Other infections	95% Confidence Intervals	Cot death	95% Confidence Intervals	Ear infections	95% Confidence Intervals	Diabetes	95% Confidence Intervals
Sex												
Men	NS		NS		1.17 *	(1.02–1.34)	0.55 **	(0.48–0.63)	0.73 **	(0.63–0.85)	NS	
Women (reference group)					1		1		1			
Age												
16–24	4.25 **	(2.51–7.21)	2.16 **	(1.44–3.24)	2.67 **	(1.97–3.64)	1.46 *	(1.06–2.02)	0.69 *	(0.48–0.99)	NS	
25–34	3.42 **	(2.27–5.17)	2.53 **	(1.80–3.58)	2.73 **	(2.10–3.54)	2.98 **	(2.24–3.96)	1.33	(0.99–1.78)		
35–44	3.64 **	(2.43–5.46)	1.88 **	(1.37–2.59)	2.21 **	(1.72–2.83)	2.43 **	(1.83–3.23)	1.23	(0.91–1.66)		
45–54	2.42 **	(1.64–3.56)	1.67 **	(1.21–2.31)	2.05 **	(1.59–2.64)	1.88 **	(1.45–2.44)	1.29	(0.97–1.70)		
55–64	2.04 **	(1.40–2.96)	1.31	(0.96–1.79)	1.73 **	(1.34–2.22)	1.47 **	(1.14–1.90)	1.04	(0.79–1.38)		
65–74	1.19	(0.84–1.70)	1.13	(0.83–1.56)	1.17	(0.90–1.51)	1.19	(0.91–1.54)	0.91	(0.68–1.22)		
75 and over (reference group)	1		1		1		1		1		1	
Smoking status												
Heavy smoker	0.21 **	(0.15–0.29)	0.17 **	(0.13–0.22)	0.34 **	(0.26–0.44)	0.39 **	(0.30–0.50)	0.37 **	(0.26–0.51)	0.42 **	(0.27–0.64)
Light smoker	0.38 **	(0.28–0.50)	0.36 **	(0.29–0.46)	0.50 **	(0.42–0.60)	0.53 **	(0.44–0.64)	0.75 **	(0.61–0.92)	0.51 **	(0.38–0.68)
Ex-regular smoker	0.97	(0.73–1.29)	0.70 **	(0.56–0.87)	0.80 **	(0.68–0.95)	0.99	(0.84–1.17)	0.80 *	(0.67–0.95)	0.9	(0.73–1.10)
Never smoked (reference group)	1		1		1		1		1		1	
Age of youngest child in household												
Less than 5	NS		NS		NS		2.16 **	(1.67–2.78)	1.39 **	(1.09–1.77)		
5–10							1.52 **	(1.17–1.98)	0.94	(0.72–1.23)		
11–15							1.05	(0.79–1.39)	0.92	(0.68–1.24)		
No children in household (reference group)							1		1			
Number of adults in the household	NS		NS		NS		NS		NS		NS	
Social-economic classification												
Managerial and professional occupations	2.17 **	(1.36–3.45)	NS		NS		1.16	(0.85–1.57)	0.85	(0.62–1.17)	NS	
Intermediate occupations	1.54	(0.97–2.45)					1.07	(0.78–1.46)	0.68 *	(0.49–0.95)		
Routine and non-manual occupations	1.54	(1.00–2.37)					0.88	(0.66–1.19)	0.71 *	(0.53–0.97)		
Never worked and long-term unemployed (reference group)	1		1		1		1		1			

* p < 0.05,   ** p < 0.01   NS = the variable did not enter the model

Table C5.2 Odds of saying passive smoking increases the risk of a non-smoking adult getting certain medical conditions

All respondents

Variables in the model	Odds ratios for saying passive smoking increases the risk of a non-smoking adult getting											
	Lung cancer	95% Confidence Intervals	Bronchitis	95% Confidence Intervals	Asthma	95% Confidence Intervals	Heart disease	95% Confidence Intervals	Coughs and colds	95% Confidence Intervals	Diabetes	95% Confidence Intervals
Sex												
Men	NS		NS		NS		1.38 **	(1.19–1.59)	NS		1.29 **	(1.08–1.54)
Women (reference group)							1				1	
Age												
16-24	3.24 **	(2.07–5.09)	1.01	(0.66–1.55)	1.48	(1.00–2.19)	1.50 *	(1.08–2.07)	1.21	(0.89–1.66)	NS	
25-34	4.11 **	(2.80–6.03)	1.63 *	(1.11–2.41)	1.77 **	(1.28–2.44)	1.62 **	(1.21–2.17)	1.50 **	(1.14–1.97)		
35-44	2.45 **	(1.75–3.45)	1.24	(0.86–1.79)	1.47 *	(1.09–2.00)	1.42 *	(1.06–1.90)	1.29	(0.99–1.67)		
45-54	1.91 **	(1.36–2.67)	0.98	(0.68–1.41)	1.36	(0.99–1.86)	1.08	(0.82–1.41)	1.08	(0.83–1.40)		
55-64	1.93 **	(1.38–2.71)	0.94	(0.66–1.35)	1.16	(0.86–1.58)	1.27	(0.98–1.66)	1.1	(0.84–1.43)		
65-74	1.37	(0.98–1.91)	0.78	(0.54–1.12)	1.18	(0.86–1.62)	1.04	(0.79–1.37)	1.08	(0.82–1.42)		
75 and over (reference group)	1		1		1		1		1		1	
Smoking status												
Heavy smoker	0.15 **	(0.11–0.20)	0.20 **	(0.15–0.26)	0.21 **	(0.16–0.27)	0.35 **	(0.27–0.45)	0.32 **	(0.25–0.41)	0.48 **	(0.32–0.72)
Light smoker	0.25 **	(0.19–0.32)	0.35 **	(0.27–0.44)	0.40 **	(0.32–0.50)	0.62 **	(0.51–0.75)	0.56 **	(0.46–0.67)	0.65 **	(0.50–0.85)
Ex-regular smoker	0.74 *	(0.58–0.95)	0.88	(0.69–1.13)	0.91	(0.74–1.13)	1.02	(0.85–1.21)	0.95	(0.80–1.13)	0.89	(0.73–1.10)
Never smoked (reference group)	1		1		1		1		1		1	
Age of youngest child in household												
Less than 5	NS		NS		NS		0.70 **	(0.55–0.89)	NS		NS	
5-10							0.99	(0.75–1.29)				
11-15							1.06	(0.78–1.42)				
No children in household (reference group)							1					
Number of adults in the household	NS		NS		1.13 *	(1.02–1.26)	NS		NS		NS	
Social-economic classification												
Managerial and professional occupations	1.53	(0.99–2.35)	1.57 *	(1.05–2.36)	NS		NS		NS		NS	
Intermediate occupations	1.06	(0.69–1.64)	1.04	(0.69–1.56)								
Routine and non-manual occupations	1.09	(0.73–1.64)	1.07	(0.73–1.56)								
Never worked and long-term unemployed (reference group)	1		1									

* p < 0.05, ** p < 0.01   NS = the variable did not enter the model

Table C6.1   Odds of tolerance of smoking

All non-smokers

Variables in the model	Odds ratios for tolerance of smoking	
	Non-smokers who mind if someone smokes near them	95% confidence intervals
Sex		
Men	0.83 *	(0.70–0.98)
Women (reference group)	1	
Age		
16–24	0.22 **	(0.15–0.35)
25–34	0.29 **	(0.21–0.40)
35–44	0.46 **	(0.34–0.62)
45–54	0.54 **	(0.39–0.73)
55–64	0.68 *	(0.50–0.92)
65–74	0.73 *	(0.54–0.98)
75 and over (reference group)	1	
Smoking status		
Ex-regular smoker	0.47 **	(0.40–0.56)
Never smoked (reference group)	1	
Age of youngest child in household		
Less than 5	NS	
5–10		
11–15		
No children in household (reference group)		
Number of adults in the household	1.16 **	(1.04–1.29)
Social-economic classifiction		
Managerial and professional occupations	1.40	(0.96–2.03)
Intermediate occupations	1.00	(0.68–1.47)
Routine and non-manual occupations	0.88	(0.61–1.26)
Never worked and long-term unemployed (reference group)	1	
Said smoking did not increase the risk of a child getting:†		
Chest infection	NS	
Asthma	0.61 **	(0.46–0.79)
Other infections	0.71 **	(0.59–0.86)
Cot death	0.64 **	(0.54–0.76)
Ear infections	0.76 **	(0.63–0.91)
Said smoking did not increase the risk of a non-smoking adult getting:†		
Lung cancer	0.52 **	(0.38–0.71)
Bronchitis	NS	
Asthma	NS	
Heart disease	0.68 **	(0.56–0.83)
Coughs & colds	NS	

* p < 0.05,   ** p < 0.01   NS = the variable did not enter the model
† Reference group is people who said smoking did increase the risk of a child or non-smoking adult getting the medical condition.

Table C6.2 Odds of having certain views on smoking restrictions

All respondents

Variables in the model	Odds ratios for views on smoking restrictions							
	Support restrictions on smoking at work	95% Confidence Intervals	Support restrictions on smoking in restaurants	95% Confidence Intervals	Support restrictions on smoking in pubs	95% Confidence Intervals	Support restrictions on smoking in other public places	95% Confidence Intervals
Sex								
Men	0.76 **	(0.62–0.93)	NS		1.17 *	(1.01–1.35)	NS	
Women (reference group)	1				1			
Age								
16–24	0.70	(0.46–1.05)	0.42 **	(0.26–0.66)	0.46 **	(0.33–0.65)	1.90 **	(1.23–2.94)
25–34	1.25	(0.86–1.84)	0.62 *	(0.41–0.95)	0.61 **	(0.47–0.81)	1.51 *	(1.06–2.16)
35–44	1.60 *	(1.10–2.33)	0.82	(0.54–1.26)	1.01	(0.77–1.32)	1.71 **	(1.21–2.42)
45–54	1.78 **	(1.21–2.61)	0.96	(0.62–1.48)	1.28	(0.97–1.68)	1.50 *	(1.06–2.12)
55–64	1.39	(0.96–2.01)	0.98	(0.63–1.52)	1.40 *	(1.07–1.84)	1.33	(0.95–1.87)
65–74	2.32 **	(1.55–3.47)	1.10	(0.70–1.73)	1.36 *	(1.04–1.80)	1.56 *	(1.10–2.23)
75 and over (reference group)	1		1		1		1	
Smoking status								
Heavy smoker	0.22 **	(0.16–0.30)	0.15 **	(0.11–0.20)	0.19 **	(0.14–0.26)	NS	
Light smoker	0.36 **	(0.27–0.46)	0.28 **	(0.22–0.37)	0.28 **	(0.22–0.34)		
Ex-regular smoker	0.61 **	(0.47–0.80)	0.55 **	(0.42–0.74)	0.54 **	(0.45–0.63)		
Never smoked (reference group)	1		1		1			
Age of youngest child in household								
Less than 5	NS		NS		NS		NS	
5–10								
11–15								
No children in household (reference group)								
Number of adults in the household	NS		NS		NS		NS	
Social-economic classification								
Managerial and professional occupations	3.00 **	(1.97–4.56)	NS		1.52 *	(1.11–2.09)	2.06 **	(1.38–3.07)
Intermediate occupations	1.85 **	(1.22–2.79)			1.2	(0.87–1.67)	2.49 **	(1.63–3.79)
Routine and non-manual occupations	1.11	(0.77–1.60)			0.95	(0.70–1.29)	1.63 *	(1.12–2.38)
Never worked and long-term unemployed (reference group)	1				1		1	
Said smoking did not increase the risk of a child getting:†								
Chest infection	NS		0.63 **	(0.45–0.87)	NS		NS	
Asthma	0.55 **	(0.42–0.70)	0.66 **	(0.50–0.88)	0.73 **	(0.59–0.91)	NS	
Other infections	NS		NS		0.84 *	(0.71–0.98)	NS	
Cot death	0.70 **	(0.56–0.88)	NS		0.79 **	(0.67–0.92)	0.73 **	(0.59–0.91)
Ear infections	NS		NS		NS		0.73 *	(0.56–0.93)
Said smoking did not increase the risk of a non-smoking adult getting:†								
Lung cancer	0.55 **	(0.42–0.73)	NS		0.68 **	(0.53–0.86)	0.47 **	(0.36–0.61)
Bronchitis	NS		0.62 **	(0.46–0.83)	NS		NS	
Asthma	NS		NS		NS		0.67 **	(0.52–0.87)
Heart disease	0.72 *	(0.56–0.92)	0.66 **	(0.52–0.85)	0.80 *	(0.67–0.96)	NS	
Coughs & colds	0.74 *	(0.58–0.93)	NS		0.72 **	(0.60–0.85)	0.76 *	(0.60–0.95)

* $p < 0.05$. ** $p < 0.01$ NS = the variable did not enter the model

Table C6.3 Odds of taking account of the provision of no-smoking area when selecting somewhere to go for a meal or drink

All respondents

Variables in the model	Odds ratios for taking account of provision of non-smoking area			
	when selecting a place to go for a drink	95% Confidence Intervals	when selecting a place to go for a meal	95% Confidence Intervals
Sex				
Men	0.80 *	(0.67–0.96)	NS	
Women (reference group)	1			
Age				
16–24	0.51 **	(0.31–0.85)	0.26 **	(0.18–0.39)
25–34	0.94	(0.66–1.36)	0.48 **	(0.36–0.65)
35–44	1.32	(0.95–1.85)	0.68 *	(0.50–0.92)
45–54	1.59 **	(1.14–2.22)	0.84	(0.63–1.11)
55–64	1.36	(0.97–1.92)	0.90	(0.68–1.19)
65–74	1.54 *	(1.09–2.16)	1.13	(0.86–1.50)
75 and over (reference group)	1		1	
Smoking status				
Heavy smoker	0.12 **	(0.05–0.27)	0.20 **	(0.13–0.29)
Light smoker	0.13 **	(0.08–0.21)	0.22 **	(0.17–0.28)
Ex–regular smoker	0.79 *	(0.65–0.97)	0.75 **	(0.63–0.89)
Never smoked (reference group)	1		1	
Age of youngest child in household				
Less than 5	NS		1.38 *	(1.06–1.79)
5–10			1.36 *	(1.03–1.80)
11–15			1.12	(0.82–1.53)
No children in household (reference group)			1	
Number of adults in the household	NS		1.10 *	(1.00–1.21)
Social-economic classifiction				
Managerial and professional occupations	NS		NS	
Intermediate occupations				
Routine and non-manual occupations				
Never worked and long-term unemployed (reference group)				
Said smoking did not increase the risk of a child getting:[†]				
Chest infection	NS		NS	
Asthma	NS		0.58 **	(0.46–0.74)
Other infections	0.72 **	(0.59–0.89)	0.70 **	(0.59–0.82)
Cot death	NS		NS	
Ear infections	NS		NS	
Said smoking did not increase the risk of a non-smoking adult getting:[†]				
Lung cancer	NS		0.72 *	(0.55–0.93)
Bronchitis	NS		NS	
Asthma	0.61 **	(0.45–0.84)	NS	
Heart disease	0.73 **	(0.58–0.92)	NS	
Coughs & colds	NS		NS	
Did not support smoking restrictions:[††]				
at work	NS		0.72 *	(0.54–0.95)
in restaurants	0.52 *	(0.30–0.90)	0.44 **	(0.32–0.61)
in pubs	0.43 **	(0.34–0.53)	0.64 **	(0.54–0.75)
in other public places	0.58 **	(0.39–0.84)	0.65 **	(0.50–0.84)

* $p < 0.05$, ** $p < 0.01$ NS = the variable did not enter the model

† reference group is people who said smoking did increase the risk of a child or non-smoking adult getting the medical condition.

†† reference group is people who did support smoking restrictions.

Residual Medicines. Myra Woolf. HMSO (1996)

Smoking-related behaviour and attitudes. Fiona Dawe and Eileen Goddard. TSO (1997)

Drinking: adults' behaviour and knowledge. Eileen Goddard. TSO (1997)

The prevalence of back pain in Great Britain, 1996. Tricia Dodd. TSO (1997)

Smoking-related behaviour and attitudes, 1997. Stephanie Freeth. Office for National Statistics (1998)

Drinking: adults' behaviour and knowledge in 1998. Eileen Goddard. Office for National Statistics (1998)

Contraception and Sexual Health, 1997. Tricia Dodd and Stephanie Freeth. Office for National Statistics (1999)

Food safety in the home, 1998. Deborah Lader. Office for National Statistics (1999)

Contraception and Sexual Health, 1998. Laura Rainford and Howard Meltzer. Office for National Statistics (2000)

Smoking Related Behaviour and Attitudes, 1999. Deborah Lader and Howard Meltzer. Office for National Statistics (2000)

Drinking: adults' behaviour and knowledge in 2000. Deborah Lader and Howard Meltzer. Office for National Statistics (2001)

Contraception and Sexual Health, 1999. Fiona Dawe and Howard Meltzer. Office for National Statistics (2001)

Smoking Related Behaviour and Attitudes, 2000. Deborah Lader and Howard Meltzer. Office for National Statistics (2001)

Smoking Related Behaviour and Attitudes, 2001. Deborah Lader and Howard Meltzer. Office for National Statistics (2001)

Contraception and Sexual Health, 2000. Fiona Dawe and Howard Meltzer. Office for National Statistics (2002)

Drinking: adults' behaviour and knowledge in 2002. Deborah Lader and Howard Meltzer. Office for National Statistics (2002)

Contraception and Sexual Health, 2001. Fiona Dawe and Howard Meltzer. Office for National Statistics (2003)